THE INTERNATIONAL COVENANT
ON CIVIL AND POLITICAL RIGHTS

THE INTERNATIONAL COVENANT ON CIVIL AND POLITICAL RIGHTS

Cases, Materials, and Commentary

SARAH JOSEPH, JENNY SCHULTZ, and MELISSA CASTAN

FOREWORD BY ELIZABETH EVATT AC

OXFORD

UNIVERSITY PRESS

OXFORD
UNIVERSITY PRESS

Great Clarendon Street, Oxford OX2 6DP

Oxford University Press is a department of the University of Oxford.
It furthers the University's objective of excellence in research, scholarship,
and education by publishing worldwide in

Oxford New York

Auckland Bangkok Buenos Aires Cape Town Chennai
Dar es Salaam Delhi Hong Kong Istanbul Karachi Kolkata
Kuala Lumpur Madrid Melbourne Mexico City Mumbai Nairobi
São Paulo Shanghai Singapore Taipei Tokyo Toronto

and an associated company in Berlin

Oxford is a registered trade mark of Oxford University Press
in the UK and in certain other countries

Published in the United States
by Oxford University Press Inc., New York

British Library Cataloguing in Publication Data

Data available

Library of Congress Cataloging in Publication Data
Joseph, Sarah.
The International covenant on civil and political rights: cases, materials, and
commentary/Sarah Joseph, Jenny Schultz, and Melissa Cassan.
p. cm.
Includes bibliographical references and index.
1. Civil rights. 2. Political rights. 3. Human rights. I. Schultz, Jenny. II. Castan,
Melissa. III. Title.
K3240.J67 2000 341.4'81—dc20 00–040075
ISBN 0–19–826774–6

5 7 9 10 8 6 4

Printed in Great Britain
on acid-free paper by
Biddles Ltd, *www.biddles.co.uk*

DEDICATION

This book is dedicated to the memory of
Aaron Ronald Castan AM QC
1939–1999

Foreword

This book has the most welcome aim of bringing the work of the Human Rights Committee and the other United Nations treaty bodies to a wider audience. Despite the aspirations of the UN human rights system to touch the lives of everyone, its functions and scope are not well enough known. Nor are its system of accountability, its potential, and its limits understood.

All States which have ratified UN human rights instruments, such as the International Covenant on Civil and Political Rights, are accountable to the independent 'treaty bodies' through the reporting system. Some States have also recognized the competence of the Human Rights Committee ('HRC'), Committee on the Elimination of all Forms of Racial Discrimination ('CERD'), and the Committee against Torture, Cruel, Inhuman or Degrading Treatment or Punishment ('CAT'), to consider complaints made by individuals that their rights have been violated.[1] The treaty bodies have established procedures under which States Parties are called on to engage in face to face discussions with the members of the committees and to respond to their questions about domestic laws and practices (this process is sometimes called a 'dialogue'). The instruments make no express provision for such an encounter, but States Parties have accepted the procedure, and it has proved to be of immense value. The ability of the treaty bodies to elicit specific information from States, and from other sources, has enabled them to form a realistic assessment about the level of respect for human rights in particular countries.

These accountability measures have provided a basis for the treaty bodies, in nearly thirty years of operation, to develop a significant jurisprudence, made up of several elements. In the reporting procedures, the treaty bodies receive information from a range of sources, including inter-governmental and non-governmental organizations, and they use this material to challenge States and test their responses. As a result, their Concluding Comments, prepared in response to each State Report, can be specific and pointed. Although the observations are directed to the situation in a particular State, they have wider significance as they represent a consensus view of the Committee of how particular provisions of the instrument should be interpreted and applied. Another element in the jurisprudence of the treaty bodies consists of the views expressed in individual cases decided by the HRC and other committees. Though not legally binding in themselves, these views are significant indicators as to the application of the instrument. The HRC's Concluding Comments and its views in individual cases are the main source from which it draws in drafting its General Comments on specific

---

[1] An Optional Protocol for CEDAW has been adopted by the GA, October 1999.

provisions of the Covenant. This book is to be commended for bringing together all three elements of the jurisprudence of the treaty bodies in its discussion of each right.

Equally commendable is that the views, expressed in General Comments and individual communications, of different treaty bodies on certain rights and freedoms are drawn together for comparison and comment. An example of this is the treatment of the right to participate in the conduct of public affairs on terms of equality by the HRC and by CEDAW and their different approaches to systemic discrimination. One of the problems of the UN system is that it comprises both general and specific instruments, resulting in considerable overlap of provisions. By linking the provisions of different instruments dealing with the same rights in this way, the authors have made a significant contribution to maintaining the overall consistency of the system in areas of overlapping mandates.

The treaty bodies aim at consistency in their own interpretation of the instruments and the standards they include, and consistency in the application of those standards by States Parties, whatever their region or stage of development. The HRC, for example, considers that the rights and freedoms of the Covenant are universal minimum standards, which should have the same meaning for everyone. The role of the treaty bodies in maintaining the universal application of rights is enhanced by the fact that their membership is drawn from different regions and represents different legal systems. Although neither the regional nor the gender balance is optimal, the diversity of experience, background, language, and culture of members of the treaty bodies ensures that their interpretations are not based on just one system of laws or values.

The UN instruments impose an obligation on States to take specific legal and other measures to give effect to rights and those discussed here also require remedies to be provided in case of violation of rights.[2] A key principle in each instrument is that the primary protection of rights is to be provided by domestic laws, policies, and procedures, rather than by recourse to the international body. Regrettably, the provisions and application of domestic law often fall short of the international standards; there are wide variations in the way those standards are applied, and too many individuals are left without protection or recourse. Few States have escaped criticism by the treaty bodies and nearly all have been the subject of recommendations to bring their domestic laws and practice into line with their treaty obligations.

For States Parties to comply fully with their treaty obligations, they should not only have regard to specific provisions of the particular instrument. They should also take account of and reflect in their laws and practice the views and observations of the treaty bodies. However, States do not always take the action necessary to implement the Committee's Concluding Comments or its views under the

---

[2] CERD, art. 6. CEDAW, art 2. This is not the case with the Covenant on Economic, Social and Cultural Rights.

Optional Protocol. The instruments themselves are legally binding on States Parties, but the decisions and recommendations of the treaty bodies are not directly binding as such. Although the treaty bodies insist that the instruments require States to comply with their reporting obligations, and the principle of compliance in good faith requires them to respond positively to the Committee's views and recommendations, there is no power to enforce these obligations. These weaknesses in the system of accountability under the UN instruments make the task of the treaty bodies difficult and sometimes disappointing. In addition, they have to work with a minimum of resources and without the support they need to carry out their mandate with maximum effectiveness. The problems have been recognized in many UN reports.

The gaps in the system left by the weaknesses mentioned have not been met by the States Parties themselves; for example, they have never used the inter-State complaints procedure under article 41 of the Covenant. There is a great need to support the work of the treaty bodies by action at domestic level. If domestic courts, legal practitioners, and human rights advocates were fully aware of the obligations that their States have undertaken, and how those obligations are interpreted and applied by the independent monitoring bodies, they might well be able do more to press for effective implementation and to ensure that the application of laws and policies was as far as possible consistent with treaty obligations. In this way the impact of the human rights system on the development of national laws and policies could be strengthened.

In those States where international treaties become part of domestic law when ratified, there are frequent references to the Covenant and to the jurisprudence of the Committee in court decisions. But in many countries, there is little knowledge of the instruments or the work of the treaty bodies in the legal profession or among non-governmental organizations. Little is done to disseminate relevant information. In some States, even the agencies that are directly responsible for implementation may be ill-informed. As a consequence, the courts and the legal profession may deal with civil and political rights issues without being aware that one of the treaty bodies has interpreted or applied the relevant provision. Individuals may be unaware that their rights are protected by the instruments or ignorant of how to enforce those rights or seek remedies.

It cannot be assumed that greater knowledge will necessarily lead to improved levels of implementation. But information can be an important weapon in the struggle for human rights. The domestic authorities of States responsible for implementing and protecting rights should do much more to disseminate information about the work of the treaty bodies. National non-governmental organizations should have ready access to information about the human rights standards which their governments have undertaken to respect, and be aware of how those standards should be applied so that they can be more effective in their work for implementation of human rights at national level.

UN materials are published, eventually, and many are available on the internet.

But they are not particularly reader-friendly, and lack any kind of subject index or cross-referencing. There is a great need for works such as this, which present all the relevant jurisprudence of the treaty bodies on an issue by issue basis, with illuminating commentary. This book is particularly valuable in that it includes many direct quotations from the observations, recommendations, and comments of the treaty bodies. It is to be hoped that it will lead to greater interest in and more use of human rights standards, as interpreted by the treaty bodies, in domestic jurisdictions.

The authors have made a significant contribution to the ideals of the founders of the UN human rights system, that of universal respect for the inalienable rights of all members of the human family. 'Globalization', a term often maligned in other contexts, may yet prove to be a positive force in human rights.

ELIZABETH EVATT
Member, UN Human Rights Committee
December 1999

Preface

This publication arose out of the need for a coherent and analytical collection of the jurisprudence of the Human Rights Committee. The Committee represents a very important and continuing source of guidance on the interpretation of human rights law, and in recent years the quality and quantity of interpretive pronouncements on the ICCPR has grown considerably. It was evident that the time had come to draw together the various Optional Protocol views, General Comments, and Concluding Comments on specific States Parties. It is our hope that this publication can be used by lawyers, governments, NGOs, practitioners, scholars, and students of human rights, as a comprehensive and accessible guide and a source for that material, and to advance understanding of how the UN institutions and the ICCPR can be used to develop the human rights of all peoples.

The law is correct as at 1 January 2000, though some material produced after that date is also included. In particular, General Comment 28 on Equality between Men and Women is included as an addendum towards the end of the book. Updates of the material in this book will be accessible via the publisher's website, at <http://www.oup.co.uk.>

Sarah acted as overall coordinating editor. She also took primary responsibility for Chapters 1, 6, 7–10, 13, 18, 19, 22, 23, and 25, and co-wrote Chapters 14 and 17. Jenny took primary responsibility for Chapters 2–5, 11, 15, 16, and co-wrote Chapter 14. Melissa took primary responsibility for Chapters 12, 20, 21, and 24, and co-wrote Chapter 17.

The authors would like to thank Elizabeth Evatt for the apposite and insightful foreword she kindly prepared. We must also thank the Office of the High Commissioner for Human Rights for giving us permission to publish extensive UN material, and in particular Carla Edelenbos and Marcus Schmidt for their support and provision of information. There are also many people who made invaluable contributions to the creation of this book. In particular, we must thank Keith Akers for the preparation of the indexes, James Gus Hazel for his proof-reading of the initial manuscript, and Judith Taylor for the preparation of the appendices. Julie Debeljak, Kate Lindsay, Amrita Mukherjee, and Professor Marcia Neave acted as referees on certain chapters, and we are most appreciative of their perceptive suggestions and comments. We are also grateful to John Louth and Mick Belson of Oxford University Press for their assistance during the production of the book.

Sarah must thank the Law Department at the University of Nottingham for the use of its facilities during her sabbatical in 1998. We all must acknowledge the Monash University Law Faculty, including its library and computer staff, in giving us the time, facilities, and technical support to complete this book. Indeed, the Faculty's ongoing commitment to human rights is reflected in the establishment of the Castan Centre for Human Rights Law in 2000.

Finally we would like to thank our families and friends who tolerated the protracted agonies and ecstasies that were concomitant with the production of this publication. In particular Melissa would like to thank Robert, Nellie, Madeleine and Theodore; Jenny would like to thank Scott, Michael, Thomas, and her parents; and Sarah would like to thank her parents, Margaret and Peter, as well as her mentors, Professor David Harris and Professor Robert McCorquodale.

This book is dedicated to the memory of Ron Castan, whose untimely death was a great loss to us personally and also to the struggle for human rights and justice in Australia generally. He showed us, through his advocacy and through his personal relationships, what one person can accomplish for the improvement and enforcement of fundamental human rights. For this we owe him a debt, which we feel in some part might be met by the production, and we hope, the use, of this book.

Castan Centre for Human Rights Law   SARAH JOSEPH
Monash University Law Faculty   JENNY SCHULTZ
Melbourne   MELISSA CASTAN
27 July 2000

Contents

Part IV: Alteration of ICCPR Duties

Addendum

Appendices

Table of Comments, Recommendations, etc., of the various International Committees which deal with Human Rights

Table of Abbreviations

CAT	=	Convention against Torture and Other Cruel, Inhuman or Degrading Treatment or Punishment
CEDAW	=	Convention on the Elimination of All Forms of Discrimination Against Women
CERD	=	Committee on the Elimination of Racial Discrimination
CRC	=	Convention of the Rights of the Child
CROC	=	Committee on the Rights of the Child
ECHR	=	European Convention on Human Rights
ESD	=	Right of External Self Determination
HRC	=	Human Rights Committee
ICCPR	=	International Covenant on Civil and Political Rights
ICERD	=	International Convention on the Elimination of All Forms of Racial Discrimination
ILC	=	International Law Commission
ICESCR	=	International Convenant on Economic, Social and Cultural Rights
ISD	=	Right of Internal Self Determination
OP	=	First Optional Protocol
UN	=	United Nations

Table of Treaties

This table excludes references to the International Covenant on Civil and Political Rights and its First and Second Protocols as those references are included in the Subject Index.

Table of Cases

All references are to paragraph numbers except those in italics which are to the page numbers in the addendum at the rear of the book. The references in **bold** indicate that the case is fully or partly extracted at the particular paragraph number.

All but the last few pages of this Table contain references to cases from the Human Rights Committee.

Committee against Torture

Committee for the Elimination of Racial Discrimination

European Court of Human Rights

Privy Council

A Note on Style and Citation

As there is much primary material extracted in this book, it is necessary to include an explanation about the style and citations used.

Paragraph numbers in text: The book is arranged within chapters with sequential paragraph numbers such as **[1.01]**. However, not all paragraphs have their own separate number. Indeed, each number refers to a self-contained topic rather than one paragraph. The use of these numbers has facilitated cross-referencing. A reference to paragraph **[1.01]** will appear in the text or the footnotes as [1.01].

'Authors': In extracted cases, the applicant (the person who is bringing the case) is usually referred to as an 'author', in line with the language used by the UN treaty bodies themselves.

Citation of Optional Protocol Communications: The system of citing Optional Protocol communications has been respectfully borrowed from that used by M. Nowak, in his *CCPR Commentary* of 1993. An example of a cited communication is as follows: *Lovelace v Canada* (27/77). The first number is the communication number, accorded to a case on the basis of when it was received by the UN human rights secretariat. *Lovelace* was the 27th registered communication. The latter number refers to the year of the communication's submission, 1977. It does not refer to the date of the decision, which can be discovered from Appendix I. The format of Appendix I has also been adapted from Nowak.

General Comments: The text often refers to 'General Comments'. General Comments are expanded interpretations of rights in the ICCPR, though occasionally they may concern another issue, such as reservations or denunciations. A list of General Comments may be found in Appendix J. Occasionally in the extracts, the General Comment will be referred to by two numbers: e.g. 'General Comment 20(44).' The bracketed number refers to the session in which the General Comment was adopted, and is an alternative way of citing a General Comment. We have chosen to generally cite a General Comment by its sequential number alone.

Concluding Comments: The text also often refers to Concluding Comments on States. These are comments issued by the HRC which address the ICCPR compatibility of the various States parties. The Concluding Comments are cited for their jurisprudential value—i.e. they help identify the meaning of the various ICCPR rights. They are not herein cited in order to draw particular attention to the human rights records of the States concerned. All of the Concluding Comments of all of the UN treaty bodies may be found at the treaty bodies website: <http://www.unhchr.ch/tbs/doc.nsf>

References to Committee Members: The HRC is a quasi-judicial body, so members are not referred to as 'Judge X'. Rather, HRC members are generally called Mr X, Ms Y, or Mrs Z. There are some variations, such as Lord Colville, or Mme Chanet.

Paragraph numbers within Extracts: In most extracts, the internal numbers refer to paragraph numbers in the material extracted. For example, all majority decisions by the HRC have internal paragraph numbers. In some minority decisions, however, there are no paragraph numbers, which explains their absence in some of the extracts.

Addendum: Readers are directed to the Addendum at page 634 of the book. This General Comment, on 'Equality of Rights between Men and Women', was released at a date too late for incorporation within the appropriate chapters. It is most pertinent to chapters 1, 20, 21, and 23.

Part I

Introduction

1

Introduction

[1.01] This book is designed to provide readers with the most important jurisprudential material from United Nations (UN) human rights treaty bodies on the interpretation and implementation of civil and political rights. The UN human rights treaty bodies monitor and interpret treaties which have been ratified by a large majority of all States, so their decisions have universal relevance. These treaty bodies have been operating since 1977, when the first meetings of the Human Rights Committee, which monitors the International Covenant on Civil and Political Rights, were held. In the two decades since, UN civil and political rights jurisprudence has grown in volume, significance, and sophistication. The time has come to collate and assess the UN treaty bodies' contribution to the law regarding civil and political rights.

Civil and Political Rights

[1.02] 'Civil' rights cover rights to protect physical integrity, procedural due process rights, and non-discrimination rights. 'Political rights' enable one to participate meaningfully in the political life of one's society, and include rights such as freedom of expression, assembly, and association, and the right to vote. Civil and political rights are sometimes called the 'first generation' of human rights.[1] They dominate the content of the earliest domestic Bills of Rights in the eighteenth and nineteenth centuries.[2] They are classically perceived as rights to be free from government interference. They may be contrasted with so-called 'second generation' rights, economic, social, and cultural rights, such as rights to an adequate standard of living, education, and health, which are traditionally conceived as rights requiring positive government action.

[1.03] It has always been part of UN rhetoric that civil and political rights on the one hand, and economic, social, and cultural rights on the other, are 'interdependent and indivisible'.[3] However, during the Cold War the 'difference' and 'incompatibility' of the two sets of rights was stressed, with the West championing first-generation rights while the Eastern bloc and third world advocated the primacy of economic, social, and cultural rights.[4] Despite the apparent political support for second-generation rights throughout the Cold War, there is no doubt that economic, social, and cultural rights are normatively underdeveloped compared to civil and political rights. This is not to deny the equal importance for humankind of second-generation rights compared to civil and political rights; it is simply a statement of fact.

[1.04] Economic, social, and cultural rights have however permeated interpretation of civil and political rights by the UN treaty bodies. Indeed, UN jurisprudence has to an extent succeeded in breaking down the barriers between the two sets of rights.[5] While political support for interdependence has lagged, interdependence has been stressed in the decisions of UN treaty bodies.

The ICCPR

[1.05] The most comprehensive and well-established UN treaty on civil and political rights is the International Covenant on Civil and Political Rights 1966 (ICCPR), which has yielded the lion's share of UN jurisprudence in this area. Other UN human rights treaties have generated important material on specific civil and political rights, which will be referred to in the relevant chapters. For

---

[1] L. Sohn, 'The New International Law: Protection of the Rights of Individuals rather than States' (1982) 32 *American University Law Review* 1, 32.

[2] M. Nowak, *UN Covenant on Civil and Political Rights: CCPR Commentary* (N.P. Engel, Kehl, 1993), p. xviii.

[3] See, e.g., preambles to the ICCPR and ICESCR, and Vienna Declaration on Human Rights 1993, para. 5.

[4] H. Steiner and P. Alston, *International Human Rights in Context* (Clarendon Press, Oxford, 1996), 256–7.

[5] See, e.g., below, text at [1.57–1.58].

example, the Convention against Torture and Other Cruel, Inhuman or Degrading Treatment or Punishment 1984 (CAT) has produced important material on the right to be free from torture, inhuman or degrading treatment, or punishment. The two non-discrimination treaties, the International Convention on the Elimination of All Forms of Racial Discrimination 1966 (ICERD) and the Convention on the Elimination of All Forms of Discrimination Against Women 1979 (CEDAW), have generated substantial material on the right to be free from discrimination.

[1.06] This book is therefore largely concerned with the ICCPR, and the jurisprudence of its monitoring body, the Human Rights Committee (HRC). The ICCPR is supplemented by two Optional Protocols. The First Optional Protocol grants important procedural rights for individuals to make complaints about breaches of their rights. The Second Optional Protocol provides extra protection to the right to life by prohibiting the death penalty. A State Party to the ICCPR is under no legal obligation to ratify either Optional Protocol.

RATIFICATION

[1.07] The ICCPR was adopted by the UN General Assembly in 1966, and came into force in 1976 once it had thirty-five ratifications.[6] As of July 1999, there were 145 States Parties to the ICCPR,[7] ninety-five parties to the First Optional Protocol,[8] and forty parties to the Second Optional Protocol.[9] The number of parties to both the ICCPR and the First Optional Protocol has increased markedly since the end of the Cold War, when human rights became a less politicized discipline within the United Nations. For example, the United States, a notable long-term absentee from the international human rights system, ratified the ICCPR in 1992. In the same year, the First Optional Protocol entered into force for the Russian Federation.

[1.08] The post Cold War era has also seen the creation of a number of new States, particularly in the former Soviet Union and eastern Europe. Most of these new States have replaced States which had been parties to the ICCPR. The HRC has consistently taken the view that successor States automatically succeed to their predecessors' obligations under the ICCPR and the Optional Protocols.[10] In this respect, the HRC's view has been supported by the UN Commission on Human Rights,[11] the UN Secretary General,[12] and, most importantly, the practice

---

[6] Art. 49.

[7] *Yearbook of the Human Rights Committee* (1999) UN doc. A/54/40, Annex 1A.

[8] Ibid., Annex 1B.　　　　　　　　　　　　　　　　　[9] Ibid., Annex 1C.

[10] See UN doc. CCPR/C/SR 1178 (reported at (1993) 15 EHRR 233, on the ICCPR obligations of the successor States in the territory of the former Yugoslavia. See UN doc. A/48/40 (1993 Annual Report of the HRC), para. 41, on successor obligations of States in the territory of the former USSR. See also General Comment 26, para. 4 [25.37].

[11] UN doc. E/CN.4/1995/80 (1995).　　　　　　　[12] UN doc. E/CN.4/1996/76 (1996).

of most successor States.[13] For example, the People's Republic of China (PRC) has continued to submit reports to the HRC[14] on behalf of Hong Kong since it acquired that territory from the United Kingdom (UK) in 1997, even though the PRC itself is not a party to the treaty.[15] The PRC has 'succeeded' to the UK's previous obligations under the ICCPR regarding the territory of Hong Kong.

SUBSTANTIVE RIGHTS

[1.09] The substantive guarantees of the ICCPR are contained in Part III, though article 1 is contained anomalously in Part I.[16] The substantive rights are:

Article 1:	Right of Self-determination
Article 6:	Right to Life
Article 7:	Freedom from Torture, Inhuman and Degrading Treatment or Punishment
Article 8:	Freedom from Slavery, Servitude, and Forced Labour
Article 9:	Rights to Liberty and Security of the Person
Article 10:	Right of Detained Persons to Humane Treatment
Article 11:	Freedom from Imprisonment for Inability to Fulfil a Contract
Article 12:	Freedom of Movement
Article 13:	Right of Aliens to Due Process when Expelled
Article 14:	Right to a Fair Trial
Article 15:	Freedom from Retroactive Criminal Law
Article 16:	Right to Recognition as a Person before the Law
Article 17:	Rights to Privacy
Article 18:	Freedom of Thought, Conscience, and Religion
Article 19:	Freedom of Opinion and Expression
Article 20:	Freedom from War Propaganda, and Freedom from Incitement to Racial, Religious, or National Hatred
Article 21:	Freedom of Assembly
Article 22:	Freedom of Association
Article 23:	Rights of Protection of the Family and the Right to Marry
Article 24:	Rights of Protection for the Child
Article 25:	Right of Participation in Public Life
Article 26:	Right to Equality before the Law and Rights of Non-Discrimination
Article 27:	Rights of Minorities

---

[13] See generally M. Kamminga, 'State Succession in Respect of Human Rights Treaties' (1996) 7 *European Journal of International Law* 469.

[14] See [1.25] ff. on the reporting process.

[15] See Concluding Comments on Hong Kong (China), (1999) UN doc. CCPR/C/79/Add.117, especially at para. 3. The PRC has signed but not ratified the Covenant.

[16] This may reflect its anomalous status as a non-individual right: see [7.20].

SUPPORTING GUARANTEES

[1.10] Part II of the Covenant contains supporting guarantees in articles 2 to 5.

[1.11] Article 2(1) is fundamental; it is the 'obligation' provision that directs States immediately to implement the substantive ICCPR guarantees at the municipal level. In particular, article 2(1) obliges States to 'respect and ensure enjoyment by all individuals within its territory, and subject to its jurisdiction' the substantive ICCPR rights 'without distinction of any kind'. The immediacy of the obligation facilitates the justiciability and definition of a State's ICCPR duties. A State is either fulfilling its obligations or it is not; article 2(1) seems to allow no exceptions. The importance of this immediate obligation becomes apparent when one contrasts the progressive obligation in article 2(1) of the International Covenant on Economic, Social, and Cultural Rights (ICESCR). A State, under article 2(1) ICESCR, is required 'to take steps . . . to the maximum of its available resources, with a view to achieving progressively the full realisation' of ICESCR rights. It is not easy to define the content of a progressive duty, as it is difficult to establish when a breach of this duty arises. The word 'available' leaves too much 'wiggle room for the State'.[17] The progressive nature of ICESCR duties has definitely hampered the development of ICESCR norms.

[1.12] Article 2(1) also defines the personal and territorial scope of the ICCPR; the beneficiaries of the ICCPR are 'individuals', while States Parties are responsible only for persons and events 'within its territory and subject to its jurisdiction'.[18]

[1.13] Finally, article 2(1) also contains an important guarantee of non-discrimination. Article 3 supplements this non-discrimination guarantee by specifically guaranteeing equality between men and women in the enjoyment of Covenant rights, and is arguably superfluous. Both articles 2(1) and 3 bolster the free-standing prohibition on discrimination in article 26.[19]

[1.14] Paragraphs 2 and 3 of article 2 supplement paragraph 1 by requiring specific measures of national protection of ICCPR rights. Article 2(2) obliges States to 'adopt legislative or other measures as may be necessary to give effect to' ICCPR rights. Thus, States must change their laws so as to conform to their ICCPR obligations. Article 2(3)(a) obliges States Parties to provide effective domestic remedies for persons whose ICCPR rights are violated. Article 2(3)(b) specifies that these remedies should be determined by a competent government body, ideally the judiciary, while article 2(3)(c) directs that such remedies must be enforced.

---

[17] R. Robertson, 'Measuring State Compliance with the Obligation to Devote the "Maximum Available Resources" to Realising Economic, Social and Cultural Rights' (1994) 16 *Human Rights Quarterly* 693, 694.

[18] See generally Chap. 4.

[19] See, on the non-discrimination guarantees, Chap. 23.

[1.15] Article 4 confers rights on the States Parties to derogate from their ICCPR obligations 'in time of public emergency'. However, this right of derogation is strictly limited by internal provisions of article 4, so there are in-built guarantees against its abuse by the State.[20]

[1.16] Article 5 provides that ICCPR rights must not be abused by States, groups, or persons so as to undermine the enjoyment of ICCPR rights by others. For example, individuals must not abuse their rights to promote fascist policies which call for the destruction of the rights of others.[21] Article 5(2) provides that the ICCPR must not be used as a pretext to lower the level of protection provided for civil and political rights under other international treaties, or under municipal law or custom. Article 5(2) is a 'savings' provision,[22] which preserves the sanctity of any laws that provide a higher level of protection for civil and political rights than is required by the ICCPR.[23]

[1.17] The supporting guarantees in articles 2 to 5 cannot be autonomously violated by a State Party. Violations cannot occur unless there is a simultaneous violation of a substantive right in Part III of the Covenant. For example, one cannot claim a breach of one's right to a remedy under article 2(3) without first establishing entitlement to that remedy via a breach of a substantive right. However, note must be taken of a vigorous challenge to the HRC's long-standing jurisprudence in this regard in a dissenting opinion by Mrs Evatt, Mrs Medina Quiroga, and Mme Chanet in *Kall v Poland* (552/93):[24]

¶ 3. . . . The Committee has taken the view so far that [article 2(3)] cannot be found to have been violated by a State unless a corresponding violation of another right under the Covenant has been determined. We do not think this is the proper way to read article 2(3).

¶ 4. It has to be taken into account that article 2 is not directed to the Committee, but to the States; it spells out the obligations the States undertake to ensure that rights are enjoyed by the people under their jurisdiction. Read that way it does not seem to make sense that the Covenant should tell States parties that only when the Committee has found that a violation has occurred they should provide for a remedy. This interpretation of article 2(3) would render it useless. What article 2 intends is to set forth that whenever a human right recognized by the Covenant is affected by the action of a State agent there must be a procedure established by the State allowing the person whose right has been affected to claim before a competent body that there has been a violation. This interpretation is in accordance with the whole rationale underlying the Covenant, namely that it is for the States

---

[20] See, on derogations, Chap. 25.

[21] See *M.A. v Italy* (117/81), excerpted at [18.29].

[22] Nowak, above, note 2, 100.

[23] See the dissenting opinion of Mr Lallah in *Kindler v Canada* (470/91) for an example of the invocation of art. 5(2), at [8.29].

[24] See also separate opinion of Mr Wennergren in *S.E. v Argentina* (275/88). A breach of art. 2(3) without a corresponding breach of a substantive ICCPR right could for example occur when the substantive rights breach occurred before a State's ratification of the ICCPR: see [2.10].

parties thereto to implement the Covenant and to provide suitable ways to remedy possible violations committed by State organs. It is a basic principle of international law that international supervision only comes into play when the State has failed in its duty to comply with its international obligations.

RELATIONSHIP WITH DOMESTIC LAW

[**1.18**] Though the ICCPR imposes duties upon States in the international plane of law, it is envisaged that the implementation of the rights therein is primarily a domestic matter.[25] Indeed, article 2, the general obligation provision, essentially requires States Parties effectively to protect rights at the municipal level. International enforcement measures, such as the supervisory mechanisms of the HRC, are designed to be a secondary source of ICCPR rights protection. For example, individuals cannot utilize the individual complaints mechanism until they have exhausted domestic remedies.[26] The primacy conferred on national enforcement manifests a concession to State sovereignty, as well as a recognition of the superiority of municipal enforcement systems in terms of efficiency, expediency, and effectiveness.[27]

[**1.19**] The actual domestic protection afforded to ICCPR rights depends on the legal and political system of the relevant State Party. In certain States, such as the Netherlands, the ICCPR has direct effect, and is therefore part of a State Party's domestic law. Alleged breaches can be litigated in domestic courts. In other States, the ICCPR is not self-executing, and so is not automatically part of municipal law. For example, in the UK and Australia, treaties must be specifically incorporated into domestic law before they are part of domestic law. In neither State has the ICCPR been so incorporated.[28] However, discrete ICCPR rights are protected by miscellaneous statutes in both States, such as statutes regulating the exercise of police power, or anti-discrimination statutes. Furthermore, in both States, the ICCPR has an indirect effect in that its norms are used by the judiciary to construe ambiguous statutes, and to fill lacunae in the common law.[29]

---

[25] See Nowak, above, note 2, 27. [26] See generally Chap. 6.

[27] See D. L. Donoho, 'Relativism versus Universalism in Human Rights: The Search for Meaningful Standards' (1991) 27 *Stanford Journal of International Law* 345, 372–3; see also D. Harris, 'The International Covenant on Civil and Political Rights and the United Kingdom: An Introduction', in D. Harris and S. Joseph, *The International Covenant on Civil and Political Rights and United Kingdom Law* (Clarendon Press, Oxford, 1995), 6.

[28] The UK Parliament has passed the Human Rights Act, 1998 which will incorporate the European Convention of Human Rights into UK law upon its coming into force in late 2000.

[29] See *Derbyshire County Council v Times Newspapers* [1992] QB 770 and Justice M. Kirby, 'The Australian Use of International Human Rights Norms: From Bangalore to Balliol—a View from the Antipodes' (1993) 16 *University of New South Wales Law Journal* 363.

The ICCPR

The Human Rights Committee

[1.20] The HRC is created under article 28 of the ICCPR. It is a panel of eighteen human rights experts. HRC members are nominated by the State Party of which they are nationals,[30] and elected by a ballot of all States Parties to serve four year terms.[31] Half of the HRC are elected every two years.[32] It convenes three times a year for three-week meetings.

[1.21] Article 31(2) ICCPR specifies that consideration be given to the 'equitable distribution of membership and to the representation of the different forms of civilisation and of the principal legal systems'. Thus, States Parties should endeavour to elect a fair number of HRC members from Western liberal democracies, Latin America, Africa, and Asia. The 'geographical balance' requirement may have been thrown into some disarray by the effective disappearance of the Eastern bloc as a separate political force in 1989. Indeed, a Western representative bias can be detected in recent years, with over half of the members serving from 1998 to 2000 coming from the United States, Canada, Australia, the United Kingdom, France, Italy, Israel, Finland, Germany, and Poland.

[1.22] Of particular importance is that HRC members act in their *personal* capacity.[33] Though they are nominated by their own State, they do not sit as government representatives. Thus, HRC meetings are not overtly politicized unlike, for example, meetings of the United Nations Commission on Human Rights.[34] Certain safeguards are taken to ensure political impartiality. For example, an HRC member does not participate in decisions which directly concern his/her State. However, States are of course unlikely to nominate members who are outspokenly opposed to their policies.[35] HRC members have undoubtedly been influenced, perhaps unconsciously, by the politics and culture of their respective home States.[36] Indeed, a conspicuous clash of political persuasions occurred between east and west throughout the Cold War, causing some institutional paralysis.[37] A growth in HRC initiatives has been evident in the 1990s, and has been facilitated by the greater degree of internal consensus since the end of the Cold War.

[1.23] Though its Rules of Procedure provide for majority opinions, the HRC

---

[30] Art. 29 ICCPR.   [31] Art. 32 ICCPR.
[32] This rule is necessarily implied by art. 32(1) ICCPR.   [33] Art. 28(3) ICCPR.
[34] See generally, on the Commission on Human Rights, Alston and Steiner, above, note 4, chap. 7.
[35] In this respect, note the failure in 1994 of the Federal Republic of Yugoslavia (Serbia-Montenegro) to renominate Mr Vojin Dimitrijevic as an HRC member. Mr Dimitrijevic was originally nominated by the government of the former Yugoslavia in 1982.
[36] Harris, above, note 27, 21.
[37] S. Joseph, 'New Procedures Concerning the Human Rights Committee's Examination of State Reports' (1995) 13 *Netherlands Quarterly of Human Rights* 5, 5–6. See also L. Heffernan, 'A Comparative View of Individual Petition Procedures under the European Convention on Human Rights and the International Covenant on Civil and Political Rights' (1997) 19 *HRQ* 78, 85.

endeavours to make decisions by consensus.[38] Such decisions of course carry more weight than majority opinions.[39] However, consensus occasionally necessitates unsatisfactory compromises, which can unfortunately dilute certain decisions.[40] Though consensus remains the norm, more individual opinions have emerged from the HRC in recent years.

[1.24] The HRC performs four essential functions in monitoring the ICCPR: (1) it conducts dialogues and draws conclusions from States' reports; (2) it issues General Comments which explain the meaning of the ICCPR's provisions, (3) it hears interstate complaints under article 41, and (4) it makes decisions under the First Optional Protocol. These functions are largely replicated by the other treaty bodies, though some treaty bodies have no jurisdiction to hear individual complaints.[41]

REPORTING SYSTEM AND CONCLUDING COMMENTS

[1.25] The reporting system is the only compulsory monitoring system under the ICCPR.[42] Article 40 requires a State Party to submit reports within a year of entry into force of the Covenant for that State, and thereafter when the HRC so requests. The HRC has requested that reports be presented every five years.[43] In exceptional circumstances, the HRC may call for an emergency report.[44] For example, during the height of the Balkan wars, emergency reports were requested from and submitted by the Federal Republic of Yugoslavia, Croatia, and Bosnia-Herzegovina.

[1.26] The reports are subsequently examined in a public dialogue between the HRC and representatives of the relevant State Party. Importantly, the report is not the only source of information available to the HRC during these dialogues, as reports can suffer from numerous inadequacies. For example, they can be too brief,

---

[38] Rules of Procedure of the Human Rights Committee, UN doc. CCPR/C/3/Rev. 5, 11 August 1997, Rule 51. Rule 51 permits majority voting, but footnotes 1 and 2 to rule 51 prescribe a preference for consensus votes.

[39] Joseph, above, note 37, 6.

[40] M. Schmidt, 'Individual Human Rights Complaint Procedures based on United Nations Treaties and the Need for Reform' (1992) 43 *ICLQ* 645, 656–8.

[41] No individual complaints procedure is available under the ICESCR, CEDAW, or the Convention on the Rights of the Child (CRC). Furthermore, no General Comments have as yet been issued under the CRC. An Optional Protocol to CEDAW was adopted by the UN in October 1999.

[42] See generally I. Boerefijn, 'Towards a Strong System of Supervision: The Human Rights Committee's Role in Reforming the Reports Procedure under Article 40 of the Covenant on Civil and Political Rights' (1995) 17 *HRQ* 766.

[43] See Decision on Periodicity, UN doc. CCPR/C/19/Rev. 1, 26 August 1982, para. 2.

[44] Joseph, above, note 37, 15–23.

[45] See A. Robertson and J. Merrills, *Human Rights in the World* (3rd edn., Manchester University Press, Manchester, 1992), 45.

ambiguous, or self-serving.[45] Therefore, HRC members may utilize information from alternative sources such as non-governmental organizations, the press, or UN specialized agencies, in conducting these dialogues.[46]

[1.27] At the conclusion of these dialogues, the HRC publishes 'Concluding Comments', which are always adopted by consensus. These Concluding Comments resemble a 'report card' on the relevant State and its report; they list positive and negative aspects of the State's implementation of the ICCPR.[47] These Concluding Comments provide authoritative assessments of a State's human rights record, as well as recommendations for improvement. They also provide valuable evidence of the content of ICCPR rights, and are therefore excerpted where relevant throughout the ensuing chapters.

GENERAL COMMENTS

[1.28] The HRC initially refused to interpret its article 40 mandate as authorizing the issue of a consensus evaluation on a particular State's report and subsequent dialogue. Some early HRC members, particularly those from the Eastern bloc, felt that such a practice would unduly interfere with a State's internal affairs.[48] In order to achieve consensus, the HRC initially interpreted article 40(4) as an authorization for the issue of comments addressed generally to States Parties.

[1.29] Hence, the HRC has issued numerous 'General Comments', which address matters of relevance to all States Parties. Most of these General Comments have expanded on the meaning of specific Covenant rights. Some Comments have addressed a broader range of rights under a specific theme, such as General Comment 15 on 'the position of aliens under the Covenant'. A few Comments have addressed miscellaneous issues such as reservations, denunciations, and advice to States on how to prepare reports. Generally, the older Comments, such as those on article 1 (General Comment 12 on the right of peoples to self-determination) and article 19 (General Comment 10 on freedom of expression), are less detailed and consequently less useful than the more elaborate later Comments (see, e.g., General Comment 23 on minority rights). Despite their inception as an arguably weak compromise interpretation of article 40, the HRC's General Comments have proven to be a valuable jurisprudential resource. They are extensively excerpted where relevant in the following chapters.

---

[46] Eastern bloc members had initially argued that the HRC was not authorized to use such information; see D. McGoldrick, *The Human Rights Committee* (Clarendon Press, Oxford, 1994), 77–8; see also Joseph, above, note 37, 6, note 7.

[47] Joseph, above, note 37, 7–12.

[48] See, e.g., Mr Graefrath of the German Democratic Republic, at UN doc. CCPR/C/SR 231, para. 10.

INTERSTATE COMPLAINTS

[1.30] Under article 41 ICCPR, States Parties may submit complaints about violations of the ICCPR by another State if both States have made declarations that the HRC is competent to hear such complaints. Thus the procedure is optional. Though forty-seven States had made article 41 declarations by July 1999,[49] the interstate complaints mechanism has never been utilized. Presumably this is because of the diplomatic and political implications of such an action; States fear retaliatory attacks on their own human rights records.

INDIVIDUAL COMMUNICATIONS UNDER THE FIRST OPTIONAL PROTOCOL

[1.31] The First Optional Protocol is a separate treaty from the ICCPR. If a State ratifies the Optional Protocol, individuals may submit complaints about alleged violations of their ICCPR rights by that State to the HRC.

[1.32] Until 1998, Optional Protocol communications were considered in two stages. First, the HRC considered whether the communication was admissible. The admissibility criteria are set out in articles 1 to 3 and 5 of the Optional Protocol. There are several jurisdictional admissibility criteria. First, there must be an individual victim (personal jurisdiction).[50] Ordinarily the complaint must be submitted by the victim or victim's counsel. In exceptional circumstances, the complaint may be submitted on the victim's behalf by a close relative or friend.[51] Secondly, the complaint must relate to a matter within the relevant State's jurisdiction (territorial jurisdiction).[52] Thirdly, the complaint must relate to an event which occurred after the relevant State ratified the Optional Protocol (temporal jurisdiction).[53] Procedural admissibility requirements are found in article 5 of the Optional Protocol: the complaint must not be simultaneously before another international tribunal,[54] and the complainant must exhaust domestic remedies before submitting the complaint to the HRC.[55] The complainant must also submit sufficient evidence to substantiate the complaint before the HRC will proceed. Finally, the main substantive hurdle is that the complaint must relate to a matter which arises under the ICCPR. This admissibility hurdle is construed from article 2 of the Optional Protocol, which prescribes that victims must have a claim under an enumerated ICCPR right, and article 3, which prohibits the admissibility of 'incompatible' complaints. For example, complaints alleging breach of a right to property[56] and a right to asylum[57] have been ruled inadmissible *ratione materiae*, as they failed to raise a claim under the Covenant.

---

[49] See UN doc. A/54/40, annex 1D. See Annex G for list of these States.
[50] See, on the 'victim' requirement, Chap. 3.   [51] See [3.17] ff.
[52] See, on inadmissibility *ratione loci*, Chap. 4.
[53] See, on inadmissibility *ratione temporis*, Chap. 2.
[54] See, on this admissibility hurdle, Chap. 5.   [55] See generally Chap. 6.
[56] *O.J. v Finland* (419/90).   [57] *V.M.R.B. v Canada* (236/87).

[1.33] The second stage of the individual complaints procedure was for the HRC to consider the merits of the complaint. Ultimately, the HRC issued its 'views' on the merits under article 5(4) of the Optional Protocol, in which it pronounced on whether violations of the ICCPR had taken place. HRC views are not legally binding, as the HRC is not a judicial body.[58] However, the HRC is the pre-eminent interpreter of the ICCPR which is itself legally binding. The HRC's decisions are therefore strong indicators of legal obligations, so rejection of those decisions is good evidence of a State's bad faith attitude towards its ICCPR obligations.[59]

[1.34] Indeed, HRC decisions are issued 'in a judicial spirit'.[60] Merits decisions do resemble definitive findings of breach, or non-breach, by the State concerned. The HRC will also recommend an appropriate remedy, such as the amendment of impugned legislation,[61] the payment of damages,[62] and/or the release of persons unfairly detained.[63] Furthermore, the HRC has instituted a 'follow-up' procedure that publicizes the ultimate fate of its Optional Protocol recommendations.[64] Hence, a State's failure to implement HRC views is on public record, which can potentially prompt censure and criticism. The familiar international legal sanction of bad publicity is therefore available when States are found in breach under the Optional Protocol, and when they fail to redress those breaches.

[1.35] HRC decisions have directly caused States to alter their laws and/or practices so as to conform to the ICCPR.[65] Indeed, States do endeavour to avoid the public censure entailed in adverse HRC findings. Fear of public condemnation arising from international scrutiny can often provide sufficient incentive to States to improve their human rights record.[66] Nevertheless, there is a depressing rate of

---

[58]   McGoldrick, above, note 46, 54–5, 151–2.

[59]   S. Joseph, 'Toonen v Australia: Gay Rights under the ICCPR' (1994) 13 *University of Tasmania Law Review* 392, 401; see also J.S. Davidson, 'The Procedure and Practice of the Human Rights Committee under the First Optional Protocol to the International Covenant on Civil and Political Rights' (1991) 4 *Canterbury Law Review* 337, at 353; and Heffernan, above, note 37, 102–3.

[60]   *Selected Decisions of the Human Rights Committee under the Optional Protocol*, CCPR/C/OP/2 (1988), 1.

[61]   See, e.g., *Toonen v Australia* (488/92).   [62]   See, e.g., *A v Australia* (560/93).

[63]   In numerous Jamaican death penalty cases, the HRC has found violations of art. 14 entailed in the relevant trial procedures. Its recommendations in such cases that the victims be released have been controversial, as the State Party fears releasing potentially dangerous criminals. Mr Sadi, in *Kelly v Jamaica* (253/87), stated in a dissenting opinion that he was open to other remedies, including the ordering of a new trial. In separate opinions in *McLeod v Jamaica* (734/97) and *McTaggart v Jamaica* (749/97), Mr Scheinin has lamented the HRC's failure to prescribe more specific remedies, such as specified amounts of compensation.

[64]   See, e.g., 'Follow-up Activities under the Optional Protocol', in *Annual Report of the Human Rights Committee* (UN, New York, 1998), A/53/40, i, 70–7.

[65]   For example, the decision in *Toonen v Australia* (488/92) led to the enactment of federal legislation which provided a remedy and, ultimately, the repeal of the impugned Tasmanian law; see also C. Cohn, 'The Early Harvest: Domestic Legal Changes Related to the Human Rights Committee and the Covenant on Civil and Political Rights' (1991) 13 *HRQ* 295.

[66]   R. Higgins, 'Some Thoughts on the Implementation of Human Rights' (1990) 5 *Interights Bulletin*, 52.

non-compliance with Optional Protocol decisions.[67] However, this non-compliance may be caused in large part by the weakness of enforcement mechanisms available in international law, rather than any particular disdain for the non-judicial nature of the HRC, or the quality of their decisions. This is not to say of course that States Parties always agree with the HRC's legal analysis.[68]

[1.36] In mid-1997, the HRC adopted new rules of procedure to streamline the Optional Protocol process. This was a response to the escalation in the number of submitted communications caused by a rapid growth in Optional Protocol ratifications, and increasing public awareness of the procedure.[69] Rule 91 now dictates that the HRC will consider issues of merits and admissibility together. The rules regarding admissibility however remain the same. If the case is blatantly inadmissible, such as when the communication is inadmissible *ratione temporis*, it is dismissed. Otherwise, States are given six months to respond to the allegations of violation. Only in the first two months may they submit applications to reject complaints on the grounds of inadmissibility. Such an application does not absolve the State from its obligations to submit information on the merits of the case within the allotted six months. Extensions of time may be granted only in exceptional cases.[70]

Interpretation and Development of ICCPR norms

[1.37] This book is concerned with the jurisprudence of the United Nations treaty bodies, especially that of the HRC. As the excerption and analysis of that jurisprudence are arranged in separate chapters according to the relevant substantive right, it is necessary in this introductory chapter to comment on some broad unifying themes within that jurisprudence.

GENERAL OVERVIEW

[1.38] The essential sources of HRC jurisprudence are its decisions under the Optional Protocol, its General Comments, and its Concluding Comments. Its Optional Protocol decisions apply the ICCPR in concrete situations, so they deliver the most specific interpretations of the Covenant. As is noted below, the broadbrush approach of Concluding and General Comments has its advantages when dealing with systemic violations of ICCPR rights [1.75].

---

[67] Harris, above, note 27, 38.

[68] For example, Australia has disputed the HRC's interpretation of 'lawful' in *A v Australia* (560/1993) *viz.* art. 9(4); see *Annual Report of the Human Rights Committee* (1998), A/53/40, i, 74; see [11.55] for this aspect of the *A* decision.

[69] *Annual Report of the Human Rights Committee* (1998), A/53/40, i, 61.

[70] See Rules of Procedure of the Human Rights Committee, UN doc. CCPR/C/3/Rev. 5, 11 August 1997, Rule 91.

[1.39] By the end of 1998, the HRC had completed its consideration of nearly 600 communications. It must be noted however that a disproportionate number of communications have concerned a handful of States and a narrow range of subject matters. From 1976 to about 1985, most complaints concerned gross abuses of human rights, including allegations of torture, disappearance, and extended arbitrary detention, by the military government in Uruguay. Since the mid-1980s, a very large number of cases have been submitted by death row prisoners in the Caribbean, particularly Jamaica.[71] These cases have generally concerned the fairness of trials resulting in capital sentences, though a number of these cases have also addressed the length of detention and conditions on death row.[72] This unevenness in 'complaint rate' has caused the HRC's Optional Protocol jurisprudence to be disproportionately concerned with matters pertaining to articles 7, 9, 10, and 14. In contrast, there is relatively little jurisprudence on certain rights, such as those rights enunciated in articles 21 and 22.

[1.40] Despite the disproportionate number of complaints of an essentially similar nature, the Optional Protocol has nevertheless yielded a large body of jurisprudence touching on important aspects of most ICCPR rights. The HRC has dealt with a large number of complicated issues, which have necessitated genuine findings of law rather than mere establishment of facts. For example, Optional Protocol decisions have addressed the ICCPR compatibility of laws, administrative decisions, or practices of the following type: a law that prohibited Holocaust denial,[73] the deportation or extradition of persons in various contexts,[74] passport controls on persons who have failed to perform compulsory military service,[75] detention for reasons of military discipline,[76] detention of illegal immigrants seeking asylum,[77] prohibitions on gay sex,[78] amnesty laws,[79] extended detention on death row,[80] language requirements designed to promote a certain linguistic culture,[81] commercial ventures into indigenous lands,[82] and restrictions on media access to report Parliamentary proceedings.[83]

---

[71] A statistic survey of Optional Protocol decisions on 1 September 1998, posted on the website of the UN High Commissioner for Human Rights at http://www.unhchr.ch/html/menu2/8/stat2.htm, revealed that 177 out of 829 communications concerned Jamaica.

[72] In late 1997, Jamaica took the unprecedented step of withdrawing from the Optional Protocol system. Trinidad and Tobago followed suit in 1998, though it re-acceded to the Optional Protocol on the same day, with a reservation prohibiting complaints about the application of the death sentence. See *Annual Report of the Human Rights Committee* (1998), A/53/40, i, 87, notes f and g.

[73] See *Faurisson v France* (550/93), majority decision excerpted at [18.48].

[74] See, e.g., *Kindler v Canada* (470/91) at [8.27], *Stewart v Canada* (538/93) [12.30] and [20.15]; also see [9.51]ff.

[75] *Peltonen v Finland* (492/92) [12.20].   [76] *Vuolanne v Finland* (265/87) [11.54].

[77] *A v Australia* (560/93) [11.15], [11.52], and [11.55].

[78] *Toonen v Australia* (488/92), at [16.36].   [79] *Rodriguez v Uruguay* (322/88) at [9.90].

[80] *Johnson v Jamaica* (588/94) at [9.41].

[81] *Ballantyne et al. v Canada* (359, 385/89) at [18.38].

[82] See, e.g., *Länsman v Finland* (511/92) at [24.26].

[83] *Gauthier v Canada* (633/95), at [18.27].

[1.41] Arguably the most rigorous Optional Protocol decisions have concerned article 26, the free-standing guarantee of non-discrimination.[84] In landmark decisions in 1987, *Broeks v Netherlands* (172/84) and *Zwaan-de-Vries v Netherlands* (182/84), the HRC found that article 26 guaranteed non-discrimination in relation to all rights, including economic, social, and cultural rights. In numerous subsequent communications, the HRC has had to consider the compatibility of numerous allegedly discriminatory measures in national social welfare policies.

[1.42] The Optional Protocol jurisprudence is of course supplemented by the General Comments and the Concluding Comments, which have addressed numerous issues outside the scope of submitted communications. Finally, important additional matters have been addressed by the other UN treaty bodies.

[1.43] It is generally recognized that human rights texts should be interpreted liberally, so corresponding limitations are to be construed narrowly.[85] Nevertheless, it is difficult to identify any consistent trend of liberalism, radicalism, or conservatism in the HRC's interpretations.[86] For example, the HRC's extension in 1988 of article 26 into the realm of economic, social, and cultural rights may be perceived as radical.[87] However, it has arguably been quite conservative in its subsequent consideration of complaints about discrimination in the allocation of social and economic rights, as it has rarely found actual breaches of article 26. The HRC has displayed a more conservative response to 'the death row phenomenon' than the European Court of Human Rights in *Soering v UK*.[88] Nevertheless, minority opinions in numerous 'death row' cases have been quite radical in characterizing extradition to face the death penalty as breaches of the right to life, despite the clear capital punishment exception in article 6.[89] Furthermore, the HRC has been more radical than the European bodies in its apparent rejection of the cautious doctrine of the margin of appreciation.[90] The

---

[84] Harris, above, note 27, 17; see generally, Chap. 23.

[85] See Siracusa Principles on Limitations and Derogations to the ICCPR (1985) 7 HRQ 3, 4; Nowak, above, note 2, XXIV. See also majority opinion in *Alberta Unions Case* (118/82), para. 5.

[86] Harris, above, note 27, 19–20.

[87] See T. Opsahl, 'Equality in Human Rights Law with Particular Reference to Art. 26 of the International Covenant of Civil and Political Rights' in *Festschrift für Felix Ermacora* (N.P. Engel, Kehl, 1988), at 52, describing the adverse Dutch reaction to the findings in *Broeks* and *Zwaan-de-Vries*; see also Harris, above, note 27, 18, note 92.

[88] See *Soering v UK*, No 161 (1989) II EHRR 439. See, e.g., *Johnson v Jamaica* (588/94), rejecting the *Soering* reasoning [9.41].

[89] See, e.g., minority opinions in *Kindler v Canada* (470/91), at [8.28–8.29].

[90] A doctrine analogous to that of the margin of appreciation has only been expressly used by the HRC once, in *Hertzberg v Finland* (61/79). Former HRC member Roslyn Higgins has since denied its modern-day usage by the HRC. See [18.20–18.21] for discussion of *Hertzberg* and the 'margin' doctrine. See also *Länsman v Finland* (511/92), where the HRC rejected the application of a margin of appreciation in the context of art. 27 minority rights, at para. 9.4: see [24.27]. Finally, see Heffernan, above, note 37, 91.

absence of a consistent HRC interpretative 'philosophy' may be due to the fact that new personnel join the HRC every two years.[91]

[1.44] The HRC can be criticized for occasionally delivering judgments which are accompanied by weak, sparse reasoning. For example, the parties' arguments in *Ominayak v Canada* (167/84), which concerned the ICCPR compatibility of certain commercial developments in indigenous tribal lands, continue for an unprecedented twenty-seven pages in the 1990 Annual Report.[92] The HRC's decision however is a mere five-line statement that historical inequities coupled with recent commercial developments threatened the life and culture of an indigenous Canadian tribe, thus violating the minority rights of members of that tribe. This case gives little guidance on why such an important breach of article 27 was found. The only merits decision on the article 21 guarantee of freedom of assembly, *Kivenmaa v Finland* (412/90), is completely opaque and arguably confused in its reasoning.[93] The brevity and/or tentativeness of certain decisions may well be an unfortunate consequence of the continuous search by the HRC for consensus. Indeed, dissenting opinions[94] or separate concurring opinions[95] often contain more explicit, detailed reasoning. In this respect, the increasing frequency of separate opinions is to be applauded.[96]

[1.45] Nevertheless, there is no doubt that the more recent HRC decisions, General Comments, and Concluding Comments generally exhibit more rigorous reasoning than earlier opinions. In this respect, they have been assisted by the submission of more coherent arguments from the parties. The brevity that impairs *Ominayak* and the confusion that undermines *Kivenmaa* are not traits that universally afflict Optional Protocol decisions.

THE ROLE OF PRECEDENT

[1.46] The HRC is not expressly bound by any doctrine of precedent. Indeed, in a dissenting opinion in *Thomas v Jamaica* (532/1993), Messrs Pocar and Lallah stated:

any . . . views of the Committee based on legal grounds . . . can be reversed or modified at any time, in the light of further arguments raised by Committee members during the consideration of another case.

The HRC majority did not expressly disagree on this point.

[1.47] The HRC has nevertheless expressly followed its own decisions on

---

[91] Most sitting members are usually re-elected. However, there are always a few vacancies caused by retirements, deaths, or the occasional failure to be renominated or re-elected.
[92] See UN doc. A/45/40, ii, 1–30.   [93] See [19.06].
[94] Compare dissenting opinion of Mr Herndl in *Kivenmaa* [19.07].
[95] See separate opinion of Evatt, Kretzmer, and Klein in *Faurisson v France* (550/93) [18.49].
[96] Harris, above, note 27, 37; see also Schmidt, above, note 40.

numerous occasions.[97] Its opportunities for applying its own jurisprudence have however been limited by the fact that numerous cases have evolved around findings of fact rather than law.[98] Whilst it has never expressly contradicted its own previous decisions, it has sporadically expressed inconsistent opinions. For example, the case of *Foin v France* (666/95) appears to overrule the previous decision in *Järvinen v Finland* (295/88).[99] Furthermore, it seems possible that the HRC has retreated from its strong anti-nuclear stance in General Comment 14 on the right to life.[100] Recent Concluding Comments have indicated that the ICCPR may indeed protect the right to strike, contrary to its early decision in *J.B. v Canada* (118/82).[101] The HRC's divergences from its own jurisprudence, though infrequent, are a sign that the ICCPR is a living instrument capable of dynamic development.

[1.48] The HRC has had little opportunity to refer to the decisions of its fellow UN treaty bodies, which have tended to deal with cases in different areas. Nor has it often referred to regional human rights bodies, which have produced an extensive amount of relevant jurisprudence. References to, for example, decisions of the European Court of Human Rights are sparse, and tend to be prompted by the parties' arguments.[102] More consistent reference to comparable international bodies would be preferable, in order to facilitate the development of consistent international human rights principles.[103]

RIGHTS OF INDIVIDUALS

[1.49] The ICCPR generally confers rights on individuals. However, the 'individual as right-bearer' is not a universally accepted model. It is a paradigm that reflects a Western individualistic focus, rather than the communitarian or 'collective rights' focus of certain non-Western societies.[104] Thus, the ICCPR can perhaps be fairly criticized for reflecting a Western cultural norm to the exclusion of other cultural norms.[105] However, some 'rights' within the ICCPR do not attach to individuals.[106] Furthermore, the ICCPR, by prescribing numerous

---

[97] For example, the reasoning regarding the death row phenomenon in *Johnson v Jamaica* (588/94) has been followed in numerous majority decisions, such as *Hylton v Jamaica* (600/1994), *Lewis v Jamaica* (527/1993), and *Spence v Jamaica* (59/1994).

[98] This is the case with most of the Uruguayan and Jamaican cases.

[99] See [23.47–23.48].   [100] See [8.46].

[101] The merits of this decision are excerpted at [19.19]. See also commentary on the HRC's changing jurisprudence on conscientious objection at [17.19–17.22].

[102] See Harris, above, note 27, 15, note 75.   [103] Ibid., 15.

[104] S. Joseph, 'A Rights Analysis of the Covenant on Civil and Political Rights' (1999) 5 *Journal of International Legal Studies*, 67–8. See also J. Donnelly, *Universal Human Rights in Theory and Debate* (Cornell University Press, Ithaca, NY, 1989), especially at 57–60; Donoho, above, note 27, 350, note 15 and citations therein.

[105] F. Jhabvala, 'The International Covenant on Civil and Political Rights as a Vehicle for the Global Promotion and Protection of Human Rights' (1985) 15 *Israel Yearbook on Human Rights* 184, 198.

[106] See Chap. 7 on the right of peoples to self-determination (art. 1), and below [1.75].

permissible limitations to its rights, authorizes many instances where the collective rights and probably the cultural needs of society can trump individual freedoms.[107]

LIMITATIONS TO ICCPR RIGHTS

[1.50] Some ICCPR rights are absolute. Examples of these absolute rights are article 7, which prohibits torture, inhuman and degrading treatment, or punishment; and article 8(1), which prohibits slavery. A State cannot impose limits on an absolute right unless it has entered a valid derogation under article 4,[108] or has entered a valid reservation.[109]

[1.51] Where limitations are permitted to ICCPR rights, they must generally be prescribed by national law.[110] This means that the circumstances in which the limitation will be imposed are clearly delineated in an accessible law, whether that be statute law or common law.[111] The law should not be so vague as to permit too much discretion and unpredictability in its implementation.[112]

[1.52] Some ICCPR rights (i.e. articles 12(1) and (2), 13, part of 14(1), 18(1), 19(2), 21, and 22) list permissible limitations, such as public order, national security, and protection of the rights of others.[113] All enumerated limitations must be 'necessary in a democratic society', which imports a notion of proportionality in determining the permissibility of a particular limitation.[114] Other ICCPR rights (i.e. articles 6(1), 9(1), article 12(4), and 17) permit 'non-arbitrary' limits. The notion of 'arbitrariness' also incorporates proportionality into the determination of the extent of such limits.[115] Article 25 rights, which may expressly be limited by 'reasonable' measures, and article 26 rights of non-discrimination, which may be limited, according to HRC jurisprudence,[116] by 'reasonable and objective' measures, are similarly limited by the notion of proportionality.[117] Therefore, despite the differently worded permissible limitations, most ICCPR rights may be limited by proportionate laws designed to protect a countervailing community

---

[107] Donoho, above, note 27, 378. See also Joseph, above, note 104, 68.

[108] However, most absolute rights are non-derogable. Art. 10(1) is a derogable right, despite being drafted in absolute language.

[109] See Chap. 25 on a State Party's rights of reservation.

[110] This requirement is expressed in different ways throughout the different ICCPR guarantees.

[111] See Nowak, above, note 2, 171. See also *Sunday Times v UK* (1979–80) 2 EHRR 245, para. 49, confirming that judge-made laws may constitute sufficiently prescribed 'laws' for the purposes of limitations to rights under the European Convention.

[112] See, e.g., *Pinkney v Canada* (27/78), at [16.11]. See also General Comment 27, para. 13 [12.23].

[113] These limitations have not been interpreted in the context of every relevant right. However, it seems that the terms would be interpreted in a similar manner in all contexts.

[114] See *Pietraroia v Uruguay* (44/79), para. 16, and separate opinion of Evatt, Kretzmer, and Klein in *Faurisson v France* (550/93), para. 8 of their separate opinion at [18.49].

[115] See *Toonen v Australia* (488/92), para. 8.3 [16.13].   [116] See [23.40] ff.

[117] Harris, above, note 27, 13.

benefit, such as public order, or to protect the conflicting right of another person.[118]

[1.53] The dividing line between an ICCPR right and its limitations is by no means clear, especially at the 'edges' of a right. The edges of a right may be characterized as the area between blatant conformity with the right and blatant non-conformity.[119] The compatibility of a law impacting on the edges of a human right with that human right is generally worked out on a case-by-case basis, unless there exists a highly relevant precedent. This uncertainty confirms that the abstract ICCPR rights have not been totally concretized. The process of concretization occurs over time through the growth of HRC jurisprudence, and is facilitated by municipal decisions on ICCPR rights, and academic writings.[120]

POSITIVE OBLIGATIONS

[1.54] Civil and political rights are classically perceived as freedoms from the arbitrary interference of the State.[121] Therefore, they are generally conceptualized as 'negative' rights that States refrain from certain actions. This traditional conception of civil and political rights has largely contributed to the perception that these rights are cost-free, in that it does not 'cost' a State to refrain from doing something. Cost-free rights may also more fairly be imposed immediately, which in turn renders them justiciable. These 'characteristics' of civil and political rights may be contrasted with those commonly associated with economic, social, and cultural rights. The latter rights are traditionally perceived as positive, in that States are required to take action to provide them (e.g. States are required to provide for adequate health care and standards of education). Positive rights are consequently perceived as costly, progressive, and non-justiciable. Indeed, this sharply perceived divide between civil and political rights, and economic, social, and cultural rights, largely contributed to the decision to split the two sets of rights into two Covenants.[122]

---

[118] See P. Hassan, 'International Covenant on Civil and Political Rights: Background Perspectives on Article 9(1)' (1973) 3 *Denver Journal of International Law and Policy* 153, detailing the drafting history of the inclusion of the word 'arbitrary' into art. 9(1), in place of an enumerated list of limitations to one's right to liberty. Hassan concludes that the prohibition of 'arbitrary' restrictions on liberty 'could provide better safeguards against governmental oppression of its peoples than any article with a detailed list of limitations' (at 183).

[119] See M. Delmas-Marty, 'The Richness of Underlying Legal Reasoning' in M. Delmas-Marty (ed.), *The European Convention for the Protection of Human Rights* (Martinus Nijhoff, Dordrecht, 1992), 332.

[120] Joseph, above, note 104, 80.   [121] McGoldrick, above, note 46, 11.

[122] Ibid. See also C. Scott, 'The Interdependence and Permeability of Human Rights Norms: Towards a Partial Fusion of the International Covenants on Human Rights' (1989) 27 *Osgoode Hall Law Journal* 769, 832. At 833, Scott provides a list of common perceived 'characteristics' of, on the one hand, economic, social, and cultural rights and, on the other, civil and political rights. Civil and political rights are characterized as 'immediate', 'justiciable', and 'real or legal rights', whilst economic, social, and cultural rights are characterized as 'progressive', 'non-justiciable', and 'aspirations or goals'.

[1.55] However, it is a divide that has proven simplistic and flawed. Indeed, intuition suffices to identify positive aspects within numerous ICCPR articles. For example, the article 10(1) guarantee of humane treatment in detention necessitates the construction of a sufficient number of detention centres to prevent overcrowding. The article 14(1) right to a fair trial obviously necessitates provision of independent organs of justice. The article 25(b) right to vote fundamentally involves provision of apparatus to ensure fair elections. The express duties to protect families in article 23 and children in article 24 overtly require positive measures.

[1.56] The HRC has expressly found numerous positive duties imposed on States by the various substantive ICCPR rights. It has stated that States have duties to investigate allegations of ICCPR breach,[123] and duties to provide procedures and mechanisms to prevent the occurrence of ICCPR breaches.[124] Relevant personnel should be appropriately trained so as to instil in them knowledge of how to behave in conformity with the Covenant.[125] A duty to educate the general population to imbue society with a human rights culture is mentioned in numerous Concluding Comments.[126] Finally, the HRC expressly incorporated positive obligations into its interpretation of article 27, the minority rights guarantee, in General Comment 23.[127]

[1.57] Linked to the HRC's uncovering of positive aspects to civil and political rights has been its willingness to 'permeate' ICCPR rights with significant economic, social, and cultural elements.[128] As mentioned above, article 26 has been interpreted to extend to non-discrimination in the arena of economic, social, and cultural rights [1.41]. Article 6, the right to life, has been interpreted to incorporate a duty upon States to tackle infant mortality, epidemics, and to take measures to increase life expectancy.[129] Thus, States are required to provide a certain standard of health care, which is traditionally perceived as a social right.

[1.58] HRC jurisprudence has gone some way towards undermining the traditional divide between civil and political rights, and economic, social, and cultural rights. The HRC has confirmed that all ICCPR rights impose negative duties of forbearance and positive duties of performance on States Parties.[130]

---

[123] See, e.g., General Comment 20, para. 14, on the duty to investigate allegations of breaches of art. 7 [9.83].

[124] See, e.g., ibid., para. 11 [9.76].   [125] See, e.g., ibid., para. 10 [9.75].

[126] See, e.g., Concluding Comments on Hungary, (1994) UN doc. CCPR/C/79/Add. 22, para. 11; Concluding Comments on Ecuador (1998) UN doc. CCPR/C/79/Add. 92, para. 21.

[127] See [24.36–24.37].   [128] See generally Scott, above, note 122.

[129] See General Comment 6 on art. 6, para. 5, at [8.39].

[130] Nowak, above, note 2, p. xviii.

HORIZONTAL OBLIGATIONS

[1.59] A particular type of positive ICCPR duty is a duty placed upon States Parties to protect individuals from undue interference with their ICCPR rights by other people. This type of duty refers to the 'horizontal effects' of the Covenant.[131] To what extent does the ICCPR oblige States to impose duties on private entities to respect the rights of others?

[1.60] Some ICCPR rights have an express horizontal effect. Article 20 requires States to prohibit war propaganda, and the advocacy of national, racial, or religious hatred.[132] Articles 6(1) and 17(2) state that the rights to life and privacy, respectively, shall be protected by law. Therefore, States must provide legal protection from homicides and intrusions into privacy by private entities.[133] The other UN treaties also provide that rights therein have a horizontal effect. For example, both anti-discrimination treaties require that measures be taken to combat, respectively, race and sex discrimination in the private sphere.[134] Finally, the HRC has frequently alluded to the horizontal effects of ICCPR rights in its General Comments. For example, in General Comments regarding articles 7 and 26, the HRC has stressed that States Parties should take measures to combat private acts of, respectively, torture, inhuman and degrading treatment, and discrimination.[135]

[1.61] The HRC has had little opportunity to analyse the horizontal effects of ICCPR rights in Optional Protocol cases. Its early decision in *Hertzberg v Finland* (61/79) indicated that such effects were very weak in the area of freedom of expression.[136] However, in *B.d.B. v the Netherlands* (273/88), the HRC said that a State Party is 'not relieved of obligations under the Covenant when some of its functions are delegated to other autonomous organs'.[137] The relevant 'autonomous organ' was an industrial board made up of representatives of employer and employee organizations, which had no formal connection to the government.[138] Subsequent decisions, such as *Delgado Páez v Colombia* (195/85) on the right to security of the person, and *L.K. v The Netherlands* (CERD No. 4/1991), a decision by the Committee on the Elimination of Racial Discrimination (CERD) on the ICERD obligation to prohibit racial hatred,[139] have confirmed the horizontal application of UN civil and political rights law.

---

[131] Ibid., 38.   [132] See generally Chap. 18.

[133] See, on private homicides [8.36–8.38], and on private invasions of privacy, [16.18–16.20].

[134] See, e.g., Art. 2(d) ICERD and Art. 2(e) CEDAW.   [135] See [9.19] and [23.71].

[136] See [18.23].

[137] At para. 6.6; see also *Lindgren et al. v Sweden* (298–9/88), para. 10.4.

[138] The case was inadmissible for other reasons. See also *Nahlik v Austria* (608/95), para. 8.2 [23.72].

[139] Art. 4 ICERD partially mirrors Art. 20 ICCPR; the latter goes further in requiring States to prohibit national and religious hatred, see generally Chap. 18.

[1.62] The ability to enjoy most ICCPR human rights would be totally under-mined if States had no duties to control human rights abuse in the private sector. It is therefore likely that the general duty in article 2(1) on States to 'ensure' ICCPR rights entails a duty, of perhaps varying degrees of strictness, to protect individuals from abuse of all ICCPR rights by others.[140]

ARTICLE 50: APPLICABILITY OF THE COVENANT IN FEDERAL STATES

[1.63] Article 50 ICCPR stipulates that the Covenant's guarantees 'extend to all parts of federal States without any limitations or exceptions'. Thus, central governments in federations, such as the United States, Canada, Australia, Brazil, and the Russian Federation, are required to guarantee that the laws and activities of their provincial counterparts conform to the Covenant's norms. Indeed, viola-tions of the Covenant have been found in a number of cases where the impugned law was a provincial law rather than a federal law.[141] The violation is neverthe-less attributed to the central government, as it is the government with interna-tional legal personality, and the actual treaty party.

[1.64] Article 50 is an important guarantor of ICCPR rights. The effect of the ICCPR would be considerably diminished in federations if the provincial legal realm were excluded from the Covenant's reach. However, it must be conceded that article 50 can create internal legal problems for central governments where they lack constitutional power to override or 'correct' provincial laws that breach the Covenant.[142]

CULTURAL AND ECONOMIC RELATIVISM

[1.65] The HRC has never issued a consensus opinion on the relevance of cultural relativism in its interpretation of the ICCPR. Cultural relativism pertains to the idea that human rights values, including ICCPR norms, vary across cultures. A related argument is more appropriately termed 'economic relativism', whereby it is postulated that the full exercise of certain rights is unsuitable in States with vulnerable developing economies.[143] At issue is the degree to which human rights are truly universal, or whether uniform imposition of human rights

---

[140] See also A. Clapham, *Human Rights in the Private Sphere* (Clarendon Press, Oxford, 1993), 107–12.

[141] See, e.g., *Ballantyne et al. v Canada* (359, 385/89), at [18.38] and *Toonen v Australia* (488/92), at [16.36].

[142] For example, the Canadian federal government does not necessarily have power over matters arising under international treaties, including the ICCPR; see, e.g., *Attorney-General (Canada) v Attorney-General (Ontario)* [1937] AC 326. Therefore, the federal government may have to negotiate with provincial governments in order to correct ICCPR abuses. In contrast, the Australian federal government may override State laws that contradict Australia's obligations under international treaties: see, e.g., *Commonwealth v Tasmania* (1983) 158 CLR 1.

[143] A. Pollis, 'Cultural Relativism Revisited: Through a State Prism' (1996) 18 HRQ 316, 317.

standards amounts to cultural imperialism,[144] or is economically unviable. Interpretation of the ICCPR, a universal treaty with States Parties across the cultural and economic spectrum, by the HRC with its multinational membership, should provide fertile ground for identifying and perhaps resolving cultural clashes over human rights.

[1.66] The ICCPR is generally enunciated in universalist language. For example, the preamble cites the 'inherent dignity' and the 'equal and inalienable rights of all members of the human family'. Such words do not import notions of different rights for members of different cultures. Furthermore, States Parties have freely ratified the treaty. After such consensual ratification, it perhaps seems unconvincing for a State to claim cultural exemption from certain rights. Finally, the immediacy of the article 2(1) obligation, especially when compared to the progressiveness of the ICESCR obligation, seems to confirm that ICCPR implementation cannot be 'delayed' until economic circumstances improve.[145]

[1.67] However, the ICCPR does cater to some extent for cultural differences. First, States can enter relevant reservations if they refuse to implement certain rights.[146] The HRC has however purported severely to limit State rights of reservation in its General Comment 24. The HRC listed a number of rights to which no reservation could be allowed, including some rights at the crossroads of cultural argument, such as freedom of thought, conscience, and religion (article 18(1)). Indeed, General Comment 24 has proven to be quite controversial, though 'cultural' objections to it have not been specifically raised.[147]

[1.68] Secondly, the existence of numerous limitations to certain ICCPR rights does allow some room for cultural diversity in their interpretation. For example, a number of rights may be expressly limited by proportionate measures designed to protect 'public morals', which must be a relative concept varying in its application from State to State.[148] Indeed, the uncertainty entailed in ICCPR limitations introduces flexibility to human rights interpretation, and generates ideological and cultural debate over the content of human rights guarantees.[149] It is possible that the HRC might apply these limitations differently in the context of different cultural or economic circumstances.

[1.69] So far no Optional Protocol complaints have raised crucial cultural relativist issues. In *Toonen v Australia* (488/1992), a complaint about Tasmania's prohibition on gay sex was unanimously upheld by the HRC as a breach of the article 17 right to privacy.[150] In its views, the HRC were expressly influenced by

---

[144] Donoho, above, note 27, 346.
[145] Note however the apparent progressive obligation in art. 23(4): see [20.31].
[146] Donoho, above, note 27, 364.   [147] See generally Chap. 25.
[148] See, e.g., *Delgado Páez v Colombia* (195/85), at [18.24].
[149] See Donoho, above, note 27, at 370, and 382–4.   [150] See [16.36].

evidence of tolerance and acceptance of homosexuality in Australia.[151] This may indicate that a different decision would result if an identical complaint came from a State Party with no comparable record of tolerance.[152] However, in a number of subsequent Concluding Comments, the HRC expressed concern over laws prohibiting sexual relationships between consenting adult partners of the same sex.[153] This may indicate that the *Toonen* decision does have universal application.

[1.70] The HRC has obliquely addressed the issue of cultural relativism in several Concluding Comments. It has generally exhibited little inclination to concede that ICCPR rights are culturally variable. Rather, it has recommended that States take appropriate steps to dismantle oppressive traditional or cultural structures, particularly those that perpetuate inequality between the sexes.[154] Furthermore, it has not deferred to fundamentalist Islamic laws that restrict the ability of Moslems to change their religion.[155] Regarding Senegal, it has criticized the practice of polygamy and the strict prohibition of abortion.[156] Finally, it has condemned female genital mutilation as a practice that breaches the rights to life (article 6) and freedom from cruel, inhuman, and degrading treatment (article 7), despite the cultural significance of this practice in certain societies.[157]

[1.71] However, the HRC has also recognized that the reversal of traditional attitudes cannot realistically occur overnight. For example, regarding Cameroon, the HRC has stated in relation to systemic sex discrimination:[158]

¶ 25.   The Committee invites the Government to improve the situation of women with a

---

[151] The HRC rejected arguments by Tasmania, submitted via the State Party, that the laws were indeed necessary to protect public morality in Tasmania. The HRC implicitly rejected the veracity of the Tasmanian relativist argument, rather than the validity of relativist arguments *per se*.

[152] See Joseph, above, note 59, 404–8.

[153] See, e.g., Concluding Comments on Lesotho (1999) UN doc. CCPR/C/79/Add. 106, para. 13; see also Concluding Comments on United Republic of Tanzania (1998) UN doc. CCPR/C/79/Add. 97, para. 23.

[154] See, e.g., Concluding Comments on Morocco (1996) UN doc. CCPR/C/79/Add. 4, para. 4; Concluding Comments on Yemen (1995) UN doc. CCPR/C/79/Add. 51, paras. 4 and 20; Concluding Comments on Zambia (1996) UN doc. CCPR/C/79/Add. 62, paras. 3 and 9; Concluding Comments on Cambodia (1999), UN doc. CCPR/C/79/Add, 108, para. 17; Concluding Comments on Ecuador (1998), UN doc. CCPR/C/79/Add. 92, para. 16; Concluding Comments on Sudan (1997) UN doc. CCPR/C/79/Add. 85, para. 11; Concluding Comments on the United Republic of Tanzania (1998) UN doc. CCPR/C/79/Add. 97, para. 12; Concluding Comments on Zimbabwe (1998) UN doc. CCPR/C/79/Add. 89, para. 12.

[155] See, e.g., General Comment 22, para. 5, at [17.05]; Concluding Comments on Jordan (1994) UN doc. CCPR/C/79/Add. 53, para. 10; Concluding Comments on the Islamic Republic of Iran (1993) UN doc. CCPR/C/79/Add. 25, para. 16.

[156] (1997) UN doc. CCPR/C/79/Add. 82, para. 12. See also [8.47] regarding abortion.

[157] Concluding Comments on Lesotho (1999) UN doc. CCPR/C/79/Add. 106, para. 12; Concluding Comments on Senegal (1997) UN doc. CCPR/C/79/Add. 82, para. 12; Concluding Comments on Sudan (1997) UN doc. CCPR/C.79/Add. 85, para. 10; Concluding Comments on the United Republic of Tanzania (1998) UN doc. CCPR/C/79/Add. 97, para. 11.

[158] Concluding Comments on Cameroon (1994) UN doc. CCPR/C/79/Add. 33, para. 25.

view to achieving the effective application of article 3 of the Covenant, in particular by adopting the necessary educational and other measures to overcome the weight of certain customs and traditions. . . .

Regarding Senegal, the HRC stated the following:[159]

¶ 12. . . . The Committee encourages the State party to launch a systematic campaign to promote popular awareness of persistent negative attitudes towards women . . .

The HRC's occasional emphasis on educational rather than coercive measures may signal some sort of exemption from the normal immediacy of ICCPR obligations in culturally sensitive areas.

[1.72] Some of the most acute cultural problems arise with regard to the implementation of equal rights for women. It is not surprising therefore that the CEDAW Committee has addressed the cultural dimension in some important General Recommendations.[160] The CEDAW Committee, like the HRC, has also stressed the universal application of women's rights of equality, thus rejecting contrary arguments based on cultural sanctity. For example, in its General Recommendation 14, the CEDAW Committee condemned the practice of female circumcision. However, the CEDAW Committee recommended that educative measures be taken to combat the continued practice of female circumcision, rather than the immediate implementation of coercive laws to punish perpetrators.[161] The CEDAW Committee recognizes that it necessarily takes time to eradicate abusive practices that have a cultural base.

[1.73] The HRC has not generally accepted economic relativist arguments. For example, in *Mukong v Cameroon* (458/91), it refused to accept that economic hardship and budgetary considerations could excuse the State from liability for the atrocious prison conditions suffered by the author.[162] In *Lubuto v Zambia* (390/90), economic hardship could not justify the delay in the complainant's appeal.[163] Finally, in its General Comment 21 on article 10, the HRC noted that the obligation to treat detainees with respect for their dignity 'cannot be dependent on the material resources available in the State party'.[164] Underdevelopment cannot therefore justify overcrowding in prisons, or the failure to provide adequate resources to detainees. On the other hand, in *Aumeeruddy-Sziffra et al. v Mauritius* (35/78), the HRC did state that the level of protection required for families under article 23 may vary according to 'different social, economic, political and cultural conditions and traditions'.[165] This may indicate that economic

---

[159] (1997) UN doc. CCPR/C/79/Add. 82.

[160] General Recommendations are the CEDAW equivalent of HRC General Comments.

[161] In contrast, the HRC recommended 'that the practice be made punishable under law' in Comments on Lesotho and Sudan, above, note 157. However, note that CEDAW obligations are not expressly immediate, unlike ICCPR obligations under art. 2(1).

[162] See [9.27] and [9.67].

[163] See [14.73]; see also HRC decision in *Fillastre and Bizouarn v Bolivia* (336/88) [11.34].

[164] See General Comment 21, para. 4 [9.100].   [165] Para. 9.2.(b) 2 (ii) 1: see [20.05].

relativism does apply to the level of entitlement entailed in article 23 rights. However, economic relativism does not generally apply to ICCPR rights, unlike the rights in the ICESCR.[166]

SYSTEMIC HUMAN RIGHTS ABUSE

[1.74] Although ICCPR rights are essentially bestowed on individuals, certain civil and political rights abuses are so endemic that they cannot realistically be addressed at an individual level. For example, systemic inequality may arise where certain groups have been oppressed in a certain society for centuries. Yet it is hard to prove that one is an individual victim of 'systemic inequality'.[167] Such systemic abuses of civil and political rights are not so easily identifiable or rectifiable under the individualistic Optional Protocol procedure.

[1.75] The prevalence of systemic human rights abuse demonstrates the fallacy in conceiving all human rights in terms of individual rights. Some of the more 'systemic' human rights duties of States are better viewed conceptually as people's rights. For example, the right of self-determination in article 1 expressly belongs to peoples, and cannot in fact be enforced under the individual complaints mechanism.[168] In this respect, the General Comments and Concluding Comments provide important consensus interpretations of ICCPR rights, particularly in regard to complex issues at a macro level.

Conclusion

[1.76] The ICCPR is probably the most important human rights treaty in the world. Unlike the regional treaties, it is open to a universal membership. It covers a wide range of rights, and thus offers much broader protection than the single-issue treaties like CAT. Unlike its sister Covenant, the ICESCR, there now exists a large body of jurisprudence that gives meaningful content to its norms.

[1.77] There are significant deficiencies in the ICCPR system. Most obviously, the enforcement mechanisms are extremely weak. ICCPR violations probably occur without remedy within all States Parties. Concluding Comments and adverse Optional Protocol decisions are too often ignored, especially by the worst violators. However, weak enforcement characterizes the entire system of international law, rather than just human rights.

[1.78] The work of the HRC has been hampered by a lack of resources. It is

---

[166] The ICESCR implicitly recognizes that poorer States cannot guarantee ICESCR rights to the same extent as richer States in its progressive obligation provision; art. 2(1).
[167] See [23.77] ff.
[168] See, e.g., *Kitok v Sweden* (197/85), at para. [7.20].

largely reliant upon the good will of States and/or NGOs for much of its information. Its annual sitting time of nine weeks is far too short, leading to long
delays in the issue of OP views, and long intervals between the submission of a
State report and the subsequent examination of that report by the HRC.

[1.79] Despite these deficiencies, the civil and political rights norms developed
under the ICCPR and other UN treaties are of obvious relevance to the interpretation of these rights by judges, lawyers, government officials, and human rights
advocates in all municipal jurisdictions due to their universal applicability. Those
norms, as well as the strengths and shortcomings of the jurisprudence of the HRC
and the other treaty bodies, are explored in excerpts and accompanying commen-
taries in the following chapters.

Postscript: Please note that General Comment 28 on 'Equality of Rights
Between Men and Women', contained in the Addendum at page 634, contains
extra information on some of the material in this chapter.

Part II

Admissibility
under the ICCPR

2

The 'Ratione Temporis' Rule

Introduction

[2.01] Under article 1 of the First Optional Protocol (OP), a claim can only be brought by an individual against a State Party to the Covenant which is also a party to the Protocol. Under article 3 OP, no communication may be submitted which is 'incompatible with the provisions of the Covenant'. Under these two provisions, the Committee is precluded from adjudicating on a matter if it is inadmissible *ratione temporis* (by reason of time). If the facts complained of date from a period prior to that on which the OP entered into force with respect to the State Party concerned, the Committee is incompetent *ratione temporis* to consider the application. The basis of this rule flows from the generally recognized principle of international law, that treaties will not have a retroactive effect.[1]

[2.02] *Kim v Republic of Korea* (574/94) demonstrates that it is important to know what event has given rise to the complaint. The author complained here of his conviction under a National Security Law for his expression of certain political opinions. The State Party argued that, as the author's violations of the National Security Law occurred before entry into force of the OP, the complaint was inadmissible *ratione temporis*. The HRC disagreed, as 'the violation alleged by the author was his *conviction* under the National Security Law', rather than the events giving rise to the conviction. The conviction occurred after entry into force of the OP.[2] Furthermore, in *Somers v Hungary* (566/93), the complaint concerned, in part, the expropriation of the author's parent's property by the Hungarian Communist government in 1951. This complaint was obviously inadmissible *ratione temporis*.[3] However, the complaint also concerned subsequent restitution legislation adopted by the new Hungarian government in 1991 and

---

[1] See J. S. Davidson, 'Admissibility under the Optional Protocol to the International Covenant on Civil and Political Rights' (1991) 4 *Canterbury Law Review* 337, at 342, citing arts. 4 and 28 of the Vienna Convention on the Law of Treaties.

[2] See also *Holland v Ireland* (593/1994), para. 9.2. See also T. Zwart, *The Admissibility of Human Rights Petitions* (Martinus Nijhoff, Dordrecht, 1994), 125–6.

[3] It was also inadmissible *ratione materiae* as the ICCPR does not guarantee a right to property.

1992, after the entry into force of the OP for Hungary. As the 1991–2 legislation redressed the losses of only some victims of the communist expropriations but not others, it could be challenged as a breach of the article 26 guarantee of non-discrimination.[4]

When does Time Begin?

[2.03] One issue is whether the Committee may examine violations of the Covenant that occurred after entry into force of the Covenant but prior to entry into force of the OP. This issue has been addressed by the Committee in numerous cases, including *Könye and Könye v Hungary* (520/92).

KÖNYE and KÖNYE v HUNGARY (520/92)

¶ 6.4. The Committee begins by noting that the State party's obligations under the Covenant apply as of the date of its entry into force for the State party. There is, however, a different issue as to when the Committee's competence to consider complaints about alleged violations of the Covenant under the Optional Protocol is engaged. In its jurisprudence under the Optional Protocol, the Committee has held that it cannot consider alleged violations of the Covenant which occurred before the entry into force of the Optional Protocol for the State party, unless the violations complained of continue after the entry into force of the Optional Protocol. . . .

This view has been upheld consistently by the Committee.[5]

[2.04] Only one member of the Committee has ever questioned the rule that cases are inadmissible if they concern events that arise after the relevant State has ratified the Covenant, but before that State's ratification of the Optional Protocol. This dissenting opinion arose in the following case.

ADUAYOM et al. v TOGO (422/90)

In this case, the Committee majority found that the complainants' allegations regarding breaches of article 9 were inadmissible *ratione temporis*. Mr Pocar dissented in the following terms:

[I]t is my personal view that the claim under article 9, paragraph 1, could have been considered by the Committee even if the alleged facts occurred prior to the entry into force of the Optional Protocol for Togo. As I had the opportunity to indicate with regard to other communications, and in more general terms when the Committee discussed its General Comment on reservations (see CCPR/C/SR.1369, page 6, paragraph 31), the Optional

---

⁴ Paras. 6.3–6.4; the case was subsequently dismissed on the merits.
⁵ See also *M.T. v Spain* (310/88), *A.I.E. v Libya Arab Jamahiriya* (457/91), *Perera v Australia* (536/93), *K.L.B.W. v Australia* (499/92), and *A.S. and L.S. v Australia* (490/92).

Protocol provides for a procedure which enables the Committee to monitor the implementation of the obligations assumed by States parties to the Covenant, but it has no substantive impact on the obligations as such, which must be observed as from the entry into force of the Covenant. In other words, it enables the Committee to consider violations of such obligations not only within the reporting procedure established under article 40 of the Covenant, but also in the context of the consideration of individual communications. From the merely procedural nature of the Optional Protocol it follows that, unless a reservation is entered by a State party upon accession to the Protocol, the Committee's competence also extends to events that occurred before the entry into force of the Optional Protocol for that State, provided such events occurred or continued to have effects after the entry into force of the Covenant.

No other Committee member has expressly supported Mr Pocar's view. However, a violation of the Covenant constitutes a breach of the ICCPR whether a State has ratified the OP or not. Nowak therefore argues that 'the date of entry into force of the OP is relevant only for the submission of the communication but not for the violations it alleges'.[6] It is therefore submitted that Pocar's questioning of the Committee's stance on this issue is legally persuasive.[7]

[2.05] In *Párkányi v Hungary* (410/90), the State Party failed to object to the Committee's competence to hear a claim concerning the author's detention, despite the fact that the impugned events occurred after entry into force of the Covenant for Hungary, but prior to entry into force of the OP. Indeed, the State Party expressly conceded that the communication was admissible *ratione temporis*.[8] The Committee majority, in considering itself competent to hear the claim, implicitly found that Hungary had validly waived its rights in this respect.[9] *Párkányi* is the only case where the Committee has not strictly applied the *ratione temporis* rule.[10]

Continuing Violations

[2.06] As specified in *Könye and Könye v Hungary* (520/1992) [2.03] and other cases, there is an exception to the rule of *ratione temporis,* which is where the alleged violation is a continuing violation. The Committee can consider a communication concerning an alleged violation occurring before the date of entry into force of the OP, where the alleged violation continues or has effects which themselves constitute violations after that date.

---

[6] M. Nowak, *CCPR Commentary* (N.P. Engel, Kehl, 1993), at 679.

[7] See also Zwart, above, note 2, 135–7; P. R. Ghandhi, *The Human Rights Committee and the Right of Individual Communication* (Ashgate, Brookfield, Vermont, 1998), 156–7.

[8] Para. 4.

[9] Mr Wennergren dissented, finding that the HRC had no competence in international law to examine such complaints, regardless of any consent on behalf of the State Party.

[10] See also Zwart, above, note 2, 137–8. Cf., e.g., *Mukunto v Zambia* (768/97), where certain allegations were inadmissible *ratione temporis* despite the State Party's failure to raise the issue (para. 6.3).

[2.07]   *LOVELACE v CANADA (24/77)*

In this case the author, Sandra Lovelace, married a non-Indian on 23 May 1970 and consequently lost her status as a Maliseet Indian under the Indian Act, approximately six years before entry into force of the Optional Protocol in Canada. She challenged this circumstance as a breach of her minority rights under article 27. Although the State Party did not raise any objections in this respect to admissibility, the Committee *ex officio* examined whether it had competence *ratione temporis* to hear the communication.

¶ 7.3. In regard to the present communication, however, the Human Rights Committee must also take into account that the Covenant entered into force in respect of Canada on 19 August 1976, several years after the marriage of Mrs. Lovelace. She consequently lost her status as an Indian at a time when Canada was not bound by the Covenant. The Human Rights Committee has held that it is empowered to consider a communication when the measures complained of, although they occurred before the entry into force of the Covenant, continued to have effects which themselves constitute a violation of the Covenant after that date. It is therefore relevant for the Committee to know whether the marriage of Mrs. Lovelace in 1970 has had any such effects.

¶ 7.4. Since the author of the communication is ethnically an Indian, some persisting effects of her loss of legal status as an Indian may, as from the entry into force of the Covenant for Canada, amount to a violation of rights protected by the Covenant. The Human Rights Committee has been informed that persons in her situation are denied the right to live on an Indian reserve with resultant separation from the Indian community and members of their families. Such prohibition may affect rights which the Covenant guarantees in articles 12 (1), 17, 23 (1), 24 and 27. There may be other such effects of her loss of status. . . .

¶ 10. The Human Rights Committee, in the examination of the communication before it, has to proceed from the basic fact that Sandra Lovelace married a non Indian on 23 May 1970 and consequently lost her status as a Maliseet Indian under section 12 (1) (b) of the Indian Act. This provision was, and still is, based on a distinction *de jure* on the ground of sex. However, neither its application to her marriage as the cause of her loss of Indian status nor its effects could at that time amount to a violation of the Covenant, because this instrument did not come into force for Canada until 19 August 1976. Moreover, the Committee is not competent, as a rule, to examine allegations relating to events having taken place before the entry into force of the Covenant and the Optional Protocol. Therefore as regards Canada it can only consider alleged violations of human rights occurring on or after 19 August 1976. In the case of a particular individual claiming to be a victim of a violation, it cannot express its view on the law in the abstract, without regard to the date on which this law was applied to the alleged victim. In the case of Sandra Lovelace it follows that the Committee is not competent to express any view on the original cause of her loss of Indian status, i.e. the Indian Act as applied to her at the time of her marriage in 1970.

¶ 11. The Committee recognizes, however, that the situation may be different if the alleged violations, although relating to events occurring before 19 August 1976, continue, or have effects which themselves constitute violations, after that date. In examining the situation of Sandra Lovelace in this respect, the Committee must have regard to all relevant provisions of the Covenant. It has considered, in particular, the extent to which the general provisions in articles 2 and 3 as well as the rights in articles 12 (1), 17 (1), 23 (1), 24, 26 and 27, may be applicable to the facts of her present situation.

The Committee came to the conclusion that the communication was admissible *ratione temporis*:[11]

¶ 13.1. The Committee considers that the essence of the present complaint concerns the continuing effect of the Indian Act, in denying Sandra Lovelace legal status as an Indian, in particular because she cannot for this reason claim a legal right to reside where she wishes to, on the Tobique Reserve. This fact persists after the entry into force of the Covenant, and its effects have to be examined, without regard to their original cause. . . .

[2.08] *J.L. v AUSTRALIA (491/92)*

In this case the complainant was a solicitor who had not been willing to pay the annual fee required by the Law Institute of Victoria to renew his practising certificate. As a consequence the Law Institute refused to issue his practising certificate and he continued to practise without the certificate. At the application of the Institute the Supreme Court fined the author, struck his name off the roll of barristers and solicitors, and ordered that he be imprisoned for contempt of court. The author complained to the Committee that he had been denied proceedings before an independent and impartial tribunal, contrary to article 14. He made the following comments regarding the issue of *ratione temporis*:

¶ 3.3. With respect to the date of entry into force of the Optional Protocol for Australia, it is claimed that the violation of article 14 of the Covenant has continuing effects, in that the author remains struck off the roll of solicitors of the Supreme Court, without any prospect of being reinstated.

The Committee agreed with the author:

¶ 4.2. The Committee has noted the author's claim that his detention between 1 September and 29 November 1991 was unlawful. It observes that this event occurred prior to the entry into force of the Optional Protocol for Australia (25 December 1991), and that it does not have consequences which in themselves constitute a violation of any of the provisions of the Covenant. Accordingly, this part of the communication is inadmissible *ratione temporis*. As to the author's contention that he was denied a fair and impartial hearing, the Committee notes that although the relevant court hearings took place before 25 December 1991, the effects of the decisions taken by the Supreme Court continue until the present time. Accordingly, complaints about violations of the author's rights allegedly ensuing from these decisions are not in principle excluded *ratione temporis*.

However, the Committee found the case inadmissible for other reasons.[12]

---

[11] On the merits decision, see [24.12].

[12] The communication was ultimately found to be incompatible with the provisions of the Covenant. See also *M.A. v Italy* (117/81), para. 13.2.

[2.09] The Committee has found continuing violations, enabling communications to be found admissible *ratione temporis*, in numerous other cases, including *Kulomin v Hungary* (521/1991) and *Gueye et al. v France* (196/1989).

[2.10]   *S.E. v ARGENTINA (275/88)*

The authors complained about the 'disappearance' of their relatives at the hands of State agents. These disappearances, and any consequent violations, were however found to have occurred before 1986, the date of entry into force of the OP for Argentina. The authors further claimed that the enactment of the Due Obedience Act of 1987, which commenced after entry into force of the OP for Argentina, itself violated a number of articles of the Covenant. The law effectively conferred impunity on military personnel for potentially gross violations of human rights. The Committee made the following comments regarding inadmissibility.

¶ 5.3. . . . The author has invoked article 2 of the Covenant and claimed a violation of the right to a remedy. In this contest the Committee recalls its prior jurisprudence that article 2 of the Covenant constitutes a general undertaking by States and cannot be invoked, in isolation, by individuals under the Optional Protocol (*M.G.B. and S.P. v Trinidad and Tobago*, communication No. 268/1987, para. 6.2, declared inadmissible on 3 November 1989). Bearing in mind that article 2 can only be invoked by individuals in conjunction with other articles of the Covenant, the Committee observes that article 2, paragraph 3 (a), of the Covenant stipulates that each State party undertakes 'to ensure that any person whose rights or freedoms are violated shall have an effective remedy' . . . Thus, under article 2 the right to a remedy arises only after a violation of a Covenant right has been established. However, the events which could have constituted violations of several articles of the Covenant and in respect of which remedies could have been invoked, occurred prior to the entry into force of the Covenant and of the Optional Protocol for Argentina. Therefore, the matter cannot be considered by the Committee, as this aspect of the communication is inadmissible *ratione temporis*.

¶ 5.4. The Committee finds it necessary to remind the State party that it is under obligation, in respect of violations occurring or continuing after the entry into force of the Covenant, thoroughly to investigate alleged violations and to provide remedies where applicable, for victims or their dependants.

Article 2(3) provides victims of ICCPR violations with a right to a remedy. However, as is confirmed in *S.E. v Argentina*, article 2(3) does not provide an autonomous right.[13] One cannot claim a violation of article 2(3) unless it is accompanied by a violation of a substantive Covenant right. In this case, the author was precluded from claiming substantive rights violations, as any such violations occurred before entry into force of the OP for Argentina.[14]

---

[13] See also *R.A.V.N. v Argentina* (343–5/88), *Atkinson v Canada* (573/94), para. 8.2. See also [1.17].
[14] See also *Inostroza et al. v Chile* (717/96) [10.13], *Vargas v Chile* (718/96); in contrast, see decision in *Rodriguez v Uruguay* (322/88), at [9.90].

[2.11] *KÖNYE and KÖNYE v HUNGARY (520/92)*

The authors' property was expropriated by the State prior to the Optional Protocol entering into force for Hungary in December 1988. The authors claimed that the State's failure to compensate them represented a continuing violation of article 17, guaranteeing them rights of privacy within the family and the home. They also claimed the State's rejection of the authors' request for new compensation hearings after 1988 breached article 14, as this rejection had not taken place in a 'public hearing'. The HRC disagreed, and stated the following on continuing violations:

¶ 6.4. . . . A continuing violation is to be interpreted as an affirmation, after the entry into force of the Optional Protocol, by act or by clear implication, of the previous violations of the State party.

[2.12] Mme Chanet dissented regarding the admissibility of the article 14 complaint. Indeed, as the article 14 complaint related to alleged failures in the Hungarian administration of justice after 1988, the allegation seemed clearly admissible *ratione temporis*: there was possibly no need even to refer to the 'continuing violations' doctrine. Chanet concluded with the following admonition of the HRC majority:

Finally, it is my view that when the Committee considers a communication under the Optional Protocol, its decisions should be guided only by the legal principles found in the provisions of the Covenant itself, and not by political considerations, even of a general nature, or the fear of a flood of communications from countries that have changed their system of Government.

[2.13] Ghandhi argues that the HRC incorporated a stricter test of continuing violation in the *Könye* case, in its reference to a need for some 'affirmation', by act or clear implication, of the previous violations after the entry into force of the Optional Protocol.[15] Indeed, the need for 'affirmation' arguably precludes admissibility of cases where the continuing effects of a violation persist without any State exacerbation of those violations after entry into force of the Optional Protocol. Application of such a test would have led to an inadmissibility finding in the *Lovelace* case [2.07]. This 'affirmation' test has been reiterated in *Aduayom et al. v Togo* (422/90)[16] and *Julian and Drake v New Zealand* (601/94).[17] In neither case, however, was the test applied in a particularly controversial way. It may be that the *Könye* decision was an aberration, and the 'affirmation' test a mere semantic change in the doctrine of continuing violations.

---

[15] See Ghandhi, above, note 7, 147–50.

[16] In this case, the previous violations were 'affirmed' by the State Party's refusal to reinstate the authors to their previous posts (para. 8.2), see [22.46].

[17] Here, the State Party had not reaffirmed violations allegedly entailed in the 1952 Peace Treaty between New Zealand and Japan.

Conclusion

[2.14] The *ratione temporis* rule applies so as to preclude admissibility of cases where the impugned events occurred before entry into force of the Optional Protocol for the relevant State Party. However, when a violation has begun before that date and continues after that date, or where effects continue after that date which of themselves constitute violations, the complaint will not be precluded from admissibility by application of the *ratione temporis* rule.

3

The 'Victim' Requirement

The 'Victim' Requirement for Optional Protocol Admissibility

[3.01] Article 1 of the Optional Protocol (OP) states that petitions must be submitted by individuals who believe themselves to be victims of a breach of the ICCPR. In the *Mauritian Women's Case* (35/78), the Committee made the following oft-quoted statement:

¶ 9.2. .... A person can only claim to be a victim in the sense of article 1 of the Optional Protocol if he or she is actually affected. It is a matter of degree how concretely this requirement should be taken. However, no individual can in the abstract, by way of an *actio popularis*, challenge a law or practice claimed to be contrary to the Covenant. ...

Therefore, a petitioner may claim to be a victim only if he or she is personally affected by the act or omission which is at issue. The Committee will dismiss the communication as inadmissible if the petitioner cannot show this victim status. Exceptionally, a third party may submit the communication on behalf of a victim [3.17]. However, a victim must always be involved in the communication. This is illustrated in the following case.

[3.02] *POONGAVANAM v MAURITIUS (567/93)*

The author in this case was convicted of murder and sentenced to death in the Assizes Court of Mauritius. He was tried before a judge and a jury of nine men, whose verdict was unanimous. He challenged the Jury Act as incompatible with the Covenant. His arguments were as follows:

¶ 3.2. The author claims that Section 42 of the Courts Act, which provides for a jury 'consisting of nine men qualified as provided in the Jury Act' violates article 3 of the Covenant, as it is discriminatory vis-à-vis women, who remain in practice excluded from jury service.

¶ 3.3. It is further submitted that article 25(c) of the Covenant was violated, as Mauritian women did not and in practice do not have access, on general terms of equality, to public service, service in a trial jury being interpreted as constituting public service.

¶ 3.4. The author contends that the State party violated article 26 of the Covenant, as the exclusion of women from jury service in fact means that their equality before the law is not guaranteed.

The Committee held that the author's claim was inadmissible in the following terms:

¶ 4.2. The Committee has noted the author's claim that he is a victim of violations by Mauritius of articles 3, 25(c) and 26, because women were excluded from jury service at the time of his trial. The author has failed to show, however, how the absence of women on the jury actually prejudiced the enjoyment of his rights under the Covenant. Therefore, he cannot claim to be a 'victim' within the meaning of article 1 of the Optional Protocol.

[3.03] In *Morrison v Jamaica* (663/95), the author, a prisoner in Jamaica, found the correspondence of fellow prisoners dumped in an abandoned cell, which would indicate that his own correspondence had been similarly discarded before proper delivery. The HRC however found the author had no claim in this respect, as there was no evidence that he had found 'letters or documents addressed by or to himself'.[1]

[3.04] In *Van Duzen v Canada* (50/79), the HRC found against the author on the merits, on the basis that post-admissibility developments had remedied his grievance. However, one does not necessarily have to remain a 'victim' throughout the entire period of deliberation of one's complaint. The *Van Duzen* facts were exceptional, as the author could not even claim that his rights were ever violated.[2] By comparison, the author in *A v Australia* (560/93) could claim to be a relevant 'victim' of article 9, even though he had been released by the time the HRC came to its merits decision.[3] 'A' was nevertheless entitled to compensation for his arbitrary detention.

[3.05] In *Hill and Hill v Spain* (526/93), the HRC confirmed that one may bring an OP case even if one's own behaviour is tainted. The fact that the authors had fled Spain, in breach of Spanish bail conditions, did not affect their standing to bring an OP complaint.[4]

---

[1] Para. 6.7.   [2] See discussion of this case at [15.06].
[3] See discussion of *A v Australia* (560/93) at [11.15], [11.52], and [11.55].   [4] Para. 12.1.

Victim must be an Individual

[3.06] The 'victim' must be a natural rather than an artificial person.

NON-GOVERNMENTAL ORGANIZATIONS

[3.07]   *HARTIKAINEN v FINLAND (40/78)*

The author of the communication was a Finnish schoolteacher who submitted the communication on his own behalf and also in his capacity as General Secretary of the Union of Free Thinkers in Finland. The Committee made the following comments in regard to the author's attempt to represent an organization:

¶ 3. On 27 October 1978, the Committee on Human Rights decided: (a) to transmit the communication to the State party under rule 91 of the provisional rules of procedure, requesting information and observations relevant to the question of admissibility of the communication in so far as it related to the author in his personal capacity, and . . . (b) to inform the author that it could not consider the communication in so far as it had been submitted by him in his capacity as General Secretary of the Union of Free Thinkers in Finland, unless he furnished the names and addresses of the persons he claimed to represent together with information as to his authority for acting on their behalf.

¶ 4. In December 1978 and January 1979, the author submitted the signatures and other details of 56 individuals authorising him to act on their behalf as alleged victims.

Hence, non-governmental organizations (NGOs) have no standing to submit cases on their own behalf.[5] The Committee will however allow NGOs to assist authors in their communications, as they did, for example, in *Hertzberg et al. v Finland* (61/79) and *Inostroza et al. v Chile* (717/96).

POLITICAL PARTIES

[3.08] In *J.R.T. and the W.G. Party v Canada* (104/81) the communication was submitted by a Canadian citizen and by the W.G. Party, an unincorporated political party. The Committee held that:

¶ 8(a). . . . the W.G. Party was an association and not an individual and as such cannot submit a communication to the Committee under the Optional Protocol. Therefore the communication is inadmissible under article 1 of the Optional Protocol in so far as it concerns the W.G. Party.

---

[5] See also *Coordinamento v Italy* (163/84).

CORPORATIONS

[3.09] In *A Newspaper Publishing Company v Trinidad and Tobago* (360/89) and *A Publication and Printing Company v Trinidad and Tobago* (361/89), complaints were submitted by corporations on their own behalf. They were deemed inadmissible as corporations have no standing before the Committee.

[3.10] In neither of the Trinidadian cases was it claimed that the alleged violations of the company's rights constituted simultaneous violations of the rights of individuals, such as the shareholders. This issue arose in the following case.

S.M. v BARBADOS (502/92)

The author was the owner and sole shareholder of a Barbadian company. He submitted a complaint to the Committee, arguing that he had been denied a fair and public hearing in a case involving an insurance claim. The Committee found the true 'victim' was in fact the company. It made the following comments:

¶ 6.2. The Committee notes that the author has submitted the communication claiming to be a victim of a violation of his right under article 14, paragraph 1, to have access to court, because the judge at first instance ordered the company of which he is the owner and sole shareholder to pay security and then stayed the proceeding until payment. The author is essentially claiming before the Committee violations of rights of his company. Notwithstanding that he is the sole shareholder, the company has its own legal personality. All domestic remedies referred to in the present case were in fact brought in the name of the company, and not of the author.

¶ 6.3. Under article 1 of the Optional Protocol only individuals may submit a communication to the Human Rights Committee. The Committee considers that the author, by claiming violations of his company's rights, which are not protected by the covenant, has no standing under article 1 of the Optional Protocol.

S.M. v Barbados may be contrasted with the following case.

[3.11]   SINGER v CANADA (455/91)

Allan Singer operated a stationery and printing business and had a clientele that was predominantly English-speaking. He brought a complaint about Quebec laws that prohibited outdoor advertising in a language other than French.[6] The State Party challenged the standing of the author to bring the complaint, noting that the real 'victim' was the author's company, Allan Singer Limited.[7] The Committee nevertheless found the complaint admissible in the following terms:

---

[6] See [18.38] for discussion of the merits of the similar case of *Ballantyne et al. v Canada* (359, 385/89).   [7] Para. 8.1.

¶ 11.2. The State party has contended that the author is claiming violations of rights of his company, and that a company has no standing under article 1 of the Optional Protocol. The Committee notes that the Covenant rights which are at issue in the present communication, and in particular the right of freedom of expression, are by their nature inalienably linked to the person. The author has the freedom to impart information concerning his business in the language of his choice. The Committee therefore considers that the author himself, and not only his company, has been personally affected by the contested provisions of Bills Nos. 101 and 178.

[3.12] In *Singer*, the restriction of the rights of commercial expression of Singer's company naturally impacted on Singer's own rights to freedom of expression.[8] It may be that in many instances, a violation against a corporation would also entail a violation of the rights of its shareholders or employees, who are of course able to bring a complaint on their own behalf. However, the HRC's assertion that 'freedom of expression' is 'inalienably linked to the person' may go too far in implying that restriction on corporate expression may always be characterized as a restriction of an individual's expression. It must be noted that Singer's company was a small family corporation. Suppose a law restricted the advertising rights of a large publicly listed company, whose shareholders had no real influence on the running of its business. Could it realistically be said that such a law restricted the freedom of expression of those shareholders, or employees, or even the directors?[9]

COLLECTIVE RIGHTS

[3.13] In *Ominayak, Chief of the Lubicon Lake Band v Canada* (167/87) the Committee stated:

¶ 32.1. . . . The Optional Protocol provides a procedure under which individuals can claim their individual rights have been violated. These rights are set out in part III of the Covenant, articles 6 to 27, inclusive. There is, however, no objection to a group of individuals, who claim to be similarly affected, collectively to submit a communication about alleged breaches of their rights.

[3.14] It should be noted that the right to self-determination found in article 1 of the ICCPR is in an anomalous position as it is a people's right and thus it is not a right that is justiciable under the OP.[10]

---

[8] This finding would be of particular importance to newspaper editors and journalists.

[9] In *RJR-MacDonald v Canada (Attorney-General)* (1995) 3 SCR 199, the Supreme Court of Canada found Canadian laws which prescribed compulsory health warnings on cigarette packets, and which prohibited certain other writing on the packet, violated a corporation's rights of free expression. Could such a complaint ever be grounded on the art. 19 rights of the shareholders, or directors, given the huge conglomerate nature of the cigarette manufacturer? See also A.C. Hutchinson, 'Supreme Court Inc: The Business of Democracy and Rights' in G.W. Anderson (ed.), *Rights and Democracy: Essays in UK–Canadian Constitutionalism* (Blackstone Press, London, 1999), 33, criticizing the 'abuse' of the Canadian Charter of Rights by corporate plaintiffs.

[10] See [7.20].

[3.15] In *E.W. et al. v The Netherlands* (429/90) the Committee noted, with regard to 6,588 authors, that:

¶ 6.3. The Committee has considered the claim of the State party that the communication is in fact an *actio popularis*. The Committee notes that, provided each of the authors is a victim within the meaning of article 1 of the Optional Protocol, nothing precludes large numbers of persons from bringing a case under the Optional Protocol. The mere fact of large numbers of petitioners does not render their communication an *actio popularis*, and the Committee finds that the communication does not fail on this ground.

Therefore, when there are a number of victims with the same complaint, the victims can group their cases together into the one case.

Standing for Third Parties

[3.16] Ordinarily, victims are obliged to bring an OP complaint themselves. For example, in *Fei v Colombia* (514/92), the author alleged that there had been a violation of article 24, entailed in her children's presumed right to acquire Italian nationality and their right to equal access to both parents.[11] The HRC held this part of the complaint to be inadmissible because 'this violation would have had to be claimed on behalf of the author's children, in whose name the communication had not been submitted'.[12]

[3.17] There are however some exceptions to the basic principle that only the victims themselves can bring a claim. There are a number of situations in which the Committee will permit a third party to submit a communication. First, the alleged victim may appoint a representative to conduct the communication on his/her behalf. Secondly, a third party may submit the communication when the alleged victim is unable to do so. Thirdly, if the author of the communication dies during the proceedings, the author's heirs may continue the case on his/her behalf.[13]

REPRESENTATION

[3.18] Rule 90(b) of the Committee's rules of procedure allows for the possibility of calling a representative to act on the victim's behalf in a communication. In essence the representative acts like an attorney for the victim, and in most cases these representatives have been legal counsel. In order to satisfy the Committee that the author is acting as an authorized representative, written evidence of a representative's authority to act, such as a power of attorney, must be submitted.

---

[11] On this case, see [20.40].   [12] Para. 5.2.
[13] T. Zwart, *The Admissibility of Human Rights Petitions* (Martinus Nijhoff, Dordrecht, 1994), 71.

[3.19] *SOLÍS PALMA v PANAMA (436/90)*

The facts are evident from the excerpts below.

¶ **1.** The author of the communication is Renato Pereira, a Panamanian attorney born in 1936 and a resident of Paris at the time of submission of the communication. He acts on behalf of Manuel Solís Palma, a Panamanian citizen born in 1917 and formerly the President of the Republic of Panama. He contends that at the time of submission of the complaint, Mr. Solís Palma was unable to submit the communication himself, as he was prosecuted by the current Government of Panama and hiding from its agents. It is submitted that Mr. Solís Palma is a victim of violations by Panama of articles 9 and 10 of the International Covenant on Civil and Political Rights.

The HRC refused to accept Mr Pereira as Mr Solís Palma's representative:

¶ 5.2. The Committee has noted Mr. Pereira's claim that as a personal friend of Mr. Solís Palma, he acted in the latter's best interest by filing a claim on his behalf under the Optional Protocol, and that he should be deemed to have standing within the meaning of article 1 of the Protocol. It further observes that on two occasions, by letters of 21 February 1991 and 25 August 1992, Mr. Pereira was requested to provide a copy of a power of attorney duly signed by the alleged victim or a member of his family. He did not comply with this request, despite the fact that, by the summer of 1992, Mr. Solís Palma had been granted political asylum in Venezuela and therefore would have been in a position to authorise Mr. Pereira to represent him before the Committee.

¶ 5.3. In the light of the above and in the absence of a power of attorney or other documented proof that the author is authorised to act on behalf of Mr. Solís Palma, the Committee concludes that the author has no standing before the Committee, within the meaning of article 1 of the Optional Protocol.

Similar decisions have been issued in a number of cases, including *A.D. v Canada* (78/80) and *R. and M. H. v Italy* (565/93), and the decision of the Committee Against Torture in *Barakat v Tunisia* (CAT 14/94).

[3.20] The HRC has recognized the right of minors to bring cases before it, though in most cases minors are represented by their parents.[14]

P. S. v DENMARK (397/90)

¶ 5.2. The Committee has taken notice of the State party's contention that the author has no standing to act on behalf of his son [T.S.], as Danish law limits this right to the custodial parent. The Committee observes that standing under the Optional Protocol may be determined independently of national regulations and legislation governing an individual's

---

[14] Ibid., 43–4, 78; P.R. Ghandhi, *The Human Rights Committee and the Right of Individual Communication* (Ashgate, Dartmouth, 1998), 89. Note that in *Yutronic v Chile* (740/97), a complaint on behalf of the victim's adult sons was inadmissible, as the sons could have submitted the complaint themselves, and there was no evidence of the sons authorizing the complaint (para. 6.2).

standing before a domestic court of law. In the present case, it is clear that T.S. cannot himself submit a complaint to the Committee; the relationship between father and son and the nature of the allegations must be deemed sufficient to justify representation of T.S. before the Committee by his father.[15]

VICTIM IS UNABLE TO SUBMIT THE COMMUNICATION PERSONALLY

[3.21] There may be circumstances in which it is impossible for the victim personally to bring the communication, for example where the victim has been killed, or has disappeared, or is being held incommunicado.[16] In such cases, the Committee requires a sufficient link to exist between the author and the victim. It must appear likely that the alleged victim would consent to submission of the complaint by the representative.[17]

[3.22] The HRC has confirmed that a close family connection will be a sufficient link to justify an author acting on behalf of an alleged victim.[18] 'Close family members' have included persons beyond the nuclear family, such as aunts, uncles, nephews, nieces, and cousins.[19] The HRC has been less inclined to allow submission by representatives outside the victim's family.[20] For example, in *Mbenge v Zaire* (16/77), the HRC found that the author could represent his relatives, but not his driver or his pharmacist.[21]

[3.23] Once the alleged victim is in a position to communicate directly with the Committee, he/she must confirm an intention to pursue the complaint or the communication will be declared inadmissible. For example, in *Mpandanjila v Zaire* (138/83), the original complaint was submitted on behalf of thirteen people allegedly detained incommunicado. The thirteen were subsequently released and thus in a position to communicate with the Committee. Four of the original thirteen victims were subsequently dropped as parties to the communication due to their failure to confirm their intention to continue with the complaint.

[3.24]   *E.H.P. v CANADA (67/80)*

The author submitted a complaint on her own behalf, as well as on the behalf of 'present and future generations' of Port Hope, Ontario. She claimed that the dumping of toxic waste within Port Hope threatened her life, and the life of present and future generations.[22] The Committee stated the following with regard to the standing of the author:

---

[15] Note however that the HRC ultimately held that the complaint was inadmissible because domestic remedies had not been exhausted.

[16] Many of the early Uruguayan cases concerned such circumstances.

[17] Zwart, above, note 13, 76.   [18] Ibid.   [19] Ibid.

[20] M. Nowak, *CCPR Commentary* (N.P. Engel, Kehl, 1993), 663.   [21] Para. 5(d).

[22] See further [8.40].

¶ 8(a). The Committee considers that the author of the communication has the standing to submit the communication both on her own behalf and also on behalf of those residents of Port Hope who have specifically authorised her to do so. Consequently, the question as to whether a communication can be submitted on behalf of 'future generations' does not have to be resolved in the circumstances of the present case. The Committee will treat the author's reference to 'future generations' as an expression of concern purporting to put into due perspective the importance of the matter raised in the communication.

The complaint was found inadmissible for failure to exhaust domestic remedies.[23] However, the Committee's ambivalence at striking out the reference to 'future generations' is interesting. Perhaps one can make a complaint about the rights of an unborn baby. Such a complaint could relate to abortion (e.g. an allegation regarding breach of the alleged right to life of a foetus)[24] or freedom from inhuman and degrading treatment (e.g. an allegation regarding an assault on a pregnant woman, which could severely harm her unborn baby). The Port Hope complaint went further however, as the author claimed standing in respect of people who had not even been conceived. Even if such complaints were admissible, one cannot imagine many instances where breaches of the 'rights' of future generations would be foreseeable enough to establish admissibility.[25]

VICTIM IS REPRESENTED BY HIS SUCCESSORS

[3.25] In *Croes v The Netherlands* (164/84), the Committee allowed the author's heirs to continue to proceed with the communication after the author died whilst his case was still being considered by the Committee. However, if no instructions come forth from the author's heirs, the case may be discontinued, as occurred in *Wallen v Trinidad and Tobago* (576/94).[26]

Potential Violations

FUTURE VIOLATIONS MUST BE REASONABLY FORESEEABLE

[3.26] The Committee has received a number of complaints relating to ICCPR violations that had not actually occurred, but which the author alleged would occur in the future. This issue arose in the following case.

A.R.S. v CANADA (91/81)

The author was a Canadian citizen serving a prison sentence in a Canadian prison. His prison term was set to expire in 1988, but he had been informed in writing

---

[23] See generally Chap. 6.
[25] See [3.26] ff. on foreseeable violations.
[24] See, on abortion, [8.47].
[26] Para. 6.2.

that he had earned remission and could be released in 1982. The author objected to certain provisions of the Parole Act 1970 which had come into force after he had committed the offences for which he was sentenced. The author claimed that he should not be subject to the new parole system, as it imposed a heavier burden than the old parole system, contrary to article 15.[27] The Committee noted that the author's complaint, submitted in 1981, was about hypothetical events and therefore was inadmissible.[28] It made the following comments:

¶ 5.1. The author's principal complaint is against the introduction by the Parole Act 1970, in August 1970, after the commission of the punishable acts for which he was convicted, of a system of mandatory supervision for all prisoners benefiting from remission of sentence. However, the Committee is of the view that no action taken before the entry into force of the Covenant for the State party concerned can, as such, be judged in the light of the obligations deriving from the Covenant. Moreover, individuals may not criticize national laws in the abstract, since the Optional Protocol gives them the right to bring the matter before the Committee only where they claim to be victims of a violation of the Covenant.

¶ 5.2. With regard to the actual implementation of the mandatory supervision, which might give the author cause for complaint, the Committee notes that the author has not yet served the two thirds of his sentence for which he is not entitled to remission and that in addition his release, due on 8 September 1982, depends on his good conduct up to that date. The mandatory supervision system is therefore not yet applicable to him. The possibility of the remission he has earned being cancelled after his release is still more hypothetical. In the present situation, therefore, he has no actual grievance such as is required for the admissibility of a communication by an individual under articles 1 and 2 of the Optional Protocol.

[3.27]   *AUMEERUDDY-CZIFFRA et al. v MAURITIUS (35/78)*

Under Mauritian law, alien wives of Mauritian men were automatically eligible for Mauritian residence status, while alien husbands of Mauritian women were not. The petitioners were a number of Mauritian women, who claimed that these laws violated the Covenant as they discriminated on the basis of sex. The Committee made the following comments regarding admissibility:

¶ 9.2. In the first place, a distinction has to be made between the different groups of the authors of the present communication. A person can only claim to be a victim in the sense of article 1 of the Optional Protocol if he or she is actually affected. It is a matter of degree how concretely this requirement should be taken. However, no individual can in the abstract, by way of an *actio popularis*, challenge a law or practice claimed to be contrary

---

[27] See [15.05].

[28] See also the decision in *MacIsaac v Canada* (55/79), where the HRC could not ultimately decide that the author was a victim, as it would have required several questionable presumptions on its part: see [15.07].

to the Covenant. If the law or practice has not already been concretely applied to the detriment of that individual, it must in any event be applicable in such a way that the alleged victim's risk of being affected is more than a theoretical possibility.

¶ 9.2(a). In this respect the Committee notes that in the case of the 17 unmarried co-authors there is no question of actual interference with, or failure to ensure equal protection by the law to any family. Furthermore there is no evidence that any of them is actually facing a personal risk of being thus affected in the enjoyment of this or any other rights set forth in the Covenant by the laws complained against. In particular it cannot be said that their right to marry under article 23 (2) or the right to equality of spouses under article 23 (4) are affected by such laws.

Hence, the case was only admissible in so far as it concerned the rights of the three married authors.

[3.28] *KINDLER v CANADA (470/91)*

The author in this communication was detained in a jail in Canada at the time of his submission and subsequently extradited to the United States, where he faced the threat of capital punishment.[29] He made the following claims before the Committee:

¶ 3. The author claims that the decision to extradite him violates articles 6, 7, 9, 14 and 26 of the Covenant. He submits that the death penalty *per se* constitutes cruel and inhuman treatment or punishment, and that conditions on death row are cruel, inhuman and degrading. . . .

The State Party objected to the admissibility of the complaint on a number of grounds. It disputed, *inter alia*, the author's status as a 'victim' of an ICCPR violation:

¶ 4.2. It is argued that the author cannot be considered a victim within the meaning of the Optional Protocol, since his allegations are derived from assumptions about possible future events, which may not materialize and which are dependent on the law and actions of the authorities of the United States. . . .

The Committee found the complaint admissible as the extradition potentially exposed Kindler to a real risk of violation of his ICCPR rights by the United States:[30]

¶ 13.2. If a State Party extradites a person within its jurisdiction in circumstances such that as a result there is a real risk that his or her rights under the Covenant will be violated in another jurisdiction, the State party itself may be in violation of the Covenant.

---

[29] See, on the merits, [8.27].
[30] See also [4.12], regarding the question of Canada's territorial jurisdiction in this case. Ultimately, Kindler lost on the merits, see [8.27].

[3.29]   *COX v CANADA (539/93)*

The author in this case made a very similar complaint to that made in *Kindler*. The majority found the case to be similarly admissible. The following excerpts are from a dissenting opinion on admissibility submitted by Mrs Higgins, co-signed by Messrs Francis, Herndl, Mavrommatis, Ndiaye, and Sadi.

[In *Kindler v Canada*, the Committee] observed that 'if a State party takes a decision relating to a person within its jurisdiction, and the necessary and foreseeable consequence is that the person's rights under the Covenant will be violated in another jurisdiction, the State party itself may be in violation of the Covenant'. . . .

The above test is relevant also to the admissibility requirement, under article 1 of the Optional Protocol, that an author be a 'victim' of a violation in respect of which he brings a claim. In other words, it is not always necessary that a violation already have occurred for an action to come within the scope of article 1. But the violation that will affect him personally must be a 'necessary and foreseeable consequence' of the action of the defendant State.

It is clear that in the case of Mr. Cox, unlike in the case of Mr. Kindler, this test is not met. Mr. Kindler had, at the time of the Canadian decision to extradite him, been tried in the United States for murder, found guilty as charged and recommended to the death sentence by the jury. Mr. Cox, by contrast, has not yet been tried and *a fortiori* has not been found guilty or recommended to the death penalty. Already it is clear that his extradition would not entail the possibility of a 'necessary and foreseeable consequence of a violation of his rights' that would require examination on the merits. This failure to meet the test of 'prospective victim' within the meaning of article 1 of the Optional Protocol is emphasized by the fact that Mr. Cox's two co-defendants in the case in which he has been charged have already been tried in the State of Pennsylvania, and sentenced not to death but to a term of life imprisonment. The fact that the Committee—and rightly so in our view—found that Kindler raised issues that needed to be considered on their merits, and that the admissibility criteria were there met, does not mean that every extradition case of this nature is necessarily admissible. In every case, the tests relevant to articles 1, 2, 3 and 5, paragraph 2, of the Optional Protocol must be applied to the particular facts of the case.

The Committee has not at all addressed the requirements of article 1 of the Optional Protocol, that is, whether Mr. Cox may be considered a 'victim' by reference to his claims under articles 14, 26, 6 or 7 of the Covenant.

We therefore believe that Mr. Cox was not a 'victim' within the meaning of article 1 of the Optional Protocol, and that his communication to the Human Rights Committee is inadmissible.

The duty to address carefully the requirements for admissibility under the Optional Protocol is not made the less necessary because capital punishment is somehow involved in a complaint.

[3.30]   *E.W. et al. v THE NETHERLANDS (429/90)*

The facts of the case are outlined in the Committee's admissibility decision, excerpted directly below:

¶ 6.2. The authors claim that the State party's preparations for the deployment of cruise missiles in Woensdrecht and the presence in the Netherlands of other nuclear weapons violate their rights under article 6 of the Covenant. The Committee recalls in this context its second General Comment on article 6, where it observed that 'the designing, testing, manufacture, possession and deployment of nuclear weapons are among the greatest threats to the right to life which confront mankind today'. (General Comment 14(23), adopted on 2 November 1984.) At the same time, the Committee notes that the procedure laid down in the Optional Protocol was not designed for conducting public debate over matters of public policy, such as support for disarmament and issues concerning nuclear and other weapons of mass destruction. . . .

¶ 6.4. The Committee next considers whether the authors are victims within the meaning of the Optional Protocol. For a person to claim to be a victim of a violation of a right protected by the Covenant, he or she must show either that an act or an omission of a State party has already adversely affected his or her enjoyment of such right, or that such an effect is imminent, for example on the basis of existing law and/or judicial or administrative decision or practice. The issue in this case is whether the preparation for the deployment or the actual deployment of nuclear weapons presented the authors with an existing or imminent violation of their right to life, specific to each of them. The Committee finds that the preparations for deployment of cruise missiles between 1 June 1984 and 8 December 1987 and the continuing deployment of other nuclear weapons in the Netherlands did not, at the relevant period of time, place the authors in the position to claim to be victims whose right to life was then violated or under imminent prospect of violation. Accordingly, after careful examination of the arguments and materials before it, the Committee finds that the authors cannot claim to be victims within the meaning of article 1 of the Optional Protocol.

[3.31]   *BORDES and TEMEHARO v FRANCE (645/95)*

The authors complained of violations of their rights to life and freedom from interference in their family life entailed in the underground detonation of nuclear bombs by France in the South Pacific in 1995.[31] In response, the State Party submitted evidence of the apparent safety of the nuclear tests. It concluded the following:

¶ 3.6 . . . the State party affirms that the authors have failed to discharge the burden of proof that they are 'victims' within the meaning of article 1 of the Optional Protocol. It notes that the authors cannot argue that the risk to which they might be exposed through the nuclear tests would be such as to render imminent a violation of their rights under articles 6 and 17 of the Covenant. Purely theoretical and hypothetical violations, however, do not suffice to make them 'victims' within the meaning of the Optional Protocol.

---

[31] See also [8.45].

The Committee agreed with the State Party that the case was inadmissible:

¶ 5.4. The Committee has noted the State party's contention that the authors do not qualify as 'victims' within the meaning of article 1 of the Optional Protocol. It recalls that for a person to claim to be a victim of a violation of a right protected by the Covenant, he or she must show either that an act or omission of a State party has already adversely affected his or her enjoyment of such right, or that there is a real threat of such result.

¶ 5.5. The issue in the present case therefore is whether the announcement and subsequent conduct of underground nuclear tests by France on Mururoa and Fangataufa resulted in a violation of their right to life and their right to their family life, specific to Ms. Bordes and Mr. Temeharo, or presented an imminent threat to their enjoyment of such rights. The Committee observes that, on the basis of the information presented by the parties, the authors have not substantiated their claim that the conduct of nuclear tests between September 1995 and the beginning of 1996 did not place them in a position in which they could justifiably claim to be victims whose right to life and to family life was then violated or was under a real threat of violation.

¶ 5.6. Finally, as to the authors' contention that the nuclear tests will further deteriorate the geological structure of the atolls on which the tests are carried out, further fissurate the limestone caps of the atolls, etc., and thereby increase the likelihood of an accident of catastrophic proportions, the Committee notes that this contention is highly controversial even in concerned scientific circles; it is not possible for the Committee to ascertain its validity or correctness.

¶ 5.7. On the basis of the above considerations and after careful examination of the arguments and materials before it, the Committee is not satisfied that the authors can claim to be victims within the meaning of article 1 of the Optional Protocol.

LEGISLATION MAY VIOLATE ICCPR IN THE ABSENCE OF ENFORCEMENT

[3.32] The HRC has also found that domestic legislation may be incompatible with the Covenant even where it has not been directly implemented in relation to the particular author.

AUMEERUDDY-CZIFFRA et al. v MAURITIUS (35/78)

The facts of this case are outlined above [3.27]. After rejecting the standing of a number of the complainants, the Committee considered whether the remaining authors could be considered victims, in the absence of the enforcement of the impugned law.

¶ 9.2(b) 1. The Committee will next examine that part of the communication which relates to the effect of the laws of 1977 on the family life of the three married women.

¶ 9.2(b) 2(i) 3. In the present cases, not only the future possibility of deportation, but the existing precarious residence situation of foreign husbands in Mauritius represents, in the opinion of the Committee, an interference by the authorities of the State party with the family life of the Mauritian wives and their husbands. The statutes in question have rendered it uncertain for the families concerned whether and for how long it will be possible for them to continue their family life by residing together in Mauritius. Moreover, as described . . . in one of the cases, even the delay for years, and the absence of a positive decision granting a residence permit, must be seen as a considerable inconvenience, among other reasons because the granting of a work permit, and hence the possibility of the husband to contribute to supporting the family, depends on the residence permit, and because deportation without judicial review is possible at any time.

The Committee accordingly decided that the remaining three authors could be deemed 'victims'.[32]

[3.33]   *BALLANTYNE et al. v CANADA (359 and 387/89)*

In this case the authors challenged a provision in the Charter of the French Language, enacted by the Provincial government of Quebec, stating that only French could be used in public bill-posting and in commercial advertising outdoors.[33] The Committee found the communication admissible, despite the fact that the law had not been officially enforced against two of the authors. Its comments were as follows:

¶ 10.4. The Committee has further reconsidered, *eo volonte*, whether all the authors are properly to be considered victims within the meaning of article 1 of the Optional Protocol. In that context, it has noted that Mr. Ballantyne and Ms. Davidson have not received warning notices from the Commissioner-Enquirer of the 'Commission de protection de la langue française' nor been subjected to any penalty. However, it is the position of the Committee that where an individual is in a category of persons whose activities are, by virtue of the relevant legislation, regarded as contrary to law, they may have a claim as 'victims' within the meaning of article 1 of the Optional Protocol.

[3.34]   *TOONEN v AUSTRALIA (488/92)*

This case concerned a challenge to Tasmanian laws which criminalized sexual relations between consenting males.[34] Although the Tasmanian police had not charged anyone under this law for many years, the author argued that the stigmatizing effects of the law nevertheless rendered him a victim. His arguments were as follows:

¶ 2.3. Although in practice the Tasmanian police have not charged anyone either with 'unnatural sexual intercourse' or 'intercourse against nature' (Section 122) nor with 'indecent practice between male persons' (Section 123) for several years, the author argues that because of his long-term relationship with another man, his active lobbying of Tasmanian politicians and the reports about his activities in the local media, and because of his activities as a gay rights

---

[32] See, on the merits, [16.22], [20.13], and [23.42].   [33] See also [18.38].
[34] See [16.36] for the merits decision.

activist and gay HIV/AIDS worker, his private life and his liberty are threatened by the continued existence of Sections 122(a), (c) and 123 of the Criminal Code.

¶ 2.4. Mr. Toonen further argues that the criminalization of homosexuality in private has not permitted him to expose openly his sexuality and to publicize his views on reform of the relevant laws on sexual matters, as he felt that this would have been extremely prejudicial to his employment. In this context, he contends that Sections 122(a), (c) and 123 have created the conditions for discrimination in employment, constant stigmatization, vilification, threats of physical violence and the violation of basic democratic rights.

¶ 2.5. The author observes that numerous 'figures of authority' in Tasmania have made either derogatory or downright insulting remarks about homosexual men and women over the past few years. These include statements made by members of the Lower House of Parliament, municipal councillors (such as 'representatives of the gay community are no better than Saddam Hussein'; 'the act of homosexuality is unacceptable in any society, let alone a civilized society'), of the church and of members of the general public, whose statements have been directed against the integrity and welfare of homosexual men and women in Tasmania (such as '[g]ays want to lower society to their level'; 'You are 15 times more likely to be murdered by a homosexual than a heterosexual . . .'). In some public meetings, it has been suggested that all Tasmanian homosexuals should be rounded up and 'dumped' on an uninhabited island, or be subjected to compulsory sterilization. Remarks such as these, the author affirms, have had the effect of creating constant stress and suspicion in what ought to be routine contacts with the authorities in Tasmania.

¶ 2.6. The author further argues that Tasmania has witnessed, and continues to witness, a 'campaign of official and unofficial hatred' against homosexuals and lesbians. This campaign has made it difficult for the Tasmanian Gay Law Reform Group to disseminate information about its activities and advocate the decriminalization of homosexuality. Thus, in September 1988, for example, the TGLRG was refused permission to put up a stand in a public square in the city of Hobart, and the author claims that he, as a leading protester against the ban, was subjected to police intimidation.

¶ 2.7. Finally, the author argues that the continued existence of Sections 122(a), (c) and 123 of the Criminal Code of Tasmania continue to have profound and harmful impacts on many people in Tasmania, including himself, in that it fuels discrimination and harassment of, and violence against, the homosexual community of Tasmania.

The HRC agreed that the author could be deemed a victim within the meaning of article 1 OP. It made the following comments on the issue of admissibility:

¶ 5.1. During its forty-sixth session, the Committee considered the admissibility of the communication. As to whether the author could be deemed a 'victim' within the meaning of article 1 of the Optional Protocol, it noted that the legislative provisions challenged by the author had not been enforced by the judicial authorities of Tasmania for a number of years. It considered, however, that the author had made reasonable efforts to demonstrate that the threat of enforcement and the pervasive impact of the continued existence of these provisions on administrative practices and public opinion had affected him and continued to affect him personally, and that they could raise issues under articles 17 and 26 of the Covenant. Accordingly, the Committee was satisfied that the author could be deemed a victim within the meaning of article 1 of the Optional Protocol, and that his claims were admissible *ratione temporis*.

The HRC agreed that the very existence of the laws breached or at least imminently threatened Toonen's rights. Toonen could therefore claim 'victim' status, even in the absence of the enforcement of the impugned laws.

Conclusion

[**3.35**] The HRC has interpreted the OP 'victim' requirement quite strictly. Generally, one's communication will not be admissible unless one is an individual victim of an ICCPR rights abuse, or if one is in foreseeable danger of an ICCPR violation. Exceptions do apply, where one may submit a communication on behalf of another, or where one is designated a victim of legislation despite its non-enforcement.

4

Territorial and Jurisdictional Limits

Introduction

[4.01] Article 2(1) of the ICCPR limits a State's liability to 'persons subject to a State's jurisdiction and within its territory'. Article 1 of the Optional Protocol (OP) also limits the liability of a State to 'persons subject to its jurisdiction'. This chapter addresses the territorial and jurisdictional limits of State ICCPR and OP obligations.

[4.02] The HRC has interpreted this requirement so that a person can complain of a violation within jurisdiction even though he/she is no longer within the jurisdiction. For example, in *Massiotti and Baristussio v Uruguay* (25/78), the authors were residing, respectively, in the Netherlands and Sweden at the time they lodged their communications. Despite the State Party's argument that the HRC would be exceeding its competence if it heard the matter, the HRC clearly stated that the authors were victims under the jurisdiction of Uruguay when the alleged violations actually took place.[1] This rule applies regardless of whether the author is a citizen of the relevant State.[2]

[4.03] *Mbenge v Zaire* (16/77) demonstrates that an intra-territorial violation can occur to someone who is outside a State's territory. Mbenge was tried *in absentia* in contravention of article 14(3)(d)[3] even though, at the time of the impugned trial, Mbenge was in Belgium.[4]

[4.04] In *Quinteros v Uruguay* (107/81), the author complained of the severe mental anguish caused to her by the disappearance of her daughter at the hands of Uruguayan agents. The HRC agreed that the author was a victim of a violation of article 7.[5] However, its finding was prefaced by an observation that the author

---

[1] Paras. 7.1–7.2.   [2] See *Miha v Equatorial Guinea* (414/90).
[3] See [14.75].
[4] See also P.R. Ghandhi, *The Human Rights Committee and the Right of Individual Petition* (Ashgate, Dartmouth, 1998), 133.   [5] See [9.37].

was 'in Uruguay at the time of the incident regarding her daughter'.[6] However, the relevance of the location of the author at the time of her daughter's kidnapping must be questionable; distance would not normally decrease the mental anguish. Zwart and Ghandhi argue that a stricter territorial test may apply where the facts concern an 'indirect' victim as opposed to a direct victim.[7] The 'direct' victim in *Quinteros* was the author's daughter, whereas the violation of the author's rights was totally contingent upon a finding of violation regarding the daughter.[8]

Extraterritorial State Responsibility

[4.05] States Parties are required to ensure the implementation of ICCPR rights within their sovereign territory, and within territory over which they have effective control. For example, Israel bears responsibility for implementation of the ICCPR within Israel, as well as the Occupied Territories, southern Lebanon, and West Bekaa.[9] The text of article 2(1) of the ICCPR seems expressly to exclude liability for a State Party for acts which occur outside its territory. The HRC addressed this issue in the following cases, where the complaints alleged ICCPR violations entailed in the extraterritorial activities of State agents.

LÓPEZ BURGOS v URUGUAY (52/79)

¶ 2.2. The author claims that on 13 July 1976 her husband was kidnapped in Buenos Aires [Argentina] by members of the 'Uruguayan security and intelligence forces' who were aided by Argentine para-military groups, and was secretly detained in Buenos Aires for about two weeks. On 26 July 1976 Mr. López Burgos, together with several other Uruguayan nationals, was illegally and clandestinely transported to Uruguay, where he was detained incommunicado by the special security forces at a secret prison for three months. During his detention of approximately four months both in Argentina and Uruguay, he was continuously subjected to physical and mental torture and other cruel, inhuman or degrading treatment.

The Committee made the following comments regarding admissibility:

¶ 12.1. The Human Rights Committee . . . observes that although the arrest and initial detention and mistreatment of López Burgos allegedly took place on foreign territory, the Committee is not barred either by virtue of article 1 of the Optional Protocol ('. . . individuals subject to its jurisdiction . . .') or by virtue of article 2(1) of the Covenant

---

[6] Para. 14.

[7] See Ghandhi, above, note 4, 126; T. Zwart, *The Admissibility of Human Rights Petitions* (Martinus Nijhoff, Dordrecht, 1994), at 97.

[8] Zwart, above, note 7, 169–71; Ghandhi, above, note 4, 104.

[9] See Concluding Comments on Israel, (1999) UN doc. CCPR/C/79/Add. 93), paragraph 10.

('. . . individuals within its territory and subject to its jurisdiction . . .') from considering these allegations, together with the claim of subsequent abduction into Uruguayan territory, inasmuch as these acts were perpetrated by Uruguayan agents acting on foreign soil.

¶ 12.2. The reference in article 1 of the Optional Protocol to 'individuals subject to its jurisdiction' does not affect the above conclusion because the reference in that article is not to the place where the violation occurred, but rather to the relationship between the individual and the State in relation to a violation of any of the rights set forth in the Covenant, wherever they occurred.

¶ 12.3. Article 2 (1) of the Covenant places an obligation upon a State party to respect and to ensure rights 'to all individuals within its territory and subject to its jurisdiction', but it does not imply that the State Party concerned cannot be held accountable for violations of rights under the Covenant which its agents commit upon the territory of another State, whether with the acquiescence of the Government of that State or in opposition to it. According to article 5 (1) of the Covenant:

> 'Nothing in the present Covenant may be interpreted as implying for any State, group or person any right to engage in any activity or perform any act aimed at the destruction of any of the rights and freedoms recognized herein or at their limitation to a greater extent than is provided for in the present Covenant.'

In line with this, it would be unconscionable to so interpret the responsibility under article 2 of the Covenant as to permit a State party to perpetrate violations of the Covenant on the territory of another State, which violations it could not perpetrate on its own territory.

Mr Tomuschat appended a concurring opinion which offered more persuasive reasoning. He made the following comments:

I concur in the views expressed by the majority. None the less, the arguments set out in paragraph 12 for affirming the applicability of the Covenant also with regard to those events which have taken place outside Uruguay need to be clarified and expanded. Indeed, the first sentence in paragraph 12.3, according to which article 2 (1) of the Covenant does not imply that a State party 'cannot be held accountable for violations of rights under the Covenant which its agents commit upon the territory of another State', is too broadly framed and might therefore give rise to misleading conclusions. In principle, the scope of application of the Covenant is not susceptible to being extended by reference to article 5, a provision designed to cover instances where formally rules under the Covenant seem to legitimize actions which substantially run counter to its purposes and general spirit. Thus, Governments may never use the limitation clauses supplementing the protected rights and freedoms to such an extent that the very substance of those rights and freedom would be annihilated: individuals are legally barred from availing themselves of the same rights and freedoms with a view to overthrowing the regime of the rule of law which constitutes the basic philosophy of the Covenant. In the present case, however, the Covenant does not even provide the pretext for a 'right' to perpetrate the criminal acts which, according to the Committee's conviction, have been perpetrated by the Uruguayan authorities.

To construe the words 'within its territory' pursuant to their strict literal meaning as excluding any responsibility for conduct occurring beyond the national boundaries would, however, lead to utterly absurd results. The formula was intended to take care of objective difficulties which might impede the implementation of the Covenant in specific situations. Thus, a State party is normally unable to ensure the effective enjoyment of the rights under the Covenant to its citizens abroad, having at its disposal only the tools of diplomatic protection with their limited potential. Instances of occupation of foreign territory offer another example of situations which the drafters of the Covenant had in mind when they confined the obligation of States parties to their own territory. All these factual patterns have in common, however, that they provide plausible grounds for denying the protection of the Covenant. It may be concluded, therefore, that it was the intention of the drafters, whose sovereign decision cannot be challenged, to restrict the territorial scope of the Covenant in view of such situations where enforcing the Covenant would be likely to encounter exceptional obstacles. Never was it envisaged, however, to grant States parties unfettered discretionary power to carry out wilful and deliberate attacks against the freedom and personal integrity of their citizens living abroad. Consequently, despite the wording of article 2 (l), the events which took place outside Uruguay come within the purview of the Covenant.

A similar conclusion was reached by the Committee in the case of *Celiberti de Casariego v Uruguay* (56/1979).

[4.06]   *MONTERO v URUGUAY (106/81)*

In this case the petitioner's Uruguayan passport was confiscated by the Uruguayan consulate in Germany. The author alleged that this amounted to a breach of article 12 which guarantees freedom of movement.[10] Despite the fact that the confiscation took place in Germany the HRC held that the impugned act was within the jurisdiction of Uruguay. It made the following comments on this issue:

¶ 5. Before taking its decision on the admissibility of the communication, the Human Rights Committee examined, *ex officio*, whether the fact that Mabel Pereira Montero resides abroad affects the competence of the Committee to receive and consider the communication under article 1 of the Optional Protocol, taking into account the provisions of article 2(1) of the Covenant. In that context, the Committee made the following observations: article 1 of the Optional Protocol applies to individuals subject to the jurisdiction of the State concerned who claim to be victims of a violation by that State of any of the Covenant rights. The issue of a passport to a Uruguayan citizen is clearly a matter within the jurisdiction of the Uruguayan authorities and he is 'subject to the jurisdiction' of Uruguay for that purpose. Moreover, a passport is a means of enabling him 'to leave any country including his own', as required by article 12(2) of the Covenant. Consequently, the Committee found that it followed from the very nature of that right that, in the case of a citizen resident abroad, it imposed obligations both on the State of residence and on the State of nationality and that, therefore, article 2(1) of the Covenant could not be interpreted as limiting the obligations of Uruguay under article 12(2) to citizens within its own territory.

---

[10] See discussion of the merits of the similar case of *Vidal Martins v Uruguay* (57/79) at [12.16].

[4.07] States Parties are therefore obliged to prevent their agents from violating the ICCPR rights of persons abroad. The HRC has interpreted the jurisdictional limits of State responsibility broadly to apply extraterritorially, despite the wording of article 2(1) ICCPR. This interpretation has important ramifications for States with armed forces stationed abroad, such as Australia with its forces in East Timor in late 1999, and the allied forces in northern Iraq and Kosovo.[11] Indeed, the HRC has stated, with regard to Belgium:[12]

¶ 14. The Committee is concerned about the behaviour of Belgian soldiers in Somalia under the aegis of the United Nations Operation in Somalia (UNOSOM II), and acknowledges that the State Party has recognized the applicability of the Covenant in this respect and opened 270 files for purposes of investigation. The Committee regrets that it has not received further information on the results of the investigations and adjudication of cases and requests the State party to submit this information.

[4.08] As States Parties are generally required to prevent private citizens from abusing the rights of others within jurisdiction, it is worth speculating whether a State Party could ever be held responsible for the actions of its nationals acting abroad in a private capacity.[13] For example, could a State Party be held liable for a failure to prevent egregious human rights abuse by its corporate citizens abroad? This is a compelling issue, as some transnational corporations are more politically and economically powerful than some of the host States (especially developing nations) in which they operate, so compulsory 'home State' regulation may be highly desirable.[14]

State Liability for the Acts of International Organizations

[4.09]   *H.v.d.P v THE NETHERLANDS (217/86)*

The author of this communication complained about the recruitment policies of his employer, the European Patent Office:

¶ 2.3. The author then turned to the Human Rights Committee, which he considers competent to consider the case, since five States parties (France, Italy, Luxembourg, the Netherlands and Sweden) to the European Patent Convention are also parties to the Optional Protocol to the International Covenant on Civil and Political Rights. He argues that 'pursuant to article 25(c), every citizen shall have access, on general terms of equality, to public service in his country. The EPO, though a public body common to the

---

[11] See T. Meron, 'Extraterritoriality of Human Rights Treaties: The 1994 US Action in Haiti' (1995) 89 *AJIL* 78.

[12] UN doc. CCPR/C/79/Add. 99.

[13] See generally Zwart, above, note 7, 87–90. See also Draft Articles on State Responsibility [1980] 2 *Yearbook of the International Law Commission*, pt. 2, at 30–4; UN doc. A/CN.4/SER.A/1980/Add.1. See also [1.59–1.62].

[14] See S. Joseph, 'Taming the Leviathans: Multinational Enterprises and Human Rights' (1999) 46 *Netherlands International Law Review* 171, at 175–8, and 183–4.

Contracting States, constitutes a body exercising Dutch public authority'.[15] The appeal to the President of EPO and the opinion given by the Internal Appeals Committee, the author argues, do not constitute an effective remedy within the meaning of article 2 of the Covenant against violations of article 25(c) of the Covenant. Moreover, 'the Internal Appeals Committee is a travesty of competence, independence and impartiality as required by article 14 of the Covenant.[16] IAC declines to adjudicate on the basis of public international law invoked by the applicant, i.e. law which the Contracting States undertook solemnly to observe'. . . .

The HRC found the case inadmissible for the following reasons:

¶ 3.2. The Human Rights Committee observes in this connection that it can only receive and consider communications in respect of claims that come under the jurisdiction of a State party to the Covenant. The author's grievances, however, concern the recruitment policies of an international organization, which cannot, in any way, be construed as coming within the jurisdiction of the Netherlands or of any other State party to the International Covenant on Civil and Political Rights and the Optional Protocol thereto. Accordingly, the author has no claim under the Optional Protocol.

[4.10] It is not surprising that the HRC has no jurisdiction over international organizations, as they are not parties to the ICCPR. However, the power and influence of modern international organizations, such as the European Union and its many organs, the World Trade Organization, the International Monetary Fund, the World Bank, and the United Nations itself, has expanded to the extent where they perhaps should be expressly bound by new human rights treaties.

However, note the HRC's comments regarding the Belgian contingent of the UN operation in Somalia [4.07], which seemed to imply that a State Party retains ICCPR responsibility for its armed forces even when they are under UN command. Is the Belgian comment consistent with the decision in *H.v.d.P.*?

Liability with Regard to the Acts of Other States

[4.11] Article 1 of the OP specifies that complaints must be submitted by victims of violations 'by that State party'. States Parties are not therefore generally liable for violations of ICCPR rights by other States.[17]

[4.12] *KINDLER v CANADA (470/91)*

The author alleged that his planned extradition by the State Party to the United States, where he faced the possibility of the death penalty, violated the ICCPR.[18]

---

[15] See generally on art. 25(c) Chap. 22.
[16] See generally on art. 14 Chap. 14.
[17] See, e.g., *E.M.E.H. v France* (409/90). See, however, [7.19] on the jurisdictional limits of art. 1(3). [18] See on the merits [8.27].

The State Party argued that the claim was inadmissible *ratione loci*, as it essentially concerned the anticipated actions of another State (which was, at the time, not even a State Party to the ICCPR). The HRC disagreed in the following terms:

¶ 6.2. The Committee considered the contention of the State party that the claim is inadmissible *ratione loci*. Article 2 of the Covenant requires States parties to guarantee the rights of persons within their jurisdiction. If a person is lawfully expelled or extradited, the State party concerned will not generally have responsibility under the Covenant for any violations of that person's rights that may later occur in the other jurisdiction. In that sense a State party clearly is not required to guarantee the rights of persons within another jurisdiction. However, if a State party takes a decision relating to a person within its jurisdiction, and the necessary and foreseeable consequence is that that person's rights under the Covenant will be violated in another jurisdiction, the State party itself may be in violation of the Covenant. That follows from the fact that a State party's duty under article 2 of the Covenant would be negated by the handing over of a person to another State (whether a State party to the Covenant or not) where treatment contrary to the Covenant is certain or is the very purpose of the handing over. For example, a State party would itself be in violation of the Covenant if it handed over a person to another State in circumstances in which it was foreseeable that torture would take place. The foreseeability of the consequence would mean that there was a present violation by the State party, even though the consequence would not occur until later on.

¶ 6.3. The Committee therefore considered itself competent to examine whether the State party is in violation of the Covenant by virtue of its decision to extradite the author under the Extradition Treaty of 1976 between the United States and Canada, and the Extradition Act of 1985.

[4.13] The HRC has found a number of cases admissible where authors alleged that their deportations to other States would result in a foreseeable breach of their article 6 right to life[19] or article 7 freedom from torture by that other State.[20] However, the HRC has never considered a complaint regarding deportation of a person who feared a 'lesser' human rights violation (e.g. violation of a derogable right) by the receiving State.

[4.14]   *T.T. v AUSTRALIA (706/96)*

The author complained that his proposed deportation to Malaysia would expose him to foreseeable breaches of his rights under articles 6 (possible imposition of the death penalty) and 14 (right to a fair trial). The State Party made the following arguments.

¶ 5.13. The State party argues that its obligation in relation to future violations of human rights by another State arises only in cases involving a potential violation of the most fundamental human rights and does not arise in relation to allegations under article 14, paragraph 3. It recalls that the Committee's jurisprudence so far has been confined to cases

---

[19] See [8.27–8.31].   [20] See [9.51] ff.

where the alleged victim faced extradition and where the claims related to violations of articles 6 and 7. . . .

In *T.T.*, the HRC did not address Australia's arguments in this respect as they found an article 14 breach was not foreseeable.[21] The HRC did however reiterate the *Kindler* test of State responsibility for the foreseeable actions:

¶ 8.1. What is at issue is, whether by deporting T. to Malaysia, Australia exposes him to a real risk (that is, a necessary and foreseeable consequence) of violation of his rights under the Covenant.

This principle does not appear to limit a State's potential liability regarding the actions of other States to only violations by the latter of the 'most fundamental' ICCPR rights. For example, could a pornographer complain that his/her deportation to a certain State would breach his/her article 19 freedom of expression if that State had overly restrictive obscenity laws? If this 'extraterritorial' responsibility extends to all ICCPR rights, it is indeed a very broad and onerous responsibility.

Conclusion

[4.15] The HRC has taken an expansive view of the territorial and jurisdictional limits of a State's responsibilities under the ICCPR. This is evinced by its decisions regarding location of the complainant at the time of the complaint, responsibility for the extraterritorial actions of State agents, and a State's responsibility for the extraterritorial consequences of its intra-territorial decisions. States have however not been held to have any jurisdiction over the actions of international organizations. Whilst a State's jurisdictional responsibility over individuals within jurisdiction has been established, it is perhaps doubtful whether States have any responsibility for the actions of their nationals abroad, when these nationals act in a private capacity.

---

[21] A similar scenario arose in *A.R.J. v Australia* (692/96).

5

Consideration Under Another International Procedure

ARTICLE 5(2)(a), OPTIONAL PROTOCOL

The Committee shall not consider any communication from an individual unless it has ascertained that:

(a) the same matter is not being examined under another procedure of international investigation or settlement.

[5.01] Article 5(2)(a) only precludes the admissibility of complaints under the First Optional Protocol (OP) that are being *concurrently* considered by an international body that is comparable to the HRC. For example, in *L.E.S.K. v The Netherlands* (381/89), the same matter had previously been considered by the European Commission on Human Rights. As the case was not under simultaneous examination elsewhere, it did not matter that it had previously been declared inadmissible by another body.[1] Furthermore, article 5(2)(a) will not apply where the complaint laid before the other international body has been withdrawn.[2]

[5.02] Nor does it matter if the other body has concluded its merits decision; this will not preclude admissibility before the HRC.[3] Davidson disapproves, arguing that this interpretation increases the likelihood of divergent international human rights opinions, which might lead to human rights 'forum shopping', and a loss of respect for international human rights bodies.[4] However, the HRC's interpretation accords with a literal interpretation of article 5(2)(a): a concluded case '*is not being examined*' within the wording of article 5(2)(a).

---

[1] See, e.g., *H. d. P v The Netherlands* (217/86); *R.L.A. W. v The Netherlands* (372/89); *C.B.D. v The Netherlands* (394/90)

[2] See *Millán Sequeira v Uruguay* (6/77), para. 6; *Torres Ramirez v Uruguay* (4/77), para. 9, and *Thomas v Jamaica* (321/88), para. 5.1.

[3] See *Wright v Jamaica* (349/89), where the author's situation had previously been found to violate the Inter-American Convention on Human Rights.

[4] J.S. Davidson, 'The Procedure and Practice of the Human Rights Committee under the First Optional Protocol to the International Covenant on Civil and Political Rights' (1991) 4 *Canterbury Law Review* 337, at 348.

What Constitutes Another International Procedure?

[5.03] *BABOERAM et al. v SURINAME (146, 148–154/83)*

In this case the Committee considered a number of communications jointly as they related to the same events. In each instance the State Party objected to the admissibility of the claims on the basis that the communications were allegedly being considered under another international procedure. The HRC found all of the cases admissible in the following terms:

¶ 9.1. With respect to the admissibility of the communications the Human Rights Committee observed first that a study by an intergovernmental organization either of the human rights situation in a given country (such as that by [the Inter-American Commission on Human Rights] in respect of Suriname) or a study of the trade union rights situation in a given country (such as the issues examined by the Committee on Freedom of Association of the ILO in respect of Suriname), or of a human rights problem of a more global character (such as that of the Special Rapporteur of the Commission on Human Rights on summary or arbitrary executions), although such studies might refer to or draw on information concerning individuals, cannot be seen as being the same matter as the examination of an individual case within the meaning of article 5, paragraph 2(a), of the Optional Protocol. Secondly, a procedure established by non-governmental organizations (such as Amnesty International, the International Commission of Jurists or the [International Committee of the Red Cross], irrespective of the latter's standing in international law) does not constitute a procedure of international investigation or settlement within the meaning of article 5, paragraph 2 (a), of the Optional Protocol. Thirdly, the Human Rights Committee ascertained that, although the individual cases of the alleged victims had been submitted to IACHR (by an unrelated third party) and registered before that body, collectively, as case No. 9015, that case was no longer under consideration. Accordingly, the Human Rights Committee concluded that it was not barred by the provisions of article 5, paragraph 2 (a), of the Optional Protocol from considering the communications.

[5.04] In *A v S* (1/76) the Committee held that the ECOSOC Resolution 1503 procedure was not classified as a procedure within the meaning of article 5(2)(a); it was not designed to redress individual claims, but rather to redress more large scale systemic abuses, in particular 'consistent patterns of human rights violations'.[5] Similarly, admissibility in *Celis Laureano v Peru* (540/93) was not precluded by its simultaneous consideration by a United Nations Working Group on Enforced and Involuntary Disappearances.[6]

[5.05] In *Polay de Campos v Peru* (577/94), the case was admissible despite its registration before the Inter-American Commission on Human Rights. The Commission however 'had no plans to prepare a report on the case within the next twelve months'. As the Inter-American proceedings were dormant, the HRC found the case was not precluded from admissibility by article 5(2)(a).

---

[5] See, on the 1503 procedure, A.H. Robertson and J.H. Merrills, *Human Rights in the World* (3rd edn., Manchester University Press, Manchester, 1994), 74–8. [6] Para. 7.1.

[5.06] Therefore, it seems that only individual complaints proceedings before other United Nations human rights treaty bodies, like the Committee Against Torture, or individual proceedings before regional human rights bodies, namely the bodies under the European and Inter-American Conventions on Human Rights, and the African Charter, will constitute relevant 'procedures of international investigation or settlement' for the purposes of article 5(2)(a), OP.[7]

What is Examination of the 'Same Matter'?

[5.07]   *FANALI v ITALY (75/80)*

In this case the Committee was asked to decide on the admissibility of a communication where the author's co-defendants in a prior domestic trial had already raised similar issues to the author before the European Commission of Human Rights. The Committee found the case admissible, and gave a very clear indication of what constituted the 'same matter' for the purposes of article 5(2)(a) OP in their admissibility decision:

¶ 7.2. With regard to article 5 (2) (a) of the Optional Protocol, the Committee did not agree with the State party's contention that 'the same matter' had been brought before the European Commission on Human Rights since other individuals had brought their own cases before that body concerning claims which appeared to arise from the same incident. The Committee held that the concept of 'the same matter' within the meaning of article 5 (2) (a) of the Optional Protocol had to be understood as including the same claim concerning the same individual, submitted by him or someone else who has the standing to act on his behalf before the other international body. Since the State party itself recognized that the author of the present communication had not submitted his specific case to the European Commission of Human Rights, the Human Rights Committee concluded that the communication was not inadmissible under article 5 (2) (a) of the Optional Protocol.

The *Fanali* case was followed in *Blom v Sweden* (191/85) and *Sánchez López v Spain* (777/97).

[5.08]   *MILLÁN SEQUEIRA v URUGUAY (6/77)*

¶ 9. In a decision adopted on 25 July 1978, the Human Rights Committee concluded:

(a) That the two-line reference to Millán Sequeira in case No. 2109 before the Inter-American Commission on Human Rights—which case lists in a similar manner the names of hundreds of other persons allegedly detained in Uruguay—did not constitute the same matter as that described in detail by the author in his communication to the Human Rights Committee. Accordingly, the communication was not inadmissible under article 5 (2) (a) of the Optional Protocol. . . .

---

[7] See also T. Zwart, *The Admissibility of Human Rights Petitions* (Martinus Nijhoff, Dordrecht, 1994), 175.

[5.09] If the complaint before the other international body was made prior to the date of entry into force of the OP in the country concerned, the communication is never inadmissible under article 5(2)(a) OP.[8] For example, in *Grille Motta v Uruguay* (11/77), the HRC reasoned that the alternative complaints could not concern 'the same matter' as they related to events which took place before entry into force of the OP.[9]

Reservations by European Parties

[5.10] The crux of article 5(2)(a) is that the Committee cannot consider communications which are simultaneously being heard by another international body. The Optional Protocol does not preclude the Committee from examining communications which have been previously considered by another body. However, many European parties have made a reservation which denies the HRC competence to re-examine communications which have been considered under an alternative international procedure. The obvious intent behind these reservations is to prevent the possibility of 'appeal' from the European Convention (ECHR) bodies to the HRC.[10] These reservations have been considered in a number of cases.

[5.11]   *A.M. v DENMARK (121/82)*

¶ 5. Before considering any claims contained in a communication, the Human Rights Committee must decide whether the communication is admissible under the Optional Protocol to the International Covenant on Civil and Political Rights. The Committee observes in this connection that, when ratifying the Optional Protocol and recognizing the competence of the Committee to receive and consider communications from individuals subject to its jurisdiction, the State party Denmark made a reservation, with reference to article 5 (2) (a) of the Optional Protocol, in respect of the competence of the Committee to consider a communication from an individual if the matter has already been considered under other procedures of international investigation.

¶ 6. In the light of the above-mentioned reservation and observing that the same matter has already been considered [and declared inadmissible] by the European Commission of Human Rights and therefore by another procedure of international investigation within the meaning of article 5(2) (a) of the Optional Protocol to the International Covenant on Civil and Political Rights, the Committee concludes that it is not competent to consider the present communication.

[5.12] Mr Graefrath wrote a strong dissent.

---

[8] Ibid., 175–6; see also P.R. Ghandhi, *The Human Rights Committee and the Right of Individual Communication* (Ashgate, Dartmouth, 1998), 226–7.

[9] Para. 5(a).

[10] Ghandhi, above, note 8, 228. See Chap. 25 generally on reservations, and especially [25.30].

I cannot . . . share the view that the Committee is barred from considering the communication by the reservation of Denmark relating to article 5 (2) (a) of the Optional Protocol. That reservation refers to matters that have already been considered under other procedures of international investigation. It does not in my opinion refer to matters, the consideration of which has been denied under any other procedure by a decision of inadmissibility.

In the case of the author of communication No. 121/82, the European Commission of Human Rights has declared his application inadmissible as being manifestly ill-founded. It has thereby found that it has no competence to consider the matter within the legal framework of the European Convention. An application that has been declared inadmissible has not, in the meaning of the reservation, been 'considered' in such a way that the Human Rights Committee is precluded from considering it.

The reservation aims at preventing the Human Rights Committee from reviewing cases that have been considered by another international organ of investigation. It does not seek to limit the competence of the Human Rights Committee to deal with communications merely on the ground that the rights of the Covenant allegedly violated may also be covered by the European Convention and its procedural requirements. If that had been the aim of the reservation, it would, in my opinion, have been incompatible with the Optional Protocol.

If the Committee interprets the reservation in such a way that it would be excluded from considering a communication when a complaint referring to the same facts has been declared inadmissible under the procedure of the European Convention, the effect would be that any complaint that has been declared inadmissible under that procedure could later on not be considered by the Human Rights Committee, despite the fact that the conditions for admissibility of communications are set out in a separate international instrument and are different from those under the Optional Protocol.

An application that has been declared inadmissible under the system of the European Convention is not necessarily inadmissible under the system of the Covenant and the Optional Protocol, even if it refers to the same facts. This is also true in relation to an application that has been declared inadmissible by the European Commission as being manifestly ill-founded. The decision that an application is manifestly ill-founded can necessarily be taken only in relation to rights set forth in the European Convention. These rights, however, differ in substance and in regard to their implementation procedures from the rights set forth in the Covenant. They, as well as the competence of the European Commission, derive from a separate and independent international instrument. A decision on non-admissibility of the European Commission, therefore, has no impact on a matter before the Human Rights Committee and cannot hinder the Human Rights Committee from reviewing the facts of a communication on its own legal basis and under its own procedure and from ascertaining whether they are compatible with the provisions of the Covenant. This might lead to a similar result as under the European Convention, but not necessarily so.

The reservation of Denmark was intended to avoid the same matter being considered twice. It did not aim at closing the door for a communication that might be admissible under the Optional Protocol despite the fact that it has been declared inadmissible by the European Commission.

A number of commentators have expressed a preference for Graefrath's dissent over the decision of the majority.[11]

[5.13] *V.Ø. v NORWAY (168/84)*

In this case the author had already made a prior application to the European Commission of Human Rights. The Committee therefore focused on the effect of a relevant Norwegian reservation on the author's communication. It made the following comments:

¶ 2.5. With regard to his prior application to the European Commission of Human Rights, the author submits in his communication to the Human Rights Committee (a) that the European Commission focused mainly on the question of the alleged tardiness of the court procedures, to the detriment of the main issues complained of and (b) . . . that the provisions of the European Convention invoked before the European Commission of Human Rights differ in several areas from those of the Covenant invoked in the present communication to the Human Rights Committee. He maintains that the relevant provisions of the Covenant are better suited to protect his rights in the matter complained of than those earlier invoked before the European Commission of Human Rights.

¶ 2.6. In the author's subsequent submission of 1 July 1984 he further explained that his application to the Human Rights Committee is no 'appeal' over the decision by the European Commission, but concerns only the Norwegian court decision. 'The European Convention for the Protection of Human Rights and Fundamental Freedoms, article 6, reads that 'everyone is entitled to a fair and public hearing within a reasonable time by an independent and impartial tribunal established by law'. It follows from this that the European Convention has a limited mandate with respect to the issue of equality before the law. Furthermore, the European Convention does not cover the areas which come under articles 23 and 26 of the Covenant.[12] Thus, in the case of the applicant, the International Covenant is of considerably more interest than the European Convention.' . . .

¶ 2.7. The author further argues that 'the same matter has not already been properly examined under any other procedures of international investigation or settlement. Certainly, the same matter has not been examined anywhere with regard to the International Covenant, articles 3, 14, 23 and 26.'

The HRC found the case inadmissible, due to the Norwegian reservation. It stated that the two letters, to the European Commission and the HRC, were 'almost identical', and referred to the same facts and same legal arguments.[13] The fact that some provisions of the ICCPR may have offered more relevant protection than the ECHR was irrelevant.

[5.14] In the more recent decision of *Linderholm v Croatia* (744/97), the complaint was again inadmissible due to a declaration that precluded OP examination of cases

---

[11] See, e.g., Ghandhi, above, note 8, 230.
[12] See, on art. 23, Chap. 20, and on art. 26, Chap. 23.
[13] Para. 4.2.

previously examined by the European Commission. The HRC did specifically note that the scope of the non-discrimination provisions in the European Convention and in the ICCPR was different,[14] but concluded that these distinctions would have made no difference to the resolution of the case at hand.[15] This may indicate that the HRC will in the future be reluctant to apply the European reservations to preclude the admissibility of cases that concern ICCPR rights which are fundamentally different from those in the ECHR.[16]

[5.15]   *CASANOVAS v FRANCE (441/90)*

In this case the French government argued that the complaint be declared inadmissible on the basis that the author's claim had already been declared inadmissible by the European Commission on Human Rights. The Committee made the following finding in favour of the author regarding admissibility:

¶ 5.1. At its 48th session, the Committee considered the admissibility of the communication. It noted the State party's contention that the communication was inadmissible because of the reservation made by the State party to article 5, paragraph 2, of the Optional Protocol. The Committee observed that the European Commission had declared the author's application inadmissible as incompatible *ratione materiae* with the European Convention. The Committee considered that, since the rights of the European Convention differed in substance and in regard of their implementation procedures from the rights set forth in the Covenant, a matter that had been declared inadmissible *ratione materiae* had not, in the meaning of the reservation, been 'considered' in such a way that the Committee was precluded from examining it.

[5.16] In *Casanovas*, the relevant French reservation precluded HRC examination of a matter if it had been 'examined' by a comparable human rights body. In the same session,[17] the HRC considered a complaint in *V.E.M. v Spain* (467/91). The relevant Spanish reservation precluded OP admissibility where the same matter had been 'submitted' to another body. As the Spanish reservation was ostensibly broader, it precluded admissibility in the case, which otherwise had very similar facts to *Casanovas*.

[5.17] In *Trébutien v France* (421/90), *Glaziou v France* (452/91), and *Valentijn v France* (584/94), previous European submissions were found inadmissible as 'manifestly ill-founded'; the cases were subsequently inadmissible under the OP due to the French reservation. These cases may be distinguished from *Casanovas* as 'manifestly ill-founded' inadmissibility may be distinguished from a finding of inadmissibility *ratione materiae*; the former finding entails some evaluation of the complaint's merits and relevant evidence by the European Commission or Court, whereas the latter does not.

---

[14] Art. 26 ICCPR is a more comprehensive guarantee of non-discrimination than art. 14 ECHR: see [23.11].   [15] Para. 4.2.
[16] The ICCPR offers different protection from the ECHR under a number of arts., including arts. 14, 23, 24, and 25.   [17] 48th session in July 1993.

[5.18] *PAUGER v AUSTRIA (716/96)*

¶ 6.4. .... The Committee observed that the European Commission had declared the author's application inadmissible on procedural grounds, without examining in any way the merits of the author's claim. .... On this basis, the Committee considered that the European Commission did not 'examine' the author's complaint, since it declared it inadmissible on procedural grounds. ....

Thus, substantive inadmissibility (e.g. no claim under the ECHR) is distinguished from procedural inadmissibility under the ECHR (e.g. non-exhaustion of domestic remedies), for the purposes of deciding whether the standard European reservation has precluded Optional Protocol inadmissibility.[18]

Conclusion

[5.19] Article 5(2)(a) of the OP precludes the admissibility of cases which are being simultaneously considered by a comparable human rights body, in a procedure which is analogous to the OP procedure. Once such consideration has ceased, article 5(2)(a) poses no obstacle to admissibility. However, a number of European parties have entered a reservation to the OP, precluding admissibility where the matter has been considered by a comparable human rights body, even where such consideration is complete. These reservations have effectively blocked the HRC from acting as an 'appeals' body from the European Convention bodies.

---

[18] The Austrian reservation precluded OP examination where the case had been 'examined' by another body. In *O.F. v Norway* (158/83), a similar Norwegian reservation did not preclude admissibility where the Secretariat of the European Commission had merely advised the author that his application would be outside the six-month time-limit. In that case the application had not even been registered at the Commission. See Zwart, above, note 7, 179–80.

6

Exhaustion of Domestic Remedies

ARTICLE 5(2)(b), FIRST OPTIONAL PROTOCOL

The Committee shall not consider any communication from an individual unless it has ascertained that . . . the individual has exhausted all available domestic remedies. This shall not be the rule where the application of the remedies is unreasonably prolonged.

[6.01] The domestic remedies rule also applies to constrain admissibility under the International Convention on the Elimination of all Forms of Racial Discrimination (ICERD)[1] and the Convention against Torture and other Cruel, Inhuman, or Degrading Treatment or Punishment (CAT).[2] This rule ensures that States Parties are furnished with an opportunity to correct any municipal human rights abuses before the matter is addressed at the international level. The HRC spelt out the rationale behind article 5(2)(b) in *T.K. v France*:[3]

¶ 8.3. The purpose of article 5(2)(b) of the Optional Protocol is, *inter alia*, to direct possible victims of violations of the provisions of the Covenant to seek, in the first place, satisfaction from the competent State party authorities and, at the same time, to enable State parties to examine, on the basis of individual complaints, the implementation, within their territory and by their organs, of the provisions of the Covenant and, if necessary, remedy the violations occurring, before the Committee is seized of the matter.

What Sort of Remedies must be Exhausted?

[6.02]   *R.T. v FRANCE (262/87)*

¶ 7.4. . . . The Committee observes that article 5, paragraph 2 (b), of the Optional Protocol, by referring to 'all available domestic remedies', clearly refers in the first place to judicial remedies. . . .

---

[1] Art. 14(7)(a).   [2] Art. 22(5)(b).
[3] See also *M.K. v France* (222/87), para. 8.3.

Therefore, local remedies are usually deemed to be exhausted when a final judicial decision has been rendered, and there remains no available appeal.[4]

PATIÑO v PANAMA (437/90)[5]

¶ 5.2. . . . For the purposes of article 5(2)(b) of the Optional Protocol, an applicant must make use of all judicial or administrative avenues that offer him a reasonable prospect of redress.

VICENTE et al. v COLOMBIA (612/95)

¶ 5.2. . . . The Committee considered that the effectiveness of a remedy also depended on the nature of the alleged violation. In other words, if the alleged offence is particularly serious, as in the case of violations of basic human rights, in particular the right to life, purely administrative and disciplinary measures cannot be considered adequate and effective. . . .

Whilst the *Patiño* statement confirms that non-judicial remedies may occasionally have to be exhausted, *R.T.* correctly indicates that judicial remedies are considered the remedies most likely to be effective, and are therefore the most relevant remedies for the purposes of article 5(2)(b). *Vicente* confirms that judicial remedies are essential for allegations of extremely serious abuse. The HRC has evinced greater suspicion of the efficacy of executive remedies, and are less likely to require their exhaustion. For example, in *Ellis v Jamaica* (276/88), the HRC found that the availability to a prisoner on death row of a petition for mercy to the Governor-General was not a 'domestic remedy within the meaning of article 5(2)(b)'.[6] Similarly, as indicated in *Muhonen v Finland* (89/81), the HRC is suspicious of the efficacy of 'extraordinary remedies' [6.32].

[6.03] In *Pereira Montero v Uruguay* (106/81), the author complained of the refusal by the State Party's German consulate to renew her passport. The HRC refused to accept the contention that she should have returned home to Uruguay in order to have her passport renewed.[7] Such an imposition did not constitute a remedy which had to be exhausted for the purposes of admissibility.

[6.04]   C.F. v CANADA (118/81)

¶ 6.2. . . . The Covenant provides that a remedy shall be granted whenever a violation of one of the rights guaranteed by it has occurred; consequently, it does not generally

---

[4] A. Conçado Trindade, *The Application of the Rule of Exhaustion of Local Remedies in International Law: Its Rationale in the International Protection of Individual Rights* (Cambridge University Press, Cambridge, 1983), 58.

[5] See also *Thompson v Panama* (438/90), para. 5.2.   [6] Para. 9.1.

[7] See also [12.15–12.16].

prescribe preventive protection, but confines itself to requiring effective redress *ex post facto*. . . .

Whilst *ex post facto* remedies are generally accepted as remedies which must be exhausted before recourse may be had to the HRC via the Optional Protocol (OP), there are occasions where such remedies will be deemed ineffective, as in the case of *Ominayak v Canada* (167/84) [6.14].

How Must Remedies be Exhausted?

[6.05] A prospective OP complainant is required to have raised the substance of his/her ICCPR complaint before local authorities, before his/her OP complaint will be held admissible. This principle is evinced in the following case excerpts.

GRANT v JAMAICA (353/88)

¶ 5.1. . . . With regard to the author's claims concerning the conditions of detention on death row, the Committee noted that he had not indicated what steps, if any, he had taken to submit his grievances to the competent prison authorities, and what investigations, if any, had been carried out. Accordingly, the Committee found that in this respect domestic remedies had not been exhausted.

PERERA v AUSTRALIA (541/93)

¶ 6.5. With regard to the author's claim that the appeal against his retrial was unfair, because one of the judges had participated in his prior appeal against the first conviction, the Committee notes that the judge's participation on appeal was not challenged by the defence and that domestic remedies with respect to this matter have thus not been exhausted. This part of the communication is therefore inadmissible.

¶ 6.6. As regards the author's claim about the failure to provide him with the services of an interpreter, the Committee notes that this issue was never brought to the attention of the courts, neither during the trial, nor at appeal. This part of the communication is therefore inadmissible for failure to exhaust domestic remedies, under article 5, paragraph 2(b), of the Optional Protocol.

[6.06]   *B.D.B. v NETHERLANDS (273/89)*

¶ 6.3. . . . The Committee observes that whereas authors must invoke the substantive rights contained in the Covenant, they are not required, for the purposes of the Optional Protocol, necessarily to do so by reference to specific articles of the Covenant.

This aspect of the *B.d.B.* decision has been followed in *Van Alphen v Netherlands*

(305/88), *Henry v Jamaica* (230/87), and *Little v Jamaica* (283/88). Thus, the semantics of one's domestic complaint are not decisive in determining whether one has properly alerted domestic authorities to potential breaches of one's ICCPR rights. For example, a complaint to the HRC regarding the arbitrariness of an arrest will not be inadmissible under article 5(2)(b) if that arrest has been challenged in domestic forums; there is no necessity for the complainant specifically to invoke article 9 ICCPR. Furthermore, an OP author is only required to raise ICCPR issues before domestic forums; it is not necessary for the author to ensure the due consideration of those issues by such forums.[8]

[6.07] Certain domestic remedies may have to be implemented within a certain time period. For example, a person may only have a limited time in which they can seek to appeal a lower court's decision to a higher court. In general, it is up to the author to ensure his/her compliance with domestic procedural requirements.

A.P.A. v SPAIN (433/90)

The author was complaining about alleged breaches of his right to a fair trial. He details his attempts to exhaust domestic remedies below.

¶ 2.3. The author appealed to the Supreme Court of Spain on procedural grounds. On 2 June 1989, the Supreme Court confirmed the judgement of first instance. Allegedly because of summer holidays, the author was not notified of the Supreme Court's decision until 11 September 1989, that is considerably after the expiration of the deadline of 20 working days allowed for the filing of a constitutional motion against the decision (*recurso de amparo*).

¶ 2.4. On 15 January 1990, A.P.A. appealed to the Constitutional Tribunal, alleging a breach of article 24 of the Constitution, which guarantees the right to a fair trial. On 26 February 1990, the Constitutional Tribunal declared the *amparo* inadmissible, as statutory deadlines for the filing of the motion had expired.

¶ 2.5. In the above context, the author notes that during the month of August, the Spanish judicial system is virtually paralysed because of summer holidays. For this reason, article 304 of the Spanish Civil Code stipulates that the month of August is not counted for the purpose of determining deadlines for the filing of appeals. Article 2 of an agreement (*Acuerdo de Pleno*) of 15 June 1982, however, stipulates that for the purpose of a number of procedures before the Constitutional Tribunal, including *amparo* proceedings, August does count for the determination of such deadlines.

The HRC nevertheless found that the author had failed to exhaust domestic remedies.

---

[8] See, e.g., *Henry v Jamaica* (230/87), para. 7.2; *Little v Jamaica* (283/88).

¶ 6.2. The Committee has noted the parties' arguments relating to the question of exhaustion of domestic remedies. It notes that while the month of August does not count for the determination of deadlines in the filing of most criminal appeals, it does count under regulations governing *amparo* proceedings before the Constitutional Tribunal. While it is true that local remedies within the meaning of article 5, paragraph 2 (b), of the Optional Protocol must only be exhausted to the extent that they are both available and effective, it is an established principle that an accused must exercise due diligence in the pursuit of available remedies. In this context, the principle that ignorance of the law excuses no one—*ignorantia iuris neminem excusat*—also applies to article 5, paragraph 2(b), of the Optional Protocol.

¶ 6.3. In the instant case, the decision of the Supreme Court of 2 June 1989 was duly notified to the author's counsel. The author claims that counsel did not inform him of this notification until after the expiration of the *amparo* proceedings deadline. Nothing in the file before the Committee indicates that author's counsel was not privately retained. In the circumstances, counsel's inaction or neglect in communicating the Supreme Court's judgement to his client cannot be attributed to the State party but must be attributed to the author; the Committee does not consider that, under article 14 of the Covenant, it was incumbent upon the Supreme Court's registry or upon the Prosecutor's office to directly notify the author personally of the decision of 2 June 1989 in the circumstances of the case. It must, accordingly, be concluded that local remedies were not pursued with the requisite diligence and, therefore, that the requirements of article 5, paragraph 2(b), of the Optional Protocol have not been met.

In a minority concurring opinion, Mr Aguilar Urbina further explained the HRC's reasoning:

¶ 2.2. The author concedes, moreover, that there was negligence or omission on the part of his counsel, but holds that that conduct cannot be imputed to himself. However, it cannot be maintained that the supposed negligence of the author's lawyer can be ascribed to the State party and not to the author himself, who should have made the necessary arrangements to take the requisite steps within the time-periods established by law.

A similar decision was reached by the Committee on the Elimination of Racial Discrimination under ICERD in *C.P. and M.P. v Denmark* (CERD 5/1994); the negligence of the authors' private counsel in failing to file an appeal within statutory time-limits meant that available domestic remedies had not been exhausted, so the communication was consequently inadmissible.[9] In *Barbaro v Australia* (CERD 7/95), the failure of the author's privately retained lawyer to inform him of appeal possibilities before the expiration of statutory time-limits similarly meant that the author had failed properly to exhaust domestic remedies.[10]

[6.08] In contrast, in *Griffin v Spain* (493/92), the author's failure to seek a relevant remedy within a statutory time period was not held against him, as his court-appointed lawyer had failed to inform him of this remedy (indeed, the lawyer had

---

[9] Para. 6.2.   [10] Para. 10.4.

not contacted him at all).[11] *Griffin* indicates that authors may be excused from exhausting domestic remedies where their failure to do so has resulted from the negligence or incompetence of State-provided lawyers, as opposed to privately retained counsel.[12]

[6.09] In *Muhonen v Finland* (89/81), the author had 'clearly been given to understand that there was no further remedy',[13] and thus was not required to pursue the outstanding remedy.[14]

[6.10]   *J.R.T. and the W.G. PARTY v CANADA (104/81)*

With regard to one of the author's complaints in this case, the HRC noted:

¶ 8(b). As to the author's claim that section 13(1) of the Canadian Human Rights Act, under which his use of the telephone service has been curtailed, has been applied against him in violation of article 19 of the Covenant, the Committee notes that he failed to file his application for judicial review within the time-limits prescribed by law. It appears, however, in view of the ambiguity ensuing from the conflicting time-limits laid down in the laws in question, that a reasonable effort was indeed made to exhaust domestic remedies in this respect and, therefore, the Committee does not consider that, as to this claim, the communication should be declared inadmissible under article 5(2)(b) of the Optional Protocol.

[6.11]   *MPANDANJILA et al. v ZAIRE (138/83)*

¶ 2.4. On 7 July 1982, the [victims' Belgian] lawyers filed appeals with the Supreme Court of Justice . . . on behalf of their clients against the judgment on 1 July 1982. By decision of 26 October 1982, . . . the Supreme Court declined to consider the appeals because the court fees had not been paid. In this connection, the lawyers point out that they had taken steps to ensure that the requirement of payment of the court fees be complied with. They state that, since their clients were scattered among several detention centres, and it was impossible to communicate with them, a Zairian lawyer, Maître Mukendi . . . was asked to carry out the necessary formalities for depositing the fees. By a letter dated 15 September 1982, they urged Maître Mukendi to contact Mrs Birindwa (the wife of one of the alleged victims), who was supposed to collect the necessary funds. At the same time, they wrote to the Chief Justice of the Supreme Court to inform the Court of the steps taken to comply with the necessary formalities. It later transpired that Mrs Birindwa had not been in Kinshasa at the time in question and that the intended collection and payment of the court fees had not been made. The lawyers contend, however, that the efforts made to comply with the formalities, although unsuccessful, should be considered as satisfactory, in particular as

---

[11] Para. 6.1.

[12] However, in its jurisprudence on the right to a fair trial, the HRC has possibly adopted uniform rules regarding a State's responsibility for the conduct of all lawyers, whether privately retained or not. See [14.95].   [13] Para. 6.1.

[14] See also the minority opinion in *Y.L. v Canada* (112/81), para. 2.

the decision not to take action on the appeals was taken relatively shortly after the Supreme Court was informed of the efforts made to collect and deposit the fees. . . .

The HRC agreed that the case was admissible:

¶ 5.2. . . . The Committee noted the particular difficulties facing the authors, who were allegedly scattered among different detention centres, in paying their court fees in timely fashion. The Committee also noted the speed of the Supreme Court's decision, against which there was no appeal, to dismiss the case on that ground. . . . In the circumstances, the Committee concluded that the communication was not inadmissible . . . by virtue of article 5, paragraph 2(b) of the Optional Protocol. . . .

Thus, the article 5(2)(b) OP requirement will be fulfilled if the author, or author's counsel, has made an unsuccessful yet genuine attempt to comply with procedural formalities in order to exhaust local remedies.

No Requirement to Exhaust Futile Remedies

[6.12]   *PRATT and MORGAN v JAMAICA (210/86, 225/87)*

¶ 12.3. . . . That the local remedies rule does not require resort to appeals that objectively have no prospect of success, is a well established principle of international law and of the Committee's jurisprudence.

Complainants are not required to pursue remedies that are objectively futile. However, as evinced in numerous cases, such as *R.T. v France* (262/87) and *Kaaber v Iceland* (674/95), a complainant's subjective belief in the futility of domestic remedies does not *per se* absolve him/her of the requirement that such remedies be exhausted.

[6.13]   *DERMIT BARBATO v URUGUAY (84/81)*

¶ 9.4. As to the question of exhaustion of domestic remedies in the case of Guillermo Dermit, the Committee also takes into account the following considerations: the remedies listed by the State party as unexhausted cannot be considered available to the alleged victim in the circumstances of his case. They are either inapplicable *de jure* or *de facto* and do not constitute an effective remedy, within the meaning of article 2 (3) of the Covenant, for the matters complained of. There are therefore no grounds to alter the conclusion reached in the Committee's decision of 28 October 1981, that the communication is not inadmissible under article 5 (2) (b) of the Optional Protocol.

In a number of similar cases against the military regime in Uruguay in the Committee's early years,[15] the HRC found that the State Party had not shown that

---

[15] See, e.g., *Torres Ramírez v Uruguay* (4/77), *Grille Motta et al. v Uruguay* (11/77), and *Martínez Machado v Uruguay* (83/80)

allegedly available remedies would be effective.[16] These cases involved allegations of egregious human rights abuses, such as breaches of the right to life, and
freedom from torture and/or arbitrary detention. In many such cases, the State
security forces were essentially acting with impunity, without regard for any
notion of the rule of law. Such is indicated by the reference in *Dermit Barbato* to
the lack of remedies '*de jure* or *de facto*'. In such situations, it seems the HRC
will recognize that pursuit of domestic remedies under such a regime is likely to
be futile, so a high burden of proof will be placed on the State Party to prove the
efficacy of unexhausted remedies. This contention is supported by the decision in
Arzuaga Gilboa v Uruguay (147/83), where the HRC stated that 'effective' remedies entailed 'procedural guarantees for a "fair and public hearing by a competent, independent and impartial tribunal" '.[17] A State which does not provide for
such a system for the administration of justice is unlikely to offer effective
enforceable remedies, particularly against its own officers, as the system does not
accord with the rule of law.[18]

[6.14] *OMINAYAK et al. v CANADA (167/84)*

This case concerned a complaint by the chief of an indigenous Canadian tribe, the
Lubicon Lake Band, regarding the rights of himself and his people.[19] The main
allegation concerned an alleged breach of the Band members' article 27 minority
rights, entailed in the destructive effect on Lubicon culture of various acts of the
provincial government of Alberta, including expropriation of Lubicon land for the
benefit of private corporate interests, and its authorization of energy exploration
in their homelands.[20] Regarding exhaustion of domestic remedies, the author
stated the following:

¶ 3.2. With respect to the exhaustion of domestic remedies, it is stated that the Lubicon
Lake Band has been pursuing its claims through domestic political and legal avenues. It is
alleged that the domestic political and legal process in Canada is being used by government officials and energy corporation representatives to thwart and delay the Band's
actions until, ultimately, the Band becomes incapable of pursuing them, because industrial
development at the current rate in the area, accompanied by the destruction of the environmental and economic base of the Band, would make it impossible for the Band to
survive as a people for many more years. . . .

¶ 3.5. On 16 February 1982, an action was filed in the Court of Queen's Bench of Alberta

---

[16] See, generally, P.R. Ghandhi, *The Human Rights Committee and the Right of Individual Communication: Law and Practice* (Ashgate, Dartmouth, 1998), 240–9.

[17] Para. 7.2.

[18] The *Arzuaga Gilboa* statement does not however require domestic remedies to conform with all of the due process guarantees in art. 14. See D. McGoldrick, *The Human Rights Committee* (Clarendon Press, Oxford, 1994), 193. Indeed, the HRC has conceded that non-judicial remedies may occasionally be effective [6.02].

[19] The case is otherwise known as the *Lubicon Lake Band Case*.

[20] The merits of this case are considered at [24.24].

requesting an interim injunction to halt development in the area until issues raised by the Band's land and natural resource claims were settled. The main purpose of the interim injunction, the author states, was to prevent the Alberta government and the oil companies (the 'defendants') from further destroying the traditional hunting and trapping territory of the Lubicon Lake people. This would have permitted the Band members to continue to hunt and trap for their livelihood and subsistence as a part of their aboriginal way of life. The provincial court did not render its decision for almost two years, during which time oil and gas development continued, along with rapid destruction of the Band's economic base. On 17 November 1983, the request for an interim injunction was denied and the Band, although financially destitute, was subsequently held liable for all court costs and attorneys' fees associated with the action.

¶ 3.6. The decision of the Court of Queen's Bench was appealed to the Court of Appeal of Alberta: it was dismissed on 11 January 1985. In reaching its decision, the Court of Appeal agreed with the lower court's finding that the Band's claim of aboriginal title to the land presented a serious question of law to be decided at trial. None the less, the Court of Appeal found that the Lubicon Lake Band would suffer no irreparable harm if resource development continued fully and that the balance of convenience, therefore, favoured denial of the injunction.

The State Party disputed that effective remedies had been exhausted:

¶ 5.4. Rather than proceed with a trial on the merits, the Band appealed against the dismissal of the interim application. Its appeal was dismissed by the Alberta Court of Appeal of 11 January 1985. The Band's application for leave to appeal the dismissal of the interim injunction to the Supreme Court of Canada was refused on 14 March 1985. Almost two months later, on 13 May 1985, the State party adds, the Supreme Court of Canada denied another request by the Band that the Court bend its own rules to rehear the application. Thus, the State party states, the Court upheld its well-established rule prohibiting the rehearing of applications for leave to appeal.

¶ 5.5. The State party submits that, after such extensive delays caused by interim proceedings and the contesting of clearly settled procedural matters of law, the author's claim that the application of domestic remedies is being unreasonably prolonged has no merit. It submits that it has been open to the Band as plaintiff to press on with the substantive steps in either of its legal actions so as to bring the matters to trial.

The HRC found in favour of the complainant on this point:[21]

¶ 13.2. With regard to the requirement, in article 5, paragraph 2 (b), of the Optional Protocol, that authors must exhaust domestic remedies before submitting a communication to the Human Rights Committee, the author of the present communication had invoked the qualification that this requirement should be waived 'where the application of the remedies is unreasonably prolonged'. The Committee noted that the author had argued that the only effective remedy in the circumstances of the case was to seek an interim injunction, because 'without the preservation of the status quo, a final judgement on the merits, even if favourable to the Band, would be rendered ineffectual', in so far as

---

[21] Mr Wennergren dissented on this point.

'any final judgement recognizing aboriginal rights, or alternatively treaty rights, [could] never restore the way of life, livelihood and means of subsistence of the Band'. Referring to its established jurisprudence that 'exhaustion of domestic remedies can be required only to the extent that these remedies are effective and available', the Committee found that, in the circumstances of the case, there were no effective remedies still available to the Lubicon Lake Band. . . .

¶ 31.1. The Committee has seriously considered the State party's request that it review its decision declaring the communication admissible under the Optional Protocol 'in so far as it may raise issues under article 27 or other articles of the Covenant'. In the light of the information now before it, the Committee notes that the State party has argued convincingly that, by actively pursuing matters before the appropriate courts, delays, which appeared to be unreasonably prolonged, could have been reduced by the Lubicon Lake Band. At issue, however, is the question of whether the road of litigation would have represented an effective method of saving or restoring the traditional or cultural livelihood of the Lubicon Lake Band, which, at the material time, was allegedly at the brink of collapse. The Committee is not persuaded that that would have constituted an effective remedy within the meaning of article 5, paragraph 2 (b), of the Optional Protocol. In the circumstances, the Committee upholds its earlier decision on admissibility.

Though the domestic remedies rule generally will be satisfied by the provision of *ex post facto* remedies [6.04], the *Ominayak* decision confirms that it is unreasonable to expect authors to seek remedies that will not crystallize until after irreparable damage to their ICCPR rights has occurred. In some cases, *ex post facto* remedies, particularly prolonged ones, will not be able to provide meaningful redress. For example, as demonstrated in *Ominayak*, the destruction of one's culture in breach of article 27 minority rights cannot be adequately redressed by *ex post facto* remedies, such as the payment of compensation or legislative reform.[22] In such cases, it is nevertheless incumbent upon the author to seek injunctive relief before seeking a remedy under the OP.[23]

---

[22] In *A and S.N. v Norway* (224/87), the State Party pointed out that the length of the HRC's own deliberations can result in its views being delivered too late to assist the author (para. 4.3). The HRC did not address this point in this case. However, the HRC may request States Parties, under Rule 86 of its Rules of Procedure, to institute interim measures to prevent potential irreparable damage to the authors' rights whilst the case is being considered by the HRC. Such measures have been requested, for example, in *Ominayak*, as well as a large number of Caribbean cases where the HRC requested that the authors, prisoners on death row, not be executed whilst the HRC was considering the prisoners' complaints about the fairness of their trials. Unfortunately, States Parties may exceptionally breach these interim orders, as occurred in *Ashley v Trinidad and Tobago* (580/94) (when the author was executed despite a Rule 86 request). See also [8.26].

[23] In *E.H.P. v Canada* (67/80), the author claimed that the storage of radioactive waste nearby endangered her right to life (see [3.24] and [8.40]). She also claimed that the exhaustion of remedies would take too long, and irreparable harm would occur in the meantime. The HRC found the case inadmissible under art. 5(2)(b) OP. Zwart suggests that '[t]hings might have been different if the author had sought injunctive relief instead of completely bypassing local remedies', in T. Zwart, *The Admissibility of Human Rights Petitions* (Martinus Nijhoff, Dordrecht/Boston/London, 1994), 197.

[6.15]   *P.M.P.K. v SWEDEN (CAT 30/95)*

The author complained that her proposed expulsion from Sweden to Zaire breached her rights under article 3 CAT,[24] as the expulsion would expose her to a real chance of torture in Zaire. The author's first two applications for asylum, including one 'new application', had been refused. The State Party argued that she could submit another 'new application' for asylum as she could submit new evidence of her medical condition. The author argued that pursuit of this remedy would be futile.

¶ 5. By submission of 10 November 1995, counsel claims that a 'new application' under chapter 2, section 5, of the Aliens Act would not be successful. In this connection, she points out that an application has to be based on new circumstances not previously considered and that only 5% of 'new applications' succeed. Since the author's [first 'new application'] was refused on the basis that the situation in Zaire had improved, she argues that a 'new application' on the basis of the new medical evidence would be rejected on the same grounds.

The CAT Committee nevertheless could not 'conclude that the available remedy of a 'new application' would be *a priori* ineffective'.[25] The *P.M.P.K.* decision indicates that UN human rights treaty bodies will not easily presume available remedies to be futile.

[6.16] The following cases address the effect of the doctrine of precedent on the determination of a remedy's potential effectiveness.

LÄNSMAN et al. v FINLAND (511/92)

¶ 6.1. . . . wherever the jurisprudence of the highest domestic tribunal has decided the matter at issue, thereby eliminating any prospect of success of an appeal to the domestic courts, authors are not required to exhaust domestic remedies, for the purposes of the Optional Protocol.

PRATT and MORGAN v JAMAICA (210/86, 225/87)

In this case, the authors were prisoners on death row in Jamaica. They claimed, *inter alia*, that their execution after a very long period of detention on death row would breach the ICCPR. The State Party claimed, in this respect, that the authors could still appeal to the Supreme Court of Jamaica on the issue of whether their execution would breach the Jamaican Constitution. The authors justified their failure to pursue this remedy in the following terms:

¶ 7.1. In their comments dated 29 October 1987, the authors contend that . . . they have

---

[24] See discussion of art. 3 CAT at [9.51] ff.   [25] Para. 7.

indeed exhausted all available legal remedies. They refer to the decision of the Judicial Committee of the Privy Council in *Noel Riley et al. v the Attorney-General* (1981), where it was decided by a majority (3/2) that whatever the reasons for, or length of, delay in executing a sentence of death lawfully imposed, the delay can afford no ground for holding the execution to be in contravention of section 17 of the Jamaican Constitution. Accordingly there are no grounds upon which an application by way of constitutional motion to the Supreme Court of Jamaica could successfully be brought. Any such motion must inevitably fail and be decided against the applicants: in consequence, this is not a domestic remedy available to the applicants. On 17 July 1986, the Judicial Committee of the Privy Council refused the applicants' petition for special leave to appeal.

The State Party responded:

¶ 11.2. The State party rejects the argument that 'an application to the Supreme Court, in respect of section 17 of the Jamaican Constitution, must inevitably fail by reason of the Privy Council's decision in Riley's case'. It contends that while it is true that the doctrine of precedent is generally applicable, it is equally true that this doctrine may be set aside on the grounds that a previous decision had been arrived at *per incuriam* (through inadvertence). Thus, it would be open to the authors to argue that the decision in *Riley v the Attorney-General* was the result of inadvertence, especially in the light of the dissenting opinions given by Lord Scarman and Lord Brightman. For this reason, the State party contends that there are no grounds for disregarding its contention that the communications are inadmissible in so far as they relate to article 7.

The HRC decided in favour of the authors on this point:

¶ 12.5. A thorough consideration of the judgment of the Privy Council in the case of *Riley* does not lend itself to the conclusion that it was arrived at *per incuriam*. . . . In these circumstances, authors' counsel was objectively entitled to take the view that, on the basis of the doctrine of precedent, a constitutional motion in the cases of Mr Pratt and Mr Morgan would be bound to fail and there was thus no effective remedy still to exhaust.[26]

SOHN v REPUBLIC OF KOREA (518/92)

The complaint concerned the compatibility of a local law which prohibited third-party intervention in labour disputes with article 19 ICCPR, which guarantees freedom of expression.[27] The State Party argued that the author had not exhausted domestic remedies:

¶ 4.2. As regards the author's argument that he has exhausted domestic remedies because the Constitutional Court has already declared that article 13(2) of the Labour Dispute Adjustment Act, on which his conviction was based, is constitutional, the State party

---

[26] In the Jamaican legal system, the Judicial Committee of the Privy Council is a higher court than the Jamaican Supreme Court. The authors in the *Pratt and Morgan* case ultimately did appeal to the Privy Council in *Pratt and Another v Jamaica* [1993] 3 WLR 995. Ironically, the Privy Council in that case overturned the *Riley* precedent. Excessively long detentions on death row and the substantive ICCPR compatibility of the 'death row phenomenon' are discussed at [9.39] ff.

[27] See [18.34] on the merits of this case.

contends that the prior decision of the Constitutional Court only examined the compatibility of the provision with the right to work, the right to equality and the principle of legality, as protected by the Constitution. It did not address the question of whether the article was in compliance with the right to freedom of expression.

¶ 4.3. The State party argues, therefore, that the author should have requested a review of the law in the light of the right to freedom of expression, as protected by the Constitution. Since he failed to do so, the State party argues that he has not exhausted domestic remedies.

The author responded thus:

¶ 5.1. In his comments on the State party's submission, the author maintains that he has exhausted all domestic remedies and that it would be futile to request the Constitutional Court to pronounce itself on the constitutionality of the Labour Dispute Adjustment Act when it has done so in the recent past.

¶ 5.2. The author submits that if the question of constitutionality of a legal provision is brought before the Constitutional Court, the Court is legally obliged to take into account all possible grounds that may invalidate the law. As a result, the author argues that it is futile to bring the same question to the Court again.

¶ 5.3. In this context, the author notes that, although the majority opinion in the judgement of the Constitutional Court of 15 January 1990 did not refer to the right to freedom of expression, two concurring opinions and one dissenting opinion did. He submits that it is clear therefore that the Court did in fact consider all the grounds for possible unconstitutionality of the Labour Dispute Adjustment Act, including a possible violation of the constitutional right to freedom of expression.

The HRC found in favour of the author on this point:

¶ 6.1. At its 50th session, the Committee considered the admissibility of the communication. After having examined the submissions of both the State party and the author concerning the constitutional remedy, the Committee found that the compatibility of article 13(2) of the Labour Dispute Adjustment Act with the Constitution, including the constitutional right to freedom of expression, had necessarily been before the Constitutional Court in January 1990, even though the majority judgement chose not to refer to the right to freedom of expression. In the circumstances, the Committee considered that a further request to the Constitutional Court to review article 13(2) of the Act, by reference to freedom of expression, did not constitute a remedy which the author still needed to exhaust under article 5, paragraph 2, of the Optional Protocol.

The cases confirm that authors are not expected to appeal points of law in the face of contrary superior court precedent.[28] Similarly, one is not required to challenge an action that is clearly authorized by domestic legislation,[29] especially if such authorization is contained in the domestic constitution.[30]

---

[28] In *Faurisson v France* (550/93), para. 6.1, the author was not required to appeal his case to the French Court of Appeal ('Court of Cassation') when his co-accused had already lost his appeal. See also *Johannes Vos v Netherlands* (786/97), para. 6.2.

[29] See *A v Australia* (560/93), para. 5.6.   [30] See *Barzhig v France* (327/88), para. 5.1.

[6.17] *BARBARO v AUSTRALIA (CERD 7/95)*

The author alleged he was a victim of racial discrimination contrary to ICERD, as he had been denied a permanent employment licence by the Liquor Licensing Commissioner (LLC) of South Australia. The author argued that the LLC's decision had been motivated by racial discrimination. The author had not sought judicial review of the LLC decision, though he had pursued relevant administrative remedies without success. The Committee found that the author had failed to exhaust domestic remedies.

¶ 10.3. The State party has also claimed that the author has failed to exhaust domestic remedies which were both available and effective, since he could have challenged the . . . decision of the LLC [in the] Supreme Court of South Australia. The author has replied that . . . the precedent established by the judgment in *Alvaro's* case would have made an appeal to the Supreme Court of South Australia futile. . . .

¶ 10.5. The Committee further does not consider that the judgment of the Supreme Court of South Australia in *Alvaro's* case was necessarily dispositive of the author's own case. Firstly, the judgment in *Alvaro's* case was a majority and not a unanimous judgment. Secondly, the judgment was delivered in respect of legal issues which were, as the State party points out, largely uncharted. In the circumstances, the existence of one judgment, albeit on issues similar to those in the author's case, did not absolve Mr. Barbaro from attempting to avail himself of the remedy under Rule 98.01 of the Supreme Court Rules. . . .

The *Barbaro* decision indicates that authors are required to appeal points of law against contrary precedent where the relevant precedent is weak and therefore assailable.[31]

[6.18] In *Phillip v Jamaica* (594/92), the author was not required to have alerted prison authorities to the poor state of his conditions of detention, 'given that he had not filed a complaint because of his fears of the warders'.[32] Therefore, one is not required to pursue remedies which may foreseeably result in one's victimization.

Must Authors Exhaust Costly Remedies?

[6.19] *P.S. v DENMARK (397/90)*

¶ 5.4. . . . The Committee recalls the State party's contention that judicial review of administrative regulations and decisions, pursuant to section 63 of the Danish Constitutional Act, would be an effective remedy available to the author. The Committee notes that the author has refused to avail himself of these remedies, because of considerations of principle and

---

[31] The *Alvaro* decision could itself have been appealed to the Full Court of the South Australian Supreme Court, and then perhaps to the High Court of Australia.   [32] Para. 6.4.

in view of the costs involved. The Committee finds, however, that financial considerations and doubts about the effectiveness of domestic remedies do not absolve the author from exhausting them. Accordingly, the author has failed to meet the requirements of article 5, paragraph 2(b), in this respect.

[6.20]   *HENRY v JAMAICA (230/88)*

In this case, the State Party claimed that the author could have pursued constitutional remedies in the Jamaican Supreme Constitutional Court regarding his allegations over the fairness of his trial. The author claimed that he could not exhaust this remedy due to lack of funds, and the lack of availability of legal aid for constitutional motions. The State Party responded:

¶ 6.4. In respect of the absence of legal aid for the filing of constitutional motions, the State party submits that nothing in the Optional Protocol or in customary international law would support the contention that an individual is relieved of the obligation to exhaust domestic remedies on the grounds that there is no provision for legal aid and that his indigence has prevented him from resorting to an available remedy. In this connection, the State party observes that the Covenant only imposes a duty to provide legal aid in respect of criminal offences (article 14, paragraph 3(d)). Furthermore, international conventions dealing with economic, social and cultural rights do not impose an unqualified obligation on States to implement such rights: article 2 of the International Covenant on Economic, Social and Cultural Rights, for instance, provides for the progressive realization of economic rights and relates to the 'capacity of implementation' of States. In the circumstances, the State party argues that it is incorrect to infer from the author's indigence and the absence of legal aid in respect of the right to apply for constitutional redress that the remedy is necessarily nonexistent or unavailable. . . .

The HRC found in favour of the author on this point:

¶ 7.3. The Committee recalls that by submission of 10 October 1991 in a different case, the State party indicated that legal aid is not provided for constitutional motions. In the view of the Committee, this supports the finding . . . that a constitutional motion is not an available remedy which must be exhausted for purposes of the Optional Protocol. In this context, the Committee observes that it is not the author's indigence which absolves him from pursuing constitutional remedies, but the State party's unwillingness or inability to provide legal aid for this purpose.

¶ 7.4. The State party claims that it has no obligation under the Covenant to make legal aid available in respect of constitutional motions, as such motions do not involve the determination of a criminal charge, as required by article 14, paragraph 3(d), of the Covenant. But the issue before the Committee has not been raised in the context of article 14, paragraph 3(d), but only in the context of whether domestic remedies have been exhausted. . . .

¶ 7.6. For the above reasons, the Committee maintains that a constitutional motion does not constitute a remedy which is both available and effective within the meaning of article 5, paragraph 2(b), of the Optional Protocol. . . .

This reasoning in *Henry* has been consistently supported in subsequent cases.[33] The HRC further stated in *Douglas et al. v Jamaica* (352/89):

¶ 9.2. ... As to the State party's argument that international conventions dealing with economic, social and cultural rights do not impose an unqualified obligation on States to implement such rights, the Committee observes that the question of whether remedies remain available to the author within the meaning of article 5, paragraph 2(b), of the Optional Protocol is entirely distinct from and has no bearing on the issue of progressive realization of economic, social and cultural rights.

The *Henry* and *Douglas* decisions confirm that the non-availability of legal aid to indigent persons is relevant in determining whether the author has overcome procedural admissibility barriers under the OP. The decision in *Currie v Jamaica* (377/89) takes the *Henry* and *Douglas* reasoning further, as the non-availability of legal aid for constitutional motions was there found to constitute a substantive breach of the ICCPR, namely the article 14(1) guarantee of a fair trial.[34]

[6.21] A literal reading of the HRC's decision in *P.S. v Denmark* [6.19] indicates that financial considerations are irrelevant in HRC determinations regarding the effectiveness of a remedy. *Henry* and its successors confirm that this is not the case. *P.S.* may be distinguished on the basis that the author had not attempted to pursue any judicial remedies, nor, perhaps more importantly, had he indicated any inability to afford to pursue such remedies. Indeed, financial considerations do not absolve an author from pursuing a costly remedy if he/she has the means to secure legal assistance for such a purpose. For example, in *R.W. v Jamaica* (340/88),[35] the author was able to afford legal representation for a constitutional motion, so the non-availability of legal aid in Jamaica for such motions was irrelevant in this case for the purposes of article 5(2)(b) OP. Furthermore, an author is not absolved from seeking a costly local remedy that he/she cannot afford if he/she has not yet sought legal aid.[36]

Unreasonable Prolongation of Remedies

[6.22] Article 5(2)(b) of the OP expressly exempts complainants from having to pursue 'unreasonably prolonged' remedies. The *Ominayak* case demonstrates how unreasonable delay can also lead to a finding that the remedy at issue is ineffective [6.14].

---

[33] See, e.g., *Campbell v Jamaica* (248/87), *Little v Jamaica* (283/88), *Ellis v Jamaica* (276/88), *Hibbert v Jamaica* (293/88), *Thomas v Jamaica* (321/88), *Wright v Jamaica* (349/89), *Hylton v Jamaica* (600/94), and *Gallimore v Jamaica* (680/96).
[34] See [14.13].   [35] Para. 6.2.
[36] *Faurisson v France* (550/93), para. 6.1; *G.T. v Canada* (420/90), para. 6.3.

[6.23] **FILLASTRE and BIZOARN v BOLIVIA (336/88)**

The complaint concerned the arrest and prolonged detention of two French private detectives by Bolivian authorities. The HRC found in favour of the authors in its admissibility decision:

¶ 5.2. During its 40th session, the Committee considered the admissibility of the communication. It took note of the State party's observations and clarifications concerning the current status of the case before the Bolivian courts, observing that the victims were still awaiting the outcome of the proceedings instituted against them in September 1987, that is, more than three years after their arrest. In the circumstances, the Committee considered that a delay of over three years for the adjudication of the case at first instance, discounting the availability of subsequent appeals, was 'unreasonably prolonged' within the meaning of article 5, paragraph 2(b), of the Optional Protocol. From the available information, the Committee deduced that such delays as had been encountered were neither attributable to the alleged victims nor explained by the complexity of the case. It therefore concluded that the requirements of article 5, paragraph 2(b), had been met.

The *Fillastre* decision indicates that the unreasonableness of potential delays varies according to the complexities of the case.[37]

[6.24] **HENDRIKS v THE NETHERLANDS (201/85)**

This case concerned allegations that Dutch family courts had unfairly favoured the author's ex-wife with regard to the custody of the author's son, thereby breaching article 23(4).[38] The HRC, in finding the complaint admissible, made the following comments regarding the exhaustion of domestic remedies:

¶ 6.3. Article 5, paragraph 2 (b), of the Optional Protocol precludes the Committee from considering a communication unless domestic remedies have been exhausted. In that connection, the Committee noted that, in its submission of 9 July 1986, the State party had informed the Committee that nothing would prevent Mr. Hendriks from once again requesting the Netherlands courts to issue an access order. The Committee observed, however, that Mr. Hendriks' claim, initiated before the Netherlands courts 12 years earlier, had been adjudicated by the Supreme Court in 1980. Taking into account the provision of article 5, paragraph 2 (b) . . . of the Optional Protocol regarding unreasonably prolonged remedies, the author could not be expected to continue to request the same courts to issue an access order on the basis of 'changed circumstances', notwithstanding the procedural change in domestic law (enacted in 1982) which would now require [the author's son] to be heard. The Committee observed that, although in family law disputes, such as custody cases of that nature, changed circumstances might often justify new proceedings, it was satisfied that the requirement of exhaustion of domestic remedies had been met in the case before it.

---

[37] Freedom from unreasonable delay before the conclusion of one's trial is also a substantive guarantee in the Covenant in art. 14(3)(c) [14.65–14.73]. Indeed, a violation of this guarantee was found in *Fillastre*.

[38] The merits of this case are considered at [20.35–20.39].

[6.25] *BLANCO v NICARAGUA (328/88)*

The author complained of various egregious human rights abuses entailed in his treatment by the Nicaraguan government. Whilst his communication was pending, a new government came to power, and argued that the author now had recourse to a number of newly available remedies. The HRC nevertheless found that the complaint was admissible:

¶ 9.1. The Committee has taken due note of the State party's submission that the author has failed to exhaust domestic remedies, since he can now address his complaints to the competent courts of the present Nicaraguan Government.

¶ 9.2. The Committee welcomes the State party's readiness to examine the author's complaints and considers that such examination could be seen as a remedy under article 2, paragraph 3, of the Covenant. However, for purposes of article 5, paragraph 2(b), of the Optional Protocol, the Committee considers that the author, who was arrested in 1979 and spent ten years in detention, cannot be at this stage required to engage the Nicaraguan courts of the present administration before his case can be examined under the Optional Protocol. In this context the Committee recalls that the communication was submitted to the Committee in 1988, at a time when domestic remedies were not available or not effective. Even if domestic remedies may now be available, the application of such remedies would entail an unreasonable prolongation of the author's quest to be vindicated for his detention and alleged ill-treatment; the Committee concludes that the Optional Protocol does not require the author, in the circumstances of his case, to further engage the Nicaraguan courts. Moreover, the Committee reiterates its finding that the criteria of admissibility under the Optional Protocol were satisfied at the time of submission of the communication. . . .

[6.26] *H.S. v FRANCE (184/84)*

The HRC found this complaint inadmissible in the following terms:

¶ 9.4. The Committee is aware that the proceedings before the Tribunal de grande instance de Bobigny lasted for more than six and a half years. However, the Committee finds that the delays in the proceedings in 1984 and 1985 were caused by the author himself. For that reason the Committee is unable to conclude that the domestic remedies, which, according to both parties, are in progress, have been unduly prolonged in a manner that would exempt the author from exhausting them under article 5, paragraph 2 (b), of the Optional Protocol.

The case concerned the State Party's failure to recognize the alleged French nationality of the author. The author was found personally responsible for delays of two years out of a six and a half year process; the HRC implicitly recognizes that four and a half years for immigration proceedings is 'reasonable', presumably due to the complexities of such proceedings [6.23].

The principle in *H.S.*, that domestic remedies will not be deemed unreasonably prolonged if such prolongation is the fault of the author, has been confirmed in a number of cases, including *N.A.J v Jamaica* (246/87). In *N.A.J.*, an appeal to the Judicial Committee of the Privy Council remained available to the author; the thirteen-year delay was largely due to the author's failure to pursue this avenue.

[6.27] The HRC has stated in a number of cases, such as *R.L. et al. v Canada* (358/89), that 'fears about the length of proceedings do not absolve authors from the requirement of at least making a reasonable effort to exhaust domestic remedies'.[39] This mirrors the rule regarding an author's fears over the futility of domestic remedies [6.12]. Of course, in some cases, the complainant may objectively justify his or her fear of unreasonable delay, as in *Ominayak v Canada* (167/84) [6.14].

Burden of Proof

[6.28] The availability of domestic remedies may raise extremely technical questions regarding the municipal law of the relevant State, which are outside the expertise of the HRC. Therefore, it is important to know where the burden of proof lies in proving the availability, or non-availability, of effective domestic remedies.

[6.29]   *C.F. v CANADA (118/81)*

The complaint in this case concerned the inability of the authors, inmates in Canadian federal penitentiaries, to vote in provincial elections in Quebec. The State Party argued that the authors had failed to exhaust domestic remedies.

¶ 4.2. As regards the non-exhaustion of domestic remedies, the State party argues that the authors, by seeking an interlocutory decision against the Solicitor General's negative reply, had chosen an inappropriate remedy and that instead they should have applied for a declaratory judgement as to their right to vote. The State party claims that such a declaration would have been an 'effective and sufficient' remedy according to international jurisprudence and Canadian legal practice. The State party admits that it could be argued that there was not sufficient time to get a declaratory judgement before the Quebec provincial elections of 1981 were held and that therefore a declaration was not an effective remedy in regard to the present communication. The State party, however, argues that the real object of the communication is to assert the right of inmates in federal penitentiaries in relation to future elections . . . and therefore concludes that it was not 'too late' for the authors to seek a declaration of their rights in the domestic courts to achieve this object of their claim. Consequently, domestic remedies had not been exhausted.

In subsequent submissions, the authors disputed the effectiveness of the alleged remedy. The HRC initially found in favour of the authors on this point.

---

[39] Para. 6.4.

¶ 6.2. With regard to article 5, paragraph 2(b), of the Optional Protocol the Committee observed that, although the authors might not have been able to obtain a declaratory judgement before the elections of 13 April 1981, a subsequent judgement could nevertheless in principle have been an effective remedy in the meaning contemplated by article 2, paragraph 3, of the Covenant and article 5, paragraph 2(b), of the Optional Protocol. The Covenant provides that a remedy shall be granted whenever a violation of one of the rights guaranteed by it has occurred; consequently, it does not generally prescribe preventive protection, but confines itself to requiring effective redress *ex post facto*. However, the Committee was of the view that the Canadian Government had not shown that an action for a declaratory judgement would have constituted an effective remedy either with regard to the elections of 13 April 1981 or with regard to any future elections. On the basis of the Government's submission of 20 August 1982, it was not clear whether an action seeking to have declared unlawful the refusal of the competent prison authorities to let the alleged victims participate in the elections of 13 April 1981 would have been admissible. On the other hand, taking into account the authors' submission received on 7 June 1983, the Committee expressed doubt as to whether, and to what extent, executive authorities in Canada are bound to give effect to a declaratory judgement in similar circumstances arising in the future. Since it is incumbent on the State party concerned to prove the effectiveness of remedies which it claims have not been exhausted, the Committee concluded that article 5, paragraph 2(b), of the Optional Protocol did not preclude the admissibility of the communication.

The State Party went on to submit extremely detailed evidence regarding the effectiveness of declaratory judgments in Canada. The HRC subsequently reversed its admissibility finding in the following terms:[40]

¶ 10.1. Pursuant to rule 93, paragraph 4, of its provisional rules of procedure the Human Rights Committee has reviewed its decision on admissibility of 25 July 1983. . . . According to the detailed explanations contained in the submission of 17 February 1984, however, the legal position appears to be sufficiently clear in that the specific remedy of a declaratory judgement was available and, if granted, would have been an effective remedy against the authorities concerned. In drawing this conclusion, the Committee also takes note of the fact that the authors were represented by legal counsel.

[6.30] The *C.F.* case clearly indicates that States Parties bear a substantial burden in proving the existence and efficacy of relevant domestic remedies. However, the HRC's adherence to this 'rule' regarding burden of proof is inconsistent, as is perhaps indicated in the next case.

S.H.B. v CANADA (192/85)

The author submitted a complaint regarding his treatment by local courts. In particular, the local court in family law proceedings had awarded custody of the

---

[40] Zwart, above, note 23, criticizes this reversal at 202, as the remedy would only have related to forthcoming elections, rather than redress the denial of the authors' right to vote in the 1981 election. Indeed, see the HRC's own comment in *C.F.* at [6.04].

author's child to the complainant's ex-wife, and had ordered that he pay his ex-wife substantial alimony. The complainant alleged that the orders breached several provisions of the ICCPR.[41] With regard to the exhaustion of domestic remedies, the complainant submitted the following:

¶ 2.4. With regard to the exhaustion of domestic remedies, the author states that he has appealed to the Supreme Court of Alberta, but that the court of appeals refused to investigate the trial judge's use of discretion and that no written reasons were given for refusing to consider the appeal. The author has also addressed himself to the Chief Justice of Alberta, the Judicial Council, the Minister of Justice of Canada, the Minister of Justice of Alberta, and the Provincial Ombudsman of Alberta, without success, because the judge's power of discretion is considered beyond challenge and thus no investigations were conducted. The author indicates that he could still make an appeal to the Supreme Court of Canada, but explains that this would not be a practical option because the main issue is the judge's use of discretion and the current law provides that the judge has absolute discretion in matters of awarding child custody and division of matrimonial property, and thus the Supreme Court could not overturn the lower court's decision without a legislative change. Moreover, even if the issue could be examined by the Supreme Court of Canada, the backlog of cases is such that review of his case would be impossible within a reasonable time. . . .

¶ 6.3. With regard to the State party's contention that he has not exhausted domestic remedies with respect to the issue of custody, the author submits that 'it has been the unanimous advice of several legal experts that the awarding of child custody is entirely within the discretion of the judge' and that therefore an appeal to the Court of Appeal would be totally futile. He could not, he argues, obtain a new evaluation of the facts by the Court of Appeal, and the only possibility of challenging the lower court's decision would be by establishing bias or misconduct on the part of the judge or of the Amicus Curiae. In pursuing this 'unconventional means', he requested the Provincial Ombudsman in Alberta to conduct an investigation into the way the department of Amicus Curiae in Alberta is run. However, the author alleges that the Attorney-General of Alberta invoked technical objections, thus denying the ombudsman the opportunity to investigate the matter and to establish the author's allegations. He also reported the lower court judge to the Chief Justice of Alberta and to the Judicial Council. However, 'the Judicial Council refused to conduct an investigation, thus effectively denying me the opportunity to prove my allegations of bias and denying me the means to ask for a new trial on the issue of custody.' The author also forwards press reports showing that recently many other divorced fathers have unsuccessfully attempted to sue the Amicus Curiae, but that the Master in Chambers (who is not a judge) has blocked the legal action, 'thus denying citizens of this province the fundamental constitutional right of having their cases determined in court.'

¶ 6.4. The author concludes that domestic remedies, to the extent that they can be considered effective, have been exhausted. He further emphasizes the time factor 'since the harm to my son continues until a solution is reached.'

The State Party had argued the following:

---

[41] The complainant cited arts. 2, 3, 7, 8(2), 14, 15, 23(4), and 26.

¶ 5.2. With regard to the author's claim concerning custody, the State party points out that while he appealed to the Court of Appeal of Alberta on the issues of maintenance and division of matrimonial property, he did not appeal on the issue of custody, although he could have done so pursuant to the Alberta Judicature Act of 1980. . . .

¶ 5.4. With regard to maintenance and division of property, the State party notes that the author has failed to seek leave to appeal the judgement of the Alberta Court of Appeal to the Supreme Court of Canada. It is submitted that leave to appeal in at least 18 maintenance and/or matrimonial property cases has been granted by the Supreme Court of Canada since 1975 and that in eight of these cases the appeal was allowed. Thus, 'leave to appeal to the Supreme Court of Canada on these matters is an effective and sufficient domestic remedy, although of course the relative merits of the case will affect the likelihood of relief being granted. Certain delays are inevitably involved in invoking the appellate jurisdiction of the highest court of any country, but Canada submits that the time periods involved in proceedings before the Supreme Court of Canada are not untoward in this regard, and that they are least prejudicial in matters such as the present, involving solely financial and property interests.'

The HRC found in favour of the State Party on this point:

¶ 7.2. The Committee observes in this respect, on the basis of the information available to it, that the author has failed to pursue remedies which the State party has submitted were available to him, namely, an appeal to the Court of Appeal on the issue of custody and an application for leave to appeal to the Supreme Court of Canada on the issues of maintenance and division of matrimonial property. The Committee has noted the author's belief that a further appeal on the issue of custody would be futile and that a procedure before the Supreme Court of Canada would entail a further delay. The Committee finds, however, that, in the particular circumstances disclosed by the communication, the author's doubts about the effectiveness of these remedies are not warranted and do not absolve him from exhausting them, as required by article 5, paragraph 2 (b), of the Optional Protocol. The Committee accordingly concludes that domestic remedies have not been exhausted.

The State Party did not address the author's arguments that decisions regarding child custody are essentially within the discretion of the trial judge. In this respect, the strict burden of proof imposed in the *C.F.* case does not appear to have been fulfilled.

[6.31] Indeed, McGoldrick argues convincingly that it is 'difficult to establish whether the initial burden is on the author to provide evidence that he has satisfied domestic remedies or on the State party to prove that domestic remedies are available and effective'.[42] He suggests that the initial burden is probably with the author, though that burden is 'probably not too heavy'.[43] Conçado Trindade, writing in the very early years of the HRC, also felt that the Committee had taken a

---

[42] McGoldrick, above, note 18, 189.
[43] Ibid. See also comments at [6.13] regarding burden of proof in some of the 'Uruguayan' cases.

'flexible' approach by sharing and distributing the burden of proof between the State and the complainant.[44]

[6.32] In *Muhonen v Finland* (89/81), the author alleged violations of his rights under articles 14(6). The State Party alleged that he could have sought an 'extraordinary remedy', seeking to annul an impugned decision of the Minister of Justice.[45] Despite the State Party's submission of detailed evidence of the mechanics of this extraordinary remedy, the HRC found that it was not a remedy that had to be exhausted by the author.[46] This indicates that States Parties bear a heavy onus of proof in proving the effectiveness of remedies outside the judicial mainstream. Indeed, the apparent difference between the *C.F. v Canada* [6.29] and *S.H.B. v Canada* [6.30] decisions may be explained by the fact that the available remedy in *S.H.B.* involved the ordinary passage of appeal from a lower court to a higher court, whereas *C.F.* concerned the more unusual remedy of a judicial declaration.[47]

Conclusion

[6.33] The HRC has been fairly strict in implementing the domestic remedies rule: it is probably the most common reason for rejecting the admissibility of communications. However, it has demonstrated some flexibility regarding the futility of remedies which may, for example, be demonstrated by a State Party's continuous failure to implement apparently available remedies, adverse higher court precedents, the unreasonable prolongation of available remedies, and occasionally the costliness of available remedies. The HRC has also been flexible in its allocation of the burden of proof between the author and the State Party with regard to questions of the proper exhaustion of effective local remedies.

---

[44] See A. Conçado Trindade, 'Exhaustion of Local Remedies under the UN Covenant on Civil and Political Rights and its Optional Protocol' (1979) 28 *ICLQ* 734, at 758–9, 762, and 764.

[45] Paras. 4.2–5.2.

[46] Para. 6.1.

[47] For example, the State Party conceded at para. 7.3 in *C.F.* that a declaration 'does not pronounce any direct sanction against a defendant if he or she fails to respect it'. Rather, a declaration represented judicial guidance for the legality of future actions.

Part III
Civil and Political Rights

Right of Self-determination—Article 1

ARTICLE 1

1. All peoples have the right of self-determination. By virtue of that right they freely determine their political status and freely pursue their economic, social and cultural development.

2. All peoples may, for their own ends, freely dispose of their natural wealth and resources without prejudice to any obligations arising out of international economic cooperation, based upon the principle of mutual benefits, and international law. In no case may a people be deprived of its own means of subsistence.

3. The States Parties to the present Covenant, including those having responsibility for the administration of Non-Self-Governing and Trust Territories, shall promote the realization of the right of self-determination, and shall respect that right, in conformity with the provisions of the Charter of the United Nations.

[7.01] Article 1 is common to both the ICCPR and the International Covenant on Economic, Social, and Cultural Rights, highlighting the complex nature of the right of self-determination, and its importance for the achievement of all first and second generation rights.

GENERAL COMMENT 12

¶ 1. . . . The right of self-determination is of particular importance because its realization is an essential condition for the effective guarantee and observance of individual human rights and for the promotion and strengthening of those rights. It is for that reason that States set forth the right of self-determination in a provision of positive law in both Covenants and placed this provision as article 1 apart from and before all of the other rights in the two Covenants.

[7.02] The Committee on the Elimination of Racial Discrimination (CERD), along with the HRC, has issued a general comment on the topic. The CERD General Recommendation is far more detailed and useful than the HRC Comment.

Definition of Self-determination

[7.03] The HRC has issued very little jurisprudence on the meaning of self-determination for the purposes of the ICCPR. This is partly due to its refusal to admit article 1 complaints under the First Optional Protocol [7.20]. Furthermore, its General Comment on article 1 fails to give any clear definition beyond reiteration of the express words of article 1.

[7.04]   *GENERAL COMMENT 12*

¶ 2. Article 1 enshrines an inalienable right of all peoples as described in its paragraphs 1 and 2. By virtue of that right they freely 'determine their political status and freely pursue their economic, social and cultural development'. The article imposes on all States parties corresponding obligations. This right and the corresponding obligations concerning its implementation are interrelated with other provisions of the Covenant and rules of international law. . . .

¶ 7. In connection with article 1 of the Covenant, the Committee refers to other international instruments concerning the right of all peoples to self-determination, in particular the Declaration on Principles of International Law concerning Friendly Relations and Co-operation among States in accordance with the Charter of the United Nations, adopted by the General Assembly on 24 October 1970 (General Assembly Resolution 2625 (XXV)).

[7.05] The Comment obliquely refers to other 'international law' obligations, indicating that the ICCPR meaning accords with the international legal meaning of self-determination.[1] The most important international law document in this respect is, as indicated in paragraph 7, General Assembly Resolution 2625, the 'Declaration on Friendly Relations'.[2] The Declaration describes the right of self-determination as 'the right of peoples to be free from alien subjugation, domination and exploitation'. However, the interpretation of 'peoples' and 'alien subjugation' remains controversial.

PEOPLES

[7.06] Self-determination is the collective right of 'peoples'. Various conditions or characteristics of 'peoples' have been put forward, including common historical tradition, racial or ethnic identity, cultural homogeneity, linguistic unity, religious or ideological affinity, territorial connection, common economic life, and consisting of a certain minimum number.[3] However, no permanent, universally

---

[1] However, see D. McGoldrick, *The Human Rights Committee* (Clarendon Press, Oxford, 1993), 248.

[2] H. Hannum, 'Rethinking Self-Determination' (1993) 34 *Virginia Journal of International Law* 1, 14. The CERD General Recommendation 21 on Self-determination also endorses the Declaration on Friendly Relations at para. 3.

[3] See R. McCorquodale, 'Self-Determination: A Human Rights Approach' (1994) 43 *ICLQ* 857,

acceptable list of criteria for a 'people' exists.[4] Neither the HRC nor the CERD Committee has postulated a definition.

[7.07] Much contemporary scholarship on self-determination divides the right into a right of external self-determination (ESD) and a right of internal self-determination (ISD).[5] The definition of 'peoples' in terms of the ICCPR becomes less contentious if one recognizes that all peoples are entitled to some form of self-determination, though not all peoples are entitled to the most radical manifestation of the right, ESD. In this respect, a 'people' may be broadly defined as a group with a common racial or ethnic identity, or a cultural identity (which could incorporate political, religious, or linguistic elements) built up over a long period of time.[6]

EXTERNAL SELF-DETERMINATION

[7.08]   *CERD GENERAL RECOMMENDATION 21*

¶ 4. . . . The external aspect of self-determination implies that all peoples have the right to determine freely their political status and their place in the international community based upon the principle of equal rights and exemplified by the liberation of peoples from colonialism and by the prohibition to subject peoples to alien subjugation, domination, and exploitation.

[7.09] A claim of ESD equates with a claim by a people to a certain territory.[7] ESD is exercised by maintaining existing State boundaries, or changing the boundaries of existing States. The first form of ESD arises where the relevant 'self determination unit' is the population of an existing State. The latter arises where the relevant 'self determination unit' wishes to break away from an existing State. The most controversial mode of exercising ESD is by way of secession.[8] During the 1950s and 1960s, the right of secession, and indeed the notion of self-determination, was intertwined with the notion of decolonization.[9]

866, note 52, and R. White, 'Self-Determination: Time for a Re-Assessment?' (1981) 28 *Netherlands International Law Review* 147, 163, note 52, quoting a report by the International Commission of Jurists, *The Events in East Pakistan* (ICJ, Geneva, 1972), at 70.

[4] McCorquodale, above, note 3, 865; M. Koskenniemi, 'National Self-Determination Today: Problems of Legal Theory and Practice' (1994) 43 *ICLQ* 241, 261.

[5] See, e.g., R. McCorquodale, above, note 3, 863; M. Pomerance, *Self-Determination in Law and Practice* (Hague/Boston/London, Martinus Nijhoff, 1982), 37–42.

[6] S. Joseph, 'Resolving Conflicting Claims of Territorial Sovereignty and External Self-Determination, Part 1' (1999) 3(1) *International Journal of Human Rights* 40, 42–5.

[7] L. Brilmayer, 'Secession and Self-Determination: A Territorial Interpretation' (1991) 16 *Yale Journal of International Law* 177.

[8] The Declaration on Friendly Relations specifies other modes: free association or integration with another independent State.

[9] See *Western Sahara Advisory Opinion* [1975] ICJ Rep. 12, 37. See also G. Simpson, 'The Diffusion of Sovereignty: Self-Determination in the Post-Colonial Age' (1996) 32 *Stanford Journal of International Law* 255, 265; and R. McCorquodale, 'South Africa and the Right of Self-Determination'

However, in the post-Cold War era, a number of non-colonial peoples have successfully seceded, including the peoples of the former USSR, the former Czechoslovakia, the former Yugoslavia, Eritrea, and, imminently, East Timor. Furthermore, the text of article 1 does not expressly confine the right to colonial peoples. Indeed, the HRC has now confirmed that the principle of self-determination, and possibly the right of secession in some instances, 'applies to all peoples, and not merely to colonised peoples'.[10]

[7.10] The right of ESD is politically controversial, as it clearly threatens the territorial integrity of States.

CERD GENERAL RECOMMENDATION 21

¶ 1. The Committee notes that ethnic or religious groups or minorities frequently refer to the right of self-determination as a basis for an alleged right to secession. . . .

¶ 6. The Committee emphasizes that, in accordance with the Declaration of the General Assembly on Friendly Relations, none of the Committee's actions shall be construed as authorizing or encouraging any action which would dismember or impair, totally or in part, the territorial integrity or political unity of sovereign and independent states conducting themselves in compliance with the principle of equal rights and self-determination of peoples and possessing a government representing the whole people belonging to the territory without distinction as to race, creed or colour. In view of the Committee international law has not recognized a general right of peoples to unilaterally declare secession from a state. In this respect, the Committee follows the views expressed in the Agenda for Peace (paras. 17 et seq.), namely that a fragmentation of States may be detrimental to the protection of human rights as well as to the preservation of peace and security. This does not, however, exclude the possibility of arrangements reached by free agreements of all parties concerned.[11]

[7.11] The HRC has largely avoided consensus comments on the territorial aspirations of secessionist groups within existing States Parties. Future potential candidates for secession include the Chechens, the Québecois, and the Kosovars, though the existence of an international right of secession for such peoples would likely be opposed by, respectively, the Russian Federation, Canada, and the Federal Republic of Yugoslavia. The HRC has however criticized Morocco's policies regarding the Western Sahara:[12]

¶ 9. The Committee remains concerned about the very slow pace of the preparations towards a referendum in Western Sahara on the question of self-determination, and at the

(1994) 10 *South African Journal on Human Rights* 4, 6. See also CERD General Recommendation 21, para. 4 [7.08].

[10] Concluding Comments on Azerbaijan (1994) UN doc. CCPR/C/79/Add. 38, para. 6.
[11] The 'Agenda for Peace' was issued in 1992 by Secretary General Boutros Boutros Ghali (1992) UN doc. A/47/277–S/24111.
[12] (1999) UN doc. CCPR/C/79/Add. 113.

lack of information on the implementation of human rights in that region. The State party should move expeditiously and cooperate fully in the completion of the necessary preparations for the referendum. . . .

As the International Court of Justice has ruled that the peoples of the Western Sahara have a right of external self-determination,[13] it is not surprising that the HRC has singled out their secessionist aspirations for explicit endorsement.

INTERNAL SELF-DETERMINATION

[7.12] ISD refers to the right of peoples to choose their political status within a State,[14] or of exercising a right of meaningful political participation. For example, the institution of democratic rule in South Africa constituted an exercise of ISD by the black majority in South Africa. The notion of ISD overlaps considerably with the rights guaranteed in articles 25 (right of political participation)[15] and 27 (minority rights)[16] of the ICCPR. Indeed, Cassese describes ISD as a 'manifestation of the totality of rights embodied in the Covenant'.[17]

[7.13]   *CERD GENERAL RECOMMENDATION 21*

¶ 4. . . . The right to self-determination of peoples has an internal aspect, i.e. the rights of all peoples to pursue freely their economic, social and cultural development without outside interference. In that respect there exists a link with the right of every citizen to take part in the conduct of public affairs at any level as referred to in article 5 (c) of the International Convention on the Elimination of All Forms of Racial Discrimination. In consequence, governments are to represent the whole population without distinction as to race, colour, descent, national, or ethnic origins.

¶ 5. In order to respect fully the rights of all peoples within a state, governments are again called upon to adhere to and implement fully the international human rights instruments and in particular the International Convention on the Elimination of All Forms of Racial Discrimination. Concern for the protection of individual rights without discrimination on racial, ethnic, tribal, religious, or other grounds must guide the policies of governments. In accordance with article 2 of the International Convention on the Elimination of All Forms of Racial Discrimination and other relevant international documents, governments should be sensitive towards the rights of persons of ethnic groups, particularly their right to lead lives of dignity, to preserve their culture, to share equitably in the fruits of national growth, and to play their part in the government of the country of which its members are citizens. Also, governments should consider, within their respective constitutional frameworks, vesting persons of ethnic or linguistic groups comprised of their citizens, where appropriate, with the right to engage in such activities which are particularly relevant to the preservation of the identity of such persons or groups.

---

[13] *Western Sahara Advisory Opinion* [1975] ICJ Rep. 12.
[14] McCorquodale, above, note 3, at 864.
[15] See generally Chap. 22.   [16] See generally Chap. 24.
[17] A. Cassese, *Self-Determination of Peoples* (Cambridge University Press, Cambridge, 1995), 53.

[7.14] Self-determination is therefore a complex right, entailing an 'internal' and an 'external' form. The right can be conceptualized as a sliding scale of different levels of entitlement to political emancipation, constituting various forms of ISD up to the apex of the right, the right of ESD, which vests only in exceptional circumstances.[18] Different 'peoples' are entitled to different 'levels' of self-determination.

[7.15] It is contended that a people is entitled to ESD,[19] by way of secession, when it lives under colonial[20] or neo-colonial domination,[21] or when it is so severely persecuted, and its human rights so systematically abused, that ESD is necessary to remedy such abuse, and preserve its long-term viability as a people.[22] Alternatively, peoples may reach free agreements to secede from each other,[23] as occurred when Czechoslovakia peacefully split into the Czech and Slovak Republics in 1993. Finally, peoples which are not entitled to ESD are nevertheless entitled to ISD.

Article 1(2)

[7.16] Article 1(2) sounds like a very important right. For example, its terms suggest that a government cannot permit mining on a people's land without its approval.[24] The right is tempered by the saving of certain 'international obligations arising out of international economic cooperation'. However, this tempering may be undone by article 47 of the Covenant,[25] which provides:

---

[18] See F. Kirgis Jr., 'The Degrees of Self-Determination in the United Nations Era' (1994) 88 *American Journal of International Law* 304, 306, and B. Kingsbury, 'Claims by Non-State Groups in International Law' (1992) 25 *Cornell International Law Journal* 481, 503.

[19] See generally on situations where peoples should be recognized as having a right of ESD, Joseph, above, note 6, and S. Joseph, 'Resolving Conflicting Claims of Territorial Sovereignty and External Self-Determination, Part 2' (1999) 3 (2) *International Journal of Human Rights* 49.

[20] See above, [7.09].

[21] Post-World War II invasions can be termed 'neo-colonial situations', and have rarely been recognized as valid by the international community. See, e.g., regarding the Indonesian invasion of East Timor, G.A. Resolution 3485 (XXX) and SC Resolution 384 (1975). See, regarding the Chinese invasion of Tibet, G.A. Resolution 1723/16 (20 December 1961). See, e.g., regarding the Israeli Occupied Territories, UN doc. A/RES/ES–7/2, GAOR, 7th Emergency Session, Supp. 1, 3 (1980). See, regarding the Turkish invasion of northern Cyprus, SC Res 353 (1974), SC Res 440 (1978), and SC Res 541, 18 November 1983. See also Joseph, above, note 19, 52–3.

[22] Numerous commentators have recognised a right of 'remedial ESD' such as L. Buchheit, *Secession: The Legitimacy of Self-Determination* (New Haven, Conn., Yale University Press 1978), 220, and R. White, above, note 3, 160. Its existence is also implied by the Declaration on Friendly Relations, which guarantees territorial integrity only to States which are 'conducting themselves in compliance with the principles of equal rights and self-determination of people'. See also CERD General Recommendation 21, para. 6 [7.10].

[23] See, e.g., CERD General Recommendation 21, para. 6 [7.10].

[24] See, in this respect, [24.24–24.30].

[25] McGoldrick, above, note 1, 15 and 251.

Nothing in the present Covenant shall be interpreted as impairing the inherent right of all peoples to enjoy and utilise fully their natural wealth and resources.

[7.17] Unfortunately, the HRC has shed very little light on the terms of article 1(2). Its most significant statements came in its recent Concluding Comments on Canada, where it stated:[26]

¶ 8. The Committee notes that, as the State party acknowledged, the situation of the aboriginal peoples remains 'the most pressing human rights issue facing Canadians'. In this connection, the Committee is particularly concerned that the State party has not yet implemented the recommendations of the Royal Commission on Aboriginal Peoples (RCAP). With reference to the conclusion by RCAP that without a greater share of lands and resources institutions of aboriginal self-government will fail, the Committee emphasizes that the right to self-determination requires, *inter alia*, that all peoples must be able to freely dispose of their natural wealth and resources and that they may not be deprived of their own means of subsistence (art. 1, para. 2). The Committee recommends that decisive and urgent action be taken towards the full implementation of the RCAP recommendations on land and resource allocation. The Committee also recommends that the practice of extinguishing inherent aboriginal rights be abandoned as incompatible with article 1 of the Covenant.

Thus, the extinguishment and presumably the diminution of aboriginal native title rights breaches article 1(2).[27]

Article 1(3)

[7.18]   *GENERAL COMMENT 12*

¶ 6. Paragraph 3, in the Committee's opinion, is particularly important in that it imposes specific obligations on States parties, not only in relation to their own peoples but vis-à-vis all peoples which have not been able to exercise or have been deprived of the possibility of exercising their right to self-determination. The general nature of this paragraph is confirmed by its drafting history. . . . The obligations exist irrespective of whether a people entitled to self-determination depends on a State party to the Covenant or not. It follows that all States parties to the Covenant should take positive action to facilitate realization of and respect for the right of peoples to self-determination. Such positive action must be consistent with the States' obligations under the Charter of the United Nations and under international law: in particular, States must refrain from interfering in the internal affairs of other States and thereby adversely affecting the exercise of the right to self-determination. . . .

---

[26] (1999) UN doc. CCPR/C/79/Add. 105.

[27] The CERD Committee found the diminution of native title rights to breach the CERD Convention, as they were racially discriminatory in Concluding Comments on Australia (1999) UN doc. CERD/C/54/Misc.40/Rev.2. See [24.18]. On the nature of self-determination and its relationship with economic and social aspects of subsistence, see S. J. Anaya, *Indigenous People and International Law* (Oxford University Press, New York, 1996).

[7.19] Article 1(3) is unusual as it imposes duties on States with regard to persons outside their jurisdiction, indeed even if those people are within the jurisdiction of another State Party.[28] This goes beyond the standard obligation in article 2(1) to respect and ensure the Covenant's rights to persons *within* jurisdiction.[29] States Parties are expected to take positive measures to 'promote' rights of self-determination where they have been denied. Such measures may include the termination of diplomatic relations with States that deny self-determination rights.[30] States must however conform to the UN Charter, and not 'interfere in the internal affairs of other States', and are therefore prohibited from using force to assist an oppressed people to achieve self-determination in a foreign State.[31]

Non-justiciability under the First Optional Protocol

[7.20] Despite the undoubted importance of article 1, the HRC has paradoxically decided that it is not justiciable under the First Optional Protocol.

KITOK v SWEDEN (197/85)

This case involved a complaint about denial of reindeer husbandry rights to the author, a member of the Sami people of northern Scandinavia, in alleged breach of, *inter alia*, article 1.[32] The HRC ruled the article 1 complaint inadmissible in the following terms:

¶ 6.3. . . . the Committee observed that the author, as an individual, could not claim to be the victim of a violation of the right of self-determination, enshrined in article 1 of the Covenant. Whereas the Optional Protocol provides a recourse procedure for individuals claiming that their rights have been violated, article 1 . . . deals with rights conferred upon peoples, as such. . . .

The *Kitok* decision in respect of the non-justiciability of article 1 has been followed in *Ominayak v Canada* (167/84)[33] and *Marshall v Canada* (205/86).[34]

---

[28] McGoldrick, above, note 1, 253. See also Chap. 4, on territorial limits to a State Party's responsibility.   [29] McGoldrick, above, note 1, 253.

[30] In the 1980s, before the advent of Concluding Comments, individual HRC members questioned States Parties' representatives regarding relations with Israel (due to its occupation of Palestinian territories) and South Africa (due to its apartheid system); ibid., 251–2.

[31] See J. Crawford, *The Creation of States in International Law* (Clarendon Press, Oxford, 1979), 114–18. Note that no general doctrine of unilateral humanitarian intervention has yet been formally accepted in international law: see, e.g., B. Simma, 'NATO, the UN, and the Use of Force: Legal Aspects' (1999) 10 *European Journal of International Law* 1.

[32] See, on the art. 27 aspect of this complaint, [24.21].

[33] Para. 13.3. Though the Lubicon Lake Band could be termed a 'people' for the purposes of art. 1, only individuals, rather than peoples, have standing under the OP: see [3.13–3.15].

[34] Para. 5.1 (also known as *Mikmaq Tribal Society v Canada*).

[7.21] It is regrettable that the HRC has adopted such a narrow interpretation of the 'victim' requirement in the Optional Protocol,[35] so as to preclude article 1 complaints.[36] Certain complaints could perhaps have been more successful if the authors could have relied on article 1 rather than the Covenant's individual rights. For example, the authors in *Bordes and Temeharo v France* (645/95) unsuccessfully complained that French nuclear tests in the vicinity of their islands breached their rights to life and family life.[37] Perhaps a complaint under article 1, as the tests were conducted without the consent of the islanders and may have severely harmed the natural environment, would have been more viable.

Conclusion

[7.22] Article 1 jurisprudence under the ICCPR has been brief and disappointing. It is time for the HRC to issue more significant contributions to the law surrounding this most controversial of rights. It is also recommended that the Committee on Economic, Social, and Cultural Rights issue a General Comment on common article 1.

---

[35] See also [3.13–3.15].

[36] Cassese, above, note 17, persuasively argues for a more liberal interpretation of the Optional Protocol in this regard at 141–6, and 345–6.

[37] See [3.31] on this case.

8

The Right to Life—Article 6

ARTICLE 6

1. Every human being has the inherent right to life. This right shall be protected by law. No one shall be arbitrarily deprived of his life.

2. In countries which have not abolished the death penalty, sentence of death may be imposed only for the most serious crimes in accordance with the law in force at the time of the commission of the crime and not contrary to the provisions of the present Covenant and to the Convention on the Prevention and Punishment of the Crime of Genocide. This penalty can only be carried out pursuant to a final judgement rendered by a competent court.

3. When deprivation of life constitutes the crime of genocide, it is understood that nothing in this article shall authorize any State Party to the present Covenant to derogate in any way from any obligation assumed under the provisions of the Convention on the Prevention and Punishment of the Crime of Genocide.

4. Anyone sentenced to death shall have the right to seek pardon or commutation of the sentence. Amnesty, pardon or commutation of the sentence of death may be granted in all cases.

5. Sentence of death shall not be imposed for crimes committed by persons below eighteen years of age and shall not be carried out on pregnant women.

6. Nothing in this article shall be invoked to delay or to prevent the abolition of capital punishment by any State Party to the present Covenant.

[8.01] Article 6 protects the right to life, which has been described by the HRC as 'the supreme right'.[1] Article 6 has both a negative component, as in a right not to be arbitrarily or unlawfully deprived of life by the State or its agents, and a positive component, in that the State must adopt measures that are conducive to allowing one to live.

Right not to be Killed by the State

[8.02]   *GENERAL COMMENT 6*

¶ 3. The protection against arbitrary deprivation of life which is explicitly required by the third sentence of article 6(1) is of paramount importance. The Committee considers that States parties should take measures not only to prevent and punish deprivation of life by criminal acts, but also to prevent arbitrary killing by their own security forces. The deprivation of life by the authorities of the State is a matter of the utmost gravity. Therefore, the law must strictly control and limit the circumstances in which a person may be deprived of his life by such authorities.

[8.03]   *SUÁREZ de GUERRERO v COLOMBIA (45/79)*

The HRC based its view on the following facts. On 13 April 1978, a police raid was carried out on a house in Bogotá, in the belief that a kidnapped former Ambassador was being held prisoner there. The Ambassador was not found. However, the police hid in the house and awaited the arrival of the suspected kidnappers. Seven persons subsequently entered the house. They were shot and killed by the police.

¶ 11.5. Although the police initially stated that the victims had died while resisting arrest, brandishing and even firing various weapons, the report of the Institute of Forensic Medicine . . . together with the ballistics reports and the results of the paraffin test, showed that none of the victims had fired a shot and that they had all been killed at point-blank range, some of them shot in the back or in the head. It was also established that the victims were not all killed at the same time, but at intervals, as they arrived at the house, and that most of them had been shot while trying to save themselves from the unexpected attack. . . .

The police involved in the operation were acquitted on charges of causing violent death. This acquittal was directed by a Colombian statute, Article 1 of Decree No. 0070 of 20 January 1978.

¶ 11.2. Legislative Decree No. 0070 of 20 January 1978 amended article 25 of the Penal Code 'for so long as the public order remains disturbed and the national territory is in a state of siege'. . . . The Decree established a new ground of defence that may be pleaded by members of the police force to exonerate them if an otherwise punishable act was committed 'in the course of operations planned with the object of preventing and curbing

---

[1] General Comment 6, para. 1

the offences of extortion and kidnapping, and the production and processing of and trafficking in narcotic drugs'.

Despite the fact that the killings were deemed 'lawful' in Colombian municipal law, the HRC found that María Fanny Suárez de Guerrero had been 'arbitrarily' deprived of her life in contravention of Article 6(1).

¶ 13.2. In the present case it is evident from the fact that seven persons lost their lives as a result of the deliberate action of the police that the deprivation of life was intentional. Moreover, the police action was apparently taken without warning to the victims and without giving them any opportunity to surrender to the police patrol or to offer any explanation of their presence or intentions. There is no evidence that the action of the police was necessary in their own defence or that of others, or that it was necessary to effect the arrest or prevent the escape of the persons concerned. Moreover, the victims were no more than suspects of the kidnapping which had occurred some days earlier and their killing by the police deprived them of all the protections of due process of law laid down by the Covenant. . . .

¶ 13.3. For these reasons it is the Committee's view that the action of the police resulting in the death of Mrs. María Fanny Suárez de Guerrero was disproportionate to the requirements of law enforcement in the circumstances of the case and that she was arbitrarily deprived of her life contrary to article 6 (1) of the International Covenant on Civil and Political Rights. Inasmuch as the police action was made justifiable as a matter of Colombian law by Legislative Decree No. 0070 of 20 January 1978, the right to life was not adequately protected by the law of Colombia as required by article 6 (1).

[8.04] The *Suárez de Guerrero* case confirms that 'arbitrary' is a broader concept than 'unlawful'. That is, a killing may breach article 6 even though it is authorized by domestic law. The prohibition on the 'arbitrary' deprivation of life signifies that life must not be taken in unreasonable or disproportionate circumstances. Some indicators of the arbitrariness of a homicidal act are the intention behind and the necessity for that action.[2]

[8.05] In paragraph 13.3, the HRC confirms that the proportionate requirements of law enforcement will justify the use of lethal force by the State. The HRC describes some relevant law enforcement requirements at paragraph 13.2 in stating that the killings were not perpetrated for the purposes of the defence of self or others, the execution of an arrest, or the prevention of an escape. These exceptions mirror the express 'law enforcement' exceptions to the right to life in article 2(2) of the European Convention of Human Rights.[3]

---

[2] See D. McGoldrick, *The Human Rights Committee* (Clarendon, Oxford, 1994), 342. See also how the word 'arbitrary' has been interpreted in the context of other guarantees, such as arts. 9(1) [11.12 ff] and 17 [16.13].

[3] On art. 2(2) of the ECHR, see *McCann and Others v UK*, Series A, No. 324, Judgment of 27 September 1995, and *Andronicou v Cyprus,* Case 86/1996/705/897, Judgment of 25 August 1997, reported in (1998) 3 *Butterworths Human Rights Reports* 389. See also S. Joseph, 'Denouement of the Deaths on the Rock: The Right to Life of Terrorists' (1995) 14 *Netherlands Quarterly of Human Rights* 5.

[8.06] In its Concluding Comments on Cyprus in 1994, the HRC was concerned about the 'wide discretion' given to police officers regarding 'the use of force'.[4] The HRC recommended that Cyprus redraft the relevant instructions in accordance with the UN's Basic Principles on the Use of Force and Firearms by Law Enforcement Officials.[5] Similar recommendations were made to the United States of America.[6] The UN Basic Principles, and therefore article 6 by implication, strictly limit the use of potentially lethal force. In particular, Basic Principle 9 recommends the use of firearms only 'when strictly unavoidable in order to protect life'.[7]

[8.07] Note the ostensible importance of the fact that the *Suárez de Guerrero* killings were 'intentional'.[8] Do unintentional or negligent killings by State agents breach article 6(1)? This question is addressed in the following case.

BURRELL v JAMAICA (546/93)

Rickly Burrell was a prisoner on death row in Jamaica who was killed by a warder during a disturbance at the prison in October 1993. Counsel for Burrell submitted evidence that Burrell was shot 'in cold blood'. The State responded as follows:

¶ 4.1. By submission of 22 July 1994, the State party provides a copy of a report, dated 15 May 1994, from Senior Inspector B.R. Newman about the circumstances of Mr. Burrell's death. The report states that Mr. Burrell occupied cell No. 10 at Gibraltar 1 in St. Catherine Prison. Gibraltar Block is a two-storey-high building divided into four sections, each section containing about 26 cells without any functioning sanitary facilities. Each section is supervised by a different team of warders. Sanitary facilities are found in the yard. Inmates are unlocked, five at a time, to slop and to exercise and also for meals.

¶ 4.2. The report states that on 31 October 1993 the serving of lunch was at its final stage by about 12.30 p.m. Some inmates, including Mr. Burrell, were still in the passage of Gibraltar 1 and the four warders on duty were engaged in locking them in their cells. Unknown to them, an altercation between two inmates from Gibraltar 2 and the members of a patrol party had occurred in the yard. These inmates suddenly rushed from outside into the passage and overpowered the warders. The report states that other inmates, including Mr. Burrell, joined them in relieving the warders of their batons and their keys, and in opening some of the cells. The warders were dragged into cells 9 and 10, where they were assaulted. Other warders quickly appeared on the scene and ordered the inmates to release their hostages. The inmates reportedly refused, whereupon shots were fired. The injured

---

[4] (1995) UN doc. CCPR/C/79/Add.39, para. 6.

[5] Ibid., para. 18. The Basic Principles are reprinted in *UN Human Rights—A Compilation of International Instruments*, UN doc.A/CONF.144/28(1990).

[6] (1995) UN doc. CCPR/C/79/Add.50, para. 32.

[7] See also N. Rodley, 'Rights and Responses to Terrorism in Northern Ireland' in D. Harris and S. Joseph (eds.), *The International Covenant on Civil and Political Rights and United Kingdom Law* (Clarendon Press, Oxford, 1995), 142–3.   [8] Para. 13.2.

warders and inmates were taken to Spanish Town Hospital, where Mr. Burrell and three other inmates were pronounced dead.

¶ 4.3. The State party states that the post-mortem report shows that Mr. Burrell died as a result of shotgun and blunt force injuries. It is also stated that according to eyewitnesses, the shooting continued after the warders were rescued.

¶ 4.4. The State party submits that it is evident that the death of Rickly Burrell was the sequel to altercations between two death-row prisoners from Gibraltar 2 and certain warders of the patrol party. The State party states that it appears that Mr. Burrell was not aware of this incident, which seems to have ignited hostile reactions in the inmates, who then turned against the four warders in Gibraltar 1. The State party submits that the warders were in serious danger, since one of the prisoners tried to cut a warder's throat and others tried to hang a warder by a towel. The State party submits that the other warders, apparently after having ordered the inmates to release their colleagues, panicked upon realizing that their colleagues were in danger of losing their lives and opened fire. The State party submits that the use of necessary force may have been justified under section 15 (3) of the Corrections Act (1985), which reads: 'Every correctional officer may use force against any inmate using violence to any person, if such officer has reasonable grounds to believe that such a person is in danger of life or limb, or that other grievous bodily hurt is likely to be caused by him.' In this context, the State party submits that, although none of the warders was hospitalized, two of them were rendered unfit for work for two months, as a result of the injuries received. One of them is said to have a long scar at his throat, where an inmate cut him. The State party concludes: 'Like Burrell, none of these four warders was involved in the commencement of the altercation, but became victims. For Burrell, it was fatal.'

Counsel for Burrell responded:

¶ 5.1. In his comments on the State party's submission, counsel points out that the State party has failed to indicate what role Mr. Burrell played in the incident which led to his death. In this context, counsel notes that only one of the three warders refers to Mr. Burrell in his statement, saying that he was among the inmates who pushed him into the cell. In Inspector Newman's report it is stated that Mr. Burrell joined in with the others who were trying to overpower the warders. No further reference to Mr. Burrell's conduct is made. Counsel further notes that the Inspector's report was drawn up more than six months after the incident, and that the only disclosed sources of information are statements by three of the four warders who were kept in the cell by the inmates, although it seems that other sources were also used. In particular, counsel asserts that no statement has been submitted from the fourth warder involved in the incident nor from the Staff Warder who was in charge on 31 October 1993. Nor have statements been taken from any of the warders who came to their colleagues' rescue.

¶ 5.2. As to the cause of Mr. Burrell's death, counsel notes that the pathologist's report, of which the State party has provided no copy, states that he died of shotgun and blunt force injuries, but that the State party has given no details as to how Mr. Burrell was killed. Counsel notes that the Inspector's report states that warders panicked and opened fire; he argues that if Mr. Burrell's death resulted from this, it would constitute a violation of article 6 of the Covenant. Furthermore, counsel submits that if the State party contends that

Mr. Burrell was shot to prevent further injuries to the warders in the cell, the pathologist's evidence would suggest that he was beaten to death after there was no longer any danger, in flagrant breach of article 6 of the Covenant.

¶ 5.3. Counsel further submits that there is evidence which indicates that Mr. Burrell was not shot to prevent injury to the warders in the cell, but that he was shot after there was no more threat. In this context, counsel refers to statements from inmates and to press articles. He claims that relatives of some of the prisoners killed saw that the shot wounds were at the back of the body, and that the body showed signs of heavy beating. Inmates who survived further allege that they were brutally assaulted by the warders and shot at after the four warders were released. It is also alleged that the supervisor told the investigating police that he had not been consulted about the use of guns and that the warders had taken the guns without his permission. Finally, counsel also refers to the report of Amnesty International, in which it was stated that it was difficult to see how the inmates could have been shot dead in such a confined space without warders also being injured if they were still being held at that time.

¶ 5.4. Counsel also submits that the regulations for the use of force would have required the use of non-lethal force.

¶ 5.5. Counsel further notes that the Inspector's report suggests that the warders did not obtain the consent of the senior officer before fetching firearms. Counsel refers to article 2 of the Principles on the Effective Prevention and Investigation of Extra-legal, Arbitrary and Summary Executions which requires a clear chain of command over all officials authorized by law to use force and firearms. Counsel argues that the incident of 31 October 1993 and previous incidents at St. Catherine's District Prison show that there was no such clear chain of command or that it was utterly ineffective. In this context, counsel also argues that if the warders had received proper training in control and restraint techniques, they might not have panicked and shot Mr. Burrell and three other inmates.

¶ 5.6. Counsel argues that the State party's investigation falls short of its obligations under the Covenant. In this context, he notes that he has never received a reply from the Parliamentary Ombudsman, that the report of the Forensic Pathologist has not been submitted to the Committee and that the State party does not refer to the coroner's inquest, although section 79 of the Corrections Act (1985) requires that a coroner's inquest be held on the death of any inmate in a correctional institution. Counsel refers to the Committee's jurisprudence in the Uruguayan cases and argues that the State party is under the obligation to make a full and thorough inquiry.[9]

¶ 5.7. Finally, counsel refers to a letter, dated 16 June 1994, from the Jamaican Ministry of National Security and Justice to Amnesty International, in which the Ministry states that the Inspectorate's report on the incident of October 1993 has been referred to the Director of Public Prosecutions for a ruling on the question of criminal responsibility and that it is not considered necessary to set up an independent commission of inquiry. In this connection, counsel notes with concern that the Director of Public Prosecutions has not yet made a decision in relation to a report concerning disturbances in 1991.

---

[9] See below, [8.08–8.13].

Counsel had also made the following comment in an earlier submission:

¶ 2.12. Counsel contends that many incidents of excessive violence by prison warders have occurred in the past years and that complaints are not adequately dealt with but that, on the contrary, prisoners who complain about maltreatment are subjected to threats by warders. If investigations are held, the results are not made public. It is further submitted that the Parliamentary Ombudsman, although constituting the main independent procedure for investigation of complaints from inmates, has no powers of enforcement and his recommendations are not binding. Counsel points out that the last annual report from the Ombudsman to Parliament dates from 1988.

The HRC found against the State Party:

¶ 9.5. The Committee has carefully examined all information forwarded by both counsel and the State party in relation to Mr. Burrell's death following the hostage taking of some warders at St. Catherine prison's death row section, on 31 October 1993. It regrets that the State party has not made available the autopsy report nor the results of the Coroner's inquest in the case. The Committee notes that counsel has alleged, on the basis of letters received from other inmates in St. Catherine Prison, that Mr. Burrell was shot after the warders were already released, and thus the need for force no longer existed. The Committee notes that the State party itself has acknowledged that Mr. Burrell's death was the unfortunate result of confusion on the side of the warders, who panicked when seeing some of their colleagues being threatened by the inmates, and that the report submitted by the State party acknowledges that the shooting continued after the warders were rescued. In the circumstances, the Committee concludes that the State party has failed in taking effective measures to protect Mr. Burrell's life, in violation of article 6, paragraph 1, of the Covenant.

It appears as if the HRC gave the State Party the benefit of the doubt and accepted its contention that Burrell's killing was not intentional. The HRC nevertheless found that the killing was a breach of article 6. The State failed in its negative duty not to kill arbitrarily, and failed in its positive duty to protect Burrell's life whilst he was in State custody.[10]

DUTY TO INVESTIGATE STATE KILLINGS[11]

[8.08]   *GENERAL COMMENT 6*

¶ 4. States parties should also take specific and effective measures to prevent the disappearance of individuals, something which unfortunately has become all too frequent and leads too often to arbitrary deprivation of life. Furthermore, States should establish effective facilities and procedures to investigate thoroughly cases of missing and disappeared persons in circumstances which may involve a violation of the right to life.

[8.09] In *Baboeram et al. v Suriname* (146, 148–154/83), the Committee found

---

[10] See also *Dermit Barbato v Uruguay* [8.34]
[11] See also the similar duty regarding art. 7, [9.83] ff.

a violation of article 6(1) entailed in the arrest and killing of fifteen persons by Surinamese military police. The HRC recommended the appropriate remedy:

¶ 16. The Committee therefore urges the State party to take effective steps (i) to investigate the killings of December 1982; (ii) to bring to justice any persons found to be responsible for the death of the victims; (iii) to pay compensation to the surviving families; and (iv) to ensure that the right to life is duly protected in Suriname.

Therefore, States Parties have positive duties to investigate all State killings, and to provide redress with regard to those that breach article 6, including those arising from 'disappearances'.

[8.10] *HERRERA RUBIO V COLOMBIA (161/83)*

The facts are outlined immediately below.

¶ 10.2. Joaquín Herrera Rubio was arrested on 17 March 1981 by members of the Colombian armed forces on suspicion of being a 'guerrillero'. He claims that he was tortured ('submarine', 'hanging' and beatings) by Colombian military authorities who also threatened him that unless he signed a confession his parents would be killed. On 27 March 1981, several individuals wearing military uniforms, identifying themselves as members of the counter-guerrilla, came to the home of the author's parents and led them away by force. One week later the bodies of José Herrera and Emma Rubio de Herrera were found in the vicinity. At that time the District of Caquetá is reported to have been the scene of a military counter-insurgency operation, during which most villages in the area were subjected to stringent controls by the armed forces. The State party has shown that a judicial investigation of the killings was carried out from 24 September 1982 to 25 January 1983, and claims that it was established that no member of the armed forces had taken part in the killings.

Colombia submitted the following information regarding its investigation into the killings.

¶ 6.1. In its submission . . ., the State party indicates that the killings of José Herrera and Emma Rubio de Herrera were duly investigated and that no evidence was found to support charges against military personnel. The investigation was therefore closed by order of the Attorney-General delegate for the Armed Forces, dated 15 August 1984. . . .

¶ 6.2. The State party also forwarded the text of a decision of the Penal Chamber of the Superior Court of Florencia, dated 18 February 1983, finding, after a judicial investigation lasting from 24 September 1982 to 25 January 1983, that the killings had been perpetrated by armed persons, without, however, being able to determine to which group they belonged.

The State Party later confirmed that no new investigations in the case were pending due to a lack of sufficient evidence. The HRC found a violation of article 6 despite the apparent efforts to investigate the matter by Colombian officials.

¶ 10.3. Whereas the Committee considers that there is reason to believe, in the light of the author's allegations, that Colombian military persons bear responsibility for the deaths of José Herrera and Emma Rubio de Herrera, no conclusive evidence has been produced to establish the identity of the murderers. In this connection the Committee refers to its general comment No. 6 (16) concerning article 6 of the Covenant, which provides, *inter alia*, that States parties should take specific and effective measures to prevent the disappearance of individuals and establish effective facilities and procedures to investigate thoroughly, by an appropriate impartial body, cases of missing and disappeared persons in circumstances which may involve a violation of the right to life. The Committee has duly noted the State party's submissions concerning the investigations carried out in this case, which, however, appear to have been inadequate in the light of the State party's obligations under article 2 of the Covenant.

McGoldrick has criticized the *Herrera Rubio* decision 'for not being more specific as to the particular inadequacies of the investigation'.[12] The HRC did not take the opportunity to spell out how the investigation could have been improved so as to comply with article 6.

[8.11] *Sanjuán Arévalo v Colombia* (181/84) contained very similar facts to the *Herrera Rubio* case. The HRC majority again found Colombia had violated article 6(1) in failing properly to investigate the disappearances and assumed deaths of the Sanjuán brothers, especially considering the strong implication of government involvement in their disappearances. Mr Nisuke Ando delivered a dissenting opinion, exhibiting sympathy for the problems governments can encounter in attempting to control rampant security forces which simply ignore the rule of law:

the finding that '[in] all these circumstances . . . the right to life . . . and the right to liberty and security of the person . . . have not been effectively protected by the State of Colombia' is, in my opinion, too sweeping. It is true that many cases of disappearances, including this one, are reported to have occurred in Colombia, and that the investigations of these cases seem to have encountered a number of difficulties. This situation is indeed deplorable. Nevertheless, considering the efforts made by the Colombian Government, which can be ascertained from its replies to the Committee's requests for clarification, I am unable to persuade myself that the Committee's sweeping finding is justified.

[8.12] In *Sanjuán Arévalo*, the HRC majority found that it had not been suggested that the disappearances were 'caused by persons other than Government officials'.[13] In contrast, Ando found that there was insufficient evidence for the HRC to assume government collusion in the disappearances. These comments possibly imply that States have no duty to investigate private killings or disappearances. However, paragraph 3 of General Comment 6 confirms that States must 'prevent and punish deprivation of life by criminal acts' [8.02]. It is however possible that the duty of a State to investigate a death is more onerous when evidence indicates that government officials are involved in that death.

---

[12] See McGoldrick, above, note 2, 344.
[13] Para. 11.

[8.13] The strict duty of States Parties to prevent and otherwise investigate disappearances and deaths was confirmed unanimously in *Miango Muiyo v Zaire* (194/85), *Mojica v Dominican Republic* (449/91), and *Laureano v Peru* (540/93). The evidence in all of these cases indicated official involvement in the disappearances and deaths.

DUTY TO PUNISH OFFENDERS FOR STATE KILLINGS

[8.14] In *Suárez de Guerrero v Colombia* (45/79), the Columbian security forces were acquitted of using excessive force under an impunity statute [8.03]. The statute itself was found to constitute a breach of article 6(1).[14] It manifested the State Party's failure adequately to protect life by punishing the perpetrators of arbitrary killings.[15]

[8.15]   *BAUTISTA de ARELLANA v COLOMBIA (563/93)*[16]

N.E. Bautista de Arellana was abducted from her home on 30 August 1987. Her body was discovered on 12 September 1987, though it was not officially identified until 11 September 1990. In subsequent administrative proceedings, named State agents were found responsible for Ms Bautista's disappearance and death. In finding a violation of article 6, the HRC stated the following:

¶ 8.2. In its submission of 14 July 1995, the State party indicates that Resolution 13 of 5 July 1995 pronounced disciplinary sanctions against Messrs. Velandia Hurtado and Ortega Araque, and that the judgment of the Administrative Tribunal of Cundinamarca of 22 June 1995 granted the claim for compensation filed by the family of Nydia Bautista. The State party equally reiterates its desire to guarantee fully the exercise of human rights and fundamental freedoms. These observations would appear to indicate that, in the State party's opinion, the above-mentioned decisions constitute an effective remedy for the family of Nydia Bautista. The Committee does not share this view, because purely disciplinary and administrative remedies cannot be deemed to constitute adequate and effective remedies within the meaning of article 2, paragraph 3, of the Covenant, in the event of particularly serious violations of human rights, notably in the event of an alleged violation of the right to life. . . .

¶ 10. . . . the Committee urges the State party to expedite the criminal proceedings leading to the prompt prosecution and conviction of the persons responsible for the abduction, torture and death of Nydia Bautista.

[8.16] The emphasis placed by the HRC on criminal law 'remedies' for State killings in *Bautista de Arellana* is possibly at odds with its decision in the following case.

---

[14] Para. 13.3.
[15] See also generally on the issue of remedies and impunity [9.88–9.93].
[16] See also, in a similar vein, *Vicente et al. v Colombia* (612/95), paras. 8.2–8.3.

CROES v THE NETHERLANDS (164/84)

The author was the leader of a political party, the People's Electoral Movement (known as the 'MEP') promoting independence for the island of Aruba. At an MEP parade in 1983, the author was allegedly shot by a police officer. He did not die, but submitted a complaint that the State had threatened his right to life. The HRC eventually found the complaint inadmissible for failure to exhaust domestic remedies.

¶ 10. . . . It would have been open to Mr. Croes to institute civil proceedings against the State party and to claim compensation for the damages suffered as a result of the alleged failure of the State party to fulfil its obligations under the International Covenant on Civil and Political Rights. It is true that he claimed that this type of recourse would not address his concerns. In this context, the Committee observes that although States parties are obliged to investigate in good faith allegations of human rights violations, criminal proceedings would not be the only available remedy. Accordingly, the Committee cannot accept the argument of the author and his heirs[17] that proceedings before the Aruban courts, other than those leading to the criminal prosecution of the policeman, do not constitute effective remedies within the meaning of article 5, paragraph 2 (b), of the Optional Protocol. The Committee adds that the authors' complaint could be directed, in all of its aspects, against the Aruban authorities in general and that he and his heirs have failed to pursue all avenues of judicial recourse open to them.

[8.17] It has been confirmed in numerous cases that the ICCPR contains no independent right to see another prosecuted.[18] However, it seems that the duty to investigate alleged violations of the ICCPR in good faith may occasionally entail a duty to prosecute a certain person, as occurred in *Bautista de Arellana*. On the other hand, a State's performance of an adequate investigation provides evidence that a State's decision not to prosecute was justified, as occurred in *Croes*, where the Dutch investigation of Croes's shooting uncovered no evidence of police misbehaviour.[19]

Capital Punishment

[8.18] Articles 6(2) to 6(6) are concerned with an exception to the right to life, the judicial imposition of a sentence of death.

---

[17] Mr Croes died in an accidental car crash whilst the communication was being considered, so his heirs continued the complaint.

[18] See, e.g., *H.C.M.A. v The Netherlands* (213/86), *S.E. v Argentina* (275/88).

[19] Para. 8.2. See also *I.M. v Italy* (266/87), where the communication regarding I.M.'s death was inadmissible as civil domestic remedies had not yet been exhausted against doctors allegedly responsible for that death.

GENERAL COMMENT 6

¶ 6. While it follows from article 6 (2) to (6) that States parties are not obliged to abolish the death penalty totally they are obliged to limit its use and, in particular, to abolish it for other than the 'most serious crimes'. Accordingly, they ought to consider reviewing their criminal laws in this light and, in any event, are obliged to restrict the application of the death penalty to the 'most serious crimes'. The article also refers generally to abolition in terms which strongly suggest (paragraphs 2 (2) and (6)) that abolition is desirable. The Committee concludes that all measures of abolition should be considered as progress in the enjoyment of the right to life within the meaning of article 40, and should as such be reported to the Committee. The Committee notes that a number of States have already abolished the death penalty or suspended its application. Nevertheless, States' reports show that progress made towards abolishing or limiting the application of the death penalty is quite inadequate.

¶ 7. The Committee is of the opinion that the expression 'most serious crimes' must be read restrictively to mean that the death penalty should be a quite exceptional measure. It also follows from the express terms of article 6 that it can only be imposed in accordance with the law in force at the time of the commission of the crime and not contrary to the Covenant. The procedural guarantees therein prescribed must be observed, including the right to a fair hearing by an independent tribunal, the presumption of innocence, the minimum guarantees for the defence, and the right to review by a higher tribunal. These rights are applicable in addition to the particular right to seek pardon or commutation of the sentence.

[8.19] Imposition of the death penalty is prohibited in States Parties which have ratified the Second Optional Protocol.[20] By October 1999, only forty States had done so, though the HRC vigorously encourages such ratification in its dialogues with States Parties to the ICCPR.

[8.20]   *LUBUTO v ZAMBIA (390/90)*

The HRC considered the meaning of 'most serious crimes' in article 6(2) in this case.

¶ 7.2. The Committee notes that the author was convicted and sentenced to death under a law that provides for the imposition of the death penalty for aggravated robbery in which firearms are used. The issue that must accordingly be decided is whether the sentence in the instant case is compatible with article 6, paragraph 2, of the Covenant, which allows for the imposition of the death penalty only 'for the most serious crimes'. Considering that in this case use of firearms did not produce the death or wounding of any person and that the court could not under the law take these elements into account in imposing sentence, the Committee is of the view that the mandatory imposition of the death sentence under these circumstances violates article 6, paragraph 2, of the Covenant.

---

[20] See Appendices C and F.

Mr Ando concurred, but added that some crimes could be serious enough to attract the death penalty even if they injured no one, such as 'bombing of busy quarters, destruction of reservoirs, poisoning of drinking water, gassing in subway stations and probably espionage in war-time'. This is because some crimes 'create a grave danger which may result in death or irreparable harm to many and unspecified persons', and should thus be severely punished regardless of their ultimate consequences.

[8.21] The HRC has also confirmed that the following are not 'most serious crimes', and cannot therefore attract the death penalty without violating article 6: robbery,[21] traffic in toxic or dangerous wastes,[22] abetting suicide, drug-related offences, property offences,[23] multiple evasion of military service,[24] apostasy, committing a third homosexual act, embezzlement by officials, theft by force,[25] crimes of an economic nature, adultery, corruption, and 'crimes that do not result in the loss of life'.[26] Messrs Klein and Kretzmer, in the minority in *T.T. v Australia* (706/96), implied that drug offences were not serious enough to attract the death penalty.[27] In Concluding Comments on Iraq, the HRC strongly implied that 'non-violent' infringements are not serious enough to attract the death penalty.[28] The HRC has also stated that 'political and economic' offences are not 'most serious crimes' for the purposes of article 6(2).[29] Finally, retribution cannot be legally accepted as a ground for imposition of the death penalty.[30] In summary, it appears that only intentional killings or attempted killings, or the intentional infliction of grievous bodily harm, may permissibly attract the death penalty under article 6(2).

[8.22]   *MBENGE v ZAIRE (16/77)*

In this case, the HRC found that Daniel Monguya Mbenge had been twice sentenced to death in trials which had breached various sub-paragraphs of article 14(3).[31]

¶ 17. Daniel Monguya Mbenge also alleges a breach of article 6 of the Covenant. Paragraph 2 of that article provides that sentence of death may be imposed only 'in accordance with the

---

[21] Concluding Comments on Republic of Korea (1992) UN doc. A/47/40, 122–4, para. 9.

[22] Concluding Comments on Cameroon (1994) UN doc. CCPR/C/79/Add.33, para. 9.

[23] Concluding Comments on Sri Lanka (1996) UN doc. CCPR/C/79/Add.56, para. 14.

[24] Concluding Comments on Iraq (1997) UN doc. CCPR/79/Add. 84, para. 11.

[25] Concluding Comments on Sudan (1997) UN doc. CCPR/C/79/Add. 85, para. 8.

[26] Concluding Comments on the Islamic Republic of Iran (1995) UN Doc CCPR/C/79/Add. 25, para. 8.

[27] The complaint related to the author's extradition to Malaysia where, it was alleged, he faced the possibility of the death penalty for a drugs offence. The majority found that it was unlikely he would even be tried for the drugs offence upon his return.

[28] (1997) UN doc. CCPR/79/Add. 84, para. 10.

[29] Concluding Comments on Libyan Arab Jamahiriya (1998) UN doc. CCPR/C/79/Add. 101, para. 8.   [30] Ibid.

[31] Art. 14 guarantees the right to a fair trial and the fair administration of justice. See generally Chap. 14.

law (of the State party) in force at the time of the commission of the crime and not contrary to the provisions of the Covenant'. This requires that both the substantive and the procedural law in the application of which the death penalty was imposed was not contrary to the provisions of the Covenant, and also that the death penalty was imposed in accordance with that law and therefore in accordance with the provisions of the Covenant. Consequently, the failure of the State party to respect the relevant requirements of article 14 (3) [relating to fairness of the trial] leads to the conclusion that the death sentences pronounced against the author of the communication were imposed contrary to the provisions of the Covenant, and therefore in violation of article 6 (2).

[8.23] The HRC has entertained a large number of complaints from the Caribbean from prisoners on death row, alleging procedural defects in their trials. As in the *Mbenge* case, and as foreshadowed by General Comment 6, the HRC has continued to find concurrent breaches of article 6(2) where a death sentence is imposed following judicial proceedings which do not comply with article 14.[32] However, it must be noted that not all violations of article 14 in capital trials give rise to concurrent breaches of article 6(2). In particular, breaches of the guarantees of expeditious criminal trials and appeals (articles 14(3)(c) and 14(5)) do not concurrently breach article 6(2).[33] Whilst an unreasonable delay constitutes unfair treatment of the defendant, it does not mean that the actual trial is conducted in an unjust manner, so any resultant capital sentence is not so open to challenge.

[8.24] Article 6(5) prohibits the execution of pregnant women, and persons who were under 18 at the time they committed the relevant crime.[34] In addition, the HRC has hinted that mentally retarded persons should also be immune from execution, by 'regretting' the failure of the United States to protect such persons from the death penalty.[35] In *Williams v Jamaica* (609/95), the HRC did not consider a complaint about the proposed execution of a 'mentally disturbed' individual as his sentence was commuted to life imprisonment during consideration of the complaint.[36]

[8.25] In Concluding Comments on Lebanon, the HRC was:[37]

¶ 20. . . . deeply concerned at the Government's extension of the number of crimes carrying the death penalty which, bearing in mind that article 6 of the Covenant limits the

---

[32] See, e.g., *Pinto v Trinidad & Tobago* (232/87), *Reid v Jamaica* (250/87), *Kelly v Jamaica* (253/87), *Wright v Jamaica* (349/89), *Henry v Jamaica* (230/87), *Campbell v Jamaica* (248/87), *Burrell v Jamaica* (546/93), and *Price v Jamaica* (572/94)). Mr Wennergren dissented on this point in both *Pinto* and *Reid*, but the HRC has been unanimous on this point ever since.

[33] See, e.g., *Brown and Parish v Jamaica* (665/95), para. 9.2.

[34] See, e.g., *Johnson v Jamaica* (592/94), para. 10.3, where the author was only 17 years of age when he committed the alleged crime, and was sentenced to death in contravention of art. 6(5).

[35] Concluding Comments on the USA, UN doc. CCPR/C/79/Add.50, para. 16

[36] Para. 6.2.

[37] (1997) UN doc. CCPR/C/79/Add. 78, para. 20; see also Concluding Comments on Peru (1996) UN doc. CCPR/C/79/Add.67, para. 15.

circumstances under which capital punishment may be imposed, suggesting that they be submitted to continuing review with a view to the abolition of capital punishment, is not compatible with that article.

Therefore, any expansion of a State Party's list of capital crimes, including presumably reintroduction of the death penalty,[38] appears to breach article 6, even if such expansion applies only to the 'most serious crimes'.

[8.26] Obviously, a violation concerning the imposition of capital punishment will not be effectively remedied if the relevant person is executed whilst the HRC is deliberating. Therefore, the HRC frequently requests States to undertake interim protection measures (e.g. refrain from executing the complainant) under Rule 86 of the Committee's rules of procedure. States Parties usually comply with these requests. With regard to the complaints in *Kandu-Bo et al. v Sierra Leone* (839–841/98), the State Party executed twelve persons in violation of the Rule 86 request. The HRC formally condemned Sierra Leone's action, and resolved to continue its examinations of the original complaints, despite the authors' deaths.

Extradition to a State with Capital Punishment[39]

[8.27]   *KINDLER v CANADA (470/91)*

One of the most controversial issues before the HRC has arisen in the Canadian 'extradition' cases, of which *Kindler* was the first merits decision.

¶ 2.1. In November 1983 the author was convicted in the State of Pennsylvania, United States, of first degree murder and kidnapping; the jury recommended the death sentence. According to the author, this recommendation is binding on the court. In September 1984, prior to sentencing, the author escaped from custody. He was arrested in the province of Quebec in April 1985. In July 1985 the United States requested and in August 1985 the Superior Court of Quebec ordered his extradition.

¶ 2.2. Article 6 of the 1976 Extradition Treaty between Canada and the United States provides:

'When the offence for which extradition is requested is punishable by death under the laws of the requesting State and the laws of the requested State do not permit such punishment for that offence, extradition may be refused unless the requesting State provides such assurances as the requested State considers sufficient that the death penalty shall not be imposed or, if imposed, shall not be executed'.

Canada abolished the death penalty in 1976, except in the case of certain military offences.

¶ 2.3. The power to seek assurances that the death penalty will not be imposed is conferred on the Minister of Justice pursuant to section 25 of the 1985 Extradition Act. On

---

[38] See, in this regard, minority opinions in *Kindler v Canada* (470/91) at [8.28–8.29].
[39] See [9.51] ff. on the related issue of deportation and refoulement of someone to States in which his/her art. 7 rights might be breached.

January 17, 1986, after hearing the author's counsel, the Minister of Justice decided not to seek these assurances.

¶ 2.4. The author filed an application for review of the Minister's decision with the Federal Court, which dismissed the application in January 1987. The author's appeal to the Court of Appeal was rejected in December 1988. The matter then came before the Supreme Court of Canada, which decided on 26 September 1991 that the extradition of Mr. Kindler would not violate his rights under the Canadian Charter of Human Rights. The author was extradited on the same day.

Kindler claimed, *inter alia*, that the decision to extradite him violated article 6, in that it subjected him to a risk of capital punishment in the United States. The United States, at the time of the communication, was not a party to the ICCPR. The HRC dismissed Canadian arguments that the communication was inadmissible *ratione loci*.[40] On the merits, the HRC founded in favour of the State Party in the following terms:

¶ 13.1. Before examining the merits of this communication, the Committee observes that, as indicated in the admissibility decision, what is at issue is not whether Mr. Kindler's rights have been or are likely to be violated by the United States, which is not a party to the Optional Protocol, but whether by extraditing Mr. Kindler to the United States, Canada exposed him to a real risk of a violation of his rights under the Covenant. States parties to the Covenant will often also be party to various bilateral obligations, including those under extradition treaties. A State party to the Covenant is required to ensure that it carries out all its other legal commitments in a manner consistent with the Covenant. The starting point for an examination of this issue must be the obligation of the State party under article 2, paragraph 1, of the Covenant, namely, to ensure to all individuals within its territory and subject to its jurisdiction the rights recognized in the Covenant. The right to life is the most essential of these rights. . . .

¶ 13.2. If a State party extradites a person within its jurisdiction in circumstances such that as a result there is a real risk that his or her rights under the Covenant will be violated in another jurisdiction, the State party itself may be in violation of the Covenant.

¶ 14.1. With regard to a possible violation by Canada of article 6 the Covenant by its decision to extradite the author, two related questions arise:

(a) Did the requirement under article 6, paragraph 1, to protect the right to life prohibit Canada from exposing a person within its jurisdiction to the real risk (that is to say, a necessary and foreseeable consequence) of losing his life in circumstances incompatible with article 6 of the Covenant as a consequence of extradition to the United States?

(b) Did the fact that Canada had abolished capital punishment except for certain military offences require Canada to refuse extradition or request assurances from the United States, as it was entitled to do under article 6 of the Extradition Treaty, that the death penalty would not be imposed against Mr. Kindler?

---

[40] See [4.12].

¶ 14.2. As to (a), the Committee recalls its General Comment on Article 6 . . . which provides that while States parties are not obliged to abolish the death penalty totally, they are obliged to limit its use. The General Comment further notes that the terms of article 6 also point to the desirability of abolition of the death penalty. This is an object towards which ratifying parties should strive: 'All measures of abolition should be considered as progress in the enjoyment of the right to life'. Moreover, the Committee notes the evolution of international law and the trend towards abolition, as illustrated by the adoption by the United Nations General Assembly of the Second Optional Protocol to the International Covenant on Civil and Political Rights. Furthermore, even where capital punishment is retained by States in their legislation, many of them do not exercise it in practice.

¶ 14.3. The Committee notes that article 6, paragraph 1, must be read together with article 6, paragraph 2, which does not prohibit the imposition of the death penalty for the most serious crimes. Canada itself did not impose the death penalty on Mr. Kindler, but extradited him to the United States, where he faced capital punishment. If Mr. Kindler had been exposed, through extradition from Canada, to a real risk of a violation of article 6, paragraph 2, in the United States, that would have entailed a violation by Canada of its obligations under article 6, paragraph 1. Among the requirements of article 6, paragraph 2, is that capital punishment be imposed only for the most serious crimes, in circumstances not contrary to the Covenant and other instruments, and that it be carried out pursuant to a final judgment rendered by a competent court. The Committee notes that Mr. Kindler was convicted of premeditated murder, undoubtedly a very serious crime. He was over 18 years of age when the crime was committed. The author has not claimed before the Canadian courts or before the Committee that the conduct of the trial in the Pennsylvania court violated his rights to a fair hearing under article 14 of the Covenant.

¶ 14.4. Moreover, the Committee observes that Mr. Kindler was extradited to the United States following extensive proceedings in the Canadian Courts, which reviewed all the evidence submitted concerning Mr. Kindler's trial and conviction. In the circumstances, the Committee finds that the obligations arising under article 6, paragraph 1, did not require Canada to refuse the author's extradition.

¶ 14.5. The Committee notes that Canada has itself, save for certain categories of military offences, abolished capital punishment; it is not, however, a party to the Second Optional Protocol to the Covenant. As to question (b), namely whether the fact that Canada has generally abolished capital punishment, taken together with its obligations under the Covenant, required it to refuse extradition or to seek the assurances it was entitled to seek under the extradition treaty, the Committee observes that the abolition of capital punishment does not release Canada of its obligations under extradition treaties. However, it is in principle to be expected that, when exercising a permitted discretion under an extradition treaty (namely, whether or not to seek assurances that capital punishment will not be imposed) a State which has itself abandoned capital punishment would give serious consideration to its own chosen policy in making its decision. The Committee observes, however, that the State party has indicated that the possibility to seek assurances would normally be exercised where exceptional circumstances existed. Careful consideration was given to this possibility.

¶ 14.6. While States must be mindful of the possibilities for the protection of life when exercising their discretion in the application of extradition treaties, the Committee does not find that the terms of article 6 of the Covenant necessarily require Canada to refuse to extradite or to seek assurances. The Committee notes that the extradition of Mr. Kindler would have violated Canada's obligations under article 6 of the Covenant, if the decision to extradite without assurances would have been taken arbitrarily or summarily. The evidence before the Committee reveals, however, that the Minister of Justice reached a decision after hearing argument in favour of seeking assurances. The Committee further takes note of the reasons given by Canada not to seek assurances in Mr. Kindler's case, in particular, the absence of exceptional circumstances, the availability of due process, and the importance of not providing a safe haven for those accused of or found guilty of murder.

[8.28] Mr Pocar issued the following dissent:

Regarding the death penalty, it has to be recalled that, although article 6 of the Covenant does not prescribe categorically the abolition of capital punishment, it imposes a set of obligations on States parties that have not yet abolished it. As the Committee has pointed out in its General Comment 6(16), 'the article also refers generally to abolition in terms which strongly suggest that abolition is desirable.' Furthermore, the wording of paragraphs 2 and 6 clearly indicates that article 6 tolerates—within certain limits and in view of a future abolition—the existence of capital punishment in States parties that have not yet abolished it, but may by no means be interpreted as implying for any State party an authorization to delay its abolition or, *a fiori*, [*sic*] to enlarge its scope or to introduce or reintroduce it. Consequently, a State party that has abolished the death penalty is in my view under the legal obligation, according to article 6 of the Covenant, not to reintroduce it. This obligation must refer both to a direct reintroduction within the State's jurisdiction, and to an indirect one, as it is the case when the State acts—through extradition, expulsion or compulsory return—in such a way that an individual within its territory and subject to its jurisdiction may be exposed to capital punishment in another State. I therefore conclude that in the present case there has been a violation of article 6 of the Covenant.

[8.29] Mr Lallah, with whom Mme Chanet and Mr Aguilar Urbina agreed, issued a more detailed dissent:

¶ 1. I am unable to subscribe to the Committee's Views to the effect that the facts before it do not disclose a violation by Canada of any provision of the Covenant. . . .

¶ 2.3. The question which arises is what exactly are the obligations of Canada with regard to the right to life guaranteed under article 6 of the Covenant even if read alone and, perhaps and possibly, in the light of other relevant provisions of the Covenant, such as equality of treatment before the law under article 26 and the obligations deriving from article 5(2) which prevents restrictions or derogations from Covenant rights on the pretext that the Covenant recognizes them to a lesser extent. The latter feature of the Covenant would have, in my view, importance since the right to life is one to which Canada gives greater protection than might be thought to be required, on a minimal interpretation, under article 6 of the Covenant.

¶ 2.4. It would be useful to examine, in turn, the requirements of articles 6, 26 and 5(2) of the Covenant and their relevance to the facts before the Committee.

¶ 3.1. Article 6(1) of the Covenant proclaims that everyone has the inherent right to life. It requires that this right shall be protected by law. It also provides that no one shall be arbitrarily deprived of his life. Undoubtedly, in pursuance of article 2 of the Covenant, domestic law will normally provide that the unlawful violation of that right will give rise to penal sanctions as well as civil remedies. A State party may further give appropriate protection to that right by outlawing the deprivation of life by the State itself as a method of punishment where the law previously provided for such a method of punishment. Or, with the same end in view, the State party which has not abolished the death penalty is required to restrict its application to the extent permissible under the remaining paragraphs of article 6, in particular, paragraph 2. But, significantly, paragraph 6 has an object to prevent States from invoking the limitations in article 6 to delay or to prevent the abolition of capital punishment. And Canada has decided to abolish this form of punishment for civil, as opposed to military, offences. It can be said that, in so far as civil offences are concerned, paragraph 2 is not applicable to Canada, because Canada is not a State which, in the words of that paragraph, has not abolished the death penalty.

¶ 3.2. It seems to me, in any event, that the provisions of article 6(2) are in the nature of a derogation from the inherent right to life proclaimed in article 6(1) and must therefore be strictly construed. Those provisions cannot justifiably be resorted to in order to have an adverse impact on the level of respect for, and the protection of, that inherent right which Canada has undertaken under the Covenant 'to respect and to ensure to all individuals within its territory and subject to its jurisdiction'. In furtherance of this undertaking, Canada has enacted legislative measures to do so, going to the extent of abolishing the death penalty for civil offences. In relation to the matter in hand, three observations are called for.

¶ 3.3. First, the obligations of Canada under article 2 of the Covenant have effect with respect to 'all individuals within its territory and subject to its jurisdiction', irrespective of the fact that Mr. Kindler is not a citizen of Canada. The obligations towards him are those that must avail to him in his quality as a human being on Canadian soil. Secondly, the very notion of 'protection' requires prior preventive measures, particularly in the case of a deprivation of life. Once an individual is deprived of his life, it cannot be restored to him. These preventive measures necessarily include the prevention of any real risk of the deprivation of life. By extraditing Mr. Kindler without seeking assurances, as Canada was entitled to do under the Extradition Treaty, that the death sentence would not be applied to him, Canada put his life at real risk. Thirdly, it cannot be said that unequal standards are being expected of Canada as opposed to other States. In its very terms, some provisions of article 6 apply to States which do not have the death penalty and other provisions apply to those States which have not yet abolished that penalty. Besides, unequal standards may, unfortunately, be the result of reservations which States may make to particular articles of the Covenant though, I hasten to add, it is questionable whether all reservations may be held to be valid.

¶ 3.4. A further question arises under article 6(1), which requires that no one shall be arbitrarily deprived of his life. The question is whether the granting of the same and equal level of respect and protection is consistent with the attitude that, so long as the individual is within Canada's territory, that right will be fully respected and protected to that level, under Canadian law viewed in its total effect even though expressed in different enactments (penal law and extradition law), whereas Canada might be free to abrogate that level of respect and protection by the deliberate and coercive act of sending that individual away from its territory to another State where the fatal act runs the real risk of being perpetrated. Could this inconsistency be held to amount to a real risk of an 'arbitrary' deprivation of life within the terms of article 6(1) in that unequal treatment is in effect meted out to different individuals within the same jurisdiction? A positive answer would seem to suggest itself as Canada, through its judicial arm, could not sentence an individual to death under Canadian law whereas Canada, through its executive arm, found it possible under its extradition law to extradite him to face the real risk of such a sentence.

¶ 3.5. For the above reasons, there was, in my view, a case before the Committee to find a violation by Canada of article 6 of the Covenant.

¶ 4. Consideration of the possible application of articles 26 and 5 of the Covenant would, in my view, lend further support to the case for a violation of article 6.

¶ 5. In the light of the considerations discussed in paragraph 3.4 above, it would seem that article 26 of the Covenant which guarantees equality before the law has been breached.[41] Equality under this article, in my view, includes substantive equality under a State party's law viewed in its totality and its effect on the individual. Effectively, different and unequal treatment may be said to have been meted out to Mr. Kindler when compared with the treatment which an individual having committed the same offence would have received in Canada. It does not matter, for this purpose, whether Canada metes out this unequal treatment by reason of the particular arm of the State through which it acts, that is to say, through its judicial arm or through its executive arm. Article 26 regulates a State party's legislative, executive as well as judicial behaviour. That, in my view, is the prime principle, in questions of equality and non-discrimination under the Covenant, guaranteeing the application of the rule of law to a State party.

¶ 6. I have grave doubts as to whether, in deciding to extradite Mr. Kindler, Canada would have reached the same decision if it had properly directed itself on its obligations deriving from article 5(2), in conjunction with articles 2, 6 and 26, of the Covenant. It would appear that Canada rather considered, in effect, the question whether there were, or there were not, special circumstances justifying the application of the death sentence to Mr. Kindler, well realising that, by virtue of Canadian law, the death sentence could not have been imposed in Canada itself on Mr. Kindler on conviction there for the kind of offence he had committed. Canada had exercised its sovereign decision to abolish the death penalty for civil, as distinct from military, offences, thereby ensuring greater respect for, and protection of the individual's inherent right to life. Article 5(2) would, even if article 6 of the Covenant were given a minimal interpretation, have prevented Canada from invoking that minimal interpretation to restrict or give lesser protection to that right by an executive act of extradition though, in principle, permissible under Canadian extradition law.

[8.30] Similar majority decisions and similar dissents regarding article 6 were delivered in the cases of *Ng v Canada* (469/91) and *Cox v Canada* (539/93).

[8.31] Compare the reasoning in paragraphs 14.5 to 14.6 of *Kindler* to the

---

[41] See generally on art. 26, Chap. 23.

reasoning of the dissenters in *Kindler*. The minority generally contend that 'States which have abolished the death penalty' cannot benefit from the capital punishment exception in article 6(2), due to that article's opening words. Therefore, Canada cannot extradite persons to a State where they might foreseeably be executed, without breaching article 6(1). This is so even if the execution itself would not constitute a violation of article 6 by the executing State. This is possible as the latter State can benefit from the defence in article 6(2). Mr Wennergen's dissent was even more extreme, holding that article 6(2) does not apply in the context of extradition at all, so all extraditions of persons who might subsequently be executed would breach article 6(1).[42] The minority's contention is attacked in a separate opinion in *Cox v Canada* (539/93) by Messrs Herndl and Sadi:

Had the drafters of article 6 intended to preclude all extradition to face the death penalty, they could have done so. Considering that article 6 consists of six paragraphs, it is unlikely that such an important matter would have been left for future interpretation.[43]

[8.32] Despite the majority's decision in *Kindler* and similar cases, the HRC remains ideologically opposed to capital punishment. For example, the HRC 'noted with appreciation' a change in Portuguese Macau's laws which prohibited extradition of someone to a State where that person might face the death penalty.[44]

Positive Right to Life

DUTY TO TRAIN RELEVANT PERSONNEL

[8.33] With regard to other ICCPR rights, the HRC has stressed that there exists a duty upon the State Party to train relevant personnel, such as police officers and prison guards, to minimize the chance of violation.[45] Such a duty can be assumed to exist with regard to article 6. For example, with regard to Romania, the HRC recommended the close regulation of the use of firearms by police.[46] Close regulation would presumably include the provision of appropriate firearms instruction. In Concluding Comments on the United Republic of Tanzania, the HRC regretted 'the absence of training for the police in human rights and in the proper use of riot equipment, such as rubber bullets'.[47]

---

[42] See W. Schabas, 'Soering's Legacy: The Human Rights Committee and the Judicial Committee of the Privy Council take a walk down Death Row' (1994) 43 *ICLQ* 913, at 918.

[43] Indeed, Schabas states that 'the dissenters may well be letting their abolitionist hopes colour their reading of art. 6 of the Covenant': ibid.

[44] (1997) UN doc. CCPR/C/79/Add.76, para. 5.

[45] See, e.g., with regard to art. 7, [9.75].

[46] (1999) UN doc. CCPR/C/79/Add. 111, para. 12.

[47] (1998) UN doc. CCPR/C/79/Add. 97, para. 18. In respect of the negligent use of firearms, see also *Burrell v Jamaica* (546/93) [8.07].

DUTY TO PROTECT DETAINEES

[8.34]   *DERMIT BARBATO v URUGUAY (84/81)*

The HRC received a complaint regarding the death of one Hugo Haraldo Dermit Barbato, who had been a prisoner held by Uruguayan authorities.

¶ 9.2. The State party has not submitted any report on the circumstances in which Hugo Dermit died or any information as to what inquiries have been made or the outcome of such inquiries. Consequently the Committee cannot help but give appropriate weight to the information submitted by the author, indicating that a few days before Hugo's death he had been seen by other prisoners and was reported to have been in good spirits, in spite of the interruption of the preparations for his release and departure from Uruguay. While the Committee cannot arrive at a definite conclusion as to whether Hugo Dermit committed suicide, was driven to suicide or was killed by others while in custody, the inescapable conclusion is that in all the circumstances, the Uruguayan authorities either by act or by omission were responsible for not taking adequate measures to protect his life, as required by article 6 (1) of the Covenant.

¶ 10. The Human Rights Committee, acting under article 5(4) of the Optional Protocol to the International Covenant on Civil and Political Rights is of the view that the communication discloses violations of the Covenant, in particular: (a) with respect to Hugo Haroldo Dermit Barbato: Of article 6, because the Uruguayan authorities failed to take appropriate measures to protect his life while he was in custody. . . .

¶ 11. The Committee, accordingly, is of the view that the State party is under an obligation to take effective steps (a) to establish the facts of Hugo Dermit's death, to bring to justice any persons found to be responsible for his death and to pay appropriate compensation to his family. . . .

[8.35] There were strong indications that State authorities had killed Mr Dermit Barbato. Nevertheless, the HRC was unwilling to make such a finding. It found a breach of article 6(1) entailed in the State's failure to take adequate measures to prevent the victim's death while he was in their custody. In a similar vein, the UK was criticized in 1995 for the 'high number of suicides among prisoners, especially among juveniles'.[48] States therefore have positive duties to ensure that persons do not die in State custody. This complements a State's negative duty not to kill.

DUTY TO CONTROL PRIVATE ENTITIES

[8.36] The positive right to life includes a duty to prevent and punish killings and disappearances by private actors [8.02].[49] Indeed, this duty is clearly provided for

---

[48] (1996) UN doc. CCPR/C/79/Add.55, para. 13.
[49] See also H. Kabaalioglu, 'The Obligations to "Respect" and "Ensure" the Right to Life' in B. Ramcharan (ed.), *The Right to Life in International Law* (Martinus Nijhoff, Dordrecht, 1985), 160 at 179.

in article 6(1), which obliges the protection of people's lives 'by law'.[50] Mr Wennergren briefly discussed this aspect of article 6 in his separate opinion in *Kindler v Canada* (470/91):

The standard way to ensure the protection of the right to life is to criminalize the killing of human beings. The act of taking human life is normally subsumed under terms such as 'manslaughter', 'homicide' or 'murder'. Moreover, there may be omissions which can be subsumed under crimes involving the intentional taking of life, inaction or omission that causes the loss of a person's life, such as a doctor's failure to save the life of a patient by intentionally failing to activate life-support equipment, or failure to come to the rescue of a person in a life-threatening situation of distress. Criminal responsibility for the deprivation of life lies with private persons and representatives of the State alike. The methodology of criminal legislation provides some guidance when assessing the limits for a State party's obligations under article 2, paragraph 1, of the Covenant, to protect the right to life within its jurisdiction.

[8.37] The HRC has addressed this duty in a number of Concluding Comments. Paraguay has been criticized in this respect for having lenient laws regarding infanticide.[51] A number of African States have been censured for their tolerance of the practice of female genital mutilation, due to the threat posed by the practice to the lives of young victims.[52] The USA was censured for 'the easy availability of firearms' which threatened 'the protection and enjoyment of the right to life'.[53] Regarding Guatemala, the HRC was concerned at the serious violations of the rights of street children, including their right to life, by 'public and private police',[54] the latter referring to organized vigilante groups. 'Stern measures must be taken to punish those found guilty of committing any kind of violence against minors, especially against those who endure hard living.'[55]

[8.38] States Parties are also required to prevent and punish deaths caused by negligence or recklessness in both the public and private sectors. For example, the Ukraine was commended for its establishment of laws penalizing the preparation and sale of radiation-contaminated products.[56]

SOCIO-ECONOMIC ASPECTS OF ARTICLE 6

[8.39] Ramcharan has stated that a 'survival requirement', such as a right to live, must be envisaged as part of the right to life, '[s]ince more people die on account

---

[50] See M. Nowak, *CCPR Commentary* (N. P. Engel, Kehl, 1993), 105–6.

[51] (1995) UN doc. CCPR/C/79/Add.48, para. 16.

[52] Concluding Comments on Lesotho (1999) UN doc. CCPR/C/79/Add. 106, para. 12; Concluding Comments on Senegal (1997) UN doc. CCPR/C/79/Add. 82, para. 12; Concluding Comments on Sudan (1997) UN doc. CCPR/C.79/Add. 85, para. 10.

[53] (1995) UN doc. CCPR/C/79/Add.50, para. 17.

[54] (1996) UN doc. CCPR/C/79/Add.63, para. 20.

[55] Ibid., para. 32. Algeria has also been criticized for its apparent tolerance of vigilante groups, (1998) UN doc. CCPR/C/79/Add. 95, para. 8.

[56] (1996) UN doc. CCPR/C/79/Add.52, para. 6.

of hunger and disease than are killed'.[57] The HRC has confirmed that article 6 has a socio-economic aspect in General Comment 6.

GENERAL COMMENT 6

¶ 5. Moreover, the Committee has noted that the right to life has been too often narrowly interpreted. The expression 'inherent right to life' cannot properly be understood in a restrictive manner, and the protection of this right requires that States adopt positive measures. In this connection, the Committee considers that it would be desirable for States parties to take all possible measures to reduce infant mortality and to increase life expectancy, especially in adopting measures to eliminate malnutrition and epidemics.

The reference to 'desirability' may indicate that States have a moral 'soft law' obligation, rather than a legal 'hard law' duty, to tackle problems such as high infant mortality and low life expectancy.[58]

[8.40] *E.H.P. v CANADA (67/80)*

¶ 1.1. The author of the communication (initial letter dated 11 April 1980, and further letter dated 4 February 1981) is a Canadian citizen. She submitted the communication on her own behalf and, as Chairman of the Port Hope Environmental Group, on behalf of present and future generations of Port Hope, Ontario, Canada, including 129 Port Hope residents who have specifically authorized the author to act on their behalf. The author describes the facts as follows.

¶ 1.2. During the years 1945 to 1952, the Eldorado Nuclear Ltd., a Federal Crown Corporation and Canada's only radium and uranium refinery, disposed of nuclear waste in dumpsites within the confines of Port Hope, Ontario, a town of 10,000 inhabitants, located in an area which is planned to become among those most densely populated in North America. In 1975, large-scale pollution of residences and other buildings was discovered (unsuspecting citizens had used material from the dumpsites as fill or building material for their houses). The Atomic Energy Control Board (AECB), a Federal Government licensing and regulating agency with all responsibility regarding nuclear matters in Canada, initiated a cleaning operation and, from 1976 to 1980, the excavated waste material from approximately 400 locations was removed and relocated elsewhere (at distances ranging from 6 miles to 200 miles away from Port Hope). These new dumpsites have now been closed for further removal of radio-active waste from Port Hope. The author claims that the reasons are political, that is, that no other constituency wishes to accept the waste and that the Federal Government is unwilling to come to grips with the problem. In the meantime, approximately 200,000 tons (AECB estimate) of radio-active waste remains in Port Hope and is being stored, in the continuing clean-up process, in eight 'temporary' disposal sites in Port Hope, near or directly beside residences (one approximately 100 yards from the

---

[57] B. Ramcharan, 'The Right to Life' (1983) 30 *NILR* 297, 305; cf Y. Dinstein, 'The Right to Life, Physical Integrity, and Liberty' in L. Henkin (ed.), *The International Bill of Rights* (Columbia University Press, New York, 1981), at 115.
[58] Nowak, above, note 50, 107, note 17.

public swimming pool). The author maintains that this temporary solution is unacceptable and points out that large 'temporary' disposal sites still exist around town more than 30 years after they were licensed. The author claims that the Atomic Energy Control Board is hampered in its efforts on behalf of the inhabitants of Port Hope by the failure of the Federal Government to make alternative dumpsites available. Federal and provincial governments cannot be compelled by the AECB to provide such sites.

¶ 1.3. The author claims that the current state of affairs is a threat to the life of present and future generations of Port Hope, considering that excessive exposure to radio-activity is known to cause cancer and genetic defects, and that present health hazards for Port Hope residents include alpha, beta and gamma emissions and radon gas emissions above the approved levels of safety, that is the safety levels approved by AECB, based on the standards of safety set by the International Commission on Radiological Protection. . . .

In its admissibility decision, the HRC 'observe[d] that the present communication raise[d] serious issues, with regard to the obligation of States parties to protect human life'.[59] It also found that the author had standing to submit the communication on her own behalf, and was authorized to do so on behalf of other residents of Port Hope. She and the other residents could legitimately claim to be victims of a potential breach of article 6.[60] The HRC did not decide whether she could submit the complaint on behalf of future generations. The communication was however declared inadmissible due to failure to exhaust domestic remedies.[61]

[8.41]   *PLOTNIKOV v RUSSIAN FEDERATION (784/97)*

The author submitted the following complaint:

¶ 3. The author complains that his life is threatened because of lack of money for medicine, caused by a wrong indexing law regarding savings accounts, in violation of article 6 of the Covenant.

The HRC found the complaint inadmissible:

¶ 4.2. The Committee notes that the author's claim is based on the level of hyperinflation in the State party and on the indexing law which reduced the value of his savings, thus preventing the author from buying medicine. The Committee notes that the arguments advanced by the author do not substantiate, for the purposes of admissibility, that the occurrence of hyperinflation or the failure of the indexing law to counterbalance the inflation would amount to a violation of any of the author's Covenant rights for which the State party can be held accountable.

The *Plotnikov* admissibility decision confirms that it will be difficult to prove that one is a victim of an article 6 violation entailed in socio-economic deprivation. Indeed, the HRC also appears to recognize that, in a globalized world, a State's economic collapse can be triggered by external factors as well as internal ones.

---

[59] Para. 8.   [60] See also [3.24].   [61] See generally Chap. 6.

[8.42] Given that the Optional Protocol is perhaps a deficient mechanism for redressing socio-economic deprivation, it is encouraging that the HRC has addressed the socio-economic aspect of article 6 in several Concluding Comments. For example, regarding Canada:[62]

¶ 12. The Committee is concerned that homelessness has led to serious health problems and even to death. The Committee recommends that the State party take positive measures required by article 6 to address this serious problem.

The HRC has also cited 'the increasing rate of infant mortality' in Romania,[63] and the shorter life expectancy of women in Nepal, as 'principal subjects of concern'.[64] The HRC commended Jordan for 'its notable achievements in the field of life expectancy together with reduction of child mortality rates'.[65] It has also commended Zimbabwe on its efforts to incorporate HIV/AIDS awareness into school curricula.[66]

Participation in War

[8.43] *GENERAL COMMENT 6*

The HRC has confirmed that Article 6 obliges States to minimize war and armed conflict.

¶ 2. The Committee observes that war and other acts of mass violence continue to be a scourge of humanity and take the lives of thousands of innocent human beings every year. Under the Charter of the United Nations the threat or use of force by any State against another State, except in exercise of the inherent right of self-defence, is already prohibited. The Committee considers that States have the supreme duty to prevent wars, acts of genocide and other acts of mass violence causing arbitrary loss of life. Every effort they make to avert the danger of war, especially thermonuclear war, and to strengthen international peace and security would constitute the most important condition and guarantee for the safeguarding of the right to life. In this respect, the Committee notes, in particular, a connection between article 6 and article 20, which states that the law shall prohibit any propaganda for war (para. 1) or incitement to violence (para. 2) as therein described.[67]

No consensus HRC comment has specifically criticized a State for participating in a war. States have been criticized for their use of disproportionate force during war.[68]

---

[62] (1999) UN doc. CCPR/C/79/Add. 105.
[63] (1994) UN doc. CCPR/C/79/Add.30, para. 11; see also Concluding Comments on Brazil (1996) UN doc. CCPR/C/79/Add. 66, para. 23.
[64] (1995) UN doc. CCPR/C/79/Add.42, para. 8.
[65] (1995) UN doc. CCPR/C/79/Add.35, para. 4.
[66] (1998) UN doc. CCPR/C/79/Add. 89, para. 7.   [67] See, on art. 20, Chap. 18.
[68] See, e.g., Concluding Comments on the Federal Republic of Yugoslavia (Serbia and Montenegro) (1992) UN Doc A/48/40, 86–8, paras. 6–7, and Concluding Comments on the Russian Federation (1996) UN Doc. CCPR/C/79/Add. 54, paras. 26–30.

Nuclear Capability[69]

[8.44] The HRC's denunciation of armed conflict went a step further in its adoption of General Comment 14, which censured States with nuclear capabilities.

GENERAL COMMENT 14

¶ 3. While remaining deeply concerned by the toll of human life taken by conventional weapons in armed conflicts, the Committee has noted that, during successive sessions of the General Assembly, representatives from all geographical regions have expressed their growing concern at the development and proliferation of increasingly awesome weapons of mass destruction, which not only threaten human life but also absorb resources that could otherwise be used for vital economic and social purposes, particularly for the benefit of developing countries, and thereby for promoting and securing the enjoyment of human rights for all.

¶ 4. The Committee associates itself with this concern. It is evident that the designing, testing, manufacture, possession and deployment of nuclear weapons are among the greatest threats to the right to life which confront mankind today. This threat is compounded by the danger that the actual use of such weapons may be brought about, not only in the event of war, but even through human or mechanical error or failure.

¶ 5. Furthermore, the very existence and gravity of this threat generates a climate of suspicion and fear between States, which is in itself antagonistic to the promotion of universal respect for and observance of human rights and fundamental freedoms in accordance with the Charter of the United Nations and the International Covenants on Human Rights.

¶ 6. The production, testing, possession, deployment and use of nuclear weapons should be prohibited and recognized as crimes against humanity.

¶ 7. The Committee accordingly, in the interest of mankind, calls upon all States, whether Parties to the Covenant or not, to take urgent steps, unilaterally and by agreement, to rid the world of this menace.

[8.45] In *E.W. et al. v The Netherlands* (429/90), the 6,588 authors submitted a complaint that deployment of nuclear weapons within the Netherlands threatened their right to life. The authors extensively cited General Comment 14 in their submissions. The HRC however found that the authors could not establish that they were 'victims' of any article 6 breach.[70] *Bordes and Temeharo v France* (645/95) concerned the compatibility of French nuclear testing with the article 6 rights of the authors, who lived in the vicinity of the South Pacific tests. Both parties had submitted detailed evidence on the effect of nuclear testing on human beings in the area. The HRC accepted the French argument that the authors had

---

[69] See also *Advisory Opinion of the International Court of Justice on the Legality of the Threat or Use of Force of Nuclear Weapons*, 8 July 1996 (1996) 4 ILM 809. The majority judges were ultimately unable to reach a conclusion that the use of nuclear weapons was illegal in all circumstances.

[70] See [3.30].

not proven that there was a 'real and immediate threat' to their lives, so again the authors failed to establish their status as 'victims'.[71]

In *E.C.W. v The Netherlands* (524/92), the author was arrested during a demonstration against the deployment of cruise missiles. The HRC denied that this circumstance raised issues under Article 6. In *A.R.U. v The Netherlands* (509/92), the HRC denied that the author's conscription into the Dutch military service, which entailed participation in the NATO defence strategy 'which is based on a threat with and the use of nuclear weapons', was a breach of article 6. In *Lindon v Australia* (646/95), the author's protestations over Australia's maintenance of a nuclear defence research facility at Pine Gap again raised no issues under article 6.[72] The HRC came to similar decisions in *C.B.D. v The Netherlands* (394/90), *J.P.K. v The Netherlands* (401/90), *T.W.M.B. v The Netherlands* (403/90), and *Brinkhof v The Netherlands* (402/90).

[8.46] General Comment 14 is one of the more controversial HRC comments.[73] Though the subsequent decisions under the Optional Protocol may indicate that the HRC no longer adheres to its sentiments, the HRC reiterated its support for the General Comment in *Bordes and Temeharo v France* (645/95).[74] Perhaps nuclear issues are too difficult to address under the Optional Protocol, as it is difficult to prove that one is a victim of nuclear deployment. Whilst no consensus HRC comment has criticized a specific State's nuclear policies, the HRC did applaud the Ukraine's accession to the Nuclear Non-proliferation Treaties.[75]

Abortion and Euthanasia

[8.47] Anti-abortion advocates argue that abortion constitutes a breach of the right to life of an unborn baby.[76] However, the HRC has not adopted this position. Rather, it has focused on the human rights detriment of anti-abortion laws. For example, regarding Lesotho, the HRC recommended that:

¶ 11. . . . the State party . . . review the law of abortion to provide for situations where the life of the woman is in danger.

Regarding Peru, the HRC stated:[77]

¶ 15. The Committee is also concerned that abortion gives rise to a criminal penalty even if a woman is pregnant as a result of rape and that clandestine abortions are the main cause

---

[71] Para. 3.9. See generally [3.31]. See also *L.C.B. v UK* (1999) 27 EHRR 212, where the European Court of Human Rights found that claims regarding the lethal effects of nuclear tests on Christmas Island were not sufficiently substantiated.   [72] Para. 6.2.

[73] See McGoldrick, above, note 2, 335–6, R. Higgins, 'The United Nations: Still a Force for Peace' (1989) 52 *MLR* 1, 4; Nowak, above, note 50, 109.   [74] Para. 5.9.

[75] (1996) UN doc. CCPR/C/79/Add.52, para. 7.

[76] See Dinstein, above, note 57, 122.

[77] Concluding Comments on Peru (1996) UN doc. CCPR/C/79/Add. 67, para. 15.

of maternal mortality. These provisions not only mean that women are subject to inhumane treatment but are possibly incompatible with articles 3, 6 and 7 of the Covenant. . . .

¶ 22. Peru . . . must take the necessary measures to ensure that women do not risk their life because of the existence of restrictive legal provisions on abortion.

Regarding Chile, it said:[78]

¶ 15. The criminalization of all abortions, without exception, raises serious issues, especially in the light of unrefuted reports that many women undergo illegal abortions that pose a threat to their lives. The legal duty imposed upon health personnel to report on cases of women who have undergone abortions may inhibit women from seeking medical treatment, thereby endangering their lives. The State party is under a duty to ensure the life of all persons, including pregnant women whose pregnancies are terminated. In this regard: the Committee recommends that the law be amended so as to introduce exceptions to the general prohibition on all abortions and to protect the confidentiality of medical information.

Regarding Ecuador it said:[79]

¶ 11. The Committee expresses its concern about the very high number of suicides of young females referred to in the report, which appear in part to be related to the prohibition of abortion. In this regard, the Committee regrets the State party's failure to address the resulting problems faced by adolescent girls, in particular rape victims, who suffer the consequences of such acts for the rest of their lives. Such situations are, from both the legal and practical standpoints, incompatible with articles 3, 6 and 7 of the Covenant, and with article 24 when female minors are involved. The Committee recommends that the State party adopt all necessary legislative and other measures to assist women, and particularly adolescent girls, faced with the problem of unwanted pregnancies to obtain access to adequate health and education facilities.

Thus, anti-abortion laws may, depending on their severity and comprehensiveness, breach not only article 6[80] but also articles 7 and 24, and women's rights of non-discrimination under articles 3 and 26.

[8.48] The UN Committee on the Elimination of All Forms of Discrimination Against Women (CEDAW Committee) cited compulsory abortion as a danger to the mental and physical health of women in its General Recommendation 19, and

---

[78] (1999) UN doc. CCPR/C/79/Add. 104.

[79] (1998) UN doc. CCPR/C/79/Add. 92.

[80] Anti-abortion laws were also cited by the HRC as a possible cause for the high rate of deaths amongst expectant mothers in Concluding Comments on Paraguay, UN doc. CCPR/C/79/Add.48, paras. 17 and 28; Bolivia (1998) UN doc. CCPR/C/79/Add.73, para. 22, Colombia (1998) UN doc. CCPR/C/79/Add.75, para. 24, Costa Rica (1999) UN doc. CCPR/C/79/Add. 107, para. 11, Senegal (1997) UN doc. CCPR/C/79/Add. 82, para. 12, the United Republic of Tanzania (1998) UN doc. CCPR/C/79/Add. 97, para. 15, and Cameroon (1999) UN doc. CCPR/C/79/Add. 116, para. 13. Furthermore, the 'risk to life and health of women' entailed by 'strict laws on abortion' in Poland constituted a breach of art. 6 (1999) UN doc. CCPR/C/79/Add. 110, para. 11. Finally, the HRC has criticized Ireland's restrictions on information about abortion (1994) UN Doc. CCPR/C/79/Add. 21, para. 15.

also condemned the criminalizing of abortion in the same General Comment.[81] The CEDAW Committee clearly endorses freedom of choice for women in the abortion debate.

[8.49] In contrast, the HRC has been conspicuously silent regarding the 'right to life' issues raised by the practice of euthanasia. Proponents of euthanasia argue that terminally ill persons should be able to die with dignity at a time of their own choice. Opponents of euthanasia argue that the deliberate termination of human life, for whatever reason, breaches the right to life. The euthanasia debate raises complex issues which have not been explored yet by the HRC.[82]

Conclusion

[8.50] The HRC has confirmed that States are under a strict duty not to kill people arbitrarily. This duty incorporates a positive obligation to investigate all State killings and punish any improper killings. The cases decided in this area have concerned blatant abuses of State power; we await HRC decisions in more borderline cases.

[8.51] Most capital punishment cases have concerned the fairness of trials that result in a sentence of death. The HRC has strictly interpreted any defects in the trial to constitute breaches of article 6 as well as the Covenant's fair trial provisions. More controversial has been the relevance of article 6 in cases concerning extradition of an alleged felon to a State where he/she might face capital punishment. The HRC majority has permitted such extradition, but a large minority has interpreted the death-penalty exception in article 6(2) narrowly so as to disallow such extradition.

[8.52] In its General Comments on article 6, the HRC has confirmed a broad positive element to the right to life. For example, States must control private entities to prevent and punish unjustifiable homicides. More radical perhaps is the incorporation of a strong socio-economic element into article 6 so as to require States to attempt to ensure that people within the jurisdiction have access to basic subsistence needs. However, no breach of these positive elements of article 6 has yet been found in Optional Protocol cases.

[8.53] Numerous complaints have concerned the threat posed to life by the deployment and testing of nuclear weapons. The HRC has dismissed these complaints, which indicates that it has retreated from the strong anti-nuclear sentiments expressed in General Comment 14.

---

[81] See paras. 22 and 24(m) of General Recommendation 19 [23.80].

[82] These issues are explored in G. Zdankowski, 'The International Covenant on Civil and Political Rights and Euthanasia' (1997) 20 *University of New South Wales Law Journal* 170.

[8.54] Finally, no cases have raised issues relating to abortion and euthanasia. The HRC has confirmed that abortion is compatible with article 6, and indeed, that anti-abortion laws may breach article 6. The HRC has however been silent on the article 6 compatibility of the practice of voluntary euthanasia.

Postscript: Please note that General Comment 28 on 'Equality of Rights Between Men and Women', contained in the Addendum at page 634, contains extra information on some of the material in this chapter.

9

Freedom from Torture and Rights to Humane Treatment—Articles 7, 10

Article 7

No one shall be subjected to torture or to cruel, inhuman or degrading treatment or punishment. In particular, no one shall be subjected without his free consent to medical or scientific experimentation.

[9.01] Article 7 prohibits torture, inhuman and degrading treatment, and punishment. It is one of the few absolute rights in the ICCPR; no restrictions are permitted. Furthermore, it is a non-derogable right. Article 7 prohibits three levels of 'bad' treatment or punishment of a person. The prohibition on heinous 'treatment' is broader than the prohibition on heinous 'punishment'; the latter is inflicted for a disciplinary purpose (however unsound) whilst treatment can be inflicted for numerous purposes. Article 7 is complemented in the ICCPR by article 10, which prohibits less serious forms of treatment than that prohibited by article 7. Article 10 is discussed below.[1]

[9.02] The United Nations Convention against Torture and Other Cruel, Inhuman or Degrading Treatment or Punishment 1984 (CAT) expands on the scope of obligations not to commit torture and, to a lesser extent, other heinous forms of punishment or treatment. One may expect HRC jurisprudence regarding torture to be consistent with that of the Committee Against Torture (CAT Committee).[2] This chapter will refer to the jurisprudence of both bodies.

DEFINITIONS

Torture

[9.03] Torture is the most reprehensible of the three standards of treatment prohibited by article 7 and CAT.[3] The definition of torture, as opposed to inhuman or degrading treatment or punishment, is important, even though perpetration of all three forms of treatment is prohibited under the treaties. Certain consequences may flow from a finding of torture which do not flow from a finding of a lesser standard of treatment. For example, only articles 10 to 13 of the CAT apply to the less heinous forms of treatment. Finally, it is of moral value to

---

[1] See [9.95]ff.

[2] See, e.g., arguments of counsel in *Cox v Canada* (539/93), para. 9.4.

[3] M. Nowak, *UN Covenant on Civil and Political Rights: CCPR Commentary* (N. P. Engel, Kehl, 1993), 129. See also arguments of the State Party in *Vuolanne v Finland* (265/87), at para. 6.4.

a State not to be branded a 'torturer' even if it is branded a sponsor of inhuman and/or degrading treatment; a special stigma attaches to torture.[4]

[9.04] In view of the universal status of CAT, article 1 therein contains a widely accepted definition of torture.

ARTICLE 1, CAT

1. For the purposes of this Convention, the term 'torture' means any act by which severe pain or suffering, whether physical or mental, is intentionally inflicted on a person for such purposes as obtaining from him or a third person information or a confession, punishing him for an act he or a third person has committed or is suspected of having committed, or intimidating or coercing him or a third person, or for any reason based on discrimination of any kind, when such pain or suffering is inflicted by or at the instigation of or with the consent or acquiescence of a public official or other person acting in an official capacity. It does not include pain or suffering arising only from, inherent in or incidental to lawful sanctions.

[9.05] This definition confirms that 'torture' entails a certain severity in pain and suffering. Importantly, this suffering can be mental as well as physical. International human rights cases have confirmed that the threshold of severity for torture is extremely high. For example, the European Court of Human Rights found that the combined effects of the following interrogation techniques, which were used on terrorist suspects in the UK in the early 1970s, constituted inhuman treatment rather than torture: hooding detainees, subjecting them to constant and intense 'white' noise, sleep deprivation, giving them insufficient food and drink, and making them stand for long periods in a painful posture ('wall-standing').[5] Indeed, the Court's first finding of torture did not occur until 1997, when it found that the repeated rape in custody of the complainant in *Aydin v Turkey* constituted torture.[6]

[9.06] Is the article 1 definition subjective? Some people have a high tolerance for the pain caused by a certain act; should this exclude the act from being classified as torture? A particularly susceptible person might suffer extreme pain and trauma from a relatively benign act. Can such circumstances give rise to a finding of 'torture'?[7]

[9.07] Under article 1, an act of torture has to be inflicted intentionally. Does this 'intention' relate to an intention to cause pain and suffering, or an intention to commit the actual act? The latter would yield a broader definition; it is quite

---

[4] Nowak, above, note 3, 129; see also *Aydin v Turkey*, Judgment of the European Court of Human Rights, 26 August 1997 (1998) 25 EHRR 251 para. 82.
[5] *Ireland v UK*, Judgment of 18 January 1978, Series A/25 (1979–80) 2 EHRR 25, para. 167. See however note 23 below.
[6] See *Aydin*, above, note 4, paras. 80–6.
[7] See *Vuolanne v Finland* (265/87), para. 9.2 [9.20].

possible not to anticipate or specifically 'intend' to induce the level of pain and suffering actually caused by a certain act. As the definition refers again twice to 'pain and suffering', it seems that the relevant intention is to cause that pain and suffering. Thus, 'negligent' infliction of pain and suffering, which is not as morally culpable as intentional infliction, does not constitute 'torture'.[8] Furthermore, acts that would not cause extreme pain and suffering to an ordinary person [9.06] are normally outside the definition. The requisite intent would be missing, unless the torturer was aware of the victim's special susceptibilities.

[9.08] Does the reference to an 'act' of torture preclude omissions from being classified as 'torture'? For example, would the deliberate withholding of food or medical attention constitute torture? Boulesbaa has persuasively argued that any failure to extend the definitions to omissions would be 'nothing less than a ploy to help States evade the provisions of the Convention', and would be contrary to the object and purpose of CAT.[9] Therefore, affirmative and negative conduct should suffice to constitute torture, if the other requisite elements of the definition are present. Indeed, the HRC has clearly found that omissions have breached article 7 (though they may not have entailed findings of 'torture').[10]

[9.09] Article 1 also prescribes that torture be inflicted for a purpose. The definition lists a number of example purposes, though the list is not exhaustive. The enumerated purposes are all linked to a desire personally to persecute the victim because of who or what they are. Do the prescribed 'purposes' have to be similar to the enumerated purposes? For example, would an act committed on a random victim solely for the self-gratification of a sadist be a torturous act committed for a relevant purpose?[11] Would a medical experiment conducted out of 'curiosity' constitute torture?[12] Any malevolent purpose should hopefully satisfy this aspect of the definition.

The requirement of a malevolent purpose saves acts committed with a benevolent purpose from being classified as torture.[13] An example of the latter act would be performance of an emergency amputation without anaesthetic. The purpose requirement in the definition of torture has been apparently endorsed by the HRC [9.16].[14]

---

[8] See J. Herman Burgers and H. Danelius, *The United Nations Convention Against Torture* (Martinus Nijhoff, Dordrecht, 1988), 118.

[9] A. Boulesbaa, *The UN Convention on Torture and the Prospects for Enforcement* (Martinus Nijhoff, The Hague, 1999), 15.   [10] See below, [9.32].

[11] See Burgers and Danelius, above, note 8, 119.   [12] See Boulesbaa, above, note 9, 21.

[13] Note however that the enumerated 'purposes' are not necessarily malevolent, in that it may be perfectly legitimate to attempt to seek information from somebody, Burgers and Danelius, above, note 8, 118.

[14] See D. Harris, M. O'Boyle, and C. Warbrick, *The Law of the European Convention on Human Rights* (Butterworths, London, 1995), 60, on how 'purpose' is probably included within the European definition. The definition of 'torture' in art. 2 of the Inter-American Convention to Prevent and Punish Torture 1985 states that torture may be committed for 'any purpose'.

[9.10] Article 1 also specifies that the pain and suffering be inflicted at the instigation of or with the consent or acquiescence of a public official or other person acting in an official capacity. Article 1 specifies a sliding scale of the required official involvement in an act, with 'acquiescence' constituting the weakest level, before that act will be defined as 'torture'. This requirement seems to exclude 'private' tortures from the purview of CAT unless public officials 'acquiesce' in their occurrence. It is uncertain how loosely the term 'acquiescence' will be interpreted by the CAT Committee. For example, does non-enforcement of a law proscribing a certain type of torture (e.g. rape) constitute acquiescence? Does weak enforcement of such a law, or the adoption of enforcement procedures which are not victim-sensitive (and thus discourage formal complaint) constitute acquiescence?[15] 'Acquiescence' perhaps denotes a more positive manifestation of approval for the torturous act by the State. The inclusion of the 'public official' requirement in the definition is designed to prevent States from being held liable for acts beyond their control. However, States should be held liable for private tortures if they fail to respond adequately to them, or fail to take reasonable measures to prevent them; this arguably requires a lower standard of State involvement than 'acquiescence'. Article 16 CAT extends the requirement of 'involvement by a public official' to the Convention's proscription of cruel, inhuman, and degrading treatment.

[9.11]   ***G.R.B. v SWEDEN (CAT 83/97)***

The author complained that her planned deportation to Peru would violate article 3 of CAT, which prohibits deportation to a State where one might be tortured [9.51], as she faced a foreseeable danger of torture upon her return to Peru. One of the author's complaints related to the anticipated danger posed to her upon her return by Sendero Luminoso ('Shining Path'), a Peruvian terrorist group. With regard to this complaint, the State Party argued:

¶ 4.14. As regards the persecution that the author fears from the Sendero Luminoso, the State party stresses that the acts of Sendero Luminoso cannot be attributable to the authorities. Nevertheless, the State Party recognizes that, depending on the circumstances in the individual case, grounds might exist to grant a person asylum although the risk of persecution is not related to a government but to a non-governmental entity. However, the State party's view in the present case is that, even if there is a risk of persecution from Sendero Luminoso, it is of local character and the author could therefore secure her safety by moving within the country.

---

[15] See C. Mackinnon, 'On Torture: A Feminist Perspective on Human Rights' in K. Mahoney and P. Mahoney (eds.), *Human Rights in the Twenty-first Century: A Global Challenge* (Martinus Nijhoff, Dordrecht, 1993). See also Boulesbaa, above, note 9, 26, noting the US understanding of the term: '[acquiescence] requires that the public official, prior to the activity constituting torture, have awareness of such activity and thereafter breach his legal responsibility to intervene to prevent such activity'.

The CAT Committee found in favour of the State Party on this point. After reiterating article 1, the Committee noted:

¶ 6.5. . . . The Committee considers that the issue whether the State party has an obligation to refrain from expelling a person who might risk pain or suffering inflicted by a non-governmental entity, without the consent or acquiescence of the Government, falls outside the scope of article 3 of the Convention.

It is notable in *G.R.B.* that the State Party appeared to adopt a more liberal interpretation of the article 1 requirement of public official involvement than the CAT Committee.

[9.12]   *ELMI v AUSTRALIA (CAT 120/98)*

The author alleged that his proposed deportation to Somalia would breach article 3 CAT, as he risked torture by Somalian militia groups. The State Party submitted the following argument:

¶ 4.4. The State party contends that this communication is inadmissible *ratione materiae* on the basis that the Convention is not applicable to the facts alleged. In particular, the kind of acts the author fears that he will be subjected to if he is returned to Somalia do not fall within the definition of 'torture' set out in article 1 of the Convention. Article 1 requires that the act of torture be 'committed by, or at the instigation of, or with the consent or acquiescence of a public official or any other person acting in an official capacity'. The author alleges that he will be subjected to torture by members of armed Somali clans. These members, however, are not 'public officials' and do not act in an 'official capacity'.

¶ 4.5. The Australian Government refers to the Committee's decision in *G.R.B. v Sweden*, in which the Committee stated that 'a State party's obligation under article 3 to refrain from forcibly returning a person to another State where there were substantial grounds to believe that he or she would be in danger of being subjected to torture was directly linked to the definition of torture as found in article 1 of the Convention.'

¶ 4.6. The State party further submits that the definition of torture in article 1 was the subject of lengthy debates during the negotiations for the Convention. On the issue of which perpetrators the Convention should cover, a number of views were expressed. For example, the delegation of France argued that 'the definition of the act of torture should be a definition of the intrinsic nature of the act of torture itself, irrespective of the status of the perpetrator'. There was little support for the French view although most States did agree that 'the Convention should not only be applicable to acts committed by public officials, but also to acts for which the public authorities could otherwise be considered to have some responsibility.'

¶ 4.7. The delegation of the United Kingdom of Great Britain and Northern Ireland made an alternative suggestion that the Convention refer to a 'public official or any other agent of the State'. By contrast, the delegation of the Federal Republic of Germany 'felt that it should be made clear that the term 'public official' referred not only to persons who, regardless of their legal status, have been assigned public authority by State organs on a permanent basis or in an individual case, but also to persons who, in certain regions or under particular conditions actually hold and exercise authority over others and whose authority is comparable to government authority or—be it only temporarily—has replaced government authority or whose authority has been derived from such persons.'

¶ 4.8. According to the State party it was ultimately 'generally agreed that the definition should be extended to cover acts committed by, or at the instigation of, or with the consent or acquiescence of a public official or any other person acting in an official capacity'. It was not agreed that the definition should extend to private individuals acting in a non-official capacity, such as members of Somali armed bands.

The author's counsel responded as follows:

¶ 5.1. As regards the *ratione materiae* admissibility of the communication, counsel submits that despite the lack of a central government, certain armed clans in effective control of territories within Somalia are covered by the terms 'public official' or 'other person acting in an official capacity' as required by article 1 of the Convention. In fact, the absence of a central government in a State increases the likelihood that other entities will exercise quasi-governmental powers.

¶ 5.2. Counsel further emphasizes that the reason for limiting the definition of torture to the acts of public officials or other persons acting in an official capacity was that the purpose of the Convention was to provide protection against acts committed on behalf of, or at least tolerated by, the public authorities, whereas the State would normally be expected to take action, in accordance with its criminal law, against private persons having committed acts of torture against other persons. Therefore, the assumption underlying this limitation was that, in all other cases, States were under the obligation by customary international law to punish acts of torture by 'non-public officials'. It is consistent with the above that the Committee stated, in *G.R.B. v Sweden*, that 'whether the State party has an obligation to refrain from expelling a person who might risk pain or suffering inflicted by a non-governmental entity, without the consent or acquiescence of the Government, falls outside the scope of article 3 of the Convention'. However, the present case is distinguishable from the latter as it concerns return to a territory where non-governmental entities themselves are in effective control in the absence of a central government, from which protection cannot be sought.

¶ 5.3. Counsel submits that when the Convention was drafted there was agreement by all States to extend the scope of the perpetrator of the act from the 'public official' referred to in the Declaration on the Protection of All Persons from Being Subjected to Torture and Other Cruel, Inhuman or Degrading Treatment or Punishment, to include 'other person[s] acting in an official capacity'. This would include persons who, in certain regions or under particular conditions, actually hold and exercise authority over others and whose authority is comparable to government authority.

¶ 5.4. According to a general principle of international law and international public policy, international and national courts and human rights supervisory bodies should give effect to the realities of administrative actions in a territory, no matter what may be the strict legal position, where those actions affect the everyday activities of private citizens. In *Ahmed v Austria*, the European Court of Human Rights, in deciding that deportation to Somalia would breach article 3 of the European Convention on Human Rights, which prohibits torture, stated that 'fighting was going on between a number of clans vying with each other for control of the country. There was no indication that the dangers to which the applicant would have been exposed to had ceased to exist or that any public authority would be able to protect [the applicant].'

¶ 5.5. In relation to Somalia, there is abundant evidence that the clans, at least since 1991, have, in certain regions, fulfilled the role, or exercised the semblance, of an authority that is comparable to government authority. These clans, in relation to their regions, have prescribed their own laws and law enforcement mechanisms and have provided their own education, health and taxation systems. The report of the independent expert of the Commission on Human Rights illustrates that States and international organizations have accepted that these activities are comparable to governmental authorities and that '[t]he international community is still negotiating with the warring factions, who ironically serve as the interlocutors of the Somali people with the outside world'.

The HRC found in favour of the author:

¶ 6.5. The Committee does not share the State party's view that the Convention is not applicable in the present case since, according to the State party, the acts of torture the author fears he would be subjected to in Somalia would not fall within the definition of torture set out in article 1 (i.e. pain or suffering inflicted by or at the instigation of or with the consent or acquiescence of a public official or other person acting in an official capacity, in this instance for discriminatory purposes). The Committee notes that for a number of years Somalia has been without a central government, that the international community negotiates with the warring factions and that some of the factions operating in Mogadishu have set up quasi-governmental institutions and are negotiating the establishment of a common administration. It follows then that, *de facto*, those factions exercise certain prerogatives that are comparable to those normally exercised by legitimate governments. Accordingly, the members of those factions can fall, for the purposes of the application of the Convention, within the phrase 'public officials or other persons acting in an official capacity' contained in article 1.

[9.13] It is arguable that in neither *G.R.B.* nor *Elmi* was the central government capable of protecting the respective author from torture by non-governmental groups. The major difference between the cases, evinced from the decisions, is that *Elmi* concerned the forced return of the author to a State (Somalia) where no central government actually existed. In *G.R.B.*, the CAT Committee would not deem Sendero Luminoso personnel to be public officials, even if they were in effective control of some areas of Peru, as 'public' power in Peru is exercised *de jure* by the Peruvian government. In the absence of any *de jure* government control, as in Somalia, the CAT Committee will be more likely to recognize persons with *de facto* power as 'public officials'.[16] It is interesting to speculate whether the CAT Committee would find rebel groups in effective control of land during a recognized state of war with a central government, such as the Tamils of Tamil Eelam in the north of Sri Lanka, to be 'public officials'.[17]

---

[16] See also Boulesbaa, above, note 9, 27–8.
[17] Radovan Karadzic, the Bosnian Serb leader during the 1991–4 Bosnian war, has been accepted

From a humanitarian point of view, the important issue is whether the person can be protected by the government from torture, whether the threat comes from government agents or private entities. 'Lack of likely protection' is perhaps more easily established when there is no central government, but can occur where recognized central governments are incapable of controlling rapacious non-governmental groups. Unfortunately, the wording of article 1 CAT seems to require the establishment of some level of government collusion in or acceptance of the relevant ill-treatment. Even though the Peruvian government, as alleged in *G.R.B.*, may have been incapable of protecting the author from torture by the Sendero Luminoso terrorist group, one cannot say the Peruvian government in any way 'acquiesced' in Sendero Luminoso abuses. A more humanitarian interpretation of 'torture', which would be particularly relevant in cases where the central government cannot control anti-government forces, may necessitate a rewriting of the article 1 definition.

[9.14] The article 1 definition excludes 'pain or suffering arising only from, inherent in or incidental to lawful sanctions'. Boulesbaa points out that the drafters deliberately omitted references to the relevance of international standards in this rider clause.[18] Thus, it may be that 'lawful sanctions' cannot amount to torture, but may still be classified under CAT as cruel, inhuman, and degrading treatment or punishment.[19] Nevertheless, it seems unlikely that the CAT Committee would interpret this rider so as to enable States totally to avoid being branded a 'torturer' simply by enacting perverse laws. 'Lawful' should be interpreted so as to permit sanctions that are otherwise permitted under CAT and other relevant international law.[20] For example, imprisonment for reasonably serious crimes comes within such a definition of 'lawful', so the pain and suffering caused by such imprisonment to an extremely claustrophobic person would be excluded from the definition. However, the rider should not exempt imprisonment from being classified as 'torture' if the conditions of such imprisonment are extremely harsh.

[9.15] The latest universal definition of torture is contained in article 7(2)(e) of the Rome Statute of the International Criminal Court 1998 (ICC Statute):

ARTICLE 7(2)(E), ICC STATUTE

'Torture' means the intentional infliction of severe pain or suffering, whether physical or mental, upon a person in the custody or under the control of the accused; except that

---

as a 'public official' for the purposes of a torture claim under the Alien Torts Claims Act 1789 in the United States in *Kadic v Karadzic* 70 F., 3d 232 (2nd Cirt., 1995).

[18] Boulesbaa, above, note 9, 29–35.

[19] A. Na'im, 'Towards a Cross-Cultural Approach to Defining International Standards of Human Rights: The Meaning of "Cruel Inhuman or Degrading Treatment" ' in A. Na'im (ed.), *Human Rights in Cross-Cultural Perspectives : A Quest for Consensus* (University of Pennsylvania Press, Philadelphia, Penn., 1992), 29–32.

[20] Compare the interpretations of 'lawful' by the HRC at [11.55–11.56] and at [16.09–16.12].

torture shall not include pain or suffering arising only from, inherent in or incidental to, lawful sanctions.

The definition of torture in the ICC Statute is ostensibly broader than that in the CAT definition. The ICC Statute definition omits any reference to 'purpose' or 'public official involvement'. However, it must be remembered, with regard to the latter omission, that the ICC Statute attributes personal, rather than State, responsibility.

[9.16] The HRC has not issued a specific definition of 'torture' for the purposes of article 7. Indeed, it has decided not to differentiate between the three levels of banned treatment/punishment in article 7.

GENERAL COMMENT 20

¶ 4. The Covenant does not contain any definition of the concepts covered by article 7, nor does the Committee consider it necessary to draw up a list of prohibited acts or to establish sharp distinctions between the different kinds of punishment or treatment; the distinctions depend on the nature, purpose and severity of the treatment applied.

In line with this comment, the HRC often fails to specify which aspect of article 7 has been breached; violations may simply be described as 'violations of article 7'. This may be contrasted with the practice of the European Court of Human Rights in its interpretation of the equivalent provision of the European Convention on Human Rights, article 3. The Court usually specifies which type of 'treatment' has occurred.[21] The HRC on the other hand has been able to elaborate and develop the scope of the prohibition without actually defining the terms.

'Article 7' Treatment: Cruel, Inhuman, and Degrading Treatment or Punishment

[9.17] In General Comment 20, the HRC made the following general statements on the definition of the acts prohibited by article 7 ('article 7 treatment'):

¶ 2. The aim of the provisions of article 7 of the International Covenant on Civil and Political Rights is to protect both the dignity and the physical and mental integrity of the individual. It is the duty of the State party to afford everyone protection through legislative and other measures as may be necessary against the acts prohibited by article 7, whether inflicted by people acting in their official capacity, outside their official capacity or in a private capacity. The prohibition in article 7 is complemented by the positive requirements of article 10, paragraph 1, of the Covenant, which stipulates that 'All persons deprived of their liberty shall be treated with humanity and with respect for the inherent dignity of the human person'.

¶ 5. The prohibition in article 7 relates not only to acts that cause physical pain but also to acts that cause mental suffering to the victim. . . .

---

[21] See Harris *et al.*, above, note 14, 56–7.

[9.18] Therefore, no specific definitions of 'cruel', 'inhuman', or 'degrading' treatment have emerged under the ICCPR or CAT. The requirements of severity, intention, and purpose are presumably applied more leniently in determining whether such treatment has occurred. For example, it may be possible negligently to inflict such treatment.

[9.19] In paragraph 2 of General Comment 20, the HRC states that States Parties have a positive duty to prohibit torture, inhuman and degrading treatment by private people. Therefore, the HRC specifically acknowledges the importance of combating 'private' assaults on bodily integrity and dignity. Perhaps the author in *G.R.B.* [9.11] would have had a better chance of successfully establishing a violation under the ICCPR than under CAT.

[9.20]   *VUOLANNE v FINLAND (265/87)*

Vuolanne was held in military detention in a small cell for ten days for disciplinary reasons. He claimed, *inter alia*, that this detention breached article 7. He described the conditions of his detention as follows:

¶ 2.6. . . . [The author] states that his punishment was enforced in two parts, during which he was locked in a cell of 2 x 3 metres with a tiny window, furnished only with a camp bed, a small table, a chair and a dim electric light. He was only allowed out of his cell for purposes of eating, going to the toilet and to take fresh air for half an hour daily. He was prohibited from talking to other detained persons and from making any noise in his cell. He claims that the isolation was almost total. He also states that in order to lessen his distress, he wrote personal notes about his relations with persons close to him, and that these notes were taken away from him one night by the guards, who read them to each other. Only after he asked for a meeting with various officials were his papers returned to him.

The HRC found in favour of the State Party on the article 7 issue, and stated the following on the content of article 7:

¶ 9.2. The Committee recalls that article 7 prohibits torture and cruel or other inhuman or degrading treatment. It observes that the assessment of what constitutes inhuman or degrading treatment falling within the meaning of article 7 depends on all the circumstances of the case, such as the duration and manner of the treatment, its physical or mental effects as well as the sex, age and state of health of the victim. A thorough examination of the present communication has not disclosed any facts in support of the author's allegations that he is a victim of a violation of his rights set forth in article 7. In no case was severe pain or suffering, whether physical or mental, inflicted upon Antti Vuolanne by or at the instigation of a public official; nor does it appear that the solitary confinement to which the author was subjected, having regard to its strictness, duration and the end pursued, produced any adverse physical or mental effects on him. Furthermore, it has not been established that Mr. Vuolanne suffered any humiliation or that his dignity was interfered with apart from the embarrassment inherent in the disciplinary measure to which he was subjected. In this connection, the Committee expresses the view that for punishment to be degrading, the humiliation or debasement involved must exceed a particular level and must, in any event, entail other elements beyond the mere fact of deprivation of liberty. Furthermore, the Committee finds that the facts before it do not substantiate the allegation that during his detention Mr. Vuolanne was treated without humanity or without respect for the inherent dignity of the person, as required under article 10, paragraph 1, of the Covenant.

[9.21] The *Vuolanne* case confirms that the determination of whether 'article 7 treatment' has occurred is in part a subjective evaluation. Factors such as the victim's age and mental health can aggravate the effect of certain treatment so as to bring that treatment within article 7.

[9.22] Note the HRC's statement that 'degrading treatment' must entail more than 'the mere deprivation of liberty'. However, it seems that the statement goes too far. Would the 'mere' detention of an extremely claustrophobic person, for no reason other than to break his or her will, breach article 7?

[9.23] More clues to the definition of impugned treatment under article 7 can be gleaned from the ensuing examination of the case law.

RESTRICTIONS ON ARTICLE 7 RIGHTS

[9.24] Article 7 is expressed in absolute terms and permits no exceptions.

GENERAL COMMENT 20

¶ 3. The text of article 7 allows of no limitation. The Committee also reaffirms that, even in situations of public emergency such as those referred to in article 4 of the Covenant, no derogation from the provision of article 7 is allowed and its provisions must remain in force. The Committee likewise observes that no justification or extenuating circumstances may be invoked to excuse a violation of article 7 for any reasons, including those based on an order from a superior officer or public authority.

This is reaffirmed in article 2, CAT, with respect to 'torture':

ARTICLE 2, CAT

2. No exceptional circumstances whatsoever, whether a state of war or a threat of war, internal political instability or any other public emergency, may be invoked as a justification of torture.

3. An order from a superior officer or a public authority may not be invoked as a justification of torture.

[9.25] Therefore, it appears that notions such as proportionality have no relevance when considering whether violations of article 7 or CAT have occurred. For example, in Israel, the law authorizes the use of 'moderate physical and psychological pressure' in interrogating suspected terrorists. In 1997, Israel claimed that the use of these techniques had thwarted ninety planned terrorist attacks, saving countless lives.[22] The CAT Committee nevertheless classified some of these interrogation techniques as 'torture' as well as 'inhuman and degrading treatment' in Concluding Comments regarding Israel in 1997. The techniques were held to breach CAT, even though they were designed to protect the population from a particularly deadly terrorist threat. The CAT Committee stated:[23]

¶ 134. The Committee acknowledges the terrible dilemma that Israel confronts in dealing with terrorist threats to its security, but as a State party to the Convention Israel is precluded from raising before this Committee exceptional circumstances as justification for acts prohibited by article 1 of the Convention. This is plainly expressed in article 2 of the Convention.

[9.26] Proportionality does however play a role in the determination of violations of article 7 ICCPR. For example, amputation of a limb in many circumstances would breach article 7. However, amputation of a limb does not *per se* constitute article 7 treatment. Amputation would not breach article 7 if it were done to save a person's life (e.g. to stop the spread of gangrene). Therefore, the 'reasonableness' of the decision to perform a certain act, even if it causes considerable pain, suffering, or indignity, may be relevant in deciding if certain treatment is in fact article 7 treatment.[24] Once a certain act is found to constitute article 7 treatment however, no justification can be raised to prevent a finding of violation. Proportionality is therefore relevant when considering the appropriate *classification* of the act as article 7 treatment, rather than in considering any alleged *justification* for engaging in article 7 treatment.

[9.27] In *Mukong v Cameroon* (458/91), the State Party attempted to justify appalling prison conditions on the basis of economic and budgetary problems caused by Cameroon's underdevelopment; the HRC nevertheless found that the conditions of Mukong's incarceration breached article 7.[25]

---

[22] See Israel's Second Periodic Report under the Convention Against Torture, CAT/C/33/Add.2/Rev. 1, especially paras. 2–3, and 24.

[23] UN doc. CAT/C/18/CRP1/Add. 4. The actual techniques used were classified so the CAT Committee relied on reports from non-governmental organizations. The techniques reported were: restraining in painful conditions; hooding; sounding of loud music for prolonged periods; prolonged sleep deprivation; threats (including death threats), violent shaking, and using 'cold air to chill'. Compare *Ireland v UK*, above, note 5. See also HRC Concluding Comments on Israel (1999) UN doc. CCPR/C/79/Add.93, paragraph 19.

[24] In this respect, note that while 'purpose' is an element of the definition of 'torture' [9.09], it does not appear to be an element of the definitions of other art. 7 treatment. This is intimated by the HRC in General Comment 20, para. 4 [9.16]. See also [9.18].

[25] See [9.67]. Indeed, economic circumstances do not generally justify digressions from Covenant norms: see [1.73].

SPECIFIC VIOLATIONS OF ARTICLE 7 AND THE CONVENTION AGAINST TORTURE

[9.28] In numerous early cases against Latin American States, the HRC found various combinations of the following acts to constitute torture:[26] systematic beatings, electroshocks, burns, extended hanging from hand and/or leg chains, repeated immersions in a mixture of blood, urine, vomit, and excrement ('submarino'), standing for great lengths, simulated executions, and amputations.[27] In *Muteba v Zaire* (124/82), *Miango Muiyo v Zaire* (194/85), and *Kanana v Zaire* (366/89), the HRC found that various combinations of the following acts constituted torture: beatings, electric shocks to the genitals, mock executions, deprivation of food and water, and thumb presses.[28]

[9.29] In *Linton v Jamaica* (255/87), the author was beaten unconscious, subjected to a mock execution, and denied appropriate medical care. In *Bailey v Jamaica* (334/88), the author, a prisoner, was beaten repeatedly with clubs, iron pipes, and batons, and then left without any medical attention for injuries to his head and hands. In *Hylton v Jamaica* (407/90), the author, a prisoner, was severely beaten by, and received repeated death threats from, prison warders. In *Deidrick v Jamaica* (619/95), the author was locked up in his cell twenty-three hours a day, without mattress or bedding, integral sanitation, natural light, recreational facilities, decent food, or adequate medical care.[29] In all cases, the HRC decided that this treatment amounted to 'cruel and inhuman treatment'.

[9.30] In *Francis v Jamaica* (320/88), the HRC found that the author had been 'assaulted by soldiers and warders, who beat him, pushed him with a bayonet, emptied a urine bucket over his head, threw his food and water on the floor and his mattress out of the cell'.[30] In *Thomas v Jamaica* (321/88), the HRC found that the author had been beaten with rifle butts and was refused medical treatment for consequent injuries.[31] In *Young v Jamaica* (615/95), the author had been detained in a tiny cell, allowed few visitors, assaulted by prison warders, had his effects stolen and his bed repeatedly soaked.[32] In *Polay Campos v Peru* (577/94), the author was displayed to the press in a cage.[33] In all four cases, the impugned treatment constituted 'degrading treatment within the meaning of article 7'.

---

[26] See also the treatment described in *Domukovsky et al. v Georgia* (623–624, 626, 627/95) at para. 18.6, which was described as both 'torture and inhuman treatment' (severe beatings and physical and moral pressure, including infliction of concussion, broken bones, burning and wounding, scarring, threats to family).

[27] Nowak, above, note 3, 131, citing *Grille Motta v Uruguay* (11/77), *López Burgos v Uruguay* (52/79), *Sendic v Uruguay* (63/79), *Angel Estrella v Uruguay* (74/80), *Arzuago Gilboa v Uruguay* (147/83), *Cariboni v Uruguay* (159/83), *Berterretche Acosta v Uruguay* (162/83), *Herrera Rubio v Colombia* (161/83), *Lafuente Peñarrieta v Bolivia* (176/84). See also P.R. Ghandhi, 'The Human Rights Committee and Articles 7 and 10(1) of the International Covenant on Civil and Political Rights, 1966' (1990) 13 *Dalhousie Law Journal* 758, 762–6.

[28] Nowak, above, note 3, 161. [29] Para. 9.3. [30] Para. 12.4.

[31] Para. 9.2. [32] Paras. 3.6, 5.2. [33] Para. 8.5.

[9.31] In many article 7 cases, the HRC has found violations of article 7 without specifying the limb of article 7 that was breached. For example, in *Wight v Madagascar* (115/82), ten months' incommunicado detention, including solitary confinement chained to a bed spring for three and a half months with minimal clothing and severe food rations, followed by a further month's incommunicado detention in a tiny cell, followed by detention with another in a three by three metre cell without external access for eighteen months, breached article 7.[34] In *Cañón García v Ecuador* (319/88), the HRC found that the rubbing of salt water into the author's nasal passages, and a night spent handcuffed to a chair 'without being given as much as a glass of water' constituted a breach of article 7.[35] In *Henry v Trinidad and Tobago* (752/97), the author was beaten so severely on the head by prison officers that he required several stitches;[36] this action breached article 7.[37] Being 'blindfold and dunked in a canal' by soldiers breached article 7 in *Vicente et al. v Colombia* (612/95).[38] Female genital mutilation has also been cited as a breach of article 7.[39] In Concluding Comments on Poland, ritual abuse and humiliation of new army recruits were also described as a breach of article 7.[40]

[9.32] The failure of the State Party to redress the serious mental deterioration of the author, a death row detainee, in *Williams v Jamaica* (609/95) also constituted degrading treatment, in breach of article 7.[41] *Williams* demonstrates that a State Party can breach article 7 by failing to act, as well as by committing acts.

[9.33] It is instructive to note the cases where violations of article 10(1) have been found rather than violations of article 7.[42] These cases describe treatment which is bad enough to breach article 10, but implicitly not so bad as to constitute 'article 7 treatment'.

Evidentiary Requirements

[9.34] Many article 7 cases have turned on questions of fact rather than law. The HRC in such cases had only to consider whether there was enough evidence that certain acts had occurred, rather than whether the alleged acts breached article 7. This is because numerous cases have raised allegations of acts that are so atrocious that they undoubtedly breach article 7.

[9.35]   *MUKONG v CAMEROON (458/91)*

This case contains some useful statements on the evidential requirements for an article 7 complaint:

---

[34] Paras. 15.2, 17.   [35] Para. 5.2.   [36] Para. 2.1.
[37] Para. 7.1.   [38] Para. 8.5.
[39] Concluding Comments on Lesotho (1999) UN doc. CCPR/C/79/Add. 106, para. 12; Concluding Comments on Sudan (1997) UN doc. CCPR/C/79/Add. 85, para. 10; Concluding Comments on Cameroon (1999) UN doc. CCPR/C/79/Add. 116, para. 12. See also [1.70].
[40] (1999) UN doc. CCPR/C/79/Add. 110, para. 15.   [41] Para. 6.5.
[42] See commentary at [9.100] ff.

¶ 9.1. The author has contended that the conditions of his detention in 1988 and 1990 amount to a violation of article 7, in particular because of insalubrious conditions of detention facilities, overcrowding of a cell at the First Police District of Yaoundé, deprivation of food and of clothing, and death threats and incommunicado detention at the Camp of the Brigade Mobile Mixte in Douala. The State party has replied that the burden of proof for these allegations lies with the author, and that as far as conditions of detention are concerned, they are a factor of the underdevelopment of Cameroon.

¶ 9.2. The Committee does not accept the State party's views. As it has held on previous occasions, the burden of proof cannot rest alone with the author of a communication, especially considering that the author and the State party do not always have equal access to the evidence and that frequently the State party alone has access to the relevant information. (See Views on communication No. 30/1978 (*Bleier v Uruguay*), adopted on 29 March 1982, paragraph 13.3.). Mr. Mukong has provided detailed information about the treatment he was subjected to; in the circumstances, it was incumbent upon the State party to refute the allegations in detail, rather than shifting the burden of proof to the author.

[9.36]   *BAILEY v JAMAICA (709/96)*

This case concerned allegations under article 10(1) rather than 7. However, one may assume that the evidential requirements are similar. In this case, the HRC majority found that the author had failed, for the purposes of admissibility, to substantiate his claims that he was being detained in inhuman conditions at St Catherine's District Prison, Jamaica. A minority view, signed by Mrs Evatt, Mrs Gaitán de Pombo, Mrs Medina Quiroga, and Mr Yalden, was more generous to the author:

The author has not given specific details of this claim, other than to refer in his submission to a report from Amnesty International based on a 1993 visit and a report called Prison Conditions in Jamaica, 1990. These reports, which are not annexed, cover a period during which the author was held at St Catherine's District Prison. Having regard to the Committee's earlier views in which it has found the conditions on death row in St Catherine's District Prison to violate article 10(1) of the Covenant,[43] and to the failure of the State party to respond to the author's allegations, I am of the view that the author's claim under article 10(1) is sufficiently substantiated for the purpose of admissibility and to support a finding of a violation of this provision.

The majority's hard line on evidence in *Bailey* was foreshadowed in earlier dissents by Mr Ando in *Morgan and Williams v Jamaica* (720/96) and *Yasseen and Thomas v Republic of Guyana* (676/96). Ando and, now, the HRC majority seem less willing to infer violations of article 7 or 10(1) from NGO evidence, in the absence of specific evidence of individual suffering by the authors. The minority view in *Bailey*, which accepts that certain prison conditions are so appalling that they surely 'affect' the author individually, is to be preferred.

---

[43] See, e.g., *McTaggart v Jamaica* (749/97), paras. 8.5–8.6, and other cases cited below at note 109.

Mental Distress

[9.37] Both the HRC and the CAT Committee have recognized that mental distress can be as cruel as the infliction of physical pain. Such mental anguish arose on the facts of the following case.

QUINTEROS v URUGUAY (107/81)

This complaint was submitted by a mother on behalf of herself and her daughter, Elena. Elena had been abducted by Uruguayan security forces. Indeed, at the time of the *Quinteros* decision, Elena had not been released, so her fate was unknown. The HRC found a violation of article 7 with regard to Elena. The mother, María, submitted the following complaint on her own behalf:

¶ 1.9. [The author] adds that she is herself a victim of violations of article 7 (psychological torture because she does not know where her daughter is) . . .

The HRC also found a breach or article 7 with regard to the mother:

¶ 14. With regard to the violations alleged by the author on her own behalf, the Committee . . . understands the anguish and stress caused to the mother by the disappearance of her daughter and by the continuing uncertainty concerning her fate and whereabouts. The author has the right to know what has happened to her daughter. In these respects, she too is a victim of the violations of the Covenant suffered by her daughter in particular, of article 7.

[9.38] In *Quinteros*, the HRC found a 'violation of article 7' with regard to the mother; it did not specify whether she had suffered torture, or inhuman treatment, or degrading treatment. Her treatment does not appear to fit within the definition of torture in article 1 CAT. Did the Uruguayan authorities have an intention to cause severe pain and suffering to the mother [9.07]?

Death Row Phenomenon

[9.39] Capital punishment is an express exception to the right to life in article 6.[44] However, an alternative route for attacking the ICCPR compatibility of the death penalty is via article 7. In particular, it has been argued in numerous cases that 'the death row phenomenon' constitutes a breach of article 7. The death row phenomenon is caused by prolonged detention on death row, which causes ever-increasing mental anxiety and mounting tension over one's impending death. The death row phenomenon therefore constitutes a form of mental distress which might raise article 7 issues. The inhuman and degrading nature of the death row phenomenon has been recognized by the European Court of Human Rights[45] and the Judicial Committee of the Privy Council.[46]

---

[44] See generally [8.18] ff.
[45] *Soering v UK*, Judgment of 7 July 1989, Series A, No 161 (1989) 11 *EHRR* 439.
[46] *Pratt and Morgan v Attorney-General for Jamaica* [1993] 2 AC 1.

[9.40] The HRC majority has consistently denied that the death row phenomenon violates article 7.[47] In *Barrett and Sutcliffe v Jamaica* (270, 271/88), where the complainants had spent ten years on death row, the HRC gave one reason why it does not tend to accept that the death row phenomenon breaches article 7:

¶ 8.4. . . . even prolonged periods of detention under a severe custodial regime on death row cannot generally be considered to constitute cruel, inhuman or degrading treatment if the convicted person is merely availing himself of appellate remedies. . . . The evidence before the Committee indicates that the . . . delay in petitioning the [appellate court] is largely attributable to the authors.

Mme Chanet disagreed on this point in *Barrett and Sutcliffe*:

Without being at all cynical, I consider that the author cannot be expected to hurry up in making appeals so that he can be executed more rapidly.

. . . A very long period on death row, even if partially due to the failure of the condemned prisoner to exercise a remedy, cannot exonerate the State party from its obligations under article 7 of the Covenant.

[9.41] The most detailed HRC views on the death row phenomenon were issued in *Johnson v Jamaica* (588/94).

JOHNSON v JAMAICA (588/94)

The facts are evident from the extract below:

¶ 8.2. The question that must be addressed is whether the mere length of the period a condemned person spends confined to death row may constitute a violation by a State party of its obligations under articles 7 and 10 not to subject persons to cruel, inhuman and degrading treatment or punishment and to treat them with humanity. In addressing this question, the following factors must be considered:

(a) The Covenant does not prohibit the death penalty, though it subjects its use to severe restrictions. As detention on death row is a necessary consequence of imposing the death penalty, no matter how cruel, degrading and inhuman it may appear to be, it cannot, of itself, be regarded as a violation of articles 7 and 10 of the Covenant.

(b) While the Covenant does not prohibit the death penalty, the Committee has taken the view, which has been reflected in the Second Optional Protocol to the Covenant, that article 6 'refers generally to abolition in terms which strongly suggest that abolition is desirable'. (See General Comment 6 (16) of 27 July 1982; also see Preamble to the Second Optional Protocol to the Covenant Aiming at the Abolition of the Death Penalty.) Reducing recourse to the death penalty may therefore be seen as one of the objects and purposes of the Covenant.

(c) The provisions of the Covenant must be interpreted in the light of the Covenant's

---

[47] See, e.g., *Kindler v Canada* (470/91), *Simms v Jamaica* (541/93), *Rogers v Jamaica* (494/92), and *Hylton v Jamaica* (600/94).

objects and purposes (article 31 of the Vienna Convention on the Law of Treaties). As one of these objects and purposes is to promote reduction in the use of the death penalty, an interpretation of a provision in the Covenant that may encourage a State party that retains the death penalty to make use of that penalty should, where possible, be avoided.

¶ 8.3. In light of these factors, we must examine the implications of holding the length of detention on death row, *per se*, to be in violation of articles 7 and 10. The first, and most serious, implication is that if a State party executes a condemned prisoner after he has spent a certain period of time on death row, it will not be in violation of its obligations under the Covenant, whereas if it refrains from doing so, it will violate the Covenant. An interpretation of the Covenant leading to this result cannot be consistent with the Covenant's object and purpose. The above implication cannot be avoided by refraining from determining a definite period of detention on death row, after which there will be a presumption that detention on death row constitutes cruel and inhuman punishment. Setting a cut-off date certainly exacerbates the problem and gives the State party a clear deadline for executing a person if it is to avoid violating its obligations under the Covenant. However, this implication is not a function of fixing the maximum permissible period of detention on death row, but of making the time factor, *per se*, the determining one. If the maximum acceptable period is left open, States parties which seek to avoid overstepping the deadline will be tempted to look to the decisions of the Committee in previous cases so as to determine what length of detention on death row the Committee has found permissible in the past.

¶ 8.4. The second implication of making the time factor *per se* the determining one, i.e. the factor that turns detention on death row into a violation of the Covenant, is that it conveys a message to States parties retaining the death penalty that they should carry out a capital sentence as expeditiously as possible after it was imposed. This is not a message the Committee would wish to convey to States parties. Life on death row, harsh as it may be, is preferable to death. Furthermore, experience shows that delays in carrying out the death penalty can be the necessary consequence of several factors, many of which may be attributable to the State party. Sometimes a moratorium is placed on executions while the whole question of the death penalty is under review. At other times the executive branch of government delays executions even though it is not feasible politically to abolish the death penalty. The Committee would wish to avoid adopting a line of jurisprudence which weakens the influence of factors that may very well lessen the number of prisoners actually executed. It should be stressed that by adopting the approach that prolonged detention on death row cannot, *per se*, be regarded as cruel and inhuman treatment or punishment under the Covenant, the Committee does not wish to convey the impression that keeping condemned prisoners on death row for many years is an acceptable way of treating them. It is not. However, the cruelty of the death row phenomenon is first and foremost a function of the permissibility of capital punishment under the Covenant. This situation has unfortunate consequences.

¶ 8.5. Finally, to hold that prolonged detention on death row does not, *per se*, constitute a violation of articles 7 and 10, does not imply that other circumstances connected with detention on death row may not turn that detention into cruel, inhuman and degrading treatment or punishment. The jurisprudence of the Committee has been that where compelling circumstances of the detention are substantiated, that detention may constitute a violation of the Covenant. This jurisprudence should be maintained in future cases.

¶ 8.6. In the present case, neither the author nor his counsel have pointed to any compelling circumstances, over and above the length of the detention on death row, that would turn Mr. Johnson's detention into a violation of articles 7 and 10. The Committee therefore concludes that there has been no violation of these provisions.

[9.42] A significant minority of members (Chanet, Aguilar Urbina, Bhagwati, Bruni Celli, and Prado Vallejo) argued that the majority opinion was too inflexible. They preferred the compatibility of the death row phenomenon to be assessed on a case-by-case basis.

[9.43] The HRC majority has occasionally found that compelling circumstances exist so as to transform the death row phenomenon into a violation of article 7.

FRANCIS v JAMAICA (606/94)

¶ 9.1. The Committee must determine whether the author's treatment in prison, particularly during the nearly 12 years that he spent on death row following his conviction on 26 January 1981 until the commutation of his death sentence on 29 December 1992 entailed violations of articles 7 and 10 of the Covenant. With regard to the 'death row phenomenon', the Committee reaffirms its well established jurisprudence that prolonged delays in the execution of a sentence of death do not *per se* constitute cruel, inhuman or degrading treatment. On the other hand, each case must be considered on its own merits, bearing in mind the imputability of delays in the administration of justice on the State party, the specific conditions of imprisonment in the particular penitentiary and their psychological impact on the person concerned.

¶ 9.2. In the instant case, the Committee finds that the failure of the Jamaican Court of Appeal to issue a written judgment over a period of more than 13 years, despite repeated requests on Mr. Francis' behalf, must be attributed to the State party. Whereas the psychological tension created by prolonged detention on death row may affect persons in different degrees, the evidence before the Committee in this case, including the author's confused and incoherent correspondence with the Committee, indicates that his mental health seriously deteriorated during incarceration on death row. Taking into consideration the author's description of the prison conditions, including his allegations about regular beatings inflicted upon him by warders, as well as the ridicule and strain to which he was subjected during the five days he spent in the death cell awaiting execution in February 1988, which the State party has not effectively contested, the Committee concludes that these circumstances reveal a violation of Jamaica's obligations under articles 7 and 10, paragraph 1, of the Covenant.

[9.44]   *CLIVE JOHNSON v JAMAICA (592/94)*

In this case, the author had been under 18 years of age at the time of his conviction, so imposition of the death penalty contravened article 6(5) of the

Covenant.[48] As his death sentence was void *ab initio*, his eight years on death row breached article 7.[49] Mr Kretzmer further explained the decision in a concurring opinion:

[W]hen a State party would violate the Covenant by imposing and carrying out the death sentence . . . the violation involved in imposing the death penalty is compounded by holding the condemned person on death row. . . . This detention on death row may certainly amount to cruel and inhuman punishment, especially when that detention lasts longer than is necessary for the domestic legal proceedings required to correct the error involved in imposing the death sentence.

[9.45] A few minority opinions have found article 7 violations on the basis of the death row phenomenon *per se*, as in the following case.

LAVENDE v TRINIDAD AND TOBAGO (554/1993)

The majority in this case followed *Johnson* in finding no violation of article 7 entailed in the complainant's eighteen years on death row. Messrs Bhagwati, Prado Vallejo, and Pocar, as well as Ms Chanet and Mrs Gaitan de Pombo, dissented in the following terms:

The Committee reiterates in the present cases the views that prolonged detention on death row cannot *per se* constitute a violation of article 7 of the Covenant. This view reflects a lack of flexibility that would not allow the Committee to examine the circumstances of each case, in order to determine whether, in a given case, prolonged detention on death row constitutes cruel, inhuman or degrading treatment within the meaning of the above-mentioned provision. This approach leads the Committee to conclude, in the present cases, that detention on death row for eighteen years after the exhaustion of local remedies does not allow a finding of violation of article 7. We cannot agree with this conclusion. Keeping a person detained on death row for so many years, after exhaustion of domestic remedies, and in the absence of any further explanation of the State party as to the reasons thereof, constitutes in itself cruel and inhuman treatment. It should have been for the State party to explain the reasons requiring or justifying such prolonged detention on death row; however, no justification was offered by the State party in the present cases.

A similar dissent was issued in *Bickaroo v Trinidad and Tobago* (555/93), where the relevant period of detention on death row was sixteen years. A sizeable minority within the HRC is therefore willing to find that extended detention on death row may *per se* breach article 7 in cases where the detention is extraordinarily long.[50]

[9.46] One's anxiety at impending execution would intensify once a warrant for execution had actually been issued. The following cases address this issue.

---

[48] See [8.24] on art. 6(5).   [49] Para. 10.4.
[50] See also the dissent of Mr Bán in *Cox v Canada* (539/93).

MARTIN v JAMAICA (317/88)

¶ 12.3. The author further alleges that the delay of 17 days between the issuing of the warrant for his execution and its stay, during which time he was detained in a special cell, constitutes a violation of article 7 of the Covenant. The Committee observes that, after the warrant had been issued, a stay of execution was requested, on the grounds that counsel would prepare a petition for leave to appeal to the Judicial Committee of the Privy Council. This stay of execution was subsequently granted. Nothing in the information before the Committee indicates that the applicable procedures were not duly followed, or that the author continued to be detained in the special cell after the stay of execution had been granted. The Committee therefore finds that the facts before it do not disclose a violation of article 7 of the Covenant.

PENNANT v JAMAICA (647/95)

¶ 8.6. . . . the author was placed in a death cell for two weeks after a warrant for execution was read to him. The Committee notes the State party's contention that it is to be expected that this would cause the author 'some anxiety', and that the time spent there was because efforts were 'presumably' being made to have his execution stayed. The Committee considers that in the absence of a detailed explanation by the State party as to the reasons for the author's two weeks' stay in a death cell, this cannot be deemed compatible with . . . article 7 of the Covenant. . . .

Despite the *Martin* decision, it now seems that the HRC accepts that detention in 'a death cell' after the issue of a warrant for execution does amount to a breach of article 7 if it is deemed unreasonably long. The imminence of anticipated execution, and the consequent increase in anxiety, distinguishes such instances from ordinary cases of the death row phenomenon. Unreasonably long detention in a death cell, according to *Pennant*, is only two weeks. States Parties should not issue warrants for execution more than a few days before the anticipated date for execution.[51]

Method of Execution

NG v CANADA (469/91)

[9.47] The author argued that his extradition to the United States, where he was to be tried for serial murder, and, if convicted, would likely receive the death penalty, violated his right to life under article 6.[52] The author also argued that the method of execution that he was likely to face, gas asphyxiation, would breach article 7. The HRC majority agreed with him on the second point:

---

[51] See also *Pratt and Morgan v Jamaica* (220/86, 225/87), para. 13.7, where a delay of 20 hours before informing the authors of a stay of their executions constituted a breach of art. 7.
[52] See [8.27–8.29] on the similar case of *Kindler v Canada* (470/91).

¶ 16.1. .... In the instant case, it is contended that execution by gas asphyxiation is contrary to internationally accepted standards of humane treatment, and that it amounts to treatment in violation of article 7 of the Covenant. The Committee begins by noting that whereas article 6, paragraph 2, allows for the imposition of the death penalty under certain limited circumstances, any method of execution provided for by law must be designed in such a way as to avoid conflict with article 7.

¶ 16.2. The Committee is aware that, by definition, every execution of a sentence of death may be considered to constitute cruel and inhuman treatment within the meaning of article 7 of the Covenant; on the other hand, article 6, paragraph 2, permits the imposition of capital punishment for the most serious crimes. Nonetheless, the Committee reaffirms, as it did in its General Comment 20[44] on article 7 of the Covenant (CCPR/C/21/Add.3, paragraph 6) that, when imposing capital punishment, the execution of the sentence '... must be carried out in such a way as to cause the least possible physical and mental suffering'.

¶ 16.3. In the present case, the author has provided detailed information that execution by gas asphyxiation may cause prolonged suffering and agony and does not result in death as swiftly as possible, as asphyxiation by cyanide gas may take over 10 minutes. ...

¶ 16.4. In the instant case and on the basis of the information before it, the Committee concludes that execution by gas asphyxiation, should the death penalty be imposed on the author, would not meet the test of 'least possible physical and mental suffering', and constitutes cruel and inhuman treatment, in violation of article 7 of the Covenant. Accordingly, Canada, which could reasonably foresee that Mr. Ng, if sentenced to death, would be executed in a way that amounts to a violation of article 7, failed to comply with its obligations under the Covenant, by extraditing Mr. Ng without having sought and received assurances that he would not be executed.

[9.48] Messrs Mavrommatis and Sadi, with whom Messrs Ando and Herndl, essentially agreed, dissented on this point in the following terms:

We do not believe that, on the basis of the material before us, execution by gas asphyxiation could constitute cruel and inhuman treatment within the meaning of article 7 of the Covenant. A method of execution such as death by stoning, which is intended to and actually inflicts prolonged pain and suffering, is contrary to article 7.

Every known method of judicial execution in use today, including execution by lethal injection, has come under criticism for causing prolonged pain or the necessity to have the process repeated. We do not believe that the Committee should look into such details in respect of execution such as whether acute pain of limited duration or less pain of longer duration is preferable and could be a criterion for a finding of violation of the Covenant.

The minority HRC members felt that a mode of execution should be 'intentionally' brutal in order for it to breach article 7. This echoes the requirement of intentionality in article 1 of CAT.

[9.49] In *Cox v Canada* (539/93), the HRC found that execution by lethal injection did not breach article 7.[53]

---

[53] Para. 17.3.

[9.50] In Concluding Comments on the Islamic Republic of Iran, the HRC 'deplore[d] that a number of executions [had] taken place in public',[54] indicating that public executions constitute 'inhuman' or at least 'degrading' treatment.

Extradition, Expulsion, Refoulement

[9.51]   ***ARTICLE 3, CAT***

1. No State Party shall expel, return (*refouler*) or extradite a person to another State where there are substantial grounds for believing that he would be in danger of being subjected to torture.

2. For the purpose of determining whether there are such grounds, the competent authorities shall take into account all relevant considerations including, where applicable, the existence in the State concerned of a consistent pattern of gross, flagrant or mass violations of human rights.

GENERAL COMMENT 20

¶ 9. In the view of the Committee, States parties must not expose individuals to the danger of torture or cruel, inhuman or degrading treatment or punishment upon return to another country by way of their extradition, expulsion or refoulement.

[9.52] Article 3 expressly applies only to prohibit refoulement to a State where one foreseeably faces torture, rather than the lesser forms of impugned treatment. General Comment 20 prohibits refoulement with regard to all article 7 treatment. Despite the greater apparent depth of the article 7 guarantee, most complaints concerning deportation and refoulement have been submitted to the CAT Committee, probably because of the express protection given to prospective deportees in article 3. Indeed, most cases before the CAT Committee have concerned alleged violations of article 3.

[9.53]   ***TALA v SWEDEN (CAT 43/1996)***

The State Party had refused the author's request for political asylum from Iran, and proposed to expel him to Iran. The CAT Committee upheld Tala's allegation that such an expulsion would breach article 3:

¶ 10.1. The Committee must decide, pursuant to paragraph 1 of article 3, whether there are substantial grounds for believing that Mr. Tala would be in danger of being subject to torture upon return to Iran. In reaching this decision, the Committee must take into account all relevant considerations, pursuant to paragraph 2 of article 3, including the existence of a consistent pattern of gross, flagrant or mass violations of human rights. The aim of the determination, however, is to establish whether the individual concerned would be person-

---

[54] (1993) UN doc. CCPR/C/79/Add. 25, para. 8.

ally at risk of being subjected to torture in the country to which he or she would return. It follows that the existence of a consistent pattern of gross, flagrant or mass violations of human rights in a country does not as such constitute a sufficient ground for determining that a particular person would be in danger of being subjected to torture upon his return to that country; additional grounds must exist to show that the individual concerned would be personally at risk. Similarly, the absence of a consistent pattern of gross violations of human rights does not mean that a person cannot be considered to be in danger of being subjected to torture in his or her specific circumstances.

¶ 10.2. The Committee has noted the State party's assertion that its authorities apply practically the same test as prescribed by article 3 of the Convention when determining whether or not a person can be deported. The Committee, however, notes that the text of the decisions taken by the Immigration Board (26 November 1990) and the Aliens Appeal Board (3 July 1992 and 25 August 1995) in the author's case does not show that the test as required by article 3 of the Convention (and as reflected in chapter 8, section 1, of the 1989 Aliens Act) was in fact applied to the author's case.

¶ 10.3. In the instant case, the Committee considers that the author's political affiliation with the People's Mujahedin Organization and activities, his history of detention and torture, should be taken into account when determining whether he would be in danger of being subjected to torture upon his return. The State party has pointed to contradictions and inconsistencies in the author's story, but the Committee considers that complete accuracy is seldom to be expected by victims of torture and that the inconsistencies as exist in the author's presentation of the facts do not raise doubts about the general veracity of his claims, especially since it has been demonstrated that the author suffers from Post Traumatic Stress Disorder. Further, the Committee has noted from the medical evidence that the scars on the author's thighs could only have been caused by a burn and that this burn could only have been inflicted intentionally by another person than the author himself.

¶ 10.4. The Committee is aware of the serious human rights situation in Iran, as reported *inter alia* to the United Nations Commission on Human Rights by the Commission's Special Representative on the situation of human rights in the Islamic Republic of Iran. The Committee notes the concern expressed by the Commission, in particular in respect of the high number of executions, instances of torture and cruel, inhuman or degrading treatment or punishment.

¶ 10.5. In the circumstances, the Committee considers that substantial grounds exist for believing that the author would be in danger of being subjected to torture if returned to Iran.

¶ 11. In the light of the above, the Committee is of the view that, in the prevailing circumstances, the State party has an obligation to refrain from forcibly returning Mr. Kaveh Yaragh Tala to Iran, or to any other country where he runs a real risk of being expelled or returned to Iran.

[9.54] CAT has come to similar decisions in *Khan v Canada* (CAT 15/94) (Canada would violate article 3 by expelling Khan to Pakistan), *Alan v Switzerland* (CAT 21/95), *Ayas v Sweden* (CAT 97/97), *Haydin v Sweden* (CAT 101/97), *H.D. v Switzerland* (CAT 112/98) (violations of article 3 would occur by expelling the respective authors to Turkey), *S.M.R. and M.M.R. v Sweden* (CAT 103/98), *Aemei v Switzerland* (CAT 34/95), *Falakaflaki v Sweden* (CAT 89/97) (violation of article 3 by expelling the respective authors to Iran), *A v The Netherlands* (CAT 91/97) (violation of article 3 entailed in deporting A to Tunisia), *X v The Netherlands* (CAT 41/96), *Kisoki v Sweden* (CAT 41/96), and *Mutombo v Switzerland* (CAT 13/93) (State Party would violate article 3 by expelling the respective authors to Zaire). All cases turned on CAT's assessment of the author's submissions that he/she would likely be tortured if expelled to the country in question. In numerous inadmissible cases under article 3, the author has been found by CAT not to have sufficiently substantiated his/her claim of foreseeable persecution upon expulsion.[55]

[9.55] CAT comprehensively addressed the issue of evidence under article 3 CAT in its General Comment 1.

CAT GENERAL COMMENT 1

¶ 5. With respect to the application of article 3 of the Convention to the merits of a case, the burden is upon the author to present an arguable case. This means that there must be a factual basis for the author's position sufficient to require a response from the State party.

¶ 6. Bearing in mind that the State party and the Committee are obliged to assess whether there are substantial grounds for believing that the author would be in danger of being subjected to torture were he/she to be expelled, returned or extradited, the risk of torture must be assessed on grounds that go beyond mere theory or suspicion. However, the risk does not have to meet the test of being highly probable.

¶ 7. The author must establish that he/she would be in danger of being tortured and that the grounds for so believing are substantial in the way described, and that such danger is personal and present. All pertinent information may be introduced by either party to bear on this matter.

¶ 8. The following information, while not exhaustive, would be pertinent:

(a) Is the State concerned one in which there is evidence of a consistent pattern of gross, flagrant or mass violations of human rights (see article 3, para. 2)?;

(b) Has the author been tortured or maltreated by or at the instigation of or with the consent or acquiescence of a public official or other person acting in an official capacity in the past? If so, was this the recent past?;

(c) Is there medical or other independent evidence to support a claim by the author that he/she has been tortured or maltreated in the past? Has the torture had after-effects?;

---

[55] See, e.g., *Y v Switzerland* (CAT 18/94), *E.A. v Switzerland* (CAT 28/95), *P.Q.L. v Canada* (CAT 57/96), *K.N. v Switzerland* (CAT 94/97), *J.U.A. v Switzerland* (CAT 100/97), *N.P. v Australia* (CAT 106/98), *A.L.N. v Switzerland* (CAT 90/97), *X,Y and Z v Sweden* (CAT 61/96).

(d) Has the situation referred to in (a) above changed? Has the internal situation in respect of human rights altered?;

(e) Has the author engaged in political or other activity within or outside the State concerned which would appear to make him/her particularly vulnerable to the risk of being placed in danger of torture were he/she to be expelled, returned or extradited to the State in question?;

(f) Is there any evidence as to the credibility of the author?;

(g) Are there factual inconsistencies in the claim of the author? If so, are they relevant?

¶ 9. Bearing in mind that the Committee against Torture is not an appellate, a quasi-judicial or an administrative body, but rather a monitoring body created by the States parties themselves with declaratory powers only, it follows that:

(a) Considerable weight will be given, in exercising the Committee's jurisdiction pursuant to article 3 of the Convention, to findings of fact that are made by organs of the State party concerned; but

(b) The Committee is not bound by such findings and instead has the power, provided by article 22, paragraph 4, of the Convention, of free assessment of the facts based upon the full set of circumstances in every case.

[9.56] The CAT Committee has been influenced in its findings of article 3 violations by the poor human rights records of the proposed 'receiving' States. In its General Comment 1, the CAT Committee extrapolated on relevant characteristics of the receiving State.

CAT GENERAL COMMENT 1

¶ 2. The Committee is of the view that the phrase 'another State' in article 3 refers to the State to which the individual concerned is being expelled, returned or extradited, as well as to any State to which the author may subsequently be expelled, returned or extradited.

¶ 3. Pursuant to article 1, the criterion, mentioned in article 3, paragraph 2, 'a consistent pattern of gross, flagrant or mass violations of human rights' refers only to violations by or at the instigation of or with the consent or acquiescence of a public official or other person acting in an official capacity.

[9.57]   KORBAN v SWEDEN (CAT 88/97)

¶ 3.1. The author claims that his return to Iraq would constitute a violation of article 3 of the Convention against Torture by Sweden, since there are risks that he would be arrested and subjected to torture in that country. He also claims that, not having a residence permit in Jordan, it is unsafe for him to return to that country from which he fears to be sent back to Iraq since the Jordan police [sic] work closely with the Iraqi authorities.

The CAT Committee subsequently found that deportation to Iraq would violate article 3 CAT. Regarding the proposed deportation to Jordan, the Committee again found in favour of the author:

¶ 6.5. The Committee notes that the Swedish immigration authorities had ordered the author's expulsion to Jordan and that the State party abstains from making an evaluation of the risk that the author will be deported to Iraq from Jordan. It appears from the parties' submissions, however, that such risk cannot be excluded, in view of the assessment made by different sources, including UNHCR, based on reports indicating that some Iraqis have been sent by the Jordanian authorities to Iraq against their will, that marriage to a Jordanian woman does not guarantee a residence permit in Jordan and that this situation has not improved after the signature of a Memorandum of Understanding between the UNHCR and the Jordanian authorities regarding the rights of refugees in Jordan. The State party itself has recognized that Iraqi citizens who are refugees in Jordan, in particular those who have been returned to Jordan from a European country, are not entirely protected from being deported to Iraq.

¶ 7. In the light of the above, the Committee is of the view that, in the prevailing circumstances, the State party has an obligation to refrain from forcibly returning the author to Iraq. It also has an obligation to refrain from forcibly returning the author to Jordan, in view of the risk he would run of being expelled from that country to Iraq. In this respect the Committee refers to paragraph 2 of its general comment on the implementation of article 3 of the Convention in the context of article 22, according to which 'the phrase 'another State' in article 3 refers to the State to which the individual concerned is being expelled, returned or extradited, as well as to any State to which the author may subsequently be expelled, returned or extradited'. Furthermore, the Committee notes that although Jordan is a party to the Convention, it has not made the declaration under article 22.[56] As a result, the author would not have the possibility of submitting a new communication to the Committee if he was threatened with deportation from Jordan to Iraq.

Hence, the deportation to Jordan would have breached article 3, even though the author never alleged that he faced the risk of torture in Jordan. Rather, he feared subsequent deportation from Jordan to Iraq.

[9.58] Generally, the CAT Committee has manifested a greater willingness than the HRC to overrule municipal findings of fact in the absence of procedural deficiencies in the relevant municipal proceedings.[57] Indeed, the HRC has found a violation only once in circumstances where the author complained about his/her deportation, in the context of the extradition in *Ng v Canada* (469/91) [9.47]. The HRC has found complaints of article 7 breaches entailed in deportation to allegedly 'unsafe' States to be unsubstantiated in *Torres v Finland* (291/88), *A.R.J. v Australia* (692/96), and *T.T. v Australia* (706/96).[58]

[9.59] Cases concerning refoulement are usually made by asylum-seekers and persons claiming refugee status. It seems that these cases may raise issues

---

[56] Art. 22 prescribes the individual complaints mechanism under CAT.
[57] See, in particular, the discussion at [14.36] and [20.39]. On procedural deficiencies in deportation cases, also see Chap. 13.
[58] A minority of Messrs Scheinin, Klein, and Kretzmer found that the author in *T.T.* had submitted sufficient evidence that there was a real risk of a violation of his ICCPR rights upon his deportation to Malaysia.

concerning rights under the United Nations Convention relating to the Status of Refugees 1951.

X v SPAIN (CAT 23/1995)

X argued that his deportation from Spain to Algeria breached article 3, as he claimed that he would be tortured upon return due to his membership of the outlawed Front Islamique du Salut (FIS). The CAT Committee found in favour of the State Party.

¶ 7.3. The Committee . . . points out that its authority does not extend to a determination of whether or not the claimant is entitled to asylum under the national laws of a country, or can invoke the protection of the Geneva Convention relating to the Status of Refugees. Under article 3 of the Convention, the Committee must decide whether expulsion or extradition might expose an individual to the risk of being tortured.

¶ 7.4. The Committee notes that throughout a year of proceedings in Spain, X's representatives based their arguments solely on asylum and did not invoke the right protected by article 3 of the Convention. Nor did they present the Committee with serious grounds for believing that X risked being tortured if he was expelled to Algeria. It is not alleged that X was detained or tortured in Algeria before leaving for Morocco and Spain; it is not indicated precisely what he did in FIS to justify his fear of being tortured. On the contrary, X said in his first statement to the Melilla authorities, with a lawyer and interpreter present, the intention was to seek work in Germany, and the truthfulness of that statement was questioned during the asylum proceedings in Spain.

¶ 7.5. The Committee concludes that the communication on behalf of X has not sufficiently [been] justified as regards the claimed violation of article 3 of the Convention but rather a matter of political asylum, making the communication incompatible with article 22 of the Convention against Torture and Other Cruel, Inhuman or Degrading Treatment or Punishment.

Similarly, CAT had no jurisdiction to determine whether the applicant was a 'refugee' under the 1951 Convention in *Mohamed v Greece* (CAT 40/96). The *X* and *Mohamed* cases confirm that determinations under article 3 CAT are conceptually separate from questions arising under the Refugee Convention.[59]

[9.60] *PAEZ v SWEDEN (CAT 39/96)*

The author challenged the State Party's decision to expel him to Peru. The author claimed that he would be tortured upon return to Peru, as he was a member of 'Sendero Luminoso' (Shining Path), an anti-government terrorist organization in Peru. The HRC delivered the following merits decision:

---

[59] For a comparison of CAT/ICCPR and Refugee Convention protection from refoulement, see S. Taylor, 'Australia's Implementation of its Non-Refoulement Obligations under the Convention Against Torture and Other Cruel Inhuman or Degrading Treatment or Punishment and the International Covenant on Civil and Political Rights' (1994) 17 *University of New South Wales Law Journal* 432.

¶ 14.3. The Committee notes that the facts on which the author's asylum claim are based are not in dispute. The author is a member of Sendero Luminoso and on 1 November 1989 participated in a demonstration where he handed out leaflets and distributed handmade bombs. Subsequently, the police searched his house and the author went into hiding and left the country to seek asylum in Sweden. It is, further, beyond dispute that the author comes from a politically active family, that one of his cousins disappeared and another was killed for political reasons, and that his mother and sisters have been granted *de facto* refugee status by Sweden.

¶ 14.4. It appears from the State party's submission and from the decisions by the immigration authorities in the instant case, that the refusal to grant the author asylum in Sweden is based on the exception clause of article 1F of the 1951 Convention relating to the Status of Refugees. This is illustrated by the fact that the author's mother and sisters were granted *de facto* asylum in Sweden, since it was feared that they may be subjected to persecution because they belong to a family which is connected to Sendero Luminoso. No ground has been invoked by the State party for its distinction between the author, on the one hand, and his mother and sisters, on the other, other than the author's activities for Sendero Luminoso.

¶ 14.5. The Committee considers that the test of article 3 of the Convention is absolute. Whenever substantial grounds exist for believing that an individual would be in danger of being subjected to torture upon expulsion to another State, the State party is under obligation not to return the person concerned to that State. The nature of the activities in which the person concerned engaged cannot be a material consideration when making a determination under article 3 of the Convention.

Article 1F of the Convention Relating to the Status of Refugees 1951 states that the following persons cannot be considered 'refugees' and are therefore entitled to no Convention protection: persons who have committed war crimes, crimes against peace, crimes against humanity, serious non-political crimes prior to admission to the country of refuge, or acts contrary to the purposes and principle of the United Nations. In contrast, article 3 CAT imposes absolute duties upon States not to extradite war criminals and mass murderers if their extradition would foreseeably result in their torture.[60]

[9.61] Article 3 CAT protects only persons who foreseeably face *torture* upon expulsion to a certain State. In *I.A.O. v Sweden* (65/97), the foreseeable risk of detention *per se* was not enough to 'trigger the protection of article 3 of the Convention'.[61]

[9.62] Article 3 CAT and article 7 ICCPR do not confer rights of asylum. CAT commented on remedies for article 3 breaches in *Aemei v Switzerland* (34/95):

¶ 11. The Committee's finding of a violation of article 3 of the Convention in no way

---

[60] Ibid., 452.
[61] Para. 14.5. Would the author have been better off submitting a complaint under the ICCPR rather than art. 3 CAT? See [4.14].

affects the decision(s) of the competent national authorities concerning the granting or refusal of asylum. The finding of a violation of article 3 has a declaratory character. Consequently, the State party is not required to modify its decision(s) concerning the granting of asylum; on the other hand, it does have a responsibility to find solutions that will enable it to take all necessary measures to comply with the provisions of article 3 of the Convention. Those solutions may be of a legal nature (e.g., a decision to admit the applicant temporarily), but also of a political nature (e.g., action to find a third State willing to admit the applicant to its territory and undertaking in its turn not to return or expel him).

[9.63] In order to protect the rights in article 3 CAT States must not institute procedures which automatically expel certain categories of persons. For example, the CAT Committee has criticized Finnish authorities for utilizing a 'list of safe countries' automatically to deny asylum to people seeking refuge from those countries; each assessment should include consideration of the possible application of article 3.[62]

[9.64] The above discussion focuses on the harshness of the reception one might receive in a receiving country, rather than the harshness involved in being forced to leave the expelling country. The latter issue arose in *Canepa v Canada* (558/93).

CANEPA v CANADA (558/93)

Canepa was an Italian citizen who had lived in Canada with his family for most of his life. Despite his ties to Canada, the Canadian authorities proposed to deport him because of his criminal record. Canepa claimed, *inter alia*, that this deportation would breach article 7:[63]

¶ 4.6. Finally, the author contends that the enforcement of the deportation order amounts to cruel, inhuman and degrading treatment within the meaning of article 7 of the Covenant. He acknowledges that the Committee has not yet considered whether the permanent separation of an individual from his family and close relatives and the effective banishment of a person from the only country which he ever knew and in which he grew up can amount to cruel, inhuman or degrading treatment; he submits, however, that this issue should be considered on the merits.

The State Party responded thus:

¶ 9.1. By submission of 21 December 1995, the State party argues that the author's allegations in respect to article 7 of the Covenant are not substantiated, since there is no evidence that the author's separation from his family poses any particular risk to his mental or physical health. The State party argues that article 7 is not as broad in scope as contended by the author and does not apply to the present situation, where the author does not face a substantial risk of torture or of serious abuse in the receiving country. The author

---

[62] CAT Concluding Comments on Finland (1997) UN doc. A/51/44, para. 62.
[63] See also [12.32–12.33] and [20.18] for other findings in this case.

has not shown that he will suffer any undue hardship as a result of his deportation. The State party adds that the author is not absolutely barred from returning to Canada. Furthermore, the author's family is apparently able to join the author in Italy, as indicated by the author's father at the Immigration Appeal Board hearing. The State party argues that the question of separation from family is rather an issue to be dealt with under articles 17 and 23 of the Covenant.

The HRC later agreed with the State Party that 'the facts of the instant case [were] not of such a nature as to raise an issue under article 7'.[64]

Corporal Punishment

[9.65]   *GENERAL COMMENT 20*

¶ 5. . . . In the Committee's view . . . the [article 7] prohibition must extend to corporal punishment, including excessive chastisement ordered as punishment for a crime or as an educative or disciplinary measure. It is appropriate to emphasize in this regard that article 7 protects, in particular, children, pupils and patients in teaching and medical institutions.

The HRC's reference to '*excessive* chastisement' indicates that corporal punishment is not *per se* a breach of article 7. However, the HRC has since stated, with regard to Cyprus, that 'corporal punishment is prohibited by the Covenant'.[65]

[9.66] In *Matthews v Trinidad and Tobago* (569/93), the HRC implied that twenty strokes with a birch, inflicted as a judicial punishment, would breach article 7.[66] Similarly, a sentence of between twenty and seventy four lashes would also breach article 7.[67] In Concluding Comments on Lesotho, the HRC recommended the abolition of all judicial corporal punishment, disregarding the fact that such punishment was supervised by medical doctors.[68] Finally, in Concluding Comments on Iraq, the HRC was deeply concerned about the amputation of hands and branding of convicts in Iraq.[69] The comments regarding amputation as a punishment in an Islamic State indicate that 'cultural' defences to article 7 allegations will not be accepted by UN human rights treaty bodies.[70]

---

[64] A similar complaint in *Stewart v Canada* (538/93) was also found inadmissible in respect of art. 7, at para. 11.2.

[65] Concluding Comments on Cyprus (1998) UN doc. CCPR/C/79/Add. 88, para. 16.

[66] See para. 6.5; no violation of art. 7 was found as there was insufficient evidence that the punishment had ever been carried out (para. 7.2).

[67] This is implied in *A.R.J. v Australia* (692/96), para. 6.14. The author alleged his deportation to Iran subjected him to a foreseeable risk of such punishment. The HRC found the risk was not sufficiently foreseeable so no breach of art. 7 arose. See also Concluding Comments on Libyan Arab Jamahiriya (1998) UN doc. CCPR/C/79/Add. 101, para. 11, where the HRC condemned 'flogging' as a penalty for criminal offences.

[68] (1999) UN doc. CCPR/C/79/Add. 106, para. 20.

[69] (1997) UN doc. CCPR/C/79/Add. 84, para. 12.

[70] See also the condemnation of amputation as a punishment in Concluding Comments on Libyan Arab Jamahiriya (1998) UN doc. CCPR/C/79/Add. 101, para. 11. See also [1.70].

Conditions of Detention

[9.67]   *PORTORREAL v DOMINICAN REPUBLIC (188/84)*

¶ 9.2. Mr. Ramon B. Martinez Portorreal is a national of the Dominican Republic, a lawyer and Executive Secretary of the Comite Dominicano de los Derechos Humanos. On 14 June 1984 at 6 a.m., he was arrested at his home, according to the author, because of his activities as a leader of a human rights association, and taken to a cell at the secret service police headquarters, from where he was transferred to another cell measuring 20 by 5 metres, where approximately 125 persons accused of common crimes were being held, and where, owing to lack of space, some detainees had to sit on excrement. He received no food or water until the following day. On 16 June 1984, after 50 hours of detention, he was released. At no time during his detention was he informed of the reasons for his arrest. . . .

¶ 11. The Human Rights Committee . . . is of the view that these facts disclose violations of the Covenant, with respect to: Articles 7 and 10, paragraph 1, because Ramon Martinez Portorreal was subjected to inhuman and degrading treatment and to lack of respect for his inherent human dignity during his detention . . .

MUKONG v CAMEROON (458/91)

In this case, the conditions of Mukong's detention in prison entailed a violation of article 7.

¶ 9.3. As to the conditions of detention in general, the Committee observes that certain minimum standards regarding the conditions of detention must be observed regardless of a State party's level of development. These include, in accordance with Rules 10, 12, 17, 19 and 20 of the U.N. Standard Minimum Rules for the Treatment of Prisoners,[71] minimum floor space and cubic content of air for each prisoner, adequate sanitary facilities, clothing which shall be in no manner degrading or humiliating, provision of a separate bed, and provision of food of nutritional value adequate for health and strength. It should be noted that these are minimum requirements which the Committee considers should always be observed, even if economic or budgetary considerations may make compliance with these obligations difficult. It transpires from the file that these requirements were not met during the author's detention in the summer of 1988 and in February/March 1990.

¶ 9.4. The Committee further notes that quite apart from the general conditions of detention, the author has been singled out for exceptionally harsh and degrading treatment. Thus, he was kept detained incommunicado, was threatened with torture and death and intimidated, deprived of food, and kept locked in his cell for several days on end without the possibility of recreation. In this context, the Committee recalls its General Comment 20[44] which recommends that States parties should make provision against incommunicado detention[72] and notes that total isolation of a detained or imprisoned person may amount to acts prohibited by article 7. . . . In view of the above, the Committee finds that

---

[71] See [9.108] for a discussion of these Standard Minimum Rules.
[72] See [9.71] and [9.76].

Mr. Mukong has been subjected to cruel, inhuman and degrading treatment, in violation of article 7 of the Covenant.

EDWARDS v JAMAICA (529/93)

¶ 8.3. With regard to the conditions of detention at St. Catherine's District Prison, the Committee notes that in his original communication the author made specific allegations, in respect of the deplorable conditions of detention. He alleged that he was held for the period of 10 years alone in a cell measuring 6 feet by 14 feet, let out only for three and half hours a day, was provided with no recreational facilities and received no books. The State party made no attempt to refute these specific allegations. In these circumstances, the Committee takes the allegations as proven. It finds that holding a prisoner in such conditions of detention constitutes not only a violation of article 10, paragraph 1, but, because of the length of time in which the author was kept in these conditions, also a violation of article 7.

BROWN v JAMAICA (775/97)

¶ 6.13. The author has, however, also complained about the circumstances of his detention at St. Catherine's District Prison, which have not been addressed by the State party. In particular, he has stated that he is locked up in his cell for 23 hours a day, that he has no mattress or other bedding, no adequate sanitation, ventilation or electric lighting, and that he is denied exercise as well as medical treatment, adequate nutrition and clean drinking water. The author has also claimed that his belongings, including an asthma pump and other medication, were destroyed by the warders in March 1997, and that he has been denied prompt assistance in case of an asthma-attack. Although the State party has promised to investigate certain of these claims, the Committee notes with concern that the results of the State party's investigation have never been communicated. In the circumstances, due weight must be given to the author's uncontested allegations to the extent that they are substantiated. The Committee finds that the above constitute violations of articles 7 and 10, paragraph 1, of the Covenant.

SMITH and STEWART v JAMAICA (668/95)

¶ 7.5. [The author] states that the sanitary conditions of the prison are dreadful, that the quality and quantity of food is grossly inadequate and that he has been denied access to non-legal mail. Furthermore, he states that he has been subjected to inadequate medical attention, which has caused the loss of his sight in one eye. The State party has not refuted these allegations. . . . The Committee finds that these circumstances disclose a violation of articles 7 and 10, paragraph 1, of the Covenant.

[9.68] In Concluding Comments on Japan, the HRC stated the following:[73]

---

[73] (1998) UN doc. CCPR/C/79/Add. 102.

¶ 27. The Committee is deeply concerned at many aspects of the prison system in Japan which raise serious questions of compliance with articles 2, paragraph 3 (a), 7 and 10 of the Covenant. Specifically, the Committee is concerned with the following:

(a) Harsh rules of conduct in prisons that restrict the fundamental rights of prisoners, including freedom of speech, freedom of association and privacy;

(b) Use of harsh punitive measures, including frequent resort to solitary confinement;

(c) Lack of fair and open procedures for deciding on disciplinary measures against prisoners accused of breaking the rules;

(d) Inadequate protection for prisoners who complain of reprisals by prison warders;

(e) Lack of a credible system for investigating complaints by prisoners; and

(f) Frequent use of protective measures, such as leather handcuffs, that may constitute cruel and inhuman treatment.

[9.69] In one of the HRC's first merits decision, *Massera v Uruguay* (5/77), the HRC found that 'detention in conditions detrimental to [one's] health' constituted a breach of article 7. Nevertheless, the HRC has dealt with most cases regarding poor general conditions of detention under article 10(1), indicating that it has retreated from its *Massera* position.[74]

Solitary Confinement and Incommunicado Detention

[9.70] In General Comment 20, the HRC states that 'prolonged solitary confinement of the detained or imprisoned person may amount to acts prohibited by article 7'.[75]

[9.71] Incommunicado detention is an aggravated form of detention where one is not necessarily in solitary confinement, but one is denied access to family, friends, and others (e.g. lawyers). In *Laureano v Peru* (540/1993) and *Tshishimbi v Zaire* (542/1993), the forced disappearance of the victims, depriving them of contact with the outside world, entailed 'cruel and inhuman treatment'. In *Polay Campos v Peru* (577/94), incommunicado detention for one year constituted 'inhuman treatment',[76] while continued solitary confinement for over three years also breached article 7.[77] Finally, eight months' incommunicado detention in overcrowded, damp conditions in *Shaw v Jamaica* (704/96) constituted 'inhuman and degrading treatment'.[78] *Shaw* concerned the shortest period for which a period of incommunicado detention has been found to breach article 7. Other cases of incommunicado detention have been dealt with under article 10 [9.109].

---

[74] Ghandhi, above, note 27, 769. See [9.101–9.103] below.
[75] Para. 6. See also para. 11 [9.76].   [76] Para. 8.6.
[77] Para. 8.7. See also *Marais v Madagascar* (49/79) and *El-Megreisi v Libyan Arab Jamahiriya* (440/90).   [78] Para. 7.1.

Unauthorized Medical Experimentation

[9.72] The last sentence of article 7 specifically prohibits subjection to medical or scientific experimentation without consent. This specific prohibition was a response to the atrocities of Nazi doctors in concentration camps during World War II.[79]

GENERAL COMMENT 20

¶ 7. Article 7 expressly prohibits medical or scientific experimentation without the free consent of the person concerned. . . . The Committee . . . observes that special protection in regard to such experiments is necessary in the case of persons not capable of giving valid consent, and in particular those under any form of detention or imprisonment. Such persons should not be subjected to any medical or scientific experimentation that may be detrimental to their health.

The HRC has therefore indicated that vulnerable persons, like prisoners or other detainees, should never be subjected to potentially detrimental medical experimentation, as any consent given by such people is inherently suspect.

[9.73] In Concluding Comments on the USA, the HRC stated the following:[80]

¶ 21. The Committee is concerned that, in some states, non-therapeutic research may be conducted on minors or mentally-ill patients on the basis of surrogate consent, in violation of the provisions in article 7 of the Covenant.

[9.74] A prohibition on 'medical experimentation' is considerably narrower than a prohibition on medical 'treatment'. Non-experimental medical treatment, even if rendered without consent, will have to reach a certain level of severity before violating article 7. Certainly, the sterilization of disabled women without consent is a breach of article 7.[81]

DUTIES TO TRAIN APPROPRIATE PERSONNEL

[9.75]   *GENERAL COMMENT 20*

¶ 10. The Committee should be informed how States parties disseminate, to the population at large, relevant information concerning the ban on torture and the treatment prohibited by article 7. Enforcement personnel, medical personnel, police officers and any other persons involved in the custody or treatment of any individual subjected to any form of arrest, detention or imprisonment must receive appropriate instruction and training. States parties should inform the Committee of the instruction and training given and the way in which the prohibition of article 7 forms an integral part of the operational rules and ethical standards to be followed by such persons.

Article 10 CAT reflects a similar duty.

---

[79] Nowak, above, note 3, 137–8, citing UN doc. A/2929, 31, para. 14.
[80] (1995) UN doc. CCPR/C/79/Add.50.
[81] Concluding Comments on Japan (1998) UN doc. CCPR/C/79/Add. 102, para. 31.

DUTIES TO INSTITUTE PROCEDURES TO MINIMIZE RISKS OF 'ARTICLE 7 TREATMENT'

[9.76] *GENERAL COMMENT 20*

¶ 11. In addition to describing steps to provide the general protection against acts prohibited under article 7 to which anyone is entitled, the State party should provide detailed information on safeguards for the special protection of particularly vulnerable persons. It should be noted that keeping under systematic review interrogation rules, instructions, methods and practices as well as arrangements for the custody and treatment of persons subjected to any form of arrest, detention or imprisonment is an effective means of preventing cases of torture and ill-treatment. To guarantee the effective protection of detained persons, provisions should be made for detainees to be held in places officially recognized as places of detention and for their names and places of detention, as well as for the names of persons responsible for their detention, to be kept in registers readily available and accessible to those concerned, including relatives and friends. To the same effect, the time and place of all interrogations should be recorded, together with the names of all those present and this information should also be available for purposes of judicial or administrative proceedings. Provisions should also be made against incommunicado detention. In that connection, States parties should ensure that any places of detention be free from any equipment liable to be used for inflicting torture or ill-treatment. The protection of the detainee also requires that prompt and regular access be given to doctors and lawyers and, under appropriate supervision when the investigation so requires, to family members.

[9.77] A corresponding duty is found in article 11 CAT. The HRC's description of these duties and the above-mentioned training duties [9.75] indicates the sort of evidence States should produce to refute allegations of article 7 violations. Fulfilment of these essentially procedural duties, helps to ensure that substantive violations of article 7 do not occur, and provides evidence that they have not occurred.[82]

Duty to Prevent Incommunicado Detention

[9.78] In paragraph 11 of the General Comment, the HRC recognizes that incommunicado detention must be prevented in order to minimize the risks of breach of article 7 [9.76]. People who are detained incommunicado are highly vulnerable to 'article 7 treatment' as there are no procedural safeguards to ensure accountability and thus deter the perpetration of article 7 treatment. Continued incommunicado detention essentially amounts to a 'disappearance'; the link between disappearances and article 7 was noted in the following case.

MOJICA v DOMINICAN REPUBLIC (449/91)

The HRC found that the State had failed to take specific and effective measures to prevent the disappearance of the author's son. Indeed, there was strong

---

[82] See commentary on *Hill and Hill v Spain* (526/93) below [9.116].

evidence of State involvement in the disappearance. This case entailed numerous violations of the ICCPR,[83] including a breach of article 7:

¶ 5.7. The circumstances surrounding Rafael Mojica's disappearance, including the threats made against him, give rise to a strong inference that he was tortured or subjected to cruel and inhuman treatment. Nothing has been submitted to the Committee by the State party to dispel or counter this inference. Aware of the nature of enforced or involuntary disappearances in many countries, the Committee feels confident to conclude that the disappearance of persons is inseparably linked to treatment that amounts to a violation of article 7.

[9.79] A distinction may be drawn between the *Mojica* decision, and those in *Laureano v Peru* (540/93), *Tshishimbi v Zaire* (542/93), and *Shaw v Jamaica* (704/96) [9.71]. The latter cases involved findings that incommunicado detention itself breached article 7, whereas in *Mojica* the article 7 finding was linked to acts which presumably occurred during such detention.

NON-USE OF STATEMENTS OBTAINED AFTER ARTICLE 7 TREATMENT IN JUDICIAL PROCEEDINGS

[9.80]   *GENERAL COMMENT 20*

¶ 12. It is important for the discouragement of violations under article 7 that the law must prohibit the use or admissibility in judicial proceedings of statements or confessions obtained through torture or other prohibited treatment.

Article 7 in this respect complements article 14(3)(g).[84] The corresponding guarantee in CAT is in article 15.

DUTIES TO REMEDY BREACHES OF ARTICLE 7

Duty to Pass and Enforce Legislation

[9.81]   *GENERAL COMMENT 20*

¶ 13. States parties should indicate when presenting their reports the provisions of their criminal law which penalize torture and cruel, inhuman and degrading treatment or punishment, specifying the penalties applicable to such acts, whether committed by public officials or other persons acting on behalf of the State, or by private persons. Those who violate article 7, whether by encouraging, ordering, tolerating or perpetrating prohibited acts, must be held responsible. Consequently, those who have refused to obey orders must not be punished or subjected to any adverse treatment.

The duty to pass and enforce appropriate laws is also reflected in articles 2(1) and 4 of CAT.

---

[83] See [8.13].   [84] See [14.103–14.106].

[9.82] Paragraph 13 of the General Comment again stresses the obligation for States to proscribe 'article 7' treatment by private persons [9.19]. For example, regarding Yemen, the HRC expressed concern about the State Party's lack of laws dealing with domestic violence.[85] States Parties must also ensure that their laws do not permit unjustified defences for perpetrators of article 7 treatment, and that the gravity of an offence is sufficiently recognized in law. For example, regarding Peru, the HRC stated:[86]

¶ 15. The Committee notes with concern that the law still contains a provision exempting a rapist from punishment if he marries his victim and another which classifies rape as an offence prosecutable privately.

Duty to Investigate Allegations of Article 7 Treatment

[9.83]   *GENERAL COMMENT 20*

¶ 14. Article 7 should be read in conjunction with article 2, paragraph 3, of the Covenant. In their reports, States parties should indicate how their legal system effectively guarantees the immediate termination of all the acts prohibited by article 7 as well as appropriate redress. The right to lodge complaints against maltreatment prohibited by article 7 must be recognized in the domestic law. Complaints must be investigated promptly and impartially by competent authorities so as to make the remedy effective. The reports of States parties should provide specific information on the remedies available to victims of maltreatment and the procedure that complainants must follow, and statistics on the number of complaints and how they have been dealt with.

The corresponding duty in CAT is reflected in articles 12 to 14.

[9.84]   *HERRERA RUBIO v COLOMBIA (161/83)*

The duty to investigate specific allegations of torture and other ill treatment was confirmed in this case.

¶ 10.5. It is implicit in article 4, paragraph 2, of the Optional Protocol that the State party has the duty to investigate in good faith all allegations of violation of the Covenant made against it and its authorities, and to furnish to the Committee the information available to it. In no circumstances should a State party fail to investigate fully allegations of ill-treatment when the person or persons allegedly responsible for the ill-treatment are identified by the author of a communication. The State party has in this matter provided no precise information and reports, *inter alia*, on the questioning of military officials accused of maltreatment of prisoners, or on the questioning of their superiors.

---

[85] (1995) UN doc. CCPR/C/79/Add.51, para. 14.
[86] Concluding Comments on Peru (1996) UN doc. CCPR/C/79/Add. 67.

[9.85]   *HALIMI-NEDZIBI v AUSTRIA (CAT 8/91)*

The author was arrested in April 1988 and charged with drug-trafficking. The author made various allegations of torture and other ill-treatment by police during their investigations. The author also made the following complaint:

¶ 3. The author claims that the failure of the Austrian authorities promptly to investigate his allegations of torture and the refusal of the courts of first and second instance to exclude as evidence against him statements allegedly made by him and several witnesses as a result of torture constitute a violation of articles 12 and 15 of the Convention.

On the merits, the CAT Committee agreed with the author that the State Party had failed adequately to investigate his allegations of ill-treatment.

¶ 13.5. It remains to be determined whether the State party complied with its duty to proceed to a prompt and impartial investigation of the author's allegations that he had been subjected to torture, as provided in article 12 of the Convention. The Committee notes that the author made his allegations before the investigating judge on 5 December 1988. Although the investigating judge questioned the police officers about the allegations on 16 February 1989, no investigation took place until 5 March 1990, when criminal proceedings against the police officers were instituted. The Committee considers that a delay of 15 months before an investigation of allegations of torture is initiated, is unreasonably long and not in compliance with the requirement of article 12 of the Convention.

The *Halimi-Nedzibi* decision is particularly interesting, as the CAT Committee had earlier found that the actual allegations of ill-treatment were not sustained.[87] Thus, the duty to investigate allegations of torture under CAT is completely independent of the duty not to torture.

[9.86] The HRC has stressed the need for impartial, preferably external, investigations of allegations of brutality by the military and/or the police in a number of Concluding Comments.[88] Regarding Hong Kong, the HRC stated the following:

¶ 11. [The HRC] notes that the investigation of [complaints of human rights abuses by police] rests within the Police Force itself rather than being carried out in a manner that ensures its independence and credibility. In light of the high proportion of complaints against police officers which are found by investigating police to be unsubstantiated, the Committee expresses concern about the credibility of the investigation process and takes the view that investigation into complaints of abuse of authority by members of the Police Force must be, and must appear to be, fair and independent and therefore must be entrusted to an independent mechanism.[89]

The HRC made similar recommendations to the government of Brazil:[90]

---

[87] Para. 13.4.

[88] See, e.g., Concluding Comments on the United Kingdom (1995) UN Doc. CCPR/C/79/Add.5, para. 14; Concluding Comments on Chile (1999) UN doc. CCPR/C/79/Add. 104, para. 10.

[89] (1996) UN Doc. CCPR/C/79/Add.57. See also Concluding Comments on Zambia (1996) UN doc. CCPR/C/79/Add.62, para. 12.

[90] (1996) UN doc. CCPR/C/79/Add. 66.

¶ 22. The Committee strongly recommends that all complaints of misconduct by members of security forces be investigated by an independent body and not by the security forces themselves. Formal mechanisms for receipt and investigation of such complaints should be established in all areas of the country and their existence publicized. Such mechanisms must make provision for effective protection of complainants and witnesses against intimidation and reprisals.

[9.87] Of course, one should not be subject to victimization because one has made a complaint about one's treatment. In this respect, the HRC noted with concern that in Brazil:[91]

¶ 12. . . . [w]here members of State security forces are accused of human rights violations witnesses are not afforded protection against reprisals, intimidation, threats and harassment. . . .

Duty to Punish Offenders

[9.88] It is implicit in the duty to pass and enforce legislation that perpetrators of torture, or cruel, inhuman, or degrading treatment, be appropriately punished. Such a duty is explicit in article 4 CAT.

GENERAL COMMENT 20

¶ 15. The Committee has noted that some States have granted amnesty in respect of acts of torture. Amnesties are generally incompatible with the duty of States to investigate such acts; to guarantee freedom from such acts within their jurisdiction; and to ensure that they do not occur in the future. States may not deprive individuals of the right to an effective remedy, including compensation and such full rehabilitation as may be possible.

[9.89] The HRC's condemnation of amnesties expressly applies only in regard to torturers, rather than perpetrators of other article 7 treatment. However, the obligation to provide redress for victims, and to punish their tormentors,[92] may effectively prohibit amnesties for persons who have treated others in an inhuman or degrading fashion. The issue of amnesty laws arose in the following case.

[9.90]   *RODRIGUEZ v URUGUAY (322/88)*

The author submitted that he had been subjected to torture by Uruguayan police in June 1983. He was detained from June 1983 to December 1984. In 1985, a new government replaced the military junta in Uruguay. The author complained about the failure of this new government to provide him with any redress for the human rights violations that had occurred under the previous regime.

¶ 2.2. The author states that during his detention and even thereafter, until the transition from military to civilian rule, no judicial investigation of his case could be initiated. After

---

[91] (1996) UN doc. CCPR/C/79/Add. 66.   [92] See [9.81] ff.

the reintroduction of constitutional guarantees in March 1985, a formal complaint was filed with the competent authorities. On 27 September 1985, a class action was brought before the Court of First Instance (Juzgado Letrado de Primera Instancia en lo Penal de 4 Turno) denouncing the torture, including that suffered by the author, perpetrated on the premises of the secret police. The judicial investigation was not, however, initiated because of a dispute over the court's jurisdiction, as the military insisted that only military courts could legitimately carry out the investigations. At the end of 1986, the Supreme Court of Uruguay held that the civilian courts were competent, but in the meantime, the Parliament had enacted, on 22 December 1986, Law No. 15,848, the Limitations Act or Law of Expiry (Ley de Caducidad) which effectively provided for the immediate end of judicial investigation into such matters and made impossible the pursuit of this category of crimes committed during the years of military rule.

The complaint:

¶ 3. The author denounces the acts of torture to which he was subjected as a violation of article 7 of the Covenant and contends that he and others have been denied appropriate redress in the form of investigation of the abuses allegedly committed by the military authorities, punishment of those held responsible and compensation to the victims. In this context, he notes that the State party has systematically instructed judges to apply Law No. 15,848 uniformly and close pending investigations; the President of the Republic himself allegedly advised that this procedure should be applied without exceptions. The author further contends that the State party cannot, by simple legislative act, violate its international commitments and thus deny justice to all the victims of human rights abuses committed under the previous military régime.

The State Party defended its amnesty law:

¶ 8.1. On 3 November 1992 the State party submitted [that] the State's power to declare an amnesty or to bar criminal proceedings are 'matters pertaining exclusively to its domestic legal system, which by definition have constitutional precedence'.

¶ 8.2. The State party emphasizes that Law No. 15,848 on the lapsing of State prosecutions was endorsed in 1989 by referendum, 'an exemplary expression of direct democracy on the part of the Uruguayan people'. Moreover, by decision of 2 May 1988, the Supreme Court declared the Law to be constitutional. It maintains that the law constitutes a sovereign act of clemency that is fully in accord and harmony with the international instruments on human rights.

¶ 8.3. It is argued that notions of democracy and reconciliation ought to be taken into account when considering laws on amnesty and on the lapsing of prosecutions. In this context, the State party indicates that other relevant laws were adopted, including Law No. 15,737, adopted on 15 March 1985, which decreed an amnesty for all ordinary political and related military offences committed since 1 January 1962, and which recognizes the right of all Uruguayans wishing to return to the country to do so, and the right of all public officials dismissed by the military government to be reinstated in their respective positions. This law expressly excluded from the amnesty offences involving inhuman or degrading treatment or the disappearance of persons under the responsibility of police officers or members of the armed forces. By Law No. 15,783 of 28 November 1985, persons who had been arbitrarily dismissed for political, ideological or trade-union reasons were entitled to reinstatement.

¶ 8.4. With regard to the right to judicial safeguards and the obligation to investigate, the State party asserts that Law No. 15,848 in no way restricts the system of judicial remedies established in article 2, paragraph 3, of the Covenant. Pursuant to this Law only the State's right to bring criminal charges lapsed. The law did not eliminate the legal effects of offences in areas outside the sphere of criminal law. Moreover, the State argues, its position is consistent with the judgment of the Inter-American Court of Human Rights in the case of *Velasquez Rodríguez* that the international protection of human rights should not be confused with criminal justice (paragraph 174).

¶ 8.5. In this connection, the State party contends that 'to investigate past events . . . is tantamount to reviving the confrontation between persons and groups. This certainly will not contribute to reconciliation, pacification and the strengthening of democratic institutions'. Moreover, 'the duty to investigate' does not appear in the Covenant or any express provision and there are consequently no rules governing the way this function is to be exercised. Nor is there any indication in the Convention text concerning its precedence or superiority over other duties—such as the duty to punish—nor, of course, concerning any sort of independent legal life detached from the legal and political context within which human rights as a whole come into play . . . the State can, subject to the law and in certain circumstances, refrain from making available to the person concerned the means of establishing the truth formally and officially in a criminal court, which is governed by public, not private interest. This, of course, does not prevent or limit the free exercise by such a person of his individual rights, such as the right to information, which in many cases in themselves lead to the discovery of the truth, even if it is not the public authorities themselves that concern themselves with the matter'.

¶ 8.6. With regard to the author's contention that Law No. 15,848 'frustrates any attempt to obtain compensation, as the enforcement of the law bars an official investigation of his allegations' the State party asserts that there have been many cases in which claims similar to that of the author have succeeded in civil actions and that payment has been obtained.

On the merits, the HRC initially found that the author had been tortured by the military regime in Uruguay in violation of article 7. It made the following comments about the State's amnesty law:

¶ 12.2. As to the appropriate remedy that the author may claim pursuant to article 2, paragraph 3, of the Covenant, the Committee finds that the adoption of Law No. 15,848 and subsequent practice in Uruguay have rendered the realization of the author's right to an adequate remedy extremely difficult.

¶ 12.3. The Committee cannot agree with the State party that it has no obligation to investigate violations of Covenant rights by a prior régime, especially when these include crimes as serious as torture. Article 2, paragraph 3(a) of the Covenant clearly stipulates that each State party undertakes 'to ensure that any person whose rights or freedoms as herein recognised are violated shall have an effective remedy, notwithstanding that the violation has been committed by persons acting in an official capacity'. In this context the Committee refers to its General Comment No. 20 on article 7 . . . which provides that allegations of torture must be fully investigated by the State. . . . The State party has suggested that the author may still conduct private investigations into his torture. The Committee finds that the responsibility for investigations falls under the State party's obligation to grant an effective remedy. Having examined the specific circumstances of this case, the Committee finds that the author has not had an effective remedy.

¶ 12.4. The Committee moreover reaffirms its position that amnesties for gross violations of human rights and legislation such as the Law No. 15,848, Ley de Caducidad de la Pretensión Punitiva del Estado are incompatible with the obligations of the State party under the Covenant. The Committee notes with deep concern that the adoption of this law effectively excludes in a number of cases the possibility of investigation into past human rights abuses and thereby prevents the State party from discharging its responsibility to provide effective remedies to the victims of those abuses. Moreover, the Committee is concerned that, in adopting this law, the State party has contributed to an atmosphere of impunity which may undermine the democratic order and give rise to further grave human rights violations. . . .

¶ 13. The Human Rights Committee, acting under article 5, paragraph 4, of the Optional Protocol, is of the view that the facts before it disclose a violation of article 7, in connection with article 2, paragraph 3, of the Covenant.

¶ 14. The Committee is of the view that Mr. Hugo Rodríguez is entitled, under article 2, paragraph 3(a), of the Covenant, to an effective remedy. It urges the State party to take effective measures (a) to carry out an official investigation into the author's allegations of torture, in order to identify the persons responsible for torture and ill-treatment and to enable the author to seek civil redress; (b) to grant appropriate compensation to Mr. Rodríguez, and (c) to ensure that similar violations do not occur in the future.

[9.91] It has been confirmed in numerous cases that the ICCPR contains no independent right to see another prosecuted.[93] However, it seems that the duty to investigate alleged violations of the ICCPR[94] may on occasion entail a duty to prosecute a certain person.[95]

[9.92] The HRC have consistently condemned impunity statutes in its Concluding Comments on numerous States Parties.[96] CAT have similarly condemned amnesty statutes[97] and States with a culture of impunity.[98]

[9.93] In its Concluding Comments regarding Spain in 1996, the HRC was

---

[93] See, e.g., *H.C.M.A. v The Netherlands* (213/1986), *S.E. v Argentina* (275/1988).

[94] This duty has been confirmed expressly with regard to art. 6 (see [8.08–8.13]) as well as art. 7 [9.83–9.87]. Presumably the duty could arise with regard to other ICCPR violations.

[95] In this respect, see [8.15–8.17]; see also *Vicente et al. v Colombia* (612/95), paras. 8.2–8.3.

[96] See Concluding Comments on El Salvador (1994) UN doc. CCPR/C/79/Add.34, para. 7; Concluding Comments on Bolivia (1998) UN doc. CCPR/C/79/Add.73, para. 15; Concluding Comments on Lebanon (1998) UN doc. CCPR/C/79/Add.78, para. 12; Concluding Comments on Chile (1999) UN doc. CCPR/C/79/Add. 104, para. 7; Concluding Comments on Sudan (1997) UN doc. CCPR/C/79/Add. 85, para. 17; Concluding Comments on Cambodia (1999) UN doc. CCPR/C/79/Add. 108, para. 6.

[97] See, e.g., CAT Concluding Comments on Senegal, UN doc. A/51/44, para. 112.

[98] See, e.g., CAT Concluding Comments on Colombia, UN doc. A/51/44, para. 80.

concerned over the lenient sentences given to police officers convicted of human rights abuses.

¶ 10. [W]hen members of the security forces are found guilty of [ill-treatment and even torture] and sentenced to deprivation of liberty, they are often pardoned or released early, or simply do not serve their sentences. Moreover, those who perpetrate such deeds are seldom suspended from their functions for any length of time.[99]

Thus, perpetrators of article 7 treatment must not only be punished, but must incur adequate penalties.[100]

DUTY TO PROSECUTE OR EXTRADITE TORTURERS

[9.94] Articles 4 to 9 of CAT prescribe duties with respect to the exercise of State jurisdiction over alleged torturers caught within their territorial jurisdiction. First, these articles confer universal jurisdiction upon States Parties with regard to the crime of torture. Thus, States Parties may exercise jurisdiction to prosecute an alleged torturer, even in the absence of a territorial or personal link to the crime.[101] Secondly, the CAT *requires* States Parties either to exercise its jurisdiction to refer the case of an alleged torturer to its competent authorities for the purpose of prosecution, or to extradite that person to a State where he/she will be prosecuted.[102] Of course, certain procedural safeguards are guaranteed to the alleged torturer. For example, a State Party would not be required to prosecute or extradite an alleged torturer in the absence of adequate evidence of that person's guilt.

It is uncertain, and perhaps unlikely, that the ICCPR confers any duties upon States with regard to the exercise of universal jurisdiction over alleged torturers.

Article 10

1. All persons deprived of their liberty shall be treated with humanity and with respect for the inherent dignity of the human person.

---

[99] UN doc. CCPR/C/79/Add.61.

[100] See also the criticism of 'inadequacy of sanctions against police and prison officers' in Concluding Comments on Italy (1998) CCPR/C/79/Add. 94, para. 13.

[101] A territorial link arises where the crime occurs within a State's territory. A personal link arises where the victim or perpetrator is a national of that State. See M. Lippman, 'The Development and Drafting of the United Nations Convention Against Torture and other Cruel, Inhuman and Degrading Treatment or Punishment' (1994) 17 *Boston College International and Comparative Law Review* 275, 316–17. See, on universal jurisdiction, H. Steiner and P. Alston, *International Human Rights in Context* (Clarendon Press, Oxford, 1996) 1021–40. See also *R. v Bartle and the Commissioner of Police for the Metropolis and others, ex parte Pinochet* [1999] 2 WLR 827, where the House of Lords decided that the UK could extradite the General to Spain to face charges of torture as the UK's domestic incorporation of CAT had displaced Pinochet's pre-existing sovereign immunity from prosecution. Ultimately, the UK allowed Pinochet to return to Chile, due to the General's ill health and presumed incapacity to stand trial fairly. The General may now face prosecution in Chile.

[102] See also Boulesbaa, above, n. 9, 177–235; Burgers and Danelius, above, note 8, 129–41.

2. (a) Accused persons shall, save in exceptional circumstances, be segregated from convicted persons and shall be subject to separate treatment appropriate to their status as unconvicted persons;

(b) Accused juvenile persons shall be separated from adults and brought as speedily as possible for adjudication.

3. The penitentiary system shall comprise treatment of prisoners the essential aim of which shall be their reformation and social rehabilitation. Juvenile offenders shall be segregated from adults and be accorded treatment appropriate to their age and legal status.

[9.95] Article 10(1) of the ICCPR guarantees that States treat persons in detention with humanity and dignity. Article 10(2) and (3) reinforces specific aspects of this right. Article 10 seems to prohibit a less serious form of treatment than that prohibited by article 7. It provides extra protection for a particularly vulnerable group, persons deprived of their liberty. Finally, an important distinction between articles 7 and 10 is that the latter is a derogable right.

[9.96] Article 10 complements article 9. While the latter article regulates the reasons for which one may be detained,[103] article 10 regulates the conditions of such detention.

MEANING OF 'PERSONS DEPRIVED OF THEIR LIBERTY'

[9.97]   *GENERAL COMMENT 21*

¶ 2. Article 10, paragraph 1, of the International Covenant on Civil and Political Rights applies to anyone deprived of liberty under the laws and authority of the State who is held in prisons, hospitals—particularly psychiatric hospitals—detention camps or correctional institutions or elsewhere. States parties should ensure that the principle stipulated therein is observed in all institutions and establishments within their jurisdiction where persons are being held.

Paragraph 2 of the General Comment confirms that article 10(1) regulates conditions in all forms of detention. In *Mpandanjila et al. v Zaire* (138/83), the HRC even found a breach of article 10(1) entailed in ill-treatment suffered during a 'period of banishment'. Nowak has noted with regard to *Mpandanjila* that the 'supervision and isolation from the environment were so severe that the situation was more comparable to detention than banishment'.[104]

PRIVATE DETENTION INSTITUTIONS

[9.98] Article 10(1) obviously applies to State-run detention institutions. However, numerous States, such as the UK and Australia, now authorize the

---

[103] See Chap. 11 on art. 9.   [104] Nowak, above, note 3, 186.

detention of persons in privately-run institutions. As such detention is still 'under the law and authority of the State', it is presumed that such detentions are within the ambit of article 10(1).[105]

[9.99] The HRC has quizzed the United Kingdom on the 'contracting out' of operations dealing with detainees:

¶ 17. The Committee is concerned that the practice of the State party in contracting out to the private commercial sector core State activities which involve the use of force and the detention of persons weakens the protection of rights under the Covenant. The Committee stresses that the State party remains responsible in all circumstances for adherence to all articles of the Covenant.

¶ 26. The Committee recommends that the use of the private commercial sector in the detention, transport and deportation of prisoners be reviewed and that, pending its termination, no further detention tasks be contracted out by the Government. The State party should ensure that all those who are involved in the detention of prisoners be made fully aware of the international obligations on the State party concerning the treatment of detainees, including the United Nations Standard Minimum Rules for the Treatment of Prisoners.

This comment implies that article 10(1) rights apply in privately-run institutions of detention. However, the HRC recognized that less State control can be realistically exercised over such institutions, and it therefore expressed a preference that States do not 'privatize' operations dealing with detainees.

MINIMUM CONDITIONS OF DETENTION

[9.100]   *GENERAL COMMENT 21*

¶ 3. Article 10, paragraph 1, imposes on States parties a positive obligation towards persons who are particularly vulnerable because of their status as persons deprived of liberty, and complements for them the ban on torture or other cruel, inhuman or degrading treatment or punishment contained in article 7 of the Covenant. Thus, not only may persons deprived of their liberty not be subjected to treatment that is contrary to article 7, including medical or scientific experimentation, but neither may they be subjected to any hardship or constraint other than that resulting from the deprivation of liberty; respect for the dignity of such persons must be guaranteed under the same conditions as for that of free persons. Persons deprived of their liberty enjoy all the rights set forth in the Covenant, subject to the restrictions that are unavoidable in a closed environment.

¶ 4. Treating all persons deprived of their liberty with humanity and with respect for their dignity is a fundamental and universally applicable rule. Consequently, the application of this rule, as a minimum, cannot be dependent on the material resources available in the State party.[106] This rule must be applied without distinction of any kind, such as race, colour, sex, language, religion, political or other opinion, national or social origin, property, birth or other status.

---

[105] See also [22.44].   [106] See also [1.73] and [9.27].

¶ 5. States parties are invited to indicate in their reports to what extent they are applying the relevant United Nations standards applicable to the treatment of prisoners: the Standard Minimum Rules for the Treatment of Prisoners (1957), the Body of Principles for the Protection of All Persons under Any Form of Detention or Imprisonment (1988), the Code of Conduct for Law Enforcement Officials (1978) and the Principles of Medical Ethics relevant to the Role of Health Personnel, particularly Physicians, in the Protection of Prisoners and Detainees against Torture and Other Cruel, Inhuman or Degrading Treatment or Punishment (1982).

[9.101] Paragraph 3 implies that article 10 prohibits a less serious form of treatment than that prohibited by article 7.[107] This has been confirmed in the following cases.

KELLY v JAMAICA (253/1987)

¶ 5.7. Inasmuch as the author's claim under article 10 is concerned, the Committee reaffirms that the obligation to treat individuals with respect for the inherent dignity of the human person encompasses the provision of, *inter alia*, adequate medical care during detention. The provision of basic sanitary facilities to detained persons equally falls within the ambit of article 10. The Committee further considers that the provision of inadequate food to detained individuals and the total absence of recreational facilities does not, save under exceptional circumstances, meet the requirements of article 10.[108] In the author's case, the State party has not refuted the author's allegation that he has contracted health problems as a result of a lack of basic medical care, and that he is only allowed out of his cell for 30 minutes each day. As a result, his right under article 10, paragraph 1, of the Covenant has been violated.

The silence regarding article 7 may be interpreted as meaning that the conditions of Kelly's detention did not breach that provision. Compare the *Kelly* decision with the early decision in *Massera v Uruguay* (5/77) [9.69].

GRIFFIN v SPAIN (493/92)

¶ 3.1. The author claims that he has been subjected to cruel, inhuman and degrading treatment and punishment during his incarceration at the prison of Melilla. The living conditions in this prison are said to be 'worse than those depicted in the film "Midnight Express" '; a 500-year old prison, virtually unchanged, infested with rats, lice, cockroaches and diseases; 30 persons per cell, among them old men, women, adolescents and an eight-month old baby; no windows, but only steel bars open to the cold and the wind; high incidence of suicide, selfmutilation, violent fights and beatings; human faeces all over the floor as the toilet, a hole in the ground, was flowing over; sea water for showers and often for drink as well; urine soaked blankets and mattresses to sleep on in spite of the fact that the supply rooms were full of new bed linen, clothes etc. He adds that he has learned that the prison

---

[107] See also Ghandhi, above, note 27, 763.

[108] The HRC's implicit recognition that 'exceptional circumstances' may justify the absence of recreation facilities, and the failure to provide adequate food to detainees is worrying. However, the comment may simply acknowledge the status of art. 10(1) as a derogable right.

has been 'cleaned up' since the riots, but that he can provide the Committee with a list of witnesses and with a more detailed account of conditions and events in the said prison.

At the admissibility stage, the HRC stated:

¶ 6.3. The Committee noted that the author had invoked article 7 in respect of his allegations concerning the events and conditions of the prison of Melilla. It found, however, that the facts as described by the author fell rather within the scope of article 10.

Ultimately, the HRC found that the detention conditions as outlined by Griffin amounted to a breach of article 10(1).

TAYLOR v JAMAICA (707/96)

¶ 3.7. Counsel submits that the conditions at St. Catherine District Prison amount to a violation of the author's rights under articles 7 and 10, paragraph 1. Reference is made to the findings of various reports by non-governmental organizations on the conditions of St. Catherine's Prison. The actual conditions which are said by counsel to apply to the author on death row include being confined in the cell for 23 hours each day, no provision of mattress or bedding for the concrete bunk, no integral sanitation, inadequate ventilation and no natural lighting. In addition, the general conditions of the prison are also claimed to affect the author. Counsel contends that the author's rights as an individual under the Covenant are being violated, notwithstanding the fact that he is a member of a class—those on death row—whose rights are also being violated through being detained in similar conditions. In this respect, counsel contends that a violation of the Covenant does not cease to be a violation merely because others suffer the same deprivation at the same time. The conditions under which the author is detained at St. Catherine District Prison are said to amount to cruel, inhuman and degrading treatment within the meaning of articles 7 and 10. paragraph 1, of the Covenant.

¶ 3.8. Furthermore, counsel submits that the cells and prison conditions do not meet the fundamental and basic requirements of the United Nations Standard Minimum Rules for the Treatment of Prisoners and amount to violations of articles 7 and 10, paragraph 1, of the Covenant. ....

¶ 8.1. ... In the Committee's opinion, the [prison] conditions described therein and which affect the author directly are such as to violate his right to be treated with humanity and with respect for the inherent dignity of the human person, and are therefore contrary to article 10, paragraph 1.

[9.102] The above cases concerned complaints about the general conditions of detention. Perhaps article 10 applies when conditions of detention are generally poor, while article 7 applies where the author is specifically treated worse than others. Some support for this notion comes from the following case.

PINTO v TRINDIDAD and TOBAGO (512/92)

¶ 8.3. The author has complained about appalling conditions of detention and harassment at the Carrera Convict Prison. The State party has only refuted this allegation in general terms; on the other hand, the author has failed to provide details on the treatment he was subject to, other than by reference to conditions of detention that affected all inmates equally. On the basis of the material before it, the Committee concludes that there has been no violation of article 7.

Note, in particular, the reference in *Pinto* to 'conditions of detention that affected all inmates equally'. Do those words indicate that treatment, no matter how appalling, will fall outside article 7 if it is applied equally to all detainees? The HRC did not specifically say that the appalling prison conditions amounted to a breach of article 10(1), though this was possibly an oversight, as a violation of article 10(1) was found with regard to other allegations [9.112].

[9.103] In the very early case of *Massera v Uruguay* (5/77), the HRC found that 'detention in conditions detrimental to [one's] health' constituted a breach of article 7 [9.69]. However, subsequent cases, such as those excerpted directly above, indicate that the HRC has abandoned this early position. Indeed, Nowak contends that article 10(1) is primarily aimed at redressing a poor 'general state or a detention facility',[109] whereas article 7 is designed to redress 'specific, usually violent attacks on personal integrity'.[110] The above cases at [9.101–9.102] support Nowak's contention.

[9.104] However, the line between the two provisions is often blurred in HRC jurisprudence. In some cases, general conditions of detention have been so severe as to reach the threshold of severity for a violation of article 7 [9.67]. Furthermore, breaches of article 10 have been found in cases of specific attacks on people, as in the following case.

WALKER and RICHARDS v JAMAICA (639/95)

¶ 8.1. With regard to the alleged violation of article 10, paragraph 1, of the Covenant for ill-treatment in detention on death row, the Committee notes that in respect of Mr. Walker's complaint that he was beaten in May of 1990, which required five stitches for his injury, the State party admitted that these injuries occurred during the prison riots in May 1990

---

[109] See also *Párkányi v Hungary* (410/1990), para. 8.2; *Bennett v Jamaica* (590/94), para. 10.8; *Henry v Jamaica* (752/97), paras. 7.3–7.4, *Morgan and Williams v Jamaica* (720/96), para. 7.2; *Blaine v Jamaica* (696/96), para. 8.4; *Levy v Jamaica* (719/96), para. 7.4; *Taylor v Jamaica* (705/96), para. 7.4; *Shaw v Jamaica* (704/96), para. 7.2; *McTaggart v Jamaica* (749/97), paras. 8.5–8.6; *Yasseen and Thomas v Republic of Guyana* (676/96), paras. 7.4, 7.6; *Matthews v Trinidad and Tobago* (569/93), para. 7.3; *McLeod v Jamaica* (734/96), para. 6.4; *Polay Campos v Peru* (577/94), para. 8.4; *Johnson v Jamaica* (653/95), para. 8.2; *Campbell v Jamaica* (618/95), para. 7.2; *Phillip v Jamaica* (594/92), para. 7.4, *Pennant v Jamaica* (647/95), para. 8.4, *Forbes v Jamaica* (649/95), para. 7.5, where the HRC found a violation of art. 10(1) but not art. 7 entailed in awful prison conditions.

[110] Nowak, above, note 3, 188; Ghandhi, above, note 27, 769–71. See also *Chung v Jamaica* (591/94), where the author's 'beatings at the hands of warders' violated both arts. 7 and 10(1) (para. 8.2), and *McTaggart v Jamaica* (749/97) (author beaten and had belongings burnt), para. 8.7; *Johnson v Jamaica* (653/95) (beatings and threats, no medical treatment), para. 8.1; *Morrison v Jamaica* (663/95) (beatings), para. 8.3, *Pennant v Jamaica* (647/95), para. 8.3 (beatings by police); *Gallimore v Jamaica* (680/96), para. 7.1.

riots and that it would investigate the matter and inform the Committee. The Committee further notes that 20 months after the communication was brought to the attention of the State party and over 7 years after the events, no information has been received to explain the matter. In the circumstances and in the absence of information from the State party, the Committee finds that the treatment received by Mr. Walker on death row constitutes a violation of article 10, paragraph 1, of the Covenant.

Therefore, article 10 also redresses personal attacks which fall short of article 7 severity.[111]

[9.105] Often simultaneous breaches of both articles 7 and 10 are found.[112] This is not surprising, as treatment which violates article 7 will likely violate article 10 if the victim is a detainee. For example, in *Linton v Jamaica* (255/1987), the impugned treatment was found to constitute cruel and inhuman treatment contrary to article 7 [9.29]. The HRC then stated that this finding '*therefore* also entailed a violation of article 10, paragraph 1'.[113] Often, however, the article 7 finding will suffice and article 10 will not be specifically invoked or considered by the HRC.[114]

[9.106] In Concluding Comments on Cambodia, the HRC requested the State Party to ensure that 'women prisoners are guarded only by female warders'.[115] Many States Parties would breach the Covenant if male warders were totally prohibited from female prisons. The comment could have been motivated by evidence of widespread rape in Cambodian women's prisons.[116]

[9.107] The United Nations has adopted a number of non-binding codes regarding the treatment of detainees.[117] The HRC implicitly endorsed these UN Codes in its General Comment 21, at paragraph 5 [9.100].[118] Furthermore, in cases such as *Mukong v Cameroon*,[119] the HRC indicated that the norms found in the most famous of the UN codes, the Standard Minimum Rules for the Treatment of Prisoners 1957,[120] are incorporated into the article 10 guarantee.[121] The HRC has

---

[111] The victims in *Solórzano v Venezuela* (156/83), paras. 10.2, 12, *Chaplin v Jamaica* (596/94), para. 8.2, *Elahie v Jamaica* (553/93), para. 8.3, *Brown v Jamaica* (775/97), paras. 3.2, 6.5, *Jones v Jamaica* (585/94), para. 9.4, and *Marshall v Jamaica* (730/96), para. 6.7, also suffered from personal attacks on their person.

[112] See, e.g., *Francis v Jamaica* (320/1988), *Bailey v Jamaica* (334/1988), *Soogrim v Trinidad and Tobago* (362/1989), *Thomas v Jamaica* (321/1988), *Kanana v Zaire* (366/1989), *El-Megreisi v Libyan Arab Jamahiriya* (440/1990), *Bozize v Central African Republic* (428/1990), *Blanco v Nicaragua* (328/1988), *Reynolds v Jamaica* (587/1994), *Ortega v Ecuador* (481/1991).

[113] Para. 8.5, emphasis added.

[114] For example, this arguably occurred in *Rodriguez v Uruguay* (322/1988), where the art. 10 claim was inexplicably ignored at the admissibility stage. In *Mukong v Cameroon* (458/1991) [9.67], both the HRC and the complainant seemed to ignore the art. 10 implications of the facts.

[115] (1999) UN doc. CCPR/C/79/Add.108. [116] Ibid., para. 13.

[117] See generally S.M. Bernard, 'An Eye for an Eye: The Current Status of International Law on the Humane Treatment of Prisoners' (1994) 25 *Rutgers Law Journal* 759, 770–80.

[118] See also para. 13 [9.120]. [119] Para. 9.3 [9.67].

[120] ECOSOC Resolution 662 (XXIV).

[121] See also *Potter v New Zealand* (632/95), para. 6.3, stating that the Standard Minimum Rules 'constitute valuable guidelines for the interpretation of the Covenant'.

adopted a similar position in a significant number of Concluding Comments. For example, regarding the USA, the HRC stated:[122]

¶ 34. . . . Conditions of detention in prisons, in particular in maximum security prisons, should be scrutinized with a view to . . . implementing the Standard Minimum Rules for the Treatment of Prisoners and the Code of Conduct for Law Enforcement Officials therein.

Thus, it can be safely assumed that the Standard Minimum Rules, and possibly norms in other UN codes, have been elevated to norms of international treaty law in article 10(1) of the Covenant.

[9.108] The Standard Minimum Rules overlap to some extent with the express requirements of article 10. For example, Rule 8 provides for the separation of convicted and remand prisoners, and of juvenile and adult prisoners. The Standard Minimum Rules are most useful in identifying standards for 'humane' treatment.[123] For example, each prisoner should generally have his or her own cell, though some exceptions are permitted.[124] Lighting, heating, and ventilation, as well as work and sleep arrangements, should 'meet all the requirement of health'.[125] 'Adequate' bedding, clothing, food, and hygiene facilities must be supplied.[126] Rules 22 to 26 specify requisite medical services for prisoners. Rules 31 to 34 regulate disciplinary measures. Prisoners must also be permitted access to the outside world,[127] receive information concerning their rights,[128] have access to a prison library,[129] have a reasonable opportunity to practise their religion,[130] and have any confiscated property returned upon release.[131] Finally, prison wardens must inform a prisoner's family or designated representative if that prisoner dies or is seriously injured.[132] The prisoner must also be allowed to inform his/her family or representative of his or her imprisonment, and of any subsequent transfer to another institution.[133] Finally, the Rules must be applied without discrimination.[134]

Incommunicado Detention

[9.109] In a number of early cases against Uruguay, the HRC found that incommunicado detention 'for months' constituted a breach of article 10(1).[135] The shortest period of such detention which constituted a breach was fifteen days in *Arzuaga Gilboa v Uruguay* (147/83).[136] The Committee has not been called upon

---

[122] UN Doc. CCPR/C/79/Add.50 (1995) 2 IHRR 638; see also Concluding Comments on the Ukraine (1996) UN Doc. CCPR/C/79/Add.52, para. 24; Concluding Comments on Morocco (1995) UN Doc. CCPR/C/79/Add.44, para. 21, and Concluding Comments on the UK [9.99].
[123] See Bernard, above, note 117, 770–3.   [124] Rule 9.
[125] Rules 10–11.   [126] Rules 15–21.   [127] Rules 38–39.
[128] Rules 35–36.   [129] Rule 40.   [130] Rules 41–42.
[131] Rule 43.   [132] Rule 44. See also [8.34–8.35].   [133] Rule 44(3).
[134] Rule 6.
[135] See, e.g., *Valentini de Bazzano v Uruguay* (5/77), *Pietraroia v Uruguay* (44/79), *Cubas Simones v Uruguay* (70/80). See also *Peñarietta v Bolivia* (176/84).   [136] Para. 14.

to decide on the compatibility of shorter periods.[137] By the time such detention has lasted eight months, the incommunicado detention will amount to a breach of article 7.[138]

Communication with Family and Friends

[9.110] Much of the 'inhumanity' of incommunicado detention arises from the inability of the detainee to contact family and friends. The importance of family contact was clarified in the following case in the context of unreasonable censorship of a prisoner's mail.

ANGEL ESTRELLA v URUGUAY (74/80)

¶ 9.2. With regard to the censorship of Miguel Angel Estrella's correspondence, the Committee accepts that it is normal for prison authorities to exercise measures of control and censorship over prisoners' correspondence. Nevertheless, article 17 of the Covenant provides that 'no one shall be subjected to arbitrary or unlawful interference with his correspondence'. This requires that any such measures of control or censorship shall be subject to satisfactory legal safeguards against arbitrary application. . . . Furthermore, the degree of restriction must be consistent with the standard of humane treatment of detained persons required by article 10 (1) of the Covenant. In particular, prisoners should be allowed under necessary supervision to communicate with their family and reputable friends at regular intervals, by correspondence as well as by receiving visits. On the basis of the information before it, the Committee finds that Miguel Angel Estrella's correspondence was censored and restricted at Libertad prison to an extent which the State party has not justified as compatible with article 17 read in conjunction with article 10 (1) of the Covenant.[139]

A similar violation of article 10(1), entailed in a refusal to allow a prisoner to correspond with his family and friends, was found in *Kulomin v Hungary* (521/92).

Death Row Phenomenon

[9.111] With regard to the death row phenomenon, the comments above regarding article 7 apply equally to article 10(1).[140] Current jurisprudence indicates that the death row phenomenon *per se* is not a breach of article 10(1).

Victimization

[9.112] The author in *Pinto v Trinidad and Tobago* (512/92) had successfully challenged the fairness of his trial in the earlier communication of *Pinto v Trinidad and Tobago* (232/87). In the later case, the HRC found a violation of article 10(1) entailed in the consequent victimization of the author:[141]

---

[137] N. Rodley, 'Rights and Responses to Terrorism in Northern Ireland' in D. Harris and S. Joseph (eds.), *The International Covenant on Civil and Political Rights and United Kingdom Law* (Clarendon Press, Oxford, 1995), 130. [138] See *Shaw v Jamaica* (704/96) [9.71].
[139] See also [16.26]. [140] See [9.39] ff.
[141] Victimization also occurred on the facts of *Elahie v Trinidad and Tobago* (553/93) and *Wolf v Panama* (289/88), para. 2.8.

¶ 8.3. [T]o convey to the author that the prerogative of mercy would not be exercised and his early release denied because of his human rights complaints reveal lack of humanity and amount to treatment that fails to respect the author's dignity, in violation of article 10, paragraph 1.

INCONSISTENCIES BETWEEN ARTICLES 7 AND 10(1)

[9.113] Some HRC cases on articles 7 and 10(1), particularly cases involving allegations of numerous human rights violations, evince inconsistencies. Indeed, some article 7 violations do not seem to involve human rights abuses which are objectively worse than in other cases where only article 10(1) has been violated.[142] Furthermore, the prison conditions described in *Deidrick v Jamaica* [9.29] seem virtually identical to those in *Taylor v Jamaica* [9.101]; article 7 was breached in the former case but not the latter. A recent example of apparent HRC confusion over articles 7 and 10(1) arose in *Mojica v Dominican Republic* (449/91). In that case, the HRC found that, in the light of Mojica's disappearance, they could assume that violations of article 7 had occurred [9.78]. However, they had earlier found an article 10(1) claim inadmissible for non-substantiation; 'it related to what might hypothetically have happened to Rafael Mojica after his disappearance'.[143]

It may be argued that a State is sufficiently rebuked if it is found to have violated either article 7 or 10(1). However, breaches of article 7 undoubtedly impact more on a State's reputation than violations of article 10(1). It is hoped that future HRC jurisprudence regarding articles 7 and 10(1) is more consistent and uniformly coherent.

POSITIVE DUTIES UNDER ARTICLE 10(1)

[9.114]   *GENERAL COMMENT 21*

¶ 6. The Committee recalls that reports should provide detailed information on national legislative and administrative provisions that have a bearing on the right provided for in article 10, paragraph 1. The Committee also considers that it is necessary for reports to specify what concrete measures have been taken by the competent authorities to monitor the effective application of the rules regarding the treatment of persons deprived of their liberty. States parties should include in their reports information concerning the system for supervising penitentiary establishments, the specific measures to prevent torture and cruel, inhuman or degrading treatment, and how impartial supervision is ensured.

---

[142] Compare the violations of art. 7 in *Young v Jamaica* [9.30], *Massera v Uruguay* [9.69], *Portorreal v Dominican Republic* [9.67], *Edwards v Jamaica* [9.67], with those in *Griffin v Spain* [9.101]; see also *Cámpora Schweizer v Uruguay* (66/80) for an art. 10(1) violation which resembled earlier art. 7 violations.

[143] Para. 4.2.

¶ 7. Furthermore, the Committee recalls that reports should indicate whether the various applicable provisions form an integral part of the instruction and training of the personnel who have authority over persons deprived of their liberty and whether they are strictly adhered to by such personnel in the discharge of their duties. It would also be appropriate to specify whether arrested or detained persons have access to such information and have effective legal means enabling them to ensure that those rules are respected, to complain if the rules are ignored and to obtain adequate compensation in the event of a violation.

[9.115] Paragraphs 6 and 7 mirror obligations outlined with regard to article 7.[144] The HRC has expressed concern about Sri Lanka's failure to observe its positive obligations under article 10:[145]

¶ 18. The Committee . . . regrets that conditions in places of detention other than prisons are not regulated by law and that prisons and other places of detention are not regularly visited by magistrates or other independent bodies.

[9.116] Fulfilment of procedural duties regarding humane treatment of detainees assists in the prevention of substantive article 10 rights. Inadequate procedures can mean that a State will find it difficult to refute allegations of breaches of article 10. An example of the evidential consequences of a State's failure to keep adequate prison records is found in the following case.

HILL and HILL v SPAIN (526/93)

The authors claimed, *inter alia*, that they were denied food for five of the ten days they were kept in police custody. The State Party submitted records, allegedly signed by the authors, to refute this allegation. The Hills challenged the adequacy of the State Party's evidence:

¶ 10.4. They reaffirm that they did not receive any food or drink for a period of five days and very little thereafter, because the allocation of funds specifically for this purpose were misappropriated. They point out that the State party's list does not refer to the first five days, when they allege to have been totally deprived of subsistence. The lists presented by the State refer to 11 days, and only two of these, the 21st and 24th July, show their signature.

On the merits, the HRC found in favour of the Hill brothers regarding the article 10 allegation:

¶ 13. With respect to the authors' allegations regarding their treatment during detention, particularly during the first 10 days when they were in police custody . . ., the Committee notes that the information and documents submitted by the State party do not refute the authors' claim that they were not given any food during the first five days of police detention. The Committee concludes that such treatment amounts to a violation of article 10 of the Covenant.

---

[144] See [9.75–9.93].
[145] Concluding Comments on Sri Lanka (1996) UN doc. CCPR/C/79/Add.56.

ARTICLE 10(2)(A)—SEGREGATION OF ACCUSED PERSONS FROM CONVICTED PERSONS

[9.117]   *GENERAL COMMENT 21*

¶ 9. Article 10, paragraph 2 (a), provides for the segregation, save in exceptional circumstances, of accused persons from convicted ones. Such segregation is required in order to emphasize their status as unconvicted persons who at the same time enjoy the right to be presumed innocent as stated in article 14, paragraph 2. The reports of States parties should indicate how the separation of accused persons from convicted persons is effected and explain how the treatment of accused persons differs from that of convicted persons.

[9.118]   *PINKNEY v CANADA (27/78)*

Pinkney was a prisoner on remand in Canada. Though his cell was in a separate area from those of convicted prisoner, convicted prisoners did serve food and work as cleaners in the remand unit. The HRC found that this arrangement did not breach article 10(2)(a):

¶ 30. The Committee is of the opinion that the requirement of article 10(2)(a) of the Covenant that 'accused persons shall, save in exceptional circumstances, be segregated from convicted persons' means that they shall be kept in separate quarters (but not necessarily in separate buildings). The Committee would not regard the arrangements described by the State party whereby convicted persons work as food servers and cleaners in the remand area of the prison as being incompatible with article 10 (2) (a), provided that contacts between the two classes of prisoners are kept strictly to a minimum necessary for the performance of those tasks.

[9.119] A breach of article 10(2)(a) was found on the facts in *Wolf v Panama* (289/88) as the author was housed in a prison for convicted offenders.[146]

ARTICLE 10(2)(B) AND 10(3)—PROTECTION FOR JUVENILE DETAINEES

[9.120]   *GENERAL COMMENT 21*

¶ 13. Article 10, paragraph 2 (b), provides that accused juvenile persons shall be separated from adults. The text also provides that cases involving juveniles must be considered as speedily as possible. Reports should specify the measures taken by States parties to give effect to that provision. Lastly, under article 10, paragraph 3, juvenile offenders shall be segregated from adults and be accorded treatment appropriate to their age and legal status in so far as conditions of detention are concerned, such as shorter working hours and contact with relatives, with the aim of furthering their reformation and rehabilitation. Article 10 does not indicate any limits of juvenile age. While this is to be determined by each State party in the light of relevant social, cultural and other conditions, the Committee is

---

[146] Para. 6.8; see also *Morrison v Jamaica* (663/95), para. 8.3.

of the opinion that article 6, paragraph 5, suggests that all persons under the age of 18 should be treated as juveniles, at least in matters relating to criminal justice. States should give relevant information about the age groups of persons treated as juveniles. In that regard, States parties are invited to indicate whether they are applying the United Nations Standard Minimum Rules for the Administration of Juvenile Justice, known as the Beijing Rules (1987).

Article 10 reinforces article 24 ICCPR which provides general protection for children's rights.[147]

[9.121] In *Thomas v Jamaica* (800/98), the detention of the author from the ages of 15 and 17 with adult prisoners breached article 10(2)(b) and (3).[148] Furthermore, the HRC has expressed concern over laws and practices in Cyprus:[149]

¶ 13. The Committee is concerned . . . that persons between the age of sixteen and eighteen are not considered child or youthful offenders and are subject to penal sanction.

ARTICLE 10(3)—REHABILITATIVE PURPOSE FOR DETENTION

[9.122]   *GENERAL COMMENT 21*

¶ 10. As to article 10, paragraph 3, which concerns convicted persons, the Committee wishes to have detailed information on the operation of the penitentiary system of the State party. No penitentiary system should be only retributory; it should essentially seek the reformation and social rehabilitation of the prisoner. States parties are invited to specify whether they have a system to provide assistance after release and to give information as to its success.

¶ 11. . . . The Committee requests specific information concerning the measures taken to provide teaching, education and re-education, vocational guidance and training and also concerning work programmes for prisoners inside the penitentiary establishment as well as outside.

¶ 12. In order to determine whether the principle set forth in article 10, paragraph 3, is being fully respected, the Committee also requests information on the specific measures applied during detention, e.g., how convicted persons are dealt with individually and how they are categorized, the disciplinary system, solitary confinement and high-security detention and the conditions under which contacts are ensured with the outside world (family, lawyer, social and medical services, and non-governmental organizations).

[9.123] Article 10(3) seems a controversial inclusion in the ICCPR, as it purports to dictate the policy States should adopt with regard to the treatment of offenders. The preponderance of 'law and order' campaigns throughout the world indicates

---

[147] See Chap. 21. See also R. Levesque, 'Future Visions of Juvenile Justice: Lessons from International and Comparative Law' (1996) 29 *Creighton Law Review* 1563.

[148] Para. 6.5.

[149] Concluding Comments on Cyprus (1994) UN doc. CCPR/C/79/Add.39.

that prison policy has become a highly politicized area in recent years.[150] The 'rehabilitation' paradigm was more prevalent, at least in Western criminal justice systems, when the ICCPR was adopted in 1966. In more recent times in many States there has been a trend towards harsher penalties and prison conditions, evincing a shift towards the 'retribution' model of criminal sociology. It is possible that the 'rehabilitation' aspect of article 10(3) has become an anachronism at the beginning of the twenty-first century.[151]

[9.124] Article 10(3) has arisen in very few Optional Protocol cases. Indeed, it seems very difficult to establish that one was a specific 'victim' of a State's failure to adopt a rehabilitation model of criminal justice.[152] Only Mme Chanet has found an article 10(3) issue to be admissible. In *Hankle v Jamaica* (710/96), the author claimed that his life sentence for murder, which included a twenty-year non-parole period, breached article 7.[153] The HRC majority found this claim to be unsubstantiated.[154] Mme Chanet felt that the rehabilitation aspect of article 10(3) should have rendered this complaint admissible, as it should have:

. . . prompted the Committee to admit the communication and examine on its merits the compatibility of a mandatory penalty of 20 years with a text stipulating that the aim of that penalty is to rehabilitate the offender.

The question to be argued should have been the following: does not the inability to modify the penalty for such a long period constitute an obstacle to the social rehabilitation of the prisoner?

Mme Chanet's dissent indicates that mandatory sentencing regimes are incompatible with article 10(3). The HRC's failure to consider the issue on the merits indicates that the 'rehabilitation' aspect of article 10(3) is a weak and perhaps empty guarantee.

[9.125] The HRC has referred to article 10(3) in its Concluding Comments on Belgium:[155]

¶ 16. [A]lternative sentencing, including community service, should be encouraged in view of its rehabilitative function. . . .

¶ 19. Bearing in mind that pursuant to article 10, paragraph 3, of the Covenant, the essential aim of incarceration should be the reformation and social rehabilitation of offenders, the Committee urges the State party to develop rehabilitation programmes both for the time during imprisonment and for the period after release, when ex-offenders must be reintegrated into society if they are not to become recidivists.

---

[150] 'Law and order' has, for example, been a major electoral issue in recent years in the USA, the UK, and various States in Australia.

[151] See, e.g., P. Roberts, 'Recent Trends in English Penal Policy' in A. Kwak and R. Dingwall (eds.), *Social Chance, Social Policy and Social Work in the New Europe* (Ashgate, Aldershot, 1998).

[152] The art. 10(3) complaint in *Lewis v Jamaica* (708/96) was inadmissible as the author could not establish 'victimhood'.   [153] Para. 3.1.

[154] Para. 6.3.   [155] (1998) UN doc. CCPR/C/79/Add. 99.

[9.126] Besides the Belgian comment, the rehabilitation aspect of article 10(3) has been ignored in HRC Concluding Comments, which may prompt speculation that its specific 'rehabilitation obligation' has become largely a dead letter. However, proper adherence to the other aspects of article 10, which have been vigorously monitored by the HRC, would result in a humane penitentiary system which would aid the reformation and rehabilitation of inmates.[156]

Conclusion

[9.127] The HRC and the CAT Committee have generated a rich jurisprudence relating to the prohibition of torture, cruel, inhuman, and degrading treatment, and punishment. The HRC has also developed jurisprudence under article 10, which provides additional protection for persons in detention.

[9.128] Numerous cases, such as the early complaints against Uruguay, have concerned factual situations which gave rise to obvious violations of articles 7 and/or 10. However, cases have also concerned more borderline situations, such as the ICCPR/CAT compatibility of the infliction of psychological anxiety, the death row phenomenon, and the deportations of asylum-seekers.

[9.129] HRC jurisprudence indicates that inadequate prison conditions, which affect the general prison population, tend to give rise to breaches of article 10 rather than article 7. Article 7 is more likely to be relevant in cases where the complainant has been singled out for especially bad treatment. However, the HRC has unfortunately not been totally clear in defining the line between breaches of article 7 and breaches of article 10.

Finally, articles 7 and 10 of the ICCPR, as well as CAT, impose numerous positive duties on States Parties to train relevant personnel, to implement procedures to guard against violations, and to investigate and punish breaches.

Postscript: Please note that General Comment 28 on 'Equality of Rights Between Men and Women', contained in the Addendum at page 634, contains extra information on some of the material in this chapter.

---

[156] Nowak, above, note 3, 192.

10

Miscellaneous Rights—Articles 8, 11, and 16

Though the rights are not similar in nature, articles 8, 11, and 16 are grouped together in this chapter due to the virtual absence of jurisprudence under these articles.

Article 8: Freedom from Slavery, Servitude, and Forced Labour

1. No one shall be held in slavery; slavery and the slave-trade in all their forms shall be prohibited.

2. No one shall be held in servitude.

3. (a) No one shall be required to perform forced or compulsory labour;

(b) Paragraph 3(a) shall not be held to preclude, in countries where imprisonment with hard labour may be imposed as a punishment for a crime, the performance of hard labour in pursuance of a sentence to such punishment by a competent court.

(c) For the purpose of this paragraph the term 'forced or compulsory labour' shall not include

(i) Any work or service, not referred to in subparagraph (b), normally required of a person who is under detention in consequence of a lawful order of a court, or of a person during conditional release from such detention;

(ii) Any service of a military character and, in countries where conscientious objection is recognized, any national service required by law of conscientious objectors;

(iii) Any service exacted in cases of emergency or calamity threatening the life or well-being of the community;

(iv) Any work or service which forms part of normal civil obligations.

[10.01] Article 8 guarantees some of the most fundamental human rights: freedom from slavery, servitude, and forced or compulsory labour. Indeed, the world-wide fight against slavery was one of the first 'human rights' campaigns. Freedom from slavery and servitude is now recognized as part of customary international law.[1] Furthermore, the ICCPR freedoms from slavery and servitude are non-derogable rights.

[10.02] Article 8(1) prohibits slavery. Slavery occurs where one human being effectively 'owns' another,[2] so that the former person can thoroughly exploit the latter with impunity. Article 8(2) guarantees freedom from servitude, which is a broader concept than slavery. 'Servitude' refers to other forms of egregious economic exploitation or dominance exercised by one person over another, or 'slavery-like' practices.[3]

[10.03] Article 8(3)(a) prohibits forced or compulsory labour, which is essentially defined in ILO Convention 29 as 'all work or service which is extracted from any person under the menace of any penalty and for which the said person has not offered himself voluntarily'.[4] However, paragraphs 8(3)(b) to (c) contain a number of exceptions, or qualifications, to this rule. The HRC has unfortunately issued few consensus comments on the extent of these exceptions. In *Wolf v Panama* (289/88), the HRC inferred that the exception regarding prison labour, in article 8(3)(c)(i), does not apply until a sentence has been pronounced against a prisoner.[5] Article 8(3)(c)(ii) has been used to deny the existence in the Covenant of a freedom for conscientious objectors from compulsory military service, despite arguments to the contrary based on article 18 (freedom of conscience).[6] More recent HRC jurisprudence has however intimated that the Committee now recognizes a right of conscientious objection in article 18.[7]

[10.04] Bonded labour, or debt bondage, is a condition arising from a debtor's pledge of his/her personal services, or those of one under the debtor's control (often a child), as security for a debt, if the reasonable value of those services is not applied towards liquidation of the debt, or the length and nature of the personal services is not defined.[8] In Concluding Comments on India, the HRC made the following comments about 'bonded' labour:[9]

---

[1] See American Law Institute, *Restatement (Third) of Foreign Relations Law*, para. 702. Note that the *Restatement* does not refer to the prohibitions on servitude or forced labour.

[2] Y. Dinstein, 'The Right to Life, Physical Integrity, and Liberty' in L. Henkin (ed.), *The International Bill of Rights* (Columbia University Press, New York, 1981), at 126. See Slavery Convention 1926, 60 LNTS 253, art. 1(1).

[3] See Supplementary Convention on the Abolition of Slavery, the Slave Trade, and Institutions and Practices Similar to Slavery 1956, 266 UNTS 3, Section III. Also see M. Nowak, *CCPR Commentary* (N.P. Engel, Kehl/Strasbourg/Arlington, 1993), at 148.

[4] *ILO Convention Concerning Forced or Compulsory Labour* 1930, 39 UNTS 55, art. 2(1).

[5] The author had alleged that he had performed forced labour even though no sentence had yet been imposed on him. The HRC found the allegation unsubstantiated at para. 6.8.

[6] See *L.T.K. v Finland* (185/84), para. 5.2.

[7] See commentary at [17.19–17.22].

[8] Supplementary Convention on the Abolition of Slavery, the Slave Trade, and Institutions and Practices Similar to Slavery 1956, 266 UNTS 3, art. 1(b).

[9] (1997) UN doc. CCPR/C/79/Add. 81.

¶ 29. The Committee expresses concern at the extent of bonded labour, as well as the fact that the incidence of this practice reported to the Supreme Court is far higher than is mentioned in the report. The Committee also notes with concern that eradication measures which have been taken do not appear to be effective in achieving real progress in the release and rehabilitation of bonded labourers. Therefore: the Committee recommends that a thorough study be urgently undertaken to identify the extent of bonded labour and that more effective measures be taken to eradicate this practice, in accordance with the Bonded Labour System (Abolition) Act of 1976 and article 8 of the Covenant.

[10.05] Forced prostitution is an egregious form of article 8 abuse, as confirmed in Concluding Comments on Portugal (Macau):[10]

¶ 13. The Committee is particularly concerned at reports on the extent of trafficking in women in Macau and on the large numbers of women from different countries who are being brought into Macau for the purpose of prostitution. The Committee is extremely concerned at the inaction by the authorities in preventing and penalizing exploitation of these women and that, in particular, immigration and police officials are not taking effective measures to protect these women and to impose sanctions on those who are exploiting women through prostitution in violation of article 8 of the Covenant. . . .

¶ 19. The Committee further recommends that the Government should initiate or strengthen programmes aimed at providing assistance to women in difficult circumstances, particularly those coming from other countries who are brought into Macau for the purpose of prostitution. Strong measures should be taken to prevent this form of trafficking and to impose sanctions on those who exploit women in this way. Protection should be extended to women who are the victims of this kind of trafficking so that they may have a place of refuge and an opportunity to stay in order to give evidence against the person responsible in criminal or civil proceedings.

Regarding Italy, the HRC stated:[11]

¶ 5. It is noted with appreciation that the judiciary has begun to treat offences concerning trafficking of women and others for the purpose of prostitution as acts which can be assimilated to slavery and contrary to international and national law.

[10.06] In Concluding Comments on Brazil, the HRC confirmed that there is a positive element to article 8 protection:[12]

¶ 31. The Committee urges the State party to enforce laws prohibiting forced labour, child labour and child prostitution and to implement programmes to prevent and combat such human rights abuses. In addition, the Committee exhorts the State party to establish more effective supervisory mechanisms to ensure compliance with the provisions of national legislation and relevant international standards. It is imperative that persons who are responsible for, or who directly profit from, forced labour, child labour and child prostitution, be severely punished under law.[13]

---

[10] (1997) UN doc. CCPR/C/79/Add. 77; see also Concluding Comments on Cambodia (1999) UN doc. CCPR/C/79/Add. 16.   [11] (1995) UN doc. CCPR/C/79/Add.37.
[12] (1996) UN doc. CCPR/C/79/Add. 66; see also Concluding Comments on Dominican Republic (1993) UN doc. CCPR/C/79/Add. 18, para. 5.
[13] On prohibitions of child labour and child prostitution, see [21.34–21.35] and [21.39–21.40].

A State Party must protect all persons within jurisdiction from article 8 abuse by private bodies, as well as refraining from engaging in such abuse itself. Indeed, it is likely that private economic interests generate most article 8 abuses these days.[14] A further concern is the treatment of domestic servants, especially illegal aliens, by employers in numerous States Parties.[15]

Article 11: Freedom from Imprisonment for Inability to Fulfil a Contract

No one shall be imprisoned merely on the ground of inability to fulfil a contractual obligation.

[10.07] Article 11 protects against imprisonment as a punishment for inability to fulfil a contractual obligation. The 'contractual obligations' envisaged in article 11 are private law civil obligations, rather than, for example, statutory obligations.[16] As the guarantee was primarily designed to tackle the phenomenon of 'debtor's prisons', 'contractual obligations' obviously include monetary debts.[17] However, article 11 could apply to other contractual obligations, such as performance of services or delivery of goods.[18] The reference to 'inability' indicates that the person must be incapable of fulfilling the relevant contractual obligation, rather than simply unwilling to do so.[19] The word 'merely' indicates that the guarantee does not protect persons who have committed some other offence over and above the contractual breach. For example, if one intentionally manufactures one's 'inability' and commits fraud, one is not protected from imprisonment by article 11.[20]

Article 11 is a non-derogable right, which has generated no meaningful jurisprudence, so its parameters remain largely undefined.

Article 16: Right to Recognition as a Person before the Law

Everyone shall have the right to recognition everywhere as a person before the law.

[10.08] Article 16 guarantees one a basic human right to be legally recognized as a person. If one's humanity is not legally recognized, one will lose legal recognition of, and therefore be effectively denied, one's other human rights. For example, Jews in Nazi Germany were deprived of legal recognition; this denial was a

---

[14] See Nowak, above, note 3, 145.
[15] See, e.g., N. Mole, 'Immigration and Freedom of Movement' in D. Harris and S. Joseph, *The International Covenant on Civil and Political Rights and United Kingdom Law* (Clarendon Press, Oxford, 1995), 319–20.　　　　　　　　　　　　　　[16] Nowak, above, note 3, 194.
[17] Ibid., 193.　　　　　　　　　　　　　　　　　　　　　　[18] Ibid., 194.
[19] Dinstein, above, note 2, 136.　　　　　　　　　[20] Nowak, above, note 3, 195.

precursor to denial of all of their other human rights. Article 16 is a non-derogable right.

[10.09] Volio states that article 16 requires States Parties to treat all humans within the jurisdiction as persons enjoying the protection of the law, and being subject to legal obligations. Thus, all humans can enter into contracts, sue, and be sued.[21] Nowak, on the other hand, adopts a more conservative interpretation of article 16, and argues that it does not protect one's legal capacity to act or to pursue legal proceedings. Therefore, for example, limitations on the legal capacities of children or mentally ill persons, or even vexatious litigants, do not breach article 16.[22] Article 16 is written in absolute language, and appears to brook no exception. Given the widespread limitations to the legal capacities of certain persons that do exist, Nowak's minimalist interpretation appears to be correct.

[10.10]   *AVELLANAL v PERU (202/86)*

¶ 2.1. The author is the owner of two apartment buildings in Lima, which she acquired in 1974. It appears that a number of tenants . . . cease[d] paying rent for their apartments. . . . [T]he author sued the tenants on 13 September 1978. The court of first instance found in her favour and ordered the tenants to pay her the rent due since 1974. The Superior Court reversed the judgement on 21 November 1980 on the procedural ground that the author was not entitled to sue, because, according to article 168 of the Peruvian Civil Code, when a woman is married only the husband is entitled to represent matrimonial property before the Courts. . . . [O]n 15 February 1984 the Supreme Court upheld the decision of the Superior Court.

The author claimed that the above facts breached, *inter alia*, article 16. The HRC found the case admissible in respect of article 16, but inexplicably ignored this article in its merits decision. On the merits, it found breaches of articles 14(1) (right of access to courts), 3, and 26 (prohibitions of sex discrimination).[23]

[10.11] In *De Gallicchio and Vicario v Argentina* (400/90), the author sought to be recognized as her granddaughter's guardian, so she could have standing to represent her granddaughter in various proceedings. No complaint was issued regarding the granddaughter's inability to represent herself, nor did the HRC raise the issue itself. By implication, the granddaughter's inability to represent herself, because she was a minor, was not a breach of article 16. Furthermore, the local court's failure to recognize the grandmother's standing on behalf of the granddaughter in certain proceedings did not breach article 16 either; the HRC noted that the grandmother had been granted standing in certain other proceedings.[24]

---

[21] F. Volio, 'Legal Personality, Privacy, and the Family' in Henkin, above, note 2, at 188.
[22] Nowak, above, note 3, 283.
[23] See also [14.12].
[24] Para. 10.3; see generally on this case [21.48].

[10.12] The HRC's views in the *Vicario* and *Avellanal* cases support Nowak's minimalist interpretation of article 16 [10.09]. A more expansive approach may be evident from the minority decisions in the following case.

[10.13]   *INOSTROZA et al. v CHILE (717/96)*

On the facts of this case, the authors' relatives had allegedly been murdered by Chilean soldiers in 1973. Their bodies were never recovered. Complaints about these murders would have been inadmissible *ratione temporis*, as Chile did not ratify the Optional Protocol until 1992.[25] The authors complained of a decision by the Chilean Supreme Court, in 1995, not to overrule a decision by Chilean military tribunals not to investigate the deaths. This decision was prompted by an Amnesty Decree of 1978, which conferred impunity on the Chilean military for such acts as the murders in question. The authors put forward the following argument:

¶ 3.4. . . . the decision of the military tribunals not to investigate the victims' deaths amounts to a violation of article 16 of the Covenant, i.e. failure to recognize the victims as persons before the law.

The HRC majority found the complaint inadmissible *ratione temporis*, as the Supreme Court judgment 'could not be regarded as a new event that could affect the rights of a person who was killed in 1973'.[26] Mme Chanet stated the following in an individual opinion:

I challenge the decision taken by the Committee, which, in dealing with the two communications, dismissed the applicants on the grounds of the *ratione temporis* reservation lodged by Chile at the time of its accession to the Optional Protocol.

In my view the question could not be addressed in this manner, in view of the fact that judicial decisions taken by the State party were adopted after the date it had [ratified the Optional Protocol] and that the problem raised in connection with article 16 of the Covenant relates to a situation which, as long as it is not permanently ended, has long-term consequences.

In the case in question, even if the actual circumstances referred to in the two communications diverge, the attitude of the State regarding the consequences to be drawn from the disappearances necessarily raised a question as regards article 16 of the Covenant.

Under article 16, everyone has the right to recognition as a person before the law.

While this right is extinguished on the death of the individual, it has effects which last beyond his or her death; this applies in particular to wills, or the thorny issue of organ donation.

---

[25] See generally, on the *ratione temporis* rule, Chap. 2.
[26] Para. 6.4; see the comparable case of *S.E. v Argentina* (275/88) at [2.10].

This right survives *a fortiori* when the absence of the person is surrounded by uncertainty; he or she may reappear, and even if not present, does not cease to exist under the law; it is not possible to substitute civil death for confirmed natural death.

These observations do not imply that this right is of unlimited duration: either the identification of the body is incontestable and a declaration of death can be made, or uncertainty remains concerning the absence or the identification of the person and the State must lay down rules applicable to all these cases; it may, for example, specify a period after which the disappeared person is regarded as dead.

This is what the Committee should have sought to find out in this particular case by examining the matters in depth.

Mr Solari Yrigoyen also dissented, in the following terms:

. . . [T]he communication concerns the violation of the author's right to recognition everywhere as a person before the law, as a consequence of the lack of investigation of his whereabouts or location of the body. [Article 16] is a fundamental right to which anyone is entitled, even after his death, and one that should be protected whenever its recognition is sought. [The Committee] is not precluded *ratione temporis* from examining the author's communication on the matter. . . .

Vargas v Chile (718/96) was a very similar case to *Inostroza*. The HRC issued a similar majority opinion. Mme Chanet issued a dissent in identical terms, which was co-signed by Mr Pocar.

[10.14] In recent Concluding Comments on Israel, the HRC stated:[27]

¶ 21. . . . A specific concern of the Committee is that at least some of the persons kept in administrative detention for reasons of State security (and in particular some Lebanese) do not personally threaten State security but are kept as 'bargaining chips' in order to promote negotiations with other parties on releasing detained Israeli soldiers or the bodies of deceased soldiers. The Committee considers the present application of administrative detention to be incompatible with articles 7 and 16 of the Covenant. . . .

This comment, along with the minority opinions in the recent *Inostroza* and *Vargas* decisions, indicate that at least some HRC members are starting to pay attention to the article 16 guarantee.

Conclusion

[10.15] Articles 8, 11, and 16 have generated little jurisprudence. Articles 11 and 16 are of limited scope, which may explain their absence from HRC consideration. These rights also substantially overlap with other rights that have been more prevalent in HRC jurisprudence, such as freedoms from discrimination (articles

---

[27] (1999) UN doc. CCPR/C/79/Add. 93.

2, 3, and 26), the right to a fair trial (article 14), and the right of children to freedom from exploitation (article 24), so it is possible that the HRC simply chooses to deal with relevant complaints under other ICCPR provisions. The HRC's silence could also indicate that these rights are no longer breached on a common basis, though that may be wishful thinking. It may also be that victims of breaches of these provisions are so disempowered that they are unable to access, and are even unaware of international avenues of redress. These rights are nevertheless important guarantees of human dignity. Indeed, except for article 8(3), they are all non-derogable.

Postscript: Please note that General Comment 28 on 'Equality of Rights Between Men and Women', contained in the Addendum at page 634, contains extra information on some of the material in this chapter.

11

Freedom from Arbitrary Detention—Article 9

ARTICLE 9

1. Everyone has the right to liberty and security of person. No one shall be subjected to arbitrary arrest or detention. No one shall be deprived of his liberty except on such grounds and in accordance with such procedure as are established by law.

2. Anyone who is arrested shall be informed, at the time of arrest, of the reasons for his arrest and shall be promptly informed of any charges against him.

3. Anyone arrested or detained on a criminal charge shall be brought promptly before a judge or other officer authorized by law to exercise judicial power and shall be entitled to trial within a reasonable time or to release. It shall not be the general rule that persons awaiting trial shall be detained in custody, but release may be subject to guarantees to appear for trial, at any other stage of the judicial proceedings, and, should occasion arise, for execution of the judgement.

4. Anyone who is deprived of his liberty by arrest or detention shall be entitled to take proceedings before a court, in order that that court may decide without delay on the lawfulness of his detention and order his release if the detention is not lawful.

5. Anyone who has been the victim of unlawful arrest or detention shall have an enforceable right to compensation.

[11.01] The liberty and security of the person are protected by article 9 of the ICCPR. In relation to the right to liberty, article 9 does not grant complete freedom from arrest or detention. Deprivation of liberty has always been and will continue to be a legitimate form of State control over persons within the jurisdiction.[1] Instead article 9(1) acts as a substantive guarantee that arrest or detention will not be arbitrary or unlawful. Article 9(2) to (5) provides procedural guarantees that help ensure enjoyment of the substantive guarantee in article 9(1).

[11.02] Article 9 has usually been invoked in the context of deprivations of liberty. However, the article also guards the right to security of the person. This right applies to persons in and out of detention.

The Right to Security of the Person

[11.03] The issue of the right to the security of person was discussed in the following case.

DELGADO PÁEZ v COLOMBIA (195/85)

The author in this case was a Colombian teacher of religion and ethics who had made complaints against the Apostolic Prefect and the education authorities concerning discrimination against him. The author received death threats as a result of these complaints and was attacked in the city of Bogotá. After a work colleague was shot dead by unknown assailants, the author fled the country and obtained political asylum in France. The author filed a complaint alleging that the Colombian government had violated its obligation to protect his rights to equality, justice, and life, and as such he had been forced to leave the country. Although not initially invoked by the author, the Committee found a violation of article 9(1) in the following terms:

¶ 5.5. The first sentence of article 9 does not stand as a separate paragraph. Its location as a part of that paragraph could lead one to the view that the right to security arises only in the context of arrest and detention. The *travaux préparatoires* indicate that the discussions of the first sentence did indeed focus on matters dealt with in the other provisions of article 9. The Universal Declaration of Human Rights, in article 3, refers to the right to life, the right to liberty and the right to security of the person. These elements have been dealt with in separate clauses in the Covenant. Although in the Covenant the only reference to the right to security of the person is to be found in article 9, there is no evidence that it was intended to narrow the concept of the right to security only to situations of formal deprivation of liberty. At the same time, States parties have undertaken to guarantee the rights enshrined in the Covenant. It cannot be the case that, as a matter of law, States can ignore known threats to the life of persons under their jurisdiction, just because he or she is not arrested or otherwise detained. States parties are under an obligation to take reasonable and appropriate measures to protect them. An interpretation of article 9 which would allow a

---

[1] Indeed, Nowak states that imprisonment has grown in significance due to 'gradual displacement of other forms of punishment, such as the death penalty and corporal punishment': M. Nowak, *CCPR Commentary* (N.P. Engel, Kehl, 1993), 159.

State party to ignore threats to the personal security of non-detained persons within its jurisdiction would render totally ineffective the guarantees of the Covenant.

¶ 5.6. There remains the question of the application of this finding to the facts of the case under consideration. There appears to have been an objective need for Mr. Delgado to be provided by the State with protective measures to guarantee his security, given the threats made against him, including the attack on his person, and the murder of a close colleague. It is arguable that, in seeking to ensure this protection, Mr. Delgado failed to address the competent authorities, making his complaints to the military authorities in Leticia, the teachers' union, the Ministry of Education and the President of Colombia, rather than to the general prosecutor or the judiciary. It is unclear to the Committee whether these matters were reported to the police. It does not know either with certainty whether any measures were taken by the Government. However, the Committee cannot but note that the author claims that there was no response to his request to have these threats investigated and to receive protection, and that the State party has not informed the Committee otherwise. Indeed, the State party has failed to comply with the request by the Committee to provide it with information on any of the issues relevant to article 9 of the Covenant. Whereas the Committee is reluctant to make a finding of a violation in the absence of compelling evidence as to the facts, it is for the State party to inform the Committee if alleged facts are incorrect, or if they would not, in any event, indicate a violation of the Covenant. The Committee has, in its past jurisprudence, made clear that circumstances may cause it to assume facts in the author's favour if the State party fails to reply or to address them. The pertinent factors in this case are that Mr. Delgado had been engaged in a protracted confrontation with the authorities over his teaching and his employment. Criminal charges, later determined unfounded, had been brought against him and he had been suspended, with salary frozen. . . . Further, he was known to have instituted a variety of complaints against the ecclesiastical and scholastical authorities in Leticia. . . . Coupled with these factors were threats to his life. If the State party neither denies the threats nor co-operates with the Committee to explain whether the relevant authorities were aware of them, and, if so, what was done about them, the Committee must necessarily treat as correct allegations that the threats were known and that nothing was done. Accordingly, while fully understanding the situation in Colombia, the Committee finds that the State party has not taken, or has been unable to take, appropriate measures to ensure Mr. Delgado's right to security of his person under article 9, paragraph 1.

Note that the HRC recognized the appalling security situation in Colombia which would have impacted on the Colombian government's ability to provide protection for individuals. In particular, it 'fully understood the situation in Colombia' and noted that Colombia may have been 'unable to take' the appropriate measures to protect Mr. Delgado. Nevertheless, Colombia was found to have violated article 9(1).[2]

[11.04] The Committee's decision in *Delgado Páez* illustrates that the right to personal security is independent of the guarantee of liberty. It also reveals that the

---

[2] Compare, in this respect, the dissenting opinion of Mr Ando in *Sanjuán Arévalo v Colombia* (181/84) in the context of a violation of the right to life, art. 6, at [8.11–8.12].

State is under an obligation to protect a person's right to personal security against attacks by private persons. This is of importance, for example, to people who are being stalked, or are under genuine risk of attack, such as habitually battered spouses.[3] The *Delgado Páez* decision regarding security of the person has been followed in *Bwalya v Zambia* (314/88) and *Bahamonde v Equatorial Guinea* (468/91).

[11.05]   ***TSHISHIMBI v ZAIRE (542/93)***

In this case Mr Tshishimbi had participated in a failed coup attempt against President Mobutu of Zaire. He was also a supporter of the democratic movement in Zaire and was appointed as a military adviser to the Tshisekedi government when it took office. He was then abducted during the night in unknown circumstances. After his abduction his family, relatives, and colleagues had no news from him. It was believed that he was detained at the headquarters of the National Intelligence Service which remained loyal to President Mobutu. His wife submitted the communication on behalf of her husband. It was submitted that the facts revealed violations by Zaire of a number of articles including article 9(1). The Committee agreed with the contention that Zaire had violated Mr Tshishimbi's rights under article 9(1):[4]

¶ 5.4. The first sentence of article 9, paragraph 1, guarantees to everyone the right to liberty and security of person. In its prior jurisprudence, the Committee has held that this right may be invoked not only in the context of arrest and detention, and that an interpretation which would allow States parties to tolerate, condone or ignore threats made by persons in authority to the personal liberty and security of non-detained individuals within the State party's jurisdiction would render ineffective the guarantees of the Covenant. In the circumstances of this case, the Committee concludes that the State party has failed to ensure Mr. Tshishimbi's right to liberty and security of person, in violation of article 9, paragraph 1 of the Covenant.[5]

[11.06]   ***LEEHONG v JAMAICA (613/95)***

¶ 9.3. With respect to the author's claim that he was shot by the police from behind before being arrested, the Committee reiterates its jurisprudence where it has held that it is insufficient for the State party to simply say that there has been no breach of the Covenant. Consequently, the Committee finds that in the circumstances the State party not having provided any evidence in respect of the investigation it alleges to have carried out the shooting remains uncontested and due weight must be given to the author's allegations.

---

[3] See, in this respect, the concern expressed in Concluding Comments on Poland on the level of domestic violence, and 'the shortage of provision of hostels and refuges for family members suffering from domestic violence': (1999) UN doc. CCPR/C/79/Add. 110, para. 14.

[4] Numerous violations of ICCPR rights were in fact found in this case, see, e.g., [9.71].

[5] See also *Mojica v Dominican Republic* (449/91), para. 5.4.

Accordingly, the Committee finds that there has been a violation of article 9, paragraph 1, with respect to the author's right to security of the person.

The 'investigation' duty entailed in article 9(1) mirrors similar duties of investigation regarding the right to life[6] and freedom from torture, inhuman, and degrading treatment.[7]

[11.07]   **The Right to 'Liberty'**

General Comment 8 expands on the meaning of the right to liberty in article 9(1):

GENERAL COMMENT 8

¶ 1. Article 9 which deals with the right to liberty and security of persons has often been somewhat narrowly understood in reports by States parties, and they have therefore given incomplete information. The Committee points out that paragraph 1 is applicable to all deprivations of liberty, whether in criminal cases or in other cases such as, for example, mental illness, vagrancy, drug addiction, educational purposes, immigration control, etc. It is true that some of the provisions of article 9 (part of para. 2 and the whole of para. 3) are only applicable to persons against whom criminal charges are brought. But the rest, and in particular the important guarantee laid down in paragraph 4, i.e. the right to control by a court of the legality of the detention, applies to all persons deprived of their liberty by arrest or detention. Furthermore, States parties have in accordance with article 2 (3) also to ensure that an effective remedy is provided in other cases in which an individual claims to be deprived of his liberty in violation of the Covenant. . . .

¶ 4. Also if so-called preventive detention is used, for reasons of public security, it must be controlled by these same provisions, i.e. it must not be arbitrary, and must be based on grounds and procedures established by law (para. 1), information of the reasons must be given (para. 2) and court control of the detention must be available (para. 4) as well as compensation in the case of a breach (para. 5). And if, in addition, criminal charges are brought in such cases, the full protection of article 9 (2) and (3), as well as article 14, must also be granted.

[11.08] Most cases have concerned detention for the purposes of criminal justice. However, a number of cases have concerned detention for the purposes of immigration, such as *Torres v Finland* (291/88) [11.46] and *A v Australia* (560/93) [11.15]. *Vuolanne v Finland* (265/87) concerned detention for the purposes of military discipline [11.54]. *A v New Zealand* (754/97) concerned enforced detention for psychiatric treatment [11.18].

---

[6] See [8.08–8.13].   [7] See [9.83–9.87].

[11.09] *CELEPLI v SWEDEN (456/91)*

In this case, Celepli was prohibited from travelling freely throughout the State, as he was confined to certain city limits. The State Party submitted the following:

¶ 4.5. The State party argues that article 9 of the Covenant, protecting the right to liberty and security of the person, prohibits unlawful arrest and detention, but does not apply to mere restrictions on liberty of movement which are covered by article 12. The State party argues that the restrictions on his freedom of movement were not so severe that his situation could be characterized as a deprivation of liberty within the meaning of article 9 of the Covenant. Moreover, the author was free to leave Sweden to go to another country of his choice.

The author responded:

¶ 5.3. With regard to the State party's arguments that the restrictions on his freedom of movement cannot be considered to be so severe as to constitute a deprivation of liberty, the author argues that a residence restriction can be considered a deprivation of liberty when it is of considerable duration or when it has serious consequences. He claims that his condition, being under residence restriction for nearly seven years and having to report to the police three times a week for five years, was so severe as to amount to a deprivation of liberty, within the meaning of article 9 of the Covenant.

The Committee found the article 9 complaint 'incompatible' with the Covenant,[8] so it apparently agreed with the State Party. It seems that article 9 therefore applies only to severe deprivations of liberty, such as incarceration within a certain building (e.g. prison, psychiatric institution, immigration detention centre),[9] rather than restrictions on one's ability to move freely around a State, or an even smaller locality. The latter circumstances raise issues with regard to article 12 rather than article 9.[10]

The Requirement of Legality and the Prohibition of Arbitrariness

[11.10] There are two permissible limitations to one's right to liberty under article 9. First the deprivation of liberty is permissible only if it is 'in accordance with procedures as are established by law'. Hence, arrest and subsequent detention must be specifically authorized and sufficiently circumscribed by law.[11] Secondly the law itself and the enforcement of that law must not be arbitrary. As in other contexts under the ICCPR, the prohibition of 'arbitrary' deprivations of liberty

---

[8] Para. 6.1.

[9] Nowak refers to detention in a 'narrowly bounded location', above, note 1, 160.

[10] The facts of *Celepli* are outlined more thoroughly at [12.10].

[11] Y. Dinstein, 'Right to Life, Physical Integrity, and Liberty' in L. Henkin (ed.), *The International Bill of Rights* (Columbia University Press, New York, 1981), 130; see also [16.09–16.12].

goes further than the prohibition of 'unlawful' deprivations, as 'arbitrariness' is a principle *above* rather than *within* the law.[12]

[11.11] An example of an 'unlawful' arrest occurred in *Domukovsky et al. v Georgia* (623–624/95, 626–627/95). One of the authors was kidnapped from Azerbaijani territory by Georgian agents, in breach of Azerbaijani law and article 9.[13] Indeed, this case appears to confirm that an arrest must be 'lawful' within the law of both the arresting State and the State where the arrest takes place. Of course, in most cases, these States will be one and the same.[14]

[11.12] The meaning of arbitrariness in the context of article 9(1) was considered in the following case.

VAN ALPHEN v THE NETHERLANDS (305/88)

The author was a Dutch solicitor who was arrested on suspicion of having been an accessory or accomplice to forgery and of filing false income tax returns. The author was detained for over nine weeks in an attempt to force him to provide information in relation to certain clients to the authorities. The author alleged that his arrest and detention were arbitrary and in violation of, *inter alia*, article 9(1) of the Covenant. In his opinion his arrest and detention were used deliberately to pressure him to give information that could be used in investigations against himself or his clients. In finding a breach of article 9(1) of the Covenant, the Committee made the following comments:

¶ 5.6. The principal issue before the Committee is whether the author's detention from 5 December 1983 to 9 February 1984 was arbitrary. It is uncontested that the Netherlands judicial authorities, in determining repeatedly whether to prolong the author's detention, observed the rules governing pre-trial detention laid down in the Code of Criminal Procedure. It remains to be determined whether other factors may render an otherwise lawful detention arbitrary, and whether the author enjoys an absolute right to invoke his professional obligation to secrecy regardless of the circumstances of a criminal investigation.

¶ 5.7. In the instant case, the Committee has examined the reasons adduced by the State party for a prolongation of the author's detention for a period of nine weeks. The Committee observes that the privilege that protects a lawyer–client relationship belongs to the tenets of most legal systems. But this privilege is intended to protect the client. In the case under consideration the client had waived the privilege. The Committee does not know the circumstances of the client's decision to withdraw the duty of confidentiality in the case. However, the author himself was a suspect, and although he was freed from his duty of confidentiality, he was not obliged to assist the State in mounting a case against him.

---

[12] See also, on the meaning of 'arbitrary', [8.04] and [16.13]. However, see the Committee's decision regarding the meaning of 'lawful', virtually equating it with 'arbitrary', in *A v Australia* in respect of art. 9(4) [11.55–11.56].

[13] See para. 18.2.

[14] See generally Chap. 4 on the territorial jurisdiction of States.

¶ 5.8. The drafting history of article 9, paragraph 1, confirms that 'arbitrariness' is not to be equated with 'against the law', but must be interpreted more broadly to include elements of inappropriateness, injustice and lack of predictability. This means that remand in custody pursuant to lawful arrest must not only be lawful but reasonable in all the circumstances. Further, remand in custody must be necessary in all the circumstances, for example, to prevent flight, interference with evidence or the recurrence of crime. The State party has not shown that these factors were present in the instant case. It has, in fact, stated that the reason for the duration of the author's detention 'was that the applicant continued to invoke his obligation to maintain confidentiality despite the fact that the interested party had released him from his obligations in this respect', and that 'the importance of the criminal investigation necessitated detaining the applicant for reasons of accessibility'. Notwithstanding the waiver of the author's professional duty of confidentiality, he was not obliged to provide such co-operation. The Committee therefore finds that the facts as submitted disclose a violation of article 9, paragraph 1, of the Covenant.

[11.13] Even if one's initial arrest is not arbitrary, the subsequent period of detention may breach article 9(1). In *Spakmo v Norway* (631/95), the author was twice arrested for failure to abide by a police order to cease demolition work on a particular site. Both arrests conformed to article 9(1). However, the State Party failed to demonstrate that Spakmo's detention for eight hours after the second arrest was reasonable, so that detention breached article 9(1).[15]

[11.14] Other examples of violations of article 9(1) include cases where prisoners are kept in detention after their sentences have been served[16] or after their release has been judicially ordered,[17] instances of illegal abduction by State actors,[18] cases where the detention contravenes municipal law,[19] and cases where people are arrested for their political views.[20] In *Tshionga a Minanga v Zaire* (366/89), the author was detained for half a day, apparently for the purposes of political persecution. This detention, despite its relative brevity, breached article 9(1).[21] Furthermore, the HRC has criticized the Islamic Republic of Iran for 'requiring repentance from detainees as a condition of their release from custody'.[22] In Concluding Comments on the Ukraine, the HRC condemned the practice of 'administrative detention' of vagrants.[23] Regarding Peru, the HRC

---

[15] Para. 6.3.   [16] See, e.g., *Weismann and Perdomo v Uruguay* (8/77).

[17] See, e.g., *Bazzano v Uruguay* (5/77), *Ramirez v Uruguay* (4/77), *Carballal v Uruguay* (33/78), *de Bouton v Uruguay* (37/78), *Jijón v Ecuador* (277/88).

[18] *Lopez Burgós v Uruguay* (52/79), *Casariego v Uruguay* (56/79).

[19] *Bolaños v Ecuador* (238/87).

[20] See, e.g., *Portorreal v Dominican Republic* (188/84), *Mukong v Cameroon* (458/91), *Blanco v Nicaragua* (328/88). Political persecution also seemed to be the motive behind many of the detentions in early cases against Uruguay.

[21] See also minority opinion in *Giry v Dominican Republic* (193/85), finding a breach of art. 9(1) where the author was detained for two hours and forty minutes prior to being forced aboard a flight to the United States. The majority dealt with this case under art. 13: see [13.20].

[22] Concluding Comments on the Islamic Republic of Iran (1993) UN doc. CCPR/C/79/Add. 25, para. 11.

[23] (1995) UN doc. CCPR/C/79/Add. 52, para. 13.

criticized laws which authorized the 'preventive detention' of persons for up to fifteen days, with a possibility of extension by another fifteen days, in cases of suspected terrorism, espionage, and illicit drug trafficking.[24]

[11.15]   *A v AUSTRALIA (560/93)*

The author was a Cambodian national who together with twenty-five other Cambodian nationals, had landed illegally in Australia by boat on 25 November 1989. Shortly after his arrival he applied for refugee status. This application was rejected by the Determination of Refugee Status Committee in 1990. The author continued to appeal his refugee status, whilst using legal mechanisms to restrain the government from deporting him. The author was detained for the entire time that his refugee status was being determined, a period of over four years. Ultimately, the author was released and given an entry permit in January 1994 on humanitarian grounds.

The author argued first that he had been detained arbitrarily within the meaning of article 9(1).

¶ 3.3. It is contended that the State party's policy of detaining boat people is inappropriate, unjustified and arbitrary, as its principal purpose is to deter other boat people from coming to Australia, and to deter those already in the country from continuing with applications for refugee status. The application of the new legislation is said to amount to 'human deterrence', based on the practice of rigidly detaining asylum-seekers under such conditions and for periods so prolonged that prospective asylum-seekers are deterred from even applying for refugee status, and current asylum-seekers lose all hope and return home.

¶ 3.4. No valid grounds are said to exist for the detention of the author . . . Furthermore, the length of detention—1,299 days or three years and 204 days as at 20 June 1993—is said to amount to a breach of article 9, paragraph 1.

Australia submitted the following arguments in justification of the author's detention:

¶ 7.1. [The State party] recalls that Australia's policy of detention of unauthorized arrivals is part of its immigration policy. Its rationale is to ensure that unauthorized entrants do not enter the Australian community until their alleged entitlement to do so has been properly assessed and found to justify entry. Detention seeks to ensure that whoever enters Australian territory without authorization can have any claim to remain in the country examined and if the claim is rejected, will be available for removal. The State party notes that from late 1989, there was a sudden and unprecedented increase of applications for refugee status from individuals who had landed on the country's shores. This led to severe delays in the length of detention of applicants, as well as to reforms in the law and procedures for determination of on-shore applications for protection visas.

---

[24] (1996) UN doc. CCPR/C/79/Add. 67, para. 18.

¶ 7.2. As to the necessity of detention, the State party recalls that unauthorized arrivals who landed on Australian shores in 1990 and early 1991 were held in unfenced migrant accommodation hostels with a reporting requirement. However, security arrangements had to be upgraded, as a result of the number of detainees who absconded and the difficulty in obtaining cooperation from local ethnic communities to recover individuals who had not met their reporting obligations; 59 persons who had arrived by boat escaped from detention between 1991 and October 1993. Of the individuals who were allowed to reside in the community while their refugee status applications were being determined, it is noted that out of a group of 8,000 individuals who had been refused refugee status, some 27% remained unlawfully on Australian territory, without any authority to remain.

¶ 7.3. The State party points out that its policy of mandatory detention for certain border claimants should be considered in the light of its full and detailed consideration of refugee claims, and its extensive opportunities to challenge adverse decisions on claims to refugee status. Given the complexity of the case, the time it took to collect information on the continuously changing situation in Cambodia and for A's legal advisers to make submissions, the duration of the author's detention was not abusively long. Furthermore, the conditions of detention of A were not harsh, prison-like or otherwise unduly restrictive. . . .

¶ 7.5. As to the claim under article 9, paragraph 1, the State party argues that the author's detention was lawful and not arbitrary on any ground. A entered Australia without authorization, and subsequently applied for the right to remain on refugee status basis. Initially, he was held pending examination of his application. His subsequent detention was related to his appeals against the decisions refusing his application, which made him liable to deportation. Detention was considered necessary primarily to prevent him from absconding into the Australian community.

¶ 7.6. The State party notes that the *travaux préparatoires* to article 9, paragraph 1, show that the drafters of the Covenant considered that the notion of 'arbitrariness' included 'incompatibility with the principles of justice or with the dignity of the human person'. Furthermore, it refers to the Committee's jurisprudence according to which the notion of arbitrariness must not be equated with 'against the law', but must be interpreted more broadly as encompassing elements of inappropriateness, injustice and lack of predictability. Against this background, the State party contends, detention in a case such as the author's was not disproportionate nor unjust; it was also predictable, in that the applicable Australian law had been widely publicized. To the State party, counsel's argument that it is inappropriate *per se* to detain individuals entering Australia in an unauthorized manner is not borne out by any of the provisions of the Covenant.

Counsel for the author responded with the following arguments:

¶ 8.1. In his comments, dated 22 August 1996, counsel takes issue with the State party's explanation of the rationale for immigration detention. At the time of the author's detention, the only category of unauthorized border arrivals in Australia who were mandatorily detained were so-called 'boat people'. He submits that the Australian authorities had an unjustified fear of a flood of unauthorized boat arrivals, and that the policy of mandatory detention was used as a form of deterrence. As to the argument that there was an 'unprecedented influx' of boat people into Australia from the end of 1989, counsel notes that the

33,414 refugee applications from 1989 to 1993 must be put into perspective—the figure pales in comparison to the number of refugee applications filed in many Western European countries over the same period. Australia remains the only Western asylum country with a policy of mandatory, non-reviewable detention.

¶ 8.2. In any way, counsel adds, lack of preparedness and adequate resources cannot justify a continued breach of the right to be free from arbitrary detention; he refers to the Committee's jurisprudence that lack of budgetary appropriations for the administration of criminal justice does not justify a four-year period of pre-trial detention.[25] It is submitted that the 77-week period it took for the primary processing of the author's asylum application, while he was detained, was due to inadequate resources.

¶ 8.7. On the issue of the 'arbitrariness' of the author's detention, counsel notes that the State party incorrectly seeks to blame the author for the prolongation of his detention. In this context, he argues that A should not have been penalized by prolonged detention for the exercise of his legal rights. He further denies that the detention was justified because of a perceived likelihood that the author might abscond from the detention centre; he points out that the State party has been unable to make more than generalized assertions on this issue. Indeed, he submits, the consequences of long-term custody are so severe that the burden of proof for the justification of detention lies with the State authority in the particular circumstances of each case; the burden of proof is not met on the basis of generalized claims that the individual may abscond if released.

The Committee delivered the following judgment in favour of the author:

¶ 9.2. On the first question, the Committee recalls that the notion of 'arbitrariness' must not be equated with 'against the law' but be interpreted more broadly to include such elements as inappropriateness and injustice. Furthermore, remand in custody could be considered arbitrary if it is not necessary in all the circumstances of the case, for example to prevent flight or interference with evidence: the element of proportionality becomes relevant in this context. The State party however, seeks to justify the author's detention by the fact that he entered Australia unlawfully and by the perceived incentive for the applicant to abscond if left in liberty. The question for the Committee is whether these grounds are sufficient to justify indefinite and prolonged detention.

¶ 9.3. The Committee agrees that there is no basis for the author's claim that it is *per se* arbitrary to detain individuals requesting asylum. Nor can it find any support for the contention that there is a rule of customary international law which would render all such detention arbitrary.

¶ 9.4. The Committee observes however, that every decision to keep a person in detention should be open to review periodically so that the grounds justifying the detention can be assessed. In any event, detention should not continue beyond the period for which the State can provide appropriate justification. For example, the fact of illegal entry may indicate a need for investigation and there may be other factors particular to the individuals, such as

---

[25] Indeed, economic hardship does not generally justify ICCPR violation: see [1.73] and also [11.34].

the likelihood of absconding and lack of cooperation, which may justify detention for a period. Without such factors detention may be considered arbitrary, even if entry was illegal. In the instant case, the State party has not advanced any grounds particular to the author's case, which would justify his continued detention for a period of four years, during which he was shifted around between different detention centres. The Committee therefore concludes that the author's detention for a period of over four years was arbitrary within the meaning of article 9, paragraph 1.

The Committee did not condemn the notion of immigration detention *per se*, nor did it specifically condemn the extraordinary length of the author's detention. The Committee was particularly concerned that the author was not apparently afforded any individual consideration with regard to the need to detain him pending deportation. The Committee essentially condemned the State Party's blanket policy of detaining all persons in the author's circumstances (so-called 'boat people').[26]

[11.16] The Committee has expressed concern over the extended detention of immigrants in a number of Concluding Comments. For example, in its 1998 Comments on Japan, the HRC expressed concern that asylum-seekers were held for 'periods of up to six months and, in some cases, even up to two years'.[27] Regarding Switzerland, the Committee seemed to adopt an even stricter approach:[28]

¶ 15. The Committee notes with concern that [Swiss law] permits the administrative detention of foreign nationals without a temporary or permanent residence permit, including asylum-seekers and minors over the age of 15, for three months while the decision on the right of temporary residence is being prepared, and for a further six months, and even one year with the agreement of the judicial authority, pending expulsion. The Committee notes that these time-limits are considerably in excess of what is necessary, particularly in the case of detention pending expulsion. . . .

[11.17] In *A v Australia*, the HRC clearly indicated that detention is arbitrary if disproportionate in the prevailing circumstances. Therefore, a gaol term must not be totally disproportionate to the severity of the crime committed. Punishment must fit the crime. In this respect, certain sentences imposed under 'mandatory sentencing' regimes in Australia and the USA may breach article 9(1) when such sentences are imposed according to the number of crimes committed, rather than the gravity of the crimes at issue. It must however be noted that the HRC has been

---

[26] In this regard, see also the HRC's condemnation of the practice of 'collective punishment for those found guilty of collective crimes': Concluding Comments on Libyan Arab Jamahiriya (1999) UN doc. CCPR/C/79/Add. 101, para. 12.

[27] (1998) UN doc. CCPR/C/79/Add. 102, para. 19; see also Concluding Comments on the UK (Hong Kong) (1995) UN doc. CCPR/C/79/Add.57, para. 17; Concluding Comments on the UK, (1995) UN doc. CCPR/C/79/Add.55, para. 16; Concluding Comments on the USA (1995) UN doc. CCPR/C/79/Add. 50, paras. 18 and 33; Concluding Comments on Sweden (1995) UN doc. CCPR/C/79/Add. 58, para. 15.

[28] (1996) UN doc. CCPR/C/79/Add. 70.

largely silent on the application of article 9(1) in the context of a sentence for a crime, as opposed to detention prior to or without sentence.[29]

A v NEW ZEALAND (754/97)

[11.18] In this case, the author was originally sentenced to imprisonment on charges of assault and intimidation. Whilst imprisoned, he was committed under the New Zealand Mental Health Act 1969 for detention in the maximum security section of a hospital. The author argued that the State was guilty of violations of article 9(1) because he was unlawfully and arbitrarily imprisoned from 1984 to 1993 in mental institutions. In particular he made the following claims:

¶ 3.1. The author claims that his original detention under the Mental Health Act was unlawful, and that judge Unwin, not being convinced that he was mentally disordered, acted arbitrarily and unlawfully in not discharging him.

¶ 3.2. He further contends that the yearly review hearings by a panel of psychiatrists were unfair, in that he had no access to the documents they based themselves on and could not call any witnesses on his behalf. In his opinion, the hearings were orchestrated to continue his unlawful detention.

¶ 3.3. In support, the author states that numerous psychiatrists testified that he was not mentally ill and not committable. He emphasizes that his incarceration continued in spite of medical evidence that his mental state did not warrant continued detention and in spite of the fact that he had not committed any act of violence. He argues that, if at any point after the beginning of his detention at Lake Alice Hospital, he suffered from a mental disorder, this was caused by his unlawful and unjustified detention among mentally ill people with a history of violence by whom he felt threatened.

The HRC found that there was no violation of article 9(1):

¶ 7.2. The main issue before the Committee is whether the author's detention under the Mental Health Act from 1984 to 1993 constituted a violation of the Covenant, in particular of article 9. The Committee notes that the author's assessment under the Mental Health Act followed threatening and aggressive behaviour on the author's part, and that the committal order was issued according to law, based on an opinion of three psychiatrists. Further, a panel of psychiatrists continued to review the author's situation periodically. The Committee is therefore of the opinion that the deprivation of the author's liberty was neither unlawful nor arbitrary and thus not in violation of article 9, paragraph 1, of the Covenant.

In a separate opinion, Messrs Pocar and Scheinin agreed that there had been no violation of article 9(1):

We associate ourselves with the general points of departure taken by the Committee. Treatment in a psychiatric institution against the will of the patient is a form of deprivation of

---

[29] See [11.19] for one of the HRC's rare comments about sentencing and article 9.

liberty that falls under the terms of article 9 of the Covenant. In an individual case there might well be a legitimate ground for such detention, and domestic law should prescribe both the criteria and procedures for assigning a person to compulsory psychiatric treatment. As a consequence, such treatment can be seen as a legitimate deprivation of liberty under the terms of article 9, paragraph 1.

The special nature of compulsory psychiatric treatment as a form of deprivation of liberty lies in the fact that the treatment is legitimate only as long as the medical criteria necessitating it exist. In order to avoid compulsory psychiatric treatment from becoming arbitrary detention prohibited by article 9, paragraph 1, there must be a system of mandatory and periodic review of the medical-scientific grounds for continuing the detention.

In the present case we are satisfied that the law of New Zealand, as applied in the case, met with the requirements of article 9, paragraph 1. The author was subject to a system of periodic expert review by a board of psychiatrists. Although the periodicity of one year appears to be rather infrequent, the facts of the case do not support a conclusion that this in itself resulted in a violation of the Covenant.

[11.19] In Concluding Comments on New Zealand, the HRC stated:[30]

¶ 14. The Committee is concerned about provisions in the Criminal Justice Amendment Act which provide for a sentence of indeterminate detention for offenders convicted even once of serious crimes who are likely to re-offend in a similar manner. The imposition of punishment in respect of possible future offences is inconsistent with articles 9 and 14 of the Covenant.

Thus, it is not compatible with article 9 for persons to be sentenced and detained on the basis that they are perceived to be likely to reoffend.[31] One cannot be detained *and sentenced* on the basis of likely future 'dangerousness'. However, perceived dangerousness may be a factor in justifying a person's enforced detention in a psychiatric institution.

The Right to be Informed of a Criminal Charge—Article 9(2)

[11.20] Article 9(2) provides that every person who is arrested on a criminal charge must be informed promptly of the charges against him (or her). One must be reasonably aware of the precise reasons for one's arrest. It is not, for example, sufficient to be informed that one is being arrested 'under prompt security measures without any indication of the substance' of the reasons for the arrest.[32]

---

[30] (1995) UN doc. CCPR/C/79/Add. 47, para. 14.

[31] See, in this respect, the judgment of the High Court of Australia in *Kable v Director of Public Prosecutions (NSW)* (1996) 189 CLR 51. See also Concluding Comments on Portugal (Macau) (1999) UN doc. CCPR/C/79/Add. 115, para. 12.

[32] *Drescher Caldas v Uruguay* (43/79), para. 13.2.

[11.21]　　　　　　　　***KELLY v JAMAICA (253/87)***

This case concerned numerous breaches of the ICCPR.[33] One violation concerned the fact that Kelly was not informed of his charge for twenty-six days. The Committee made the following comments about the relationship between article 9(2) and article 14(3)(a):[34]

¶ 5.8. Article 14, paragraph 3(a), requires that any individual under criminal charges shall be informed promptly and in detail of the nature and the charges against him. The requirement of prompt information, however, only applies once the individual has been formally charged with a criminal offence. It does not apply to those remanded in custody pending the result of police investigations; the latter situation is covered by article 9, paragraph 2, of the Covenant. In the present case, the State party has not denied that the author was not apprised in any detail of the reasons for his arrest for the several weeks following his apprehension and that he was not informed about the facts of the crime in connection with which he was detained or about the identity of the victim. The Committee concludes that the requirements of article 9, paragraph 2, were not met.

[11.22]　　　　　　　　***GRANT v JAMAICA (597/94)***

The pertinent facts are evident from the HRC's finding of a violation of article 9(2):

¶ 8.1. With regard to the author's allegations concerning a violation of article 9, the Committee observes that the State party is not absolved from its obligation under article 9, paragraph 2, of the Covenant to inform someone of the reasons of his arrest and of the charges against him, because of the arresting officer's opinion that the arrested person is aware of them. In the instant case, the author was arrested some weeks after the murder with which he was subsequently charged, and the State party has not contested that he was not informed of the reasons for his arrest until seven days later. In the circumstances, the Committee concludes that there has been a violation of article 9, paragraph 2.

[11.23] Compare the finding in *Grant* to those in *Stephens v Jamaica* (373/89) and *Griffin v Spain* (493/92). In *Stephens v Jamaica*, the Committee rejected an allegation of a violation of article 9(2) on the basis that the author was fully aware of the reasons for his detention as he had surrendered himself to the police and a detective had cautioned the author whilst he was in custody.

GRIFFIN v SPAIN (493/92)

¶ 9.2. With regard to the author's claim that, as there was no interpreter present at the time of his arrest, he was not informed of the reasons for his arrest and of the charges against him, the Committee notes from the information before it that the author was arrested and

---

[33]　See, e.g., [14.63] and [14.88].
[34]　See generally, on art. 14(3)(a), [14.56–14.57].

taken into custody at 11:30 p.m. on 17 April 1991, after the police, in the presence of the author, had searched the camper and discovered the drugs. The police reports further reveal that the police refrained from taking his statement in the absence of an interpreter, and that the following morning the drugs were weighed in the presence of the author. He was then brought before the examining magistrate and, with the use of an interpreter, he was informed of the charges against him. The Committee observes that, although no interpreter was present during the arrest, it is wholly unreasonable to argue that the author was unaware of the reasons for his arrest. In any event, he was promptly informed, in his own language, of the charges held against him. The Committee therefore finds no violation of article 9, paragraph 2, of the Covenant.

[11.24]   *HILL and HILL v SPAIN (526/93)*

The Committee found in favour of the State Party with regard to an allegation of a violation of article 9(2):

¶ 12.2. With regard to the authors' allegations of violations of article 9 of the Covenant, the Committee considers that the authors' arrest was not illegal or arbitrary. Article 9, paragraph 2, of the Covenant requires that anyone who is arrested shall be informed, at the time of arrest, of the reasons for his arrest and shall be promptly informed of any charges against him. The authors specifically allege that seven and eight hours, respectively, elapsed before they were informed of the reason for their arrest, and complain that they did not understand the charges because of the lack of a competent interpreter. The documents submitted by the State party show that police formalities were suspended from 6 a.m. until 9 a.m., when the interpreter arrived, so that the accused could be duly informed in the presence of legal counsel. Furthermore, from the documents sent by the State it appears that the interpreter was not an *ad hoc* interpreter but an official interpreter appointed according to rules that should ensure her competence. In these circumstances, the Committee finds that the facts before it do not reveal a violation of article 9, paragraph 2, of the Covenant.

The Hill brothers had contended that eight hours had passed before they were informed of the reason for their arrest. The Committee chose to accept the State's evidence that this period of time was only three hours, as well as the evidence that the interpreter was sufficiently competent. It is therefore uncertain whether eight hours' delay would have constituted a breach of article 9(2).[35] The shortest delay which has been found actually to breach article 9(2) remains the seven-day delay in *Grant* [11.22].[36]

[11.25]   *LEEHONG v JAMAICA (613/95)*

¶ 9.4. The author has claimed a violation of articles 9, paragraph 2, and 14, paragraph 3(a), since he was not informed of the charges against him at the time of his arrest. After a police officer was killed, the author was charged and arrested. Later after an investigation, the

---

[35] At least nine hours had passed in the *Griffin* case, but the HRC there assumed that Griffin was fully aware of the reasons for his arrest. See [11.23].

[36] Nine days' delay constituted a violation of art. 9(2) in *Morrison v Jamaica* (663/95).

original charge was dropped for lack of evidence, but it appears that the author was the suspect of another murder and was kept in detention [for over three months] before being charged . . . for the second crime. In the circumstance of the case and on the basis of the information before it, the Committee finds that there has been no violation of the articles 9, paragraph 2, and 14, paragraph 3, of the Covenant.

Whilst the *Leehong* decision seems correct regarding article 14(3)(a) (as he was told of the correct charges upon being formally charged), the article 9(2) decision may pave the way for police abuse of power. Police should be required to inform a detainee of the reason for his/her arrest, and the reason for his/her continued detention after arrest if those reasons should differ.[37]

Rights of Persons Detained on Criminal Charges—Article 9(3)

'PROMPT' PRESENTATION BEFORE A JUDICIAL OFFICER

[11.26] Persons detained on criminal charges must be brought promptly before a judicial officer who rules on whether the detention will continue.

GENERAL COMMENT 8

¶ 2. Paragraph 3 of article 9 requires that in criminal cases any person arrested or detained has to be brought 'promptly' before a judge or other officer authorized by law to exercise judicial power. More precise time-limits are fixed by law in most States parties and, in the view of the Committee, delays must not exceed a few days. . . .

[11.27] One of the keys to interpretation of article 9(3) is the meaning of the word 'promptly'. The General Comment is quite vague, specifying a period of 'a few days'. In *Kelly v Jamaica* (253/87), Mr Wennergren, in a separate opinion, expressed the view that 'the word "promptly" does not permit a delay of more than two to three days'. However, in *Portorreal v Dominican Republic* (188/84) the Committee found that there was no breach of article 9(3) even though the author was held for fifty hours before being brought before a judge.[38] In *Van der Houwen v The Netherlands* (583/94), seventy-three hours of detention without being brought before a judge was held not to be a violation of article 9(3).[39] Finally, while the eight-hour detention in *Spakmo v Norway* (631/95) was found to have breached article 9(1), article 9(3) was not mentioned in the case [11.13].

On the other hand, in *Jijón v Ecuador* (277/88) the Committee found a violation of article 9(3) when the author was held incommunicado for five days without being brought before a judge and without having access to counsel. Similarly in

---

[37] There was however a breach of art. 9(3) in this case entailed in the delay in bringing Leehong before a magistrate, see below, on 'promptness', [11.26–11.28].

[38] Para. 10.2.

[39] Para. 4.3.

Grant v Jamaica (597/94), a delay of at least seven days before the accused was brought before a magistrate constituted a violation of article 9(3). Another seven-day delay in *McLawrence v Jamaica* (702/96) also breached article 9(3).[40]

HRC jurisprudence therefore indicates that the limit of 'promptness' for the purposes of the article 9(3) guarantee of judicial review lies somewhere between seventy-three hours (in *Van der Houwen v The Netherlands* (583/94)), where no violation arose, and five days (*Jijón v Ecuador* (277/88)), where article 9(3) was violated.

[11.28] However, it may be that the HRC are beginning to take a stricter view. In its 1998 Comments on Zimbabwe, the HRC stated the following:[41]

¶ 17. With regard to pre-trial detention, the Committee expresses concern that under the Criminal Justice and Procedure Act the maximum period of detention of 48 hours before being brought to a judge or magistrate may be extended to 96 hours by a senior police officer, a practice which is incompatible with article 9 of the Covenant. The Committee is especially concerned that this practice provides opportunity for ill treatment and intimidation of detainees. The law relating to arrest and detention should be reviewed to bring it into conformity with article 9 of the Covenant and to ensure that individuals are not held in pre-trial custody for longer than 48 hours without court order. . . .

'JUDGE OR OTHER OFFICER AUTHORIZED BY LAW'

[11.29] *KULOMIN v HUNGARY (521/92)*

The author, a Russian citizen living in Hungary, was arrested for murder. He was detained for over a year before he was brought to trial. The State Party explained that his arrest and detention were regulated by legislation which gave the public prosecutor authority to extend a person's pre-trial detention. In this case the author's pre-trial detention was ordered and subsequently renewed on several occasions by the public prosecutor. The State claimed that there was no violation of article 9(3) as the accused had been brought promptly before an 'other officer authorized by law'. In this case the State made the argument that the public prosecutor fell within the meaning of this term:

¶ 10.4. As regards the compatibility of the procedure with the requirements of article 9, paragraph 3, the State party interprets the term 'other officers authorized by law' as meaning officers with the same independence towards the executive as the Courts. In this connection, the State party notes that the law in force in Hungary in 1988 provided that the Chief Public Prosecutor was elected by and responsible to Parliament. All other public prosecutors were subordinate to the Chief Public Prosecutor. The State party concludes that the prosecutor's organization at the time had no link whatsoever with the executive and

---

[40] Para. 5.6.
[41] (1998) UN doc. CCPR/C/79/Add. 89; see also Concluding Comments on Lesotho (1999) UN doc. CCPR/C/79/Add. 106, para. 18.

was independent from it. The State party therefore argues that the prosecutors who decided on the continued detention of Mr. Kulomin can be regarded as other officers authorized by law to exercise judicial power within the meaning of article 9, paragraph 3, and that no violation of the Covenant has occurred.

The Committee rejected the State Party's arguments in relation to article 9(3), making the following comments:

¶ 11.3. The Committee notes that, after his arrest on 20 August 1988, the author's pre-trial detention was ordered and subsequently renewed on several occasions by the public prosecutor, until the author was brought before a judge on 29 May 1989. The Committee considers that it is inherent to the proper exercise of judicial power, that it be exercised by an authority which is independent, objective and impartial in relation to the issues dealt with. In the circumstances of the instant case, the Committee is not satisfied that the public prosecutor could be regarded as having the institutional objectivity and impartiality necessary to be considered an 'officer authorized to exercise judicial power' within the meaning of article 9(3).

[11.30] Mr Ando dissented in the following terms:

Article 9, paragraph 3, of the International Covenant on Civil and Political Rights stipulates: anyone arrested or detained on a criminal charge shall be brought promptly before a judge or other officer authorized by law to exercise judicial power . . . The State party interprets the term 'other officer authorized by law' as meaning an officer with the same independence towards the executive as a court. . . .

As a matter of fact, in the domestic law of many States parties, public prosecutors are granted certain judicial power, including the power to investigate and prosecute suspects in criminal cases. In the case of Hungarian law in 1988, this power included the power to extend the detention of suspects up to one year before they were committed to trial. . . .

In my opinion, the pre-trial detention of suspects for the period of one year seems to be too long. In addition, while I do understand that under the Hungarian law of 1988 the Public Prosecutor who should decide on the extension of detention was to be different from the one who requested the extension, excessive detention was likely to occur in that type of system.

Nevertheless, I am unable to accept the categorical statement of the Committee . . . to the effect that in the Hungarian type of system the Public Prosecutor necessarily lacks the institutional objectivity and impartiality necessary to be considered as an 'officer authorized to exercise judicial power' within the meaning of article 9, paragraph 3. Even in that type of system, a prosecutor's decision on the extension of the detention of a particular suspect in a given case may well be impartial and objectively justifiable. To deny such impartiality and objectivity, the Committee needs to clarify the detailed circumstances of the instant case on which it bases its finding, but such clarification is totally lacking in the Committee's Views.

[11.31] Ando is correct in criticizing the vagueness of the majority's decision regarding article 9(3), which does little to illuminate the words 'or other officer authorized by law to exercise judicial power'. The majority should have specified how the Hungarian public prosecutor lacked sufficient 'institutional objectivity and impartiality'. However, Ando's own decision may be criticized. He characterizes the power to 'investigate' and 'prosecute suspects' as judicial power. These powers seem more concomitant with executive powers.[42]

LENGTH OF PRE-TRIAL DETENTION

[11.32] In relation to pre-trial detention, article 9(3) states that persons shall be entitled to trial within a reasonable time or release.

GENERAL COMMENT 8

¶ 3. Another matter is the total length of detention pending trial. In certain categories of criminal cases in some countries this matter has caused some concern within the Committee, and members have questioned whether their practices have been in conformity with the entitlement 'to trial within a reasonable time or to release' under paragraph 3. Pre-trial detention should be an exception and as short as possible. The Committee would welcome information concerning mechanisms existing and measures taken with a view to reducing the duration of such detention.

[11.33] Article 9(3) overlaps considerably with article 14(3)(c). Whilst the latter provision guarantees that one's criminal trial will be held within a reasonable period of time after one's charge, the former guarantees that one will not be held in detention for an unreasonable period of time prior to one's trial. Therefore, article 9(3) regulates the length of pre-trial *detention*, whereas article 14(3) regulates the total length of time that passes before one's trial. Most breaches of article 14(3)(c) have concerned persons who have been held in detention for the entire time before trial, so they have *a fortiori* also concerned breaches of article 9(3).[43]

[11.34] *FILLASTRE and BIZOUARN v BOLIVIA (336/88)*

This case involved the treatment of two French private detectives who were arrested and detained in Bolivia for a number of offences. The communication was brought by one of the victim's wives. It was submitted that the two men were held in custody for ten days without being informed of the charges against them and that there was a delay of over three years for the adjudication of the case at first instance. The State responded:

¶ 4.6. As to the author's complaint about undue delays in the judicial proceedings, the State party points out that criminal investigations under Bolivian law are carried out in

---

[42] See, e.g., P. Hanks and D. Cass, *Australian Constitutional Law: Commentary and Materials* (6th edn., Butterworths, Sydney, 1999), 395.
[43] See generally [14.65] ff.

written form, which implies that administrative and other delays may occur. Furthermore, the absence of an adequate budget for a proper administration of justice means that a number of criminal cases and certain specific procedural phases of criminal proceedings have experienced delays.

The Committee found that there was a violation of both article 9(2) and (3). It made the following comments regarding the State's claims about budgetary constraints:

¶ 6.4. . . . The pertinent factor in this case is that both Mr. Fillastre and Mr. Bizouarn allegedly were held in custody for 10 days before being brought before any judicial instance and without being informed of the charges against them. Accordingly, while not unsympathetic to the State party's claim that budgetary constraints may cause impediments to the proper administration of justice in Bolivia, the Committee concludes that the right of Mr. Fillastre and Mr. Bizouarn under article 9, paragraphs 2 and 3, have not been observed.

¶ 6.5. Under article 9, paragraph 3, anyone arrested or detained on a criminal charge 'shall be entitled to trial within a reasonable time . . .'. What constitutes 'reasonable time' is a matter of assessment for each particular case. The lack of adequate budgetary appropriations for the administration of criminal justice alluded to by the State party does not justify unreasonable delays in the adjudication of criminal cases. Nor does the fact that investigations into a criminal case are, in their essence, carried out by way of written proceedings, justify such delays. In the present case, the Committee has not been informed that a decision at first instance had been reached some four years after the victims' arrest. Considerations of evidence-gathering do not justify such prolonged detention. The Committee concludes that there has been, in this respect, a violation of article 9, paragraph 3.

[11.35]   *LEWIS v JAMAICA (708/96)*

The author, in this case, claimed to be a victim of a number of articles including article 9(3). It was alleged that there was a delay of three and a half months' between the author's arrest and the preliminary enquiry, sixteen months delay between his arrest and the arraignment, and nearly two years between his arrest and the trial.[44] The HRC in finding for the author on this issue made the following comments:

¶ 8.1. The author has argued that the 23 months' delay between his arrest and trial was unduly long and constitutes a violation of articles 9, paragraph 3, and 14, paragraph 3 (c), of the Covenant. Article 9, paragraph 3, entitles an arrested person to trial within a reasonable time or to release. The Committee notes that the arguments forwarded by the State party do not give an adequate explanation why the author, if not released on bail, was not brought to trial for 23 months. The Committee is of the view that in the context of article 9, paragraph 3, and in the absence of any satisfactory explanation for the delay by the State

---

[44] Para. 3.4.

party, a delay of 23 months during which the author was in detention is unreasonable and therefore constitutes a violation of this provision. The Committee does not, in the circumstances, consider it necessary to consider the question of violation of article 14, paragraph 3 (c).

[11.36] A number of the members of the HRC dissented on the finding of an article 9(3) violation. Lord Colville, with whom Mr Ando agreed, stated the following:

¶ 1. I am unable to agree that the delay of 23 months which elapsed between the author's arrest and trial constitutes a violation, on the facts of this case, of articles 9, paragraph 3, of the Covenant. The crucial matter is that concerning his statement, which in paragraphs 2.2 and 3.1 of the Views he complains was falsely obtained after his being beaten by the police.

¶ 2. This statement, which contained his confession to an involvement in the killing of the victim, was central to the author's defence at his trial, and was always so intended. Contrary to his claim, a study of the trial transcript shows that the statement was taken voluntarily, in the presence of a Magistrate who attended for this purpose at the request of the police officer in charge of his case. It was confirmed at the trial, by his counsel (p. 92) and by the author in the course of his sworn evidence, to be true: he never complained that it had been extracted from him in the manner now claimed. To the contrary, it was an essential part of his defence, in his attempt to ensure that his conviction (which was virtually certain) was for non-capital murder under section 2(2) of the Offences against the Person (Amendment) Act 1992, in that, he claimed, he had 'not himself used violence on that person in the course or furtherance of an attack' on him—see Court of Appeal judgement, 31 July 1995, pp. 17 & 18. The author's defence was, and had always been, to transfer the blame for all application of violence to his co-defendant, Peter Blaine. Such a line of defence (colloquially known to common lawyers as a 'cut-throat' defence) would have stood very little chance of success unless the same jury was also engaged in the decision whether they could convict Peter Blaine, in accordance with the proper rules of procedure, exemplified in article 14, paragraph 2, of the Covenant.

¶ 3. In the event the author's defence on these lines was not successful, possibly because of major inconsistencies between what he had said in the statement before the Magistrate and the evidence he gave during the trial. Nevertheless it was sufficiently important to him to give sworn evidence, and to subject himself to cross-examination by the prosecution and also counsel for his co-defendant (which did occur), in order to seek to obtain a non-capital verdict.

¶ 4. The author's co-defendant, Peter Blaine, had gone into hiding after the murder and there was a police block on Jamaican ports to prevent his leaving the jurisdiction. It was not open to the author to assist in his apprehension but it was essential to the author that he should not be tried alone, by a jury not also seized of the case of Peter Blaine. No complaint is made that the author sought release on bail, whatever the probabilities of such an application being successful, and he gives no information in that respect.

¶ 5. As for the author's claim, in paragraph 3.1 of the Views, that there was insufficient evidence, without that of Peter Blaine, to bring him to trial, this is wholly inconsistent with

(i) his initial statement, (ii) his sworn evidence at the trial and (iii) his own adopted line of defence which was to transfer any liability for capital (as opposed to non-capital) murder on to his co-defendant, Peter Blaine.

¶ 6. Accordingly I am of the opinion that the author's substantive rights under the Covenant were neither invoked nor violated in the respect set out above.

Mr. Lallah agreed with Lord Colville, and added the following:

The State party did provide some explanations which, in my view, were quite relevant. These could legitimately be considered in the context of other relevant factors shown in the case record. Those explanations and the record indicate the following: the police first conducted an enquiry; on the basis of that enquiry, a preliminary enquiry was held before a court and the author appeared several times in court; at the close of the committal proceedings, the author was committed by the court for eventual trial; the trial did not take place in the normal course since the police then succeeded in arresting a co-accused, and it must be assumed that a preliminary enquiry had to be held with regard to the participation of the co-accused, so that there could be a joint trial of the author and his co-accused in respect of a joint offence. It would seem to me that, in these circumstances, it could not be said that the time that elapsed between the committal of the author and beginning of his trial, though *ex facie* somewhat long, was unreasonable.

RIGHT TO RELEASE PENDING TRIAL

[11.37] Article 9(3) prescribes that 'the general rule' for persons awaiting trial is that they should not be detained in custody. In the following case, the HRC discussed instances where departure from this norm would be permissible.

W.B.E. v THE NETHERLANDS (432/90)

The author claimed his pre-trial detention of three months, on a charge of drug smuggling, breached article 9(3). The Committee found the allegation inadmissible, and made the following comments regarding the permissibility of pre-trial detention:

¶ 6.3. With regard to the author's allegation that his pre-trial detention was in violation of article 9 of the Covenant, the Committee observes that article 9, paragraph 3, allows pre-trial detention as an exception; pre-trial detention may be necessary, for example, to ensure the presence of the accused at the trial, avert interference with witnesses and other evidence, or the commission of other offences. On the basis of the information before the Committee, it appears that the author's detention was based on considerations that there was a serious risk that, if released, he might interfere with the evidence against him.

¶ 6.4. The Committee considers that, since pre-trial detention to prevent interference with evidence is, as such, compatible with article 9, paragraph 3, . . . and since the author has not substantiated, for purposes of admissibility, his claim that there was no lawful reason to extend his detention, this part of the communication is inadmissible under articles 2 and 3 of the Optional Protocol.

[11.38] *HILL and HILL v SPAIN (526/93)*

The authors, who were British citizens, were arrested in Spain on suspicion of having firebombed a car. One of the claims made by the authors was that the State Party had violated article 9(3) as they were not released on bail after their arrest. The State Party justified the authors' extended pre-trial detention as follows:

¶ 9.7. The State party submits that the duration of 16 months of pre-trial detention was not unusual. It was justified in view of the complexities of the case; bail was not granted because of the danger that the authors would leave Spanish territory, which they did as soon as release was granted.

In its merits decision against the State Party, the Committee made the following comments:

¶ 12.3. As for article 9, paragraph 3, of the Covenant, which stipulates that it shall not be the general rule that persons awaiting trial shall be detained in custody, the authors complain that they were not granted bail and that, because they could not return to the United Kingdom, their construction firm was declared bankrupt. The Committee reaffirms its prior jurisprudence that pre-trial detention should be the exception and that bail should be granted, except in situations where the likelihood exists that the accused would abscond or destroy evidence, influence witnesses or flee from the jurisdiction of the State party. The mere fact that the accused is a foreigner does not of itself imply that he may be held in detention pending trial. The State party has indeed argued that there was a well-founded concern that the authors would leave Spanish territory if released on bail. However, it has provided no information on what this concern was based and why it could not be addressed by setting an appropriate sum of bail and other conditions of release. The mere conjecture of a State party that a foreigner might leave its jurisdiction if released on bail does not justify an exception to the rule laid down in article 9, paragraph 3, of the Covenant. In these circumstances, the Committee finds that this right in respect of the authors has been violated.

[11.39] The Committee, in its Concluding Comments on Argentina, reiterated the requirement that bail be reasonably available as an alternative to pre-trial detention.[45]

¶ 14. The Committee further notes that bail is established according to the economic consequences of the crime committed and not by reference to the probability that the defendant will not appear in court or otherwise impede due process of law. Nor is it compatible with the presumption of innocence that the length of pre-trial detention is not a product of the complexity of the case but is set by reference to the possible length of sentence.

Therefore, article 9(3) prescribes that bail be ordinarily available to detainees.

---

[45] (1995) UN doc. CCPR/C/79/Add. 46. See also Concluding Comments on Ecuador (1998) UN doc. CCPR/C/79/Add. 92, para. 13.

Presumably, bail should not be set at an excessively high figure which might preclude a detainee from being able to raise bail.[46]

[11.40]   *KONÉ v SENEGAL (386/89)*

¶ 8.6. . . . What constitutes 'reasonable time' within the meaning of article 9, paragraph 3, must be assessed on a case-by-case basis.

¶ 8.7. A delay of four years and four months during which the author was kept in custody . . . cannot be deemed compatible with article 9, paragraph 3, in the absence of special circumstances justifying such delay, such as that there were, or had been, impediments to the investigations attributable to the accused or to his representative. No such circumstances are discernible in the present case. Accordingly, the author's detention was incompatible with article 9, paragraph 3. . . .

Koné confirms that there is no set period of permissible pre-trial detention under article 9(3). However, it must be doubted whether pre-trial detention of four years could ever be justified.[47]

[11.41] Long periods of pre-trial detention may be permitted when the detainee is charged with a very serious offence. There is a higher risk that such people will escape, or pose a danger to society, if released pending trial. Pre-trial detention for fourteen months, for a trial for capital murder, did not breach article 9(3) in *Thomas v Jamaica* (614/95).[48]

Right of Habeas Corpus—Article 9(4)

[11.42] Article 9(4) entitles any person who has been arrested or detained for whatever reason to challenge the lawfulness of his/her detention in a court without delay. This right stems from the Anglo-American legal principle of *habeas corpus*, and exists regardless of whether deprivation of liberty is actually unlawful.[49]

[11.43]   *STEPHENS v JAMAICA (373/89)*

This decision confirms that the right of access to court in article 9(4), unlike article 9(3), does not have to be performed *ex officio* by the State. Instead it occurs at the instigation of the author or his/her representatives. The State cannot be held

---

[46] Dinstein, above, note 11, 134.

[47] On the other hand, a four-year delay in bringing someone to trial (so long as they have not been detained the whole time) may be justified by the complexities of the case, or by obstruction on the part of the accused: see [14.67].

[48] Para. 9.6. A twelve-month delay on a capital murder charge in *McTaggart v Jamaica* (743/97) did not breach art. 9(3), para. 8.2.

[49] Nowak, above, note 1, 178.

responsible for the author's failure to seek review of the lawfulness of his/her detention.

¶ 9.7. With respect to the alleged violation of article 9(4), it should be noted that the author did not himself apply for *habeas corpus*. He could have, after being informed on 2 March 1983 that he was suspected of having murdered Mr. Lawrence, requested a prompt decision on the lawfulness of his detention. There is no evidence that he or his legal representative did do so. It cannot, therefore, be concluded that Mr. Stephens was denied the opportunity to have the lawfulness of his detention reviewed in court without delay.

REVIEW WITHOUT DELAY

[11.44] In *Hammel v Madagascar* (155/83), incommunicado detention for three days, during which time it was impossible for the author to gain access to a court to challenge his detention, was held to breach article 9(4). On the other hand, in *Portorreal v Dominican Republic* (188/84), the Committee found, perhaps surprisingly, no breach of article 9(4) when the author was held for fifty hours without having the opportunity to challenge his detention.

[11.45] The following cases concern the permissible delay in a court issuing a decision on the lawfulness of one's detention, as opposed to the delay in actually accessing that court.

[11.46]   *TORRES v FINLAND (291/88)*

Torres was earmarked for deportation from Finland. He had challenged the legality of his detention under Finnish migration and extradition laws. His challenge failed. He argued that his detention breached article 9(4), due to the delay in the publication of the court's decision regarding the legality of his detention.[50]

¶ 7.3. . . . [T]he Committee emphasizes that, as a matter of principle, the adjudication of a case by any court of law should take place as expeditiously as possible. This does not mean, however, that precise deadlines for the handing down of judgments may be set which, if not observed, would necessarily justify the conclusion that a decision was not reached 'without delay'. Rather, the question of whether a decision was reached without delay must be assessed on a case by case basis. The Committee notes that almost three months passed between the filing of the author's appeal, under the Aliens Act, against the decision of the Ministry of the Interior and the decision of the Supreme Administrative Court. This period is in principle too extended, but as the Committee does not know the reasons for the judgment being issued only on 4 March 1988, it makes no finding under article 9, paragraph 4, of the Covenant.

[11.47] This seems to be a very timid judgment in respect of the delay in the delivery of the court's judgment regarding the legality of Torres' detention. It

---

[50] See also [11.53].

seems incumbent upon the State Party to inform the Committee of the reasons for such a delay. It should not benefit from its failure to do so. Finland apparently did benefit here, as no violation was found in respect of the delayed judgment, even though 'in principle, the period [was] too extended'.

[11.48]   *A v NEW ZEALAND (754/97)*

The facts of this case are outlined above at [11.18]. A further complaint of the author was that he was not afforded frequent opportunity to challenge his detention in a maximum security wing of a psychiatric hospital. The HRC majority found no violation of article 9(4) on the facts:

¶ 7.3. The Committee further notes that the author's continued detention was regularly reviewed by the Courts and that the facts of the communication thus do not disclose a violation of article 9, paragraph 4, of the Covenant. In this context, the Committee has noted the author's argument that the decision by Unwin J not to dismiss him from compulsory status was arbitrary. The Committee observes, however, that this decision and the author's continued detention were reviewed by other courts, which confirmed Unwin J's findings and the necessity of continuation of compulsory status for the author. The Committee refers to its constant jurisprudence, that it is for the courts of States parties concerned to review the evaluation of the facts as well as the application of the law in a particular case, and not for the Committee, unless the Courts' decisions are manifestly arbitrary or amount to a denial of justice. On the basis of the material before it, the Committee finds that the Courts' reviews of the author's compulsory status under the Mental Health Act did not suffer from such defects.

[11.49] Messrs Pocar and Scheinin dissented, finding a violation of article 9(4). They made the following comments:

Our concern lies in the fact that although there was periodic expert review of the author's status,[51] his continued detention was not subject to effective and regular judicial review. In order for the author's treatment to meet the requirements of article 9, paragraph 4, not only the psychiatric review but also its judicial control should have been regular.

We find a violation of article 9, paragraph 4, in the case. Various mechanisms of judicial review on the lawfulness of the author's continued detention were provided by the law of New Zealand, but none of them was effective enough to provide for judicial review 'without delay'. Although there were several instances of judicial review, they were too irregular and too slow to meet the requirements of the Covenant. As the following account of the various instances of judicial review will show, this conclusion does not depend on the position one takes on the effect of the entry into force of the Optional Protocol in respect of New Zealand on 26 August 1989.

Between the original committal to compulsory psychiatric treatment in November 1984 and the decision by the Medical Health Review Tribunal, in February 1993, to discharge

---

[51] See their concurring opinion on this point at [11.18].

the author from compulsory status (before which decision he had already been released from a closed institution), there appears not to have been a single instance of judicial review that would have met the standards of article 9, paragraph 4, of the Covenant.

On 9 August 1985, the author submitted a writ of *habeas corpus*. Instead of resulting in a decision without delay, this writ was incorporated into another procedure of judicial review that ended in the judicial determination of the author's continued detention as late as 21 April 1986.

Another set of judicial proceedings to review the author's detention was initiated by the author in early December 1987. Although the author himself contributed to the delay by, *inter alia*, escaping from an institution, he was rearrested on 9 August 1989, after which date it took still until 15 August 1990 before the proceedings ended in a judicial determination by the High Court.

A third set of judicial proceedings were completed by a High Court Decision on 24 April 1991. It is unclear from the file when the proceedings in question were initiated, but from the decision itself it transpires that the review was based on 'an urgent enquiry' by the author and that a hearing had been conducted on 22 February 1991, i.e. a little more than two months prior to the decision.

Our conclusion of a violation by New Zealand of the author's rights under article 9, paragraph 4, is based on the fact that prior to the author's provisional release in April 1992, the author's requests for a judicial determination of the lawfulness of his detention were not decided without delay. Consequently, the author has a right to compensation under article 9, paragraph 5.

[11.50] As the Optional Protocol did not enter into force for New Zealand until 26 August 1989, complaints about delays in habeas corpus decisions occurring before that date would be inadmissible *ratione temporis*. However, the minority's detailed chronology of events indicates that two significant delays in issuing habeas corpus judgments occurred after August 1989, lasting, respectively, about one year, and over two months. It is regrettable that the HRC majority let the State party get away with such long delays in issuing judgments regarding the legality of a person's detention. The HRC's jurisprudence in this respect, bearing in mind its decisions in *A v New Zealand* and *Torres* [11.46], has been disappointing.

ACCESS TO LAWYERS

[11.51]   *BERRY v JAMAICA (330/88)*

In this case, the Committee clearly links access to legal representation with enjoyment of the right in article 9(4). In practice, it is virtually impossible for people to challenge their detention without legal representation.

¶ 11.1. In respect of the allegations pertaining to article 9, paragraphs 3 and 4, the State party has not contested that the author was detained for two and a half months before he was brought before a judge or judicial officer authorized to decide on the lawfulness of his detention. Instead, the State party has confined itself to the contention that, during his detention, the author could have applied to the courts for a writ of *habeas corpus*. The Committee notes, however, the author's claim, which remains unchallenged, that throughout this period he had no access to legal representation. The Committee considers that a delay of over two months violates the requirement, in article 9, paragraph 3, that anyone arrested on a criminal charge shall be brought 'promptly' before a judge or other officer authorized by law to exercise judicial power. In the circumstances, the Committee concludes that the author's right under article 9, paragraph 4, was also violated, since he was not, in due time, afforded the opportunity to obtain, on his own initiative, a decision by a court on the lawfulness of his detention.

Similarly, in *Hammel v Madagascar* (155/83) [11.44], incommunicado detention rendered a habeas corpus action impossible. Five days' incommunicado detention was identified as a breach of article 9 in Concluding Comments on Spain.[52]

[11.52]   *A v AUSTRALIA (560/93)*

The author, an illegal immigrant, was held in detention pending determination of his application for asylum [11.15]. The author's initial detention was served in a detention centre in Sydney in New South Wales. He was then transferred several thousand kilometres away to Darwin in the Northern Territory. Whilst in the Northern Territory he was moved between two refugee camps. Eventually he was moved to a detention centre in Port Hedland in Western Australia. Initially the author was receiving legal advice from lawyers at the New South Wales Legal Aid Commission but this contact was cut off as a result of the move to the Northern Territory. He then received legal advice from the Northern Territory Legal Aid Commission but he lost contact with his legal representatives in that office when he was moved to Port Hedland. Counsel claimed that the author's constant removal to different detention centres around the country effectively denied him access to his lawyers, which entailed a breach of article 9(4).

¶ 5.7. Counsel insists that an entitlement to take proceedings before a court under article 9, paragraph 4, necessarily requires that an individual have access to legal advice. Wherever a person is under detention, access to the courts can generally only be achieved through assistance of counsel. In this context, counsel disputes that his client had adequate access to legal advice. . . .

¶ 5.8. Author's counsel adds that on two occasions his client was forcibly removed from a State jurisdiction and therefore from access to his lawyers. On neither occasion was adequate notice of his removal given to his lawyers. It is submitted that these events constitute a denial of the author's access to his legal advisers.

On this issue, the Committee found in favour of the State Party:

¶ 9.6. . . . That A was moved repeatedly between detention centres and was obliged to

---

[52] (1996) UN doc. CCPR/C/79/Add. 61, para. 12.

change his legal representatives cannot detract from the fact that he retained access to legal advisers; that this access was inconvenient, notably because of the remote location of Port Hedland, does not, in the Committee's opinion, raise an issue under article 9, paragraph 4.

The Committee evidently did not find that A's access to lawyers was so badly jeopardized as to deny him an effective right of access to a court for the purposes of challenging his detention.

PROCEEDINGS MUST BE BEFORE A 'COURT'

[11.53]   *TORRES v FINLAND (291/88)*

In this case, the author, an alien earmarked for extradition, was held in detention for seven days without being given an opportunity to have recourse to a court in order to decide upon the legality of his detention. Under the relevant legislation, Torres was only entitled to review by the relevant Ministry.

¶ 7.2. [T]he Committee has taken note of the State party's contention that the author could have appealed the detention orders of 7 October, 3 December 1987 and 5 January 1988 pursuant to section 32 of the Aliens Act to the Ministry of the Interior. In the Committee's opinion, this possibility, while providing for some measure of protection and review of the legality of detention, does not satisfy the requirements of article 9, paragraph 4, which envisages that the legality of detention will be determined by a court so as to ensure a higher degree of objectivity and independence in such control. The Committee further notes that while the author was detained under orders of the police, he could not have the lawfulness of his detention reviewed by a court. Review before a court of law was possible only when, after seven days, the detention was confirmed by order of the Minister. As no challenge could have been made until the second week of detention, the author's detention from 8 to 15 October 1987, from 3 to 10 December 1987 and from 5 to 10 January 1988 violated the requirement of article 9, paragraph 4, of the Covenant that a detained person be able 'to take proceedings before a court, in order that that court may decide *without delay* on the lawfulness of his detention and order his release if the detention is not lawful' (emphasis added).

[11.54]   *VUOLANNE v FINLAND (265/87)*

In this case the author was given military disciplinary punishment of ten days' close arrest (confinement in the guardhouse without service duties) for having left his garrison without permission. The author was locked in a cell alone and was prohibited from communicating with other detainees. He requested that his detention be reviewed by a higher military officer. However the decision to detain him was upheld without a hearing. The author argued that there was a breach of article 9(4) as he was detained without being given recourse to a court of law. The State Party made a number of comments about article 9(4):

¶ 6.3. With regard to the applicability of article 9, paragraph 4, of the Covenant to the facts of this case, the State party submits:

'It is not open for somebody detained on the basis of military disciplinary procedure, as outlined above, to take proceedings in a court. The only relief is granted by the system of request for review. In other words, it has been the view of Finnish authorities that article 9, paragraph 4, of the Covenant on Civil and Political Rights does not apply to detention in military procedure. . . .

'In its General Comment 8 (16) of 27 July 1982, regarding article 9, the Committee had occasion to single out what types of detention were covered by article 9, paragraph 4. It listed detentions on grounds such as 'mental illness, vagrancy, drug addiction, educational purposes, immigration control, etc.'. Significantly, the Committee omitted deprivation of liberty in military disciplinary procedure from this list. What is common to the forms of detention listed by the Committee is that they involve the possibility of prolonged, unlimited detention. Also in most cases these forms of detention are not strictly regulated but the manner of detention is made dependent on its purpose (cure of illness, for example) and engages a wide degree of discretion on the part of the detaining authority. However, this is in striking contrast with the process of detention in military disciplinary procedure, where the grounds for detention, the length of detention and the manner of conducting the detention are clearly laid down in military law. In the event that the military authorities overstep the boundaries set by the law, the normal ways of judicial appeal are open. In other words, it might be that the Committee did not include military disciplinary process in its list of different kinds of 'detention' because it realized the material difference between it and those other forms of detention from the point of view of an individual's need of protection.

'It is clearly the case that an official—a commander—is acting in a judicial or at least quasi-judicial capacity as he, under military disciplinary procedure, orders detention. Likewise, the consideration of a request for review is comparable to judicial scrutiny of an appeal. As explained, the conditions and manner of carrying out military disciplinary detention are clearly set down by law. The discretion they imply is significantly less than discretion in some of the cases listed by the Committee. In this respect, too, the need for judicial control, if not strictly superfluous, is significantly less in military disciplinary procedure than in detention on, say, grounds of mental illness.'

The author responded as follows:

¶ 7.2. With respect to article 9, paragraph 4, the author comments on the State party's reference to the Committee's General Comment No. 8 (16) on article 9, and notes that the State party does not mention that, according to the General Comment, article 9, paragraph 4, applies to all persons deprived of their liberty by arrest or detention. He further submits:

'Military confinement is a punishment that can be ordered either by a court or in military disciplinary procedure. The duration of the punishment is comparable to the shortest prison sentences under normal criminal law (14 days is the Finnish minimum) and exceeds the length of pre-trial detention acceptable in the light of the Covenant. This shows that there is no substantial difference between these forms of detention from the point of view of an individual's need of protection. . . .'

The author then offers the following comments in order to show that the Finnish military disciplinary procedure does not correspond to the requirements of article 2, paragraph 3, either:

'(a) According to the State party, 'the normal ways of judicial appeal are open in case the military authorities overstep the boundaries set by the law'. This statement is misleading. There is no way a person punished with military confinement can bring the legality of the punishment before a court. What can in principle be challenged is the behaviour of the military authorities in question. This would mean instituting a civil charge in court, not any kind of an 'appeal'. This kind of a procedure is in no way 'normal' and even if the procedure were instituted, the court could not order the release of the victim;

'(b) Also some other statements are misleading. An official ordering detention and another officer considering the request for review are not acting in a 'judicial or at least quasi-judicial capacity'. The officers have no legal education. The procedure lacks even the most elementary requirements of a judicial process: the applicant is not heard and the final decision is made by a person who is not independent, but has been consulted already before ordering the punishment. . . .'

The Committee made the following finding in favour of the author:

¶ 9.3. The Committee has noted the contention of the State party that the case of Mr. Vuolanne does not fall within the ambit of article 9, paragraph 4, of the Covenant. The Committee considers that this question must be answered by reference to the express terms of the Covenant as well as its purpose. It observes that as a general proposition, the Covenant does not contain any provision exempting from its application certain categories of persons. According to article 2, paragraph 1, 'each State party to the present Covenant undertakes to respect and to ensure to all individuals within its territory and subject to its jurisdiction the rights recognized in the present Covenant, without distinction of any kind, such as race, colour, sex, language, religion, political or other opinion, national or social origin, property, birth or other status'. The allencompassing character of the terms of this article leaves no room for distinguishing between different categories of persons, such as civilians and members of the military, to the extent of holding the Covenant to be applicable in one case but not in the other. Furthermore, the *travaux préparatoires* as well as the Committee's general comments indicate that the purpose of the Covenant was to proclaim and define certain human rights for all and to guarantee their enjoyment. It is, therefore, clear that the Covenant is not, and should not be conceived of in terms of whose rights shall be protected but in terms of what rights shall be guaranteed and to what extent. As a consequence the application of article 9, paragraph 4, cannot be excluded in the present case.

¶ 9.4. The Committee acknowledges that it is normal for individuals performing military service to be subjected to restrictions in their freedom of movement. It is self-evident that this does not fall within the purview of article 9, paragraph 4. Furthermore, the Committee agrees that a disciplinary penalty or measure which would be deemed a deprivation of liberty by detention, were it to be applied to a civilian, may not be termed such when imposed upon a serviceman. Nevertheless, such penalty or measure may fall within the scope of application of article 9, paragraph 4, if it takes the form of restrictions that are imposed over and above the exigencies of normal military service and deviate from the normal conditions of life within the armed forces of the State party concerned. In order to establish whether this is so, account should be taken of a whole range of factors such as the nature, duration, effects and manner of the execution of the penalty or measure in question.

¶ 9.5. In the implementation of the disciplinary measure imposed on him, Mr. Vuolanne was excluded from performing his normal duties and had to spend day and night for a period of 10 days in a cell measuring 2 x 3 metres. He was allowed out of his cell solely for purposes of eating, going to the toilet and taking air for half an hour every day. He was prohibited from talking to other detainees and from making any noise in his cell. His correspondence and personal notes were interfered with. He served a sentence in the same way as a prisoner would. The sentence imposed on the author is of a significant length, approaching that of the shortest prison sentence that may be imposed under Finnish criminal law. In the light of the circumstances, the Committee is of the view that this sort of solitary confinement in a cell for 10 days and nights is in itself outside the usual service and exceeds the normal restrictions that military life entails. The specific disciplinary punishment led to a degree of social isolation normally associated with arrest and detention within the meaning of article 9, paragraph 4. It must, therefore, be considered a deprivation of liberty by detention in the sense of article 9, paragraph 4. In this connection, the Committee recalls its General Comment No. 8 (16) according to which most of the provisions of article 9 apply to all deprivations of liberty, whether in criminal cases or in other cases of detention as, for example, for mental illness, vagrancy, drug addiction, educational purposes and immigration control. The Committee cannot accept the State party's contention that because military disciplinary detention is firmly regulated by law, it does not necessitate the legal and procedural safeguards stipulated in article 9, paragraph 4.

¶ 9.6. The Committee further notes that whenever a decision depriving a person of his liberty is taken by an administrative body or authority, there is no doubt that article 9, paragraph 4, obliges the State party concerned to make available to the person detained the right of recourse to a court of law. In this particular case it matters not whether the court would be civilian or military. The Committee does not accept the contention of the State party that the request for review before a superior military officer according to the Law on Military Disciplinary Procedure currently in effect in Finland is comparable to judicial scrutiny of an appeal and that the officials ordering detention act in a judicial or quasi-judicial manner. The procedure followed in the case of Mr. Vuolanne did not have a judicial character, and the supervisory military officer who upheld the decision of 17 July 1987 against Mr. Vuolanne cannot be deemed to be a 'court' within the meaning of article 9, paragraph 4; therefore, the obligations laid down therein have not been complied with by the authorities of the State party.

Vuolanne confirms that military detentions must comply with the procedural safeguards stipulated in article 9(4). The Committee was not prepared to accept that a review of the decision to detain by a superior officer was comparable to the judicial scrutiny required by article 9(4). Such an officer does not have the requisite judicial or quasi-judicial role or status. This decision has considerable ramifications for States Parties which strictly separate the administration of justice for civilians and members of the military.

EFFECTIVENESS OF RIGHT TO CHALLENGE DETENTION

[11.55]   *A v AUSTRALIA (560/93)*

The author was held in custody for over four years whilst seeking asylum in

Australia from Cambodia [11.15]. In May 1992 the Australian Commonwealth Parliament passed the Migration Amendment Act 1992 (Cth) which inserted a new Division 4B into the Migration Act 1958. The effect of the division was that the relevant minister could authorize the detention of 'designated persons' until they left Australia or were given an entry permit. The author and other 'boat people' in similar situations were defined as 'designated persons'. The author argued that he was denied his rights under article 9(4), as the Australian legislation denied him an effective right to challenge his detention. Any challenge would have been futile, as his detention was automatically legal under the broad powers of detention conferred by the legislation.

¶ 3.5. Counsel further contends that article 9, paragraph 4, has been violated in the author's case. The effect of division 4B of the Migration Amendment Act is that once a person is qualified as a 'designated person', there is no alternative to detention, and the detention may not be reviewed effectively by a court, as the courts have no discretion to order the person's release.

¶ 5.5. Concerning the claim under article 9, paragraph 4, counsel submits that, where discretion under division 4B of the Migration Act 1958 to release a designated person does not exist, the option to take proceedings for release in court is meaningless. . . .

The State Party responded as follows with regard to article 9(4):

¶ 4.6. To the extent that the communication seeks to establish a violation of article 9, paragraph 4, on the ground that the reasonableness or appropriateness of detention cannot be challenged in court, the State party considers that the absence of discretion for a court to order a person's release falls in no way within the scope of application of article 9, paragraph 4, which only concerns review of lawfulness of detention. . . .

¶ 7.8. As to the claim under Article 9, paragraph 4, the State party reaffirms that it was always open to the author to file an action challenging the lawfulness of his detention, e.g. by seeking a ruling from the courts as to whether his detention was compatible with Australian law. The courts had the power to release A if they determined that he was being unlawfully detained. . . . For the State party, this provision does not require that State party courts must always be free to substitute their discretion for the discretion of Parliament, in as much as detention is concerned: '[T]he Covenant does not require that a court must be able to order the release of a detainee, even if the detention was according to law'.

The Committee examined in some detail the requirements laid down in Article 9(4) in its merits judgment in favour of the author:

¶ 9.5. The Committee observes that the author could, in principle, have applied to the court for review of the grounds of his detention before the enactment of the Migration Amendment Act of 5 May 1992; after that date, the domestic courts retained that power with a view to ordering the release of a person if they found the detention to be unlawful under Australian law. In effect, however, the courts' control and power to order the release of an individual was limited to an assessment of whether this individual was a 'designated person' within the meaning of the Migration Amendment Act. If the criteria for such determination were met, the courts had no power to review the continued detention of an individual and to order his/her release. In the Committee's opinion, court review of the lawfulness of detention under article 9, paragraph 4, which must include the possibility of ordering release, is not limited to mere compliance of the detention with domestic law. While domestic legal systems may institute differing methods for ensuring court review of administrative detention, what is decisive for the purposes of article 9, paragraph 4, is that such review is, in its effects, real and not merely formal. By stipulating that the court must have the power to order release 'if the detention is not lawful', article 9, paragraph 4, requires that the court be empowered to order release, if the detention is incompatible with the requirements in article 9, paragraph 1, or in other provisions of the Covenant. This conclusion is supported by article 9, paragraph 5, which obviously governs the granting of compensation for detention that is 'unlawful' either under the terms of domestic law or within the meaning of the Covenant. As the State party's submissions in the instant case show that court review available to A was, in fact, limited to a formal assessment of the self-evident fact that he was indeed a 'designated person' within the meaning of the Migration Amendment Act, the Committee concludes that the author's right, under article 9, paragraph 4, to have his detention reviewed by a court, was violated.

Mr Bhagwati submitted a concurring individual opinion on this point:

. . . it was argued on behalf of the State that all that article 9, paragraph 4, of the Covenant requires is that the person detained must have the right and opportunity to take proceedings before a court for review of lawfulness of his/her detention and lawfulness must be limited merely to compliance of the detention with domestic law. The only inquiry which the detained person should be entitled to ask the court to make under article 9, paragraph 4, is whether the detention is in accordance with domestic law, whatever the domestic law may be. But this would be placing too narrow an interpretation on the language of article 9, paragraph 4, which embodies a human right. It would not be right to adopt an interpretation which will attenuate a human right. It must be interpreted broadly and expansively. The interpretation contended for by the State will make it possible for the State to pass a domestic law virtually negating the right under article 9, paragraph 4, and making nonsense of it. The State could, in that event, pass a domestic law validating a particular category of detentions and a detained person falling within that category would be effectively deprived of his/her right under article 9, paragraph 4. I would therefore place a broad interpretation on the word 'lawful' which would carry out the object and purpose of the Covenant and in my view, article 9, paragraph 4, requires that the court be empowered to order release 'if the detention is not lawful', that is, the detention is arbitrary or incompatible with the requirement of article 9, paragraph 1, or with other provisions of the Covenant. It is no doubt true that the drafters of the Covenant have used the word 'arbitrary' along with 'unlawful' in article 17 while the word 'arbitrary' is absent in article 9, paragraph 4. But it is elementary that detention which is arbitrary is unlawful or in other words, unjustified by law. Moreover the word 'lawfulness' which calls for interpretation in article 9, paragraph 4, occurs in the Covenant and must therefore be interpreted in the context of the provisions of the Covenant and having regard to the object and purpose of the Covenant. This conclusion is furthermore supported by article 9, paragraph 5, which governs the granting of compensation for detention 'unlawful' either under the terms of the domestic law or within the meaning of the Covenant or as being arbitrary. . . .

[11.56] The text of article 9(4) requires that one must have an opportunity to challenge the 'lawfulness' of one's detention before a court. The author in this case did have such an opportunity. However, the relevant Australian legislation, which essentially authorized the detention of aliens in A's position, precluded any chance of success; A's detention was automatically lawful in municipal law. The Committee's finding of a violation of article 9(4) confirms that 'lawfulness' in article 9(4) means 'lawfulness' under the Covenant, rather than 'lawfulness' in municipal law. In this sense, 'lawful' in article 9(4) seems to equate with 'not arbitrary'; this conclusion is reinforced by the Committee's reference in paragraph 9.5 to article 9(1), and by Mr Bhagwati's separate concurring opinion. The Committee's decision here seems to redress a drafting flaw in article 9(4). A narrow reading of 'lawful' would have meant that States could reduce the Covenant's right of habeas corpus to a mere formal provision with little substantive value by passing laws which authorize broad powers to detain persons on any grounds.[53]

Right to Compensation—Article 9(5)

[11.57] Article 9(5) provides for a right of compensation to all who have been unlawfully deprived of their liberty of person. Numerous cases have confirmed that article 9(5) compensation is payable when there is a breach of any provision of article 9.[54]

[11.58] Article 9(5) prescribes the payment of compensation for 'unlawful' detentions. This must include detentions which are unlawful under a State's own domestic law, even if they are permitted under article 9 itself.[55] However, the HRC in *A v Australia* (560/93) confirmed that article 9(5) also prescribes the payment of compensation when the detention is 'lawful' within domestic law, but contrary to the Covenant.[56] Thus, as with article 9(4) [11.56], the HRC has imported a sanction for 'arbitrary yet lawful detentions' into article 9(5) despite the omission of any reference to 'arbitrary detentions' in the provision.[57]

---

[53] Compare the prevailing interpretation of 'lawful' in the context of art. 17 at [16.09–16.12] and [16.34]. The Australian government responded to the *A* decision with a vigorous rejection of the Committee's broad interpretation of 'lawful': see R. Piotrowicz, 'The Detention of Boat People and Australia's Human Rights Obligations' (1998) 72 *Australian Law Journal* 417, at 423–5.

[54] In *Santullo Valcada v Uruguay* (9/77), compensation was payable for a breach of art. 9(4). In *Portorreal v Dominican Republic* (188/84) the Committee found that art. 9(5) compensation was payable for breaches of art. 9(1) and (2). In *Bolaños v Ecuador* (23/87) compensation was held payable for violations of art. 9(1) and (3).

[55] See, in this respect, art. 5(1) ICCPR. See also decision of Mr Pocar in *Aduayom v Togo* (422/90) [11.59].

[56] See para. 9.5 and Mr Bhagwati's concurring opinion in *A* [11.55].

[57] See also Nowak, above, note 1, at 181.

[11.59]   *ADUAYOM v TOGO (422/90)*

In this case the Committee was precluded *ratione temporis* from examining the article 9 complaint as the authors' claims were based on events that occurred prior to the entry into force of the Optional Protocol for Togo. The Committee therefore held that it was precluded from examining the claim under article 9(1) and also article 9(5). However Mr Pocar dissented in the following terms:[58]

. . . assuming, as the majority view does, that the Committee was precluded *ratione temporis* from considering the authors' claim under article 9, paragraph 1, of the Covenant, it would still be incorrect to conclude that it is equally precluded, *ratione temporis*, from examining their claim under article 9, paragraph 5. Although the right to compensation, to which any person unlawfully arrested or detained is entitled, may also be construed as a specification of the remedy within the meaning of article 2, paragraph 3, i.e. the remedy for the violation of the right set forth in article 9, paragraph 1, the Covenant does not establish a causal link between the two provisions contained in article 9. Rather, the wording of article 9, paragraph 5, suggests that its applicability does not depend on a finding of violation of article 9, paragraph 1; indeed, the unlawfulness of an arrest or detention may derive not only from a violation of the provisions of the Covenant, but also from a violation of a provision of domestic law. In this latter case, the right to compensation may exist independently of whether the arrest or detention can be regarded as the basis for a claim under article 9, paragraph 1, provided that it is unlawful under domestic law. In other words, for the purpose of the application of article 9, paragraph 5, the Committee is not precluded from considering the unlawfulness of an arrest or detention, even if it might be precluded from examining it under other provisions of the Covenant. This also applies when the impossibility to invoke other provisions is due to the fact that arrest or detention occurred prior to the entry into force of the . . . Optional Protocol. Since in the present case the unlawfulness of the authors' arrest and detention under domestic law is undisputed, I conclude that their right to compensation under article 9, paragraph 5, of the Covenant has been violated, and that the Committee should have made a finding to this effect.

[11.60] Mr Pocar draws attention to the inclusion in the Covenant of article 9(5), as well as the general right to a remedy for violation of any Covenant provision in article 2(3). Article 2(3) is not an autonomous Covenant 'right' [1.17]. One is not entitled to a remedy under article 2(3) in the absence of a violation of a substantive Covenant right.[59] Mr Pocar argues that, in contrast, article 9(5) is an autonomous right. A finding of violation of article 9(5) should not therefore be dependent upon a violation of another Covenant right, specifically another right in article 9. Pocar's contention is supported contextually by the separate inclusion of article 9(5) in Part III of the Covenant. Indeed, it seems unlikely that article 9(5) was designed merely to replicate article 2(3) in the limited context of article 9. The majority in *Aduayom* was silent on this point, but its inadmissibility decision may imply that article 9(5) is not an autonomous right. Alternatively, its decision may

---

[58] See also [2.04].
[59] See, e.g., *M.G.B. and S.P. v Trinidad and Tobago* (268/87) and *S.E. v Argentina* (275/88).

merely indicate that it will not consider the 'lawfulness' of a detention under the Covenant *or under municipal law* which occurred prior to entry into force of the Optional Protocol. Therefore, it cannot determine in such circumstances whether a breach of article 9(5) has occurred.

Conclusion

[11.61] The HRC has issued a large number of Optional Protocol decisions regarding most aspects of the provisions in article 9. The large majority have concerned detention for the purposes of criminal justice, though other types of detention (such as detention of aliens and detention for the reason of enforced psychiatric treatment) have arisen. A number of uncertainties regarding the interpretation of the article 9 provisions nevertheless remain, such as the exact definition of 'promptness' within article 9(3), and the permissible length of time which may be taken before a court must render its decision in a habeas corpus application.

Postscript: Please note that General Comment 28 on 'Equality of Rights Between Men and Women', contained in the Addendum at page 634, contains extra information on some of the material in this chapter.

Freedom of Movement—Article 12

ARTICLE 12

1. Everyone lawfully within the territory of a State shall, within that territory, have the right to liberty of movement and freedom to choose his residence.

2. Everyone shall be free to leave any country, including his own.

3. The abovementioned rights shall not be subject to any restrictions except those which are provided by law, are necessary to protect national security, public order (*ordre public*), public health or morals or the rights and freedoms of others, and are consistent with the other rights recognized in the present Covenant.

4. No one shall be arbitrarily deprived of the right to enter his own country.

[12.01] Article 12 protects the freedom of movement of persons, including the rights to move freely and to reside within the state, and the right to traverse state borders in order both to enter and leave the country.

Freedom of Movement within the Territory of a State

[12.02]   ***GENERAL COMMENT 27***

¶ 5. The right to move freely relates to the whole territory of a State, including all parts of federal States. According to article 12, paragraph 1, persons are entitled to move from one place to another and to establish themselves in a place of their choice. The enjoyment of this right must not be made dependent on any particular purpose or reason for the person wanting to move or to stay in a place. Any restrictions must be in conformity with paragraph 3. . . .

¶ 7. Subject to the provisions of article 12, paragraph 3, the right to reside in a place of one's choice within the territory includes protection against all forms of forced internal displacement. It also precludes preventing the entry or stay of persons in a defined part of the territory. Lawful detention, however, affects more specifically the right to personal liberty and is covered by article 9 of the Covenant. In some circumstances, articles 12 and 9 may come into play together.

[12.03] The reference to liberty of movement is understood to pertain to the right to move unhindered throughout the territory of the state. This involves some overlap with the guarantee of personal liberty contained in article 9. In *Celepli v Sweden* (456/91), the HRC confirmed that article 9 applies to more severe restrictions on movement than those that are prohibited by article 12 [11.09]. Of course, article 12 is not breached where a deprivation of liberty is authorized under article 9.

[12.04]   *ACKLA v TOGO (505/92)*

The following HRC decision is representative of the cases that have dealt with internal restrictions on movement.

¶ 10. The Committee notes . . . the author's uncontested allegation that he is under prohibition of entering the district of La Kozah and his native village which forms part of this district. Article 12 of the Covenant establishes the right to liberty of movement and freedom to choose residence for everyone lawfully within the territory of the State. In the absence of any explanation from the State party justifying the restrictions to which the author has been subjected, pursuant to paragraph 3 of article 12, the Committee is of the opinion that the restriction of the author's freedom of movement and residence is in violation of article 12 (1), of the Covenant.

Similar cases include *Mpaka-Nsusu v Zaire* (157/1983) and *Mpandanjila v Zaire* (138/1983), which both concerned arbitrary banishment measures that breached article 12(1).[1]

[12.05]   *GENERAL COMMENT 27*

¶ 6. The State party must ensure that the rights guaranteed in article 12 are protected not only from public but also from private interference. In the case of women, this obligation to protect is particularly pertinent. For example, it is incompatible with article 12, paragraph 1, that the right of a woman to move freely and to choose her residence be made subject, by law or practice, to the decision of another person, including a relative.

General Comment 27 confirms that article 12, like probably all Covenant guarantees, has a 'horizontal effect'. States must not only refrain from interfering with a person's freedom of movement; they must also ensure that one's freedom of movement is not unduly restricted by other persons.[2]

Freedom of Choice of Residence

[12.06] The right to choose one's residence is a freedom to set up permanent or temporary residence within the territory. Of course, there are a number of limitations

---

[1] See also Concluding Comments on the Islamic Republic of Iran (1993) UN doc. CCPR/C/79/Add. 25, para. 14.

[2] See discussion of horizontal obligations at [1.59–1.62].

to a person's right to reside wherever he or she wants, as illustrated in the following case.

[12.07]   *LOVELACE v CANADA (24/77)*

The matter concerned the author's loss of her rights as a Maliseet Indian to reside on a Canadian Indian reservation.

¶ 15. . . . The Committee recognizes the need to define the category of persons entitled to live on a reserve, for such purposes as those explained by the Government regarding protection of its resources and preservation of the identity of its people. . . .

The Committee here indicates that rights of residence can be validly restricted in order to reserve land for special minority groups. The facts of *Lovelace* however concerned the denial of those rights to a member of the relevant minority group. The Committee went on to make its decision under article 27 of the Covenant (the minority rights provision) [24.12], rather than article 12.[3]

Application of Article 12(1) to Aliens

[12.08] Article 12(1) applies to all persons 'lawfully within the territory of a State'. Therefore, a State may impose restrictions on entry, so the Covenant does not guarantee a right to residency *per se*:

GENERAL COMMENT 15

¶ 5. The Covenant does not recognize the right of aliens to enter or reside in the territory of a State party. It is in principle a matter for the State to decide who it will admit to its territory. However, in certain circumstances, an alien may enjoy the protection of the Covenant even in relation to entry or residence, for example, when considerations of non-discrimination, prohibition of inhuman treatment and respect for family life arise.[4]

¶ 6. Consent for entry may be given subject to conditions relating, for example, to movement, residence and employment . . . However once aliens are allowed to enter the territory of a State party they are entitled to the rights set out in the Covenant.

[12.09]   *GENERAL COMMENT 27*

¶ 4. Everyone lawfully within the territory of a State enjoys, within that territory, the right to move freely and to choose his or her place of residence. In principle, citizens of a State are always lawfully within the territory of that State. The question whether an alien is 'lawfully' within the territory of a State is a matter governed by domestic law, which may

[3] See also General Comment 27, para. 16 [12.23].
[4] Indeed, see [9.51] ff. See also [20.14].

subject the entry of an alien to the territory of a State to restrictions, provided they are in compliance with the State's international obligations. In that connection, the Committee has held that an alien who entered the State illegally, but whose status has been regularized, must be considered to be lawfully within the territory for the purposes of article 12.[5] Once a person is lawfully within a State, any restrictions on his or her rights guaranteed by article 12, paragraphs 1 and 2, as well as any treatment different from that accorded to nationals, have to be justified under the rules provided for by article 12, paragraph 3. It is, therefore, important that States parties indicate in their reports the circumstances in which they treat aliens differently from their nationals in this regard and how they justify this difference in treatment.

The HRC therefore recognizes that aliens 'lawfully within the country' may potentially be granted different, usually lesser, rights of freedom of movement to citizens. Such a situation arose in the following case.

[12.10] *CELEPLI v SWEDEN (456/91)*

The facts are evident from the excerpts below:

¶ 1. The author of the communication is Ismet Celepli, a Turkish citizen of Kurdish origin living in Sweden. He claims to be the victim of violations of his human rights by Sweden.

¶ 2.1. In 1975, the author arrived in Sweden, fleeing political persecution in Turkey; he obtained permission to stay in Sweden but was not granted refugee status. Following the murder of a former member of the Workers Party of Kurdistan (PKK), in June 1984 at Uppsala, suspicions of the author's involvement in terrorist activities arose. On 18 September 1984, the author was arrested and taken into custody under the Aliens Act; he was not charged with any offence. On 10 December 1984, an expulsion order against him and eight other Kurds was issued, pursuant to sections 30 and 47 of the Swedish Aliens Act. The expulsion order was not, however, enforced as it was believed that the Kurds could be exposed to political persecution in Turkey in the event of their return. Instead, the Swedish authorities prescribed limitations and conditions concerning the Kurds' place of residence.

¶ 2.2. Under these restrictions, the author was confined to his home municipality (Västerhaninge, a town of 10,000 inhabitants, 25 kilometres south of Stockholm) and had to report to the police three times a week; he could not leave or change his town of residence nor change employment without prior permission from the police.

¶ 2.3. Under Swedish law, there exists no right to appeal against a decision to expel a suspected terrorist or to impose restrictions on his freedom of movement. The restrictions of the author's freedom of movement were alleviated in August 1989 and the obligation to report to the police was reduced to once a week. On 5 September 1991 the expulsion order was revoked; the restrictions on his liberty of movement and the reporting obligations were abolished.

¶ 3.1. It is submitted that the Government reached its decision to expel the author after an

---

[5] See *Celepli v Sweden* (456/91) [12.10].

inquiry by the Municipal Court of Stockholm, which allegedly obtained its information mainly from the Swedish security police. The author claims that the hearing before the Court, which took place *in camera*, was more like an interrogation than an investigation. A request for information about the basis of the suspicions against the nine Kurds was refused on grounds of national security. The author, who states that he was never involved in terrorist activities, claims that he was subjected to a regime of residence restrictions, although the grounds for this measure were not disclosed to him, and although he was not given an opportunity to prove his innocence and to defend himself before an independent and impartial tribunal. Moreover, he claims that he was not afforded the right to a review of the Government's decision. He emphasizes that he was never charged with a crime. . . .

The State Party submitted the following arguments:

¶ 4.2. The State party submits that the restrictions placed upon the author were in conformity with the 1980 Aliens Act, article 48(1) of which read: 'Where it is required for reasons of national security, the Government may expel an alien or prescribe restrictions and conditions regarding his place of residence, change of domicile and employment, as well as duty to report'. In July 1989, this Act was replaced by the 1989 Aliens Act. According to a recent amendment to this Act, the possibility to prescribe an alien's place of residence no longer exists. The State party emphasizes that the measures against aliens suspected of belonging to terrorist organizations were introduced in 1973 as a reaction to increased terrorist activities in Sweden; they were only applied in exceptional cases, where there were substantial grounds to fear that the person in question played an active role in planning or executing terrorist activities.

¶ 4.3. The State party submits that, on 31 August 1989, a decision was taken to allow the author to stay within the boundaries of the whole county of Stockholm; his obligation to report to the police was reduced to once a week. On 5 September 1991, the expulsion order against the author was revoked. . . .

¶ 4.6. With regard to the author's claim that he is a victim of a violation of article 12 of the Covenant, the State party submits that the freedom of movement protected by this article is subject to the condition that the individual is 'lawfully within the territory of a State'. The State party contends that the author's stay in Sweden, after the decision was taken to expel him on 10 December 1984, was only lawful within the boundaries of the Haninge municipality and later, after 31 August 1989, within the boundaries of the county of Stockholm. The State party argues that the author's claim under article 12 is incompatible with the provisions of the Covenant, since the author can only be regarded as having been lawfully in the country to the extent that he complied with the restrictions imposed upon him.

¶ 4.7. Moreover, the State party invokes article 12, paragraph 3, which provides that restrictions may be imposed upon the enjoyment of article 12 rights, if they are provided by law and necessary for the protection of national security and public order, as in the present case. The State party argues therefore that these restrictions are compatible with article 12, paragraph 3, and that the author's claim is unsubstantiated within the meaning of article 2 of the Optional Protocol.

On the merits, the Committee supported the State Party:

¶ 9.2. The Committee notes that the author's expulsion was ordered on 10 December 1984, but that this order was not enforced and that the author was allowed to stay in Sweden, subject to restrictions on his freedom of movement. The Committee is of the view that, following the expulsion order, the author was lawfully in the territory of Sweden, for purposes of article 12, paragraph 1, of the Covenant, only under the restrictions placed upon him by the State party. Moreover, bearing in mind that the State party has invoked reasons of national security to justify the restrictions on the author's freedom of movement, the Committee finds that the restrictions to which the author was subjected were compatible with those allowed pursuant to article 12, paragraph 3, of the Covenant. In this connection, the Committee also notes that the State party *motu proprio* reviewed said restrictions and ultimately lifted them.

[12.11] With regard to Lithuania, the HRC has stated the following:[6]

¶ 15. ... Furthermore, the Committee expresses its concern that restrictions are imposed on the freedom of movement of asylum-seekers with temporary refugee status and that failure to observe those restrictions may result in the rejection of the claim for asylum.

This comment may be condemning blanket rules which restrict the movement of all asylum-seekers, indicating that such restrictions can be imposed only after consideration of each particular asylum-seeker's situation.[7] The comment also suggests that aliens should not face disproportionate punishment for failure to comply with restrictions on their freedom of movement.

[12.12] In Concluding Comments on Mexico, the HRC stated:[8]

¶ 13. The Committee is concerned at the obstacles to the free movement of foreigners, especially the members of non-governmental organizations investigating human rights violations on Mexican territory, and in particular the fact that residence permits have been cancelled and visas refused for the same reasons. The State party should lift the restrictions on the access and activities of persons entering Mexico to investigate human rights violations.

The HRC's criticism of the refusal by Mexico to grant visas to foreign human rights investigators is interesting, as it questions the sanctity of a State's sovereign right to determine which foreigners may enter its territory.[9]

Freedom to Leave a Country—Article 12(2)

[12.13]   *GENERAL COMMENT 27*

¶ 8. Freedom to leave the territory of a State may not be made dependent on any specific purpose or on the period of time the individual chooses to stay outside the country. Thus travelling abroad is covered, as well as departure for permanent emigration. Likewise, the

---

[6] (1997) UN doc. CCPR/C/79/Add. 87.
[7] Compare, in this respect, the decision in *A v Australia* (560/93) [11.15].
[8] (1999) UN doc. CCPR/C/79/Add. 109.
[9] See also General Comment 27, para. 5 [12.08].

right of the individual to determine the State of destination is part of the legal guarantee. As the scope of article 12, paragraph 2, is not restricted to persons lawfully within the territory of a State, an alien being legally expelled from the country is likewise entitled to elect the State of destination, subject to the agreement of that State. . . .

¶ 10. The practice of States often shows that legal rules and administrative measures adversely affect the right to leave, in particular, a person's own country. It is therefore of the utmost importance that States parties report on all legal and practical restrictions on the right to leave which they apply both to nationals and to foreigners, in order to enable the Committee to assess the conformity of these rules and practices with article 12, paragraph 3. States parties should also include information in their reports on measures that impose sanctions on international carriers which bring to their territory persons without required documents, where those measures affect the right to leave another country.[10]

[12.14] The right to leave one's country pertains both to short or longer visits and the freedom to leave, semi-permanently, or to emigrate. It is available to both citizens and aliens, even those unlawfully in the country. For example, in *Oló Bahamonde v Equatorial Guinea* (468/91), the unexplained denial of a passport to the author was deemed a breach of article 12(2), as the author was arbitrarily denied his right to leave Equatorial Guinea. Iraq has been criticized for the high administrative costs entailed in the issue of a passport.[11] Furthermore, in Concluding Comments on Gabon, the HRC condemned the requirement that foreign workers obtain exit visas before being permitted to leave.[12]

[12.15]   *GENERAL COMMENT 27*

¶ 9. In order to enable the individual to enjoy the rights guaranteed by article 12, paragraph 2, obligations are imposed both on the State of residence and on the State of nationality. Since international travel usually requires appropriate documents, in particular a passport, the right to leave a country must include the right to obtain the necessary travel documents. The issuing of passports is normally incumbent on the State of nationality of the individual. The refusal by a State to issue a passport or prolong its validity for a national residing abroad may deprive this person of the right to leave the country of residence and to travel elsewhere. It is no justification for the State to claim that its national would be able to return to its territory without a passport.

Citizens therefore have a right to obtain travel documents from their own State.

[12.16]   *VIDAL MARTINS v URUGUAY (57/79)*

¶ 6.2. The Committee decides to base its views on the following facts that can be deduced from the author's submissions which also include official documents issued by the Uruguayan authorities in the case: Sophie Vital Martins, a Uruguayan citizen residing at

---

[10] See Concluding Comments on Austria (1998) UN doc. CCPR/CD/79/Add. 103, para. 11.
[11] Concluding Comments on Iraq (1997) UN doc. CCPR/C/79/Add. 84, para. 14.
[12] (1996) UN doc. CCPR/C/79/Add. 71, para. 16.

present in Mexico, and holder of a passport issued in 1971 in Sweden with a 10 years' validity upon condition that its validity be confirmed after five years, was refused such confirmation by the Uruguayan authorities without explanation several times between 1975 and 1977. In 1978 the author then applied for a new passport at the Uruguayan consulate in Mexico. According to the author, issuance of a passport is subject to the approval of the Ministry of Defence and the Ministry of the Interior. Two months after her application, Sophie Vidal Martins was informed that the Ministry of the Interior had refused to approve the issue to her of a new passport. She then appealed against this decision which later was officially reconfirmed by the Uruguayan Foreign Ministry without any reasons given. The author was offered a document which would have entitled her to travel to Uruguay, but not to leave the country again. The author declined this offer for reasons of personal security. . . .

¶ 9. The Human Rights Committee, acting under article 5 (4) of the Optional Protocol to the International Covenant on Civil and Political Rights, is of the view that the facts as found by it, in so far as they have occurred after 23 March 1976 (the date on which the Covenant entered into force in respect of Uruguay), disclose a violation of article 12 (2) of the Covenant, because Sophie Vidal Martins was refused the issuance of a passport without any justification therefore, thereby preventing her from leaving any country including her own.

A similar analysis is found in the other Uruguayan 'passport cases': *Montero v Uruguay* (106/81), *Lichtensztein v Uruguay* (77/80), and *Varel Nuñez v Uruguay* (108/81). These cases confirmed that States have a duty to provide passports to people within and outside their own territory.

[12.17] In *Lichtensztein v Uruguay* (77/1980) and *Varel Nuñez v Uruguay* (108/1981), the authors had been provided with alternative travel documents for humanitarian reasons by, respectively, Mexico and Italy. The Committee found that the issue of these alternative travel documents could not be regarded as sufficient substitutes for Uruguayan passports. For example, the authors had no guarantee that the documents would be renewed. Therefore, the issue by a second State of alternative documents does not relieve the original State from its obligations to provide a passport. The situation is probably different where a person is provided with another *passport* by a second State, as this would indicate dual nationality.[13]

GONZÁLEZ DEL RÍO v PERU (263/87)

[12.18] The author had an order for his arrest which remained pending against him for over seven years. This prevented him from leaving Peruvian territory. In relation to article 12(2), the Committee made the following comments:

¶ 5.3. Article 12, paragraph 2, protects an individual's right to leave any country, including his own. The author claims that because of the arrest warrant still pending, he is

---

[13] Notably, numerous States Parties prohibit dual nationality on a variety of bases.

prevented from leaving Peruvian territory. Pursuant to paragraph 3 of article 12, the right to leave any country may be restricted, primarily, on grounds of national security and public order *(ordre public)*. The Committee considers that pending judicial proceedings may justify restrictions on an individual's right to leave his country. But where the judicial proceedings are unduly delayed, a constraint upon the right to leave the country is thus not justified. In this case, the restriction on Mr. González' freedom to leave Peru has been in force for seven years, and the date of its termination remains uncertain. The Committee considers that this situation violates the author's rights under article 12, paragraph 2; in this context, it observes that the violation of the author's rights under article 12 may be linked to the violation of his right, under article 14, to a fair trial.

[12.19] The rights in article 12(2), like those in article 12(1), have a horizontal effect [12.05]. For example, the HRC has condemned a Lebanese law that restricted the right of women to leave the country in the absence of the consent of their husbands.[14] It also stated:[15]

¶ 22. The Committee has noted with concern the difficulties faced by many foreign workers in Lebanon whose passports were confiscated by their employers. This practice, which the Government has conceded must be addressed more satisfactorily, is not compatible with article 12 of the Covenant. The Committee recommends that the State party take effective measures to protect the rights of these foreign workers by preventing such confiscation and by providing an accessible and effective means for the recovery of passports.

[12.20] Of course, there are limits to one's rights to leave a country, as is specified in article 12(3). Public order limitations are demonstrated in the following case.

PELTONEN v FINLAND (492/92)

The facts are evident from the following excerpts:

¶ 2.1. In June 1990, the author applied for a passport at the Finnish Embassy in Stockholm. The Embassy refused to issue a passport, on the ground that Mr. Peltonen had failed to report for his military service in Finland on a specified date. Under Section 9, subsection 1(6), of the Passport Act of 1986, delivery of a passport 'may be denied' to persons aged 17 to 30 if they are unable to demonstrate that the performance of military service is not an obstacle to the issuance of a passport. . . .

¶ 2.3. The author notes that the administrative and judicial instances seized of his case did not justify the denial of a passport. In its decision, the Supreme Administrative Court merely observed that the Embassy had the right, under Section 9, subsection 1(6), not to issue a passport to the author because he was a conscript and had failed to prove that military service was no obstacle for obtaining a passport. In this context, it is noted that the Finnish government stated during the examination of its third periodic report under article

---

[14] See Concluding Comments on Lebanon (1997) UN doc. CCPR/C/79/Add. 78, para. 18; see also Concluding Comments on Sudan (1997) UN doc. CCPR/C/79/Add. 85, para. 14.
[15] (1997) UN doc. CCPR/C/79/Add. 78.

40 of the Covenant in October 1990 that 'there might have been some misunderstanding concerning the question of obligation of military service. A passport could be issued to a person under duty of performing his military service and conscription, but its validity must temporarily expire during the period of military service. There is no *de facto* possibility for a conscript to leave the country during his military service and accordingly there will be no derogation from article 12 by withholding a valid passport during that period, which is only . . . 8 to 11 months.'

¶ 2.4. The author contends that the interpretation by the Supreme Court of the words 'may be denied' in Section 9, subsection 1(6), means that Finnish Embassies around the world have full discretion to deny passports to Finnish citizens until they reach the age of 30. The duration of the denial of a passport is likely to exceed by far the period of 'eight to eleven months', as it did in this case. The author acknowledges that failure to report for military service is an offence under the Finnish Military Service Act. He observes, however, that the authorities could have instituted criminal or disciplinary proceedings against him; failure to do so is said to further underline that the denial of a passport was and continues to be used as a *de facto* punishment.

¶ 3. It is submitted [by the author] that the denial of a passport is (a) a disproportionate punishment in relation to the offence of failure to report for military service, (b) a violation of the author's right, under article 12 of the Covenant, to leave any country, and (c) a punishment not prescribed by law.

The State Party responded as follows:

¶ 6.1. . . .The State party explains the operation of the relevant Finnish law [which] provides for the right of a Finnish citizen to leave his/her own country; this is further spelled out in the Passport Act (642/1986) and Passport Decree (643/86), which regulate the right to travel abroad. The Constitution Act regulates the obligation of Finnish citizens to participate in the defence of the country; this is spelled out in the Military Service Act and the Non-Military Service Act. In relation to the legal obligation of military service, both Acts contain certain restrictions on a conscript's freedom of movement. The State party adds that the Nordic States have agreed that their citizens do not need a passport to travel within the area of the Nordic States, and that passport inspections on their borders have been abolished.

¶ 6.2. . . . The Passport Act provides that a Finnish citizen shall obtain a passport, unless otherwise stipulated in the Act. As stated above (see para. 2.1), a passport may be denied to persons aged 17 to 30 if they are unable to demonstrate that the performance of military service is not an obstacle to the issuance of a passport (Section 9, subsection 1(6)). In such cases, a request for a passport should be accompanied, e.g. with a police clearance certificate, a military passport, a call-up certificate, an order to enter into military service, a call-up certificate exempting the applicant from active military service during peace-time, a call-up certificate entirely exempting him from active military service or a certificate of non-military service (Section 4 of the Passport Decree). A Finnish citizen living abroad, and falling into the category of Section 9(1)(6), must obtain a statement from the police of his last place of residence in Finland, showing that he is not liable for military service.

¶ 6.3. As to the authorities' discretion to deny a person a passport or not, the State party points out that, when considering a passport application from a person falling within the category of Section 9(1), consideration must be given to 'the significance of travel related to the applicant's family relations, state of health, subsistence, profession and other circumstances', in accordance with Section 10 of the Act. . . . Thus, the Embassy's discretion to grant a passport is not unlimited, since the Passport Act contains clearly specified grounds for rejecting a request for a passport.

¶ 6.4. As regards the time dimension, it is submitted that the application of Section 9(1)(6) of the Passport Act cannot be limited solely to the period of a person's actual military service, but that it necessarily covers a more extensive period before and after such service, in order to secure that a conscript really performs his military service. The State party explains that, for a person who has participated in his call-up for military or alternative service, and who has been granted a deferral, e.g. for up to three years, of performance of such service, a passport is generally granted up to 28 years of age. Once the person liable for military service has reached the age of 28, the passport is generally granted for a shorter period of time, so that by the age of 30, he must perform his military service. Generally, citizens are not called for military service after the age of 30.

¶ 6.5. The State party notes that Mr. Peltonen did not react to his military call-up in 1987, and that he has disregarded all subsequent call-ups. . . . The State party further notes that the author did not show that his liability for military service did not constitute a bar to the issuing of a passport, and that there were no changes in his situation which would have warranted another conclusion. Furthermore, no mention was made in his request of any of the grounds referred to in Section 10. In this context, the State party emphasizes that the author does not require a passport e.g. for professional reasons and that he merely needed one for holiday travels.

¶ 6.6. The State party dismisses as groundless the claim that the denial of a passport is used as a *de facto* punishment for the author's failure to report for military service. It submits that the denial of the passport is based on considerations which are specified in the Constitution Act, Passport Act and Passport Decree, and which are related to the Military Service Act; the denial of a passport neither constitutes a punishment nor in any other way replaces the investigation of, and the corresponding punishment for, the offence of failing to report for military service. If the author returns to Finland [from Sweden] and is arrested, his failure to attend the call-ups will be investigated and sanctioned. However, the offence cannot serve as a basis for an extradition request.

¶ 6.7. The State party notes that, pursuant to article 12, paragraph 3, of the Covenant, the right to leave any country may be subject to restrictions which are provided for by law, are necessary to protect e.g. national security and public order (*ordre public*), and are consistent with the other rights recognized in the Covenant. For the State party, it is clear from the above that the Passport Act, which was passed by Parliament, is based on the Constitution Act and is linked to the Military Service Act, fulfils the requirement of 'provided by law'. The State party further submits that the competent authorities and tribunals have affirmed that the provisions of the Passport Act are an adequate legal basis in the author's case, and that their assessment of the case is neither arbitrary nor unreasonable.

¶ 6.8. As regards the legitimate aim of the restriction, the State party asserts that the denial of a passport falls under the notion of 'public order (*ordre public*)', within the meaning of article 12, paragraph 3; the denial of a passport to a conscript has additional, even if indirect, links to the notion of 'national security'. It argues that the authorities' decision to reject the author's application for a passport was necessary for the protection of public order, and constituted an interference by the public authorities with the author's right to leave the country under the relevant provisions of the Passport Act, which was however justified. It concludes that the denial of a passport in the case was also proportional in relation to the author's right to leave any country, and that the restriction is consistent with the other rights recognized by the Covenant.

The Committee found in favour of the State Party and made the following comments:

¶ 8.2. . . . There are . . . circumstances in which a State, if its law so provides, may refuse a passport to one of its citizens.

¶ 8.3. The *travaux préparatoires* to article 12, paragraph 3, of the Covenant reveal that it was agreed upon that the right to leave the country could not be claimed, *inter alia*, in order to avoid such obligations as national service. [See E/CN.4/SR.106, page 4 (USA); E/CN.4/SR.150, paragraph 41 (DK); E/CN.4/SR.151, paragraph 4 (U); E/CN.4/SR.315, page 12 (USA).] Thus, States parties to the Covenant, whose laws institute a system of mandatory national service, may impose reasonable restrictions on the rights of individuals, who have not yet performed such service, to leave the country until service is completed, provided that all the conditions laid down in article 12, paragraph 3, are complied with.

¶ 8.4. In the present case, the Committee notes that the refusal by the Finnish authorities to issue a passport to the author, indirectly affects the author's right under article 12, paragraph 2, to leave any country, since he cannot leave his country of residence, Sweden, except to enter countries that do not require a valid passport. The Committee further notes that the Finnish authorities, when denying the author a passport, acted in accordance with Section 9, subsection 1(6), of the Passport Act, and that the restrictions on the author's right were thus provided by law. The Committee observes that restrictions of the freedom of movement of individuals who have not yet performed their military service are in principle to be considered necessary for the protection of national security and public order. The Committee notes that the author has stated that he needs his passport for holiday-travelling and that he has not claimed that the authorities' decision not to provide him with a passport was discriminatory or that it infringed any of his other rights under the Covenant. In the circumstances of the present case, therefore, the Committee finds that the restrictions placed upon the author's right to leave any country are in accordance with article 12, paragraph 3, of the Covenant.

[12.21] Nowak, in a convincing argument which undermines the *Peltonen* reasoning, has stated that:[16]

[I]t is doubtful whether . . . an individual's freedom to leave the country may be restricted on account of mere civil-law obligations vis-à-vis private persons or the State or due to tax

---

[16] M. Nowak, *CCPR Commentary* (N.P. Engel, Kehl, 1993), 214. Nowak wrote before *Peltonen* was decided. See also the dissent of Mr Wennergren in *Peltonen*.

liabilities, as long as there is no suspicion that the person has committed a crime (tax evasion, fraudulent bankruptcy). Once obligations to the State of nationality or residence are viewed to be a legitimate reason of public order for prohibiting . . . [people] from leaving the country, the floodgates are open to wide abuse and to the complete undermining of this right. . . . It is always possible [for the State] to come up with some sort of 'debt' owed to the State, perhaps simply the costs that the State has 'invested' in educating these persons.

Indeed, the HRC's own jurisprudence on this matter has been inconsistent. In Concluding Comments on the Russian Federation, issued a year after the *Peltonen* decision, the HRC stated:[17]

¶ 20. . . . The Committee . . . regrets that all individuals not having yet performed their national service are excluded in principle from enjoying their right to leave the country.

Article 12(3)—Limits to Freedom of Movement

[12.22] Article 12(3) contains permissible limitations to the exercise of 'the above-mentioned rights', being article 12(1) and 12(2). Article 12(4) contains its own limitation measures, which specifies that the rights contained therein may be limited by 'non-arbitrary' measures.[18]

[12.23]   *GENERAL COMMENT 27*

The HRC has recently issued detailed guidelines regarding the application of the permissible limitations to article 12 rights in article 12(3).

¶ 2. The permissible limitations which may be imposed on the rights protected under article 12 must not nullify the principle of liberty of movement, and are governed by the requirement of necessity provided for in article 12, paragraph 3, and by the need for consistency with the other rights recognized in the Covenant. . . .

¶ 11. Article 12, paragraph 3, provides for exceptional circumstances in which rights under paragraphs 1 and 2 may be restricted. This provision authorizes the State to restrict these rights only to protect national security, public order (*ordre public*), public health or morals and the rights and freedoms of others. To be permissible, restrictions must be provided by law, must be necessary in a democratic society for the protection of these purposes and must be consistent with all other rights recognized in the Covenant (see para. 18 below).

¶ 12. The law itself has to establish the conditions under which the rights may be limited. State reports should therefore specify the legal norms upon which restrictions are founded. Restrictions which are not provided for in the law or are not in conformity with

---

[17] (1995) UN doc. CCPR/C/79/Add. 54.
[18] Art. 12(4) is discussed below at [12.26] ff.

the requirements of article 12, paragraph 3, would violate the rights guaranteed by paragraphs 1 and 2.

¶ 13. In adopting laws providing for restrictions permitted by article 12, paragraph 3, States should always be guided by the principle that the restrictions must not impair the essence of the right (cf. art. 5, para. 1); the relation between right and restriction, between norm and exception, must not be reversed. The laws authorizing the application of restrictions should use precise criteria and may not confer unfettered discretion on those charged with their execution. [19]

¶ 14. Article 12, paragraph 3, clearly indicates that it is not sufficient that the restrictions serve the permissible purposes; they must also be necessary to protect them. Restrictive measures must conform to the principle of proportionality; they must be appropriate to achieve their protective function; they must be the least intrusive instrument amongst those which might achieve the desired result; and they must be proportionate to the interest to be protected.

¶ 15. The principle of proportionality has to be respected not only in the law that frames the restrictions, but also by the administrative and judicial authorities in applying the law. States should ensure that any proceedings relating to the exercise or restriction of these rights are expeditious and that reasons for the application of restrictive measures are provided.

¶ 16. States have often failed to show that the application of their laws restricting the rights enshrined in article 12, paragraphs 1 and 2, are in conformity with all requirements referred to in article 12, paragraph 3. The application of restrictions in any individual case must be based on clear legal grounds and meet the test of necessity and the requirements of proportionality. These conditions would not be met, for example, if an individual were prevented from leaving a country merely on the ground that he or she is the holder of 'State secrets', or if an individual were prevented from travelling internally without a specific permit.[20] On the other hand, the conditions could be met by restrictions on access to military zones on national security grounds, or limitations on the freedom to settle in areas inhabited by indigenous or minorities communities [12.07].

¶ 17. A major source of concern is the manifold legal and bureaucratic barriers unnecessarily affecting the full enjoyment of the rights of the individuals to move freely, to leave a country, including their own, and to take up residence. Regarding the right to movement within a country, the Committee has criticized provisions requiring individuals to apply for permission to change their residence or to seek the approval of the local authorities of the place of destination, as well as delays in processing such written applications. States' practice presents an even richer array of obstacles making it more difficult to leave the country, in particular for their own nationals. These rules and practices include, *inter alia*, lack

---

[19] See criticism of Sudan regarding the restrictions on freedom of movement imposed by 'various executive agencies without meeting any defined legal criteria', UN doc. CCPR/C/79/Add. 85, para. 14. See also *Pinkney v Canada* (27/78) [16.11].

[20] See also Concluding Comments on Belarus (1992) UN doc. CCPR.C/79/Add. 5, para. 6; Concluding Comments on Russian Federation (1995) UN doc. CCPR/C/79/Add. 54, paras. 20 and 37; Concluding Comments on the Ukraine (1995) UN doc. CCPR/C/79/Add. 52, para. 16; Concluding Comments on Lithuania (1997) UN doc. CCPR/C/79/Add. 87, para. 15.

of access for applicants to the competent authorities and lack of information regarding requirements; the requirement to apply for special forms through which the proper application documents for the issuance of a passport can be obtained; the need for supportive statements from employers or family members; exact description of the travel route; issuance of passports only on payment of high fees substantially exceeding the cost of the service rendered by the administration; unreasonable delays in the issuance of travel documents; restrictions on family members travelling together; requirement of a repatriation deposit or a return ticket; requirement of an invitation from the State of destination or from people living there; harassment of applicants, for example by physical intimidation, arrest, loss of employment or expulsion of their children from school or university; refusal to issue a passport because the applicant is said to harm the good name of the country. In the light of these practices, States parties should make sure that all restrictions imposed by them are in full compliance with article 12, paragraph 3.

¶ 18. The application of the restrictions permissible under article 12, paragraph 3, needs to be consistent with the other rights guaranteed in the Covenant and with the fundamental principles of equality and non-discrimination. Thus, it would be a clear violation of the Covenant if the rights enshrined in article 12, paragraphs 1 and 2, were restricted by making distinctions of any kind, such as on the basis of race, colour, sex, language, religion, political or other opinion, national or social origin, property, birth or other status. In examining State reports, the Committee has on several occasions found that measures preventing women from moving freely or from leaving the country by requiring them to have the consent or the escort of a male person constitute a violation of article 12.

[12.24] The limitations listed in article 12(3) reflect those enumerated in articles 18, 19, 21, and 22. The case law on article 12, and therefore its limitations, is relatively scarce. *Celepli v Sweden* (456/1991) provides an example of the national security limitation [12.10], while *Peltonen v Finland* (492/1992) provides an example of the public order limitation [12.20].[21] The Committee made it clear in *Gonzáles del Río v Peru* (263/87) that pending judicial proceedings may justify restrictions on an individual's right to leave a country, presumably on the basis of public order, but not if such proceedings are unduly delayed [12.18]. It can be surmised that the other relevant limitations of public health,[22] public morals,[23] and the rights and freedoms of others,[24] will be interpreted in a similar manner to the way they have been in the context of other ICCPR rights.[25]

[12.25] The following common measures would most likely constitute permissible restrictions on freedom of movement: traffic safety rules, reasonable restrictions on

---

[21] See also Concluding Comments on Israel, (1999) UN doc. CCPR/C/79/Add. 93, paragraphs 22–3. See [18.26–18.35] for examples of how the Committee has dealt with national security and public order limitations in the context of freedom of expression.

[22] See *Singh Bhinder v Canada* (208/86) at [17.14].

[23] See, e.g., *Hertzberg v Finland* (61/79) at [18.20] and ensuing commentary.

[24] See [18.36] ff.

[25] See General Comment 27, para. 2 [12.23]; see also 'Siracusa Principles on the Limitation and Derogation Provisions in the International Covenant on Civil and Political Rights' (1985) 7 *HRQ* 3, which indicates that all limitation clauses in the ICCPR are to be interpreted in the same way with regard to each right.

access to nature reserves or animal sanctuaries, earthquake or avalanche zones, quarantine zones, or areas of civil unrest,[26] and, of course, prohibitions on unlicensed access to private property.[27] Furthermore, certain persons may be legitimately subjected to limits on their freedom of movement, such as convicted criminals, and individuals performing military service.[28]

Article 12(4)—Right to Enter One's Own Country

[12.26] *GENERAL COMMENT 27*

¶ 19. The right of a person to enter his or her own country recognizes the special relationship of a person to that country. The right has various facets. It implies the right to remain in one's own country. It includes not only the right to return after having left one's own country; it may also entitle a person to come to the country for the first time if he or she was born outside the country (for example, if that country is the person's State of nationality). The right to return is of the utmost importance for refugees seeking voluntary repatriation. It also implies prohibition of enforced population transfers or mass expulsions to other countries. . . .

¶ 21. In no case may a person be arbitrarily deprived of the right to enter his or her own country. The reference to the concept of arbitrariness in this context is intended to emphasize that it applies to all State action, legislative, administrative and judicial; it guarantees that even interference provided for by law should be in accordance with the provisions, aims and objectives of the Covenant and should be, in any event, reasonable in the particular circumstances. The Committee considers that there are few, if any, circumstances in which deprivation of the right to enter one's own country could be reasonable. A State party must not, by stripping a person of nationality or by expelling an individual to a third country, arbitrarily prevent this person from returning to his or her own country.

[12.27] In Concluding Comments on the Dominican Republic, the HRC stated that 'punishment by exile is not compatible with the Covenant'.[29]

[12.28] *J.M. v JAMAICA (165/84)*

The facts of this case are described in the excerpts:

¶ 1.2. The facts are described as follows: upon losing his passport on 22 June 1983, J. M. obtained, on the same day, a certificate from the Jamaican Consulate in Paris confirming his identity. The certificate was issued for the purpose of facilitating his travel to the Jamaican Embassy in Brussels, Belgium, where he hoped to obtain a new passport. On 7

---

[26] Alternatively, a derogation from art. 12 could be entered during times of public emergency.

[27] Nowak, above, note 16, 213, 215–16. Indeed, such access must be restrained by the property owner's rights of privacy; see [16.18–16.20].

[28] See *Vuolanne v Finland* (265/87), para. 9.4. See [11.54].

[29] (1993) UN doc. CCPR/C/790/Add. 18, para. 6.

July 1983, J. M. was denied a new passport at the Jamaican Embassy in Brussels because he was not in possession of a birth certificate. He allegedly requested the responsible officer at the Embassy to contact the competent services in Kingston in order to provide a birth certificate. Allegedly, however, the Jamaican Embassy had him evicted from the Embassy and he was arrested by the Belgian police. From 8 to 27 July 1983, he was detained in various prisons in Belgium and then deported to France. He went back to the Jamaican Consulate in Paris which, at that stage, also refused to help him and had him arrested by the French police, who kept him under detention for two days. On 18 August 1983, he flew back to Kingston, Jamaica, but he was refused entry because he did not have a passport and, allegedly, because the only documents in his possession were in French and not in English. He was then made to board an Aeroflot flight to Moscow. The following day, having landed at Moscow airport, he was put on a flight to Luxembourg, from where he flew to Paris. On 23 August 1983, he returned to Brussels and was given refuge at FEU. All his subsequent efforts during the months of August to December 1983 and in January 1984 to obtain a passport, including the intervention of a Belgian attorney, were in vain.

The author claimed that the above facts constituted a breach of article 12(4) by Jamaica. The State Party responded as follows:

¶ 5.2. As to the substance of the author's claim, the State party explained that 'although the onus would clearly be on a person claiming to be a citizen of a country to furnish evidence in support of that claim, the Government has carried out the most intensive investigations possible with a view to discovering whether [J. M.] was born in Jamaica. This search of the relevant records does not disclose the registration of the birth of [J. M.] in Jamaica. A search of relevant records does not disclose that a Jamaican passport was ever issued to [J. M.]'.

¶ 5.3. The State party further explained that J. M. 'arrived in Jamaica on 18 August 1983 and was refused leave to land because he was unable to substantiate his claim that he was Jamaican'. The State party added 'that [J. M.], who said he had lost his Jamaican passport and also told the Immigration Officers that he had lived in Jamaica up to three years prior to the date of his arrival in Jamaica, was unable to provide even the most basic information about Jamaica. For example, he could not say where he was born, where he had lived prior to leaving Jamaica, what school he had attended or give the names of anybody who knew him'.

The Committee evidently accepted the State Party's arguments, and found the complaint inadmissible. This case may indicate that an alleged victim must provide evidence that a State is in fact his/her 'own country' before gaining rights under article 12(4). One must note however that Jamaica apparently made significant efforts to ascertain J.M.'s status, so Jamaica had discharged any burden of proof it may have had.

[12.29]   *GENERAL COMMENT 27*

¶ 20. The wording of article 12, paragraph 4, does not distinguish between nationals and aliens ('no one'). Thus, the persons entitled to exercise this right can be identified only by interpreting the meaning of the phrase 'his own country'. The scope of 'his own country' is broader than the concept 'country of his nationality'. It is not limited to nationality in a formal sense, that is, nationality acquired at birth or by conferral; it embraces, at the very least, an individual who, because of his or her special ties to or claims in relation to a given country, cannot be considered to be a mere alien. This would be the case, for example, of nationals of a country who have there been stripped of their nationality in violation of international law, and of individuals whose country of nationality has been incorporated in or transferred to another national entity, whose nationality is being denied them. The language of article 12, paragraph 4, moreover, permits a broader interpretation that might embrace other categories of long-term residents, including but not limited to stateless persons arbitrarily deprived of the right to acquire the nationality of the country of such residence. Since other factors may in certain circumstances result in the establishment of close and enduring connections between a person and a country, States parties should include in their reports information on the rights of permanent residents to return to their country of residence.

[12.30] *STEWART v CANADA (538/93)*

The author was a British citizen, residing in Ontario, having emigrated there at the age of seven. He lived with his sick mother and handicapped brother, and had two young children who resided with his former wife. He faced deportation under Canada's Immigration Act because he had been convicted of forty-two petty crimes, including drug possession, one count of bodily harm, and traffic offences. Counsel argued that these crimes were mainly attributable to the author's drug dependency, for which he was seeking help. In response to the author's criminal record, the State Party issued a deportation order against the author, which could be enforced. The author argued that he would face an absolute statutory bar from re-entering Canada if he was deported. The State Party denied he faced an absolute bar. Nevertheless, his re-entry would be dependent upon the benevolence of the State Party, so he would have no 'right' of re-entry.

The author submitted the following argument regarding article 12(4):

¶ 3.4. The author submits that article 12, paragraph 4, is applicable to his situation since, for all practical purposes, Canada is his own country. His deportation from Canada would result in an absolute statutory bar from reentering Canada. It is noted in this context that article 12(4) does not indicate that everyone has the right to enter his country of nationality or of birth but only 'his own country'. Counsel argues that the U.K. is no longer the author's 'own country', since he left it at the age of seven and his entire life is now centred upon his family in Canada—thus, although not Canadian in a formal sense, he must be considered *de facto* a Canadian citizen.

In response, the State Party argued the following:

¶ 5.3. While the State party concedes that the right to remain in a country might exceptionally fall within the scope of application of the Covenant, it is submitted that there are no such circumstances in the case: the decision to deport Mr. Stewart is said to be 'justified by the facts of the case and by Canada's duty to enforce public interest statutes and

protect society. Canadian courts have held that the most important objective for a government is to protect the security of its nationals. This is consistent with the view expressed
by the Supreme Court of Canada that the executive arm of government is pre-eminent in
matters concerning the security of its citizens . . . and that the most fundamental principle
of immigration law is that non-citizens do not have an unqualified right to enter or remain
in the country'.

The Committee found in favour of the State Party:

¶ 12.2. Article 12, paragraph 4, of the Covenant provides: 'No one shall be arbitrarily
deprived of the right to enter his own country'. This article does not refer directly to expulsion or deportation of a person. It may, of course, be argued that the duty of a State party
to refrain from deporting persons is a direct function of this provision and that a State party
that is under an obligation to allow entry of a person is also prohibited from deporting that
person. Given its conclusion regarding article 12, paragraph 4, that will be explained
below, the Committee does not have to rule on that argument in the present case. It will
merely assume that if article 12, paragraph 4, were to apply to the author, the State party
would be precluded from deporting him.

¶ 12.3. It must now be asked whether Canada qualifies as being Mr. Stewart's country. In
interpreting article 12, paragraph 4, it is important to note that the scope of the phrase 'his
own country' is broader than the concept 'country of his nationality', which it embraces
and which some regional human rights treaties use in guaranteeing the right to enter a
country. Moreover, in seeking to understand the meaning of article 12, paragraph 4,
account must also be had of the language of article 13 of the Covenant. That provision
speaks of 'an alien lawfully in the territory of a State party' in limiting the rights of States
to expel an individual categorized as an 'alien'. It would thus appear that 'his own country' as a concept applies to individuals who are nationals and to certain categories of individuals who, while not nationals in a formal sense, are also not 'aliens' within the meaning
of article 13, although they may be considered as aliens for other purposes.[30]

¶ 12.4. Since the concept 'his own country' is not limited to nationality in a formal sense,
that is, nationality acquired on birth or by conferral, it embraces, at the very least, an individual who, because of his special ties to or claims in relation to a given country cannot
there be considered to be a mere alien. This would be the case, for example, of nationals
of a country who have there been stripped of their nationality in violation of international
law and of individuals whose country of nationality has been incorporated into or transferred to another national entity whose nationality is being denied them. In short, while
these individuals may not be nationals in the formal sense, neither are they aliens within
the meaning of article 13. The language of article 12, paragraph 4, permits a broader interpretation, moreover, that might embrace other categories of long-term residents, particularly stateless persons arbitrarily deprived of the right to acquire the nationality of the
country of such residence. . . .

¶ 12.5. The question in the present case is whether a person who enters a given State under
that State's immigration laws, and subject to the conditions of those laws, can regard that
State as his own country when he has not acquired its nationality and continues to retain

---

[30] See, on art. 13, Chap. 13.

the nationality of his country of origin. The answer could possibly be positive were the country of immigration to place unreasonable impediments on the acquiring of nationality by new immigrants. But when, as in the present case, the country of immigration facilitates acquiring its nationality, and the immigrant refrains from doing so, either by choice or by committing acts that will disqualify him from acquiring that nationality, the country of immigration does not become 'his own country' within the meaning of article 12, paragraph 4, of the Covenant. In this regard it is to be noted that while in the drafting of article 12, paragraph 4, of the Covenant the term 'country of nationality' was rejected, so was the suggestion to refer to the country of one's permanent home.

¶ 12.6. Mr. Stewart is a British national both by birth and by virtue of the nationality of his parents. While he has lived in Canada for most of his life he never applied for Canadian nationality. It is true that his criminal record might have kept him from acquiring Canadian nationality by the time he was old enough to do so on his own. The fact is, however, that he never attempted to acquire such nationality. Furthermore, even had he applied and been denied nationality because of his criminal record, this disability was of his own making. It cannot be said that Canada's immigration legislation is arbitrary or unreasonable in denying Canadian nationality to individuals who have criminal records.

¶ 12.7. This case would not raise the obvious human problems Mr. Stewart's deportation from Canada presents were it not for the fact that he was not deported much earlier. Were the Committee to rely on this argument to prevent Canada from now deporting him, it would establish a principle that might adversely affect immigrants all over the world whose first brush with the law would trigger their deportation lest their continued residence in the country convert them into individuals entitled to the protection of article 12 (4).

¶ 12.8. Countries like Canada, which enable immigrants to become nationals after a reasonable period of residence, have a right to expect that such immigrants will in due course acquire all the rights and assume all the obligations that nationality entails. Individuals who do not take advantage of this opportunity and thus escape the obligations nationality imposes can be deemed to have opted to remain aliens in Canada. They have every right to do so, but must also bear the consequences. The fact that Mr. Stewart's criminal record disqualified him from becoming a Canadian national cannot confer on him greater rights than would be enjoyed by any other alien who, for whatever reasons, opted not to become a Canadian national. Individuals in these situations must be distinguished from the categories of persons described in paragraph 12.4 above.

¶ 12.9. The Committee concludes that as Canada cannot be regarded as Mr. Stewart's country for the purposes of article 12, paragraph 4, of the Covenant, there could not have been a violation of that article by the State party.

The Committee went on to find that the interference with Mr Stewart's family relations that inevitably would flow from the deportation could not be regarded as violations of articles 17 and 23 of the Covenant.[31]

[12.31] Mrs Evatt and Mrs Medina Quiroga, with whom Mme Chanet and Mr

---

[31] See [20.15–20.18].

Prado Vallejo essentially agreed, issued a dissenting opinion, co-signed by Mr Aguilar Urbina:

¶ 1. We are unable to agree with the Committee's conclusion that the author cannot claim the protection of article 12, paragraph 4.

¶ 2. A preliminary issue is whether the arbitrary deportation of a person from his/her own country should be equated with arbitrary deprivation of the right to enter that country, in circumstances where there has as yet been no attempt to enter or re-enter the country. The Committee does not reach a conclusion on this issue; it merely assumes that if article 12, paragraph 4, were to apply to the author, the State would be precluded from deporting him (paragraph 12.2). The effect of the various proceedings taken by Canada, and the orders made, is that the author's right of residence has been taken away and his deportation ordered. He can no longer enter Canada as of right, and the prospects of his ever being able to secure permission to enter for more than a short period, if at all, seem remote. In our view, the right to enter a country is as much a prospective as a present right, and the deprivation of that right can occur, as in the circumstances of this case, whether or not there has been any actual refusal of entry. If a State party is under an obligation to allow entry of a person it is prohibited from deporting that person. In our opinion the author has been deprived of the right to enter Canada, whether he remains in Canada awaiting deportation or whether he has already been deported.

¶ 3. The author's communication under article 13 was found inadmissible, and no issue arises for consideration under that provision. The Committee's view is, however, that article 12, paragraph 4 applies only to persons who are nationals, or who, while not nationals in a formal sense, are also not aliens within the meaning of article 13 (paragraph 12.3). Two consequences appear to follow from this view. The first one is that the relationship between an individual and a State may be not only that of national or alien (including stateless) but may also fall into a further, undefined, category. We do not think this is supported either by article 12 of the Covenant or by general international law. As a consequence of the Committee's view it would also appear to follow that a person could not claim the protection of both article 13 and 12, paragraph 4. We do not agree. In our view article 13 provides a minimum level of protection in respect of expulsion for any alien, that is any non-national, lawfully in a State. Furthermore, there is nothing in the language of article 13 which suggests that it is intended to be the exclusive source of rights for aliens, or that an alien who is lawfully within the territory of a State may not also claim the protection of article 12, paragraph 4, if he or she can establish that it is his/her own country. Each provision should be given its full meaning.

¶ 4. The Committee attempts to identify the further category of individuals who could make use of article 12, paragraph 4, by stating that a person cannot claim that a State is his or her own country, within the meaning of article 12, paragraph 4, unless that person is a national of that State, or has been stripped of his or her nationality, or denied nationality by that State in the circumstances described (paragraph 12.4). The Committee is also of the view that unless unreasonable impediments have been placed in the way of an immigrant acquiring nationality, a person who enters a given State under its immigration laws, and who had the opportunity to acquire its nationality, cannot regard that State as his own country when he has failed to acquire its nationality (paragraph 12.5).

¶ 5. In our opinion, the Committee has taken too narrow a view of article 12, paragraph 4, and has not considered the *raison d'être* of its formulation. Individuals cannot be deprived of the right to enter 'their own country' because it is deemed unacceptable to deprive any person of close contact with his family, or his friends or, put in general terms, with the web of relationships that form his or her social environment. This is the reason why this right is set forth in article 12, which addresses individuals lawfully within the territory of a State, not those who have formal links to that State. For the rights set forth in article 12, the existence of a formal link to the State is irrelevant; the Covenant is here concerned with the strong personal and emotional links an individual may have with the territory where he lives and with the social circumstances obtaining in it. This is what article 12, paragraph 4, protects.

¶ 6. The object and purpose of the right set forth in article 12, paragraph 4, are reaffirmed by its wording. Nothing in it or in article 12 generally suggests that its application should be restricted in the manner suggested by the Committee. While a person's 'own country' would certainly include the country of nationality, there are factors other than nationality which may establish close and enduring connections between a person and a country, connections which may be stronger than those of nationality. After all, a person may have several nationalities, and yet have only the slightest or no actual connections of home and family with one or more of the States in question. The words 'his own country' on the face of it invite consideration of such matters as long standing residence, close personal and family ties and intentions to remain (as well as to the absence of such ties elsewhere). Where a person is not a citizen of the country in question, the connections would need to be strong to support a finding that it is his 'own country'. Nevertheless our view is that it is open to an alien to show that there are such well established links with a State that he or she is entitled to claim the protection of article 12, paragraph 4.

¶ 7. The circumstances relied on by the author to establish that Canada is his own country are that he had lived in Canada for over thirty years, was brought up in Canada from the age of seven, had married and divorced there. His children, mother, and handicapped brother continue to reside there. He had no ties with any other country, other than that he was a citizen of the UK; his elder brother had been deported to the UK some years before. The circumstances of his offences are set out in paragraph 2.2; as a result of these offences it is not clear if the author was ever entitled to apply for citizenship. Underlying the connections mentioned is the fact that the author and his family were accepted by Canada as immigrants when he was a child and that he became in practical terms a member of the Canadian community. He knows no other country. In all the circumstances, our view is that the author has established that Canada is his own country.

¶ 8. Was the deprivation of the author's right to enter Canada arbitrary? In another context, the Committee has taken the view that 'arbitrary' means unreasonable in the particular circumstances, or contrary to the aims and objectives of the Covenant (General Comment on article 17).[32] That approach also appears to be appropriate in the context of article 12, paragraph 4. In the case of citizens, there are likely to be few if any situations when deportation would not be considered arbitrary in the sense outlined. In the case of an alien such as the author, deportation could be considered arbitrary if the grounds relied on to deprive

---

[32] See [16.13]; see also General Comment 27, para. 21 [12.26].

him of his right to enter and remain in the country were, in the circumstances, unreasonable, when weighed against the circumstances which make that country his 'own country'.

¶ 9. The grounds relied on by the State party to justify the expulsion of the author are his criminal activities. It must be doubted whether the commission of criminal offences alone could justify the expulsion of a person from his own country, unless the State could show that there are compelling reasons of national security or public order which require such a course. The nature of the offences committed by the author do not lead readily to that conclusion. In any event, Canada can hardly claim that these grounds were compelling in the case of the author when it has in another context argued that the author might well be granted an entry visa for a short period to enable him to visit his family. Furthermore, while the deportation proceedings were not unfair in procedural terms, the issue which arose for determination in those proceedings was whether the author could show reasons against his deportation, not whether there were grounds for taking away his right to enter 'his own country'. The onus was put on the author rather than on the State. In these circumstances, we conclude that the decision to deport the author was arbitrary, and thus a violation of his rights under article 12, paragraph 4.

[12.32]   *CANEPA v CANADA (558/93)*

This case had very similar facts to *Stewart*. The author, who had emigrated to Canada with his family at the age of five, was to be deported to Italy after committing a number of drug-related offences. He had never taken the opportunity to obtain Canadian citizenship. In this case, the majority found in favour of the State Party and stated:

¶ 11.3. As to the author's claim that his expulsion from Canada violates article 12, paragraph 4, of the Covenant, the Committee recalls that in its prior jurisprudence [in *Stewart*], it expressed the view that a person who enters a State under the State's immigration laws, and subject to the conditions of those laws, cannot regard that State as his own country when he has not acquired its nationality and continues to retain the nationality of his country of origin. An exception might only arise in limited circumstances, such as where unreasonable impediments are placed on the acquisition of nationality. No such circumstances arose in the prior case the Committee dealt with, nor do they arise in the present case. The author was not impeded in acquiring Canadian citizenship, nor was he deprived of his original citizenship arbitrarily. In the circumstances, the Committee concludes that the author cannot claim that Canada is his own country, for purposes of article 12, paragraph 4, of the Covenant.

Mr Scheinin added a concurring opinion, though he seemed more willing than the majority to foresee circumstances where an alien could be granted rights of re-entry. He noted, for example, that it would be arbitrary to deport 'a blind or deaf person who knows the language used in the country of residence, but not the language of his or her [*de jure*] nationality'.

[12.33] Mrs Evatt and Mrs Medina Quiroga again dissented, referring to their opinion in *Stewart*. Mme Chanet also dissented again, and added the following attack on the reasoning of the majority.

Rendering the application of article 12, paragraph 4, of the Covenant indissociable from nationality, or indeed naturalization, is in my view too easy a solution and is not in keeping with the actual letter of the text, which, had it been intended to be so restrictive, would have employed appropriate terms relating to nationality, a legal notion that is easier to define. The deliberate use of a vaguer and hence broader term indicates that the drafters of the Covenant did not wish to limit the scope of the text in the manner decided by the Committee.

[12.34] In General Comment 27, the HRC states that 'individuals whose country of nationality has been incorporated in or transferred to another national entity, whose nationality is being denied them' have article 12(4) rights [12.29]. Such individuals could include colonial peoples[33] and peoples on land occupied belligerently by another State, such as the Palestinians of the Gaza strip.

Conclusion

[12.35] The HRC has decided few cases on article 12. General Comment 27 was a welcome addition to article 12 jurisprudence in late 1999. Despite the prescription that limits to freedom of movement and the right to leave a country be interpreted narrowly, States Parties have successfully raised these limitations to justify restrictions on these rights in *Celepli v Sweden* (456/91) and *Peltonen v Finland* (492/92). The HRC's most controversial jurisprudence under article 12 has concerned the right to enter one's 'own country' under article 12(4). The prevailing majority interpretation of 'own country' in *Stewart v Canada* (538/93) seems quite harsh to a State's long-term alien residents.

Postscript: Please note that General Comment 28 on 'Equality of Rights Between Men and Women', contained in the Addendum at page 634, contains extra information on some of the material in this chapter.

---

[33] See also Nowak, above, note 16, 220–1.

13

Procedural Rights Against Expulsion—Article 13

ARTICLE 13

An alien lawfully in the territory of a State party to the present Covenant may be expelled therefrom only in pursuance of a decision reached in accordance with law and shall, except where compelling reasons of national security otherwise require, be allowed to submit the reasons against his expulsion and to have his case reviewed by, and be represented for the purpose before, the competent authority or a person or persons especially designated by the competent authority.

[13.01] Article 13 gives aliens, who are lawfully within the territory of a State Party, procedural rights to protect them from expulsion. Expulsion of such aliens must accord with the State Party's own law. Such aliens also have a right to present arguments against expulsion and to have their cases reviewed by competent State authorities. These 'review' rights may be abrogated 'where compelling reasons of national security' so require.

Scope of Rights under Article 13

[13.02] Article 13 does not provide for substantive freedom from expulsion. Thus article 13 does not strictly protect an alien from expulsion, so long as procedural guarantees to challenge expulsion are available. Adherence to procedural safeguards helps ensure that the State Party's substantive law regarding expulsion is not being administered in an arbitrary manner. However, it is doubtful whether article 13 prohibits the adoption and implementation by States Parties of laws which authorize expulsion on arbitrary grounds. For example, article 13 may not prohibit the adoption of expulsion laws which discriminate on the basis of race, even though this could render the article 13 procedural safeguards essentially useless for aliens expelled on those grounds.[1] Other ICCPR provisions act to

---

[1] However, see [13.04] and [13.06].

constrain the adoption by States Parties of arbitrary laws regarding expulsion. For example, article 26 prevents the adoption of blatantly discriminatory laws regarding expulsion. Article 12(4) prohibits the expulsion of certain aliens who can claim the expelling State as their 'own country'.[2]

[13.03] *GENERAL COMMENT 15*

¶ 9. . . . [Article 13] is applicable to all procedures aimed at the obligatory departure of an alien, whether described in national law as expulsion or otherwise. If such procedures entail arrest, the safeguards of the Covenant relating to deprivation of liberty (articles 9 and 10) may also be applicable. If the arrest is for the particular purpose of extradition, other provisions of national and international law may apply. Normally an alien who is expelled must be allowed to leave for any country that agrees to take him. . . .

¶ 10. Article 13 directly regulates only the procedure and not the substantive grounds for expulsion. However, by allowing only those carried out 'in pursuance of a decision reached in accordance with law', its purpose is clearly to prevent arbitrary expulsions. On the other hand, it entitles each alien to a decision in his own case and, hence, article 13 would not be satisfied with laws or decisions providing for collective or mass expulsions. This understanding, in the opinion of the Committee, is confirmed by further provisions concerning the right to submit reasons against expulsion and to have the decision reviewed by and to be represented before the competent authority or someone designated by it. . . .

[13.04] Note the reference in paragraph 10 to the incompatibility of mass expulsions with article 13. The HRC here recognizes that mass expulsions cannot satisfy the procedural requirements of article 13, which compel consideration of each prospective deportee's case. This demonstrates how procedural guarantees import at least some degree of substantive accountability. Indeed, would this prohibition of mass expulsion protect against the adoption of a law which expelled people on the basis of an inherent immutable characteristic, such as race?

[13.05] Note the reference in paragraph 9 of the General Comment to 'extradition' [13.03]. The HRC majority in *Giry v Dominican Republic* (193/85) and *Kindler v Canada* (470/91) confirmed that article 13 rights did apply in the context of extradition. For example, the majority in *Kindler* noted that:[3]

¶ 6.6. The Committee also found that it is clear from the *travaux préparatoires* that it was not intended that article 13 of the Covenant . . . should detract from normal extradition arrangements. Nonetheless, whether an alien is required to leave the territory through expulsion or extradition, the general guarantees of article 13 in principle apply, as do the requirements of the Covenant as a whole. . . .

[13.06] In *Hammel v Madagascar* (155/83), the HRC notes that the State Party's decision to expel Hammel was:

---

[2] See [12.26] ff.
[3] Mr Aguilar Urbina dissented on this point in *Kindler*.

¶ 19.3. . . . linked to the fact that he had represented persons before the Human Rights Committee. Were that to be the case, the Committee observes that it would be both untenable and incompatible with the spirit of the International Covenant on Civil and Political Rights. . . .

In *Hammel*, the HRC indicates that Hammel's expulsion breached the Covenant as it was prompted by unacceptable reasons. If article 13 is the source for such incompatibility, there is then a substantive element to the article 13 guarantee. However, it is possible that such incompatibility stems from other ICCPR rights, such as the article 19 guarantee of freedom of expression.

Aliens Eligible for Article 13 Protection

[13.07]   *GENERAL COMMENT 15*

¶ 9. . . . The particular rights of article 13 only protect those aliens who are lawfully in the territory of a State party. This means that national law concerning the requirements for entry and stay must be taken into account in determining the scope of that protection, and that illegal entrants and aliens who have stayed longer than the law or their permits allow, in particular, are not covered by its provisions. However, if the legality of an alien's entry or stay is in dispute, any decision on this point leading to his expulsion or deportation ought to be taken in accordance with article 13. It is for the competent authorities of the State party, in good faith and in the exercise of their powers, to apply and interpret the domestic law, observing, however, such requirements under the Covenant as equality before the law (article 26).

Article 13 is probably of little use to the many asylum-seekers who are forced to flee their home States suddenly, and traverse State borders illegally. Such asylum-seekers may attempt to invoke article 7 to prevent their deportation. Article 7 prohibits expulsion to a State where the person is likely to be tortured or subjected to inhuman or degrading treatment.[4]

Expulsion in Accordance 'with Law'

[13.08]   *MAROUFIDOU v SWEDEN (58/79)*

The facts are outlined immediately below.

¶ 8. The Committee considering the present communication in the light of all information made available to it by the parties as provided for in article 5 (1) of the Optional Protocol, hereby decides to base its views on the following facts which have been essentially confirmed by the State party: Anna Maroufidou, a Greek citizen, who came to Sweden seeking asylum, was granted a residence permit in 1976. Subsequently on 4 April 1977 she was arrested on suspicion of being involved in a plan of a terrorist group to abduct a former member of the Swedish Government. In these circumstances the Central Immigration

---

[4] See [9.51] ff.

Authority on 28 April 1977 raised the question of her expulsion from Sweden on the ground that there was good reason to believe that she belonged to, or worked for, a terrorist organization or group, and that there was a danger that she would participate in Sweden in a terrorist act of the kind referred to in sections 20 and 29 of the Aliens Act. A lawyer was appointed to represent her in the proceedings under the Act. On 5 May 1977 the Swedish Government decided to expel her and the decision was immediately executed. . . .

¶ 9.2. [I]t is not in dispute that when the question of Anna Maroufidou's expulsion arose in April 1977 she was lawfully resident in Sweden. Nor is there any dispute in this case concerning the due observance by the State of the procedural safeguards laid down in article 13. The only question is whether the expulsion was 'in accordance with law'.

¶ 9.3. The reference to 'law' in this context is to the domestic law of the State party concerned, which in the present case is Swedish law, though of course the relevant provisions of domestic law must in themselves be compatible with the provisions of the Covenant. Article 13 requires compliance with both the substantive and the procedural requirements of the law.

¶ 10.1. Anna Maroufidou claims that the decision to expel her was in violation of article 13 of the Covenant because it was not 'in accordance with law'. In her submission it was based on an incorrect interpretation of the Swedish Aliens Act. The Committee takes the view that the interpretation of domestic law is essentially a matter for the courts and authorities of the State party concerned. It is not within the powers or functions of the Committee to evaluate whether the competent authorities of the State party in question have interpreted and applied the domestic law correctly in the case before it under the Optional Protocol, unless it is established that they have not interpreted and applied it in good faith or that it is evident that there has been an abuse of power.

¶ 10.2. In the light of all written information made available to it by the individual and the explanations and observations of the State party concerned, the Committee is satisfied that in reaching the decision to expel Anna Maroufidou the Swedish authorities did interpret and apply the relevant provisions of Swedish law in good faith and in a reasonable manner and consequently that the decision was made 'in accordance with law' as required by article 13 of the Covenant.

¶ 11. The Human Rights Committee acting under article 5 (4) of the Optional Protocol to the International Covenant on Civil and Political Rights is therefore of the view that the above facts do not disclose any violation of the Covenant and in particular of article 13.

The *Maroufidou* decision reflects the HRC's general unwillingness to overturn municipal court decisions in the absence of clear procedural defects.[5]

[13.09] The decision also reinforces the procedural nature of article 13. As 'law' is interpreted to mean a State's municipal law, it does not seem to prevent the adoption by the State of a perverse substantive law.[6]

---

[5] See also, in this respect, [14.36].

[6] The HRC's interpretation of 'law' in the context of art. 13 may be compared with its interpretation of 'law or lawful' in the context of other ICCPR guarantees: see [11.55–11.56] and [16.09–16.12].

Right to be Heard by a Competent Authority

[13.10] Article 13 does not specify that a prospective deportee has a right to be heard by a judicial body. States' practice indicates that administrative procedures are often used to consider immigration appeals matters.[7] Furthermore, administrative 'review' of the expulsion order in *Maroufidou v Sweden* (58/79) was held to comply with article 13. Any right to judicial consideration of an expulsion order would have to stem from article 14, rather than article 13. In this respect, note that the HRC expressly did not decide whether 'immigration hearings and deportation proceedings' could be considered 'suits at law' for the purposes of article 14(1) in *V.M.R.B. v Canada* (236/87).[8]

[13.11]   *GENERAL COMMENT 15*

¶ 10. . . . An alien must be given full facilities for pursuing his remedy against expulsion so that this right will in all the circumstances of his case be an effective one. The principles of article 13 relating to appeal against expulsion and the entitlement to review by a competent authority may only be departed from when 'compelling reasons of national security' so require. Discrimination may not be made between different categories of aliens in the application of article 13.

The last sentence of paragraph 10 may again indicate that article 13 prohibits the adoption of substantively discriminatory expulsion laws. However, the sentence may merely confirm that article 13 procedural rights cannot be implemented in a discriminatory manner.

[13.12]   *HAMMEL v MADAGASCAR (155/83)*

In this case, the author was given two hours' notice of his expulsion:

¶ 18.2. . . . At that time he was taken under guard to his home where he had two hours to pack his belongings. He was deported on the same evening to France . . . He was not indicted nor brought before a magistrate on any charge; he was not afforded an opportunity to challenge the expulsion order prior to his expulsion.

Hammel's expulsion was reviewed and upheld four years after his deportation. The HRC confirmed that there was a violation of article 13 in that Hammel had not been 'allowed to submit the reasons against his expulsion and to have his case reviewed by a competent authority within a reasonable time'.[9] The decision does not explicitly clarify whether it is permissible for the opportunity to submit

---

[7] See C. Avery, 'Refugee Status Decision-Making: The System of Ten Countries' (1983) 19 *Stanford Journal of International Law* 235; see also D. Campbell and J. Fisher (eds), *International Immigration and Nationality Law* (loose-leaf service) (Kluwer Law International, The Hague, 1999), for an overview of immigration law in a number of States.

[8] See [14.07–14.08] and preceding commentary.   [9] Para. 20.

reasons to arise 'within a reasonable time' *after* expulsion. After all, it is possible for a deportee to present reasons against expulsion from abroad. Nevertheless, it does not seem that reviews *in absentia* conform to the need to provide potential deportees with 'full facilities for pursuing' remedies against expulsion, in accordance with paragraph 10 of General Comment 15 [13.11].

Right to Review by a Competent Authority

[13.13] Paragraph 10 of General Comment 15 [13.11] refers to a prospective deportee's rights to 'appeal' and 'review'. It is not however clear whether this appeal/review relates to consideration of the alien's arguments against expulsion, or whether the words refer to a *subsequent* review after an initial decision has taken those arguments into account.[10] It is possible that the alien's right of review simply means a review of the initial expulsion decision, which may have been made without the furnishing of an opportunity for the alien to present counter-arguments.

[13.14] In *Maroufidou v Sweden* (58/79), the author was permitted to submit arguments against her proposed deportation. However, she was deported on the same day as the expulsion was confirmed at first instance. She did not submit an appeal from this initial decision until *after* her unlawful return to Sweden. The HRC nevertheless found that there was no question that the State Party had complied with the procedural safeguards in article 13 [13.08]. Thus, it seems that an alien's right of second review, if it does exist, may be implemented after the deportation has been effected.

Rights of Representation

[13.15] In Concluding Comments on the United Kingdom, the HRC noted with concern 'that adequate legal representation is not available for asylum-seekers effectively to challenge administrative decisions'.[11] This comment implies that article 13 entitles prospective deportees to legal representation, or at least representation by suitably qualified counsel, even though it does not entitle them to a judicial hearing [13.10].[12]

Abrogation of Article 13 Rights 'where Compelled by Reasons of National Security'

[13.16] Article 13 explicitly permits abrogation of the 'review' requirements where 'reasons of national security' compel non-compliance with those requirements.

---

[10] M. Nowak, *UN Covenant on Civil and Political Rights: CCPR Commentary* (N.P. Engel, Kehl, 1993) argues that art. 13 imports an express right to a subsequent appeal at 229.

[11] (1995) UN doc. CCPR/C/79/Add. 55, para. 16.   [12] Cf. Nowak, above, note 10, 231.

National security expulsions must still accord with the State Party's municipal law.

[13.17] *V.M.R.B. v CANADA (236/87)*

In this case, the HRC found that the author, who had been deported, had been unlawfully in Canadian territory, and therefore ineligible for article 13 protection. It also found that article 13 had in any case been complied with. Of most interest however are the following comments:

¶ 6.3. . . . Furthermore, the State party has pleaded reasons of national security in connection with the proceedings to deport him. It is not for the Committee to test a sovereign State's evaluation of an alien's security rating. . . .

This phrase was repeated verbatim in *J.R.C. v Costa Rica* (296/88).[13]

[13.18] At face value, the *V.M.R.B.* statement regarding State evaluation of the security ratings of aliens seems to render such evaluations non-justiciable under the ICCPR. If so, this could severely undermine the protection offered by article 13. It potentially invites States Parties to defend allegations of article 13 breaches with spurious claims of national security, safe in the knowledge that the HRC will not examine the merits of those claims. Furthermore, it undermines the implication in the word 'compelling' that States Parties are required to furnish persuasive evidence of serious national security dangers.[14] It must be noted, however, that the States Parties in both *V.M.R.B.* and *J.R.C.* did provide the HRC with some reasons for their national security assessments. It is perhaps not open to States to claim 'national security' as an excuse for limiting ICCPR rights limitations without providing any justificatory reason at all for that claim.[15]

[13.19] The *V.M.R.B.* statement highlights one of the dilemmas entailed in national security exceptions to human rights. National security assessments are often made by an executive government, with minimal municipal judicial review.[16] If executive governments are unprepared to reveal evidence grounding national security decisions to their own judiciary, they are extremely unlikely to reveal such evidence to an international body such as the HRC.

---

[13] Para. 8.4.

[14] See S. Jagerskiold, 'Freedom of Movement' in L. Henkin (ed.), *The International Bill of Rights: The Covenant on Civil and Political Rights* (Columbia University Press, New York, 1981), 184.

[15] National security considerations *per se* are justiciable under the ICCPR, as evinced in the HRC's decisions under art. 19 at [18.31–18.35].

[16] See, e.g., *Council of Civil Service Unions v Minister for Civil Service* [1985] AC 374 (House of Lords), and generally, H. P. Lee, P. Hanks, and V. Morabito, *In the Name of National Security* (Law Book Company, Sydney, 1995), chap. 7.

[13.20]   *GIRY v DOMINICAN REPUBLIC (193/85)*

The author presented the facts as follows, and argued, *inter alia*, that they gave rise to a violation of article 13:

¶ 3.1. According to the author, he arrived in the Dominican Republic on 2 February 1985, stayed there for two days and then, on 4 February, went to the airport to buy a ticket in order to leave the country on a flight to Saint-Barthelemy. Two agents in uniform, either belonging to the Dominican police or to the customs service, took him to the police office at the airport, where he was subjected to a thorough search. After two hours and forty minutes he was taken out by a back door leading directly to the runway and made to board an Eastern Airlines plane bound for Puerto Rico. Upon his arrival in Puerto Rico he was arrested and charged with conspiracy and attempt to smuggle drugs into the United States.

¶ 3.2. The author was tried before the United States District Court in San Juan, Puerto Rico and convicted of the offences of conspiracy to import cocaine into the United States, and of the use of a communication facility, the telephone, to commit the crime of conspiracy.

¶ 3.3. On 30 April 1986 he was sentenced to 28 years of imprisonment and fined $250,000. He is serving his term of imprisonment at the Federal Correctional Institution at Ray Brook, New York.

The State Party did not dispute the author's version of the facts. It offered the following defence to the allegations regarding article 13:

¶ 4.3. With respect to the alleged violation of article 13 of the Covenant, the State party contends that there is no violation and invokes that part of the provision that permits summary expulsions where compelling reasons of national security require. It is stated that Mr. Giry constituted a national security danger for the Dominican Republic, which, as any sovereign State, is entitled to take the necessary steps to protect national security, public order, and public health and morals.

¶ 4.4. The State party further argues that its actions must be understood in the context of the international efforts to apprehend persons involved in the illegal traffic of drugs, which must be seen as a universal crime subject to universal jurisdiction.

The HRC majority found in favour of the author with regard to article 13:[17]

¶ 5.5. . . . The Committee notes that, while the State party has specifically invoked the exception based on reasons of national security for the decision to force him to board a plane destined for the jurisdiction of the United States of America, it was the author's very intention to leave the Dominican Republic at his own volition for another destination. In spite of several invitations to do so, the State party has not furnished the text of the decision to remove the author from Dominican territory or shown that the decision to do so was reached 'in accordance with law' as required under article 13 of the Covenant. Further-

---

[17] A minority of four HRC members found that art. 13 was inapplicable, as Giry's forced deportation was not executed pursuant to any administrative decision (i.e. any legal authority) at all. It should therefore have been classified as 'an act of violence', breaching arts. 9 and 12 ICCPR.

more, it is evident that the author was not afforded an opportunity, in the circumstances of the extradition, to submit the reasons against his expulsion or to have his case reviewed by the competent authority. While finding the violation of the provision of art-icle 13 in the specific circumstances of Mr. Giry's case, the Committee stresses that States are fully entitled vigorously to protect their territory against the menace of drug dealing by entering into extradition treaties with other States. But practice under such treaties must comply with article 13 of the Covenant, as indeed would have been the case, had the relevant Dominican law been applied in the present case.

Giry appears to manifest a more vigorous approach by the HRC to supervision of national security claims under article 13 than is indicated in *V.M.R.B.* However, the facts of *Giry* certainly indicated that it was objectively disingenuous to claim that the author was expelled for compelling reasons of national security. Furthermore, no specific national security 'law' was cited as domestic authority for the extradition.

Conclusion

[13.21] Article 13 does not provide aliens with a guarantee against expulsion. Indeed, its procedural nature may mean that is not even a comprehensive guarantee against arbitrary expulsion. Nevertheless, certain ambiguous HRC statements have arguably incorporated some sort of substantive element into article 13. In any case arbitrary expulsion is probably prohibited under other ICCPR guarantees, especially article 26. The extent of article 13 procedural rights is uncertain regarding the number of 'reviews' to which an alien is entitled. Finally, the HRC has indicated it will defer to a State's judgement regarding the national security rating of an alien. This diffidence could significantly undermine article 13 rights if abused by States.

Postscript: Please note that General Comment 28 on 'Equality of Rights Between Men and Women', contained in the Addendum at page 634, contains extra information on some of the material in this chapter.

14

Right to a Fair Trial—Article 14

ARTICLE 14

1. All persons shall be equal before the courts and tribunals. In the determination of any criminal charge against him, or of his rights and obligations in a suit at law, everyone shall be entitled to a fair and public hearing by a competent, independent and impartial tribunal

established by law. The press and the public may be excluded from all or part of a trial for reasons of morals, public order (*ordre public*) or national security in a democratic society, or when the interest of the private lives of the parties so requires, or to the extent strictly necessary in the opinion of the court in special circumstances where publicity would prejudice the interests of justice; but any judgement rendered in a criminal case or in a suit at law shall be made public except where the interest of juvenile persons otherwise requires or the proceedings concern matrimonial disputes or the guardianship of children.

2. Everyone charged with a criminal offence shall have the right to be presumed innocent until proved guilty according to law.

3. In the determination of any criminal charge against him, everyone shall be entitled to the following minimum guarantees, in full equality:

(a) To be informed promptly and in detail in a language which he understands of the nature and cause of the charge against him;

(b) To have adequate time and facilities for the preparation of his defence and to communicate with counsel of his own choosing;

(c) To be tried without undue delay;

(d) To be tried in his presence, and to defend himself in person or through legal assistance of his own choosing; to be informed, if he does not have legal assistance, of this right; and to have legal assistance assigned to him, in any case where the interests of justice so require, and without payment by him in any such case if he does not have sufficient means to pay for it;

(e) To examine, or have examined, the witnesses against him and to obtain the attendance and examination of witnesses on his behalf under the same conditions as witnesses against him;

(f) To have the free assistance of an interpreter if he cannot understand or speak the language used in court;

(g) Not to be compelled to testify against himself or to confess guilt.

4. In the case of juvenile persons, the procedure shall be such as will take account of their age and the desirability of promoting their rehabilitation.

5. Everyone convicted of a crime shall have the right to his conviction and sentence being reviewed by a higher tribunal according to law.

6. When a person has by a final decision been convicted of a criminal offence and when subsequently his conviction has been reversed or he has been pardoned on the ground that a new or newly discovered fact shows conclusively that there has been a miscarriage of justice, the person who has suffered punishment as a result of such conviction shall be compensated according to law, unless it is proved that the non-disclosure of the unknown fact in time is wholly or partly attributable to him.

7. No one shall be liable to be tried or punished again for an offence for which he has already been finally convicted or acquitted in accordance with the law and penal procedure of each country.

[14.01] The rights to a fair trial and equality before the courts have historically been regarded as fundamental rules of law. Article 14 of the ICCPR sets out a series of rights which are required in both civil and criminal proceedings. The aim of the provisions is to ensure the proper administration of justice.[1] Article 14(1) outlines the general guarantee, whereas article 14(2)–(7) sets out specific guarantees in relation to criminal trials and criminal appeals. The guarantees outlined in article 14(1) apply to all stages of the proceedings in all courts. They also supplement the article 14(3) requirements by acting as a residual guarantee.[2]

[14.02]   *GENERAL COMMENT 13*

¶ 5. The second sentence of article 14, paragraph 1, provides that 'everyone shall be entitled to a fair and public hearing'. Paragraph 3 of the article elaborates on the requirements of a 'fair hearing' in regard to the determination of criminal charges. However, the requirements of paragraph 3 are minimum guarantees, the observance of which is not always sufficient to ensure the fairness of a hearing as required by paragraph 1.[3]

Article 14(1)

'SUIT AT LAW'

[14.03]   *GENERAL COMMENT 13*

¶ 2. In general, the reports of States parties fail to recognize that article 14 applies not only to procedures for the determination of criminal charges against individuals but also to procedures to determine their rights and obligations in a suit at law. Laws and practices dealing with these matters vary widely from State to State. This diversity makes it all the more necessary for States parties to provide all relevant information and to explain in greater detail how the concepts of 'criminal charge' and 'rights and obligations in a suit at law' are interpreted in relation to their respective legal systems.

[14.04] Article 14(1) guarantees various rights with regard to determinations of one's rights and obligations in criminal prosecutions, as well as in 'suits at law'. The meaning of the latter term is very important, as it is the only element of article 14 which specifically addresses non-criminal proceedings. The definition of 'suits at law' arose in the following case.

Y.L. v CANADA (112/81)

In this case the Committee dealt with the question whether the claim by a former member of the Army for a disability pension was a 'suit at law'. Y. L. was

---

[1] General Comment 13, para. 1.

[2] D. McGoldrick, *The Human Rights Committee* (Clarendon Press, Oxford, 1994), 417. See, e.g., *Maleki v Italy* (699/96) [14.76], where a breach of art. 14(1) was found even though a reservation had been entered to the relevant guarantee in art. 14(3).

[3] See also Mr Wennergren's separate opinion in *Karttunen v Finland* (387/89).

dismissed from the Canadian army due to an alleged medical condition. Y.L.'s application for a disability pension was rejected by a Pension Commission. This decision was confirmed on appeal and two subsequent applications to the Pension Commission were rejected. The applicant's application to the Entitlement Board of the Commission was also unsuccessful and his appeal to the Pension Review Board confirmed the earlier rulings. The author argued that the proceedings had been conducted unfairly, in breach of article 14(1).

The State Party argued that the complaint should be declared inadmissible for the following reasons:

¶ 4. The Canadian Government requests that the communication be declared inadmissible. As far as the proceedings before the Pension Review Board are concerned, it contends primarily that the complaints of the author are outside the scope of application of the Covenant *ratione materiae* because those proceedings did not constitute a 'suit at law' as envisaged under article 14, paragraph 1, of the Covenant. . . .

The HRC ultimately found that the author's communication was inadmissible as the availability of judicial review of the Pension Board's decision meant that he had no claim under article 2 of the Optional Protocol (OP).[4] In relation to the expression 'suit at law' the Committee made the following comments:

¶ 9.1. With regard to the alleged violation of the guarantees of 'a fair and public hearing by a competent, independent and impartial tribunal established by law', contained in article 14, paragraph 1, of the Covenant, it is correct to state that those guarantees are limited to criminal proceedings and to any 'suit at law'. The latter expression is formulated differently in the various language texts of the Covenant and each and every one of those texts is, under article 53, equally authentic.

¶ 9.2. The *travaux préparatoires* do not resolve the apparent discrepancy in the various language texts. In the view of the Committee, the concept of a 'suit at law' or its equivalent in the other language texts is based on the nature of the right in question rather than on the status of one of the parties (governmental, parastatal or autonomous statutory entities), or else on the particular forum in which individual legal systems may provide that the right in question is to be adjudicated upon, especially in common law systems where there is no inherent difference between public law and private law, and where the courts normally exercise control over the proceedings either at first instance or on appeal specifically provided by statute or else by way of judicial review. In this regard, each communication must be examined in the light of its particular features.

¶ 9.3. In the present communication, the right to a fair hearing in relation to the claim for a pension by the author must be looked at globally, irrespective of the different steps which the author had to take in order to have his claim for a pension finally adjudicated.

[14.05] In an individual opinion, Messrs Graefrath, Pocar, and Tomuschat took the position that the impugned proceedings did not constitute a 'suit at law':

---

[4] Para. 9.4. Such availability would also raise issues regarding the exhaustion of domestic remedies (see generally, Chap. 6).

¶ 3. [T]he dispute between the author and Canada does not come within the purview of article 14, paragraph 1, of the Covenant. The guarantees therein contained apply to the determination both of any criminal charge and of rights and obligations in a suit at law. Whereas this phrase in its English and Russian versions refers to proceedings, the French and the Spanish texts rely on the nature of the right or obligation which constitutes the subject-matter of the proceedings concerned. In the circumstances of the present case, there is no need to clarify the common meaning to be given to the different terms used in the various languages which, under article 53 of the Covenant, are equally authentic. It is quite clear from the submissions of both the State party and the author that in Canada the relationship between a soldier, whether in active service or retired, and the Crown has many specific features, differing essentially from a labour contract under Canadian law. In addition, it has emerged that the Pension Review Board is an administrative body functioning within the executive branch of the Government of Canada, lacking the quality of a court. Thus, in the present case, neither of the two criteria which would appear to determine conjunctively the scope of article 14, paragraph 1, of the Covenant is met. It must be concluded, therefore, that proceedings before the Pension Review Board, initiated with a view to claiming pension rights, cannot be challenged by contending that the requirements of a fair hearing as laid down in article 14, paragraph 1, of the Covenant have been violated.

[14.06] The minority view gives a much narrower scope to article 14(1) by focusing on the internal Canadian classification of the claim. In contrast, the majority, which certainly hinted that the Pension Board proceedings concerned a 'suit at law', focused on the nature of the right and whether the claim was of a kind subject to judicial supervision and control.[5] The majority view is to be preferred, as it prevents dilution of article 14(1) rights by perverse internal classifications.

[14.07]   *CASANOVAS v FRANCE (441/90)*

This case concerned the author's challenge, via administrative tribunals, to his dismissal from the French civil service.

¶ 5.2. The Committee recalled that the concept of 'suit at law' under article 14, paragraph 1, was based on the nature of the right in question rather than on the status of one of the parties. The Committee considered that a procedure concerning a dismissal from employment constituted the determination of rights and obligations in a suit at law, within the meaning of article 14, paragraph 1, of the Covenant. Accordingly, on 7 July 1993, the Committee declared the communication admissible.

In *J.L. v Australia* (491/92), the HRC was asked to consider whether the regulation of the activities of a legal professional body by the court was in breach of article 14. It found that the complaint was inadmissible. It did however note that the 'regulation of the activities of professional bodies and the scrutiny of such

---

[5] McGoldrick, above, note 2, 415.

regulations by the courts may raise issues in particular under article 14 of the Covenant'.[6] In *V.M.R.B. v Canada* (235/87) the HRC did not rule out the possibility that deportation proceedings may be 'suits at law'. In *Garcia Pons v Spain* (454/91), the HRC found a complaint about an alleged breach of article 14(1) entailed in proceedings concerning the determination of social security benefits to be admissible. Though no violation was found on the merits, it is clear that these proceedings, which had been conducted before a court, constituted a 'suit at law'.

[14.08] The cases do not provide clear guidance on the definition of a 'suit at law'. Harris persuasively argues that a 'suit at law' includes consideration of the nature of the right at issue, which brings private law rights (such as those in tort and contract) within the definition. However, determination of public law rights comes within article 14(1) if, within the relevant municipal legal system, such determination is conducted by a court of law, or if administrative determination of such rights is subject to judicial review. However, article 14(1) does not appear to guarantee a right of judicial review of public law determinations by administrators or administrative tribunals, nor does it guarantee that any such review entails evaluation of the merits of a decision.[7]

EQUALITY BEFORE THE COURTS

[14.09] Article 14(1) expressly guarantees equality before the courts, meaning that the law should be applied without discrimination by the judiciary.[8]

[14.10] In Concluding Comments on Zambia, the HRC stated:[9]

¶ 10. Section 43 of the Constitution, which restricts the right of individuals to pursue civil remedies against the President in the courts for anything done in his private capacity, is incompatible with the provisions of Article 14 of the Covenant.

Thus, it is incompatible with article 14 for persons to be vested with total immunity from suit.[10] It is uncertain whether qualified immunities, such as Presidential immunity for executive acts, are compatible with article 14(1).

---

[6] Para. 4.2.

[7] See D. Harris, *Cases and Materials on International Law* (5th edn., Sweet and Maxwell, London, 1998), 672. See also S. Bailey, 'Rights in the Administration of Justice' in D. Harris and S. Joseph (eds.), *The International Covenant on Civil and Political Rights and United Kingdom Law* (Clarendon Press, Oxford, 1995), 212–13.

[8] M. Nowak, *CCPR Commentary* (N.P. Engel, Kehl, 1993), 239.

[9] (1996) UN doc. CCPR/C/79/Add. 62.

[10] In this respect, also see the decision of the US Supreme Court in *Clinton v Jones* 117 S. Ct 1636 (1997), confirming that President Clinton had no civil immunity with regard to alleged acts taken in his unofficial capacity.

ACCESS TO COURTS

[14.11]   *BAHAMONDE V EQUATORIAL GUINEA (468/91)*

¶ 9.4. The author has contended that despite several attempts to obtain judicial redress before the courts of Equatorial Guinea, all of his *démarches* have been unsuccessful. . . . The Committee observes that the notion of equality before the courts and tribunals encompasses the very access to the courts and that a situation in which an individual's attempts to seize the competent jurisdictions of his/her grievances are systematically frustrated runs counter to the guarantees of article 14, paragraph 1. . . .

[14.12] In *Avellanal v Peru* (202/86), an obvious violation of article 14(1) was entailed in a Peruvian law which precluded access to court for married women in respect of suits regarding matrimonial property. This law also violated the article 14(1) requirement that all persons be equal before courts and tribunals.[11]

[14.13]   *CURRIE v JAMAICA (377/89)*

The author was a prisoner on death row in Jamaica. He alleged that lack of availability of legal aid for a constitutional motion, in which he proposed to challenge the fairness of his trial, constituted a breach of article 14. The author made the following submissions:

¶ 12.2. With regard to his claim under article 14, paragraph 1, of the Covenant, that he has been denied the right of access to court to seek constitutional redress for the violation of his human rights, the author submits that the high legal costs involved in seeking constitutional redress are well beyond his means and that no legal aid is provided for constitutional motions. He moreover claims that the complicated nature of the system of constitutional redress makes it inaccessible for him without legal assistance. He argues that, although the Covenant does not oblige States parties to provide legal aid in respect to civil actions, States parties are under an obligation to give effects to the rights and remedies set out in the Covenant. The author argues that the absence of legal aid for constitutional motions and the absence of a simple and accessible procedure for constitutional redress deny him effective access to the constitutional court, so that he cannot enjoy his right under article 14, paragraph 1, to a fair and public hearing for the determination of his rights and obligations.

The HRC found that there was a violation of, *inter alia*, article 14, paragraph 1:

¶ 13.2. The author has claimed that the absence of legal aid for the purpose of filing a constitutional motion itself constitutes a violation of the Covenant. The Committee notes that the Covenant does not contain an express obligation as such for a State to provide legal aid for individuals in all cases but only, in accordance with article 14 (3)(d), in the determination of a criminal charge where the interests of justice so require.

---

[11] See, for more details of this case, [10.10].

¶ 13.3. The Committee is aware that the role of the Constitutional Court is not to determine the criminal charge itself, but to ensure that applicants receive a fair trial in all cases, whether criminal or civil. The State party has an obligation, under article 2, paragraph 3, of the Covenant, to make the remedies in the Constitutional Court addressing violations of fundamental rights available and effective.

¶ 13.4. The determination of rights in proceedings in the Constitutional Court must conform with the requirements of a fair hearing in accordance with article 14, paragraph 1. In this particular case, the Constitutional Court would be called on to determine whether the author's conviction in a criminal trial has violated the guarantees of a fair trial. In such cases, the application of the requirement of a fair hearing in the Constitutional Court should be consistent with the principles in paragraph 3 (d) of article 14. It follows that where a convicted person seeking Constitutional review of irregularities in a criminal trial has not sufficient means to meet the costs of legal assistance in order to pursue his Constitutional remedy and where the interests of justice so require, legal assistance should be provided by the State. In the present case the absence of legal aid has denied to the author the opportunity to test the regularities of his criminal trial in the Constitutional Court in a fair hearing, and is thus a violation of article 14, paragraph 1, *juncto* article 2, paragraph 3.

HENRY v TRINIDAD and TOBAGO (752/97)

In this case, the author complained about his inability to pursue a constitutional motion to challenge the constitutionality of his proposed execution due to a lack of legal aid. The State Party responded:

¶ 4.10. The State party contests the author's allegation that he has been denied access to Court, because he has not been given legal aid for a constitutional motion. The State party points out that in principle legal aid is available for constitutional motions. Section 23 of the Legal Aid and Advice Act allows the Legal Aid Authority to grant aid if 'the Authority is of the opinion that the Applicant has reasonable grounds for taking the proceedings'. The author made his application for legal aid on 25 June 1987 and on 31 December 1987, legal aid was refused. According to the State party, no subsequent application for legal aid for a constitutional motion has been made by the author. Due to the legal privilege between the author and the Legal Aid Authority, the State party cannot ascertain the reasons for the refusal of legal aid. The State party submits that the author is free to apply again for legal aid if he so wishes. It considers without merit, however, his claim that he is being denied access to the courts on the basis of a legal aid application rejected in 1987.

¶ 4.11. It is the submission of the State party that all States which administer a legal aid scheme from public funds must have the right to reject applications which are frivolous, vexatious or without merit. There is no right of unlimited access to the courts at public expense in such cases. According to the State party, only if the author is able to argue that the refusal of legal aid was founded upon irregularity, irrationality or procedural impropriety should he be able to allege that he has been denied access to the courts.

The HRC upheld the author's complaint in this respect:

¶ 7.6. In this particular case, the issue which the author wished to bring in the constitutional motion was the question of whether his execution, the conditions of his detention or the length of his stay on death row amounted to cruel punishment. The Committee considers that, although article 14, paragraph 1, does not expressly require States parties to provide legal aid outside the context of the criminal trial, it does create an obligation for States to ensure to all persons equal access to courts and tribunals. The Committee considers that in the specific circumstances of the author's case, taking into account that he was in detention on death row, that he had no possibility to present a constitutional motion in person, and that the subject of the constitutional motion was the constitutionality of his execution, that is, directly affected his right to life, the State party should have taken measures to allow the author access to court, for instance through the provision of legal aid. The State party's failure to do so, was therefore in violation of article 14, paragraph 1.

The findings in *Currie* and *Henry* have been followed in a number of cases.[12] Thus, a previous decision in *Douglas, Gentles and Kerr v Jamaica* (352/89),[13] that legal aid need not be available for Jamaican constitutional challenges, has been overruled.[14]

[14.14] In *Currie* and *Henry*, the HRC was influenced by the circumstance that the author's constitutional proceedings were designed to challenge his conviction for a capital offence. Clearly, the existence of one's entitlement to legal aid for civil proceedings under article 14(1) is in part driven by the gravity of the proceedings. This mirrors the rule regarding legal aid for criminal trials in article 14(3)(d) [14.83]. The following Concluding Comments on Norway indicate that civil proceedings are serious enough to warrant an entitlement to legal aid when they concern the enforcement of any rights protected by the ICCPR:[15]

¶ 16. . . . [T]raditional Sami means of livelihood, falling under article 27 of the Covenant, do not appear to enjoy full protection in relation to various forms of competing public and private uses of land.[16] Lawsuits by private landowners leading to judicial prohibition of reindeer herding and high legal costs for Sami are a particular concern in the absence of satisfactory legal aid.

[14.15] *LINDON v AUSTRALIA (646/95)*

The author alleged that the costs order against him, in respect of an appeal he launched against a criminal trespass conviction, breached his article 14 rights.

¶ 6.4. As to the author's claim of a violation of article 14, paragraph 1, because the State party claimed costs and the courts affirmed these claims, the Committee notes that if

---

[12] See *Taylor v Jamaica* (707/96), para. 8.2; *Shaw v Jamaica* (704/96), para. 7.6.

[13] Para. 11.2; this case was decided only one session before *Currie*.

[14] However, in *Taylor v Jamaica* (705/96) and *Shaw v Jamaica* (704/96), a minority of Messrs. Ando, Bhagwati, Buergenthal, and Kretzmer rejected the idea that Jamaica had to provide legal aid for constitutional motions.

[15] (1999) UN doc. CCPR/C/79/Add. 112.   [16] See [24.20–24.22] and [24.26–24.28].

administrative, prosecutorial or judicial authorities of a State party laid such a cost burden on an individual that his access to court *de facto* would be prevented, then this might give rise to issues under article 14, paragraph 1. However, the Committee is of the opinion that in the present case the author, for purposes of admissibility, has failed to substantiate such a claim. The costs imposed on him originate mainly from legal proceedings initiated by the author himself, with no direct relationship to the author's defence against the trespassing charge. Therefore, this part of the communication is inadmissible under article 2 of the Optional Protocol.

[14.16] Does article 14(1) guarantee substantive rights of access to courts? Certainly, a person is guaranteed access to courts 'in the determination of any criminal charge against' him or her. Otherwise, it is likely that 'access' rights are intrinsically linked to the guarantee of 'equality before the courts'. All of the 'access' cases where violations have been found have dealt with situations where the author was denied an equal chance to pursue legal rights.[17] Suppose a State removed a legal right, such as a right to seek damages in tort, for all. This would remove one's substantive 'right' of access to a court to seek such damages. However, it does not seem that article 14 guarantees such rights. A number of OP communications have concerned amnesty statutes or other laws which have restricted the author's rights to seek redress for alleged human rights abuses which occurred before entry into force of the OP for the relevant State. These communications have consistently been found inadmissible *ratione temporis*.[18] A substantive right of access to courts, if it existed in article 14(1), could be triggered in respect of matters occurring prior to entry into force of the OP, so long as the date at which one sought to access the court occurred after such entry. Therefore, OP jurisprudence indicates that article 14 does not guarantee civil causes of action *per se*.[19]

[14.17] In *I.P. v Finland* (450/91), the author complained of his inability to appeal the decision of an administrative tribunal concerning his tax assessment. As those proceedings did not involve judicial review, it is uncertain whether they came within the ambit of article 14 [14.08]. The HRC stated: 'even were these matters to fall within the scope *ratione materiae* of article 14, the right to appeal relates to a criminal charge, which is not here at issue. This part of the communication is therefore inadmissible . . .'.[20] Therefore it appears that one does not have a right of appeal with regard to civil matters.

---

[17] In *Bahamonde* [14.11], the author suffered from personal political persecution, while *Avellanal* [14.12] concerned blatant sex discrimination. The legal aid cases concerned discrimination on the basis of wealth.

[18] See [2.06–2.11], especially [2.10].

[19] Access to courts in certain circumstances is guaranteed by other ICCPR rights, such as art. 9(4) (see discussion at [11.42] ff.). Furthermore, a State's failure to provide a remedy for an abuse of an ICCPR right constitutes a breach of that right in conjunction with art. 2(3) (see, e.g., *Rodriguez v Uruguay* (322/88), para. 12.3 [9.90]), rather than a breach of art. 14.

[20] Para. 6.2.

REQUISITE CHARACTERISTICS OF 'COURTS'

[14.18] *GENERAL COMMENT 13*

¶ 3. . . . States parties should specify the relevant constitutional and legislative texts which provide for the establishment of the courts and ensure that they are independent, impartial and competent, in particular with regard to the manner in which judges are appointed, the qualifications for appointment, and the duration of their terms of office; the conditions governing promotion, transfer and cessation of their functions and the actual independence of the judiciary from the executive branch and the legislative.

[14.19] *BAHAMONDE V EQUATORIAL GUINEA (468/91)*

¶ 9.4. . . . [T]he Committee has . . . noted the author's contention that the State party's president controls the judiciary in Equatorial Guinea. The Committee considers that a situation where the functions and competences of the judiciary and the executive are not clearly distinguishable or where the latter is able to control or direct the former is incompatible with the notion of an independent and impartial tribunal within the meaning of article 14, paragraph 1, of the Covenant.

The HRC again endorsed the doctrine of the separation of judicial power as an essential element of article 14 compliance in Concluding Comments on Romania. It expressed concern over the 'interference of the executive' in judicial matters, and recommended establishment of 'a clear demarcation between the competence of the executive and judicial bodies'.[21]

[14.20] In Concluding Comments on Algeria, the HRC expressed concern over the fact that 'judges enjoy immovability only after ten years of work'.[22] Similarly, in Concluding Comments on Armenia, election by popular vote for six years did 'not ensure . . . independence and impartiality'.[23] Regarding Zambia, the HRC was concerned over the President's power to remove judges, without any independent judicial oversight.[24] In Concluding Comments on the USA, the HRC stated:[25]

¶ 23. The Committee is concerned about the impact which the current system of election of judges may, in a few states, have on the implementation of the rights provided under article 14 of the Covenant and welcomes the efforts of a number of states in the adoption of a merit-selection system. It is also concerned about the fact that in many rural areas justice is administered by unqualified and untrained persons. . . .

---

[21] (1999) UN doc. CCPR/C/79/Add. 111, para. 10.
[22] (1998) UN doc. CCPR/C/79/Add. 95, para. 14.
[23] (1998) UN doc. CCPR/C/79/Add. 100, para. 8; see also Concluding Comments on Peru (1996) UN doc. CCPR/C/79/Add. 67, para. 14.
[24] (1996) UN doc. CCPR/C/79/Add. 62, para. 16.
[25] (1995) UN doc. CCPR/C/79/Add. 50.

The HRC therefore strongly endorses judicial tenure as a prerequisite for a sufficiently independent judiciary.

[14.21] In Concluding Comments on Slovakia, the HRC stated: [26]

¶ 18. The Committee notes with concern that the present rules governing the appointment of judges by the Government with the approval of Parliament could have a negative impact on the independence of the judiciary. Therefore: the Committee recommends that specific measures guaranteeing the independence of the judiciary, protecting judges from any form of political influence through the adoption of laws regulating the appointment, remuneration, tenure, dismissal and disciplining of members of the judiciary, be adopted as a matter of policy.

In the Slovakian Comments, the HRC appears to condemn the practice of judicial appointment by the Executive, which is common amongst States Parties, including Australia and the UK. In the USA, executive nominees for the Supreme Court are reviewed by the Senate. The HRC may simply be recommending that States adopt objective legal criteria for judicial appointment and tenure conditions, so as to minimize the opportunity for 'political' appointments.

[14.22] In Concluding Comments on Sudan, the HRC stated:[27]

¶ 21. The Committee is concerned that in appearance as well as in fact the judiciary is not truly independent, that many judges have not been selected primarily on the basis of their legal qualifications, that judges can be subject to pressure through a supervisory authority dominated by the Government, and that very few non-Muslims or women occupy judicial positions at all levels. Therefore: Measures should be taken to improve the independence and technical competence of the judiciary, including the appointment of qualified judges from among women and members of minorities. Training in human rights law should be given to all judges, law enforcement officers and members of the legal profession.

The HRC, in its Sudanese comment, stresses the importance of a pluralistic judiciary, ensuring the representation of diverse values within the judicial branch of government.

[14.23] Of course, the judiciary must be protected from threats and reprisals from discontented litigants.[28]

MILITARY COURTS

[14.24]   *GENERAL COMMENT 13*

¶ 4. The provisions of article 14 apply to all courts and tribunals within the scope of that article whether ordinary or specialized. The Committee notes the existence, in many countries,

---

[26] (1997) UN doc. CCPR/C/79/Add. 79.
[27] (1997) UN doc. CCPR/C/79/Add. 85.
[28] Concluding Comments on Brazil (1996) UN doc. CCPR/C/79/Add. 66, para. 11.

of military or special courts which try civilians. This could present serious problems as far as the equitable, impartial and independent administration of justice is concerned. Quite often the reason for the establishment of such courts is to enable exceptional procedures to be applied which do not comply with normal standards of justice. While the Covenant does not prohibit such categories of courts, nevertheless the conditions which it lays down clearly indicate that the trying of civilians by such courts should be very exceptional and take place under conditions which genuinely afford the full guarantees stipulated in article 14. The Committee has noted a serious lack of information in this regard in the reports of some States parties whose judicial institutions include such courts for the trying of civilians. In some countries such military and special courts do not afford the strict guarantees of the proper administration of justice in accordance with the requirements of article 14 which are essential for the effective protection of human rights. . . .

[14.25] *FALS BORDA et al. v COLOMBIA (46/79)*

The article 14 allegations are evident from the excerpts directly below:

¶ 1.5. The author alleges that [a number of Columbians, including Dr Fals Borda] have been victims of violations of article 14(1), (2), (3) and (5) of the International Covenant on Civil and Political Rights because they have been brought before military tribunals which were not competent, independent and impartial, and because they have allegedly been deprived of the procedural guarantees laid down in the Colombian Constitution and in the Covenant. . . .

¶ 9.2. . . . [The author submitted that the] subjection of Mr. and Mrs. Fals Borda to military or emergency penal procedure, in implementation of the 'Statute of Security' violated their rights under article 14 (1) of the Covenant.

In the first place, the military courts which judge civilians, as provided for in article 9 of the 'Statute of Security', as well as the judicial powers granted to army, navy and air force commanders (article 11) and police chiefs (article 12), nullify the right to a competent, independent and impartial tribunal. Articles 9, 11 and 12 of Decree No. 1923 ignore not only the universally recognized principle *nemo judex in sua causa* but also the right to a natural or judicial tribunal, provided for in article 26 of the Colombian Constitution: 'No one may be tried except in conformity with the laws in force prior to the commission of the act with which he is charged, by a court having competent jurisdiction, and in accordance with all formalities proper to each case.'

Accordingly, the only competent, independent and impartial tribunals are the courts of common jurisdiction or judiciary set up under title XV, 'the Administration of Justice', of the Colombian Constitution and in accordance with title 11, 'Jurisdiction and Competence', of the Code of Penal Procedure (Decree No. 409 of 1971). This is on the basis not only of the constitutional principle of separation of powers, but also of article 58 of the Colombian Constitution: 'Justice is administered by the Supreme Court, by superior district courts and by such other courts and tribunals as may be established by law.'

The Colombian Constitution does not allow military or emergency penal justice for citizens or civilians. Article 170 of the Colombian Constitution provides for courts menial but only for 'offences committed by military personnel on active service and in relation to that service'.

Military courts or courts martial nevertheless operate in Colombia in breach of the country's constitution and laws and of the International Covenant on Civil and Political Rights, in particular to try political opponents, under Decree No. 1923 of 1978 (the 'Statute of Security'); this is in violation of article 14 of the United Nations International Covenant on Civil and Political Rights.

Secondly, the military or emergency courts provided for in articles 9, 11 and 12 of Decree No. 1923, the 'Statute of Security', in addition to not being competent, independent and impartial (article 14 (1) of the Covenant), were not set up under a proper law passed by Congress validly amending or repealing the Code of Penal Procedure (Decree No. 409 of 1971). The 'Statute of Security' is a state-of-siege decree which violates the safeguard of legality provided in the Covenant, particularly since it is indefinite, as may be seen in article 1 of the Statute, which provides for sentences of 30 years which do not exist in the Penal Code.

The HRC found no breach of article 14. In relation to this article it made the following comments:

¶ 13.3. The allegations as to breaches of the provisions of article 14 of the Covenant concerning judicial guarantees and fair trial, seem to be based on the premise that civilians may not be subject to military penal procedures and that when civilians are nevertheless subjected to such procedures, they are in effect deprived of basic judicial guarantees aimed at ensuring fair trial, which guarantees would be afforded to them under the normal court system, because military courts are neither competent, independent and impartial. The arguments of the author in substantiation of these allegations are set out in general terms and principally linked with the question of constitutionality of Decree No. 1923. He does not, however, cite any specific incidents or facts in support of his allegations of disregard for the judicial guarantees provided for by article 14 in the application of Decree No. 1923 in the cases in question. Since the Committee does not deal with questions of constitutionality, but with the question whether a law is in conformity with the Covenant, as applied in the circumstances of this case, the Committee cannot make any finding of breaches of article 14 of the Covenant.

The *Fals Borda* decision may be fairly criticized as the HRC appears to deny the relevance of issues relating to the constitutionality of the military courts at issue. Article 14(1) stipulates that persons must be tried before tribunals 'established by law'. Therefore, the constitutionality or legality of a tribunal's existence *is* an issue with which the HRC should be concerned.

[14.26] Despite the *Fals Borda* decision, the HRC has nevertheless expressed misgivings over the broad jurisdiction of certain military courts in a number of Concluding Comments. For example, in Concluding Comments on Chile:[29]

¶ 9. The wide jurisdiction of the military courts to deal with all the cases involving prosecution of military personnel and their power to conclude cases that began in the civilian courts contribute to the impunity which such personnel enjoy against punishment for serious

---

[29] (1999) UN doc. CCPR/C/79/Add. 104.

human rights violations. Furthermore, the continuing jurisdiction of Chilean military courts to try civilians does not comply with article 14 of the Covenant. Therefore:

The Committee recommends that the law be amended so as to restrict the jurisdiction of the military courts to trial only of military personnel charged with offences of an exclusively military nature.

With regard to Lebanon the HRC stated:[30]

¶ 14. The Committee expresses concern about the broad scope of the jurisdiction of military courts in Lebanon, especially its extension beyond disciplinary matters and its application to civilians. It is also concerned about the procedures followed by these military courts, as well as the lack of supervision of the military courts' procedures and verdicts by the ordinary courts. The State party should review the jurisdiction of the military courts and transfer the competence of military courts, in all trials concerning civilians and in all cases concerning the violation of human rights by members of the military, to the ordinary courts.

The HRC was perhaps strongest in its comments regarding Slovakia:[31]

¶ 20. . . . [T]he Committee recommends that the Criminal Code be amended so as to prohibit the trial of civilians by military tribunals in any circumstances.

ELEMENTS OF A FAIR TRIAL

[14.27]   *B.D.B. v THE NETHERLANDS (273/88)*

In this case, the Committee pointed out that article 14 is concerned with procedural guarantees for trials and not with the substance of judgments handed down by the courts. It made the following comments:

¶ 6.4. With regard to an alleged violation of article 14, paragraph 1, of the Covenant, the Committee notes that while the authors have complained about the outcome of the judicial proceedings, they acknowledge that procedural guarantees were observed in their conduct. The Committee observes that article 14 of the Covenant guarantees procedural equality but cannot be interpreted as guaranteeing equality of results or absences of error on the part of the competent tribunal. Thus, this aspect of the author's communication falls outside the scope of application of article 14 and is, therefore, inadmissible under article 3 of the Optional Protocol.

[14.28]   *GENERAL COMMENT 13*

¶ 3. The Committee would find it useful if, in their future reports, States parties could provide more detailed information on the steps taken to ensure that equality before the

---

[30] (1997) UN doc. CCPR/C/79/Add. 78; see also Concluding Comments on Poland (1999) UN doc. CCPR/C/79/Add. 110, para. 21, and Concluding Comments on Cameroon (1999) UN doc. CCPR/C/79/Add. 116, para. 21.

[31] (1997) UN doc. CCPR/C/79/Add. 79.

courts, including equal access to courts, fair and public hearings and competence, impartiality and independence of the judiciary are established by law and guaranteed in practice.

Mr Ando, in a dissenting opinion in *Richards v Jamaica* (535/93), outlined the following elements of a fair criminal trial (the majority did not disagree):[32]

In my opinion, the purpose of a criminal trial is to ascertain what actually took place in the case at issue, that is, to find 'true facts' of the case, on which conviction and sentence should be based. Of course, 'true facts' as submitted by the defendant may differ from 'true facts' as submitted by the prosecution, and since defendants are generally at a disadvantage compared to the prosecution, various procedural guarantees exist to secure a fair trial. The requirement of equality of arms, rules of evidence, control of the proceedings by independent and impartial judges, deliberation and decision by neutral juries, and the system of appeals are all part of these guarantees.

[14.29]   *MORAEL v FRANCE (207/86)*

The author in this case was the managing director of a company that was in financial crisis. In subsequent civil proceedings to determine who was liable for the company's debts, the author was ordered to pay part of the company's indebtedness. In the case before the HRC the author claimed he had not been given a fair hearing as French bankruptcy law subjected directors in his position to a presumption of liability. The author also alleged that his liabilities were increased on appeal without his having a chance to challenge this increase. He made the following arguments:

¶ 2.1. With respect to article 14(1) of the Covenant, the author calls into question the French legal system, which, as it was applied to him, did not guarantee a fair hearing, in particular because there was no 'equality of arms' in the procedure whereby companies are placed under judicial supervision and because article 99 of Act No. 67–563 placed an unfair presumption of fault on company officers without requiring proof of their actual misconduct. In this connection, the author contends that the Court of Cassation wrongly interpreted the concept of due diligence by concluding that any fault committed by the author necessarily excluded diligence, even if he had not shown negligence in the exercise of his duties. The author claims that this excessively severe interpretation of 'due diligence' is discriminatory against company officials, for whom an error of judgement regarding economic developments is punished as if constituting negligence. Placing an obligation on him to achieve a desired result, the author argues, was tantamount to denying him any possibility of establishing that he had in fact exercised due diligence. The author claims that it is grossly unfair to hold him responsible for the company's financial condition, which was already disastrous at the time he was appointed Managing Director and which he sought to remedy by diligent efforts that were finally frustrated by factors beyond his control, such as the refusal by the Inspectorate of Employment of staff retrenchment measures and the ensuing strikes.

---

[32] See the majority opinion at [14.34].

¶ 2.2. Another alleged violation of article 14 (1), the author claims, consisted in the court's consideration of a new and higher amount for the company's liabilities without giving him an opportunity to challenge it. . . .

The State Party made the following arguments in reply:

¶ 4.4. In the view of the French Government, this presumption of liability attached to a company's managers is not in conflict with the principle of a fair hearing, contrary to the contention of the author. Admittedly, the liability of the persons concerned may be invoked in this type of procedure without presentation of proof of fault on the part of the managers. But that is the case in any system of liability for risk or 'objective' liability. Furthermore, the existence of such a presumption instituted by the Act is not, in itself, in any way contrary to the rule of a fair hearing inasmuch as the proceedings take place in conditions that ensure the full enjoyment of his rights by the person concerned. What is more, in the case in question, this presumption is not irrefutable, for the managers in question can in fact absolve themselves of liability by proving by whatever means that they devoted all due energy and diligence to the management of the company's affairs. The tribunal, itself supervised by the Court of Appeal, is free to evaluate such proof in the light of all the elements which had an influence on the behaviour of the managers involved.

The HRC held that there was no violation of article 14. In coming to this conclusion it made the following interpretation of the concept of a fair hearing:

¶ 9.3. The first question before the Committee is whether the author is a victim of a violation of article 14(1) of the Covenant because, as he alleges, his case did not receive a fair hearing within the meaning of that paragraph. The Committee notes in this connection that the paragraph in question applies not only to criminal matters but also to litigation concerning rights and obligations of a civil nature. Although article 14 does not explain what is meant by a 'fair hearing' in a suit at law (unlike paragraph 3 of the same article dealing with the determination of criminal charges), the concept of a fair hearing in the context of article 14 (1) of the Covenant should be interpreted as requiring a number of conditions, such as equality of arms, respect for the principle of adversary proceedings, preclusion of *ex officio reformatio in pejus*,[33] and expeditious procedure. The facts of the case should accordingly be tested against those criteria.

¶ 9.4. At issue is the application of the third paragraph of the article of the Bankruptcy Law of 13 July 1967 that established a presumption of fault on the part of managers of companies placed under judicial supervision, by requiring them to prove that they had devoted all due energy and diligence to the management of the company's affairs, failing which they could be held liable for the company's losses. The author claims in this regard that the Court of Cassation had given too severe an interpretation of due diligence, one that amounted to denying him any possibility of demonstrating that he had exercised it. It is not for the Committee, however, to pass judgement on the validity of the evidence of diligence produced by the author or to question the court's discretionary power to decide whether such evidence was sufficient to absolve him of any liability. As regards respect for the principle of adversary proceedings, the Committee notes that to its knowledge there is nothing

---

[33] *Ex officio* worsening of an earlier verdict.

in the facts concerning the proceedings to show that the author did not have the possibility of presenting evidence at his disposal or that the court based its decision on evidence
admitted without being open to challenge by the parties. As to the author's complaint that
the principle of adversary proceedings had been ignored in that the Court of Appeal had
increased the amount to be paid by the author, although the change had not been requested
by the court-appointed administrator and had not been submitted to the parties for argument, the Committee notes that the Court of Appeal fixed the amounts to be paid by the
author on the basis of the liabilities resulting from the operations of the procedure, as the
court of first instance had decided; that such verification of the statement of liabilities had
not been contested by the parties; and that the definitive amount, while equal to approximately 10 per cent of the company's indebtedness, had been charged to the author individually, whereas the court of first instance had ordered payment jointly with other
managers, which might have required the author to pay 40 per cent of the company's
indebtedness in case it proved impossible to recover the shares due from his co-debtors. In
view of the above, it is to be doubted that there was an increase in the amount charged to
the author or that the principle of adversary proceedings and preclusion of *ex officio reformatio in pejus* were ignored. . . .

Morael confirms that the placement of the burden of proof in civil cases on a
defendant is permissible under article 14(1). Indeed, later on in *Morael*, the
Committee explicitly endorsed the existence of strict liability in civil cases as a
common feature of numerous judicial systems [14.55].

[14.30]   *FEI v COLOMBIA (514/92)*

The author was involved in a custody dispute with her former husband, who had
been awarded custody of their children. She alleged, *inter alia*, that custody
proceedings in Colombia had breached article 14. Her complaints are evident
from the HRC decision in her favour on this point:

¶ 8.4. The concept of a 'fair trial' within the meaning of article 14, paragraph 1,
however, also includes other elements. Among these, as the Committee has had the
opportunity to point out (Views on Communications Nos. 203/1986 (*Muñoz v. Peru*),
para. 11.3; and 207/1986 (*Morael v France*), para. 9.3), are the respect for the principles of equality of arms, of adversary proceedings and of expeditious proceedings. In the
present case, the Committee is not satisfied that the requirement of equality of arms and
of expeditious procedure have been met. It is noteworthy that every court action instituted by the author took several years to adjudicate—and difficulties in communication
with the author, who does not reside in the State party's territory, cannot account for
such delays, as she had secured legal representation in Colombia. The State party has
failed to explain these delays. On the other hand, actions instituted by the author's ex-
husband and by or on behalf of her children were heard and determined considerably
more expeditiously. As the Committee has noted in its admissibility decision, the very
nature of custody proceedings or proceedings concerning access of a divorced parent to
his children requires that the issues complained of be adjudicated expeditiously. In the
Committee's opinion, given the delays in the determination of the author's actions, this
has not been the case.

¶ 8.5. The Committee has further noted that the State party's authorities have failed to secure the author's ex-husband's compliance with court orders granting the author access to her children, such as the court order of May 1982 or the judgement of the First Circuit Court of Bogotá of 13 March 1989. Complaints from the author about the non-enforcement of such orders apparently continue to be investigated, more than 30 months after they were filed, or remain in abeyance; this is another element indicating that the requirement of equality of arms and of expeditious procedure has not been met.

¶ 8.6. Finally, it is noteworthy that in the proceedings under article 86 of the Colombian Constitution instituted on behalf of the author's daughters in December 1993, the hearing took place, and judgement was given, on 16 December 1993, that is, before the expiration of the deadline for the submission of the author's defence statement. The State party has failed to address this point, and the author's version is thus uncontested. In the Committee's opinion, the impossibility for Mrs. Fei to present her arguments before judgement was given was incompatible with the principle of adversary proceedings, and thus contrary to article 14, paragraph 1, of the Covenant.

[14.31] In *Wolf v Panama* (289/88), an obvious violation of article 14(1) was entailed in the State's refusal to allow the author to attend relevant proceedings, and to have a chance properly to brief legal representatives.[34] *Thomas v Jamaica* (272/88) involved another blatant violation of article 14(1) in the State Party's failure to inform the author of his appeal date until after it had taken place.

[14.32] The following cases concern discrete violations of article 14(1): coercion of witnesses by the prosecution, and abuse by a prosecutor of a defendant's plea bargain.

[14.33]   *JOHN CAMPBELL v JAMAICA (307/88)*

The facts behind the HRC's finding of a violation of article 14(1) are evident below:

¶ 6.3. As regards the author's claim that his son Wayne was detained in order to force him to testify against him, the Committee observes that this is a grave allegation, which the author has endeavoured to substantiate, and which is corroborated by his son's statement. In the absence of any information from the State party, the Committee bases its decision on the facts as provided by the author.

¶ 6.4. Article 14 of the Covenant gives everyone the right to a fair and public hearing in the determination of a criminal charge against him; an indispensable aspect of the fair trial principle is the equality of arms between the prosecution and the defence. The Committee observes that the detention of witnesses in view of obtaining their testimony is an exceptional measure, which must be regulated by strict criteria in law and in practice. It is not apparent from the information before the Committee that special circumstances existed to justify the detention of the author's minor child. Moreover, in the light of his retraction, serious questions arise about possible intimidation and about the reliability of the testimony

---

[34] Para. 6.6.

obtained under these circumstances. The Committee therefore concludes that the author's right to a fair trial was violated.

In an individual opinion Wennergren extrapolated further on the reasons for finding a violation:

Testimony in a court of law is a civic duty and all legal systems provide for certain coercive measures to guarantee compliance with that duty. Subpoena and imprisonment are the most common coercive measures and should be used for the equal benefit of the prosecution and the defence, whenever deemed necessary for the presentation of evidence to the jury which, on the basis of such evidence, must determine guilt or innocence of the accused. In its Views, the Committee observes that the detention of witnesses is an exceptional measure, which must be regulated by strict criteria in practice and in law, and that it is not apparent that special circumstances existed in the author's case to justify the detention of a 13-year-old. For me, it is difficult to imagine circumstances that would justify a child's detention in order to compel him to testify against his father. In any event, this case in no way discloses such special circumstances; the judge therefore must be deemed to have violated the principle of due process of law, and the requirements of a fair hearing under article 14, paragraph 1. The violation was in fact the violation of the rights of a witness, but its negative impact on the conduct of the trial was such that it rendered it unfair within the meaning of article 14, paragraph 1, of the Covenant.[35]

[14.34]   *RICHARDS v JAMAICA (535/93)*

In this case the author was found guilty of murder and sentenced to death. The author claimed that he had been deprived of a fair trial contrary to article 14. The HRC agreed in the following terms:

¶ 7.2. The author has claimed that his trial was unfair because the prosecution entered a *nolle prosequi* plea after the author had pleaded guilty to a charge of manslaughter [and launched a fresh prosecution for murder]. The author claims that the extent of media publicity given to his guilty plea negated his right to presumption of innocence and thus denied him the right to a fair trial. The Court of Appeal of Jamaica acknowledged the possibility of disadvantage to the author at presenting his defence at the trial, but observed that nothing shows that the convicting jury was aware of this. The entry of a *nolle prosequi* was found by the Jamaican courts and the Judicial Committee of the Privy Council to be legally permissible, as under Jamaican law the author had not been finally convicted until sentence was passed. The question for the Committee is not, however, whether it was lawful, but whether its use was compatible with the guarantees of fair trial enshrined in the Covenant in the particular circumstances of the case. *Nolle prosequi* is a procedure which allows the Director of Public Prosecutions to discontinue a criminal prosecution. The State party has argued that it may be used in the interests of justice and that it was used in the present case to prevent a miscarriage of justice. The Committee observes, however, that the Prosecutor in the instant case was fully aware of the circumstances of Mr. Richards' case

---

[35] See also comments on Norway excerpted at [21.35] confirming that a State's law must provide for the appropriate treatment of child witnesses.

and had agreed to accept his manslaughter plea. The *nolle prosequi* was used not to discontinue proceedings against the author but to enable a fresh prosecution against the author to be initiated immediately, on exactly the same charge in respect of which he had already entered a plea of guilty to manslaughter, a plea which had been accepted. Thus, its purpose and effect were to circumvent the consequences of that plea, which was entered in accordance with the law and practice of Jamaica. In the Committee's opinion, the resort to a *nolle prosequi* in such circumstances, and the initiation of a further charge against the author, was incompatible with the requirements of a fair trial within the meaning of article 14, paragraph 1, of the Covenant.

JUDICIAL BIAS

[14.35] In numerous Optional Protocol cases, authors have submitted generalized complaints of unfair trials and judicial bias, such as trial by prejudiced judges or juries, deliverance of inadequate instructions to juries by judges, or faulty evaluation of fact and/or law by domestic tribunals. The HRC has usually dismissed such complaints, as is evinced from the following case excerpts.

J.K. v CANADA (174/84)

¶ 7.2. The Committee further observes that it is beyond its competence to review findings of fact made by national tribunals or to determine whether national tribunals properly evaluated new evidence submitted on appeal.

R.M. v FINLAND (301/88)

¶ 6.4. . . . The Committee further observes that it is not an appellate court and that allegations that a domestic court has committed errors of fact or law do not in themselves raise questions of violation of the Covenant unless it also appears that some of the requirements of article 14 may not have been complied with.

VAN MEURS v THE NETHERLANDS (215/86)

¶ 7.1. With respect to the author's claims that the hearing of his case was not fair, the Committee refers to its constant jurisprudence that it is not a 'fourth instance' court competent to reevaluate findings of fact or to review the application of domestic legislation. . . .

PINTO v TRINIDAD and TOBAGO (232/87)

¶ 12.3. . . . It is not, in principle, for the Committee to review specific instructions to the jury by the judge in a trial by jury, unless it can be ascertained that the instructions to the jury were clearly arbitrary or amounted to a denial of justice. In the Committee's opinion, the judge's instructions to the jury must meet particularly high standards as to their thoroughness and impartiality in cases in which a capital sentence may be pronounced on the accused. . . .

G.S. v JAMAICA (369/89)

¶ 3.2. . . . [T]he review, by the Committee, of specific instructions to the jury by the judge in a trial by jury or of generalized claims of bias is beyond the scope of application of article 14.

[14.36] The above case excerpts reinforce the fact that article 14(1) is essentially a procedural rather than a substantive right. One's right to a fair trial is guaranteed by adherence to appropriate procedures; one does not have a right that a tribunal will actually reach the correct result in one's case. There is no civil right to freedom from judicial error, so long as the appropriate procedures, usually designed to minimize error, are followed. Furthermore, the HRC will not readily presume bias or some other defect in a case in the absence of clear examples of unfairness. Indeed, the HRC has arguably been too unwilling to second-guess the decisions of domestic tribunals.[36] In a number of cases, the HRC's diffidence has prevented it from finding violations of article 14(1) in the face of apparent trial flaws. Note, for example, that more rigorous scrutiny of the circumstances of the relevant trial by Mr Scheinin in *McTaggart v Jamaica* (749/97) led him, in dissent, to find a violation of article 14. The HRC majority found most of the fair trial allegations inadmissible, and upheld no article 14 allegations on the merits.[37]

[14.37]   *HENDRIKS v THE NETHLERLANDS (201/85)*

Mr Wako issued the following separate opinion in this case, where he expressed misgivings over the HRC's deference to local courts in family court proceedings.[38]

¶ 3. My first concern is that, though the Committee's practice of not reviewing the decisions of local courts is prudent and appropriate, it is not dictated by the Optional Protocol. In cases where the facts are clear and the texts of all relevant orders and decisions have been made available by the parties, the Committee should be prepared to examine them as to their compatibility with the specific provisions of the Covenant invoked by the author. Thus, the Committee would not be acting as a 'fourth instance' in determining whether a decision of a State party's court was correct according to that State's legislation, but would only examine whether the provisions of the Covenant invoked by the alleged victim have been violated.

[14.38]   *KARTTUNEN v FINLAND (387/89)*

This is one of the few cases where judicial bias was actually established by the complainant. The author alleged that his civil trial was unfair for the following reasons:

---

[36] See P. R. Ghandhi, *The Human Rights Committee and the Right of Individual Communication* (Ashgate, Dartmouth, 1998), 216.

[37] See also the dissent of Mr Solar Yrigoyen in *Thomas v Jamaica* (614/95).

[38] See also [20.39].

¶ 2.3. In Mr. Karttunen's case, the court consisted of one career judge and five lay judges. One lay judge, V.S., was the uncle of E.M., who himself was a partner of the Säkhöjohto Ltd. Partnership Company, which appeared as a complainant against the author. While interrogating the author's wife, who testified as a witness, V.S. allegedly interrupted her by saying 'She is lying'. The remark does not, however, appear in the trial transcript or other court documents. Another lay judge, T.R., allegedly was indirectly involved in the case prior to the trial, since her brother was a member of the board of the Rääkkyla Cooperative Bank at the time when the author was a client of the bank; the brother resigned from the board with effect on 1 January 1984. In July 1986, the Bank also appeared as a complainant against the author.

¶ 2.4. The author did not challenge the two lay judges in the proceedings before the District Court; he did raise the issue before the Court of Appeal. He also requested that the proceedings at the appellate stage be public. The Court of Appeal, however, after having reevaluated the evidence *in toto*, held that whereas V.S. should have been barred from acting as a lay judge in the author's case pursuant to Section 13, paragraph 1, of the Code of Judicial Procedure, the judgement of the District Court had not been adversely affected by this defect. It moreover found that T. R. was not barred from participating in the proceedings, since her brother's resignation from the board of the Rääkkyla Cooperative Bank had been effective on 1 January 1984, long before the start of the trial. The Court of Appeal's judgement of 31 March 1988 therefore upheld the lower court's decision and dismissed the author's request for a public hearing.

¶ 3.1. The author contends that he was denied a fair hearing both by the Rääkkyla District Court and the Court of Appeal, in violation of article 14, paragraph 1, of the Covenant.

¶ 3.2. The author claims that the proceedings before the Rääkkyla District Court were not impartial, since the two lay judges, V.S. and T.R., should have been disqualified from the consideration of his case. In particular, he claims that the remark of V.S. during the testimony of Mrs. Karttunen, amounts to a violation of article 14, paragraph 1, of the Covenant. In this context, he argues that while Section 13, paragraph 1, of the Code of Judicial Procedure provides that a judge cannot sit in court if he was previously involved in the case, it does not distinguish between career and lay judges. If the court is composed of only five lay judges, as in his case, two lay judges can considerably influence the court's verdict, as every lay judge has one vote. The author further contends that the Court of Appeal erred in finding that (a) one of the lay judges, T.R., was not disqualified to consider the case, and (b) the failure of the District Court to disqualify the other lay judge because of conflict of interest had no effect on the outcome of the proceedings.

The HRC agreed with the author:

¶ 7.1. The Committee is called upon to determine whether the [non-]disqualification of lay judge V.S. and his alleged disruption of the testimony of the author's wife influenced the evaluation of evidence by, and the verdict of, the Rääkkyla District Court, in a way contrary to article 14, and whether the author was denied a fair trial on account of the Court of Appeal's refusal to grant the author's request for an oral hearing. As the two questions are closely related, the Committee will address them jointly. The Committee expresses its appreciation for the State party's frank cooperation in the consideration of the author's case.

¶ 7.2. The impartiality of the court and the publicity of proceedings are important aspects of the right to a fair trial within the meaning of article 14, paragraph 1. 'Impartiality' of the court implies that judges must not harbour preconceptions about the matter put before them, and that they must not act in ways that promote the interests of one of the parties. Where the grounds for disqualification of a judge are laid down by law, it is incumbent upon the court to consider *ex officio* these grounds and to replace members of the court falling under the disqualification criteria. A trial flawed by the participation of a judge who, under domestic statutes, should have been disqualified cannot normally be considered to be fair or impartial within the meaning of article 14.

¶ 7.3. It is possible for appellate instances to correct the irregularities of proceedings before lower court instances. In the present case, the Court of Appeal considered, on the basis of the written evidence, that the District Court's verdict had not been influenced by the presence of lay judge V.S., while admitting that V.S. manifestly should have been disqualified. The Committee considers that the author was entitled to oral proceedings before the Court of Appeal. As the State party itself concedes, only this procedure would have enabled the Court to proceed with the reevaluation of all the evidence submitted by the parties, and to determine whether the procedural flaw had indeed affected the verdict of the District Court. In the light of the above, the Committee concludes that there has been a violation of article 14, paragraph 1.

[14.39]   *GONZÁLEZ del RÍO v PERU (263/87)*

¶ 2.7. The author states that . . . [a] criminal matter remains pending since 1985, and although investigations have not resulted in any formal indictment, an order for his arrest remains pending, with the result that he cannot leave Peruvian territory. This, according to the author, is where matters currently stand. In a letter dated 20 September 1990, he states that the Supreme Court has 'buried' his file for years, and that, upon inquiry with the Court's president, he was allegedly told that the proceedings would 'be delayed to the maximum possible extent' while he [the Court's president] was in charge, since the matter was a political one and he would not like the press to question the final decision, which would obviously be adopted in Mr. González' favour . . . The author contends that the Supreme Court has no interest in admitting that its position is legally untenable, and that this explains its inaction. . . .

¶ 3.3. It is further claimed that the proceedings against the author have been neither fair nor impartial, in violation of article 14, paragraph 1, as may be seen from the politically motivated statements of magistrates and judges involved in his case. . . .

¶ 5.2. The Committee has noted the author's claim that he was not treated equally before the Peruvian courts, and that the State party has not refuted his specific allegation that some of the judges involved in the case had referred to its political implications (see paragraph 2.7 above) and justified the courts' inaction or the delays in the judicial proceedings on this ground. The Committee recalls that the right to be tried by an independent and impartial tribunal is an absolute right that may suffer no exception. It considers that the Supreme Court's position in the author's case was, and remains, incompatible with this requirement. The Committee is further of the view that the delays in the workings of the judicial system in respect of the author since 1985 violate his right, under article 14, paragraph 1, to a fair trial. In this connection, the Committee observes that no decision at first instance in this case had been reached by the autumn of 1992.

[14.40] *NARRAINEN v NORWAY (CERD 3/91)*

Narrainen is a decision by the Committee on the Elimination of Racial Discrimination, under the Convention on the Elimination of all Forms of Racial Discrimination 1966.[39] It would undoubtedly have some relevance for future HRC interpretations of article 14(1).

¶ 9.2. The Committee considers that in the present case the principal issue before it is whether the proceedings against Mr. Narrainen respected his right, under article 5(a) of the Convention, to equal treatment before the tribunals, without distinction as to race, colour or national or ethnic origin. The Committee notes that the rule laid down in article 5(a) applies to all types of judicial proceedings, including trial by jury. Other allegations put forward by the author of the communication are in the Committee's view outside the scope of the Convention.

¶ 9.3. If members of a jury are suspected of displaying or voicing racial bias against the accused, it is incumbent upon the national judicial authorities to investigate the issue and to disqualify the juror if there is a suspicion that the juror might be biased.

¶ 9.4. In the present case, the inimical remarks [alleged slurs about the author's skin colour] made by juror Ms. J. were brought to the attention of the Eidsivating High Court, which duly suspended the proceedings, investigated the issue and heard testimony about the allegedly inimical statement of Ms. J. In the view of the Committee, the statement of Ms. J. may be seen as an indication of racial prejudice and, in the light of the provision of article 5(a) of the Convention, the Committee is of the opinion that this remark might have been regarded as sufficient to disqualify the juror. However, the competent judicial bodies of Norway examined the nature of the contested remarks and their potential implications for the course of the trial.

¶ 9.5. Taking into account that it is neither the function of the Committee to interpret the Norwegian rules on criminal procedure concerning the disqualification of jurors, nor to decide as to whether the juror had to be disqualified on that basis, the Committee is unable to conclude, on the basis of the information before it, that a breach of the Convention has occurred. However, in the light of the observations made in paragraph 9.4, the Committee makes the following recommendations. . . .

¶ 10. The Committee recommends to the State party that every effort should be made to prevent any form of racial bias from entering into judicial proceedings which might result in adversely affecting the administration of justice on the basis of equality and non-discrimination. Consequently, the Committee recommends that in criminal cases like the one it has examined due attention be given to the impartiality of juries, in line with the principles underlying article 5(a) of the Convention.

[39] See generally, Chap. 23.

The *Narrainen* decision has been criticized for its deference to the Norwegian national courts: 'is not the function of an international body . . . to lend objectivity in the determination of both law and fact when there may be systemic racism in a domestic legal system?'[40]

[14.41] In *Cox v Canada* (539/93), the author alleged that the Pennsylvanian practice of requiring 'death qualified juries' in capital cases breached his right to a fair trial for a capital crime.[41] A 'death qualified jury' excludes persons who are conscientiously opposed to the death penalty, so that the jury is capable of unanimously imposing a death penalty for capital crimes. This part of Cox's complaint was held to be inadmissible.[42] It is a shame the issue was not examined on the merits.[43] 'Death qualified' juries are arguably disproportionately representative of politically conservative views, so the question of their impartiality could be raised.

[14.42]   ***WRIGHT v JAMAICA (349/89)***

This case is a rare example of a communication in which the HRC found that the domestic judge's instructions breached article 14(1). The author had been convicted of murder. His allegations are evident from the HRC's opinion:

¶ 8.1. With respect to the alleged violations of the Covenant, [a number of] issues are before the Committee: (a) whether the judge showed bias in his evaluation of the evidence or in his instructions to the jury; (b) whether the overlooking of the significance of the time of death amounted to a violation of the author's right to a fair trial. . . .

¶ 8.3. In respect of the issue of the significance of the time of death of the victim, the Committee begins by noting that the post-mortem on the deceased [the author's alleged victim] was performed on 1 September 1981 at approximately 1 p.m., and that the expert concluded that death had occurred forty-seven hours before. His conclusion, which was not challenged, implied that the author was already in police custody when the deceased was shot. The information was available to the Court; given the seriousness of its implications, the Court should have brought it to the attention of the jury, even though it was not mentioned by counsel. . . . In all the circumstances, and especially given that the trial of the author was for a capital offence, this omission must, in the Committee's view, be deemed a denial of justice and as such constitutes a violation of article 14, paragraph 1, of the Covenant. This remains so even if the placing of this evidence before the jury might not, in the event, have changed their verdict and the outcome of the case.

---

[40] F.F. Martin *et al.*, *International Human Rights Law and Practice* (Kluwer, The Hague, 1997), 543.

[41] Para. 8(2)(c). Therefore, Cox argued that, as his proposed extradition to Pennsylvania foreseeably exposed him to such a breach, the extradition itself breached art. 14. See [8.27] ff. for discussion of these types of complaints.

[42] Indeed, the HRC did not expressly address this complaint.

[43] It is uncertain whether the HRC felt that 'death qualified juries' raised no issue, or whether Cox had failed to prove that he would be unable to challenge the phenomenon of 'death qualified juries' upon return to the USA, and had therefore failed to prove the likelihood of an art. 14 breach upon extradition to the USA.

EXPEDITIOUS HEARINGS

[14.43] A specific guarantee of expeditious criminal trials is contained in article 14(3)(c). However, one of the elements of the concept of a fair civil hearing outlined by the Committee is that justice be delivered expeditiously, as is demonstrated in the following case.

MUÑOZ HERMOZA v PERU (203/86)

In this case the author was an ex-sergeant of the Guardia Civil (police) who had been dismissed from service for insulting a superior. The author unsuccessfully sought, over a ten-year period, reinstatement before various administrative and judicial authorities. The HRC held that there had been a breach of article 14:

¶ 11.3. With respect to the requirement of a fair hearing as stipulated in article 14, paragraph 1, of the Covenant, the Committee notes that the concept of a fair hearing necessarily entails that justice be rendered without undue delay. In this connection the Committee observes that the administrative review in the Muñoz case was kept pending for seven years and that it ended with a decision against the author based on the ground that he had started judicial proceedings. A delay of seven years constitutes an unreasonable delay. Furthermore, with respect to the judicial review, the Committee notes that the Tribunal of Constitutional Guarantees decided in favour of the author in 1986 and that the State party has informed the Committee that judicial remedies were exhausted with that decision . . . However, the delays in implementation have continued and two and a half years after the judgement of the Tribunal of Constitutional Guarantees, the author has still not been reinstated in his post. This delay, which the State party has not explained, constitutes a further aggravation of the violation of the principle of a fair hearing. The Committee further notes that on 24 September 1987 the Cuzco Civil Chamber, in pursuance of the decision of the Tribunal of Constitutional Guarantees, ordered that the author be reinstated; subsequently, in a written opinion dated 7 March 1988, the Public Prosecutor declared that the decision of the Cuzco Civil Chamber was valid and that the author's action of *amparo* was well founded. But even after these clear decisions, the Government of Peru has failed to reinstate the author. Instead, yet another special appeal, this time granted *ex officio* in 'Defence of the State' . . . has been allowed, which resulted in a contradictory decision by the Supreme Court of Peru on 15 April 1988, declaring that the author's action of *amparo* had not been lodged timely and was therefore inadmissible. This procedural issue, however, had already been adjudicated by the Tribunal of Constitutional Guarantees in 1986, before which the author's action is again pending. Such a seemingly endless sequence of instances and the repeated failure to implement decisions are not compatible with the principle of a fair hearing.[44]

The guarantee of expeditious hearings was also breached in *Fei v Colombia* (514/92) [14.30] and *González del Rio v Peru* (263/87) [14.39].

---

[44] See also *Mukunto v Zambia* (768/97), where the author's compensation proceedings had not been resolved after 18 years, constituting a breach of art. 14(1) (para. 6.4).

[14.44] In *Casanovas v France* (441/90), the relevant proceedings concerned the author's challenge to his dismissal from the French civil service. No breach of article 14(1) arose from the period of time, two years and nine months, that elapsed between 'the submission of the complaint of irregular dismissal to the [final] decision of reinstatement'.[45] In *Morael v France* (207/86), the HRC agreed that the length of time taken to decide the trial (just under four years) was reasonable given 'the circumstances and . . . the complexity of a bankruptcy case'.[46]

[14.45] In Concluding Comments on Brazil, the HRC stated:[47]

¶ 24. The Committee recommends that the State party continue its consideration of further ways to improve the effectiveness of the judicial process. The Government should consider the establishment of small claims courts and petty offences courts that would help to reduce the backlog of cases pending before the courts.

PUBLIC HEARINGS

[14.46] *GENERAL COMMENT 13*

¶ 6. The publicity of hearings is an important safeguard in the interest of the individual and of society at large. At the same time article 14, paragraph 1, acknowledges that courts have the power to exclude all or part of the public for reasons spelt out in that paragraph. It should be noted that, apart from such exceptional circumstances, the Committee considers that a hearing must be open to the public in general, including members of the press, and must not, for instance, be limited only to a particular category of persons. It should be noted that, even in cases in which the public is excluded from the trial, the judgement must, with certain strictly defined exceptions, be made public.

[14.47] In *Sala de Tourón v Uruguay* (32/78), the HRC implied that criminal trials at first instance must be conducted orally, rather than in writing.[48] However, in *R.M. v Finland* (301/88), the HRC confirmed that appellate proceedings may take place on the basis of written presentations, so long as proceedings and documents are open to the public.[49] Mr Wennergren, in a concurring separate opinion in *Karttunen v Finland* (387/89), stated that a 'public trial' does not *necessarily* entitle one to a public oral hearing.[50]

---

[45] Para. 7.4.   [46] Para. 9.4.

[47] (1996) UN doc. CCPR/C/79/Add. 66.

[48] The HRC failed expressly to respond to the State Party's explanation that all trials were conducted in writing, but it nevertheless found a violation of art. 14(1), entailed in the State's failure to provide a 'public trial'. See McGoldrick, above, note 2, 418–19.

[49] Para. 6.4.

[50] In *Karttunen v Finland* (387/89), one of the author's complaints concerned the Court of Appeal's failure to permit him an oral appeal. The HRC found a violation of art. 14(1) in the circumstances [14.38]. This does not however mean that one is always entitled to oral hearings.

[14.48]   ***POLAY CAMPOS v PERU (577/94)***

The communication was submitted by the alleged victim's wife. It concerned the victim's trial by a panel of 'faceless' or anonymous judges.

¶ 2.2. On 3 April 1993, Victor Alfredo Polay Campos was tried in the Yanamayo prison by a so-called 'tribunal of faceless judges' established under special anti-terrorist legislation. Such a body consists of judges who are allowed to cover their faces, so as to guarantee their anonymity and prevent them from being targeted by active members of terrorist groups. Mr. Polay Campos was convicted and sentenced to life imprisonment; it is claimed that his access to legal representation and the preparation of his defence were severely restricted. While the author does not specify the crime(s) of which her husband is convicted, it transpires from the file that he was convicted of 'aggravated terrorism'. . . .

The HRC made the following findings:

¶ 8.8. As to Mr. Polay Campos' trial and conviction on 3 April 1993 by a special tribunal of 'faceless judges', no information was made available by the State party, in spite of the Committee's request to this effect in the admissibility decision of 15 March 1996. . . . [S]uch trials by special tribunals composed of anonymous judges are incompatible with article 14 of the Covenant. It cannot be held against the author that she furnished little information about her husband's trial: In fact, the very nature of the system of trials by 'faceless judges' in a remote prison is predicated on the exclusion of the public from the proceedings. In this situation, the defendants do not know who the judges trying them are and unacceptable impediments are created to their preparation of their defence and communication with their lawyers. Moreover, this system fails to guarantee a cardinal aspect of a fair trial within the meaning of article 14 of the Covenant: that the tribunal must be, and be seen to be, independent and impartial. In a system of trial by 'faceless judges', neither the independence nor the impartiality of the judges is guaranteed, since the tribunal, being established *ad hoc*, may comprise serving members of the armed forces. In the Committee's opinion, such a system also fails to safeguard the presumption of innocence, which is guaranteed by article 14, paragraph 2. In the circumstances of the case, the Committee concludes that paragraphs 1, 2 and 3 (b) and (d) of article 14 of the Covenant were violated.

Indeed, the HRC had previously condemned the practice of trial by 'faceless judges' in Concluding Comments on Peru:[51]

¶ 12. The Committee expresses its deepest concern about Decree Law 25,475 and Decree Law 25,659 which seriously impair the protection of the rights contained in the Covenant for persons accused of terrorism and contradicts in many respects the provisions of article 14 of the Covenant. Decree Law 25,475 contains a very broad definition of terrorism under which innocent persons have been and remain detained. It establishes a system of trial by 'faceless judges', where the defendants do not know who are the judges trying them and are denied public trials, and which places serious impediments, in law and in fact, to the possibility for defendants to prepare their defence and communicate with their lawyers.

---

[51] (1996) UN doc. CCPR/C/79/Add. 67.

Under Decree Law 25,659, cases of treason are tried by military courts, regardless of whether the defendant is a civilian or a member of the military or security forces. In this connection, the Committee expresses its deep concern that persons accused of treason are being tried by the same military force that detained and charged them, that the members of the military courts are active duty officers, that most of them have not received any legal training and that, moreover, there is no provision for sentences to be reviewed by a higher tribunal. These shortcomings raise serious doubts about the independence and impartiality of the judges of military courts. The Committee emphasizes that trials of non-military persons should be conducted in civilian courts before an independent and impartial judiciary.

[14.49] Just as faceless judges are unacceptable, so are 'anonymous witnesses'.[52] It may be noted that article 68 of the Rome Statute of the International Criminal Court appears to permit the anonymity of a witness, where necessary for that witness's protection, so long as '[s]uch measures are exercised in a manner which is not prejudicial to or inconsistent with the rights of the accused to a fair and impartial trial'.[53]

[14.50]   *VAN MEURS v THE NETHERLANDS (215/86)*

¶ 6.1. With respect to the author's claim related to the publicity of the sub-district court hearing, the Committee considers that if labour disputes are argued in oral hearing before a court, they fall within the requirement, in article 14, paragraph 1, that suits at law be held in public. That is a duty upon the State that is not dependent on any request, by the interested party, that the hearing be held in public. Both domestic legislation and judicial practice must provide for the possibility of the public attending, if members of the public so wish. In the instant case, the Committee notes that while the old article 1639w of the Civil Code of the Netherlands was silent on the question of the public or non-public nature of the proceedings, it appears that in practice the public did not attend. It is far from clear in this case whether the hearing was or was not held *in camera*. The author's communication does not state that he or his counsel formally requested that the proceedings be held in public, or that the sub-district court made any determination that they be held *in camera*. On the basis of the information before it, the Committee is unable to find that the proceedings in the author's case were incompatible with the requirement of a 'public hearing' within the meaning of article 14, paragraph 1.

¶ 6.2. The Committee observes that courts must make information on time and venue of the oral hearings available to the public and provide for adequate facilities for the attendance of interested members of the public, within reasonable limits, taking into account, e.g., the potential public interest in the case, the duration of the oral hearing and the time the formal request for publicity has been made. Failure of the court to make large courtrooms available does not constitute a violation of the right to a public hearing, if in fact no interested member of the public is barred from attending an oral hearing.

---

[52] Concluding Comments on Colombia (1997) UN doc. CCPR/C/79/Add. 75, para. 21.
[53] Rome Statute of the International Criminal Court, art. 68(5).

[14.51] States Parties bear the burden of proof in justifying *in camera* trials.[54] In *Z.P. v Canada* (341/88), the author complained that his trial on charges of rape was not 'public'.[55] The State Party replied that 'the public may be excluded from all or part of a trial for reasons of morals—a request frequently made and granted in sexual abuse cases'.[56] The HRC found the author's complaint was not sufficiently substantiated.[57]

[14.52] In *McTaggart v Jamaica* (749/97), the author complained that adverse publicity had deprived him of a fair trial. As the adverse publicity occurred in another State besides Jamaica (Canada), no violation was found.[58] However, the judgment implies that adverse publicity on occasion can be so potent as irredeemably to prejudice a trial.

[14.53]   *LEVY v JAMAICA (719/96)*

¶ 7.1. As to the author's claim that the reclassification of his offence as capital murder by the single judge violated article 14, the Committee notes that pursuant to the Offences against the Persons (Amendment) Act 1992, the State party adopted a procedure to reclassify established murder convictions expeditiously by entrusting the initial review of each case to a single judge, enabling him to promptly give a decision in favour of a prisoner who in his opinion had committed a non-capital offence, and thus removing rapidly any uncertainty as to whether he was still at risk of being executed. If the single judge on the other hand found that the offence was of a capital nature, the convict was notified and was granted the right to appeal the decision to a three judge-panel, which would address the matter in a public hearing. The Committee notes that it is not disputed that all procedural safeguards contained in article 14 applied in the proceedings before the three judge-panel. The author's complaint is solely directed at the first stage of the reclassification procedure, i.e. the single judge's handling of the matter, of which the author was not notified and in which there was no public hearing where the author could comment on the relevant issues or be represented. The Committee is of the opinion that the reclassification of an offence for a convict already subject to a death sentence is not a 'determination of a criminal charge' within the meaning of article 14 of the Covenant, and consequently the provisions in article 14, paragraph 3, do not apply. The Committee considers, however, that the safeguards contained in article 14, paragraph 1, should apply also to the reclassification procedure. In this regard, the Committee notes that the system for reclassification allowed the convicts a fair and public hearing by the three judge-panel. The fact that this hearing was preceded by a screening exercise performed by a single judge in order to expedite the reclassification, does not constitute a violation of article 14.[59]

---

[54] *Estrella v Uruguay* (74/80), para. 10.   [55] Para. 3.3(j).   [56] Para. 4.6.
[57] Para. 5.6.   [58] Para. 8.4.
[59] See also *Morgan and Williams v Jamaica* (720/96), para. 7.1.

Article 14(2)—The Presumption of Innocence

[14.54] *GENERAL COMMENT 13*

¶ 7. The Committee has noted a lack of information regarding article 14, paragraph 2 and, in some cases, has even observed that the presumption of innocence, which is fundamental to the protection of human rights, is expressed in very ambiguous terms or entails conditions which render it ineffective. By reason of the presumption of innocence, the burden of proof of the charge is on the prosecution and the accused has the benefit of doubt. No guilt can be presumed until the charge has been proved beyond reasonable doubt. Further, the presumption of innocence implies a right to be treated in accordance with this principle. It is, therefore, a duty for all public authorities to refrain from prejudging the outcome of a trial.

[14.55] Article 14(2) only applies to criminal proceedings and does not apply to civil proceedings, as is demonstrated in the following case.

MORAEL v FRANCE (207/86)

The author in this case argued that the civil findings of his liability for company debts [14.29] breached article 14(2).

¶ 2.3. With respect to article 14(2), the author contends that article 99 of Act No. 67–563 had not only a civil but also a penal character, and he refers in this connection to the fact that the Public Prosecutor (*Ministère public*) was heard during the proceedings before the Tribunal of Commerce of Dunkirk. He further contends that the decision by the Court of Appeal ordering him to pay FF 3 million francs amounts to a penal sanction. He therefore claims that he should have enjoyed the presumption of innocence.

The HRC disagreed with the author's classification of his punishment as 'penal':

¶ 9.5. As to the complaint that the action for coverage of liabilities brought against the author violated the principle of presumption of innocence laid down in article 14(2) of the Covenant, the Committee points out that that provision is applicable only to persons charged with a criminal offence. Article 99 of the former bankruptcy law entailed a presumption of responsibility on the part of company managers in the absence of proof of their diligence. But that presumption did not relate to any charge of a criminal offence. On the contrary, it was a presumption relating to a system of liability for risk resulting from a person's activities—one that is well known in private law, even in the form of absolute or objective liability ruling out all evidence to the contrary. In the situation under consideration, liability was established in favour of the creditors and the amounts charged to the managers corresponded to the damages they had suffered and were to be paid in order to cover the company's liabilities. The object of article 99 of the Bankruptcy Act was to compensate creditors but it also entailed other penalties which, however, were civil-law and not criminal-law penalties. The provision concerning the presumption of innocence in article 14 (2) cannot therefore be applied in the case under consideration. That conclusion cannot be affected by the allegation that the provision of article 99 of the Bankruptcy Act was subsequently modified by elimination of the presumption of fault, considered unjust from the point of view of the material settlement of liability, for this circumstance does not of itself imply that the earlier provision contravened the above-mentioned provisions of the Convention.

Similarly in *W.J.H v The Netherlands* (408/90)[60] and *W.B.E. v The Netherlands* (432/90)[61] the HRC held that article 14(2) does not apply to proceedings for compensation for an alleged miscarriage of justice.

Article 14(3)(a)—The Right to be Informed of the Charge

[14.56] *GENERAL COMMENT 13*

¶ 8. Among the minimum guarantees in criminal proceedings prescribed by paragraph 3, the first concerns the right of everyone to be informed in a language which he understands of the charge against him (subpara. (a)). The Committee notes that State reports often do not explain how this right is respected and ensured. Article 14(3)(a) applies to all cases of criminal charges, including those of persons not in detention. The Committee notes further that the right to be informed of the charge 'promptly' requires that information is given in the manner described as soon as the charge is first made by a competent authority. In the opinion of the Committee this right must arise when in the course of an investigation a court or an authority of the prosecution decides to take procedural steps against a person suspected of a crime or publicly names him as such. The specific requirements of subparagraph 3 (a) may be met by stating the charge either orally or in writing, provided that the information indicates both the law and the alleged facts on which it is based.

[14.57] Article 14(3)(a) requires one to be informed of one's charge once the authorities have decided to issue a criminal charge. It may be distinguished from article 9(2), which applies before the issue of a charge: it requires persons to be informed of the reason for their arrest in connection with a criminal charge.[62] One may also note that the requirements of article 14(3)(a) are 'more precise' than those of article 9(2).[63] It is enough for an arrested person to be aware of the reasons for his/her arrest under article 9(2), whereas one must always be formally charged to satisfy article 14(3)(a).[64]

Article 14(3)(b)—Preparation of the Defence

[14.58] *GENERAL COMMENT 13*

¶ 9. Subparagraph 3 (b) provides that the accused must have adequate time and facilities for the preparation of his defence and to communicate with counsel of his own choosing.

---

[60] Para. 6.2. [61] Para. 6.6.
[62] See *Kelly v Jamaica* (253/87) at [11.21].
[63] *McLawrence v Jamaica* (702/96), para. 5.9.
[64] See also *Vicente et al. v Colombia* (612/95), para. 8.7.

What is 'adequate time' depends on the circumstances of each case, but the facilities must include access to documents and other evidence which the accused requires to prepare his case, as well as the opportunity to engage and communicate with counsel. When the accused does not want to defend himself in person or request a person or an association of his choice, he should be able to have recourse to a lawyer. Furthermore, this subparagraph requires counsel to communicate with the accused in conditions giving full respect for the confidentiality of their communications. Lawyers should be able to counsel and to represent their clients in accordance with their established professional standards and judgement without any restrictions, influences, pressures or undue interference from any quarter.

WHAT IS 'ADEQUATE TIME'?

[14.59]   *SMITH v JAMAICA (282/88)*

¶ 10.4. As to the author's claims that he was not allowed adequate time to prepare his defence and that, as a result, a number of key witnesses for the defence were not traced or called to give evidence, the Committee recalls its previous jurisprudence that the right of an accused person to have adequate time and facilities for the preparation of his defence is an important element of the guarantee of a fair trial and an emanation of the principle of equality of arms. [See Communications Nos. 253/1987 (*Paul Kelly v Jamaica*), Views adopted on 8 April 1991, paragraph 5.9; 283/1988 (*Aston Little v Jamaica*), Views adopted on 1 November 1991, paragraph 8.3.] The determination of what constitutes 'adequate time' requires an assessment of the circumstances of each case. In the instant case, it is uncontested that the trial defence was prepared on the first day of the trial. The material before the Committee reveals that one of the court appointed lawyers requested another lawyer to replace him. Furthermore, another attorney assigned to represent the author withdrew the day prior to the trial; when the trial was about to begin at 10 a.m., the author's counsel asked for a postponement until 2 p.m., so as to enable him to secure professional assistance and to meet with his client, as he had not been allowed by the prison authorities to visit him late at night the day before. The Committee notes that the request was granted by the judge, who was intent on absorbing the backlog on the court's agenda. Thus, after the jury was empanelled, counsel had only four hours to seek an assistant and to communicate with the author, which he could only do in a perfunctory manner. This, in the Committee's opinion, is insufficient [time] to prepare adequately the defence in a capital case. There is also, on the basis of the information available, the indication that this affected counsel's possibility of determining which witnesses to call. In the Committee's opinion, this constitutes a violation of article 14, paragraph 3(b), of the Covenant.

[14.60] *SAWYERS, MCLEAN and MCLEAN v JAMAICA (226, 256/87)*

In this case, the Committee noted that:[65]

¶ 13.6. . . . The determination of what constitutes 'adequate time' depends on an assessment of the circumstances of each case. While it is uncontested that none of the accused

---

[65] See also *Grant v Jamaica* (353/88), para. 8.4.

met with their lawyers more than twice prior to trial, the Committee cannot conclude that the lawyers were placed in a situation where they were unable properly to prepare the case for the defence. In particular, material before the Committee does not reveal that an adjournment was requested on grounds of insufficient time, nor has it been argued that the judge would have denied an adjournment. . . .

In a number of other cases, the HRC denied a breach of article 14(3)(b) where the accused had not asked for an adjournment.[66] Failure to request an adjournment is perhaps analogous to a failure to exhaust local remedies for which the State cannot be held liable.

WHAT ARE 'ADEQUATE FACILITIES'?

[14.61] *YASSEEN and THOMAS v REPUBLIC OF GUYANA (676/96)*

¶ 7.10. With regard to the missing diaries and notebooks, the Committee notes that the authors claim that these may have contained exculpatory evidence. The State party has failed to address this allegation. In the absence of any explanation by the State party, the Committee considers that due weight must be given to the authors' allegations, and that the failure to produce at the last trial (1992) police documents which were produced at the first trial (1988) and which may have contained evidence in favour of the authors, constitutes a violation of article 14, paragraph 3, (b) and (e), since it may have impeded the authors in preparation of their defence.

[14.62]   *HARWARD v NORWAY (451/91)*

¶ 9.4. Article 14 of the Covenant protects the right to a fair trial. An essential element of this right is that an accused must have adequate time and facilities to prepare his defence, as is reflected in paragraph 3(b) of article 14. Article 14, however, does not contain an explicit right of an accused to have direct access to all documents used in the preparation of the trial against him in a language he can understand. The question before the Committee is whether, in the specific circumstances of the author's case, the failure of the State party to provide written translations of all the documents used in the preparation of the trial has violated Mr. Harward's right to a fair trial, more specifically his right under article 14, paragraph 3(b), to have adequate facilities to prepare his defence.

¶ 9.5. In the opinion of the Committee, it is important for the guarantee of fair trial that the defence has the opportunity to familiarize itself with the documentary evidence against an accused. However, this does not entail that an accused who does not understand the language used in court, has the right to be furnished with translations of all relevant documents in a criminal investigation, provided that the relevant documents are made available to his counsel. The Committee notes that Mr. Harward was represented by a Norwegian lawyer of his choice, who had access to the entire file, and that the lawyer had the assistance of an interpreter in his meetings with Mr. Harward. Defence counsel therefore had

---

[66] See e.g., *Wright v Jamaica* (349/1989), para. 8.4; *Henry v Jamaica* (230/87), para. 8.2; *Thomas v Jamaica* (272/88), para. 11.4.

opportunity to familiarize himself with the file and, if he thought it necessary, to read out Norwegian documents to Mr. Harward during their meetings, so that Mr. Harward could take note of its contents through interpretation. If counsel would have deemed the time available to prepare the defence (just over six weeks) inadequate to familiarize himself with the entire file, he could have requested a postponement of the trial, which he did not do. The Committee concludes that, in the particular circumstances of the case, Mr. Harward's right to a fair trial, more specifically his right to have adequate facilities to prepare his defence, was not violated.

RIGHT TO COMMUNICATE WITH COUNSEL OF ONE'S OWN CHOOSING

[14.63] *KELLY v JAMAICA (537/93)*

¶ 9.2. . . . According to the file, . . . the author, when brought into the police station in Hanover on 24 March 1988, told the police officers that he wanted to speak to his lawyer, Mr McLeod, but the police ignored the request for five days. In the circumstances, the Committee concludes that the author's right, under article 14, paragraph 3(b), to communicate with counsel of his choice, was violated.

This right overlaps substantially with the rights contained in article 14(3)(d) and will be further considered below.

[14.64] The Committee has confirmed on numerous occasions that incommunicado detention breaches article 14(3)(b) as it renders access to legal assistance impossible. The shortest period of incommunicado detention so far found to constitute a breach of this article is forty days in *Drescher Caldas v Uruguay* (43/79).[67] Presumably, a lesser period, such as the five days prescribed in *Kelly*, would also suffice to breach the provision. Such cases have not yet come before the HRC.

Article 14(3)(c)—Trial Without Undue Delay

[14.65] *GENERAL COMMENT 13*

¶ 10. Subparagraph 3(c) provides that the accused shall be tried without undue delay. This guarantee relates not only to the time by which a trial should commence, but also the time by which it should end and judgement be rendered; all stages must take place 'without undue delay'. To make this right effective, a procedure must be available in order to ensure that the trial will proceed 'without undue delay', both in first instance and on appeal.

[14.66] Article 14(3)(c) overlaps substantially with article 9(3) which guarantees

---

[67] See N. Rodley, 'Rights and Responses to Terrorism' in D. Harris and S. Joseph (eds.), *The International Covenant on Civil and Political Rights and United Kingdom Law* (Clarendon Press, Oxford, 1995), 129. See also *Carballal v Uruguay* (33/78), *Izquierdo v Uruguay* (73/80), and *Machado v Uruguay* (83/80).

pre-trial detainees a right to be tried 'within a reasonable time'.[68] Article 9(3) however only regulates the length of detention before trial. Article 14(3)(c) regulates the actual time between arrest and trial, regardless of whether one is detained or not.

[14.67] The determination of 'undue delay' depends on the circumstances and complexity of the case. In this respect, the criminal 'expedition' rule mirrors the 'expedition' rule, incorporated into article 14(1), regarding civil trials [14.43–14.45]. In *Wolf v Panama* (289/88), a delay of four and a half years between arrest and the rendering of the judgment in a fraud case did not breach article 14(3)(c), as the HRC observed 'that investigations into allegations of fraud may be complex and the author had not shown that the facts did not necessitate prolonged proceedings'.[69]

[14.68]   *HILL and HILL v SPAIN (526/93)*

In this case the author's complaint regarding a violation of article 14(3)(c) was upheld by the HRC after a delay of three years between arrest and final appeal. The HRC's comments on this issue were as follows:

¶ 12.4. The authors were arrested on 15 July 1985 and formally charged on 19 July 1985. Their trial did not start until November 1986, and their appeal was not disposed of until July 1988. Only a minor part of this delay can be attributed to the authors' decision to change their lawyers. The State party has argued that the delay was due to 'the complexities of the case' but has provided no information showing the nature of the alleged complexities. Having examined all the information available to it, the Committee fails to see in which respect this case could be regarded as complex. The sole witness was the eyewitness who gave evidence at the hearing in July 1985, and there is no indication that any further investigation was required after that hearing was completed. In these circumstances, the Committee finds that the State party violated the authors' right, under article 14, paragraph 3(c), to be tried without undue delay.

[14.69] The Committee's decisions in *Wolf* and *Hill* do not seem compatible regarding the burden of proof. In *Wolf*, the author had been required to show that proceedings should *not* have taken so long, whereas in *Hill*, the concomitant burden was on the State to show that proceedings *should* have taken so long. The distinguishing feature may be the inherent complexity of Wolf's alleged crime, fraud, compared with the comparative 'simplicity' in investigating the Hill brothers' alleged crime, the firebombing of a car. This also demonstrates the HRC's occasional inconsistency regarding the burden of proof in Optional Protocol cases.[70]

---

[68] See [11.32–11.36].   [69] Para. 6.4.
[70] In this respect, see also [6.31] and preceding case extracts.

[14.70]   *KELLY v JAMAICA (253/87)*

¶ 5.11. . . . The author contends that his right, under article 14, paragraph (3)(c) . . . was violated because almost eighteen months elapsed between his arrest and the opening of the trial. . . . [The Committee] cannot conclude that a lapse of a year and a half between the arrest and the start of the trial constituted 'undue delay', as there is no suggestion that pre-trial investigations could have been concluded earlier, or that the author complained in this respect to the authorities.

THOMAS v JAMAICA (614/95)

¶ 9.5. The author has claimed that the period of 23 months from his conviction to the hearing of his appeal constitutes a breach of article 14, paragraph 3 (c), and 5, of the Covenant. The Committee reiterates that all guarantees under article 14 of the Covenant should be strictly observed in any criminal procedure, particularly in capital cases, and notes with regard to the period of 23 months between trial and appeal that the State party has conceded that such a delay is undesirable, but that it has not offered any further explanation. In the absence of any circumstances justifying the delay, the Committee finds that with regard to this period there has been a violation of article 14, paragraph 3 (c), in conjunction with paragraph 5, of the Covenant.

In *Brown v Jamaica* (775/97), a similar delay of twenty-three months between arrest and trial breached article 14(3)(c).[71] In *Yasseen and Thomas v Republic of Guyana* (676/96), a delay of two years between an order for retrial and the conclusion of the appeal from that retrial breached article 14(3)(c),[72] even though the authors' counsel was responsible for a delay of three months.[73] On the other hand, a fourteen-month delay in *Hankle v Jamaica* (710/96) did not constitute a breach of article 14(3)(c).[74]

Hence, a delay of twenty-three months or more between arrest and conviction at first instance,[75] and/or between conviction and the conclusion of an appeal, *prima facie* breaches article 14(3)(c). Exceptional circumstances, such as extreme complexity in the case, may justify longer delays. Shorter delays appear to be compatible with article 14(3)(c).

[14.71]   *BROWN v JAMAICA (775/97)*

¶ 6.11. . . . In respect to the alleged other delays in the criminal process, the Committee notes that the author's retrial was scheduled to begin on 23 November 1994, four months after the Court of Appeal's judgement, but that it was adjourned on several occasions upon request of the defence. In the circumstances, the Committee finds that the delay of one year

---

[71] Para. 6.11.   [72] Para. 7.11.   [73] Para. 5.7.
[74] Para. 6.6. A year's delay between arrest and trial in *McTaggart v Jamaica* (749/97), whilst 'undesirable', was not a violation (para. 8.2). See also *Campbell v Jamaica* (248/87) (no breach entailed in a ten-month delay between conviction and dismissal of the author's appeal (para. 6.8)).
[75] *Yasseen* may indicate that 21 months is enough for a violation; see text at note 71.

and nine months between the Court of Appeal's judgement and the beginning of the retrial cannot be solely attributed to the State party and that it does not disclose a violation of the Covenant.

STEPHENS v JAMAICA (373/89)

¶ 9.8. Finally, the author has alleged a violation of article 14, paragraphs 3(c) and (5), on account of the delay between his trial and his appeal. In this context, the Committee notes that during the preparation of the author's petition for special leave to appeal to the Judicial Committee of the Privy Council by a London lawyer, Mr. Stephens' legal aid representative for the trial was requested repeatedly but unsuccessfully to explain the delays between trial and the hearing of the appeal in December 1986. While a delay of almost two years and 10 months between trial and appeal in a capital case is regrettable and a matter of concern, the Committee cannot, on the basis of the material before it, conclude that this delay was primarily attributable to the State party, rather than to the author.

Thus, where the delay is attributable to the author, or author's counsel, there is no breach of article 14(3)(c).[76]

[14.72] There have been a number of Jamaican cases where the authors' rights to appeal from the Jamaican Court of Appeal to the Judicial Committee of the Privy Council have been thwarted by the failure of the Court of Appeal to produce written reasons. Privy Council appeals inevitably failed in the absence of these court documents.[77] These delays have consistently been found to constitute breaches of article 14(3)(c) as well as a breach of the right to an appeal in criminal cases in article 14(5). For example, a delay of forty-five months before production of the documents in *Pratt and Morgan v Jamaica* (210/86, 225/87) constituted breaches of both sub-paragraphs,[78] as did a delay of 'almost four years' in *Shalto v Trinidad and Tobago* (447/91).[79] On the other hand, a delay of nearly three years in producing the documents did not breach article 14(3)(c) in *Reynolds v Jamaica* (229/87). The guarantee was not even mentioned, which may indicate that this was an oversight on the part of the HRC. In view of other cases establishing that a delay of less than two years could breach article 14(3)(c), the *Reynolds* decision seems anomalous.[80]

[14.73]   *LUBUTO v ZAMBIA (390/90)*

The State Party submitted the following justification for the eight-year delay between the author's arrest and the dismissal of his final appeal:

---

[76] See also *Berry v Jamaica* (330/88), *V.B. v Trinidad & Tobago* (485/91), and *Jones v Jamaica* (585/96).

[77] See, e.g., *M.F. v Jamaica* (233/88), para. 5.2; *Reynolds v Jamaica* (229/87), para. 5.1; *Kelly v Jamaica* (253/87), para. 5.1.

[78] See also *Little v Jamaica* (283/88) (delay of five years); *Kelly v Jamaica* (253/87) (five years).

[79] Para. 7.2.

[80] The author intimated as much in a subsequent complaint, which raised new allegations about subsequent court proceedings, in *Reynolds v Jamaica* (597/94).

¶ 5.1. By submission of 29 December 1994, the State party acknowledges that the proceedings in Mr. Lubuto's case took rather long. The State party requests the Committee to take into consideration its situation as a developing country and the problems it encounters in the administration of justice. It is explained that the instant case is not an isolated one and that appeals in both civil and criminal cases take considerable time before they are disposed of by the courts. According to the State party, this is due to the lack of administrative support available to the judiciary. Judges have to write out every word verbatim during the hearings, because of the absence of transcribers. These records are later typed out and have to be proofread by the judges, causing inordinate delays. The State party also refers to the costs involved in preparing the court documents.

¶ 5.2. The State party further points out that crime has increased and the number of cases to be decided by the courts have multiplied. Due to the bad economic situation in the country, it has not been possible to ensure equipment and services in order to expedite the disposal of cases. The State party submits that it is trying to improve the situation, and that it has recently acquired nine computers and that it expects to get 40 more.

¶ 5.3. The State party concludes that the delays suffered by the author in the determination of his case are inevitable due to the situation as explained above. The State party further submits that there has been no violation of article 14, paragraph 5, in the instant case, since the author's appeal was heard by the Supreme Court, be it with delay.

The HRC found in favour of the author on this point:

¶ 7.3. The Committee has noted the State party's explanations concerning the delay in the trial proceedings against the author. The Committee acknowledges the difficult economic situation of the State party, but wishes to emphasize that the rights set forth in the Covenant constitute minimum standards which all States parties have agreed to observe. Article 14, paragraph 3(c), states that all accused shall be entitled to be tried without delay, and this requirement applies equally to the right of review of conviction and sentence guaranteed by article 14, paragraph 5. The Committee considers that the period of eight years between the author's arrest in February 1980 and the final decision of the Supreme Court, dismissing his appeal, in February 1988, is incompatible with the requirements of article 14, paragraph 3(c).

Thus, economic hardship does not excuse a State from full compliance with its article 14 obligations.[81]

Article 14(3)(d)

[14.74]   *GENERAL COMMENT 13*

¶ 11. Not all reports have dealt with all aspects of the right of defence as defined in subparagraph 3 (d). The Committee has not always received sufficient information concerning the protection of the right of the accused to be present during the determination of any charge

---

[81] See also *Mukunto v Zambia* (768/97), para. 6.4. Indeed, economic hardship rarely exempts a State from any of its ICCPR duties [1.73].

against him nor how the legal system assures his right either to defend himself in person or to be assisted by counsel of his own choosing, or what arrangements are made if a person does not have sufficient means to pay for legal assistance. The accused or his lawyer must have the right to act diligently and fearlessly in pursuing all available defences and the right to challenge the conduct of the case if they believe it to be unfair. When exceptionally for justified reasons trials *in absentia* are held, strict observance of the rights of the defence is all the more necessary.

TRIAL IN ONE'S OWN PRESENCE

[14.75]   *MBENGE v ZAIRE (16/77)*

¶ 14.1. . . . [P]roceedings *in absentia* are in some circumstances (for instance, when the accused person, although informed of the proceedings sufficiently in advance, declines to exercise his right to be present) permissible in the interest of the proper administration of justice. Nevertheless, the effective exercise of the rights under article 14 presupposes that the necessary steps should be taken to inform the accused beforehand about the proceedings against him. . . . Judgement *in absentia* requires that, notwithstanding the absence of the accused, all due notification has been made to inform him of the date and place of his trial and to request his attendance. . . .

[14.76]   *MALEKI v ITALY (699/96)*

The author was convicted *in absentia* on charges of drug trafficking. The HRC found that there had been a breach of article 14(1):

¶ 9.3. The Committee has held in the past that a trial *in absentia* is compatible with article 14, only when the accused was summoned in a timely manner and informed of the proceedings against him [Communication No. 16/79 (*Mbenge v Zaire*)]. In order for the State party to comply with the requirements of a fair trial when trying a person *in absentia* it must show that these principles were respected.

¶ 9.4. The State party has not denied that Mr. Maleki was tried *in absentia*. However, it has failed to show that the author was summoned in a timely manner and that he was informed of the proceedings against him. It merely states that it 'assumes' that the author was informed by his counsel of the proceedings against him in Italy. This is clearly insufficient to lift the burden placed on the State party if it is to justify trying an accused *in absentia*. It was incumbent on the court that tried the case to verify that the author had been informed of the pending case before proceeding to hold the trial *in absentia*. Failing evidence that the court did so, the Committee is of the opinion that the author's right to be tried in his presence was violated.

¶ 9.5. In this regard the Committee wishes to add that the violation of the author's right to be tried in his presence could have been remedied if he had been entitled to a retrial in his presence when he was apprehended in Italy. The State party described its law regarding the right of an accused who has been tried *in absentia* to apply for a retrial. It failed, however, to respond to the letter from an Italian lawyer, submitted by the author, according to which in the circumstances of the present case the author was not entitled to a retrial. The legal opinion presented in that letter must therefore be given due weight. The existence, in principle, of provisions regarding the right to a retrial, cannot be considered to have provided the author with a potential remedy in the face of unrefuted evidence that these provisions do not apply to the author's case.

¶ 10. The Human Rights Committee, acting under article 5, paragraph 4, of the Optional Protocol to the International Covenant on Civil and Political Rights, is of the view that the facts before it disclose a violation of article 14, paragraph 1, of the Covenant.

The case was decided under article 14(1) instead of the more specific article 14(3)(d) guarantee. This was because the State Party had entered a relevant reservation to 14(3)(d) [25.11].

[14.77] In Concluding Comments on Finland, the HRC stated:[82]

¶ 15. The Committee expresses concern at its understanding that, after due notice, a person charged before the Finnish courts with certain offences may be tried *in absentia*, if his or her presence was not necessary, and sentenced to a fine or up to three months' imprisonment with no possibility of retrial after 30 days. The Committee considers that unless the person has clearly agreed to this procedure, and the court is fully informed of the offender's circumstances, this method of trial could raise questions of compatibility with article 14(3)(d) and 14(3)(e) of the Covenant. The Committee suggests that this procedure be reviewed.

Thus, criminal trials *in absentia* will only be tolerated when the defendant has been given ample notice, and adequate opportunity, to attend the proceedings.[83]

RIGHT TO COUNSEL OF ONE'S OWN CHOICE

[14.78] Article 14(3)(d) overlaps to a large extent with the article 14(3)(b) guarantee, particularly regarding one's right to legal representation. Hence, simultaneous breaches of the two sub-paragraphs are often found.

[14.79] In *Estrella v Uruguay* (74/80) the author's choice of counsel was limited to one of two officially appointed defence lawyers. The author met his counsel only four times in over two years. The Committee expressed the view that there had been a breach of articles 14(3)(b) and (d). In *Lopez Burgós v Tobago* (52/79) the HRC found a violation of article 14(3)(d) when the author was forced to accept a certain person as his legal counsel even though this lawyer was connected with the government; the author had no access to a civilian lawyer unconnected with the government. Similarly, in *Pinto v Trinidad and Tobago* (232/87), the author should not have been forced to accept a court-appointed lawyer, who had performed poorly in the trial at first instance, when 'he had made the necessary arrangements to have another lawyer represent him

---

[82] (1998) UN doc. CCPR/C/79/Add. 91.
[83] See also *Wolf v Panama* (289/88), para. 6.6.

before the Court of Appeal'.[84] Thus, one cannot be forced to accept *ex officio* counsel.[85]

[14.80] Article 14(3)(d) does not entitle the accused to a choice of counsel if the author is being provided with a legal aid lawyer, and is otherwise unable to afford legal representation.[86]

[14.81] Article 14(3)(d) also gives individuals the right to defend themselves, as acknowledged by the HRC in the following case:

HILL and HILL v SPAIN (526/93)

¶ 14.2. The Committee recalls that Michael Hill insists that he wanted to defend himself, through an interpreter, and that the court denied this request. The State party has answered that the records of the hearing do not show such a request, and that Spain recognized the rights of auto defence 'pursuant to the Covenant and the European Convention of Human Rights, but that such defence should take place by competent counsel, which is paid by the State when necessary', thereby conceding that its legislation does not allow an accused person to defend himself in person, as provided for under the Covenant. The Committee accordingly concludes that Michael Hill's right to defend himself was not respected, contrary to article 14, paragraph 3(d), of the Covenant.

[14.82]   *BAILEY v JAMAICA (709/96)*

The author was convicted of capital murder in 1979. Under new legislation, his offence was reclassified as non-capital murder in 1993. He complained about the setting of a non-parole period of twenty years from the date of reclassification. The HRC upheld his complaint as a violation of article 14(1) and (3)(d):[87]

¶ 7.5. The author further claims that his rights under article 14, paragraph 1, were violated in the reclassification procedure in which the author's offence was classified as non-capital under section 7 of the Offenses Against the Person (Amendment) Act 1992 and the non-parole period was set to 20 years [from the date of reclassification]. It is submitted that the author was not provided with any reasons for the length of the non-parole period and was not given the opportunity to make any contribution to the procedure before the single judge. Even though a life sentence is prescribed by law for offences reclassified as non-capital, the Committee notes that the judge when fixing the non-parole period exercises discretionary power conferred on him by the Amendment Act 1992 and makes a decision which is separate from the decision on pardon and forms an essential part of the determination of a criminal charge. The Committee notes that the State party has not contested that the author was not afforded the opportunity to make any submissions prior to the decision

---

[84] Para. 12.5.
[85] See also *Domukovsky et al. v Georgia* (623–624, 626–627/95), para. 18.9.
[86] See *Pratt and Morgan v Jamaica* (210, 225/86). See also *Kelly v Jamaica* (253/87) [14.88].
[87] See also *Gallimore v Jamaica* (680/96), para. 7.2.

of the judge. In the circumstances, the Committee finds that article 14, paragraphs 1 and 3(d), were violated.

Thus, one has a right to representation in defending a criminal charge, and in submitting arguments regarding one's sentence and non-parole period.

RIGHTS TO LEGAL AID FOR DEFENDANTS WITH INSUFFICIENT MEANS TO PAY

[14.83]　　　　　　　　　　　*O.F. v NORWAY (158/83)*

In this case, the author was charged with a traffic speeding offence. He claimed a breach of article 14(3)(d) as he was not granted legal aid to defend these charges. The State Party argued:

¶ 3.4. . . . As far as article 14 (3) (d) is concerned, it is beyond dispute that the author was tried in his presence, defended himself in person and was aware of his right to be defended through legal assistance. Consequently, it is presumed that the author's reason for invoking this provision must be that the interests of justice required that he should have been assigned free legal assistance. The fact that the author was not assigned free legal assistance must be seen in the light of the nature of the offences with which the author was charged. Both charges were trivial and ordinary and could in practice only lead to a small fine. . . .

Even if the accused usually has no right to free legal assistance in minor cases, he is of course (section 99 of the Criminal Procedure Act) entitled to be assisted by a counsel of his own choice—paid by himself—at any stage of the prosecution, including the main hearing. . . .

Consequently, the Government are of the opinion that the facts of the case do not raise any issue under article 14(3)(d).

The HRC agreed with the State Party's contention that the case was inadmissible.[88]

LINDON v AUSTRALIA (646/95)

¶ 6.5. The Committee has considered the author's claim that he is a victim of a violation of article 14, paragraph 3(d), as he at the proceedings before the Full Court in September 1989 was denied a legal aid lawyer of his own choosing. The Committee notes that the proceedings concerned the author's interlocutory applications regarding his defence against a trespassing charge where the penalty was a fine, and in the circumstances, the Committee finds that the author, for purposes of admissibility, has failed to substantiate his claim that the interests of justice required the assignment of legal aid. Therefore, this part of the communication is inadmissible under article 2 of the Optional Protocol.

Thus, the gravity of the offence is important in deciding whether, 'in the interests of justice', an accused should be assigned legal representation at the State's expense.[89] In Concluding Comments on Slovakia, the HRC regretted the fact that

---

[88] Para. 5.6.　　　　　　　　　　　　　　　　　　　　　[89] See also [14.14].

legal aid was only available for offences which attracted a potential sentence of five years or more imprisonment.[90]

[14.84] In *Z.P. v Canada* (341/88), the author was refused legal aid by the State Party to appeal his conviction for rape. The HRC found that 'the author had not sufficiently substantiated his allegation' of a breach of article 14(3)(d), 'for the purposes of admissibility'.[91] The domestic decision to refuse legal aid was based on the perceived lack of merit in his appeal.[92] Thus, a State Party is not required to provide legal aid for a person who is appealing a serious offence unless the appeal has some objective chance of success.[93]

[14.85] This rule may however not apply to persons convicted of capital offences, who perhaps should be ensured access to all potential avenues of appeal to challenge their conviction or sentence.[94] Consider the following case.

LAVENDE v TRINIDAD and TOBAGO (554/93)

¶ 5.8. Regarding the claim under article 14, paragraph 3(d), the State party has not denied that the author was denied legal aid for the purpose of petitioning the Judicial Committee of the Privy Council for special leave to appeal. The Committee recalls that it is imperative that legal aid be available to a convicted prisoner under sentence of death, and that this applies to all stages of the legal proceedings. . . . Section 109 of the Constitution of Trinidad and Tobago provides for appeals to the Judicial Committee of the Privy Council. It is uncontested that in the present case, the Ministry of National Security denied the author legal aid to petition the Judicial Committee *in forma pauperis*, thereby effectively denying him legal assistance for a further stage of appellate judicial proceedings which is provided for constitutionally; in the Committee's opinion, this denial constituted a violation of article 14, paragraph 3(d), whose guarantees apply to all stages of appellate remedies. As a result, his right, under article 14, paragraph 5, to have his conviction and sentence reviewed 'by a higher tribunal according to law' was also violated, as the denial of legal aid for an appeal to the Judicial Committee effectively precluded the review of Mr. LaVende's conviction and sentence by that body.

Legal aid for persons convicted of a capital crime must be supplied to persons with insufficient means at preliminary hearings related to the case,[95] as well as trial and appeal.[96]

---

[90] (1997) UN doc. CCPR/C/79/Add. 79, para. 19.   [91] Para. 5.4.

[92] Para. 4.4. The accused had not informed the Montreal Legal Aid Board of any arguable grounds of appeal.

[93] See also A. De Zayas, 'The United Nations and the Guarantees of a Fair Trial in the International Covenant on Civil and Political Rights and the Convention Against Torture, and other Cruel, Inhuman and Degrading Treatment' in D. Weissbrodt and R. Wölfrum (eds.), *The Right to a Fair Trial* (Springer, New York, 1997), at 686.   [94] See also [14.14] and preceding case extracts.

[95] See *Wright and Harvey v Jamaica* (459/91), para. 10.2; *Levy v Jamaica* (719/96), para. 7.2; *Marshall v Jamaica* (730/96), para. 6.2.

[96] See also *Thomas v Jamaica* (532/93), para. 6.4; *Johnson v Jamaica* (592/94), para. 10.2 (legal aid denied in initial trial); *Robinson v Jamaica* (223/87), para. 10.4 (author entitled to legal aid though it would require an adjournment to the trial).

[14.86] The guarantee of legal aid in article 14(3)(d) applies only to criminal proceedings. However, in a few cases, such as *Currie v Jamaica* (377/89), the HRC has found that article 14(1) entitles one to legal aid in certain types of civil proceedings [14.13–14.14].

GUARANTEE OF COMPETENT REPRESENTATION

[14.87] In Concluding Comments on the USA, the HRC stated:[97]

¶ 23. . . . The Committee . . . notes the lack of effective measures to ensure that indigent defendants in serious criminal proceedings, particularly in State courts, are represented by competent counsel.

In *Vasilskis v Uruguay* (80/80), the HRC found a breach of article 14(3)(b) and (d) where the court had appointed the author a defence counsel who was not a qualified lawyer.

[14.88]   *KELLY v JAMAICA (253/87)*

¶ 5.10. . . . The Committee is of the opinion that while article 14 paragraph 3(d) does not entitle the accused to choose counsel provided to him free of charge, measures must be taken to ensure that counsel, once assigned, provides effective representation in the interest of justice. This includes consulting with, and informing, the accused if he intends to withdraw an appeal or to argue before the appeals court that the appeal has no merit.

Thus, where legal representation has been provided by the State, that representation must be 'effective'.

[14.89]   *PHILLIP v TRINIDAD and TOBAGO (594/92)*

¶ 7.2. The Committee notes that the information before it shows that the author's counsel requested the court to allow him an adjournment or to withdraw from the case, because he was unprepared to defend it, since he had been assigned the case on Friday 10 June 1988 and the trial began on Monday 13 June 1988. The judge refused to grant the request allegedly because he felt the author would be unable to afford counsel of his own choice. The Committee recalls that while article 14, paragraph 3(d), does not entitle the accused to choose counsel provided to him free of charge, the Court should ensure that the conduct of the trial by the lawyer is not incompatible with the interests of justice. The Committee considers that in a capital case, when counsel for the accused who was not experienced in such cases requests an adjournment because he is unprepared to proceed the Court must ensure that the accused is given an opportunity to prepare his defence. The Committee is of the opinion that in the instant case, Mr. Phillip's counsel should have been granted an adjournment. In the circumstances, the Committee finds that Mr. Phillip

---

97 (1995) UN doc. CCPR/C/79/Add. 50.

was not effectively represented on trial, in violation of article 14, paragraph 3 (b) and (d), of the Covenant.

[14.90] *CAMPBELL v JAMAICA (618/95)*

The author made various allegations about the incompetence of his legal aid lawyer in a capital trial. The author added:

¶ 5.3. With regard to counsel's conduct of the defence at trial or on appeal, it is argued that the State party must bear the responsibility for the conduct of counsel, since it provides legal aid at such a low rate of remuneration that the defence is inadequately resourced and counsel who accept instructions in capital cases are under such intense pressure of work that they cannot properly or adequately represent their clients.

The HRC did not find a breach entailed in the lawyers' alleged incompetence.

¶ 7.3. The author has claimed that the bad quality of the defence put forward by his counsel at trial resulted in depriving him of a fair trial. Reference has been made in particular to counsel's alleged failure to interview the author's girlfriend, and to his alleged failure to cross-examine properly the prosecution witnesses in relation to the conduct of the identification parade and in relation to the author's alleged oral statement. The Committee recalls its jurisprudence that the State party cannot be held accountable for alleged errors made by a defence lawyer, unless it was or should have been manifest to the judge that the lawyer's behaviour was incompatible with the interests of justice. The material before the Committee does not show that this was so in the instant case and consequently, there is no basis for a finding of a violation of article 14, paragraph 3(b) (d) and (e), in this respect.

[14.91] The *Campbell* decision, coupled with HRC jurisprudence under article 14(3)(e),[98] indicates that the State's guarantee of competent legal aid counsel is limited.[99] Indeed, only blatant misbehaviour or incompetence has sufficed to establish violations of article 14(3)(d), such as the withdrawal of an appeal without consultation,[100] or absence during a judge's summing up.[101] Allegations of incompetence in court strategy have not so far been upheld, with the HRC deferring to counsel's professional judgement.

[14.92] The following cases address complaints of incompetence by a privately retained lawyer.

---

[98] See below, [14.97].

[99] See also *Shaw v Jamaica* (704/96), para. 7.5; *Bailey v Jamaica* (709/96), para. 7.1.

[100] See also *Collins v Jamaica* (356/89), para. 8.2; *Steadman v Jamaica* (528/93), para. 10.3; *Smith and Stewart v Jamaica* (668/95), para. 7.3; *Morrison and Graham v Jamaica* (461/91), para. 10.3; *Morrison v Jamaica* (663/95), para. 8.6; *McLeod v Jamaica* (734/97), para. 6.3; *Jones v Jamaica* (585/94), para. 9.5.

[101] *Brown v Jamaica* (775/97), para. 6.8.

H.C. v JAMAICA (383/89)

¶ 6.3. As regards the author's claim concerning his legal representation, the Committee observes that the author's lawyer was privately retained and that his alleged failure to properly represent the author cannot be attributed to the State party. This part of the communication is therefore inadmissible.

[14.93] *H.C.* indicates that a different 'standard' may be applied to legal aid lawyers as opposed to privately retained lawyers. Perhaps the State may only fairly be obliged to guarantee a minimum level of competence from the lawyers it provides to accused persons.[102] In a dissenting opinion in *Kelly* [14.88], Mr Sadi stated the following:

While sharing the view ... that in proceedings for serious crimes, particularly capital punishment cases, a fair trial for accused persons must provide them with effective legal counsel if the accused are unable to retain private counsel, the responsibility of the State party in providing legal counsel may not go beyond the responsibility to act in good faith in assigning legal counsel to accused individuals. Any errors of judgement by court-appointed counsel cannot be attributed to the State party any more than errors by privately retained counsel can be. In an adversary system of litigation, it is an unfortunate fact that innocent people go to the gallows for mistakes made by their lawyers, just as criminals escape the gallows simply because their lawyers are clever. This flaw runs deep into the adversary system of litigation applied by most States parties to the Covenant. If court-appointed lawyers are held accountable to a higher degree of responsibility than their private counterparts, and thus the State party is made accountable for any of their errors of judgement then, I am afraid, the Committee is applying a double standard.

The State Party repeated Sadi's comments in arguments in *Grant v Jamaica* (353/88).[103]

[14.94]   TAYLOR v JAMAICA (705/96)

¶ 6.2. Regarding the claim that the author had insufficient opportunity to prepare his defence and that his representative made little effort to consult with him, take his instructions or trace and call witnesses, the Committee recalls that counsel was initially privately retained. It is of the opinion that the State party cannot be held accountable for any alleged deficiencies in the defence of the accused or alleged errors committed by the defence lawyer, unless it was manifest to the trial judge that the lawyer's behaviour was incompatible with the interests of justice. In the present case, there is no indication that author's counsel, a Queen's Counsel, was not acting other than in the exercise of his professional judgement by deciding to ignore certain of the author's instructions and not to call a witness. This claim is accordingly inadmissible under article 2 of the Optional Protocol.

[14.95] The *Taylor* decision is very similar to the above decision in *Campbell*

---

[102] See also *Henry v Jamaica* (230/87), para. 8.3; *Berry v Jamaica* (330/88), para. 11.3.
[103] Para. 6.3.

[14.90], which concerned a legal aid lawyer. It therefore seems that the HRC does not in fact require a State to guarantee a different standard of competence for private and public lawyers. Counsel's incompetence, whether he/she is privately retained or not, will ground a complaint only when his/her actions are manifestly contrary to the interests of justice.[104]

Article 14(3)(e)—Rights regarding Witness Attendance and Examination

[14.96] *GENERAL COMMENT 13*

¶ 12. Subparagraph 3 (e) states that the accused shall be entitled to examine or have examined the witnesses against him and to obtain the attendance and examination of witnesses on his behalf under the same conditions as witnesses against him. This provision is designed to guarantee to the accused the same legal powers of compelling the attendance of witnesses and of examining or cross-examining any witnesses as are available to the prosecution.

GORDON v JAMAICA (237/87)

¶ 6.3. As to the author's allegation that he was unable to have witnesses testify on his behalf, although one, Corporal Afflick, would have been readily available, it is to be noted that the Court of Appeal, as is shown in its written judgement, considered that the trial judge rightly refused to admit Corporal Afflick's evidence, since it was not part of the *res gestae*. The Committee observes that article 14, paragraph 3 (e), does not provide an unlimited right to obtain the attendance of any witness requested by the accused or his counsel. It is not apparent from the information before the Committee that the court's refusal to hear Corporal Afflick was such as to infringe the equality of arms between the prosecution and the defence. In the circumstances, the Committee is unable to conclude that article 14, paragraph 3(e), has been violated.

Thus, article 14(3)(e) is not concerned with the right to call witnesses *per se*; it is concerned with equality of rights to call witnesses as between the defence and the prosecution. It is for the author to establish that the failure of a court to permit examination of a certain witness violated his/her 'equality of arms'.[105]

[14.97] *PRATT and MORGAN v JAMAICA (210, 225/89)*

¶ 13.2. . . . [The Committee is not] in a position to ascertain whether the failure of Mr Pratt's lawyer to insist upon calling the alibi witness before the case was closed was a

---

[104] See [14.91]. See however, *Griffin v Spain* (493/92) [6.08], regarding potential different standards regarding application of the exhaustion of local remedies rule. Cf. De Zayas, above, note 93, who implies at 686 that the conduct of a privately retained lawyer does not engage the responsibility of a State. It is however arguable that the State's responsibility is engaged if a court wilfully ignores the poor conduct of a private lawyer.

[105] *Párkányi v Hungary* (410/90), para. 8.5.

matter of professional judgement or of negligence. That the Court of Appeal did not of itself insist upon the calling of this witness is not in the view of the Committee a violation of article 14, paragraph 3(e), of the Covenant.

PEART and PEART v JAMAICA (464, 482/91)

¶ 11.3. With regard to the authors' claim that the unavailability of the expert witness from the Meteorological Office constitutes a violation of article 14 of the Covenant, the Committee notes that it appears from the trial transcript that the defence had contacted the witness but had not secured his presence in court, and that, following a brief adjournment, the judge then ordered the Registrar to issue a subpoena for the witness and adjourned the trial. When the trial was resumed and the witness did not appear, counsel informed the judge that he would go ahead without the witness. In the circumstances, the Committee finds that the State party cannot be held accountable for the failure of the defence expert witness to appear.

Thus, the HRC will not address a failure by the accused's counsel to call material witnesses, even if counsel was provided by the State,[106] as this is essentially a matter for counsel's professional judgement. If counsel fails to call a witness, it is not for the domestic court to do so *ex officio*.[107]

[14.98] The following cases demonstrate violations of article 14(3)(e):

GRANT v JAMAICA (353/88)

¶ 8.5. The author . . . contends that he was unable to secure the attendance of witnesses on his behalf, in particular the attendance of his girlfriend, P.D. The Committee notes from the trial transcript that the author's attorney did contact the girlfriend, and, on the second day of the trial, made a request to the judge to have P.D. called to court. The judge then instructed the police to contact this witness, who . . . had no means to attend. The Committee is of the opinion that, in the circumstances, and bearing in mind that this is a case involving the death penalty, the judge should have adjourned the trial and issued a subpoena to secure the attendance of P.D. in court. Furthermore, the Committee considers that the police should have made transportation available to her. To the extent that P.D.'s failure to appear in court was attributable to the State party's authorities, the Committee finds that the criminal proceedings against the author were in violation of article 14, paragraphs 1 and 3 (e), of the Covenant.

[14.99]　　　*PEART and PEART v JAMAICA (464, 482/91)*

¶ 11.4. With regard to the evidence given by the main witness for the prosecution, the Committee notes that it appears from the trial transcript that, during cross-examination by the defence, the witness admitted that he had made a written statement to the police on the

---

[106] See also *Young v Jamaica* (615/95), para. 5.5; see *Perera v Australia* (536/93), para. 6.3, for a similar decision regarding privately retained counsel.
[107] See *Van Meurs v The Netherlands* (215/86), para. 7.2.

night of the incident. Counsel then requested a copy of this statement, which the prosecution refused to give; the trial judge subsequently held that defence counsel had failed to put forward any reason why a copy of the statement should be provided. The trial proceeded without a copy of the statement being made available to the defence.

¶ 11.5. From the copy of the statement, which came into counsel's possession only after the Court of Appeal had rejected the appeal and after the initial petition for special leave to appeal to the Judicial Committee of the Privy Council had been submitted, it appears that the witness named another man as the one who shot the deceased, that he implicated Andrew Peart as having had a gun in his hand, and that he did not mention Garfield Peart's participation or presence during the killing. The Committee notes that the evidence of the only eye-witness produced at the trial was of primary importance in the absence of any corroborating evidence. The Committee considers that the failure to make the police statement of the witness available to the defence seriously obstructed the defence in its cross-examination of the witness, thereby precluding a fair trial of the defendants. The Committee finds therefore that the facts before it disclose a violation of article 14, paragraph 3(e), of the Covenant.

[14.100]   *FUENZALIDA v ECUADOR (480/91)*

The author complained that his trial, at which he was convicted of rape, was unfair.

¶ 3.5. The author also claims that—in view of the submission by the victim of a laboratory report on samples (blood and semen) taken from her and samples of blood and hair taken from him against his will and showing the existence of an enzyme which the author does not have in his blood—he requested the court to order an examination of his own blood and semen, a request which the court denied. . . .

The HRC found in favour of the author on this point:

¶ 9.5. . . . The Committee has considered the legal decisions and the text of the judgement dated 30 April 1991, especially the court's refusal to order expert testimony of crucial importance to the case, and concludes that this refusal constitutes a violation of article 14, paragraphs 3 (e) and 5, of the Covenant.

Article 14(3)(f)—Right to Free Assistance of an Interpreter if Needed

[14.101]   *GENERAL COMMENT 13*

¶ 13. Subparagraph 3(f) provides that if the accused cannot understand or speak the language used in court he is entitled to the assistance of an interpreter free of any charge. This right is independent of the outcome of the proceedings and applies to aliens as well as to nationals. It is of basic importance in cases in which ignorance of the language used by a court or difficulty in understanding may constitute a major obstacle to the right of defence.

States Parties should ensure that official charge sheets and charge forms are available in all languages commonly spoken within that State.[108]

[14.102]   *GUESDON v FRANCE (219/86)*

¶ 10.2. The provision for the use of one court language does not, in the Committee's opinion, violate article 14. Nor does the requirement of a fair trial mandate States parties to make available to a citizen whose mother tongue differs from the official court language, the service of an interpreter, if this citizen is capable of expressing himself adequately in the official language. Only if the accused or the defence witnesses have difficulties in understanding, or in expressing themselves in the court language, must the services of an interpreter be made available.

The *Guesdon* decision has been affirmed in numerous cases brought by Breton activists, claiming a 'right' to speak Breton instead of French in French proceedings.[109]

Article 14(3)(g)—Freedom from Compulsory Self-incrimination

[14.103]   *GENERAL COMMENT 13*

¶ 14. Subparagraph 3(g) provides that the accused may not be compelled to testify against himself or to confess guilt. In considering this safeguard the provisions of article 7 and article 10, paragraph 1, should be borne in mind. In order to compel the accused to confess or to testify against himself, frequently methods which violate these provisions are used. The law should require that evidence provided by means of such methods or any other form of compulsion is wholly unacceptable.[110]

¶ 15. In order to safeguard the rights of the accused under paragraphs 1 and 3 of article 14, judges should have authority to consider any allegations made of violations of the rights of the accused during any stage of the prosecution.

[14.104] In Concluding Comments on Romania, the HRC stated that:[111]

¶ 13. The Committee is also concerned at the lack of legislation invalidating statements of accused persons obtained in violation of article 7 of the Covenant. The State party should adopt appropriate legislation that places the burden on the State to prove that statements made by accused persons in a criminal case have been given of their own free will, and that statements obtained in violation of article 7 of the Covenant are excluded from the evidence.

---

[108] Concluding Comments on the UK (Hong Kong) (1995) UN doc. CCPR/C/79/Add. 57, para. 13. See also [24.33].

[109] See, e.g., *Cadoret and Le Bihan v France* (221/87, 323/88), *Barzhig v France* (327/88), *C.L.D. v France* (439/90); see also *Domukovsky et al. v Georgia* (623–624. 626–627/95), para. 18.7.

[110] Arts. 7 and 10(1) prohibit various levels of inhumane treatment of persons; see generally Chap. 9. See also [9.80].

[111] (1999) UN doc. CCPR/C/79/Add. 111.

Thus, the burden of proof is on the State to prove that a confession has been obtained without duress. Implementation of certain procedures, such as the audio or video recording of police interviews, assists in alleviating such a burden.

[14.105] In Concluding Comments on the UK, the HRC stated that:[112]

¶ 28. The Committee notes with concern that the provisions of the Criminal Justice and Public Order Act of 1994, which extends legislation originally applicable in Northern Ireland, whereby inferences may be drawn from the silence of persons accused of crimes, violates various provisions of article 14 of the Covenant, despite the range of safeguards built into the legislation and rules enacted thereunder.

Restrictions on the right to silence threaten one's freedom from self-incrimination. They also arguably threaten one's right to be presumed innocent. The HRC's comments on the UK indicate that a crucial aspect of one's right to silence is the right to be free from adverse inferences drawn from one's silence.[113]

[14.106] *SÁNCHEZ LÓPEZ v SPAIN (777/97)*

The author submitted the following complaint:

¶ 2.1. On 5 May 1990, the author was driving his car at 80 km/h in an area where the speed limit was 60 km/h. The car was photographed after being detected by the police radar. The General Department of Traffic (Ministry of the Interior) asked him, as the owner of the vehicle by means of which the offence had been committed, to identify the perpetrator of the offence or driver of the vehicle, in other words, himself. This request was made on the basis of article 72 (3) of Royal Legislative Decree No. 339/1990 (Road Safety Act—Ley de Seguridad Vial (LSV)), which states: 'The owner of the vehicle, on being duly asked to do so, has the duty to identify the driver responsible for the offence; if he fails to fulfil this obligation promptly without justified cause, he shall be liable to a fine for having committed a serious misdemeanour'.

¶ 2.2. Pursuant to this request and exercising the fundamental right not to confess guilt, Mr. Sánchez López sent the traffic authorities a letter in which he stated he was not the driver of the vehicle and did not know who had been driving it since he had lent it to several people during that period. As the perpetrator of a serious misdemeanour, he was fined 50,000 pesetas (the speeding fine was 25,000 pesetas). . . .

¶ 3.1. Counsel maintains that the author has been the victim of a violation of article 14, paragraph 3 (g), of the Covenant in that he has been obliged to confess guilt to the extent that the request for identification was addressed to the owner of the vehicle, who was in fact the driver responsible for the offence. In this case he is being obliged to make a self-accusatory statement, which contravenes the right protected in the Covenant.

---

[112] (1995) UN doc. CCPR/C/79/Add. 55.

[113] See also S. Bailey, 'Rights in the Administration of Justice' in Harris and Joseph (eds.), above, note 67, 232–4. Rodley, above, note 67, argues that the abolition of the right to silence in Northern Ireland breached art. 14(3)(g) as well as the guarantee of a presumption of innocence in art. 14(2), at 137–9.

The State Party submitted the following arguments:

¶ 4.2. . . . The facts are not contested by the State party but it considers that there has not been a violation of any of the rights protected in the Covenant, since the potential danger constituted by a motor vehicle requires that road traffic should be rigorously protected.

¶ 4.3. [The State party] draws attention to the obligation under Spanish law whereby the offence should be 'personalized'. The offence cannot automatically be attributed to the owner of the vehicle, and so the law requires that the perpetrator of the offence should be personally identified. He may or may not be the owner and, if the owner of the vehicle is a juridical entity, they will certainly not be the same. . . .

The HRC found in favour of the State Party:

¶ 6.4. With regard to the claim that the author's rights to the presumption of innocence and the right not to testify against himself as protected by article 14, paragraphs 2 and 3 (g) of the Covenant were violated by the Spanish State, since he had to identify the owner of the vehicle reported for committing a traffic offence, the Committee considers that the documentation in its possession shows that the author was punished for non-cooperation with the authorities and not for the traffic offence. The Human Rights Committee considers that a penalty for failure to cooperate with the authorities in this way falls outside the scope of application of the above-mentioned paragraphs of the Covenant. Accordingly, the communication is held to be inadmissible under article 1 of the Optional Protocol.

The author was not convicted of speeding, but of failure to co-operate with the authorities. The latter conviction arose because he failed to identify the driver of a speeding vehicle, i.e. he refused to incriminate himself. The HRC's finding seems to turn on a very fine point regarding the actual charge ultimately sustained against the author. The HRC may have been swayed by the Spanish arguments, which correctly indicated that compulsory driver identification by the vehicle owner, which may occasionally result in compulsory self-incrimination, is presently the only way of identifying speeding motorists 'caught' by police radar. The HRC is then implicitly endorsing police radars and cameras as legitimate means of enforcing traffic rules. It is to be hoped that modern technology does not lead to a diminution in the scope of article 14(3)(g) with regard to more serious offences.

Article 14(4)—Rights of a Juvenile Accused

[14.107]   *GENERAL COMMENT 13*

¶ 16. Article 14, paragraph 4, provides that in the case of juvenile persons, the procedure shall be such as will take account of their age and the desirability of promoting their rehabilitation. Not many reports have furnished sufficient information concerning such relevant matters as the minimum age at which a juvenile may be charged with a criminal offence, the maximum age at which a person is still considered to be a juvenile, the existence of special courts and procedures, the laws governing procedures against juveniles and how all these special arrangements for juveniles take account of 'the desirability of promoting their rehabilitation'. Juveniles are to enjoy at least the same guarantees and protection as are accorded to adults under article 14.

Article 14(4) mirrors article 10(3), which provides for special detention facilities for juveniles.[114] Article 24 generally protects the rights of children, and probably subsumes the article 14(4) guarantee.[115]

Article 14(5)—Right to an Appeal in Criminal Cases

[14.108] *GENERAL COMMENT 13*

¶ 17. Article 14, paragraph 5, provides that everyone convicted of a crime shall have the right to his conviction and sentence being reviewed by a higher tribunal according to law. Particular attention is drawn to the other language versions of the word 'crime' (*'infraction'*, *'delito'*, *'prestuplenie'*) which show that the guarantee is not confined only to the most serious offences. In this connection, not enough information has been provided concerning the procedures of appeal, in particular the access to and the powers of reviewing tribunals, what requirements must be satisfied to appeal against a judgement, and the way in which the procedures before review tribunals take account of the fair and public hearing requirements of paragraph 1 of article 14.

Article 14(5) applies only to criminal appeals. The only potential protection for a right of appeal in civil trials derives from article 14(1). In *I.P. v Finland* (450/91), the HRC has indicated that the ICCPR does not guarantee a right of appeal in civil proceedings.[116]

[14.109] *REID v JAMAICA (355/89)*

¶ 14.3. ... The Committee considers that, while the modalities of an appeal may differ among the domestic legal systems of States parties, under article 14, paragraph 5, a State party is under an obligation to substantially review the conviction and sentence. ...

PERERA v AUSTRALIA (536/93)

¶ 6.4. ... The Committee observes that article 14, paragraph 5, does not require that a Court of Appeal proceed to a factual retrial, but that a Court conduct an evaluation of the evidence presented at the trial and of the conduct of the trial. ...

---

[114] See [9.120–9.121].

[115] See Chap. 21; see also, generally, R. Levesque, 'Future Visions of Juvenile Justice: Lessons from International and Comparative Law' (1996) 29 *Creighton Law Review* 1563. See also *V v UK* and *T v UK*, judgments of the European Court of Human Rights of 16 December 1999, regarding the rights of accused juveniles in criminal trials.

[116] See [14.17].

DOMUKOVSKY et al. v GEORGIA (623–624, 626–627/95)

¶ 18.11. The Committee notes from the information before it that the authors could not appeal their conviction and sentence, but that the law provides only for a judicial review, which apparently takes place without a hearing and is on matters of law only. The Committee is of the opinion that this kind of review falls short of the requirements of article 14, paragraph 5, of the Covenant, for a full evaluation of the evidence and the conduct of the trial and, consequently, that there was a violation of this provision in respect of each author.

H.T.B. v CANADA (534/93)

¶ 4.3. As regards the author's claim that his right to fair trial has been violated, because he was not allowed to produce evidence with regard to his defence of insanity before the Court of Appeal of Ontario, the Committee notes that this defence had already been available to the author during trial at first instance, but that he made a conscious decision not to use it. The Committee further notes that the author's conviction and sentence was reviewed by the Court of Appeal of Ontario, and that the Court decided not to admit the evidence relating to the defence of insanity, in accordance with Canadian law which prescribes that fresh evidence will generally not be admitted if it could have been adduced at trial. . . . In the circumstances of the instant case, the Committee concludes that this part of the communication is therefore inadmissible under article 3 of the Optional Protocol.

Thus, one has a right to review of one's conviction and one's sentence. One does not however have a right to a hearing *de novo*. For example, the admissibility of new evidence upon appeal can be restricted where such evidence was in fact available during the trial at first instance.[117]

[14.110] Article 14(5) guarantees a right to an appeal 'according to law', which presumably refers to the State Party's domestic law. Is it then possible for a State to undercut article 14(5) protection by adopting a perverse law, which denies access to criminal appeals?[118] This point is addressed in the next case.

SALGAR de MONTEJO v COLOMBIA (64/79)

¶ 7.1. [T]he State party [argued] that article 14 (5) of the Covenant establishes the general principle of review by a higher tribunal without making such a review mandatory in all possible cases involving a criminal offence since the phrase 'according to the law' leaves it to national law to determine in which cases and circumstances application may be made to a higher court. It explained that under the legal regime in force in Colombia, criminal offences are divided into two categories, namely *delitos* and *contravenciónes* and that convictions for all *delitos* and for almost all *contravenciónes* are subject to review by a higher court. It added that Consuelo Salgar de Montejo committed a *contravención* which

---

[117] See also *Berry v Jamaica* (330/88), para. 11.6.

[118] See also [11.56] and [16.09–16.12] on the interpretation of the word 'lawful' in the context of other ICCPR rights.

the applicable legal instrument, namely Decree No. 1923 of 1978, did not make subject to review by a higher court. . . .

The HRC found a violation of article 14(5), and replied to the State's argument as follows:

¶ 10.4. The Committee considers that the expression 'according to law' in article 14(5) is not intended to leave the very existence of the right of appeal to the discretion of the State Parties, since the rights are those recognized by the Covenant, and not merely those recognized by domestic law. Rather, what is to be determined 'according to law' is the modalities by which the review by a higher tribunal is to be carried out. It is true that the Spanish text of article 14(5) . . . refers only to *un delito*, while the English text refers to a 'crime', and the French text refers to *une infraction*. Nevertheless the Committee is of the view that the sentence of imprisonment imposed on Mrs Consuelo Salgar de Montejo, even though the offence is defined as a *contravención* in domestic law, is serious enough, in all the circumstances, to require a review by a higher tribunal as provided for in article 14, paragraph 5 of the Covenant.

The *Montejo* decision indicates that one must be allowed to appeal convictions for 'serious offences', characterized as those which result in imprisonment (Mrs Montejo's prison sentence was for one year). However, would a potential sentence of a heavy fine, or the loss of certain rights (e.g. employment) render an offence serious enough to require the availability of an appeal?[119]

[14.111] The following case addresses the article 14(5) compatibility of systems, such as common law systems, where one does not have an appeal as of right, but must seek leave to appeal.

LUMLEY v JAMAICA (662/95)

¶ 7.3. It further appears from the documents that leave to appeal was refused by a single judge whose decision was confirmed by the Court of Appeal. The judge refused leave of appeal only after a review of the evidence presented during the trial and after an evaluation of the judge's instructions to the jury. While on the basis of article 14, paragraph 5, every convicted person has the right to his conviction and sentence being reviewed by a higher tribunal according to law, a system not allowing for automatic right to appeal may still be in conformity with article 14, paragraph 5, as long as the examination of an application for leave to appeal entails a full review, that is, both on the basis of the evidence and of the law, of the conviction and sentence and as long as the procedure allows for due consideration of the nature of the case. Thus, in the circumstances, the Committee finds that no violation of article 14, paragraph 5 occurred in this respect.

[14.112] The following case addresses whether one has a right to more than one appeal under article 14(5).

---

[119] McGoldrick, above, note 2, 431.

HENRY v JAMAICA (230/87)[120]

¶ 8.4. It remains for the Committee to decide whether the failure of the Court of Appeal of Jamaica to issue a written judgement violated any of the author's rights under the Covenant. Article 14, paragraph 5, of the Covenant guarantees the right of convicted persons to have the conviction and sentence reviewed 'by a higher tribunal according to law'. In this context, the author has claimed that, because of the non-availability of the written judgement, he was denied the possibility of effectively appealing to the Judicial Committee of the Privy Council, which allegedly routinely dismisses petitions which are not accompanied by the written judgement of the lower court. In this connection, the Committee has examined the question whether article 14, paragraph 5, guarantees the right to a single appeal to a higher tribunal or whether it guarantees the possibility of further appeals when these are provided for by the law of the State concerned. The Committee observes that the Covenant does not require States parties to provide for several instances of appeal. However, the words 'according to law' in article 14, paragraph 5, are to be interpreted to mean that if domestic law provides for further instances of appeal, the convicted person must have effective access to each of them. Moreover, in order to enjoy the effective use of this right, the convicted person is entitled to have, within a reasonable time, access to written judgements, duly reasoned, for all instances of appeal. Thus, while Mr. Henry did exercise a right to appeal to 'a higher tribunal' by having the judgement of the Portland Circuit Court reviewed by the Jamaican Court of Appeal, he still has a right to a higher appeal protected by article 14, paragraph 5, of the Covenant, because article 110 of the Jamaican Constitution provides for the possibility of appealing from a decision of the Jamaican Court of Appeal to the Judicial Committee of the Privy Council in London. The Committee therefore finds that Mr. Henry's right under article 14, paragraph 5, was violated by the failure of the Court of Appeal to issue a written judgement.

Thus, one has a right to only one appeal under article 14(5). However, when a State Party's legal system provides for more appeals, the author must be given a fair opportunity to pursue those further appeals.

[14.113] *Henry* confirms that prospective appellants must have access to all judgements and documents necessary to 'enjoy the effective exercise of the right to appeal'.[121] Reasons must of course be given when an appeal is completed, or when leave to appeal has been denied.[122]

[14.114] As with a person's rights in trials at first instance, a person's right of competent counsel in criminal appeals is limited. The HRC is hesitant to find that counsel's tactics in appeals breach an accused's right to appeal; these tactics are essentially a matter of counsel's professional judgement.[123]

[14.115] Many cases regarding the article 14(3)(c) right to an expeditious crim-

---

[120] See also *Douglas, Gentles and Kerr v Jamaica* (352/89), para. 11.2.
[121] *Lumley v Jamaica* (662/95), para. 7.5.
[122] *Reid v Jamaica* (355/89), para. 14.3.
[123] See, e.g., *Tomlin v Jamaica* (589/94), para. 8.2. See also [14.91], [14.95], and [14.97].

inal trial have concerned delays occurring during the appeal process. Consequently, these cases have also entailed breaches of article 14(5).[124]

[14.116] Finally, the HRC has confirmed in *R.M. v Finland* (301/88)[125] and *Bryhn v Norway* (789/97)[126] that appeals may be conducted in writing, rather than orally.

Article 14(6)—Right to Compensation for Miscarriage of Justice

[14.117] *GENERAL COMMENT 13*

¶ 18. Article 14, paragraph 6, provides for compensation according to law in certain cases of a miscarriage of justice as described therein. It seems from many State reports that this right is often not observed or insufficiently guaranteed by domestic legislation. States should, where necessary, supplement their legislation in this area in order to bring it into line with the provisions of the Covenant.

[14.118] It is uncertain whether a 'miscarriage of justice' can occur in the absence of some form of State malfeasance, such as police or prosecutorial misbehaviour during relevant investigations or proceedings (e.g. framing the suspect, withholding evidence from the defence). Of course, an innocent person can still be found guilty in a trial where all due process rights have been complied with, and where all State agents act properly. Should a State be held accountable, by having to pay compensation to that innocent person, in such circumstances?[127] Furthermore, the level of 'innocence' that must be established before article 14(6) is triggered is uncertain. Stavros has suggested that a beneficiary of article 14(6) must be found to be 'clearly innocent', rather than one who has simply had fresh doubts raised about his/her guilt.[128]

[14.119] *MUHONEN v FINLAND (89/81)*

The author had been convicted for refusal to perform armed service in Finland. He had failed at first instance to establish that he was a conscientious objector, which would have exempted him from military duty. His second application for conscientious objector status succeeded, after he had served eight months of an eleven-month sentence. Consequently, the author was pardoned, and was released

---

[124] See, e.g., *Thomas v Jamaica* (614/95) at [14.70], and [14.72].
[125] Para. 6.4. [126] Para. 7.2; see also [14.47].
[127] See also D. Harris, 'The Right to a Fair Trial in Criminal Procedures as a Human Right' (1967) 16 *ICLQ* 352, 375. Nowak, above, note 8, 271, merely notes that art. 14(6) does not apply where non-disclosure of the fact can be attributed to the person convicted, who may conceal his/her own innocence in order to avoid betraying another.
[128] S. Stavros, *The Guarantees of Accused Persons under Article 6 of the European Convention on Human Rights* (Martinus Nijhoff, Dordrecht, 1993), 300.

two weeks later. He complained of a breach of article 14(6), entailed in the State's refusal to grant him monetary relief for time served. The HRC found in favour of the State Party in the following terms.

¶ 11.2. ... [An article 14(6)] right to compensation may arise in relation to criminal proceedings if either the conviction of a person has been reversed or if he or she 'has been pardoned on the ground that a new or newly discovered fact shows conclusively that there has been a miscarriage of justice'. As far as the first alternative is concerned, the Committee observes that Mr. Muhonen's conviction, as pronounced in the judgement of the city court of Joensuu on 13 December 1978 and confirmed by the Eastern Finland Higher Court on 26 October 1979, has never been set aside by any later judicial decision. Furthermore, Mr. Muhonen was not pardoned because it had been established that his conviction rested on a miscarriage of justice. According to the relevant Finnish statute, the law concerning the punishment of certain conscripts who decline to do military service (23/72), whoever refuses military service not having been recognized as a conscientious objector by the Examining Board commits a punishable offence. This means that the right to decline military service does not arise automatically once the prescribed substantive requirements are met, but only after due examination and recognition of the alleged ethical grounds by the competent administrative body. Consequently, the presidential pardon does not imply that there had been a miscarriage of justice. As the State party has pointed out in its submission of 22 October 1984, Mr. Muhonen's pardoning was motivated by considerations of equity.

¶ 11.3. To be sure, Mr. Muhonen's conviction came about as a result of the decision of the Examining Board of 18 October 1977, denying him the legal status of conscientious objector. This decision was based on the evidence which the Examining Board had before it at that time. Mr. Muhonen succeeded in persuading the Examining Board of his ethical objection to military service only after he had personally appeared before that body following his renewed application in the autumn of 1980, while in 1977 he had failed to avail himself of the opportunity to be present during the Examining Board's examination of his case.

¶ 12. Accordingly, the Human Rights Committee is of the view that Mr. Muhonen has no right to compensation which the Finnish authorities have failed to honour and that consequently there has been no breach of article 14 (6) of the Covenant.

[14.120]　　　　　*W.J.H v THE NETHERLANDS (408/90)*

In this case, the author was convicted at first instance of a number of offences, including forgery and fraud. However, he served no time in detention, apart from two months of pre-trial detention. Subsequent Supreme Court proceedings set aside the verdict, and the matter was sent back to the lower courts, which subsequently acquitted him on procedural grounds, as some evidence against him had been irregularly obtained.[129] He claimed, *inter alia*, a breach of article 14(6), as he was not granted compensation for the initial 'wrong' conviction. The HRC found this complaint inadmissible:

---

[129] Para. 2.2.

¶ 6.3. With regard to the author's claim for compensation under article 14, paragraph 6, . . . the Committee observes that the conditions for the application of this article are:

(a) A final conviction for a criminal offence;

(b) Suffering of punishment as a consequence of such conviction; and

(c) A subsequent reversal or pardon on the ground of a new or newly discovered fact showing conclusively that there has been a miscarriage of justice.

The Committee observes that since the final decision in this case, that of the Court of Appeal of 11 May 1988, acquitted the author, and since he did not suffer any punishment as a result of his earlier conviction of 24 December 1985, the author's claim is outside the scope of article 14, paragraph 6, of the Covenant.

Thus, a miscarriage of justice may occur only after a matter is finally disposed of by all potential appeal courts. Note that the author's conviction here was not a *final* decision; the relevant final decision was his acquittal after a number of appeals. Miscarriages of justice can therefore be distinguished from acquittals on appeal. Furthermore, pre-trial detention and the costs incurred by being forced to defend oneself in criminal proceedings do not constitute a 'punishment' for the purposes of article 14(6).[130]

Article 14(7)—Freedom from Double Jeopardy

[14.121] *GENERAL COMMENT 13*

¶ 19. In considering State reports differing views have often been expressed as to the scope of paragraph 7 of article 14. Some States parties have even felt the need to make reservations in relation to procedures for the resumption of criminal cases. It seems to the Committee that most States parties make a clear distinction between a resumption of a trial justified by exceptional circumstances and a re-trial prohibited pursuant to the principle of *ne bis in idem* as contained in paragraph 7. This understanding of the meaning of *ne bis in idem* may encourage States parties to reconsider their reservations to article 14, paragraph 7.[131]

[14.122] *A.P. v ITALY (204/86)*

The facts are outlined directly below:

¶ 2.1. The author states that he was convicted on 27 September 1979 by the Criminal Court of Lugano, Switzerland, for complicity in the crime of conspiring to exchange currency notes amounting to the sum of 297,650,000 lire, which was the ransom paid for

---

[130] Compensation for arbitrary pre-trial detention can be gained under art. 9(5). See [11.57–11.60].
[131] See, e.g., *Cámpora Schweizer v Uruguay* (66/80), where the severe delay in concluding the trial did not breach art. 14(7), though it did breach art. 14(3)(c); see also McGoldrick, above, note 2, 435.

the release of a person who had been kidnapped in Italy in 1978. He was sentenced to two years' imprisonment, which he duly served. He was subsequently expelled from Switzerland.

¶ 2.2. It is claimed that the Italian Government, in violation of the principle of *ne bis in idem*, is now seeking to punish the author for the same offence as that for which he had already been convicted in Switzerland. He was thus indicted by an Italian court in 1981 (after which he apparently left Italy for France) and on 7 March 1983 the Milan Court of Appeal convicted him *in absentia*. . . .

The HRC found that the principle in article 14(7) did not apply:

¶ 7.3. With regard to the admissibility of the communication under article 3 of the Optional Protocol, the Committee has examined the State party's objection that the communication is incompatible with the provisions of the Covenant, since article 14, paragraph 7, of the Covenant, which the author invokes, does not guarantee *ne bis in idem* with regard to the national jurisdictions of two or more States. The Committee observes that this provision prohibits double jeopardy only with regard to an offence adjudicated in a given State.

From a humanitarian point of view, the *A.P.* principle is to be regretted. If a State has imposed an adequate penalty on a person for an offence, it should not be permissible for that person to be tried for the same offence in another jurisdiction.[132] The *A.P.* decision was nevertheless followed in *A.R.J. v Australia* (692/96).[133]

[14.123] In *Jijón v Ecuador* (277/77), the author's reindictment for a charge for which he had already been convicted was ultimately quashed by the Superior Court. Thus, no breach of article 14(7) was found.[134]

Conclusion

[14.124] The HRC has issued more jurisprudence on article 14 than any other ICCPR right. This jurisprudence is however distorted by the predominance of complaints from persons on death row about the fairness of their trials. The inherent gravity of such judicial proceedings means that the jurisprudence from such cases may not be necessarily applicable in cases of considerably less gravity.

---

[132] Indeed, the *A.P.* principle does not seem to conform with the principle of *ne bis in idem* (art. 20) in the Rome Statute of the International Criminal Court, which prohibits a State from trying someone for the same crimes for which they have been tried by the International Court, and which prohibits the Court from trying someone who has already been tried by a State with respect to the same conduct (the latter principle is subject to some exceptions). See Martin *et al.*, above, note 40, 634. See generally C. van der Wyngaert and G. Stessens, 'The International *Non Bis in Idem* Principle: Resolving Some of the Unanswered Questions' (1999) 48 *ICLQ* 779.

[133] Para. 6.4.

[134] Para. 5.4.

Nevertheless, over 200 cases on article 14 have added significant flesh to the bare bones of the article 14 guarantees.

Postscript: Please note that General Comment 28 on 'Equality of Rights Between Men and Women', contained in the Addendum at page 634, contains extra information on some of the material in this chapter.

15

Prohibition of Retroactive Criminal Laws— Article 15

ARTICLE 15

1. No one shall be held guilty of any criminal offence on account of any act or omission which did not constitute a criminal offence, under national or international law, at the time when it was committed. Nor shall a heavier penalty be imposed than the one that was applicable at the time when the criminal offence was committed. If, subsequent to the commission of the offence, provision is made by law for the imposition of the lighter penalty, the offender shall benefit thereby.

2. Nothing in this article shall prejudice the trial and punishment of any person for any act or omission which, at the time when it was committed, was criminal according to the general principles of law recognized by the community of nations.

[15.01] The prohibition of retroactive criminal laws in article 15 supports the long recognized criminal law principle of *nullum crimen sine lege* (no crime except in accordance with the law), and *nulla poena sine lege* (no punishment except in accordance with the law).[1] The retroactive application of criminal law (*ex post facto* criminal laws) breaches both principles. The imposition of a heavier penalty than that which 'was applicable at the time when the criminal offence was committed' would breach the second principle. In addition, States are also obliged retroactively to apply lighter penalties. Nowak has added that article 15 prohibits punishment under extremely vague laws, which do not clearly proscribe the conduct for which one has been punished.[2]

[15.02] Article 15 is set apart from other due process rights in article 14. This is probably because article 15, but not article 14, is a non-derogable right.[3]

[15.03] There has been little jurisprudence on article 15(1). In a number of early

---

[1] M. Nowak, *CCPR Commentary* (N.P. Engel, Kehl, 1993), at 275.

[2] Ibid., 276. See also Concluding Comments on Portugal (Macau) (1999) UN doc. CCPR/C/79/Add. 115, para. 12, where the HRC criticized certain vaguely defined 'abstract' offences. An art. 15 complaint of this type was found to be unsubstantiated in *Kivenmaa v Finland* (412/90) and *Kruyt-Amesz v The Netherlands* (66/95).

[3] Ibid., 275.

cases against Uruguay, the prohibition of retroactive criminal law was clearly breached where persons were convicted and sentenced for membership of 'subversive organizations', i.e. political parties which were *subsequently* banned.[4]

Retroactive Penalties

[15.04] All of the important article 15 cases have concerned the provisions regarding retroactive penalties. The *A.R.S.* case concerned the alleged application of a retroactive heavier penalty, while the *Van Duzen* and *MacIsaac* cases concerned the alleged non-retroactive application of lighter penalties.[5]

[15.05]   *A.R.S. v CANADA (91/81)*

In this case the author claimed that the retroactive introduction of parole with mandatory supervision under the Canadian Parole Act constituted a heavier penalty in breach of article 15(1). His argument is outlined directly below:

¶ 2.2. The release of the author on 8 September 1982 is contingent on his signing the 'mandatory supervision certificate', a requirement which, he claims, did not exist at the time of commission of the offences in question. He contends that 'mandatory supervision' is therefore tantamount to a penalty heavier than the one that was applicable at the time when the criminal offences were committed and that this 'heavier penalty' constitutes in his case a violation of article 15 (1) of the Covenant. The author further maintains that 'mandatory supervision' constitutes a reimposition of punishment which should be regarded as remitted and that the demand that he sign the mandatory supervision certificate (an act, he claims, which would constitute a contract with penalties for failure of fulfilment), or else face the punishment of serving the entire sentence until 3 February 1988, constitutes a criminal action of intimidation in violation of section 382 of the Canadian Criminal Code and of article 11 of the Covenant. The author finally asserts that he is denied the right to challenge before a court the basic legal assumption that the term of imprisonment, in spite of earned remission of the sentence, continues in force after the date of release to the date of expiration, in violation of article 9 (1), (4) and (5) of the Covenant.

The HRC found the case inadmissible, primarily because they found that the author was not a relevant 'victim' of any abuse of his ICCPR rights.[6] The HRC added that mandatory supervision was not a 'penalty' within the meaning of article 15. It made the following comments in this respect:

---

[4] See, e.g., *Weinberger Weisz v Uruguay* (28/78). See also Nowak, above, note 1, 277.
[5] See T. Opsahl and A. De Zayas, 'The Uncertain Scope of Article 15(1) of the International Covenant on Civil and Political Rights' [1983] *Canadian Human Rights Yearbook* 237, for a detailed discussion of the *Van Duzen* and *MacIsaac* cases.   [6] See [3.26].

¶ 5.3. The Committee notes also that mandatory supervision cannot be considered as equivalent to a penalty, but is rather a measure of social assistance intended to provide for the rehabilitation of the convicted person, in his own interest. The fact that, even in the event of remission of the sentence being earned, the person concerned remains subject to supervision after his release and does not regain his unconditional freedom, cannot therefore be characterized as the imposition or re-imposition of a penalty incompatible with the guarantees laid down in article 15 (1) of the Covenant.

[15.06]   *VAN DUZEN v CANADA (50/79)*

The facts were not disputed and were outlined by the author as follows:

¶ 2.2. On 17 November 1967 and 12 June 1968, respectively, the author was sentenced upon conviction of different offences to a three year and a 10-year prison term. The latter term was to be served concurrently with the former, so that the combined terms were to expire on 11 June 1978. On 31 May 1971, the author was released on parole under the Parole Act 1970, then in force. On 13 December 1974, while still on parole, the author was convicted of the indictable offence of breaking and entering and, on 23 December 1974, sentenced to imprisonment for a term of three years. By application of section 17 of the Parole Act 1970 his parole was treated as forfeited on 13 December 1974. As a consequence, the author's combined terms have been calculated to expire on 4 January 1985. In 1977 several sections of the Parole Act 1970, among them section 17, were repealed. New provisions came into force on 15 October 1977 (Criminal Law Amendment Act 1977).

¶ 2.3. According to the author the combined effect of the new law was that forfeiture of parole was abolished and the penalty of committing an indictable offence while on parole was made lighter, provided the indictable offence was committed on or after 15 October 1977, because, *inter alia*, pursuant to the new provisions, time spent on parole after 15 October 1977 and before suspension of parole, was credited as time spent under sentence. Therefore, a parolee whose parole was revoked after that date was not required to spend an equivalent time in custody under the previous sentence.

¶ 2.4. The author alleges that, by not making the 'lighter penalty' retroactively applicable to persons who have committed indictable offences while on parole before 15 October 1977, the Parliament of Canada has enacted a law which deprives him of the benefit of article 15 of the Covenant and thereby failed to perform its duty, under article 2 of the Covenant, to ensure all individuals within its territory and subject to its jurisdiction are given the rights recognized in the Covenant and to take the necessary steps to adopt such legislative measures as may be necessary to give effect to those rights.

The State Party submitted the following arguments, focusing on the meaning of the word 'penalty' for the purposes of article 15(1):

¶ 8.1. In its submission under article 4 (2) of the Optional Protocol, dated 18 February 1981, the State party sets out, *inter alia,* the law relating to the Canadian parole system and asserts that it is not in breach of its obligations under the International Covenant on Civil and Political Rights. It contends:

(a) That article 15 of the International Covenant on Civil and Political Rights deals only with criminal penalties imposed by a criminal court for a particular criminal offence, pursuant to criminal proceedings;

(b) That the forfeiture of parole is not a criminal penalty within the meaning of article 15 of the Covenant;

(c) That by replacing forfeiture of parole by revocation of parole it did not substitute a 'lighter penalty' for the 'commission of an indictable offence while on parole'.

¶ 8.2. The State party further elaborates on the definition of the word 'penalty' as used in article 15 (1) of the Covenant.

¶ 8.3. The State party submits that there are various kinds of penalties: these may be criminal, civil or administrative. This distinction between criminal penalties and administrative or disciplinary ones, the State party argues, is generally accepted. Criminal penalties, it further submits, are sometimes referred to as 'formal punishment' while the administrative penalties are referred to as 'informal punishment'.

¶ 8.4. The State party adds that the setting or context of article 15 of the Covenant is criminal law. The words 'guilty', 'criminal offence' and 'offender' are evidence that when the word 'penalty' is used in the context of article 15, what is meant is 'criminal penalty'. The State party finds unacceptable Mr. Van Duzen's proposition, that the word 'penalty' in article 15 of the Covenant must be given a wide construction which would mean that article 15 would apply to administrative or disciplinary sanctions imposed by law as a consequence of criminal convictions.

The author responded as follows:

¶ 9.2. The author observes that in article 15 (1) the word 'criminal' is associated with 'offence' and not with 'penalty'. The State party's attempt to narrow the meaning of 'penalty' is not supported by the words of the article. It is submitted that if the offence is criminal within the meaning of the article, any penalty for the offence is a penalty within the meaning of the article. The State party admits that forfeiture and revocation of parole were penalties and that revocation continues to be a penalty, but tries to divide penalties into categories for which it has no authority in the words of the article, in precedent or in reason. . . .

¶ 9.6. The author further maintains that the distinction between formal punishment, which is administered through the courts, and informal punishment which is used extensively in a wide variety of inter personal and institutional contexts, misses the point of this communication. The penalty here at issue clearly entails 'punishment for crime'. The distinction does not depend on the agency that administers or imposes the penalty. The nature of the penalty, its relation to the offence, and its consequences are the critical factors, not the agency that imposes it.

In finding the case admissible, the HRC implicitly found that parole conditions could be relevant 'penalties' for the purposes of article 15.[7] However, the HRC ultimately decided that it was not necessary to determine the issue as in 1981, after the

---

[7] Opsahl and De Zayas, above, note 5, 240.

admissibility decision, the author was released on mandatory supervision instead of serving his full term.[8] It made the following comments:

¶ 10.1. The Human Rights Committee notes that the main point raised and declared admissible in the present communication is whether the provision for the retroactivity of a 'lighter penalty' in article 15 (1) of the Covenant is applicable in the circumstances of the present case. In this respect, the Committee recalls that the Canadian legislation removing the automatic forfeiture or parole for offences committed while on parole was made effective from 15 October 1977, at a time when the alleged victim was serving the sentence imposed on him under the earlier legislation. He now claims that under article 15 (1) he should benefit from this subsequent change in the law.

¶ 10.2. The Committee further notes that its interpretation and application of the International Covenant on Civil and Political Rights has to be based on the principle that the terms and concepts in the Covenant are independent of any particular national system or law and of all dictionary definitions. Although the terms of the Covenant are derived from long traditions within many nations, the Committee must now regard them as having an autonomous meaning. The parties have made extensive submissions, in particular as regards the meaning of the word 'penalty' and as regards relevant Canadian law and practice. The Committee appreciates their relevance for the light they shed on the nature of the issue in dispute.[9] On the other hand, the meaning of the word 'penalty' in Canadian law is not, as such, decisive. Whether the word 'penalty' in article 15 (1) should be interpreted narrowly or widely, and whether it applies to different kinds of penalties, 'criminal' and 'administrative', under the Covenant, must depend on other factors. Apart from the text of article 15 (1), regard must be had, *inter alia*, to its object and purpose.

¶ 10.3. However, in the opinion of the Committee, it is not necessary for the purposes of the present case to go further into the very complex issues raised concerning the interpretation and application of article 15 (1). In this respect regard must be had to the fact that the author has subsequently been released, and that this happened even before the date when he claims he should be free. Whether or not this claim should be regarded as justified under the Covenant, the Committee considers that, although his release is subject to some conditions, for practical purposes and without prejudice to the correct interpretation of article 15 (1), he has in fact obtained the benefit he has claimed. It is true that he has maintained his complaint and that his status upon release is not identical in law to the one he has claimed. However, in the view of the Committee, since the potential risk of re-imprisonment depends upon his own behaviour, this risk cannot, in the circumstances, represent any actual violation of the right invoked by him.[10]

[15.07]   *MACISAAC v CANADA (55/79)*

In this case, the HRC was again asked to consider whether the liberalization of parole laws under the Canadian criminal law should be applied retroactively.

---

[8] See *A.R.S. v Canada*, para. 5.3 [15.05], for the HRC's interpretation of the effect of 'mandatory supervision'.   [9] These submissions have not been excerpted.
[10] It is possible, perhaps, that Van Duzen could have submitted a fresh complaint about this matter if he were subsequently re-imprisoned: Opsahl and De Zayas, above, note 5, 242.

Unfortunately, the HRC was again able to sidestep the issue of law in this case, by finding that the author had failed to prove that the retroactive application of the more liberal parole laws would have resulted in him being released earlier. The HRC made the following comments:

¶ 11. In the absence of more precise submissions from the author in the present case, the Committee has attempted to examine in what way, if any, the position of the alleged victim was affected by the situation of which he basically complains. It notes that the system for dealing with recidivists was changed by the 1977 Act, to make it more flexible. The Act as amended provides, instead of the automatic forfeiture of parole, for a system of revocation at the discretion of the National Parole Board and sentencing for the recidivist offence at the discretion of the judge. However, the recidivist cannot be made to re-serve the full time spent on parole. Apparently, the author's claim in the present case is that he would have been released earlier on the hypothesis that the new provisions should have been applied to him retroactively. The Committee notes that it is not clear how this should have been done. However, here a comparison with the system existing before 1977 is necessary. Under the old system, the judge exercised his discretion in deciding the length of a penalty to be imposed. In the case of Mr. MacIsaac, whose second sentence was rendered in 1975, the recidivist offence carried a possible sentence of up to 14 years. While noting that Mr. MacIsaac's parole had been forfeited, the judge in 1975 sentenced him to 14 months. The Committee notes that one cannot focus only on the favourable aspects of a hypothetical situation and fail to take into account that the imposition of the 14-month sentence on Mr. MacIsaac for a recidivist offence was explicitly linked with the forfeiture of parole. In Canadian law there is no single fixed penalty for a recidivist offence. The law allows a scale of penalties for such offences and full judicial discretion to set the term of imprisonment (e.g. up to 14 years for the offence of breaking and entering and theft as in Mr. MacIsaac's case). It follows that Mr. MacIsaac has not established the hypothesis that if parole had not been forfeited, the judge would have imposed the same sentence of 14 months and that he would therefore have been actually released prior to May of 1979. The Committee is not in a position to know, nor is it called upon to speculate, how the fact that his earlier parole was forfeited may have influenced the penalty meted out for the offence committed while on parole. The burden of proving that in 1977 he has been denied an advantage under the new law and that he is therefore a 'victim' lies with the author. It is not the Committee's function to make a hypothetical assessment of what would have happened if the new Act had been applicable to him.

¶ 12. The Canadian Criminal Law Amendment Act 1977 in this light, and as explained by the State party, only entails a modification in the system of dealing with recidivist cases and leaves the question as to whether the total effect in the individual case will be a 'lighter penalty' to the judge who sentences the recidivist offender. The new law does not necessarily result automatically, for those to whom it is applied, in a lighter penalty compared to that under the earlier legislation. The judge entrusted with sentencing the recidivist— now as before—is bound to take into account the facts of every case, including, of course, the revocation or forfeiture of parole and exercise his discretion in sentencing within the prescribed scale of statutory minimum and maximum penalties.

¶ 13. These considerations lead to the conclusion that it cannot be established that in fact or law the alleged victim was denied the benefit of a 'lighter' penalty to which he would have been entitled under the Covenant.[11]

[15.08] In the above cases, the HRC adhered to its normal practice of deciding the legal issues only to the extent necessitated by the facts as interpreted by the HRC.[12] Therefore, a number of important questions remain unanswered. For example, it is important to know the temporal limitations to a State's duty retroactively to apply 'lighter penalties'. Opsahl and de Zayas note that no time limit is expressed in article 15(1) itself.[13] However, some time limit must be implied, otherwise article 15(1) would be creating an onerous duty that would unduly hamper law reform: 'the national legislator should not be faced with the discouraging choice between not introducing any lighter penalty or reopening the past without limit'.[14] Therefore, Opsahl and de Zayas suggest that:[15]

its minimum scope must be that it applies to cases in progress, before the sentence is passed in the first instance. Whether it also applies when the law is changed before judgement is final and after an appeal has been made seems to be an open question, but any difficulty here would still be manageable. After final judgement it could only be applied as granting a right to review of the sentence. The practical difficulties in implementing such a right then would increase considerably, at least for sentences already executed or served.

The same considerations do not arise regarding the prohibition of the imposition of retroactive heavier penalties. The time limit of such a duty is clear; the heavier penalty can only be applied with regard to crimes perpetrated after its introduction.[16]

[15.09] Another issue arises with regard to the interpretation of 'heavier' and 'lighter' penalties. It is easy to decide on the comparative severity of penalties if they are of the same type. A two-year prison sentence is obviously more severe than a one-year sentence. However, it is potentially difficult to weigh up the comparative severity of different types of penalty. Is a heavy fine less severe than a short period of imprisonment? The answer may depend on the individual circumstances of the convicted person.[17] Of course, in some circumstances, the HRC could be expected to assume the greater severity of one penalty over another, such as if capital punishment were to replace another type of punishment.[18]

---

[11] See generally, on the 'victim' requirement, Chap. 3.
[12]   Opsahl and de Zayas, above, note 5, 242.
[13] bid., 245.
[14] Ibid., 247; see also at 245.
[15] Ibid., 248; see also Nowak, above, note 1, 279.
[16] See Opsahl and de Zayas, above, note 5, 252.
[17] See Nowak, above, note 1, 278.
[18] Opsahl and De Zayas, above, note 5, 249–50.

Article 15(2)

[15.10] Article 15(2) contains an apparent exception to article 15(1), in that it expressly permits the trial and punishment of persons on charges of violations of general principles of international law, regardless of the criminal status of such acts in a State's domestic law. Article 15(2) is clearly targeting those who have committed grave breaches of international humanitarian law, such as war crimes or crimes against humanity.[19] However, article 15(1) also seems to permit such trial and punishment, as it only prohibits the trial and punishment of persons for acts or omissions which were not criminalized in *either national or international law*. Indeed, the reference to 'international law' in article 15(1) probably goes further than the exception in article 15(2), as it could refer to general and customary international law, as well as international treaty law.[20]

Conclusion

[15.11] Little jurisprudence has shed light on the duties in article 15. Changes to the Canadian parole regime prompted a number of early Optional Protocol cases, and some debate over the meaning of the word 'penalty' in article 15. There has been a dearth of article 15 complaints since. That is not to say that pertinent article 15 situations have not arisen within States Parties. For example, the convictions and punishments of East German border guards in the unified Germany appear to raise issues of retrospective criminal law. The killing of would-be defectors attempting to flee the German Democratic Republic for the Federal Republic of Germany before 1989 did not breach GDR law.[21] It is possible that such actions constituted criminal offences under international law, and may therefore be the subject of an exception under article 15(1) and (2), though this is uncertain.[22] An HRC ruling with regard to the article 15 compatibility of these convictions would be instructive.

---

[19] See H.A.N. Muhammed, 'Due Process of Law for Persons Accused of Crime' in L. Henkin (ed.), *The International Bill of Rights* (Columbia University Press, New York, 1981), 164. See also *Polyukhovich v Commonwealth of Australia* (1991) 172 CLR 501, judgment of the High Court of Australia regarding the retroactive criminalization in Australia of World War II war crimes in Europe.

[20] Nowak, above, note 1, 276. However, see also at 281, where Nowak notes that most international treaties would disallow retroactive effect.

[21] See M. Goodman, 'After the Wall: The Legal Ramifications of the East German Border Guard Trials in Unified Germany' (1996) 29 *Cornell ILJ* 727, at 744 and 765.

[22] Ibid., 744, 749–52.

16

Right to Privacy—Article 17

ARTICLE 17

1. No one shall be subjected to arbitrary or unlawful interference with his privacy, family, home or correspondence, nor to unlawful attacks on his honour and reputation.

2. Everyone has the right to the protection of the law against such interference or attacks.

The Meaning of Privacy

[16.01] Privacy is a notoriously difficult term to define.[1] Privacy has been categorized as a choice, a function, a desire, a right, a condition and/or a need.[2] Privacy has also been defined as the desire of individuals for solitude, intimacy, anonymity, and reserve.[3] It has been defined widely as 'the right to be left alone'[4] and, narrowly, as a right to control information about one's self.[5] A compromise definition could be that a right to privacy comprises 'freedom from unwarranted

---

[1] See, e.g., K. Gormley, 'One Hundred Years of Privacy' [1992] *Wisconsin Law Review* 1335, at 1397.

[2] A. Bartzis, 'Escaping the Panopticon', unpublished LLM thesis, Monash University, 1997, 26.

[3] J. Michael, 'Privacy' in D. Harris and S. Joseph (eds.), *The International Covenant on Civil and Political Rights and United Kingdom Law* (Clarendon Press, Oxford, 1995), at 333.

[4] Samuel D. Warren and Louis D. Brandeis, 'The Right to Privacy' (1890) 4 *Harvard Law Review* 193, 195.

[5] Alan F. Westin, *Privacy and Freedom* (Athenaeum, New York, 1967), 7; see also C. Fried, 'Privacy' (1968) 77 *Yale Law Journal* 475, 483.

and unreasonable intrusions into activities that society recognises as belonging to the realm of individual autonomy'.[6] The 'sphere of individual autonomy' has been described as 'the field of action [that] does not touch upon the liberty of others', where one may withdraw from others, to 'shape one's life according to one's own (egocentric) wishes and expectations'.[7]

[16.02] As far as the ICCPR is concerned, the meaning of privacy for the purposes of article 17 has not yet been thoroughly defined in either the General Comment or the case law. As Mr Herndl in his dissenting opinion in *Coeriel and Aurik v The Netherlands* (453/91) states:

The Committee itself has not really clarified the notion of privacy either in its General Comment on article 17 where it actually refrains from defining that notion. In its General Comment the Committee attempts to define all the other terms used in article 17 such as 'family', 'home', 'unlawful' and 'arbitrary'. It further refers to the protection of personal 'honour' and 'reputation' also mentioned in article 17, but it leaves open the definition of the main right enshrined in that article. i.e. the right to 'privacy'.

[16.03] *COERIEL and AURIK v THE NETHERLANDS (453/91)*

In this case, the authors wished to change their surname for religious reasons; they alleged a violation of article 17 entailed in the State Party's failure to permit them to do so. The majority of the Committee accepted that there had been a violation of article 17 of the Covenant. It made the following comments about whether a person's surname and identity came within the sphere of 'privacy'.

¶ 10.2. The first issue to be determined by the Committee is whether article 17 of the Covenant protects the right to choose and change one's own name. The Committee observes that article 17 provides, *inter alia*, that no one shall be subjected to arbitrary or unlawful interference with his privacy, family, home or correspondence. The Committee considers that the notion of privacy refers to the sphere of a person's life in which he or she can freely express his or her identity, be it by entering into relationships with others or alone. The Committee is of the view that a person's surname constitutes an important component of one's identity and that the protection against arbitrary or unlawful interference with one's privacy includes the protection against arbitrary or unlawful interference with the right to choose and change one's own name. For instance, if a State were to compel all foreigners to change their surnames, this would constitute interference in contravention of article 17. The question arises whether the refusal of the authorities to recognize a change of surname is also beyond the threshold of permissible interference within the meaning of article 17.

---

[6] S. Elizabeth Wilborn, 'Revisiting the Public/Private Distinction: Employee Monitoring in the Workplace' (1998) 32 *Georgia Law Review* 825, 833.

[7] M. Nowak, *UN Covenant on Civil and Political Rights: CCPR Commentary* (N.P. Engel, Kehl, Strasbourg, and Arlington, 1993), 288. See also F. Volio, 'Legal Personality, Privacy, and the Family' in L. Henkin (ed.), *The International Bill of Rights* (Columbia University Press, New York, 1981), listing aspects of privacy, and examples of privacy violations, at 193–5.

The Committee answered the latter question in the affirmative. Its merits decision is outlined below [16.16].

[16.04] Mr Herndl, in a dissenting opinion in *Coeriel and Aurik*, undertook a closer examination of the meaning and scope of article 17 privacy:

Article 17 is one of the more enigmatic provisions of the Covenant. In particular, the term 'privacy' would seem to be open to interpretation. What does privacy really mean? In his essay on 'Global Protection of Human Rights and Civil Rights' Lillich calls privacy 'a concept to date so amorphous as to preclude its acceptance into customary international law'. [Richard B. Lillich, 'Civil Rights', in *Human Rights in International Law, Legal and Policy Issues*, ed. T. Meron (1984), 148.] He adds, however, that in determining the meaning of privacy *stricto sensu* limited help can be obtained from European Convention practice. And there he mentions that i.e. 'the use of name' was suggested as being part of the concept of privacy. This is, by the way, a quote taken from Jacobs, who with reference to the similar provision of the European Convention (article 8) asserts that 'the organs of the Convention have not developed the concept of privacy'. (Francis G. Jacobs, *The European Convention on Human Rights* (1975), 126.)

What is true for the European Convention is equally true for the Covenant. In his commentary on the Covenant Nowak states that article 17 was the subject of virtually no debate during its drafting and that the case law on individual communications is of no assistance in ascertaining the exact meaning of the word. (Nowak, *CCPR Commentary* (1993), 294, section 15.)

It is therefore not without reason that the State party argues that article 17 would not necessarily cover the right to change one's surname (see para. 7.1 of the Views) [7.16]. . . .

The Committee itself has not really clarified the notion of privacy either in its General Comment on article 17 where it actually refrains from defining that notion. . . . While it is true that the Committee, in its General Comment, refers in various instances to 'private life' and gives examples of cases in which States must refrain from interfering with specific aspects of private life, the question whether the name of a person is indeed protected by article 17 and, in particular, whether in addition there is a right to change one's name, is not brought up at all in the General Comment.

I raise the above issues to demonstrate that the Committee is not really on safe legal ground in interpreting article 17 as it does in the present decision. I do, however, concur with the view that one's name is an important part of one's identity, the protection of which is central to article 17. Nowak is therefore correct in saying that privacy protects the special, individual qualities of human existence and a person's identity. Identity obviously includes one's name. (Nowak, loc. cit., p. 294, section 17.)

What is, therefore, protected by article 17, is an individual's name and not necessarily the individual's desire to change his/her name at whim. The Committee recognizes this, albeit indirectly, in its own decision. The example it refers to in order to illustrate a possible case of State interference with individuals' rights under article 17 in contravention of that article is: '. . . if a State were to compel all foreigners to change their surnames . . .' (see para. 10.2 of the Views). This view is correct, but obviously cannot have a bearing on a case where a State for reasons of generally applied public policy and in order to protect the existing name of individuals refuses to allow a change of name requested by an individual.

Nevertheless, it can be argued that it would be appropriate to assume that the term 'privacy' inasmuch as it covers, for the purpose of appropriate protection, an individual's name as part of his/her identity, also covers the right to change that name. . . .

Herndl's merits decision is outlined below [16.17].

[16.05] Mr Ando also delivered a dissenting judgment:

I do not consider that a family name belongs to an individual person alone, whose privacy is protected under article 17. In the Western society a family name may be regarded only as an element to ascertain one's identity, thus replaceable with other means of identification such as a number or a cipher. However, in other parts of the world, names have a variety of social, historical and cultural implications, and people do attach certain values to their names. This is particularly true with family names. Thus, if a member of a family changes his or her family name, it is likely to affect other members of the family as well as values attached thereto. Therefore, it is difficult for me to conclude that the family name of a person belongs to the exclusive sphere of privacy which is protected under article 17.

Ando's decision apparently limits 'the private sphere' to one's personal sphere as an individual, rather than as a member of a group such as a family. His definition seems unduly narrow, in light of the fact that article 17 expressly offers protection to the family.[8] Would Ando's decision have been different if the authors' families had wished collectively to change their surname?

[16.06] In *Hopu and Bessert v France* (549/93), the authors alleged that a hotel development on the sacred burial grounds of their ancestors breached, *inter alia*, their rights to privacy. The HRC majority agreed, as the authors' relationship with their ancestors constituted an important part of their identity.[9] In a dissenting opinion, Messrs Kretzmer, Buergenthal, Ando, and Lord Colville made the following comments:

¶ 6. Contrary to the Committee, we cannot accept that the authors' claim of an interference with their right to privacy has been substantiated. The only reasoning provided to support the Committee's conclusion in this matter is the authors' claim that their connection with their ancestors plays an important role in their identity. The notion of privacy revolves around protection of those aspects of a person's life, or relationships with others, which one chooses to keep from the public eye, or from outside intrusion. It does not include access to public property, whatever the nature of that property, or the purpose of the access. Furthermore, the mere fact that visits to a certain site play an important role in one's identity, does not transform such visits into part of one's right to privacy. One can think of many activities, such as participation in public worship or in cultural activities, that play important roles in persons' identities in different societies. While interference with such activities may involve violations of articles 18 or 27, it does not constitute interference with one's privacy.

---

[8] See also Michael, above, note 3, 334.   [9] See [20.10–20.11].

[16.07] In Concluding Comments on Mexico, the HRC indicated other aspects to one's 'privacy':[10]

¶ 17. The Committee is concerned by information to the effect that Mexican women seeking employment in foreign enterprises in the frontier areas of Mexico ('*maquiladoras*') are subjected to pregnancy tests and required to respond to intrusive personal questioning, and that some women employees have been administered anti-pregnancy drugs. It is also concerned that those allegations have not been seriously investigated.

Measures should be taken to investigate all such allegations with a view to ensuring that women whose rights to equality and privacy have been violated in this way have access to remedies and to preventing such violations from recurring.

The Mexican comments confirm that the article 17 guarantees rights of autonomy over one's own body.

[16.08] The Mexican comments may also imply that anti-abortion laws breach a woman's article 17 rights of privacy and autonomy.[11] However, the HRC has tended to condemn anti-abortion laws as dangers to women's rights to life and non-discrimination, rather than as breaches of rights to privacy.[12]

Limitations to Article 17 Protection—What is Meant by Arbitrary or Unlawful Interference?

[16.09] Article 17 prohibits interferences with privacy which are 'unlawful' and 'arbitrary'.

GENERAL COMMENT 16

¶ 3. The term 'unlawful' means that no interference can take place except in cases envisaged by the law. Interference authorized by States can only take place on the basis of law, which itself must comply with the provisions, aims and objectives of the Covenant.

[16.10] The Committee went on to specify that the law must be precise and circumscribed, so as not to give decision-makers too much discretion in authorizing interferences with privacy.

¶ 8. [R]elevant legislation must specify in detail the precise circumstances in which such interferences may be permitted. A decision to make use of such authorized interference must be made only by the authority designated under the law, and on a case-by-case basis.

---

[10] (1999) UN doc. CCPR/C/79/Add. 109.
[11] See, e.g., *Roe v Wade* 410 US 113 (1973), decision of the US Supreme Court.
[12] See [8.47].

For example, the Committee made the following comment in Concluding Comments on the Russian Federation:[13]

¶ 19. . . . [The Committee] is concerned that the mechanisms to intrude into private telephone communication continue to exist, without clear legislation setting out the conditions of legitimate interferences with privacy and providing for safeguards against unlawful interferences.

Similarly, Jamaica was asked to 'adopt precise legislation' governing the administration of wire-tapping.[14]

[16.11] *PINKNEY v CANADA (27/78)*

This case gives an example of how 'lawful' interferences with privacy must be sufficiently circumscribed in order to conform to the article 17 guarantee. The author, a remand prisoner, complained of censorship of his letters, and therefore a violation of his right to privacy in relation to correspondence [16.25]. The State Party explained the relevant law which governed censorship of inmates' letters.

¶ 31. . . . Mr. Pinkney, as a person awaiting trial, was entitled under section 1.21(d) of the Gaol Rules and Regulations, 1961, British Columbia Regulations 73/61, in force at the time of his detention to the 'provision of writing material for communicating by letter with (his) friends or for conducting correspondence or preparing notes in connection with (his) defence'. The Government of Canada does not deny that letters sent by Mr. Pinkney were subject to control and could even be censored. Section 2.40 *(b)* of the Gaol Rules and Regulations, 1961 is clear on that point:

> '2.40 *(b)* Every letter to or from a prisoner shall (except as hereinafter provided in these regulations in the case of certain communications to or from a legal adviser) be read by the Warden or by a responsible officer deputed by him for the purpose, and it is within the discretion of the Warden to stop or censor any letter, or any part of a letter, on the ground that its contents are objectionable or that the letter is of excessive length.'

The HRC found that section 2.40(b) violated article 17. However, its replacement by a new provision had remedied this situation.

¶ 34. No specific evidence has been submitted by Mr. Pinkney to establish that his correspondence was subjected to control or censorship which was not in accordance with the practice described by the State party. However, article 17 of the Covenant provides not only that 'No one shall be subjected to arbitrary or unlawful interference with his correspondence' but also that 'Everyone has the right to the protection of the law against such interference'. At the time when Mr. Pinkney was detained at the Lower Mainland Regional Correction Center the only law in force governing the control and censorship of prisoners' correspondence appears to have been section 2.40 *(b)* of the Gaol Rules and Regulations,

[13] (1995) UN doc. CCPR/C/79/Add. 54.
[14] (1997) UN doc. CCPR/C/79/Add. 83, para. 20.

1961. A legislative provision in the very general terms of this section did not, in the opinion of the Committee, in itself provide satisfactory legal safeguards against arbitrary application, though, as the Committee has already found, there is no evidence to establish that Mr. Pinkney was himself the victim of a violation of the Covenant as a result. The Committee also observes that section 42 of the Correction Centre Rules and Regulations that came into force on 6 July 1978 has now made the relevant law considerably more specific in its terms.

The new provision circumscribed the reasons for censoring mail; a prisoner's mail could be censored if it posed a threat to the staff or the operation of the prison. The Warden's discretion to censor, which was extremely broad under section 2.40(b), was minimized by the new section 42.

[16.12] Prohibition of 'unlawful' interferences with privacy offers only limited human rights protection, as States Parties could potentially authorize highly oppressive invasions of privacy in municipal law so long as the laws were expressed with the requisite precision.[15] Therefore, the prohibition is necessarily supplemented by the prohibition of arbitrary interferences with privacy.

[16.13]   *GENERAL COMMENT 16*

¶ 4. The expression 'arbitrary interference' is also relevant to the protection of the right provided for in article 17. In the Committee's view the expression 'arbitrary interference' can also extend to interference provided for under the law. The introduction of the concept of arbitrariness is intended to guarantee that even interference provided for by law should be in accordance with the provisions, aims and objectives of the Covenant and should be, in any event, reasonable in the particular circumstances.

Hence, the prohibition on 'arbitrary' interferences with privacy incorporates notions of reasonableness into article 17. In *Toonen v Australia* (488/92) the Committee discussed the issue of reasonableness as follows:[16]

¶ 8.3. The Committee interprets the requirement of reasonableness to imply that any interference with privacy must be proportional to the end sought and be necessary in the circumstances of any given case.

[16.14]   *GENERAL COMMENT 16*

In General Comment 16, the Committee gave an indication of how the reasonableness of interferences with privacy might be assessed.

---

[15] However, in para. 3 of General Comment 16 [16.09], the HRC does add that the law itself should comply with the Covenant. This may simply be referring to the fact that the law must not be arbitrary. Alternatively, it may mean that 'lawful' means 'lawful' in domestic and international human rights law. See [11.55–11.56].

[16] See also [8.04] and [11.12] ff. on the interpretation of 'arbitrariness' in the context of other ICCPR guarantees.

¶ 7. [T]he competent public authorities should only be able to call for such information relating to an individual's private life the knowledge of which is essential in the interests of society as understood under the Covenant. . . .

[16.15] Unlike other ICCPR provisions, permissible limitations to the right of privacy are not enumerated. This may be contrasted with other ICCPR guarantees, such as articles 12 and 19, where limitations are permitted only for specified purposes, such as protection of public order or public morals. Mr Wennergren noted in a separate concurring opinion in *Toonen v Australia* (488/92) that:

Article 17, paragraph 1, merely mandates that no one shall be subjected to arbitrary or unlawful interference with his privacy, family etc. Furthermore, the provision does not, as do other articles of the Covenant, specify on what grounds a State party may interfere by way of legislation.

A State party is therefore in principle free to interfere by law with the privacy of individuals on any discretionary grounds, not just on grounds related to public safety, order, health, morals, or the fundamental rights and freedoms of others, as spelled out in other provisions of the Covenant. However, under article 5, paragraph 1, nothing in the Covenant may be interpreted as implying for a State a right to perform any act aimed at the limitation of any of the rights and freedoms recognized therein to a greater extent than is provided for in the Covenant.

The permissible limits to the right of privacy are probably very similar to the enumerated limits found in other ICCPR guarantees.[17] All non-absolute ICCPR rights may be limited by proportionate measures designed to achieve a valid end. For example, enumerated limits to article 19 (freedom of expression) are permissible only if they are deemed to be 'necessary in a democratic society'. The latter words have been held to incorporate notions of reasonableness and proportionality into article 19,[18] which equates with the meaning given to 'arbitrary' in article 17. Whilst the permissible ends for an article 17 limitation are open, the permissible ends for article 19 are so broad (e.g. protection of 'the rights of others') as to be similarly open.

[16.16] *COERIEL and AURIK v THE NETHERLANDS (453/91)*

An example of the Committee's interpretation of 'arbitrary' interference is taken from this case. The facts are outlined by the authors directly below:

¶ 2.1. The authors have adopted the Hindu religion and state that they want to study [to become] Hindu priests ('pandits') in India. They requested the Roermond District Court (Arrondissements Rechtbank) to change their first names into Hindu names, in accordance with the requirements of their religion. This request was granted by the Court on 6 November 1986.

---

[17] See [1.52]. See also P. Hassan, 'International Covenant on Civil and Political Rights: Background Perspectives on Article 9(1)' (1973) 3 *Denver Journal of International Law and Policy* 153, detailing the drafting history of the inclusion of the word 'arbitrary' into art. 9(1).

[18] See [18.18].

¶ 2.2. Subsequently, the authors requested the Minister of Justice to have their surnames changed into Hindu names. They claimed that for individuals wishing to study and practice the Hindu religion and to become Hindu priests, it is mandatory to adopt Hindu names. By decisions of 2 August and 14 December 1988 respectively, the Minister of Justice rejected the authors' request, on the ground that their cases did not meet the requirements set out in the 'Guidelines for the change of surname' (*Richtlijnen voor geslachtsnaam-wijziging* 1976). The decision further stipulated that a positive decision would have been justified only by exceptional circumstances, which were not present in the authors' cases. The Minister considered that the authors' current surnames did not constitute an obstacle to undertake studies for the Hindu priesthood, since the authors would be able to adopt the religious names given to them by their Guru upon completion of their studies, if they so wished.

¶ 3. The authors claim that the refusal of the Dutch authorities to have their current surnames changed prevents them from furthering their studies for the Hindu priesthood and therefore violates article 18 of the Covenant.[19] They also claim that said refusal constitutes unlawful or arbitrary interference with their privacy.

The State Party submitted the following arguments in defence of its actions:

¶ 7.1. The State party, by submission of 24 February 1994, argues that article 17 of the Covenant does not protect the right to choose and change one's surname. It refers to the *travaux préparatoires*, in which no indication can be found that article 17 should be given such a broad interpretation, but on the basis of which it appears that States should be given considerable freedom to determine how the principles of article 17 should be applied. The State party also refers to the Committee's General Comment on article 17, in which it is stated that the protection of privacy is necessarily relative. . . .

¶ 7.2. Subsidiarily, the State party argues that the refusal to grant the authors a formal change of surname was neither unlawful nor arbitrary. The State party . . . submits that the decision was taken in accordance with the relevant Guidelines, which were published in the Government Gazette of 9 May 1990 and based on the provisions of the Civil Code. The decision not to grant the authors a change of surname was thus pursuant to domestic legislation and regulations.

¶ 7.3. As to a possible arbitrariness of the decision, the State party observes that the regulations referred to in the previous paragraph were issued precisely to prevent arbitrariness and to maintain the necessary stability in this field. The State party contends that it would create unnecessary uncertainty and confusion, in both a social and administrative sense, if a formal change of name could be effected too easily. In this connection, the State party invokes an obligation to protect the interests of others. The State party submits that in the present case, the authors failed to meet the criteria that would allow a change in their surname and that they wished to adopt names which have a special significance in Indian society. 'Granting a request of this kind would therefore be at odds with the policy of the Netherlands Government of refraining from any action that could be construed as interference with the internal affairs of other cultures'. The State party concludes that, taking

[19] See [17.15].

into account all interests involved, it cannot be said that the decision not to grant the change of name was arbitrary.[20]

The HRC majority found in favour of the author:

¶ 10.3. The Committee now proceeds to examine whether in the circumstances of the present case the State party's dismissal of the authors' request to have their surnames changed amounted to arbitrary or unlawful interference with their privacy. It notes that the State party's decision was based on the law and regulations in force in the Netherlands, and that the interference can therefore not be regarded as unlawful. It remains to be considered whether it is arbitrary.

¶ 10.4. The Committee notes that the circumstances in which a change of surname will be recognized are defined narrowly in the Guidelines and that the exercise of discretion in other cases is restricted to exceptional cases. The Committee recalls its General Comment on article 17, in which it observed that the notion of arbitrariness 'is intended to guarantee that even interference provided for by law should be in accordance with the provisions, aims and objectives of the Covenant and should be, in any event, reasonable in the partic-ular circumstances'. Thus, the request to have one's change of name recognized can only be refused on grounds that are reasonable in the specific circumstances of the case.

¶ 10.5. In the present case, the authors' request for recognition of the change of their first names to Hindu names in order to pursue their religious studies had been granted in 1986. The State party based its refusal of the request also to change their surnames on the grounds that the authors had not shown that the changes sought were essential to pursue their studies, that the names had religious connotations and that they were not 'Dutch sounding'. The Committee finds the grounds for so limiting the authors' rights under article 17 not to be reasonable. In the circumstances of the instant case the refusal of the authors' request was therefore arbitrary within the meaning of article 17, paragraph 1, of the Covenant.

[16.17] Mr Herndl dissented in the following terms:

(a) . . . [I]t can be argued that it would be appropriate to assume that the term 'privacy' inasmuch as it covers, for the purpose of appropriate protection, an individual's name as part of his/her identity, also covers the right to change that name. In that regard one must have a closer look at the 'Guidelines for the change of surname' published in the Nether-lands Government Gazette in 1990 and applied in the Netherlands as common policy. The Dutch policy is, as a matter of principle, based on the premise that a person should keep the name which he/she acquires at birth in order to maintain legal and social stability . . . As such, this policy can hardly be seen as violating article 17. On the contrary, it is protec-tive of acquired rights, such as the right to a certain name, and would seem to be very much in line with the precepts of article 17.

A change of name, according to the Guidelines, will be granted when the current name is a) indecent, b) ridiculous, c) so common that it has lost its distinctive character and d) not Dutch sounding. None of these grounds was invoked by the authors when they asked for authorization to change their surnames.

---

[20] Other State arguments are evident from Mr Herndl's dissent [16.17].

In accordance with the Guidelines a change of name can also be granted 'in exceptional cases', for instance 'in cases where the denial of the change of surname would threaten the applicant's mental or physical wellbeing' or 'in cases where the denial would be unreasonable, taking into account the interests of both the applicant and the State' . . . As the authors apparently could not show such 'exceptional circumstances' in the course of the proceedings before the national authorities, their request was denied. Their assertion that they needed the name change to become Hindu priests was apparently not substantiated . . . Nor can requirements imposed by Indian Hindu leaders be attributed to the Dutch authorities . . .

The request for a change of name was, therefore, legitimately turned down as the authors could not show the Dutch authorities 'exceptional circumstances' as required by law. The refusal cannot be seen as a violation of article 17. To hold otherwise would be tantamount to recognizing that an individual has an almost absolute right to have his/her name changed on request and at whim. For such a view, in my opinion, one can find no basis in the Covenant.

(b) The State party's action seen from the viewpoint of the criteria for permissible (State) interference in rights protected by article 17.

On the assumption that there exists a right of the individual to change his/her name, the question of the extent to which 'interference' with that right is still permissible, has to be examined (and is, indeed, addressed by the Committee in the present Views).

What then are the criteria laid down for (State) interference? They are two and only two. Article 17 prohibits arbitrary or unlawful interference with one's privacy.

It is obvious that the decision of the Dutch authorities not to grant a change of name cannot *per se* be regarded as constituting 'arbitrary or unlawful' interference with the authors' rights under article 17. The decision is based on the law applicable in the Netherlands. Hence it is not unlawful. The Committee itself says so (see para. 10.3 of the Views). The conditions under which a change of name will be authorized in the Netherlands are laid down in generally applicable and published 'Guidelines for the change of surname' which, in themselves, are not manifestly arbitrary. These Guidelines have been applied in the present case, and there is no indication that they were applied in a discriminatory fashion. Hence it is equally difficult to call the decision arbitrary. The Committee does so, however, 'in the circumstances of the present case' (see para. 10.5 of the Views). To arrive at that finding the Committee introduces a new notion that of 'reasonableness'. It finds 'the grounds for limiting the authors' rights under article 17 not to be reasonable' (see para. 10.5 of the Views).

The Committee thus attempts to expand the scope of article 17 by adding an element which is not part of that article. The only argument the Committee can adduce in this context is a simple reference (*renvoi*) to its own General Comment on article 17 where it stated that 'even interference provided by law . . . should be, in any event, reasonable in the particular circumstances'. It is difficult for me to go along with this argumentation and to base on such argumentation a finding that a State party violated this specific provision of the Covenant.

Herndl's well-argued analysis of the nature of identity and the issue of interference with privacy is one of the few instances where a Committee member has addressed this issue in some depth. Herndl however subscribes to a different meaning of 'arbitrary' from that adopted by the rest of the Committee. He denies that 'arbitrariness' equates with 'reasonableness'. Instead, he defines 'arbitrary' as meaning 'discriminatory'. Herndl's narrower definition has not been endorsed in any other Optional Protocol case.[21]

Obligation on the State to Take Positive Measures to Protect Privacy

[16.18] Article 17(1) obviously prohibits States from themselves invading a person's privacy. There are also positive obligations within article 17.

GENERAL COMMENT 16

¶ 1. Article 17 provides for the right of every person to be protected against arbitrary or unlawful interference with his privacy, family, home or correspondence as well as against unlawful attacks on his honour and reputation. In the view of the Committee this right is required to be guaranteed against all such interferences and attacks whether they emanate from State authorities or from natural or legal persons. The obligations imposed by this article require the State to adopt legislative and other measures to give effect to the prohibition against such interferences and attacks as well as to the protection of this right.

Furthermore, article 17(2) expressly guarantees a right to protection of the law against interference with one's privacy.

[16.19] States Parties are under an obligation to provide a remedy, either civil or criminal, for arbitrary invasions of privacy in the private sector. This is important, as many gross invasions of privacy occur at the behest of the private sector, particularly the media. No cases have so far dealt with this positive obligation.[22]

[16.20]   *GENERAL COMMENT 16*

¶ 6. The Committee considers that the reports should include information on the authorities and organs set up within the legal system of the State which are competent to authorize interference allowed by the law. It is also indispensable to have information on the authorities which are entitled to exercise control over such interference with strict regard for the law, and to know in what manner and through which organs persons concerned may complain of a violation of the right provided for in article 17 of the Covenant. States

---

[21] See also [16.13–16.14]. The majority's *Coeriel* decision contrasts with the judgment of the European Court of Human Rights in *Sjterna v Finland* (1997) 24 EHRR 195, where no ECHR violation was entailed in Finland's refusal to permit Sjterna to change his name.

[22] See [1.59–1.62] for general discussion of private sector ICCPR abuse. In *Gonzales del Rio v Peru* (263/87), the author complained about libellous attacks on himself by newspapers supported by the government. The main contention was that the State was directly responsible in promoting the attacks, rather than that the State had failed to control the newspapers. In dismissing the claim, the HRC noted that the author had failed to pursue domestic remedies against the newspapers.

should in their reports make clear the extent to which actual practice conforms to the law. State party reports should also contain information on complaints lodged in respect of arbitrary or unlawful interference, and the number of any findings in that regard, as well as the remedies provided in such cases.

Paragraph 6 of the General Comment confirms that States must have adequate complaints systems, and provide adequate remedies, for privacy violations.

Specific Aspects of Privacy

FAMILY AND HOME

[16.21]   *GENERAL COMMENT 16*

¶ 5. Regarding the term 'family', the objectives of the Covenant require that for purposes of article 17 this term be given a broad interpretation to include all those comprising the family as understood in the society of the State party concerned. The term 'home' in English, 'manzel' in Arabic, 'zhùzhái' in Chinese, 'domicile' in French, 'zhilische' in Russian and 'domicilio' in Spanish, as used in article 17 of the Covenant, is to be understood to indicate the place where a person resides or carries out his usual occupation. In this connection, the Committee invites States to indicate in their reports the meaning given in their society to the terms 'family' and 'home'.

In the General Comment, the HRC adopts a liberal interpretation of 'home', so as to include one's workplace.[23]

Most article 17 cases regarding allegations of family interferences have also concerned article 23(1), which guarantees families rights of protection.[24]

[16.22]   *AUMEERUDDY-CZIFFRA et al. v MAURITIUS (35/78)*

This complaint concerned legislation in Mauritius which provided different residential status for alien men and women married to Mauritian nationals. Alien men were placed in a more precarious residential position than alien women in Mauritius. The authors included twenty Mauritian women, three of whom were married to foreign husbands. The authors raised the following issues:

¶ 1.1. They claim that the enactment of the Immigration (Amendment) Act, 1977, and the Deportation (Amendment) Act, 1977, by Mauritius constitutes discrimination based on sex against Mauritian women, violation of the right to found a family and home, and removal of the protection of the courts of law, in breach of articles 2, 3, 4, 17, 23, 25 and 26 of the International Covenant on Civil and Political Rights. The authors claim to be victims of the alleged violations. They submit that all domestic remedies have been exhausted.

---

[23] See also Nowak, above, note 7, 302–3.
[24] See, on family rights and the rights of privacy within the family, Chap. 20.

¶ 1.2. The authors state that prior to the enactment of the laws in question, alien men and women married to Mauritian nationals enjoyed the same residence status, that is to say, by virtue of their marriage, foreign spouses of both sexes had the right, protected by law, to reside in the country with their Mauritian husbands or wives. The authors contend that, under the new laws, alien husbands of Mauritian women lost their residence status in Mauritius and must now apply for a 'residence permit' which may be refused or removed at any time by the Minister of Interior. The new laws, however, do not affect the status of alien women married to Mauritian husbands who retain their legal right to residence in the country. The authors further contend that under the new laws alien husbands of Mauritian women may be deported under a ministerial order which is not subject to judicial review.

In relation to the issue regarding article 17 the State made the following argument:

¶ 5.5. The State party further argues that nothing in the laws of Mauritius denies any citizen the right to marry whomever he may choose and to found a family. Any violation of articles 17 and 23 is denied by the State party which argues that this allegation is based on the assumption that 'husband and wife are given the right to reside together in their own countries and that this right of residence should be secure'. The State party reiterates that the right to stay in Mauritius is not one of the rights guaranteed by the provisions of the Covenant, but it admits that the exclusion of a person from a country where close members of his family are living can amount to an infringement of the person's right under article 17 of the Covenant, i.e. that no one should be subjected to arbitrary and unlawful interference with his family. The State party argues, however, that each case must be decided on its own merits.

¶ 5.7. The State party is of the opinion that if the exclusion of a non-citizen is lawful (the right to stay in a country not being one of the rights guaranteed by the provisions of the Covenant), then such an exclusion (based on grounds of security or public interest) cannot be said to be an arbitrary or unlawful interference with the family life of its nationals in breach of article 17 of the Covenant.

The HRC found a breach of article 17 in relation to the married authors[25] and it made the following comments:

¶ 9.2(b) 2(i) 1. First, their relationships to their husbands clearly belong to the area of 'family' as used in article 17 (1) of the Covenant. They are therefore protected against what that article calls 'arbitrary or unlawful interference' in this area.

¶ 9.2(b) 2(i) 2. The Committee takes the view that the common residence of husband and wife has to be considered as the normal behaviour of a family. Hence, and as the State party has admitted, the exclusion of a person from a country where close members of his family are living can amount to an interference within the meaning of article 17. In principle, article 17 (1) applies also when one of the spouses is an alien. Whether the existence and application of immigration laws affecting the residence of a family member is compatible with the Covenant depends on whether such interference is either 'arbitrary or unlawful' as stated in article 17 (1), or conflicts in any other way with the State party's obligations under the Covenant.

---

[25] The other women were found not to be relevant victims for the purposes of an OP complaint. See [3.27].

¶ 9.2(b) 2(i) 3. In the present cases, not only the future possibility of deportation, but the existing precarious residence situation of foreign husbands in Mauritius represents, in the opinion of the Committee, an interference by the authorities of the State party with the family life of the Mauritian wives and their husbands. The statutes in question have rendered it uncertain for the families concerned whether and for how long it will be possible for them to continue their family life by residing together in Mauritius. Moreover, . . . even the delay for years, and the absence of a positive decision granting a residence permit, must be seen as a considerable inconvenience, among other reasons because the granting of a work permit, and hence the possibility of the husband to contribute to supporting the family, depends on the residence permit, and because deportation without judicial review is possible at any time.

¶ 9.2(b) 2(i) 4. Since, however, this situation results from the legislation itself, there can be no question of regarding this interference as 'unlawful' within the meaning of article 17 (1) in the present cases. It remains to be considered whether it is 'arbitrary' or conflicts in any other way with the Covenant.

¶ 9.2(b) 2(i) 5. The protection owed to individuals in this respect is subject to the principle of equal treatment of the sexes which follows from several provisions of the Covenant. It is an obligation of the States parties under article 2 (1) generally to respect and ensure the rights of the Covenant 'without distinction of any kind, such as . . . (*inter alia*) sex', and more particularly under article 3 'to ensure the equal right of men and women to the enjoyment' of all these rights, as well as under article 26 to provide 'without any discrimination' for 'the equal protection of the law'.

¶ 9.2(b) 2(i) 6. The authors who are married to foreign nationals are suffering from the adverse consequences of the statutes discussed above only because they are women. The precarious residence status of their husbands, affecting their family life as described, results from the 1977 laws which do not apply the same measures of control to foreign wives. In this connection the Committee has noted that under section 16 of the Constitution of Mauritius sex is not one of the grounds on which discrimination is prohibited. . . .

¶ 9.2(b) 2(i) 8. . . . Whether or not the particular interference could as such be justified if it were applied without discrimination does not matter here. Whenever restrictions are placed on a right guaranteed by the Covenant, this has to be done without discrimination on the ground of sex. Whether the restriction in itself would be in breach of that right regarded in isolation, is not decisive in this respect. It is the enjoyment of the rights which must be secured without discrimination. Here it is sufficient, therefore, to note that in the present position an adverse distinction based on sex is made, affecting the alleged victims in their enjoyment of one of their rights. No sufficient justification for this difference has been given. The Committee must then find that there is a violation of articles 2 (1) and 3 of the Covenant, in conjunction with article 17 (1).

[16.23] The Committee's decision in the *Mauritian Women's Case* was influenced by the discriminatory character of the legislation.[26] The Committee did not decide whether legislation which restricts the residential rights of family

---

[26] See also [23.42].

members *per se* breaches article 17. However, in subsequent Concluding Comments on Zimbabwe, the HRC has confirmed that overly restrictive residential requirements for foreign spouses, even if non-discriminatory, will breach article 17 [20.14].

CORRESPONDENCE

[16.24] *GENERAL COMMENT 16*

¶ 8. Compliance with article 17 requires that the integrity and confidentiality of correspondence should be guaranteed *de jure* and *de facto*. Correspondence should be delivered to the addressee without interception and without being opened or otherwise read. Surveillance, whether electronic or otherwise, interceptions of telephonic, telegraphic and other forms of communication, wire-tapping and recording of conversations should be prohibited.

[16.25] As outlined in the General Comment, the State is obliged to provide protection in the law against interference with correspondence in order to protect its secrecy. The Committee has given some interpretation to the privacy of correspondence in cases involving the rights of prisoners to private correspondence. In *Pinkney v Canada* (27/78) the Committee found that certain legal provisions, since repealed, had not offered sufficient legal safeguards against arbitrary interference with correspondence [16.11].

[16.26] In *Angel Estrella v Uruguay* (74/80) the HRC held that prisoners should be allowed under necessary supervision to correspond with their families and reputable friends on a regular basis without interference. In this case the author had received only thirty-five out of a possible one hundred censored letters and during a seven-month period he received none. On the facts the HRC found that the author's correspondence was censored and restricted to such an extent that there was a breach of article 17 read in conjunction with article 10(1) of the Covenant, which guarantees humane treatment of detainees.[27]

[16.27] In Concluding Comments on Poland, the HRC stated:[28]

¶ 22. As regards telephone tapping, the Committee is concerned (a) that the Prosecutor (without judicial consent) may permit telephone tapping; and (b) that there is no independent monitoring of the use of the entire system of telephones.

In Concluding Comments on Zimbabwe, the HRC stated:[29]

¶ 25. The Committee notes with concern that the Postmaster-General is authorized to

---

[27] See also [9.110].
[28] (1999) UN doc. CCPR/C/79/Add. 110.
[29] (1998) UN doc. CCPR/C/79/Add. 89.

intercept any postal articles or telegrams on grounds of public security or the maintenance of law and to deliver these items to a specified State employee. The Committee recommends that steps be taken to ensure that interception be subject to strict judicial supervision and that the relevant laws be brought into compliance with the Covenant.

Thus, telephone tapping and postal interception are compatible with article 17, despite the language of General Comment 16 [16.24], so long as such practices are strictly controlled and overseen by independent, preferably judicial, bodies.[30]

SEARCHES

[16.28]   *GENERAL COMMENT 16*

¶ 8. Searches of a person's home should be restricted to a search for necessary evidence and should not be allowed to amount to harassment. So far as personal and body search is concerned, effective measures should ensure that such searches are carried out in a manner consistent with the dignity of the person who is being searched. Persons being subjected to body search by State officials, or medical personnel acting at the request of the State, should only be examined by persons of the same sex.

[16.29] In Concluding Comments on the United Kingdom, the Committee was disturbed by reports of the continuation of the practice of strip searching prisoners in Northern Ireland, 'in the context of the low security risk' that existed after the terrorist cease-fire.[31] Whilst the Committee's optimistic assessment of the terrorist security risk in 1995 may have been premature, its comment confirms that strip searches should only be conducted in proportionate circumstances.

HONOUR AND REPUTATION

[16.30]   *GENERAL COMMENT 16*

¶ 11. Article 17 affords protection to personal honour and reputation and States are under an obligation to provide adequate legislation to that end. Provision must also be made for everyone effectively to be able to protect himself against any unlawful attacks that do occur and to have an effective remedy against those responsible. States parties should indicate in their reports to what extent the honour or reputation of individuals is protected by law and how this protection is achieved according to their legal system.

Nowak suggests that 'honour' refers to one's subjective opinion of him/herself (one's self-esteem), whereas 'reputation' refers to one's appraisal by others.[32]

[16.31] The case of *Tshisekedi v Zaire* (241–242/87) concerned, *inter alia*, attacks on the reputation of Mr Tshisekedi, an opposition leader. He was arrested

---

[30] See also Concluding Comments on Lesotho (1999) UN doc. CCPR/C/79/Add. 106, para. 24.
[31] (1995) UN Doc.CCPR/C/79/Add. 55, para. 12.
[32] Nowak, above, note 7, 306.

for his involvement in demonstrations in Kinshasa. During his arrest he was given a psychiatric examination and attempts were made to have him interned in a psychiatric institution. The State party tried to justify his psychiatric assessments by submitting that as the author displayed 'signs of mental disturbance, the judicial authorities decided that he should undergo a psychiatric examination, both in the interests of his health and to ensure a fair trial'.[33] Even though its attempts to incarcerate him were unsuccessful the government continued to allege that he was insane, even though 'medical reports contradicted such diagnosis'.[34] This action by the State was found by the Committee to violate Tshisekedi's right to honour and reputation in breach of article 17. The case does not unfortunately explicitly state whether the government's action was 'unlawful' under Zairean law.

[16.32] In *I.P. v Finland* (450/91) the Committee considered whether disclosure of information about the applicant's tax status by the tax authorities amounted to an interference with his privacy and an unlawful attack on his honour and reputation. The Committee found that the claim was inadmissible as the article 17 had not been sufficiently substantiated. This case lends support for the argument that the protection for one's honour and reputation under article 17 is limited only to unlawful attacks and does not catch arbitrary attacks.[35] As there was lawful authority for the disclosure there was no breach of article 17.

[16.33] In *R.L.M. v Trinidad and Tobago* (380/89), the author, who was an attorney, argued that a judge's criticism of him whilst in court was an unlawful attack on his honour and reputation. The case was found to be inadmissible by the Committee as the criticism was not an unlawful attack. The judge's comments were privileged and therefore could not be viewed as unlawful.[36]

[16.34] Extant Optional Protocol cases indicate that 'unlawful' in the context of article 17 means 'unlawful' in domestic law. If so, the protection offered to honour and reputation is potentially very weak [16.12]. However, the HRC has more recently interpreted the word 'lawful' in the context of article 9(4) to mean more than simple compliance with municipal law.[37] This may herald broader interpretations of the word 'unlawful' in the context of article 17 protection of honour and reputation in the future.

SEXUAL PRIVACY

[16.35] Regulation of sexual behaviour that takes place in private may be an interference with privacy. In this regard, one may note the minority opinion in

---

[33] Para. 4.3.   [34] Para. 12.7.

[35] See Michael, above, note 3, 352 and Nowak, above, note 7, 305–6.

[36] See also *Simons v Panama* (460/91) where the Committee considered the author's claim that criminal proceedings against him were based on false evidence and were therefore an attack on his honour and professional reputation. The case was found to be inadmissible.

[37] See [11.55–11.56].

Hertzberg et al. v Finland (61/79), when it was stated that article 17 protects the 'right to be different and live accordingly'.[38] Sexual regulation may relate to the sexual regulation of heterosexuals, homosexuals, paedophiles, prostitutes, pornographers, and sado-masochists.[39]

[16.36]   *TOONEN v AUSTRALIA (488/92)*

This case concerned a challenge to Tasmanian laws which criminalized sexual relations between consenting males. The author submitted the following facts:

¶ 2.1. The author is an activist for the promotion of the rights of homosexuals in Tasmania, one of Australia's six constitutive states. He challenges two provisions [*sic*] of the Tasmanian Criminal Code, namely Sections 122(a) and (c) and 123, which criminalize various forms of sexual contacts between men, including all forms of sexual contacts between consenting adult homosexual men in private.

¶ 2.2. The author observes that the above sections of the Tasmanian Criminal Code empower Tasmanian police officers to investigate intimate aspects of his private life and to detain him, if they have reason to believe that he is involved in sexual activities which contravene the above sections. He adds that the Director of Public Prosecutions announced, in August 1988, that proceedings pursuant to Sections 122(a), (c) and 123 would be initiated if there was sufficient evidence of the commission of a crime.

Toonen conceded that the law had not been enforced for many years, but argued that the stigmatizing effects of the law nevertheless rendered him a victim.[40]

¶ 3.1. The author affirms that Sections 122 and 123 of the Tasmanian Criminal Code violate articles 2, paragraph 1, 17 and 26 of the Covenant because:

¶ (a) they do not distinguish between sexual activity in private and sexual activity in public and bring private activity into the public domain. In their enforcement, these provisions result in a violation of the right to privacy, since they enable the police to enter a household on the mere suspicion that two consenting adult homosexual men may be committing a criminal offence. Given the stigma attached to homosexuality in Australian society (and especially in Tasmania), the violation of the right to privacy may lead to unlawful attacks on the honour and the reputation of the individuals concerned.

(b) they distinguish between individuals in the exercise of their right to privacy on the basis of sexual activity, sexual orientation and sexual identity.

The State Party submitted its own arguments, as well as arguments put by the Tasmanian government:

¶ 6.1. . . . the State party concedes that the author has been a victim of arbitrary interfer-

---

[38] See [18.22].

[39] See Nowak, above, note 7, 298–9. See also *Leskey, Jaggard and Brown v UK* (1997) 24 EHRR 39, where UK prohibitions on certain sado-masochistic practices were found to be compatible with the ECHR guarantee of privacy (article 8 ECHR).

[40] See, on the 'victim' aspect of this case, [3.34].

ence with his privacy, and that the legislative provisions challenged by him cannot be justified on public health or moral grounds. It incorporates into its submission the observations of the government of Tasmania, which denies that the author has been the victim of a violation of the Covenant.

¶ 6.2. With regard to article 17, the Federal Government notes that the Tasmanian government submits that article 17 does not create a 'right to privacy' but only a right to freedom from arbitrary or unlawful interference with privacy, and that as the challenged laws were enacted by democratic process, they cannot be an unlawful interference with privacy. The Federal Government, after reviewing the *travaux préparatoires* of article 17, subscribes to the following definition of 'private': 'matters which are individual, personal, or confidential, or which are kept or removed from public observation'. The State party acknowledges that based on this definition, consensual sexual activity in private is encompassed by the concept of 'privacy' in article 17. . . .

¶ 6.4. As to whether the interference with the author's privacy was arbitrary or unlawful, the State party refers to the *travaux préparatoires* of article 17 and observes that the drafting history of the provision in the Commission on Human Rights appears to indicate that the term 'arbitrary' was meant to cover interferences which, under Australian law, would be covered by the concept of 'unreasonableness'. Furthermore, the Human Rights Committee, in its General Comment on article 17, states that the 'concept of arbitrariness is intended to guarantee that even interference provided for by law should be in accordance with the provisions, aims and objectives of the [Covenant] and should be . . . reasonable in the particular circumstances'. On the basis of this and the Committee's jurisprudence on the concept of 'reasonableness', the State party interprets 'reasonable' interferences with privacy as measures which are based on reasonable and objective criteria and which are proportional to the purpose for which they are adopted. . . .

¶ 6.6. None the less, the State party cautions that the formulation of article 17 allows for some infringement of the right to privacy if there are reasonable grounds, and that domestic social mores may be relevant to the reasonableness of an interference with privacy. The State party observes that while laws penalizing homosexual activity existed in the past in other Australian states, they have since been repealed with the exception of Tasmania. Furthermore, discrimination on the basis of homosexuality or sexuality is unlawful in three of six Australian states and the two self-governing internal Australian territories. The Federal Government has declared sexual preference to be a ground of discrimination that may be invoked under ILO Convention No. 111 (Discrimination in Employment or Occupation Convention), and created a mechanism through which complaints about discrimination in employment on the basis of sexual preference may be considered by the Australian Human Rights and Equal Opportunity Commission.

¶ 6.7. On the basis of the above, the State party contends that there is now a general Australian acceptance that no individual should be disadvantaged on the basis of his or her sexual orientation. Given the legal and social situation in all of Australia except Tasmania, the State party acknowledges that a complete prohibition on sexual activity between men is unnecessary to sustain the moral fabric of Australian society. On balance, the State party 'does not seek to claim that the challenged laws are based on reasonable and objective criteria'.

¶ 6.8. Finally, the State party examines, in the context of article 17, whether the challenged laws are a proportional response to the aim sought. It does not accept the argument of the Tasmanian authorities that the extent of interference with personal privacy occasioned by Sections 122 and 123 of the Tasmanian Criminal Code is a proportional response to the perceived threat to the moral standards of Tasmanian society. In this context, it notes that the very fact that the laws are not enforced against individuals engaging in private, consensual sexual activity indicates that the laws are not essential to the protection of that society's moral standards. In the light of all the above, the State party concludes that the challenged laws are not reasonable in the circumstances, and that their interference with privacy is arbitrary. It notes that the repeal of the laws has been proposed at various times in the recent past by Tasmanian governments. . . .

¶ 8.4. While the State party acknowledges that the impugned provisions constitute an arbitrary interference with Mr. Toonen's privacy, the Tasmanian authorities submit that the challenged laws are justified on public health and moral grounds, as they are intended in part to prevent the spread of HIV/AIDS in Tasmania, and because, in the absence of specific limitation clauses in article 17, moral issues must be deemed a matter for domestic decision.

The HRC found that the relevant provisions of Tasmania's Criminal Code violated Toonen's rights under article 17.

¶ 8.2. Insomuch as article 17 is concerned, it is undisputed that adult consensual sexual activity in private is covered by the concept of 'privacy', and that Mr. Toonen is actually and currently affected by the continued existence of the Tasmanian laws. The Committee considers that Sections 122(a), (c) and 123 of the Tasmanian Criminal Code 'interfere' with the author's privacy, even if these provisions have not been enforced for a decade. In this context, it notes that the policy of the Department of Public Prosecutions not to initiate criminal proceedings in respect of private homosexual conduct does not amount to a guarantee that no actions will be brought against homosexuals in the future, particularly in the light of undisputed statements of the Director of Public Prosecutions of Tasmania in 1988 and those of members of the Tasmanian Parliament. The continued existence of the challenged provisions therefore continuously and directly 'interferes' with the author's privacy.

¶ 8.3. The prohibition against private homosexual behaviour is provided for by law, namely, Sections 122 and 123 of the Tasmanian Criminal Code. As to whether it may be deemed arbitrary, the Committee recalls that pursuant to its General Comment 16(32) on article 17, the 'introduction of the concept of arbitrariness is intended to guarantee that even interference provided for by the law should be in accordance with the provisions, aims and objectives of the Covenant and should be, in any event, reasonable in the circumstances'. The Committee interprets the requirement of reasonableness to imply that any interference with privacy must be proportional to the end sought and be necessary in the circumstances of any given case. . . .

¶ 8.5. As far as the public health argument of the Tasmanian authorities is concerned, the Committee notes that the criminalization of homosexual practices cannot be considered a reasonable means or proportionate measure to achieve the aim of preventing the spread of HIV/AIDS. The Australian Government observes that statutes criminalizing homosexual activity tend to impede public health programmes 'by driving underground many of the people at the risk of infection'. Criminalization of homosexual activity thus would appear to run counter to the implementation of effective education programmes in respect of the HIV/AIDS prevention. Secondly, the Committee notes that no link has been shown between the continued criminalization of homosexual activity and the effective control of the spread of the HIV/AIDS virus.

¶ 8.6. The Committee cannot accept either that for the purposes of article 17 of the Covenant, moral issues are exclusively a matter of domestic concern, as this would open the door to withdrawing from the Committee's scrutiny a potentially large number of statutes interfering with privacy. It further notes that with the exception of Tasmania, all laws criminalizing homosexuality have been repealed throughout Australia and that, even in Tasmania, it is apparent that there is no consensus as to whether Sections 122 and 123 should not also be repealed. Considering further that these provisions are not currently enforced, which implies that they are not deemed essential to the protection of morals in Tasmania, the Committee concludes that the provisions do not meet the 'reasonableness' test in the circumstances of the case, and that they arbitrarily interfere with Mr. Toonen's right under article 17, paragraph 1.

[16.37] The Committee rejected the Tasmanian argument that public morals are exclusively a domestic matter. A contrary decision could have permitted States to justify extremely oppressive measures with potentially dubious references to public morality. 'State claims of moral justification could only [then] be investigated as to whether they were bona fide; any apparent unreasonableness entailed in the moral justification would be irrelevant.'[41] This would have drastically reduced the individual's right to privacy under the Covenant.

[16.38] At paragraph 8.6 of the decision, the Committee noted the widespread acceptance of homosexuality in Australia as evidence that prohibitions on gay sex were not necessary to protect public morals. This indicates that public morality is a relative value.[42] Hence, prohibitions on gay sex could possibly survive a challenge from a 'less tolerant' State.[43] However, the HRC has perhaps confirmed the universal application of *Toonen* in recent Concluding Comments. The HRC has criticized bans on gay sex in Lesotho[44] and Tanzania,[45] and the omission of sexuality as a prohibited ground of discrimination in the Polish Constitution[46] and in Hong Kong.[47]

---

[41] S. Joseph, 'Gay Rights Under the ICCPR—Commentary on *Toonen v Australia*' (1994) 13 *University of Tasmania Law Review* 392 at 397.

[42] See also [18.24].

[43] See Joseph, above, note 41, at 407.

[44] Concluding Comment on Lesotho (1999) UN doc. CCPR/C/79/Add. 106, para. 13.

[45] Concluding Comments on United Republic of Tanzania (1998) CCPR/C/79/Add. 97, para. 23.

[46] Concluding Comments on Poland (1999) UN doc. CCPR/C/79/Add. 110, para. 22.

[47] Concluding Comments on Hong Kong (China) (1999) UN doc. CCPR/C/79/Add. 117, para. 15. See also [23.23].

DATA PROTECTION

[16.39]   *GENERAL COMMENT 16*

¶ 10. The gathering and holding of personal information on computers, databanks and other devices, whether by public authorities or private individuals or bodies, must be regulated by law. Effective measures have to be taken by States to ensure that information concerning a person's private life does not reach the hands of persons who are not authorized by law to receive, process and use it, and is never used for purposes incompatible with the Covenant. In order to have the most effective protection of his private life, every individual should have the right to ascertain in an intelligible form, whether, and if so, what personal data is stored in automatic data files, and for what purposes. Every individual should also be able to ascertain which public authorities or private individuals or bodies control or may control their files. If such files contain incorrect personal data or have been collected or processed contrary to the provisions of the law, every individual should have the right to request rectification or elimination.[48]

Modern computer technology is capable of storing and gathering enormous amounts of personal information. The application of article 17 in the field of data protection is therefore very important.[49]

Conclusion

[16.40] The HRC has confirmed that the prohibition of 'arbitrary' interferences with privacy covers interferences which are nevertheless authorized by domestic law. Useful jurisprudence has addressed specific aspects of privacy, such as data protection, control over one's name, correspondence, sexual privacy, honour, reputation, as well as privacy within the family unit. However, numerous controversial privacy rights have not yet arisen for consideration, such as rights regarding beneficial medical treatment without consent, compulsory DNA testing, confidentiality rights (e.g. regarding medical records or 'confessions' before a priest), or the official acknowledgment of a change of sex for transsexuals.[50]

Postscript: Please note that General Comment 28 on 'Equality of Rights Between Men and Women', contained in the Addendum at page 634, contains extra information on some of the material in this chapter.

---

[48] See also Concluding Comments on the Republic of Korea (1999) UN doc. CCPR/C/79/Add. 114, para. 17, where the HRC criticized the lack of 'adequate remedies by way of correction of inaccurate information in data-bases or for their misuse or abuse'.

[49] See generally L.A. Bygrave, 'Data Protection Pursuant to the Right to Privacy in Human Rights Treaties' (1998) 6 *International Journal of Law and Information Technology* 247, especially at 252–4.

[50] See [20.20].

17

Freedom of Thought, Conscience, and Religion— Article 18

ARTICLE 18

1. Everyone shall have the right to freedom of thought, conscience and religion. This right shall include freedom to have or to adopt a religion or belief of one's choice, and freedom, either individually or in community with others and in public or private, to manifest his religion or belief in worship, observance, practice and teaching.

2. No one shall be subject to coercion which would impair his freedom to have or adopt a religion or belief of his choice.

3. Freedom to manifest one's religion or beliefs may be subject only to such limitations as are prescribed by law and are necessary to protect public safety, order, health or morals or the fundamental rights and freedoms of others.

4. The States Parties to the present Covenant undertake to have respect for the liberty of parents and where applicable, legal guardians to ensure the religious and moral education of their children in conformity with their own convictions

[17.01] The protection of freedom of religion, belief, and conscience in article 18 is supplemented by the United Nations Declaration on the Elimination of All Forms of Discrimination based on Religion or Belief 1981. However, this Declaration has failed, after eighteen years, to spawn a binding treaty in this area, comparable to the Conventions on the elimination, respectively, of race and sex discrimination.[1] However, there is no doubt that the HRC has been influenced by the Declaration, particularly in its interpretation of article 18 in General Comment 22.[2]

Definitions

FREEDOM OF THOUGHT, CONSCIENCE, AND RELIGION

[17.02]   *GENERAL COMMENT 22*

¶ 1. The right to freedom of thought, conscience and religion (which includes the freedom to hold beliefs) in article 18(1) is far-reaching and profound; it encompasses freedom of thought on all matters, personal conviction and the commitment to religion or belief, whether manifested individually or in community with others. The Committee draws the attention of States parties to the fact that the freedom of thought and the freedom of conscience are protected equally with the freedom of religion and belief. The fundamental character of these freedoms is also reflected in the fact that this provision cannot be derogated from, even in time of public emergency, as stated in article 4(2) of the Covenant.

¶ 2. Article 18 protects theistic, non-theistic and atheistic beliefs, as well as the right not to profess any religion or belief. The terms 'belief' and 'religion' are to be broadly construed. Article 18 is not limited in its application to traditional religions or to religions and beliefs with institutional characteristics or practices analogous to those of traditional religions. The Committee therefore views with concern any tendency to discriminate against any religion or belief for any reason, including the fact that they are newly established, or represent religious minorities that may be the subject of hostility on the part of a predominant religious community.

¶ 3. Article 18 distinguishes the freedom of thought, conscience, religion or belief from the freedom to manifest religion or belief. It does not permit any limitations whatsoever on the freedom of thought and conscience or on the freedom to have or adopt a religion or belief of one's choice. These freedoms are protected unconditionally, as is the right of everyone to hold opinions without interference in article 19(1). In accordance with articles 18(2) and 17, no one can be compelled to reveal his thoughts or adherence to a religion or belief.[3]

[17.03] As article 18 protects one's freedom of religion, thought, and conscience, the HRC has decided, perhaps wisely, not to define 'religion'. Therefore, it has not grappled with the relevance to that definition of such factors as: number of adherents, truth or falsity of the relevant belief, and historical foundation of the relevant movement.[4]

---

[1] See generally on these Conventions, Chap. 23.
[2] See B. Dickson, 'The United Nations and Freedom of Religion' (1995) 44 *ICLQ* 341, at 345–6.
[3] Art. 17 protects the right to privacy; see generally Chap. 16. See also [18.02].
[4] See generally W. Sadurski, 'On Legal Definitions of Religion' (1989) 63 *Australian Law Journal* 834. Regarding the 'historical basis' for religions, the HRC has recognized that 'newly estab-

[17.04] *M.A.B, W.A.T and J-A.Y.T v CANADA (570/93)*

¶ 2.1. The authors are leading members and 'plenipotentiaries' of the 'Assembly of the Church of the Universe', whose beliefs and practices involve the care, cultivation, possession, distribution, maintenance, integrity and worship of the 'Sacrament' of the Church. Whereas the authors also refer to this 'Sacrament' as 'God's tree of life', it is generally known under the designation *cannabis sativa* or marijuana.

¶ 2.2. Since the foundation of the Church, several of its members have come into conflict with the law, as their relationship with and worship of marijuana falls within the scope of application of the provisions of the Canadian Narcotic Control Act.

¶ 2.3. On 17 October 1990, a constable of the Royal Canadian Mounted Police (RCMP) entered the Church's premises in Hamilton, Ontario, under the pretext of wishing to join the Church and to purchase the 'Church Sacrament'. She was offered a few grams of marijuana, which led to the arrest and detention of W.A.T. and J.-A.Y.T. All of the marijuana and money found in their possession was confiscated and they were ordered to stand trial before a jury, under the terms of section 4 of the Narcotics Control Act. Further investigations into the activities and properties of the Church also led to the arrest and detention of M.A.B.

The authors brought a complaint before the HRC alleging, *inter alia*, that their right to freedom of religion had been violated. The HRC disposed of the matter shortly:

¶ 4.2. Taking into account the requirements laid down in articles 2 and 3 of the Optional Protocol, the Committee has examined whether the facts as submitted would raise *prima facie* issues under any provision of the Covenant. It concludes that they do not. In particular, a belief consisting primarily or exclusively in the worship and distribution of a narcotic drug cannot conceivably be brought within the scope of article 18 of the Covenant (freedom of religion and conscience); nor can arrest for possession and distribution of a narcotic drug conceivably come within the scope of article 9, paragraph 1, of the Covenant (freedom from arbitrary arrest and detention).

Narcotic consumption can be a religious canon of conduct. Indeed, Rastafarianism is a religion where the consumption of marijuana is important as it facilitates meditation and reflection on the word of God ('Jah'). Given the proliferation of cults and pseudo-religious movements in the world, it is perhaps unwise for the Committee to deny such groups the status of 'religion', especially if such denial is motivated by the Committee's disapproval of a group's activities. It may be prudent to adopt a broad definition of 'religion' for the purposes of article 18, bearing in mind that freedom to manifest religion may be subject to numerous permissible limitations.[5] For example, in this case, the HRC could have classified

---

lished' movements can constitute religions (para. 2, General Comment 22). See also P. Cumper, 'Freedom of Thought, Conscience, and Religion' in D. Harris and S. Joseph (eds.), *The International Covenant on Civil and Political Rights and United Kingdom Law* (Clarendon Press, Oxford, 1995), 359.

[5] See commentary at [17.10]ff.

the Assembly as a 'religion', but upheld the Canadian restrictions on its manifestation of that religion (marijuana consumption) as a legitimate measure to protect public health or public order.

FREEDOM TO HAVE OR ADOPT A RELIGION OR BELIEF

[17.05]   *GENERAL COMMENT 22*

¶ 5. The Committee observes that the freedom to 'have or to adopt' a religion or belief necessarily entails the freedom to choose a religion or belief, including the right to replace one's current religion or belief with another or to adopt atheistic views, as well as the right to retain one's religion or belief. Article 18(2) bars coercion that would impair the right to have or adopt a religion or belief, including the use or threat of physical force or penal sanctions to compel believers or non-believers to adhere to their religious beliefs and congregations, to recant their religion or belief or to convert. Policies or practices having the same intention or effect, such as, for example, those restricting access to education, medical care, employment or the rights guaranteed by article 25 and other provisions of the Covenant, are similarly inconsistent with article 18(2). The same protection is enjoyed by holders of all beliefs of a non-religious nature.

The HRC has stressed that one has an absolute right to change one's religion in numerous Concluding Comments,[6] contrary to the policies of a number of Moslem States.[7]

PROHIBITION OF COERCION

[17.06] Article 18(2) prohibits coercion which impairs one's right to have or adopt a certain religion or belief. Membership 'as such' of a religion is an absolute right so one should suffer no detriment due to one's adherence to a certain religion. In this respect, 'coercion' in article 18(2) means physical or indirect coercion.[8] For example, in Concluding Comments on Morocco, the HRC has condemned limitations on inter-religious marriages.[9] Regarding the Republic of Ireland, the HRC condemned the requirement that the President and judges take a religious oath before assuming office.[10] Regarding Armenia, the HRC stated:[11]

---

[6] See, e.g., Concluding Comments on Jordan (1994) UN doc. CCPR/C/79/Add. 53, para. 10; Concluding Comments on the Islamic Republic of Iran (1993) UN doc. CCPR/C/79/Add. 25, para. 16; Concluding Comments on Nepal (1994) UN doc. CCPR/C/79/Add. 42, para. 11; Concluding Comments on Libyan Arab Jamahiriya (1994) UN doc. CCPR/C/79/Add. 45, para. 13; Concluding Comments on Morocco (1994) UN doc. CCPR/C/79/Add. 44, para. 14.

[7] See also [1.70].

[8] M. Nowak, *CCPR Commentary* (N.P. Engel, Kehl, 1993), 318.

[9] (1994) UN doc. CCPR/C/79/Add. 44, para. 14.

[10] (1994) UN doc. CCPR/C/79/Add. 21, para. 15.

[11] (1998) UN doc. CCPR/C/79/Add. 100.

¶ 19. The Committee is concerned that registration of religions is required and that the number of followers required for registration has been increased. The Committee also notes that non-recognized religions are discriminated against in their entitlement to own private property and receive foreign funds.

Finally, regarding Germany, the HRC condemned the fact that membership of certain sects 'as such' disqualified a person from holding certain public service positions.[12]

[17.07] Nowak argues that article 18(1) and (2) requires States to prevent private coercion of another to have or adopt a religion, belief, conscience, or opinion.[13] Nowak's contention is most likely correct, as most other ICCPR rights have been interpreted to have 'horizontal effect'.[14] However, it is interesting to speculate how far a State would be required to intrude into the private sphere to prevent such coercion. Could a State realistically prevent parents from coercing, with threats of estrangement or disinheritance, their children into adopting their parents' religion?[15]

MANIFESTING RELIGION OR BELIEF

[17.08] *GENERAL COMMENT 22*

¶ 4. The freedom to manifest religion or belief may be exercised 'either individually or in community with others and in public or private'. The freedom to manifest religion or belief in worship, observance, practice and teaching encompasses a broad range of acts. The concept of worship extends to ritual and ceremonial acts giving direct expression to belief, as well as various practices integral to such acts, including the building of places of worship, the use of ritual formulae and objects, the display of symbols, and the observance of holidays and days of rest. The observance and practice of religion or belief may include not only ceremonial acts but also such customs as the observance of dietary regulations, the wearing of distinctive clothing or headcoverings, participation in rituals associated with certain stages of life, and the use of a particular language customarily spoken by a group. In addition, the practice and teaching of religion or belief includes acts integral to the conduct by religious groups of their basic affairs, such as the freedom to choose their religious leaders, priests and teachers, the freedom to establish seminaries or religious schools and the freedom to prepare and distribute religious texts or publications.

[17.09] Manifestation of a religion may be termed the 'active' component of one's religious freedom, as opposed to the 'passive' component, which consists of mere adherence to certain beliefs.[16] 'Manifestation' of religion or belief includes worship, teaching of the particular beliefs, and observance of specified canons of conduct or religious rituals.[17] As such activities can interfere with the

---

[12] (1996) UN doc. CCPR/C/79/Add. 73, para. 16.
[13] Ibid., 314–15.
[14] See generally [1.59–1.62].
[15] See also [23.73].
[16] Nowak, above, note 6, draws this distinction at 315–19.
[17] Ibid., 320–1.

rights of others, or even pose a danger to society, the freedom to manifest religion or belief is not absolute.

Limitations on the Freedom to Manifest One's Religion or Belief

[17.10]   *GENERAL COMMENT 22*

¶ 8. Article 18(3) permits restrictions on the freedom to manifest religion or belief only if limitations are prescribed by law and are necessary to protect public safety, order, health or morals, or the fundamental rights and freedoms of others. The freedom from coercion to have or to adopt a religion or belief and the liberty of parents and guardians to ensure religious and moral education cannot be restricted. In interpreting the scope of permissible limitation clauses, States parties should proceed from the need to protect the rights guaranteed under the Covenant, including the right to equality and non-discrimination on all grounds specified in articles 2, 3 and 26. Limitations imposed must be established by law and must not be applied in a manner that would vitiate the rights guaranteed in article 18. The Committee observes that paragraph 3 of article 18 is to be strictly interpreted: restrictions are not allowed on grounds not specified there, even if they would be allowed as restrictions to other rights protected in the Covenant, such as national security. Limitations may be applied only for those purposes for which they were prescribed and must be directly related and proportionate to the specific need on which they are predicated. Restrictions may not be imposed for discriminatory purposes or applied in a discriminatory manner. . . . Persons already subject to certain legitimate constraints, such as prisoners, continue to enjoy their rights to manifest their religion or belief to the fullest extent compatible with the specific nature of the constraint. States parties' reports should provide information on the full scope and effects of limitations under article 18(3), both as a matter of law and of their application in specific circumstances.

[17.11] The freedom to manifest one's religion may be legitimately subject to certain limitations, prescribed in article 18(3). First, the limitations must be 'prescribed by law'. This means the measures must be delineated in accessible legal instruments or decisions.[18] The term has not been extensively discussed by the HRC with regard to article 18. However, HRC jurisprudence regarding the same language in the context of other ICCPR rights gives a good indication of how the term would be interpreted in the article 18 context.[19] Secondly, the limitations must be designed to achieve an enumerated purpose: namely, 'public safety, order, health or morals or the fundamental rights and freedoms of others'. Article 18 jurisprudence has clarified only some of these limitations. The HRC could again be expected to interpret the other terms similarly to the way in which those terms have been interpreted in the context of other ICCPR rights.[20] Finally,

---

[18] See, in this regard, [12.23], [16.11], and [18.17]. See also [1.51].

[19] See 'Siracusa Principles on the Limitation and Derogation Provisions in the International Covenant on Civil and Political Rights' (1985) 7 HRQ 3, which indicates that all limitation clauses in the ICCPR are to be interpreted in the same way with regard to each right.

[20] See [12.23] and [18.16] ff.

the limiting measures must be 'necessary' to achieve an enumerated purpose. This means that the law should be 'proportionate to the specific need upon which it is predicated', according to paragraph 8 of General Comment 22.

[17.12] The HRC points out, in paragraph 8 of the General Comment, the absence of 'national security' as an enumerated limitation in article 18(3). National security is listed as a permissible limiting objective to other ICCPR rights, such as freedom of expression (article 19), assembly (article 21), and association (article 22). However, many 'national security' measures could be perhaps justified as limitations designed to achieve 'public order'.

[17.13] It is unfortunate that the HRC has issued so few consensus comments on the limits to the freedom to manifest religion or belief. It would be instructive, for example, for the HRC to issue opinions on the permissibility of restrictions of such religious activities as polygamy, animal sacrifice, or the exclusion of women from the church hierarchy.[21]

PUBLIC SAFETY AND HEALTH

[17.14]   *SINGH BHINDER v CANADA (208/86)*

The author was a Sikh, so he was religiously obliged to wear a turban. On the other hand, Canadian legislation required that he, as a federal worker, wear safety headgear (a 'hard hat') at work, to protect him from injury and electric shock. The author argued the following:

¶ 3. The author claims that his right to manifest his religious beliefs under article 18, paragraph 1, of the Covenant has been restricted by virtue of the enforcement of the hard hat regulations, and that this limitation does not meet the requirements of article 18, paragraph 3. In particular, he argues that the limitation was not necessary to protect public safety, since any safety risk ensuing from his refusal to wear safety headgear was confined to himself.

The HRC nevertheless found against the author on the merits:

¶ 6.2. Whether one approaches the issue from the perspective of article 18 or article 26, in the view of the Committee the same conclusion must be reached. If the requirement that a hard hat be worn is regarded as raising issues under article 18, then it is a limitation that is justified by reference to the grounds laid down in article 18, paragraph 3. If the requirement that a hard hat be worn is seen as a discrimination *de facto* against persons of the Sikh religion under article 26, then, applying criteria now well established in the jurisprudence of the Committee, the legislation requiring that workers in federal employment be protected from injury and electric shock by the wearing of hard hats is to be regarded as reasonable and directed towards objective purposes that are compatible with the Covenant.[22]

---

[21] See Dickson, above, note 2, 356. The HRC has indicated that the practice of polygamy breaches the Covenant: see [20.28].

[22] Art. 26 prohibits discrimination on the basis of, *inter alia*, religion. See generally, Chap. 23, and specifically, [23.33].

It is a shame that the HRC did not spell out exactly how the limitation conformed to article 18(3). Though the hard hat measure arguably protected Singh's *personal* health and safety, the Committee did not address how his non-compliance with the measure could threaten *public* safety and health. Perhaps the measure was understood as a public order measure, designed to minimize workers' compensation claims. Nevertheless, the HRC's article 18 reasoning was unconvincing, and it is arguable that the laws were not in fact proportionate to an enumerated end.[23]

PUBLIC ORDER

[17.15]   *COERIEL AND AURIK V THE NETHERLANDS (453/91)*

The authors had adopted the Hindu religion, and were studying to become Hindu priests in India. They requested the Dutch Minister of Justice to permit them to change their names, as it was compulsory to do so in order to become Hindu priests. The Minister refused, on the ground that their cases did not meet the requirements of Dutch laws regulating the change of surname.

¶ 3. The authors claim that the refusal of the Dutch authorities to have their current surnames changed prevents them from furthering their studies for the Hindu priesthood and therefore violates article 18 of the Covenant. They also claim that said refusal constitutes unlawful or arbitrary interference with their privacy.

Although the HRC majority found in favour of the authors regarding their article 17 privacy rights, it rejected the claim brought under article 18:[24]

¶ 6.1. During its 48th session, the Committee considered the admissibility of the communication. With regard to the authors' claim under article 18 of the Covenant, the Committee considered that the regulation of surnames and the change thereof was eminently a matter of public order and restrictions were therefore permissible under paragraph 3 of article 18. The Committee, moreover, considered that the State party could not be held accountable for restrictions placed upon the exercise of religious offices by religious leaders in another country. This aspect of the communication was therefore declared inadmissible.

The HRC's view that State restrictions on one's ability to change a surname were permissible for public order reasons is perhaps reasonable, as frequent surname changes could cause administrative confusion. However, the HRC's article 18 decision seemed more influenced by the fact that the relevant religious rules were imposed by religious leaders outside the country.[25] Such a principle seriously

---

[23] Note that the Canadian Human Rights Tribunal had found that the measures failed reasonably to accommodate Sikhs (see paras. 2.8–2.10). The Tribunal's decision was however overruled by the Canadian Supreme Court in *Bhinder v Canadian National Railway Co.* [1985] 2 SCR 561. See also B.G. Tahzib, *Freedom of Religion or Belief* (Martinus Nijhoff, The Hague, 1996), at 296–7 on the *Singh Bhinder* decision.

[24] See, on the 'privacy' aspect of this case, [16.03–16.05] and [16.16–16.17].

[25] Indeed, this may have been the true reason behind the art. 18 decision, given that the same restrictions were found to be 'arbitrary' interferences with privacy contrary to article 17, despite public order arguments, and therefore breaches of art. 17: ibid.

limits the effectiveness of article 18, as religious requirements are often promulgated from outside a State.[26] For example, Catholic canons of conduct are prescribed by religious authorities in the Vatican. It cannot be that restrictions on Catholic rituals by a State other than the Vatican could be justified simply because the relevant religious rules are imposed by Vatican leaders. It is hoped that this *Coeriel* principle is not followed in the future.

PUBLIC MORALS

[17.16]   *GENERAL COMMENT 22*

¶ 8. . . . The Committee observes that the concept of morals derives from many social, philosophical and religious traditions; consequently, limitations on the freedom to manifest a religion or belief for the purpose of protecting morals must be based on principles not deriving exclusively from a single tradition. . . .

Therefore, 'public morals' measures should reflect a pluralistic view of society, rather than a single religious culture.[27]

Establishment of a Religion

[17.17]   *GENERAL COMMENT 22*

¶ 9. The fact that a religion is recognized as a state religion or that it is established as official or traditional or that its followers comprise the majority of the population, shall not result in any impairment of the enjoyment of any of the rights under the Covenant, including articles 18 and 27, nor in any discrimination against adherents to other religions or non-believers. In particular, certain measures discriminating against the latter, such as measures restricting eligibility for government service to members of the predominant religion or giving economic privileges to them or imposing special restrictions on the practice of other faiths, are not in accordance with the prohibition of discrimination based on religion or belief and the guarantee of equal protection under article 26. The measures contemplated by article 20, paragraph 2 of the Covenant constitute important safeguards against infringement of the rights of religious minorities and of other religious groups to exercise the rights guaranteed by articles 18 and 27, and against acts of violence or persecution directed towards those groups. The Committee wishes to be informed of measures taken by States parties concerned to protect the practices of all religions or beliefs from infringement and to protect their followers from discrimination. Similarly, information as to respect for the rights of religious minorities under article 27 is necessary for the Committee to assess the extent to which the right to freedom of thought, conscience, religion and belief has been implemented by States parties. States parties concerned should

---

[26] F. Martin *et al.*, *International Human Rights Law and Practice* (Kluwer Law International, The Hague, 1997), 153.
[27] See *Toonen v Australia* (488/92) [16.36–16.38]. See also, however, *Delgado Páez v Colombia* (195/85), discussed at [18.24].

also include in their reports information relating to practices considered by their laws and jurisprudence to be punishable as blasphemous.[28]

¶ 10. If a set of beliefs is treated as official ideology in constitutions, statutes, proclamations of ruling parties, etc., or in actual practice, this shall not result in any impairment of the freedoms under article 18 or any other rights recognized under the Covenant nor in any discrimination against persons who do not accept the official ideology or who oppose it.

[17.18] Thus, the official 'establishment' of a State religion is compatible with article 18, so long as it does not lead to discrimination against those who have not adopted that religion.[29] In Concluding Comments on Chile, the HRC stated:[30]

¶ 24. The special status granted in public law to Roman Catholic and Orthodox churches involves discrimination between persons on account of their religion and may impede their freedom of religion. Therefore: the State party should amend the law so as to give equal status to all religious communities that exist in Chile.

In Concluding Comments on Israel, the HRC stated:[31]

¶28. The Committee is concerned at the preference given to the Jewish religion in the allocation of funding for religious bodies, to the detriment of Muslims, Christians, Druze and other religious groups. The Committee recommends that regulations and criteria for funding be published and applied to all religious groups on an equal basis.

Right of Conscientious Objection

[17.19] Numerous early cases indicated that article 18 does not guarantee a right of conscientious objection, as in a right to freedom from compulsory military service on the basis of one's conscientious objection to military force.

L.T.K. v FINLAND (185/84)

¶ 1. The author of the communication (undated), received on 18 October 1984, is L. T. K., a Finnish citizen residing in Finland. He claims to be a victim of a breach by Finland of articles 18 and 19 of the International Covenant on Civil and Political Rights, stating that his status as conscientious objector to military service has not been recognized in Finland and that he has been criminally prosecuted because of his refusal to perform military service.

The HRC found the complaint inadmissible in the following terms:

¶ 5.2. The Human Rights Committee observes in this connection that, according to the author's own account he was not prosecuted and sentenced because of his beliefs or opinions as such, but because he refused to perform military service. The Covenant does not

---

[28] See also [18.25].
[30] (1999) UN doc. CCPR/C/79/Add. 104.

[29] See also Nowak, above, note 6, 317.
[31] (1999) UN doc. CCPR/C/79/Add.93.

provide for the right to conscientious objection; neither article 18 nor article 19 of the Covenant, especially taking into account paragraph 3(c)(ii) of article 8, can be construed as implying that right.[32] The author does not claim that there were any procedural defects in the judicial proceedings against him, which themselves could have constituted a violation of any of the provisions of the Covenant, or that he was sentenced contrary to law.

¶ 6. The Human Rights Committee, after careful examination of the communication, concludes that the facts which have been submitted by the author in substantiation of his claim do not raise an issue under any of the provisions of the International Covenant on Civil and Political Rights. Accordingly, the claim is incompatible with the provisions of the Covenant.

¶ 7. The Human Rights Committee therefore decides: The communication is inadmissible.

[17.20]   *GENERAL COMMENT 22*

¶ 11. Many individuals have claimed the right to refuse to perform military service (conscientious objection) on the basis that such right derives from their freedoms under article 18. In response to such claims, a growing number of States have in their laws exempted from compulsory military service citizens who genuinely hold religious or other beliefs that forbid the performance of military service and replaced it with alternative national service. The Covenant does not explicitly refer to a right to conscientious objection, but the Committee believes that such a right can be derived from article 18, inasmuch as the obligation to use lethal force may seriously conflict with the freedom of conscience and the right to manifest one's religion or belief. When this right is recognized by law or practice, there shall be no differentiation among conscientious objectors on the basis of the nature of their particular beliefs;[33] likewise, there shall be no discrimination against conscientious objectors because they have failed to perform military service. The Committee invites States parties to report on the conditions under which persons can be exempted from military service on the basis of their rights under article 18 and on the nature and length of alternative national service.

Thus, it may be that the HRC would now overrule the early *L.T.K.* case.

[17.21] Indeed, in recent Concluding Comments, the HRC has also evinced a more sympathetic attitude to conscientious objectors. It has condemned the 'excessive period of alternative service', compared to military service, in Cyprus.[34] Regarding Libya and the Russian Federation, the HRC criticized the

---

[32] Art. 8(3)(a) prohibits forced or compulsory labour. However, art. 8(3)(c)(ii) states that para. (a) does not preclude compulsory military service or alternative service 'in countries where conscientious objection is recognized'. See generally [10.03].

[33] In this respect, see the decision in *Brinkhof v Netherlands* (402/90), where the relevant law favoured Jehovah's Witnesses over other conscientious objectors, in exempting only them from the duty to perform national service. The HRC however ultimately found that the author was not a relevant 'victim' of any discrimination.

[34] (1994) UN doc. CCPR/C/79/Add. 39, para. 10; see also Concluding Comments on Slovakia (1997) UN doc. CCPR/C/79/Add. 79, para. 12.

lack of any provision for conscientious objectors to military service.[35] In Concluding Comments on Spain, the HRC gave a clear indication that it had in fact changed its position regarding a 'right' of conscientious objection upon adoption of the General Comment:[36]

¶ 15. Finally, the Committee is greatly concerned to hear that individuals cannot claim the status of conscientious objectors once they have entered the armed forces, since that does not seem to be consistent with the requirements of article 18 of the Covenant as pointed out in General Comment No. 22. . . .

[17.22] In *Westerman v Netherlands* (682/96), the HRC found a complaint regarding the enforced military service of the author against his conscience to be admissible. The majority ultimately found in favour of the State party as the author had failed to demonstrate that he had an 'insurmountable objection of conscience to military service'.[37] Nevertheless, the admissibility decision seems to confirm that denial of conscientious objector status to a true 'objector' would breach article 18. A minority of six HRC members found that the author had demonstrated his conscientious opposition to military service, and hence found a breach of article 18 entailed in his enforced service in the French military, and his consequent punishment for failure to follow orders.

[17.23] Conscientious objection arises in forms other than refusal to perform compulsory military service. Note the following comment regarding Zambia:[38]

¶ 18. The requirement to sing the national anthem and salute the flag as a condition of attending a State school, despite conscientious objection, appear to be an unreasonable requirement and to be incompatible with articles 18 and 24 of the Covenant. [39]

[17.24]   *J.P. v CANADA (446/91)*

¶ 2.1. The author is a member of the Society of Friends (Quakers). Because of her religious convictions, she has refused to participate in any way in Canada's military efforts. Accordingly, she has refused to pay a certain percentage of her assessed taxes, equal to the amount of the Canadian federal budget earmarked for military appropriations. Taxes thus withheld have instead been deposited with the Peace Tax Fund of Conscience Canada, Inc., a non-governmental organization.

The author claimed that the enforced payment of the withheld tax would breach her freedom of conscience under article 18. The HRC disagreed, and stated the following in finding the case inadmissible:

---

[35] Concluding Comments on Libyan Arab Jamahiriya (1994) U.N. Doc. CCPR/C/79/Add.45, para. 13; Concluding Comments on Russian Federation (1995) UN doc. CCPR/C/79/Add. 54, para. 21.

[36] (1996) UN doc. CCPR/C/79/Add. 61; see also Concluding Comments on Belarus (1997) UN doc. CCPR/C/79/Add. 86, para. 16; Concluding Comments on Mexico (1999) UN doc. CCPR/C/79/Add. 109, para. 20; and Concluding Comments on Romania (1999) UN doc. CCPR/C/79/Add. 111, para. 17.   [37] Para. 9.5.

[38] (1996) U.N. Doc. CCPR/C/79/Add. 62.

[39] Art. 24 protects the rights of the child: see generally Chap. 21.

¶ 4.2. . . . Although article 18 of the Covenant certainly protects the right to hold, express and disseminate opinions and convictions, including conscientious objection to military activities and expenditures, the refusal to pay taxes on grounds of conscientious objection clearly falls outside the scope of protection of this article.

The *J.P.* decision has been upheld in *J.v.K. and C.M.G.v.K.-S. v The Netherlands* (483/91)[40] and *K.V. and C.V. v Germany* (560/93).[41]

Rights regarding Religious and Moral Education—Article 18(4)

[17.25] *GENERAL COMMENT 22*

6. The Committee is of the view that article 18(4) permits public school instruction in subjects such as the general history of religions and ethics if it is given in a neutral and objective way. The liberty of parents or legal guardians to ensure that their children receive a religious and moral education in conformity with their own convictions, set forth in article 18(4), is related to the guarantees of the freedom to teach a religion or belief stated in article 18(1). The Committee notes that public education that includes instruction in a particular religion or belief is inconsistent with article 18(4) unless provision is made for non-discriminatory exemptions or alternatives that would accommodate the wishes of parents and guardians.

[17.26] *HARTIKAINEN et al. v FINLAND (40/78)*

The facts are evident from the following excerpts:

¶ 2.1. The author claims that the School System Act of 26 July 1968, paragraph 6, of Finland is in violation of article 18 (4) of the Covenant inasmuch as it stipulates obligatory attendance in Finnish schools, by children whose parents are atheists, in classes on the history of religion and ethics. He alleges that since the textbooks on the basis of which the classes have been taught were written by Christians the teaching has unavoidably been religious in nature.

Finland defended its laws in the following terms:

¶ 7.2. Having regard to the relevant legislation, the State party submits that it can be stated that religious education is not compulsory in Finland. It adds that there is, however, the possibility that students, who by virtue of the Religious Freedom Act have been exempted from religious instruction, may receive instruction in the study of the history of religions and ethics; such instruction is designed to give the students knowledge of a general nature deemed to be useful as part of their basic education in a society in which the over-whelming majority of the population belongs to a religious denomination. The State party claims that the directives issued by the National Board of Education concerning the principal aims

---

[40] Para. 4.2.
[41] Para. 4.3. These decisions have been criticized for their lack of analysis by Tahzib, above, note 23, at 287–92.

of the instruction to be given show that the instruction is not religious in character. However, the State party explains that there have in some cases been difficulties in the practical application of the teaching plan relating to this study and that in January 1979 the National Board of Education established a working group consisting of members representing both religious and non-religious views to look into these problems and to review the curriculum.

The HRC found that there had been no violation of article 18(4):

¶ 10.4. The Committee does not consider that the requirement of the relevant provisions of Finnish legislation that instruction in the study of the history of religions and ethics should be given instead of religious instruction to students in schools whose parents or legal guardians object to religious instruction is in itself incompatible with article 18 (4), if such alternative course of instruction is given in a neutral and objective way and respects the convictions of parents and guardians who do not believe in any religion. In any event, paragraph 6 of the School System Act expressly permits any parents or guardians who do not wish their children to be given either religious instruction or instruction in the study of the history of religions and ethics to obtain exemption therefrom by arranging for them to receive comparable instruction outside of school.

¶ 10.5. The State party admits that difficulties have arisen in regard to the existing teaching plan to give effect to these provisions, (which teaching plan does appear, in part at least, to be religious in character), but the Committee believes that appropriate action is being taken to resolve the difficulties and it sees no reason to conclude that this cannot be accomplished, compatibly with the requirements of article 18 (4) of the Covenant, within the framework of the existing laws.

Therefore, compulsory religious or moral education does not conflict with article 18(4) if it provides for a pluralistic depiction of religion.[42]

[17.27] In *Delgado Páez v Colombia* (195/85), the HRC stated the following:

¶ 5.7. . . . Colombia may, without violating [article 18], allow the Church authorities to decide who may teach religion and in which manner it should be taught.

Presumably, article 18(4) would have permitted parents to withdraw their children from Colombian religious education. Nevertheless, the *Delgado Páez* statement seems to contradict the following statement regarding Costa Rica:[43]

¶ 13. The Committee recommends that the State party take steps to ensure that there is no discrimination in the exercise of the right to religious education, particularly with respect to access to religious teachings other than Catholicism. Current practices which make the selection of religious instructors subject to the authorization of the National Episcopal Conference are not in conformity with the Covenant.

[17.28] In Concluding Comments on Norway, the HRC stated the following:[44]

---

[42] Nowak, above, note 6, 333.
[43] Concluding Comments on Costa Rica (1994) U.N. Doc. CCPR/C/79/Add.31.
[44] (1993) UN doc. CCPR/C/79/Add. 27. These criticisms were repeated in the next set of Concluding Comments on Norway, at (1999) UN doc. CCPR/C/79/Add. 1112, para. 13.

¶ 10. The Committee emphasizes that article 2 of the Constitution which provides that individuals professing the Evangelical-Lutheran religion are bound to bring up their children in the same faith is in clear contradiction with article 18 of the Covenant.

The Norwegian comment seems to target laws that restricted the educational options of Evangelical Lutheran parents regarding their children. However, the Comment may also be addressing the religious rights of the children of Evangelical Lutherans. Indeed, the HRC has never explained where the article 18(4) rights of parents may end, and the article 18(1) rights of children begin, in case of conflict between such rights.[45]

[17.29] *Waldman v Canada* (694/96) concerned a complaint about preferential funding given to Roman Catholic schools compared to schools for other minority religions in Canada. The HRC chose to dispose of the case exclusively under article 26.[46]

Conclusion

[17.30] The HRC has not issued much consensus jurisprudence on the rights in article 18. Its most comprehensive statement on the topic is in General Comment 22. The General Comment manifests a more vigorous approach to protection of one's religion and belief than has been displayed in the relevant Optional Protocol cases, which have evinced a relatively conservative approach by the HRC.

Postscript: Please note that General Comment 28 on 'Equality of Rights Between Men and Women', contained in the Addendum at page 634, contains extra information on some of the material in this chapter.

---

[45] See G. Van Beuren, 'The International Protection of Family Members' Rights as the 21st Century Approaches', (1995) 17 *HRQ* 732,743–7. Nowak, above, note 6, recognizes the potential for a conflict of the religious rights of parents and children at 318. See also Tahzib, above, note 23, 364 and [17.07].
[46] See [23.54].

18

Freedom of Expression—Articles 19, 20

Article 19

1. Everyone shall have the right to hold opinions without interference.

2. Everyone shall have the right to freedom of expression; this right shall include freedom to seek, receive and impart information and ideas of all kinds, regardless of frontiers, either orally, in writing or in print, in the form of art, or through any other media of his choice.

3. The exercise of the rights provided for in paragraph 2 of this article carries with it special duties and responsibilities. It may therefore be subject to certain restrictions, but these shall only be such as are provided by law and are necessary:

   (a) For respect of the rights or reputations of others;

   (b) For the protection of national security or of public order (*ordre public*), or of public health or morals.

[18.01] Freedom of expression permits people to impart and receive ideas and information. It is a most important right for ensuring individual self-fulfilment, as well as a pluralistic, tolerant society with access to multitudes of ideas and philosophies. However, in article 19(3), it is expressly recognized that rights of free expression can be abused so as to undermine the rights of others: 'exercise of the right . . . carries with it special duties and responsibilities'. Article 19 rights may accordingly be restricted for a number of reasons. Indeed, the ICCPR provides for a compulsory restriction on a certain type of expression, namely hate speech, in article 20.[1]

---

[1] See [18.41] ff.

FREEDOM OF 'OPINION'

[18.02] *GENERAL COMMENT 10*

¶ 1. Paragraph 1 requires protection of the 'right to hold opinions without interference'. This is a right to which the Covenant permits no exception or restriction.

The holding of an opinion is passive conduct, and is an absolute freedom. The absolute nature of the right ceases once one airs or otherwise manifests one's opinions.[2] That activity is in the realm of 'freedom of expression'. However, Nowak states that it may be difficult to delineate between activity which impermissibly interferes with freedom of opinion (such as brainwashing), and activity which merely seeks to influence opinion (a possible example being bombardment by mass media propaganda).[3] Infringements may be limited to instances where one's opinion is somehow involuntarily influenced.[4]

MEANING OF 'FREEDOM OF EXPRESSION'

[18.03] *GENERAL COMMENT 10*

¶ 2. Paragraph 2 requires protection of the right to freedom of expression, which includes not only freedom to 'impart information and ideas of all kinds', but also freedom to 'seek' and 'receive' them 'regardless of frontiers' and in whatever medium, 'either orally, in writing or in print, in the form of art, or through any other media of his choice'. . . .

[18.04] Numerous cases have confirmed that protected expression includes political expression, including *Mpandanjila et al. v Zaire* (138/83), *Kalenga v Zambia* (326/88), *Jaona v Madagascar* (132/82), *Kivenmaa v Finland* (412/90) [18.06], and *Aduayom et al. v Togo* (422–424/90).[5]

[18.05] *BALLANTYNE et al. v CANADA (359, 385/89)*

This case concerned a challenge to Canadian (Quebec) laws which restricted commercial advertising in a language other than French.

¶ 11.3. Under article 19 of the Covenant, everyone shall have the right to freedom of expression; this right may be subjected to restrictions, conditions for which are set out in article 19, paragraph 3. The Government of Quebec has asserted that commercial activity such as outdoor advertising does not fall within the ambit of article 19. The Committee does not share this opinion. Article 19, paragraph 2, must be interpreted as encompassing every form of subjective ideas and opinions capable of transmission to others, which are

---

[2] See D. McGoldrick, *The Human Rights Committee* (Clarendon Press, Oxford, 1994), 460, quoting former HRC Chairman Andreas Mavrommatis.

[3] M. Nowak, *CCPR Commentary* (N.P. Engel, Kehl, 1993), 340.   [4] Ibid.

[5] *Aduayom* is discussed at [22.46]. See also cases cited at [18.31–18.34].

compatible with article 20 of the Covenant, of news and information, of commercial expression and advertising, of works of art, etc.; it should not be confined to means of political, cultural or artistic expression. In the Committee's opinion, the commercial element in an expression taking the form of outdoor advertising cannot have the effect of removing this expression from the scope of protected freedom. The Committee does not agree either that any of the above forms of expression can be subjected to varying degrees of limitation, with the result that some forms of expression may suffer broader restrictions than others.

[18.06]   *KIVENMAA v FINLAND (412/90)*

The author complained of her arrest for distributing leaflets and unfurling a banner which criticized the human rights record of a visiting head of state. Both actions occurred at a demonstration. The argument in the case centred on potential breaches of article 21, which guarantees freedom of assembly. Finland had submitted the following argument against a finding of an article 19 violation.

¶ 7.4. . . . the State party argues that a demonstration necessarily entails the expression of an opinion, but, by its specific character, is to be regarded as an exercise of the right of peaceful assembly. In this connection, the State party argues that article 21 of the Covenant must be seen as *lex specialis* in relation to article 19 and that therefore the expression of an opinion in the context of a demonstration must be considered under article 21, and not under article 19 of the Covenant.

The HRC majority found breaches of articles 19 and 21 in this case.[6] It thus confirmed that non-verbal expression is protected under article 19. On article 19, it stated:

¶ 9.3. The right for an individual to express his political opinions, including obviously his opinions on the question of human rights, forms part of the freedom of expression guaranteed by article 19 of the Covenant. In this particular case, the author of the communication exercised this right by raising a banner. It is true that article 19 authorizes the restriction by the law of freedom of expression in certain circumstances. However, in this specific case, the State party has not referred to a law allowing this freedom to be restricted or established how the restriction applied to Ms. Kivenmaa was necessary to safeguard the rights and national imperatives set forth in article 19, paragraph 2(a) and (b) of the Covenant.

Indeed, the State party was perfectly correct in earlier stating:

¶ 7.2. . . . the right to freedom of expression does not depend on the mode of expression or on the contents of the message thus expressed.

[18.07] The majority opinion in *Kivenmaa* indicates that restrictions on freedom of expression will raise independent issues under article 19, even if those restrictions

---

[6] See, on the art. 21 aspect of this case, [19.06].

necessarily raise issues under other ICCPR articles.[7] In this respect, see also *M.A. v Italy* (117/81) where M.A.'s political party was banned. This restricted his rights to freedom of expression, and also his rights of freedom of association under article 22, and right to political participation under article 25.[8]

[18.08] Rights of access to information, in the form of rights to seek and receive information, are also protected by article 19.[9] A breach of such a right was found in *Gauthier v Canada* [18.27].

[18.09] Article 19 does not go so far as to give one a right to address a court in the language of one's choice (*Guesdon v France* (219/86) if one can speak the official court language.[10] Such a right would essentially impose positive linguistic criteria upon the State in the exercise of its public functions.[11]

[18.10] In *S.G. v France* (347/88) and *G.B. v France* (348/89), the complainants were arrested for defacing roadsigns as part of an ongoing protest about the inferior status of the Breton language in France. In both cases the HRC found that 'the defacing of road signs does not raise any issues under article 19'.[12] Could graffiti ever be protected under article 19?

Freedom of the Press

[18.11] The HRC went on in the General Comment to highlight one of the most important aspects of any meaningful right to freedom of expression:

GENERAL COMMENT 10

¶ 2. . . . because of the development of modern mass media, effective measures are necessary to prevent such control of the media as would interfere with the right of everyone to freedom of expression in a way that is not provided for in paragraph 3.

[18.12] Regarding Lebanon, the HRC has stated:[13]

¶ 24. The Committee notes with concern that a number of provisions of the Media Law No. 382 of November 1994 and Decree No. 7997 of February 1996, on the basis of which the licensing of television and radio stations has been restricted to 3 and 11 stations,

---

[7] Mr Herndl dissented, finding that rights of freedom of assembly under art. 21 were *lex specialis* rights, which were not subsumed by the general art. 19 right of free expression.

[8] M.A.'s complaint was not successful: see [18.29].

[9] See generally G. Malinverni, 'Freedom of Information in the European Convention on Human Rights and in the International Covenant on Civil and Political Rights' (1983) 4 *HRLJ* 443.

[10] Para. 7.2; see also *Cadoret and Le Bihan v France* (221/87, 323/88), para. 5.2. Art. 14(3)(f) provides a right to the assistance of an interpreter if one 'cannot understand or speak the language used in court'. See [14.101–14.102].

[11] See F. De Varennes, 'Language and Freedom of Expression' (1994) 16 *HRQ* 163, 179. Such a duty may arise with regard to minority languages under art. 27: see [24.32–24.33].

[12] See *S.G. v France* at para. 5.2, and *G.B. v France* at para. 5.1.

[13] (1998) UN doc. CCPR/C/79/Add.78.

respectively, do not appear to be consistent with the guarantees enshrined in article 19 of the Covenant, as there are no reasonable and objective criteria for the award of licences. The licensing process has had the effect of restricting media pluralism and freedom of expression. In this context, the Committee also observes that the limitations placed on two different categories of radio and television stations—those that can broadcast news and political programmes and those which cannot—is unjustifiable under article 19.

¶ 25. The Committee therefore recommends that the State party review and amend the Media Law of November 1994, as well as its implementing decree, with a view to bringing it into conformity with article 19 of the Covenant. It recommends that the State party establish an independent broadcasting licensing authority, with the power to examine broadcasting applications and to grant licences in accordance with reasonable and objective criteria.

Regarding Lesotho, the HRC has stated:[14]

¶ 23. The Committee is concerned that the relevant authority under the Printing and Publishing Act has unfettered discretionary power to grant or refuse registration to a newspaper, in contravention of article 19 of the Covenant. The Committee recommends to the State party to provide for guidelines for the exercise of discretion and procedures for effective review of the validity of the grounds for refusal of registration and to bring its legislation into conformity with article 19 of the Covenant.

[18.13] In further comments on Lesotho, the HRC added:[15]

¶ 22. The Committee is seriously concerned about reports of harassment of and repeated libel suits against journalists who criticize the Government of Lesotho. The Committee is also gravely concerned about reports . . . that newspapers which adopt a negative attitude against the Government are refused advertisement by the State and parastatal companies, and that journalists working for the State who are seen at opposition demonstrations are required to submit their resignations. The Committee urges the State party to respect freedom of the press and desist from taking any action which would violate freedom of the press.

The HRC's reference to State and parastatal advertising in the Lesotho comment is interesting, as it highlights that freedom of expression can be diluted in more subtle ways than outright prohibition. For example, one can be denied opportunities to benefit from State contracts, such as advertising contracts, as a punishment for exercising freedom of expression. The Lesotho Comment confirms that one should not suffer any consequences from the State for exercising freedom of expression.

[18.14] Most of the HRC's express concerns over freedom of the press have related to overbearing government controls of the media.[16] In Concluding

---

[14] (1999) UN doc. CCPR/C/79/Add. 106.   [15] Ibid.
[16] See also Concluding Comments on Sri Lanka (1996) UN doc. CCPR/C/79/Add.56, para. 22; Concluding Comments on Armenia (1998) UN doc. CCPR/C/79/Add. 100, para. 21; Concluding Comments on Zimbabwe (1998) UN doc. CCPR/C/79/Add. 89, para. 22.

Comments on Italy, the HRC has also noted the threat to free expression posed by the concentration of media ownership in private media conglomerates:[17]

¶ 10. The Committee is concerned about the excessive concentration of the mass media in a small group of people. Furthermore, it notes that such concentration may affect the enjoyment of the right to freedom of expression and information under article 19 of the Covenant.

¶ 17. In order to avoid the inherent risks in the excessive concentration of control of the mass information media in a small group of people, the Committee emphasizes the importance of implementing measures to ensure impartial allocation of resources as well as equitable access to such media, and of adopting anti-trust legislation regulating mass media.

[18.15] Freedom of information is an important aspect of the rights of freedom of the press. The media is quite impotent if it has no 'right to know'. This aspect of press freedom has been addressed in *Gauthier v France* [18.27].

PERMISSIBLE LIMITATIONS TO FREE EXPRESSION

[18.16]   *GENERAL COMMENT 10*

¶ 4. Paragraph 3 expressly stresses that the exercise of the right to freedom of expression carries with it special duties and responsibilities and for this reason certain restrictions on the right are permitted which may relate either to the interests of other persons or to those of the community as a whole. However, when a State party imposes certain restrictions on the exercise of freedom of expression, these may not put in jeopardy the right itself. Paragraph 3 lays down conditions and it is only subject to these conditions that restrictions may be imposed: the restrictions must be 'provided by law'; they may only be imposed for one of the purposes set out in subparagraphs (a) and (b) of paragraph 3; and they must be justified as being 'necessary' for that State party for one of those purposes.

Article 19(3) permits freedom of expression to be limited by measures provided by law, and proportionately designed to protect (a) the rights or reputations of others, and/or (b) national security, public order (*ordre public*), public health or morals.

[18.17] The HRC has not so far expanded on the requirement that article 19 restrictions be 'provided by law'. Presumably this requirement would be interpreted as it has been in the context of other ICCPR guarantees, i.e. that the limitation must be sufficiently delineated in a State's law.[18] The HRC has confirmed that a relevant law can include a statutory law, the law as interpreted by the municipal judiciary,[19] and may include the law of parliamentary privilege.[20]

---

[17] (1995) UN doc. CCPR/C/79/Add.37.

[18] In particular, see *Pinkney v Canada* (27/78) re art. 17 [16.11] and [1.51].

[19] See [18.52] and preceding paras.

[20] See *Gauthier v Canada* (633/95), para. 13.5 [18.27], where the HRC stated that the restriction was 'arguably' prescribed by law.

[18.18] In a separate opinion in *Faurisson v France* (550/93), Mrs Evatt, Mrs Quiroga Medina, and Mr Klein, confirmed that the word 'necessary' imports 'an element of proportionality' into article 19(3): the law must be appropriate and adapted to achieving one of the enumerated ends.[21] In the same case, Mr Lallah issued the following warning couched in enigmatic terms:

¶ 13. Recourse to restrictions that are, in principle, permissible under article 19, paragraph 3, bristles with difficulties, tending to destroy the very existence of the right sought to be restricted. The right to freedom of opinion and expression is a most valuable right and may turn out to be too fragile for survival in the face of the too frequently professed necessity for its restriction in the wide range of areas envisaged under paragraphs (a) and (b) of article 19, paragraph 3.

Lallah is alluding to the fact that most laws which limit freedom of expression are passed in order to achieve one of the express permitted limitations. The limitations would thus destroy the right unless tightly constrained by a principle of proportionality.

[18.19] No article 19 cases have addressed the limitation of 'public health'. Presumably this limitation will be interpreted in conformity with its interpretation regarding other ICCPR rights.[22] Nowak suggests that the prohibition of misinformation about health-threatening activities, and restrictions on the advertising of dangerous substances such as tobacco are probably justified under this limitation.[23]

Public Morals

[18.20]   *HERTZBERG et al. v FINLAND (61/79)*

¶ 1. The authors of this communication . . . are five individuals, who are represented by a Finnish organization, SETA (Organization for Sexual Equality).

¶ 2.1. The facts of the five cases are essentially undisputed. The parties only disagree as to their evaluation. According to the contentions of the authors of the communication, Finnish authorities, including organs of the State-controlled Finnish Broadcasting Company (FBC), have interfered with their right of freedom of expression and information, as laid down in article 19 of the Covenant, by . . . censoring . . . radio and TV programmes dealing with homosexuality. At the heart of the dispute is paragraph 9 of chapter 20 of the Finnish Penal Code which sets forth the following:

(1) If someone publicly engages in an act violating sexual morality, thereby giving offence, he shall be sentenced for publicly violating sexual morality to imprisonment for at most six months or to a fine.

---

[21] Para. 8: see [18.49].

[22] See 'Siracusa Principles on the Limitation and Derogation Provisions in the International Covenant on Civil and Political Rights' (1985) 7 HRQ 3, which indicates that all limitation clauses in the ICCPR are to be interpreted in the same way with regard to each right. See [17.14] for a case on 'public health'.   [23] Nowak, above, note 3, 358.

(2) Anyone who publicly encourages indecent behaviour between persons of the same sex shall be sentenced for encouragement to indecent behaviour between members of the same sex as decreed in subsection 1.

The authors complained about a decision by broadcasters to censor their material (a radio programme and a TV series) on the basis that full transmission of the material would have breached paragraph 20(9)(2) of the Finnish Penal Code.

The State Party justified the law thus:

¶ 6.1. [Finland] stresses that the purpose of the prohibition of public encouragement to indecent behaviour between members of the same sex is to reflect the prevailing moral conceptions in Finland as interpreted by the Parliament and by large groups of the population. It further contends that the word 'encouragement' is to be interpreted in the narrow sense. Moreover, the Legislative Committee of the Parliament expressly provided that the law shall not hinder the presentation of factual material on homosexuality.

The HRC found in favour of the State Party:

¶ 10.2. With regard to the two censored programmes of Mrs. Nikula and of Marko and Tuovi Putkonen, the Committee accepts the contention of the authors that their rights under article 19(2) of the Covenant have been restricted. While not every individual can be deemed to hold a right to express himself through a medium like TV, whose available time is limited, the situation may be different when a programme has been produced for transmission within the framework of a broadcasting organization with the general approval of the responsible authorities. On the other hand, article 19(3) permits certain restrictions on the exercise of the rights protected by article 19(2), as are provided by law and are necessary for the protection of public order or of public health or morals. In the context of the present communication, the Finnish Government has specifically invoked public morals as justifying the actions complained of. The Committee has considered whether, in order to assess the necessity of those actions, it should invite the parties to submit the full text of the censored programmes. In fact, only on the basis of these texts could it be possible to determine whether the censored programmes were mainly or exclusively made up of factual information about issues related to homosexuality.

¶ 10.3. The Committee feels, however, that the information before it is sufficient to formulate its views on the communication. It has to be noted, first, that public morals differ widely. There is no universally applicable common standard. Consequently, in this respect, a certain margin of discretion must be accorded to the responsible national authorities.

¶ 10.4. The Committee finds that it cannot question the decision of the responsible organs of the Finnish Broadcasting Corporation that radio and TV are not the appropriate forums to discuss issues related to homosexuality, as far as a programme could be judged as encouraging homosexual behaviour. According to article 19(3), the exercise of the rights provided for in article 19(2) carries with it special duties and responsibilities for those organs. As far as radio and TV programmes are concerned, the audience cannot be controlled. In particular, harmful effects on minors cannot be excluded.

¶ 11. Accordingly, the Human Rights Committee is of the view that there has been no violation of the rights of the authors of the communication under article 19(2) of the Covenant.

[18.21] This is the only case in which the HRC has stated that States Parties to the ICCPR have a 'margin of discretion'. This 'margin' seemed to mirror the 'margin of appreciation' conferred on States Parties to the European Convention on Human Rights ('ECHR'). The margin of appreciation is akin to a benefit of the doubt given to the State, or an area in which the European Court will relax its scrutiny of the compatibility of an impugned practice with the ECHR provisions.[24] The European Court of Human Rights has confirmed that States Parties have a wide margin of appreciation when imposing limits on freedom of expression for the purpose of protecting public morals.[25]

The HRC has never disposed of any other OP case by reference to a State Party's 'margin of discretion'. Indeed, its applicability has recently been rejected in relation to other ICCPR rights.[26] Such a doctrine dilutes human rights protection. Furthermore, it may be noted that the doctrine is often applied under the ECHR when no common practice regarding the specific right at issue can be discerned throughout the States Parties to the ECHR. It is unwise to apply such a doctrine under the ICCPR, where a common practice would rarely be discerned among the very different States Parties to this universal treaty.[27]

[18.22] Mr Opsahl submitted a separate concurring opinion in *Hertzberg*, to which Messrs Lallah and Tarnopolsky agreed.

This conclusion prejudges neither the right to be different and live accordingly, protected by article 17 of the Covenant, nor the right to have general freedom of expression in this respect, protected by article 19. Under article 19(2) and subject to article 19(3), everyone must in principle have the right to impart information and ideas—positive or negative— about homosexuality and discuss any problem relating to it freely, through any media of his choice and on his own responsibility.

Moreover, in my view the conception and contents of 'public morals' referred to in article 19 (3) are relative and changing. State imposed restrictions on freedom of expression must allow for this fact and should not be applied so as to perpetuate prejudice or promote intolerance. It is of special importance to protect freedom of expression as regards minority views, including those that offend, shock or disturb the majority. Therefore, even if such laws as paragraph 9 (2) of chapter 20 of the Finnish Penal Code may reflect prevailing

---

[24] See T. Jones, 'The Devaluation of Human Rights under the European Convention' [1995] *Public Law* 430, 430–1.

[25] See *Handyside Case*, Series A, No 24, Judgment of 7 December 1976 (1979–80) 1 EHRR 737, para. 48.

[26] See *Länsman v Finland* (511/92), where the HRC rejected the application of a margin of appreciation in the context of art. 27 minority rights, at para. 9.4 [24.27]. Former HRC member Roslyn Higgins denied in 1994 that the doctrine of margin of discretion (or appreciation) operates under the ICCPR: see S. Joseph, 'Toonen v Australia: Gay Rights under the ICCPR' (1994) 13 *University of Tasmania Law Journal* 392, 406. Higgins is now a Judge on the International Court of Justice.

[27] See L. Helfer and A. Miller, 'Sexual Orientation and Human Rights: Toward a United States and Transnational Jurisprudence' (1996) 6 *Harvard Human Rights Journal* 61, at 74, arguing in 1996 that the HRC would be unlikely to follow the 1982 decision in *Hertzberg*.

moral conceptions, this is in itself not sufficient to justify it under article 19(3). It must also be shown that the application of the restriction is 'necessary'.

However, as the Committee has noted, this law has not been directly applied to any of the alleged victims. The question remains whether they have been more indirectly affected by it in a way which can be said to interfere with their freedom of expression, and if so whether the grounds were justifiable.

It is clear that nobody—and in particular no State—has any duty under the Covenant to promote publicity for information and ideas of all kinds. Access to media operated by others is always and necessarily more limited than the general freedom of expression. It follows that such access may be controlled on grounds which do not have to be justified under article 19 (3).

It is true that self-imposed restrictions on publishing, or the internal programme policy of the media, may threaten the spirit of freedom of expression. Nevertheless, it is a matter of common sense that such decisions either entirely escape control by the Committee or must be accepted to a larger extent than externally imposed restrictions such as enforcement of criminal law or official censorship, neither of which took place in the present case. Not even media controlled by the State can under the Covenant be under an obligation to publish all that may be published. It is not possible to apply the criteria of article 19 (3) to self-imposed restrictions. Quite apart from the 'public morals' issue, one cannot require that they shall be only such as are 'provided by law and are necessary' for the particular purpose. Therefore I prefer not to express any opinion on the possible reasons for the decisions complained of in the present case.

The role of mass media in public debate depends on the relationship between journalists and their superiors who decide what to publish. I agree with the authors of the communication that the freedom of journalists is important, but the issues arising here can only partly be examined under article 19 of the Covenant.

The minority decided the case on a different basis, noting the freedom media owners have to choose what to broadcast. Is their decision consistent with the concerns expressed by the HRC in its Concluding Comments on Italy [18.14]?

[18.23] The HRC majority had noted that the State Party was responsible for the censorship decisions of the Finnish Broadcasting Company, as it held a 90 per cent stake, and had placed it under specific government control.[28] The minority drew an implicit distinction between government and non-government media owners. This decision possibly highlights the relative weakness of the ICCPR in the private, as opposed to public, sector.[29]

---

[28] Para. 9.1.
[29] However, this is a very early decision. It seems that the HRC is now more aware of the possible horizontal effects of ICCPR rights: see [1.59–1.62].

[18.24]   *DELGADO PÁEZ v COLOMBIA (195/85)*

The author, a teacher, made various claims of persecution,[30] including a complaint under article 19 regarding restrictions on his academic freedom to choose how to teach religion. The HRC dismissed the article 19 complaint:

¶ 5.8. Article 19 protects, *inter alia*, the right of freedom of expression and opinion. This will usually cover the freedom of teachers to teach their subjects in accordance with their own view, without interference. However, in the particular circumstances of the case, the special relationship between Church and State in Colombia, exemplified by the applicable Concordat, the Committee finds that the requirement, by the Church, that religion be taught in a certain way does not violate article 19.

This case demonstrates how 'public morals' vary between States, and therefore that the application of this express permissible limitation to article 19 rights may also vary from State to State.[31]

[18.25] Restrictions on obscene or pornographic material would be a classic instance of an article 19(3) limitation based on protection of public morals. Prohibitions on blasphemy would also potentially be justified by 'public morals', though their justification is perhaps more contentious in many States, given the secular nature of many modern societies.[32]

Public Order and National Security

[18.26] 'Public order' may be defined as the sum of rules which ensure the peaceful and effective functioning of society.[33] *'Ordre public'* is the equivalent French concept, but it is not an exact translation, as it seems to apply more in the private law sphere than does the common law notion of public order.[34] Common 'public order' limitations on article 19 rights include prohibitions on speech which may incite crime, violence, or mass panic. Prohibition of mass broadcasting without a licence may also be justified as a public order measure, to prevent confusion of signals and blockage of the airwaves.[35]

[18.27]   *GAUTHIER v CANADA (633/95)*

The facts of this case are outlined immediately below:

¶ 2.1. The author is publisher of the National Capital News, a newspaper founded in 1982. The author applied for membership in the Parliamentary Press Gallery, a private association

---

[30] See [11.03] and [22.49] on this case.

[31] See also explanation of *Toonen v Australia* (488/92) at [16.38]. Cf. [17.16].

[32] See, on blasphemy, [17.17].   [33] See 'Siracusa Principles', above, note 22, at 5.

[34] B. Lockwood Jr., J. Finn, and G. Jubinsky, 'Working Paper for the Committee of Experts on Limitation Provisions' (1985) 7 *HRQ* 35, 57–9. For example, *ordre public* may be used to negate private law contracts 'in the interest of higher imperatives'; 'public order' is not used in the same way in common law jurisdictions.

[35] Nowak, above, note 3, 356.

that administers the accreditation for access to the precincts of Parliament. He was provided with a temporary pass that gave only limited privileges. Repeated requests for equal access on the same terms as other reporters and publishers were denied.

¶ 2.2. The author points out that a temporary pass does not provide the same access as a permanent membership, since it denies *inter alia* listing on the membership roster of the Press Gallery, as well as access to a mailbox for the receipt of press communiqués. . . .

¶ 3. The author claims that the denial of equal access to press facilities in Parliament constitutes a violation of his rights under article 19 of the Covenant.

The State provided its justification for the situation in the following terms:

¶ 11.1. By submission of 14 July 1998, the State party provides a response on the merits of the communication. It reiterates its earlier observations and explains that the Speaker of the House of Commons, by virtue of Parliamentary privilege, has control of the accommodation and services in those parts of the Parliamentary precincts that are occupied by or on behalf of the House of Commons. One of the Speaker's duties in this regard is controlling access to these areas. The State party emphasizes that the absolute authority of Parliament over its own proceedings is a crucial and fundamental principle of Canada's general constitutional framework.

¶ 11.2. With regard to the relationship between the Speaker and the Press Gallery, the State party explains that this relationship is not formal, official or legal. While the Speaker has ultimate authority over the physical access to the media facilities in Parliament, he is not involved in the general operations of these facilities which are administered and run entirely by the Press Gallery.

¶ 11.3. Press passes granting access to the media facilities of Parliament are issued to Gallery members only. The State party reiterates that the determination of membership in the Press Gallery is an internal matter and that the Speaker has always taken a position of strict non-interference. It submits that as a member of the public, the author has access to the Parliament buildings open to the public and that he can attend the public hearings of the House of Commons.

¶ 11.4. In this connection, the State party reiterates that the proceedings of the House of Commons are broadcasted on television and that any journalist can report effectively on the proceedings in the House of Commons without using the media facilities of Parliament. The State party adds that the transcripts of the House debates can be found on the Internet the following day. Speeches and press releases of the Prime Minister are deposited in a lobby open to the public, and are also posted on the Internet. Government reports and press releases are likewise posted on the Internet.

¶ 11.5. The State party argues that the author has not been deprived of his freedom to receive and impart information. Although as a member of the public, he may not take notes while sitting in the Public Gallery of the House of Commons, he may observe the proceedings in the House and report on them. The State party explains that 'Note-taking has traditionally been prohibited in the public galleries of the House of Commons as a matter of order and decorum and for security reasons (e.g. the throwing of objects at the members of Parliament from the gallery above)'. Moreover, the information he seeks is available through live broadcasting and the Internet.

¶ 11.6. Alternatively, the State party argues that any restriction on the author's ability to receive and impart information that may result from the prohibition on note-taking in the public gallery in the House of Commons is minimal and is justified to achieve a balance between the right to freedom of expression and the need to ensure both the effective and dignified operation of Parliament and the safety and security of its members. According to the State party, states should be accorded a broad flexibility in determining issues of effective governance and security since they are in the best position to assess the risks and needs.

The HRC found in favour of the author on the merits:

¶ 13.3. The issue before the Committee is thus whether the restriction of the author's access to the press facilities in Parliament amounts to a violation of his right under article 19 of the Covenant, to seek, receive and impart information.

¶ 13.4. In this connection, the Committee also refers to the right to take part in the conduct of public affairs, as laid down in article 25 of the Covenant, and in particular to General Comment No. 25 (57) which reads in part: 'In order to ensure the full enjoyment of rights protected by article 25, the free communication of information and ideas about public and political issues between citizens, candidates and elected representatives is essential. This implies a free press and other media able to comment on public issues without censorship or restraint and to inform public opinion.' General comment No. 25, paragraph 25, adopted by the Committee on 12 July 1996.[36] Read together with article 19, this implies that citizens, in particular through the media, should have wide access to information and the opportunity to disseminate information and opinions about the activities of elected bodies and their members. The Committee recognizes, however, that such access should not interfere with or obstruct the carrying out of the functions of elected bodies, and that a State party is thus entitled to limit access. However, any restrictions imposed by the State party must be compatible with the provisions of the Covenant.

¶ 13.5. In the present case, the State party has restricted the right to enjoy the publicly funded media facilities of Parliament, including the right to take notes when observing meetings of Parliament, to those media representatives who are members of a private organization, the Canadian Press Gallery. The author has been denied active (i.e. full) membership of the Press Gallery. On occasion he has held temporary membership which has given him access to some but not all facilities of the organization. When he does not hold at least temporary membership he does not have access to the media facilities nor can he take notes of Parliamentary proceedings. The Committee notes that the State party has claimed that the author does not suffer any significant disadvantage because of technological advances which make information about Parliamentary proceedings readily available to the public. The State party argues that he can report on proceedings by relying on broadcasting services, or by observing the proceedings. In view of the importance of access to information about the democratic process, however, the Committee does not accept the State party's argument and is of the opinion that the author's exclusion constitutes a restriction of his

---

[36] See generally on art. 25, Chap. 22.

right guaranteed under paragraph 2 of article 19 to have access to information. The question is whether or not this restriction is justified under paragraph 3 of article 19. The restriction is, arguably, imposed by law, in that the exclusion of persons from the precinct of Parliament or any part thereof, under the authority of the Speaker, follows from the law of parliamentary privilege.

¶ 13.6. The State party argues that the restrictions are justified to achieve a balance between the right to freedom of expression and the need to ensure both the effective and dignified operation of Parliament and the safety and security of its members, and that the State party is in the best position to assess the risks and needs involved. As indicated above, the Committee agrees that the protection of Parliamentary procedure can be seen as a legitimate goal of public order and an accreditation system can thus be a justified means of achieving this goal. However, since the accreditation system operates as a restriction of article 19 rights, its operation and application must be shown as necessary and proportionate to the goal in question and not arbitrary. The Committee does not accept that this is a matter exclusively for the State to determine. The relevant criteria for the accreditation scheme should be specific, fair and reasonable, and their application should be transparent. In the instant case, the State party has allowed a private organization to control access to the Parliamentary press facilities, without intervention. The scheme does not ensure that there will be no arbitrary exclusion from access to the Parliamentary media facilities. In the circumstances, the Committee is of the opinion that the accreditation system has not been shown to be a necessary and proportionate restriction of rights within the meaning of article 19, paragraph 3, of the Covenant, in order to ensure the effective operation of Parliament and the safety of its members. The denial of access to the author to the press facilities of Parliament for not being a member of the Canadian Press Gallery Association constitutes therefore a violation of article 19(2) of the Covenant.

¶ 13.7. In this connection, the Committee notes that there is no possibility of recourse, either to the Courts or to Parliament, to determine the legality of the exclusion or its necessity for the purposes spelled out in article 19 of the Covenant. The Committee recalls that under article 2, paragraph 3 of the Covenant, States parties have undertaken to ensure that any person whose rights are violated shall have an effective remedy, and that any person claiming such a remedy shall have his right thereto determined by competent authorities. Accordingly, whenever a right recognized by the Covenant is affected by the action of a State agent there must be a procedure established by the State allowing the person whose right has been affected to claim before a competent body that there has been a violation of his rights.

¶ 14. The Human Rights Committee, acting under article 5, paragraph 4, of the Optional Protocol to the International Covenant on Civil and Political rights, is of the view that the facts before it disclose a violation of article 19, paragraph 2, of the Covenant.

[18.28] In *Gauthier*, 'public order' was pleaded by the State, unsuccessfully, in the limited context of protecting order within the confines of the federal Parliament building. 'Public order' is usually pleaded in the broader context of protecting order in society within the whole State, as in the following cases.

[18.29]   *M.A. v ITALY (117/81)*

The facts are outlined immediately below:

¶ 1.2. The alleged victim is M. A. who at the time of submission was serving a sentence upon conviction of involvement in 'reorganizing the dissolved fascist party', which is prohibited by an Italian penal law of 20 June 1952. By order of the Court of Appeals of Florence, M. A., was conditionally released and placed under mandatory supervision on 29 July 1983.

¶ 1.3. The authors do not specify which articles of the Covenant have allegedly been violated. It is generally claimed that M. A. was condemned to prison solely for his ideas and that he has been deprived of the right to profess his political beliefs.

The HRC found M.A.'s claim inadmissible:

¶ 13.3. . . . [I]t would appear to the Committee that the acts of which M. A. was convicted (reorganizing the dissolved fascist party) were of a kind which are removed from the protection of the Covenant by article 5 thereof and which were in any event justifiably prohibited by Italian law having regard to the limitations and restrictions applicable to the rights in question under the provisions of articles 18 (3), 19 (3), 22 (2) and 25 of the Covenant. In these respects therefore the communication is inadmissible under article 3 of the Optional Protocol, as incompatible with the provisions of the Covenant, *ratione materiae*.

Article 5 prohibits interpretation of the ICCPR in such a way as to grant rights for people to engage in activities aimed at the destruction or limitation of the ICCPR rights of others. McGoldrick has correctly criticized *M.A. v Italy* (117/81) by stating that issues under articles 5 and 19(3) should have been considered at the merits stage of proceedings.[37] The HRC should have sought more information on the actual activities of the new Italian fascist party before condoning the prohibition of those activities. Italy had submitted only that the fascist party wished to 'eliminate democratic freedoms and establish a totalitarian regime'.[38] The HRC did not address M.A.'s allegation that the law was applied in a discriminatory way, being exclusively aimed at right-wing organizations, rather than all 'antidemocratic' parties, such as anarchists and Leninists.[39]

[18.30] 'National security' is invoked as a limitation when the political independence or the territorial integrity of the State is at risk.[40] Common national security restrictions include prohibitions on the transmission of 'official secrets'. 'National security' is often invoked interchangeably with 'public order' as a justification for restrictions on certain types of political speech.

---

[37] McGoldrick, above, note 2, 166–7.   [38] Para. 7.2.
[39] See para. 9(b). This allegation could have raised issues under the Covenant's non-discrimination provisions, arts. 2(1) and 26.
[40] 'Siracusa Principles', above, note 22, 6.

[18.31] *KIM v REPUBLIC OF KOREA (574/94)*

The author complained of his conviction under the 'National Security Law' for expressing opinions sympathetic to an 'anti-State organization', namely the Democratic People's Republic of Korea (North Korea). The State Party provided justifications for the author's conviction:

¶ 10.4. With regard to counsel's argument that the State party has failed to establish that a relation between the author and North Korea existed and that his actions were a serious threat to national security, the State party points out that North Korea has attempted to destabilize the country by calling for the overthrow of South Korea's 'military-fascist regime' in favour of a 'people's democratic government', which would bring about 'unification of the fatherland' and 'liberation of the people'. In the documents, distributed by the author, it was argued that the Government of South Korea was seeking the continuation of the country's division and dictatorial regime; that the Korean people had been struggling for the last half century against US and Japanese neo-colonial influence, which aims at the continued division of the Korean peninsula and the oppression of the people; that nuclear weapons and American soldiers should be withdrawn from South Korea, since their presence posed a great threat to national survival and to the people; and that joint military exercises between South Korea and the USA should be stopped.

¶ 10.5. The State party submits that it is seeking peaceful unification, and not the continuation of the division as argued by the author. The State party further takes issue with the author's subjective conviction about the presence of US forces and US and Japanese influence. It points out that the presence of US forces has been an effective deterrent to prevent North Korea from making the peninsula communist through military force.

¶ 10.6. According to the State party, it is obvious that the author's arguments are the same as that of North Korea, and that his activities thus both helped North Korea and followed its strategy and tactics. The State party agrees that democracy means allowing different voices to be heard but argues that there should be a limit to certain actions so as not to cause damage to the basic order necessary for national survival. The State party submits that it is illegal to produce and distribute printed materials that praise and promote North Korean ideology and further its strategic objective to destroy the free and democratic system of the Republic of Korea. It argues that such activities, directed at furthering these violent aims, cannot be construed as peaceful.

More justifications are evident from the dissent of Mr Ando [18.32]. Nevertheless, the HRC majority found in favour of the author:[41]

¶ 12.4. The Committee notes that the author was convicted for having read out and distributed printed material which were seen as coinciding with the policy statements of the DPRK (North Korea), with which country the State party was in a state of war. He was convicted by the courts on the basis of a finding that he had done this with the intention of siding with the activities of the DPRK. The Supreme Court held that the mere knowledge that the activity could be of benefit to North Korea was sufficient to establish guilt. Even

---

[41] See also the similar case of *Park v Republic of Korea* (628/95), paras. 10.3–10.4.

taking that matter into account, the Committee has to consider whether the author's political speech and his distribution of political documents were of a nature to attract the restriction allowed by article 19 (3) namely the protection of national security. It is plain that North Korean policies were well known within the territory of the State party and it is not clear how the (undefined) 'benefit' that might arise for the DPRK from the publication of views similar to their own created a risk to national security, nor is it clear what was the nature and extent of any such risk. There is no indication that the courts, at any level, addressed those questions or considered whether the contents of the speech or the documents had any additional effect upon the audience or readers such as to threaten public security, the protection of which would justify restriction within the terms of the Covenant as being necessary.

¶ 12.5. The Committee considers, therefore, that the State party has failed to specify the precise nature of the threat allegedly posed by the author's exercise of freedom of expression, and that the State party has not provided specific justifications as to why over and above prosecuting the author for contraventions of the Law on Assembly and Demonstration and the Law on Punishment of Violent Activities (which forms no part of the author's complaint), it was necessary for national security, also to prosecute the author for the exercise of his freedom of expression. The Committee considers therefore that the restriction of the author's right to freedom of expression was not compatible with the requirements of article 19, paragraph 3, of the Covenant.[42]

[18.32] Mr Ando dissented, in the following terms:

. . . as noted by the State party, the author was 'convicted [under the Law on Demonstration and Assembly and the Law on Punishment of Violent Activities] for organizing illegal demonstrations and instigating acts of violence on several occasions during the period from January 1989 to May 1990. During these demonstrations . . . participants "threw thousands of Molotov cocktails and rocks at police stations, and other government offices. They also set vehicles on fire and injured 134 policemen".' (para.4.2) . . .

The author's counsel argues that 'the author's conviction under the Law on Demonstration and Assembly and the Law on Punishment of Violent Activities is not the issue in this communication' and that 'the author's conviction under those laws cannot justify his [additional] conviction under the National Security Law for his allegedly enemy-benefiting expressions'. (para.9.1)

Nevertheless, the author's reading out and distributing the printed material in question, for which he was convicted under these laws, were the very acts for which he was convicted under the National Security law and which lead to the breach of public order as described by the State party. In fact, counsel fails to refute that the author's reading out and distributing the printed material in question did lead to the breach of public order, which might have been perceived by the State party as threatening national security.

I do share the concern of counsel that some provisions of the National Security Law are too broadly worded to prevent their abusive application and interpretation. Unfortunately,

---

[42] The *Kim* decision is further supported in Concluding Comments on the Republic of Korea (1999) UN doc. CCPR/C/79/Add. 114, para. 9.

however, the fact remains that South Korea was invaded by North Korea in the 1950's and the East-West détente has not fully blossomed on the Korean Peninsula yet. In any event the Committee has no information to prove that the afore-mentioned acts of the author did not entail the breach of public order, and under article 19, paragraph 3, of the Covenant the protection of 'public order' as well as the protection of 'national security' is a legitimate ground to restrict the exercise of the right to freedom of expression.

The *Kim* decision may be contrasted with the distinct lack of sympathy evinced for the author in *M.A. v Italy* (117/81). Is the HRC possibly more tolerant of left-wing antidemocratic views than of right-wing fascist views?[43]

[18.33] *MUKONG v CAMEROON (458/91)*

The facts are outlined immediately below.

¶ 2.1. The author is a journalist, writer and longtime opponent of the one-party system in Cameroon. He has frequently and publicly advocated the introduction of multiparty democracy and has worked toward the establishment of a new political party in his country. He contends that some of the books that he has written were either banned or prohibited from circulation. . . .

The author complained about a number of alleged violations of his ICCPR rights.

¶ 3.4. The author notes that his arrests on 16 June 1988 and 26 February 1990 were linked to his activities as an advocate of multiparty democracy, and claims that these were Government attempts designed to suppress any opposition activities, in violation of article 19 of the Covenant. This also applies to the Government's ban, in 1985, of a book written by the author ('Prisoner without a Crime'), in which he described his detention in local jails from 1970 to 1976.

The State Party sought to justify this apparent suppression of Mukong's expression.

¶ 6.7. In this context, the State party argues that the arrest of the author was for activities and forms of expression which are covered by the limitation clause of article 19, paragraph 3, of the Covenant. It contends that the exercise of the right to freedom of expression must take into account the political context and situation prevailing in a country at any point in time: since the independence and reunification of Cameroon, the country's history has been a constant battle to strengthen national unity, first at the level of the francophone and anglophone communities and thereafter at the level of the more than 200 ethnic groups and tribes that comprise the Cameroonian nation.

The HRC found in favour of the author:

¶ 9.6. The author has claimed a violation of his right to freedom of expression and opinion, as he was persecuted for his advocacy of multi-party democracy and the expression of opinions inimical to the State party's government. The State party has replied that

---

[43] See commentary at [18.29].

restrictions on the author's freedom of expression were justified under the terms of article 19, paragraph 3.

¶ 9.7. . . . The State party has indirectly justified its actions on grounds of national security and/or public order, by arguing that the author's right to freedom of expression was exercised without regard to the country's political context and continued struggle for unity. While the State party has indicated that the restrictions on the author's freedom of expression were provided for by law, it must still be determined whether the measures taken against the author were necessary for the safeguard of national security and/or public order. The Committee considers that it was not necessary to safeguard an alleged vulnerable state of national unity by subjecting the author to arrest, continued detention and treatment in violation of article 7. It further considers that the legitimate objective of safeguarding and indeed strengthening national unity under difficult political circumstances cannot be achieved by attempting to muzzle advocacy of multi-party democracy, democratic tenets and human rights; in this regard, the question of deciding which measures might meet the 'necessity' test in such situations does not arise. In the circumstances of the author's case, the Committee concludes that there has been a violation of article 19 of the Covenant.

It is often argued that developing nations, by virtue of their economic underdevelopment, should be permitted to 'postpone' or 'trade off' their obligations to respect certain political rights. 'This theory contends that the priority of economic development mandates political stability and thereby justifies violations of individual rights'.[44] The HRC, in its *Mukong* decision, clearly denies that underdevelopment can justify political repression and the imposition of one-party States.

[18.34]   *SOHN v REPUBLIC OF KOREA (518/92)*

The author in this case was arrested for interference in a labour dispute. The facts are outlined below.

¶ 2.1. The author has been president of the Kumho Company Trade Union since 27 September 1990 and is a founding member of the Solidarity Forum of Large Company Trade Unions. On 8 February 1991, a strike was called at the Daewoo Shipyard Company at Guhjae Island in the province of Kyungsang-Nam-Do. The Government announced that it would send in police troops to break the strike. Following that announcement, the author had a meeting, on 9 February 1991, with other members of the Solidarity Forum, in Seoul, 400 kilometres from the place where the strike took place. At the end of the meeting they issued a statement supporting the strike and condemning the Government's threat to send in troops. That statement was transmitted to the workers at the Daewoo Shipyard by facsimile. The Daewoo Shipyard strike ended peacefully on 13 February 1991.

¶ 2.2. On 10 February 1991, the author, together with some 60 other members of the Solidarity Forum, was arrested by the police when leaving the premises where the meeting had

[44] A. Pollis, 'Cultural Relativism Revisited: Through a State Prism' (1996) 18 *HRQ* 316, 317. See also J. Donnelly, 'Human Rights and Development: Complementary or Competing Concerns' (1984) 36 *World Politics* 255, 258.

been held. On 12 February 1991, he and six others were charged with contravening article 13(2) of the Labour Dispute Adjustment Act (Law No. 1327 of 13 April 1963, amended by Law No. 3967 of 28 November 1987), which prohibits others than the concerned employer, employees or trade union, or persons having legitimate authority attributed to them by law, to intervene in a labour dispute for the purpose of manipulating or influencing the parties concerned. He was also charged with contravening the Act on Assembly and Demonstration (Law No. 4095 of 29 March 1989), but notes that his communication relates only to the Labour Dispute Adjustment Act. One of the author's co-accused later died in detention, according to the author under suspicious circumstances.

The author was convicted of an offence under article 13(2) of the Labour Dispute Adjustment Act.

¶ 3.1. The author argues that article 13(2) of the Labour Dispute Adjustment Act is used to punish support for the labour movement and to isolate the workers. He argues that the provision has never been used to charge those who take the side of management in a labour dispute. He further claims that the vagueness of the provision, which prohibits any act to influence the parties, violates the principle of legality (*nullum crimen, nulla poena sine lege*).

¶ 3.2. The author further argues that the provision was incorporated into the law to deny the right to freedom of expression to supporters of labourers or trade unions. In this respect, he makes reference to the Labour Union Act, which prohibits third party support for the organization of a trade union. He concludes that any support to labourers or trade unions may thus be punished, by the Labour Dispute Adjustment Act at the time of strikes and by the Labour Union Act at other times.

¶ 3.3. The author claims that his conviction violates article 19, paragraph 2, of the Covenant. He emphasizes that the way he exercised his freedom of expression did not infringe the rights or reputations of others, nor did it threaten national security or public order, or public health or morals.

The State Party submitted its defence of the impugned provisions:

¶ 7.3. The State party explains that the articles of the Labour Dispute Adjustment Act, prohibiting intervention by third parties in a labour dispute, are meant to maintain the independent nature of a labour dispute between employees and employer. It points out that the provision does not prohibit counselling or giving advice to the parties involved.

¶ 7.4. The State party invokes article 19, paragraph 3, of the Covenant, which provides that the right to freedom of expression may be subject to certain restrictions *inter alia* for the protection of national security or of public order.

¶ 9.1. By further submission of 20 June 1995, the State party explains that the labour movement in the Republic of Korea can be generally described as being politically oriented and ideologically influenced. In this connection it is stated that labour activists in Korea do not hesitate in leading workers to extreme actions by using force and violence and engaging in illegal strikes in order to fulfil their political aims or carry out their ideological principles. Furthermore, the State party argues that there have been frequent instances where the idea of a proletarian revolution has been implanted in the minds of workers.

¶ 9.2. The State party argues that if a third party interferes in a labour dispute to the extent that the third party actually manipulates, instigates or obstructs the decisions of workers, such a dispute is being distorted towards other objectives and goals. The State party explains therefore that, in view of the general nature of the labour movement, it has felt obliged to maintain the law concerning the prohibition of third party intervention.

¶ 9.3. Moreover, the State party submits that in the instant case, the written statement distributed in February 1991 to support the Daewoo Shipyard Trade Union was used as a disguise to incite a nation-wide strike of all workers. The State party argues that 'in the case where a national strike would take place, in any country, regardless of its security situation, there is considerable reason to believe that the national security and public order of the nation would be threatened.'

¶ 9.4. As regards the enactment of the Labour Dispute Adjustment Act by the Legislative Council for National Security, the State party argues that, through the revision of the constitution, the effectiveness of the laws enacted by the Council was acknowledged by public consent. The State party moreover argues that the provision concerning the prohibition of the third party intervention is being applied fairly to both the labour and the management side of a dispute. In this connection the State party refers to a case currently before the courts against someone who intervened in a labour dispute on the side of the employer.

Mr Sohn responded:

¶ 8.4. The author denies that the statements by the Solidarity Forum posed a threat to the national security and public order of South Korea. It is stated that the author and the other members of the Solidarity Forum are fully aware of the sensitive situation in terms of South Korea's confrontation with North Korea. The author cannot see how the expression of support for the strike and criticism of the employer and the government in handling the matter could threaten national security. In this connection the author notes that none of the participants in the strike was charged with breaching the National Security Law. The author states that in the light of the constitutional right to strike, police intervention by force can be legitimately criticized. Moreover, the author argues that public order was not threatened by the statements given by the Solidarity Forum, but that, on the contrary, the right to express one's opinion freely and peacefully enhances public order in a democratic society.

¶ 8.5. The author points out that solidarity among workers is being prohibited and punished in the Republic of Korea, purportedly in order to 'maintain the independent nature of a labour dispute', but that intervention in support of the employer to suppress workers' rights is being encouraged and protected. . . .

The HRC found in favour of Mr Sohn:

¶ 10.4. . . . While the State party has stated that the restrictions were justified in order to protect national security and public order and that they were provided for by law, under article 13(2) of the Labour Dispute Adjustment Act, the Committee must still determine whether the measures taken against the author were necessary for the purpose stated. The Committee notes that the State party has invoked national security and public order by reference to the general nature of the labour movement and by alleging that the statement issued by the author in collaboration with others was a disguise for the incitement to a national strike. The Committee considers that the State party has failed to specify the precise nature of the threat which it contends that the author's exercise of freedom of expression posed and finds that none of the arguments advanced by the State party suffice to render the restriction of the author's right to freedom of expression compatible with paragraph 3 of article 19.

¶ 11. The Human Rights Committee, acting under article 5, paragraph 4, of the Optional Protocol to the International Covenant on Civil and Political Rights, finds that the facts before it disclose a violation of article 19, paragraph 2, of the Covenant.

[18.35] The above cases indicate that the HRC is reluctant to allow restrictions on free expression for the purposes of national security and public order, at least in the absence of detailed justifications by the State Party.[45] National security and public order are perhaps the limitations which are most often abused by States; they are often invoked to protect the elite position of the government, rather than truly to protect the rights of a State's population.[46]

Rights and Reputations of Others

[18.36] In article 19(3), it is expressly recognized that the exercise of freedom of expression 'carries with it special duties and responsibilities', and therefore permits various limitations to the right. Article 19(3) concedes that one's freedom of expression can clash with another's exercise of other equally important rights.[47] For example, freedom of expression can probably be limited by proportionate laws regarding defamation (which protect article 17 privacy rights and the 'reputations of others') and contempt of court (which help preserve the fair administration of justice under article 14). Another example can be taken from the above Concluding Comments on Italy [18.14] regarding abuse of power by private media interests. These can abuse their power, and indeed their own free expression, so as to inhibit the free expression, and the rights to seek information, of others.[48]

[18.37] The permissible limitation of protection of 'rights of others' is a catch-all limitation, and is potentially very broad. The HRC has never commented on its outer limits. It is to be hoped that 'rights' refers to other human rights, though not necessarily those in the ICCPR.[49] A human right of freedom of expression

---

[45] Contrast the decision of *V.M.R.B. v Canada* (236/87) at [13.17–13.19].

[46] See, e.g., 'Siracusa Principles', above, note 22, at 6, on 'national security'.

[47] The limited grant of freedom of expression in art. 19 may be contrasted with the more absolute express right in the First Amendment to the United States Bill of Rights.

[48] See Nowak, above, note 3, 350; see also D. Feldman, 'Freedom of Expression' in D. Harris and S. Joseph (eds.), *The International Covenant on Civil and Political Rights and United Kingdom Law* (Clarendon Press, Oxford, 1995), 396. See also *Faurisson v France* (550/93) [18.48] for another example of a limit on free speech imposed for the purpose of protecting the rights of others.

[49] For example, copyright protection limits freedom of expression in order to protect property rights, which are recognized in the Universal Declaration of Human Rights 1948.

should not be permissibly limited by a lesser right, such as a bare municipal legal right.[50]

[18.38]   *BALLANTYNE et al. v CANADA (359, 385/89)*

The facts of this case are outlined immediately below:

¶ 1. The authors of the communications . . . are John Ballantyne, Elizabeth Davidson and Gordon McIntyre, Canadian citizens residing in the Province of Quebec. The authors, one a painter, the second a designer and the third an undertaker by profession, have their businesses in Sutton and Huntingdon, Quebec. Their mother tongue is English, as is that of many of their clients. They allege to be victims of violations of articles 2, 19, 26 and 27 of the International Covenant on Civil and Political Rights by the Federal Government of Canada and by the Province of Quebec, because they are forbidden to use English for purposes of advertising, e.g., on commercial signs outside the business premises, or in the name of the firm.

The Quebec government, in arguments submitted through the Canadian government to the HRC, unsuccessfully argued that commercial speech was not protected by article 19 [18.05]. Quebec also argued that the measures were necessary to protect Quebec's francophile culture.

¶ 8.7. The Government of Quebec points out that in the linguistic sphere, the notion of *de facto* equality precludes purely formal equality and makes it necessary to accord different treatment in order to arrive at a result that restores the balance between different situations. It contends that the Charter of the French Language, as amended by Bill 178, 'is a measured legislative response to the particular circumstances of Quebec's society, for which, in the North American context and in the face of the domination of the English language and the ensuing cultural, socio-economic and political pressures, 'francification' ('Frenchification') is still in an exposed position'.

¶ 8.8. The requirements of Sections 58 and 68 of Bill 178 are said to be deliberately limited to the sphere of external public and commercial advertising, because it is there that the symbolic value of the language as a means of collective identification is strongest and contributes most to preserving the cultural identity of French speakers: 'the linguistic image communicated by advertising is an important factor that contributes to shaping habits and behaviour which perpetuate or influence the use of a language'. Quebec concludes on this point that Bill 178 strikes a delicate balance between two linguistic communities, one of which is in a dominant demographic position both nationally and on the continent as a whole. This aim is said to be reasonable and compatible with article 26 of the Covenant.[51]

---

[50] In this respect, see the European Commission decision in the '*Gay News*' case, *X v U.K.* (1982) 28 DR 77, where a gay magazine's right of free expression was permissibly limited by the domestic legal right of a local plaintiff (Mary Whitehouse) to pursue a private prosecution for blasphemy. It is contended that Mrs Whitehouse's right was not a human right, and should not have limited the free expression rights of Gay News.

[51] See generally [23.40] ff.

¶ 8.9. Quebec adds that the historical background and the fact that the evolution of linguistic relations in Canada constitutes a political compromise do not justify the conclusion that the requirement to carry out external commercial advertising in a certain way amounts to a violation of article 19. . . .

The HRC nevertheless found that the Quebec law constituted a breach of article 19:[52]

¶ 11.4. Any restriction of the freedom of expression must cumulatively meet the following conditions: it must be provided for by law, it must address one of the aims enumerated in paragraph 3(a) and (b) of article 19, and must be necessary to achieve the legitimate purpose. While the restrictions on outdoor advertising are indeed provided for by law, the issue to be addressed is whether they are necessary for the respect of the rights of others. The rights of others could only be the rights of the francophone minority within Canada under article 27. This is the right to use their own language, which is not jeopardized by the freedom of others to advertise in other than the French language. Nor does the Committee have reason to believe that public order would be jeopardized by commercial advertising outdoors in a language other than French. The Committee notes that the State party does not seek to defend Bill 178 on these grounds. Any constraints under paragraphs 3(a) and 3(b) of article 19 would in any event have to be shown to be necessary. The Committee believes that it is not necessary, in order to protect the vulnerable position in Canada of the francophone group, to prohibit commercial advertising in English. This protection may be achieved in other ways that do not preclude the freedom of expression, in a language of their choice, of those engaged in such fields as trade. For example, the law could have required that advertising be in both French and English. A State may choose one or more official languages, but it may not exclude, outside the spheres of public life, the freedom to express oneself in a language of one's choice. The Committee accordingly concludes that there has been a violation of article 19, paragraph 2.

The *Ballantyne* case may be distinguished from *Guesdon v France* (219/86) [18.09] in that it concerned restrictions on the use of language in the private as opposed to public spheres.[53] Restrictions on the use of one's language for private purposes, such as commercial signage, would rarely be permissible under article 19, whereas restrictions on the 'public' use of a language, such as in court proceedings, may occasionally be justified, for example, for reasons of public order.

[18.39] In *Ballantyne*, the HRC did not deny that preservation of the French language was a legitimate legislative objective. In this case however, the HRC noted that francophone culture could be preserved by a requirement of dual language signage, rather than restrictions on non-French languages. The

---

[52] Mr Ndiaye dissented on the basis that the Quebec laws supported minority rights; his dissent is excerpted at [24.35].

[53] De Varennes, above, note 11, 178–9. However, see [24.32–24.33].

Committee's decision therefore indicates that minimum impairment to freedom of expression is an element of the test of proportionality and therefore the validity of restrictions on article 19 rights.[54]

[18.40] Another challenge to the Quebec laws was brought in *Singer v Canada* (455/91). However, the laws had been amended by the time of the HRC decision, so the issue in the case was moot. However, the new provisions (which Singer did not complain about) may still pose problems under article 19, as commercial advertisements must still be in French, though this may be accompanied by an advertisement in a language other than French. Furthermore, only French advertising is permitted (a) on large roadside billboards and (b) on or in any means of public transportation, or in accesses thereto, such as bus shelters.[55] Are these laws a proportionate means of protecting francophone minority rights in Canada, and thus compatible with article 19?

Article 20 and Hate Speech

ARTICLE 20

1. Any propaganda for war shall be prohibited by law.

2. Any advocacy of national, racial or religious hatred that constitutes incitement to discrimination, hostility or violence shall be prohibited by law.

[18.41] Article 20 contains *mandatory* limitations to freedom of expression. Article 20 requires States Parties to outlaw propaganda for war, and vilification of persons on nationalist, racial, or religious grounds. Article 20 ICCPR recognizes the destructive nature of certain types of expression.

However, article 20 does conflict with the more absolutist guarantees of freedom of expression in numerous State constitutions, and the exalted position given to free speech in Western liberal theory. This has prompted numerous reservations to article 20, by States Parties such as the USA, Belgium, Denmark, Finland, and Iceland.[56]

[18.42]   *GENERAL COMMENT 11*

¶ 1. . . . In view of the nature of article 20, States parties are obliged to adopt the necessary legislative measures prohibiting the actions referred to therein. . . .

¶ 2. Article 20 of the Covenant states that any propaganda for war and any advocacy of

---

[54] The doctrine of minimum impairment is used in Canadian constitutional law in interpreting limitations to Charter rights: see, e.g., *R v Big M Drug Mart* [1985] 1 SCR 295, at 352, and *R v Oakes* [1986] 26 DLR (4d) 200, at 227 (decisions of the Canadian Supreme Court).

[55] See *Singer*, paras. 9.2–9.4.

[56] See generally on reservations Chap. 25.

national, racial or religious hatred that constitutes incitement to discrimination, hostility or violence shall be prohibited by law. In the opinion of the Committee, these required prohibitions are fully compatible with the right of freedom of expression as contained in article 19, the exercise of which carries with it special duties and responsibilities. The prohibition under paragraph 1 extends to all forms of propaganda threatening or resulting in an act of aggression or breach of the peace contrary to the Charter of the United Nations, while paragraph 2 is directed against any advocacy of national, racial or religious hatred that constitutes incitement to discrimination, hostility or violence, whether such propaganda or advocacy has aims which are internal or external to the State concerned. The provisions of article 20, paragraph 1, do not prohibit advocacy of the sovereign right of self-defence or the right of peoples to self-determination and independence in accordance with the Charter of the United Nations. For article 20 to become fully effective there ought to be a law making it clear that propaganda and advocacy as described therein are contrary to public policy and providing for an appropriate sanction in case of violation. The Committee, therefore, believes that States parties which have not yet done so should take the measures necessary to fulfil the obligations contained in article 20, and should themselves refrain from any such propaganda or advocacy.

[18.43] The General Comment indicates that 'wars' which are sanctioned under the UN Charter are not 'wars' for the purposes of article 20(1). Thus, propaganda for wars in self-defence is permissible. So, too, logically, is propaganda for wars sponsored by the Security Council under chapter VII of the Charter, such as the Allied action against Iraq in defence of Kuwait in 1990. Propaganda for illegal wars is of course caught by article 20(1). Given the dubious status of unilateral humanitarian intervention in international law, it is possible that statements of support for the NATO action against Yugoslavia (Serbia) in defence of Kosovo in early 1999 breached article 20(1).[57] Indeed, it is unfortunate that the HRC did not take the opportunity in its General Comment to define the meaning of 'propaganda for war'. Does it include information conveyed *during* a war, rather than information which precedes, supports and potentially ignites the start of a war? All States issue favourable reports of their own war efforts, which could potentially be labelled propaganda, during wars in which they are involved.

[18.44] The International Convention on the Elimination of All Forms of Racial Discrimination 1966 (ICERD) contains a more detailed obligation on States to pass and enforce racial vilification laws in article 4. The ICERD Committee has explained the *raison d'être* of article 4 in its General Recommendation 15.

CERD GENERAL RECOMMENDATION 15

¶ 1. When the International Convention on the Elimination of All Forms of Racial Discrimination was being adopted [in 1966], article 4 was regarded as central to the struggle against racial discrimination. At that time, there was a widespread fear of the

---

[57] See generally B. Simma, 'NATO, the UN, and the Use of Force: Legal Aspects' (1999) 10 *European Journal of International Law* 1.

revival of authoritarian ideologies. The proscription of the dissemination of ideas of racial superiority, and of organized activity likely to incite persons to racial violence, was properly regarded as crucial. Since that time, the Committee has received evidence of organized violence based on ethnic origin and the political exploitation of ethnic difference. As a result, implementation of article 4 is now of increased importance.

The ICERD Committee went on to explain some of the duties entailed in the proper implementation of article 4:

¶ 2. . . . To satisfy these obligations, States parties have not only to enact appropriate legislation but also to ensure that it is effectively enforced. Because threats and acts of racial violence easily lead to other such acts and generate an atmosphere of hostility, only immediate intervention can meet the obligations of effective response.

¶ 3. Article 4(a) requires States parties to penalize four categories of misconduct: (i) dissemination of ideas based upon racial superiority or hatred; (ii) incitement to racial hatred; (iii) acts of violence against any race or group of persons of another colour or ethnic origin; and (iv) incitement to such acts. . . .

¶ 5. Article 4(a) also penalizes the financing of racist activities, which the Committee takes to include all the activities mentioned in paragraph 3 above, that is to say, activities deriving from ethnic as well as racial differences. . . .

¶ 6. Some States have maintained that in their legal order it is inappropriate to declare illegal an organization before its members have promoted or incited racial discrimination. The Committee is of the opinion that article 4(b) places a greater burden upon such States to be vigilant in proceeding against such organizations at the earliest moment. These organizations, as well as organized and other propaganda activities, have to be declared illegal and prohibited. Participation in these organizations is, of itself, to be punished.

[18.45] The ICERD Committee has dealt with a complaint of a violation of article 4 in the following case.

L.K. v THE NETHERLANDS (CERD 4/91)

¶ 2.1. On 9 August 1989, the author, who is partially disabled, visited a house for which a lease had been offered to him and his family, in the Nicholas Ruychaverstraat, a street with municipal subsidized housing in Utrecht. He was accompanied by a friend, A.B. When they arrived, some 20 people had gathered outside the house. During the visit, the author heard several of them both say and shout: 'No more foreigners'. Others intimated to him that if he were to accept the house, they would set fire to it and damage his car. The author and A.B. then returned to the Municipal Housing Office and asked the official responsible for the file to accompany them to the street. There, several local inhabitants told the official that they could not accept the author as their neighbour, owing to a presumed rule that no more than 5 per cent of the street's inhabitants should be foreigners. Told that no such rule existed, street residents drafted a petition, which noted that the author could not be accepted and recommended that another house be allocated to his family.

¶ 2.2. On the same day, the author filed a complaint with the municipal police of Utrecht, on the ground that he had been the victim of racial discrimination under article 137 (*literae* (c) and (d)) of the Criminal Code (Wetboek van Strafrecht). The complaint was directed against all those who had signed the petition and those who had gathered outside the house. He submits that initially, the police officer refused to register the complaint, and that it took mediation by a local anti-discrimination group before the police agreed to prepare a report.

The author then detailed the complaint's slow passage through Dutch legal channels. Some of these details are evident from arguments excerpted directly below. L.K.'s complaint was finally dismissed by the Dutch Court of Appeal nearly two years after he filed it.

¶ 3.1. The author submits that the remarks and statements of the residents of the street constitute acts of racial discrimination within the meaning of article 1, paragraph 1, of the Convention, as well as of article 137, *literae* (c), (d), and (e), of the Dutch Criminal Code; the latter provisions prohibit public insults of a group of people solely on the basis of their race, public incitement of hatred against people on account of their race, and the publication of documents containing racial insults of a group of people.

¶ 3.2. The author contends that the judicial authorities and the public prosecutor did not properly examine all the relevant facts of the case or at least did not formulate a motivated decision in respect of his complaint. In particular, he submits that the police investigation was neither thorough nor complete. Thus, A.B. was not questioned, and street residents were only questioned in connection with the petition, not with the events outside the house visited by the author on 8/9 August 1989. Secondly, the author contends that the decision of the prosecutor not to institute criminal proceedings remained unmotivated. Thirdly, the prosecutor is said to have made misleading statements in an interview to a local newspaper in December 1989, in respect of the purported intentions of the street residents vis-à-vis the author. Fourthly, the Prosecutor-General at the Court of Appeal is said to have unjustifiably prolonged the proceedings by remaining inactive for over one year. Finally, the Court of Appeal itself is said to have relied on incomplete evidence.

¶ 3.3. Author's counsel asserts that the above reveals violations of articles 2, paragraph 1 (d), *juncto* 4 and 6; he observes that articles 4 and 6 must be read together with the first sentence and paragraph 1 litera (d) of article 2,[58] which leads to the conclusion that the obligations of States parties to the Convention are not met if racial discrimination is merely criminalized. Counsel submits that although the freedom to prosecute or not to prosecute, known as the expediency principle, is not set aside by the Convention, the State party, by ratifying the Convention, accepted to treat instances of racial discrimination with particular attention, *inter alia*, by ensuring the speedy disposal of such cases by domestic judicial instances.

The State Party submitted that its agents, such as the police, prosecutor, and courts, had acted properly with regard to the complaint.

---

[58] Art. 2(1)(d) ICERD requires States Parties to take all appropriate measures to prohibit racial discrimination by any persons, group, or organization. Art. 6 ICERD guarantees everyone within State Party jurisdiction access to effective protection and remedies for breaches of their ICERD rights.

¶ 4.5. The State party observes that the Dutch legislation meets the requirements of article 2, paragraph 1 (d), of the Convention, by making racial discrimination a criminal offence under articles 137, litera (c) *et seq.* of the Criminal Code. For any criminal offence to be prosecuted, however, there must be sufficient evidence to warrant prosecution. In the Government's opinion, there can be no question of a violation of articles 4 and 6 of the Convention because, as set out in the public prosecutor's letter of 25 June 1990, it had not been sufficiently established that any criminal offence had been committed on 8 and 9 August 1989, or who had been involved.

¶ 4.6. In the State party's opinion, the fact that racial discrimination has been criminalized under the Criminal Code is sufficient to establish compliance with the obligation in article 4 of the Convention, since this provision cannot be read to mean that proceedings are instituted in respect of every type of conduct to which the provision may apply. In this context, the State party notes that decisions to prosecute are taken in accordance with the expediency principle . . . The author was able to avail himself of an effective remedy, in accordance with article 6 of the Convention, because he could and did file a complaint pursuant to article 12 of the Code of Criminal Procedure, against the prosecutor's refusal to prosecute. The State party emphasizes that the review of the case by the Court of Appeal was comprehensive and not limited in scope.

The ICERD Committee decided in favour of L.K. in the following terms:

¶ 6.3. The Committee finds on the basis of the information before it that the remarks and threats made on 8 and 9 August 1989 to L.K. constituted incitement to racial discrimination and to acts of violence against persons of another colour or ethnic origin, contrary to article 4 (a) of the International Convention on the Elimination of All Forms of Racial Discrimination, and that the investigation into these incidents by the police and prosecution authorities was incomplete.

¶ 6.4. The Committee cannot accept any claim that the enactment of law making racial discrimination a criminal act in itself represents full compliance with the obligations of States parties under the Convention.

¶ 6.5. The Committee reaffirms its view as stated in its Opinion on Communication No. 1/1984 of 10 August 1987 (*Yilmaz-Dogan v The Netherlands*) [23.76] that 'the freedom to prosecute criminal offences—commonly known as the expediency principle—is governed by considerations of public policy and notes that the Convention cannot be interpreted as challenging the *raison d'être* of that principle. Notwithstanding, it should be applied in each case of alleged racial discrimination in the light of the guarantees laid down in the Convention'.

¶ 6.6. When threats of racial violence are made, and especially when they are made in public and by a group, it is incumbent upon the State to investigate with due diligence and expedition. In the instant case, the State party failed to do this.

¶ 6.7. The Committee finds that in view of the inadequate response to the incidents, the police and judicial proceedings in this case did not afford the applicant effective protection and remedies within the meaning of article 6 of the Convention.

¶ 6.8. The Committee recommends that the State party review its policy and procedures concerning the decision to prosecute in cases of alleged racial discrimination, in the light of its obligations under article 4 of the Convention.

¶ 6.9. The Committee further recommends that the State party provide the applicant with relief commensurate with the moral damage he has suffered.

[18.46] Cases before the HRC on racial vilification have been concerned with limits to freedom of expression rights under article 19, rather than breaches of article 20 by failure to proscribe racial vilification. The HRC, in paragraph 2 of its General Comment 11, and the ICERD Committee, in paragraph 4 of its General Recommendation 15, have confirmed the compatibility of the respective hate speech provisions with the right to freedom of expression.

[18.47]   *J.R.T. and the W.G. PARTY v CANADA (104/81)*

The facts are outlined immediately below:

¶ 1. The communication . . . is submitted by Mr. T., a 69-year old Canadian citizen, residing in Canada, and by the W.G. Party, an unincorporated political party under the leadership of Mr. T. since 1976.

¶ 2.1. The W.G. Party was founded as a political party in Toronto, Ontario, Canada, in February 1972. The Party and Mr. T. attempted over several years to attract membership and promote the Party's policies through the use of tape-recorded messages, which were recorded by Mr. T. and linked up to the Bell Telephone System in Toronto, Ontario, Canada. Any member of the public could listen to the messages by dialling the relevant telephone number. The messages were changed from time to time but the contents were basically the same, namely to warn the callers 'of the dangers of international finance and international Jewry leading the world into wars, unemployment and inflation and the collapse of world values and principles'.

¶ 2.2. The Canadian Human Rights Act was promulgated on I March 1978. Section 13 (1) of the Act reads as follows:

> It is a discriminatory practice for a person or a group of persons acting in concert to communicate telephonically or to cause to be so communicated, repeatedly, in whole or in part by means of the facilities of a telecommunication undertaking within the legislative authority of Parliament, any matter that is likely to expose a person or persons to hatred or contempt by reason of the fact that the person or those persons are identifiable on the basis of a prohibited ground of discrimination.

¶ 2.3. By application of this provision in conjunction with section 3 of the Act, which enumerates 'race, national or ethnic origin, colour, religion, age, sex, marital status, conviction for which a pardon has been granted and physical handicap' as 'prohibited grounds of discrimination', the telephone service of the W. G. Party and Mr. T. was curtailed. . . .

Mr T. claimed that the above facts violated his rights under article 19(1) and (2) ICCPR. However, the HRC found the case inadmissible in the following terms:

¶ 8(b). . . . [T]he opinions which Mr. T. seeks to disseminate through the telephone system clearly constitute the advocacy of racial or religious hatred which Canada has an obligation under article 20 (2) of the Covenant to prohibit. In the Committee's opinion, therefore, the communication is, in respect of this claim, incompatible with the provisions of the Covenant, within the meaning of article 3 of the Optional Protocol.

HOLOCAUST DENIAL

[18.48]   *FAURISSON v FRANCE (550/93)*

This case deals with the phenomenon of Holocaust denial. Faurisson was convicted under a French law, which was described as follows by the State Party:

¶ 7.10. The offence of which the author was convicted is defined in precise terms and is based on objective criteria, so as to avoid the creation of a category of offences linked merely to expression of opinions (*'délit d'opinion'*). The committal of the offence necessitates (a) the denial of crimes against humanity, as defined and recognized internationally [by the London Charter of 8 August 1945], and (b) that these crimes against humanity have been adjudicated by judicial instances [in International Military Tribunal at Nuremburg]. In other words, the Law of 13 July 1990 does not punish the expression of an opinion, but the denial of a historical reality universally recognized. The adoption of the provision was necessary in the State party's opinion, not only to protect the rights and the reputation of others, but also to protect public order and morals.

The author submitted the following complaint:

¶ 2.1. The author was a professor of literature at the Sorbonne University in Paris until 1973 and at the University of Lyon until 1991, when he was removed from his chair. Aware of the historical significance of the Holocaust, he has sought proof of the methods of killings, in particular by gas asphyxiation. While he does not contest the use of gas for purposes of disinfection, he doubts the existence of gas chambers for extermination purposes (*'chambres à gaz homicides'*) at Auschwitz and in other Nazi concentration camps. . . .

¶ 2.2. The author submits that his opinions have been rejected in numerous academic journals and ridiculed in the daily press, notably in France; nonetheless, he continues to question the existence of extermination gas chambers. As a result of public discussion of his opinions and the polemics accompanying these debates, he states that, since 1978, he has become the target of death threats and that on eight occasions he has been physically assaulted. On one occasion in 1989, he claims to have suffered serious injuries, including a broken jaw, for which he was hospitalized. He contends that although these attacks were brought to the attention of the competent judicial authorities, they were not seriously investigated and none of those responsible for the assaults has been arrested or prosecuted. On 23 November 1992, the Court of Appeal of Riom followed the request of the prosecutor of the Tribunal de Grande Instance of Cusset and decreed the closure of the proceedings (*ordonnance de non-lieu*) which the authorities had initiated against X.

¶ 2.3. On 13 July 1990, the French legislature passed the so-called 'Gayssot Act', which amends the law on the Freedom of the Press of 1881 by adding an article 24*bis*; the latter makes it an offence to contest the existence of the category of crimes against humanity as defined in the London Charter of 8 August 1945, on the basis of which Nazi leaders were tried and convicted by the International Military Tribunal at Nuremburg in 1945–1946. The author submits that, in essence, the 'Gayssot Act' promotes the Nuremburg trial and judgment to the status of dogma, by imposing criminal sanctions on those who dare to challenge its findings and premises. Mr. Faurisson contends that he has ample reason to believe that the records of the Nuremburg trial can indeed be challenged and that the evidence used against Nazi leaders is open to question, as is, according to him, the evidence about the number of victims exterminated at Auschwitz. . . .

¶ 2.5. Shortly after the enactment of the 'Gayssot Act', Mr. Faurisson was interviewed by the French monthly magazine *Le Choc du Mois*, which published the interview in its Number 32 issue of September 1990. Besides expressing his concern that the new law constituted a threat to freedom of research and freedom of expression, the author reiterated his personal conviction that there were no homicidal gas chambers for the extermination of Jews in Nazi concentration camps. Following the publication of this interview, eleven associations of French resistance fighters and of deportees to German concentration camps filed a private criminal action against Mr. Faurisson and Patrice Boizeau, the editor of the magazine *Le Choc du Mois*. By judgment of 18 April 1991, the 17th Chambre Correctionnelle du Tribunal de Grande Instance de Paris convicted Messrs. Faurisson and Boizeau of having committed the crime of '*contestation de crimes contre l'humanité*' and imposed on them fines and costs amounting to FF 326,832.

¶ 2.6. The conviction was based, *inter alia*, on the following Faurisson statements:

'. . . No one will have me admit that two plus two make five, that the earth is flat, or that the Nuremburg Tribunal was infallible. I have excellent reasons not to believe in this policy of extermination of Jews or in the magic gas chamber . . .'

'I would wish to see that 100 per cent of all French citizens realize that the myth of the gas chambers is a dishonest fabrication ("*est une gredinerie*"), endorsed by the victorious powers of Nuremburg in 1945–46 and officialized on 14 July 1990 by the current French Government, with the approval of the "court historians" '. . . .

¶ 3.1. The author contends that the 'Gayssot Act' curtails his right to freedom of expression and academic freedom in general, and considers that the law targets him personally (*'lex Faurissonia'*). He complains that the incriminated provision constitutes unacceptable censorship, obstructing and penalizing historical research. . . .

The State Party submitted the following counter-arguments:

¶ 4.1. In its submission under rule 91, the State party provides a chronological overview of the facts of the case and explains the *ratio legis* of the law of 13 July 1990. In this latter context, it observes that the law in question fills a gap in the panoply of criminal sanctions, by criminalizing the acts of those who question the genocide of the Jews and the existence of gas chambers. In the latter context, it adds that the so-called 'revisionist' theses had previously escaped any criminal qualification, in that they could not be subsumed under the prohibition of (racial) discrimination, of incitement to racial hatred, or glorification of war crimes or crimes against humanity.

¶ 4.2. The State party further observes that in order to avoid making it an offence to manifest an opinion (*'délit d'opinion'*), the legislature chose to determine precisely the material
element of the offence, by criminalizing only the negation (*'contestation'*), by one of the
means enumerated in article 23 of the law on the Freedom of the Press of 1881, of one or
several of the crimes against humanity in the sense of article 6 of the Statute of the International Military Tribunal. The role of the judge seized of allegations of facts that might
be subsumed under the new law is not to intervene in an academic or an historical debate,
but to ascertain whether the contested publications of words negate the existence of crimes
against humanity recognized by international judicial instances. The State party points out
that the law of 13 July 1990 was noted with appreciation by the Committee on the Elimination of Racial Discrimination in March 1994. . . .

¶ 7.2. . . . To the Government these revisionist theses constitute 'a subtle form of contemporary anti-semitism' . . . which, prior to 13 July 1990 could not be prosecuted under any
of the existing provisions of French criminal legislation.

¶ 7.3. The former Minister for Justice, Mr. Arpaillange, has aptly summarized the position
of the Government by stating that it was impossible not to devote oneself fully to the fight
against racism, adding that racism did not constitute an opinion but an aggression, and that
every time racism was allowed to express itself publicly, the public order was immediately
and severely threatened. . . .

¶ 7.5. . . . By challenging the reality of the extermination of Jews during the Second World
War, the author incites his readers to anti-semitic behaviour . . . contrary to the Covenant
and other international conventions ratified by France. . . .

¶ 7.13. [The State party] concludes that the author's conviction was fully justified, not
only by the necessity of securing respect for the judgment of the International Military
Tribunal at Nuremburg, and through it the memory of the survivors and the descendants of
the victims of Nazism, but also by the necessity of maintaining social cohesion and public
order.

Mr Faurisson responded in the following manner:

¶ 8.1. In his comments, the author asserts that the State party's observations are based on
a misunderstanding: he concedes that the freedoms of opinion and of expression indeed
have some limits, but that he invokes less these freedoms than the freedom to doubt and
the freedom of research which, to his mind, do not permit any restrictions. The latter freedoms are violated by the Law of 13 July 1990 which elevates to the level of only and
unchallengeable truth what a group of individuals, judges of an international military
tribunal, had decreed in advance as being authentic. Mr. Faurisson notes that the Spanish
and United Kingdom Governments have recently recognized that anti-revisionist legislation of the French model is a step backward both for the law and for history.

¶ 8.2. The author reiterates that the desire to fight anti-semitism cannot justify any limitations on the freedom of research on a subject which is of obvious interest to Jewish organizations: the author qualifies as 'exorbitant' the 'privilege of censorship' from which the
representatives of the Jewish community in France benefit. He observes that no other
subject he is aware of has ever become a virtual taboo for research, following a request by
another political or religious community. To him, no law should be allowed to prohibit the

publication of studies on any subject, under the pretext that there is nothing to research on it.

¶ 8.3. Mr. Faurisson asserts that the State party has failed to provide the slightest element of proof that his own writings and theses constitute a 'subtle form of contemporary anti-semitism' (see para. 7.2 above) or incite the public to anti-semitic behaviour (see para. 7.5 above). He accuses the State party of hubris in dismissing his research and writings as 'pseudo-scientific' (*'prétendument scientifique'*), and adds that he does not deny anything but merely challenges what the State party refers to as a 'universally recognized reality' (*'une réalité universellement reconnue'*). The author further observes that the revisionist school has, over the past two decades, been able to dismiss as doubtful or wrong so many elements of the 'universally recognized reality' that the impugned law becomes all the more unjustifiable. . . .

¶ 8.7. Mr. Faurisson argues that it would be wrong to examine his case and his situation purely in the light of legal concepts. He suggests that his case should be examined in a larger context: by way of example, he invokes the case of Galileo, whose discoveries were true, and any law, which would have enabled his conviction, would have been by its very nature wrong or absurd. . . .

The HRC found against Faurisson on the merits:

¶ 9.3. Although it does not contest that the application of the terms of the Gayssot Act, which, in their effect, make it a criminal offence to challenge the conclusions and the verdict of the International Military Tribunal at Nuremburg, may lead, under different conditions than the facts of the instant case, to decisions or measures incompatible with the Covenant, the Committee is not called upon to criticize in the abstract laws enacted by States parties. The task of the Committee under the Optional Protocol is to ascertain whether the conditions of the restrictions imposed on the right to freedom of expression are met in the communications which are brought before it.

¶ 9.4. Any restriction on the right to freedom of expression must cumulatively meet the following conditions: it must be provided by law, it must address one of the aims set out in paragraph 3 (a) and (b) of article 19, and must be necessary to achieve a legitimate purpose.

¶ 9.5. The restriction on the author's freedom of expression was indeed provided by law i.e. the Act of 13 July 1990. It is the constant jurisprudence of the Committee that the restrictive law itself must be in compliance with the provisions of the Covenant. In this regard the Committee concludes, on the basis of the reading of the judgment of the 17th Chambre correctionnelle du Tribunal de grande instance de Paris that the finding of the author's guilt was based on his following two statements: '. . . I have excellent reasons not to believe in the policy of extermination of Jews or in the magic gas chambers . . . I wish to see that 100 per cent of the French citizens realize that the myth of the gas chambers is a dishonest fabrication'. His conviction therefore did not encroach upon his right to hold and express an opinion in general, rather the court convicted Mr. Faurisson for having violated the rights and reputation of others. For these reasons the Committee is satisfied that the Gayssot Act, as read, interpreted and applied to the author's case by the French courts, is in compliance with the provisions of the Covenant.

¶ 9.6. To assess whether the restrictions placed on the author's freedom of expression by his criminal conviction were applied for the purposes provided for by the Covenant, the Committee begins by noting, as it did in its General Comment 10 that the rights for the protection of which restrictions on the freedom of expression are permitted by article 19, paragraph 3, may relate to the interests of other persons or to those of the community as a whole. Since the statements made by the author, read in their full context, were of a nature as to raise or strengthen anti-semitic feelings, the restriction served the respect of the Jewish community to live free from fear of an atmosphere of anti-semitism. The Committee therefore concludes that the restriction of the author's freedom of expression was permissible under article 19, paragraph 3 (a), of the Covenant.

¶ 9.7. Lastly the Committee needs to consider whether the restriction of the author's freedom of expression was necessary. The Committee noted the State party's argument contending that the introduction of the Gayssot Act was intended to serve the struggle against racism and anti-semitism. It also noted the statement of a member of the French Government, the then Minister of Justice, which characterized the denial of the existence of the Holocaust as the principal vehicle for anti-semitism. In the absence in the material before it of any argument undermining the validity of the State party's position as to the necessity of the restriction, the Committee is satisfied that the restriction of Mr. Faurisson's freedom of expression was necessary within the meaning of article 19, paragraph 3, of the Covenant.

¶ 10. The Human Rights Committee, acting under article 5, paragraph 4, of the Optional Protocol to the International Covenant on Civil and Political Rights, is of the view that the facts as found by the Committee do not reveal a violation by France of article 19, paragraph 3, of the Covenant.

[18.49] A number of concurring separate opinions were submitted. Mrs Evatt and Mr Kretzmer submitted the following opinion, co-signed by Mr Klein:

¶ 3. The State party has argued that the author's conviction was justified 'by the necessity of securing respect for the judgment of the International Military Tribunal at Nuremburg, and through it the memory of the survivors and the descendants of the victims of Nazism.' While we entertain no doubt whatsoever that the author's statements are highly offensive both to Holocaust survivors and to descendants of Holocaust victims (as well as to many others), the question under the Covenant is whether a restriction on freedom of expression in order to achieve this purpose may be regarded as a restriction necessary for the respect of the rights of others.

¶ 4. Every individual has the right to be free not only from discrimination on grounds of race, religion and national origins, but also from incitement to such discrimination. This is stated expressly in article 7 of the Universal Declaration of Human Rights. It is implicit in the obligation placed on States parties under article 20, paragraph 2, of the Covenant to prohibit by law any advocacy of national, racial or religious hatred that constitutes incitement to discrimination, hostility or violence. The crime for which the author was convicted under the Gayssot Act does not expressly include the element of incitement, nor do the statements which served as the basis for the conviction fall clearly within the boundaries of incitement, which the State party was bound to prohibit, in accordance with article 20, paragraph 2. However, there may be circumstances in which the right of a person to be free from incitement to discrimination on grounds of race, religion or national origins cannot be fully protected by a narrow, explicit law on incitement that falls precisely within the boundaries of article 20, paragraph 2. This is the case where, in a particular social and historical context, statements that do not meet the strict legal criteria of incitement can be shown to constitute part of a pattern of incitement against a given racial, religious or national group, or where those interested in spreading hostility and hatred adopt sophisticated forms of speech that are not punishable under the law against racial incitement, even though their effect may be as pernicious as explicit incitement, if not more so.

¶ 5. In the discussion in the French Senate on the Gayssot Act the then Minister of Justice, Mr. Arpaillange, explained that the said law, which, *inter alia*, prohibits denial of the Holocaust, was needed since Holocaust denial is a contemporary expression of racism and anti-semitism. Furthermore, the influence of the author's statements on racial or religious hatred was considered by the Paris Court of Appeal, which held that by virtue of the fact that such statements propagate ideas tending to revive Nazi doctrine and the policy of racial discrimination, they tend to disrupt the harmonious coexistence of different groups in France.

¶ 6. The notion that in the conditions of present-day France, Holocaust denial may constitute a form of incitement to anti-semitism cannot be dismissed. This is a consequence not of the mere challenge to well-documented historical facts, established both by historians of different persuasions and backgrounds as well as by international and domestic tribunals, but of the context, in which it is implied, under the guise of impartial academic research, that the victims of Nazism were guilty of dishonest fabrication, that the story of their victimization is a myth and that the gas chambers in which so many people were murdered are 'magic'.

¶ 7. The Committee correctly points out, as it did in its General Comment 10, that the right for the protection of which restrictions on freedom of expression are permitted by article 19, paragraph 3, may relate to the interests of a community as a whole. This is especially the case in which the right protected is the right to be free from racial, national or religious incitement. The French courts examined the statements made by the author and came to the conclusion that his statements were of a nature as to raise or strengthen anti-semitic tendencies. It appears therefore that the restriction on the author's freedom of expression served to protect the right of the Jewish community in France to live free from fear of incitement to anti-semitism. This leads us to the conclusion that the State party has shown that the aim of the restrictions on the author's freedom of expression was to respect the right of others, mentioned in article 19, paragraph 3. The more difficult question is whether imposing liability for such statements was necessary in order to protect that right.

¶ 8. The power given to States parties under article 19, paragraph 3, to place restrictions on freedom of expression, must not be interpreted as licence to prohibit unpopular speech, or speech which some sections of the population find offensive. Much offensive speech may be regarded as speech that impinges on one of the values mentioned in article 19, paragraph 3 (a) or (b) (the rights or reputations of others, national security, *ordre public*, public health or morals). The Covenant therefore stipulates that the purpose of protecting one of those values is not, of itself, sufficient reason to restrict expression. The restriction must be necessary to protect the given value. This requirement of necessity implies an element of proportionality. The scope of the restriction imposed on freedom of expression must be proportional to the value which the restriction serves to protect. It must not exceed that needed to protect that value. As the Committee stated in its General Comment 10, the restriction must not put the very right itself in jeopardy.

¶ 9. The Gayssot Act is phrased in the widest language and would seem to prohibit publication of *bona fide* research connected with matters decided by the Nuremburg Tribunal. Even if the purpose of this prohibition is to protect the right to be free from incitement to anti-semitism, the restrictions imposed do not meet the proportionality test. They do not link liability to the intent of the author, nor to the tendency of the publication to incite to anti-semitism. Furthermore, the legitimate object of the law could certainly have been achieved by a less drastic provision that would not imply that the State party had attempted to turn historical truths and experiences into legislative dogma that may not be challenged, no matter what the object behind that challenge, nor its likely consequences. In the present case we are not concerned, however, with the Gayssot Act, *in abstracto*, but only with the restriction placed on the freedom of expression of the author by his conviction for his statements in the interview in *Le Choc du Mois*. Does this restriction meet the proportionality test?

¶ 10. The French courts examined the author's statements in great detail. Their decisions, and the interview itself, refute the author's argument that he is only driven by his interest in historical research. In the interview the author demanded that historians 'particularly Jewish historians' ('*les historiens, en particulier juifs*') who agree that some of the findings of the Nuremburg Tribunal were mistaken be prosecuted. The author referred to the 'magic gas chamber' ('*la magique chambre à gaz*') and to 'the myth of the gas chambers' ('*le mythe des chambres à gaz*'), that was a 'dirty trick' ('*une gredinerie*') endorsed by the victors in Nuremburg. The author has, in these statements, singled out Jewish historians over others, and has clearly implied that the Jews, the victims of the Nazis, concocted the story of gas chambers for their own purposes. While there is every reason to maintain protection of *bona fide* historical research against restriction, even when it challenges accepted historical truths and by so doing offends people, anti-semitic allegations of the sort made by the author, which violate the rights of others in the way described, do not have the same claim to protection against restriction. The restrictions placed on the author did not curb the core of his right to freedom of expression, nor did they in any way affect his freedom of research; they were intimately linked to the value they were meant to protect—the right to be free from incitement to racism or anti-semitism; protecting that value could not have been achieved in the circumstances by less drastic means. It is for these reasons that we joined the Committee in concluding that, in the specific circumstances of the case, the restrictions on the author's freedom of expression met the proportionality test and were necessary in order to protect the rights of others.

Messrs Ando and Lallah, in separate concurring opinions, essentially agreed with the opinion of Mrs Evatt and Messrs Kretzmer and Klein.

[18.50] Mrs Medina Quiroga also agreed with the above opinion, and added the following observation:

¶ 2. I would like to add that a determining factor for my position is the fact that, although the wording of the Gayssot Act might, in application, constitute a clear violation of article 19 of the Covenant, the French court which tried Mr. Faurisson interpreted and applied that

Act in the light of the provisions of the Covenant, thereby adapting the Act to France's international obligations with regard to freedom of expression.

[18.51] Mr Bhagwati also submitted a separate concurring opinion:

Was the restriction on the author's freedom of expression imposed under the Gayssot Act necessary for respect of the rights and interests of the Jewish community? The answer must obviously be in the affirmative. If the restriction on freedom of expression in the manner provided under the Gayssot Act had not been imposed and statements denying the Holocaust and the extermination of Jews by asphyxiation in the gas chamber had not been made penal, the author and other revisionists like him could have gone on making statements similar to the one which invited the conviction of the author and the necessary consequence and fall-out of such statements would have been, in the context of the situation prevailing in Europe, promotion and strengthening of anti-semitic feelings, as emphatically pointed out by the State party in its submissions. Therefore, the imposition of restriction by the Gayssot Act was necessary for securing respect for the rights and interests of the Jewish community to live in society with full human dignity and free from an atmosphere of anti-semitism.

It is therefore clear that . . . the conviction of the author under the Gayssot Act was not violative of his freedom of expression guaranteed under article 19, paragraph 2. I have reached this conclusion under the greatest reluctance because I firmly believe that in a free democratic society, freedom of speech and expression is one of the most prized freedoms which must be defended and upheld at any cost and this should be particularly so in the land of Voltaire. It is indeed unfortunate that in the world of today, when science and technology have advanced the frontiers of knowledge and mankind is beginning to realize that human happiness can be realized only through inter-dependence and cooperation, the threshold of tolerance should be going down. It is high time man should realize his spiritual dimension and replace bitterness and hatred by love and compassion, tolerance and forgiveness.

[18.52] Despite the State Party's victory in *Faurisson v France*, all HRC members expressed misgivings over the wide scope of the impugned law. Whilst Mr Faurisson's interview could be legitimately censored, the law could conceivably censor expression in a way which breached article 19. Perhaps it is arguable that the restrictions on Faurisson's speech were not sufficiently circumscribed and 'provided by law', as the law itself was too broad [18.17]. However, the HRC interpreted the relevant 'law' to have been the French statute *as interpreted by the French Court.* The Court's decision had 'cured' the defects in the statute in this case.

Conclusion

[18.53] The HRC has generally been quite liberal in its interpretation of article 19, and has found numerous breaches thereof. In particular, it has generally dismissed State arguments which have sought to justify restrictions on free expression on the basis of public order or national security. States have so far had greater success in restricting speech for reasons of public morality.

[18.54] The HRC has not yet dealt with a case concerning a potential breach of article 20. In the future, it is likely to look to any precedents available from the Committee on the Elimination of Racial Discrimination under article 4 of ICERD. Article 20 has however had an influence on HRC jurisprudence, in that various restrictions on racist speech have been found to be justified under article 19(3). Indeed, the HRC's evident distaste for extreme right-wing groups (it has never upheld a complaint over the restriction of extreme right-wing views) may be fuelled by the presence in the Covenant of article 20.

Postscript: Please note that General Comment 28 on 'Equality of Rights Between Men and Women', contained in the Addendum at page 634, contains extra information on some of the material in this chapter.

19

Freedoms of Assembly and Association—
Articles 21, 22

[19.01] Article 21 guarantees freedom of peaceful assembly, while article 22 guarantees freedom of association. Both freedoms are essential to one's effective participation in civil and political society. However, neither freedom has generated much ICCPR jurisprudence.

ARTICLE 21

The right of peaceful assembly shall be recognized. No restrictions may be placed on the exercise of this right other than those imposed in conformity with the law and which are necessary in a democratic society in the interests of national security or public safety, public order (*ordre public*), the protection of public health or morals or the protection of the rights and freedoms of others.

MEANING OF 'ASSEMBLY'

[19.02] Article 21 protects the right of peaceful assembly. Nowak describes the right as one of persons to gather intentionally and temporarily for a specific purpose.[1] Certain assemblies are protected under other provisions. For example, religious assemblies are protected under article 18; purely private assemblies, such as gatherings of family and friends, are protected under article 17; and

---

[1] M. Nowak, *UN Covenant on Civil and Political Rights: CCPR Commentary* (N.P. Engel, Kehl, 1993), 373.

assemblies by associations are protected by article 22.[2] By inference, article 21 might be directed at protecting assemblies that are not covered by these other articles. Nowak suggests that article 21 is specifically directed at assemblies concerned with the discussion or proclamation of ideas.[3]

[19.03] Assemblies may occur in a variety of ways. They can be held in closed rooms, outdoors, and on public or private property. Assemblies can be mobile (as in marches and processions) or stationary. Participation may be restricted or open to all.

LIMITS TO FREEDOM OF ASSEMBLY

[19.04] Freedom of assembly is not an absolute right. First, the freedom is confined to peaceful assemblies, so assemblies must not be violent. For example, riots and affrays would not be protected. Civil disobedience manifested without force is likely to be protected under this provision.[4] However, this does not mean that States are absolved of human rights obligations in controlling violent assemblies. In Concluding Comments on Denmark, the HRC commented:[5]

¶ 14. The Committee also expresses its concern with the methods of crowd control employed by police forces, including the use of dogs, against participants in various demonstrations and gatherings which, on certain occasions, have resulted in serious injuries to persons in the crowds, including bystanders.

¶ 21. The Committee urges the Government of the State party to further the training of the police forces in methods of crowd control and handling offenders, including those suffering from mental disorder; and to keep these issues constantly under review. The Committee recommends that the authorities reconsider the use of dogs in crowd control.

The above comments may indicate that peaceful participants in a violent assembly may be protected under article 21, and/or that all participants are protected under other ICCPR provisions, such as the article 7 prohibition on inhuman and degrading treatment.

[19.05] The right of freedom of assembly is also subject to a number of express limitations. These limitations mirror those found in articles 12, 18, 19, and 22. Presumably, the limits to article 21 will be interpreted in a similar manner to relevant interpretations under other provisions.[6]

Article 21 limits must be 'in conformity with the law'. This phrase is different from that found in articles 12, 18, 19, and 22, which require limitations to be

---

[2] M. Nowak, *UN Covenant on Civil and Political Rights: CCPR Commentary*, 374.
[3] Ibid.   [4] Ibid., 375.
[5] (1997) UN Doc. CCPR/C/79/Add.68, para. 14.
[6] See [12.23] and [18.16] ff. for interpretation of identical enumerated limits. See 'Siracusa Principles on the Limitation and Derogation Provisions in the International Covenant on Civil and Political Rights' (1985) 7 HRQ 3, which indicates that all limitation clauses in the ICCPR are to be interpreted in the same way with regard to each right.

'provided' or 'prescribed' by law. Nowak believes that this difference in formulation permits the exercise of more administrative discretion in imposing limits to article 21, compared to the other mentioned articles, where restrictions should be more carefully circumscribed by law.[7]

The limits must also be 'necessary in a democratic society'. Identical words have been interpreted as incorporating a notion of proportionality into limitations to rights of freedom of expression under article 19.[8] Presumably, the words mean the same in the context of freedom of assembly.[9]

INTERPRETATION OF ARTICLE 21

[19.06] The only case on article 21 is *Kivenmaa v Finland*.

KIVENMAA v FINLAND (412/90)

The facts were outlined by the complainant as follows:

¶ 1. The author of the communication is Ms. Auli Kivenmaa, a Finnish citizen and Secretary-General of the Social Democratic Youth Organization. She claims to be a victim of a violation by Finland of articles 15 and 19, and alternatively, article 21, of the International Covenant on Civil and Political Rights. She is represented by counsel.

The facts:

¶ 2.1. On 3 September 1987, on the occasion of a visit of a foreign head of State and his meeting with the president of Finland, the author and about 25 members of her organization, amid a larger crowd, gathered across from the Presidential Palace where the leaders were meeting, distributed leaflets and raised a banner critical of the human rights record of the visiting head of State. The police immediately took the banner down and asked who was responsible. The author identified herself and was subsequently charged with violating the Act on Public Meetings by holding a 'public meeting' without prior notification.

¶ 2.2. The above-mentioned Act on Public Meetings has not been amended since 1921, nor upon entry into force of the Covenant. Section 12(1) of the Act makes it a punishable offence to call a public meeting without notification to the police at least six hours before the meeting. The requirement of prior notification applies only to public meetings in the open air (section 3). A meeting is not public if only those with personal invitations can attend (section 1(2)). Section 1(1) provides that the purpose of a 'meeting' is to discuss public matters and to make decisions on them. Section 10 of the Act extends the requirement of prior notification to public ceremonial processions and marches.

---

[7] Nowak, above, note 1, 378, and K. Partsch, 'Freedom of Conscience and Expression, and Political Freedoms' in L. Henkin (ed.), *The International Bill of Rights* (Columbia University Press, New York, 1981), 232. See, on impermissible breadth of discretion, *Pinkney v Canada* (27/78), [16.11]; see also [1.51].

[8] See [18.18]. See also [12.23].

[9] See 'Siracusa Principles', above, note 6.

¶ 2.3. Although the author argued that she did not organize a public meeting, but only demonstrated her criticism of the alleged human rights violations by the visiting head of State, the City Court, on 27 January 1988, found her guilty of the charge and fined her 438 markkaa. The Court was of the opinion that the group of 25 persons had, through their behaviour, been distinguishable from the crowd and could therefore be regarded as a public meeting. It did not address the author's defence that her conviction would be in violation of the Covenant. . . .

The main thrust of Kivenmaa's complaint was that the relevant gathering (twenty-five people protesting against a visiting head of state) did not fall within the definition of 'public meeting' in the Act on Public Meetings ('the Act'). Therefore, she argued that application of the Act in the circumstances was not 'in conformity with the law' as required by article 21.

¶ 3. . . . The author . . . argues that, even if the event could be interpreted as an exercise of the freedom of assembly, she still was not under obligation to notify the police, as the demonstration did not take the form of a public meeting, nor a public march, as defined by the said Act. . . .

¶ 8.5. In conclusion, the author states that she does not contest that restrictions on the exercise of the right of peaceful assembly may be justified, and that prior notification of public meetings is a legitimate form of such restrictions. However, the author does challenge the concrete application of the Act on Public Meetings in her case. She contends that this outdated, vague and ambiguous statute was used as the legal basis for police interference with her expressing concern about the human rights situation in the country of the visiting head of State. She claims that this interference was not in conformity with the law nor necessary in a democratic society within the meaning of article 21 of the Covenant. In this connection, it is again stressed that, by taking away the banner, the police interfered with the most effective method for the author to express her opinion.

The State Party defended its position *viz.* article 21. First, it defended the law itself.

¶ 7.6. With regard to the author's allegation that she is a victim of a violation of article 21 of the Covenant, the State party recalls that article 21 allows restrictions on the exercise of the right to peaceful assembly. In Finland, the Act on Public Meetings guarantees the right to assemble peacefully in public, while ensuring public order and safety and preventing abuse of the right of assembly. Under the Act, public assembly is understood to be the coming together of more than one person for a lawful purpose in a public place that others than those invited also have access to. The State party submits that, in the established interpretation of the Act, the Act also applies to demonstrations arranged as public meetings or street processions. Article 3 of the Act requires prior notification to the police, at least six hours before the beginning of any public meeting at a public place in the open air. The notification must include information on the time and place of the meeting as well as on its organizer. Article 12, paragraph 1, of the Act makes it a punishable offence to call a public meeting without prior notification to the police. The State party emphasizes that the Act does not apply to a peaceful demonstration by only one person.

¶ 7.7. . . . The State party submits that the prior notification requirement enables the police to take the necessary measures to make it possible for the meeting to take place, for instance by regulating the flow of traffic, and further to protect the group in their exercise of the right to freedom of assembly. In this context, the State party contends that, when a foreign head of State is involved, it is of utmost practical importance that the police be notified prior to the event.

¶ 7.8. The State party argues that the right of public assembly is not restricted by the requirement of a prior notification to the police. . . . The State party emphasizes that the prior notification is necessary to guarantee the peacefulness of the public meeting.

Secondly, the State Party defended the application of the law to Kivenmaa and her group.

¶ 7.9. As regards the specific circumstances of the present case, the State party is of the opinion that the actual behaviour of the author and her friends amounted to a public meeting within the meaning of article 1 of the Act on Public Meetings. In this context, the State party submits that, although the word 'demonstration' is not expressly named in the Act on Public Meetings, this does not signify that demonstrations are outside the scope of application of the Act. In this connection, the State party refers to general principles of legal interpretation. Furthermore, it notes that article 21 of the Covenant does not specifically refer to 'demonstrations' as a mode of assembly either. Finally, the State party argues that the requirement of prior notification is in conformity with article 21, second sentence. In this context, the State party submits that the requirement is prescribed by law, and that it is necessary in a democratic society in the interests of legitimate purposes, especially in the interest of public order.

The HRC delivered a fairly brief merits decision in favour of Kivenmaa:

¶ 9.2. The Committee finds that a requirement to notify the police of an intended demonstration in a public place six hours before its commencement may be compatible with the permitted limitations laid down in article 21 of the Covenant. In the circumstances of this specific case, it is evident from the information provided by the parties that the gathering of several individuals at the site of the welcoming ceremonies for a foreign head of State on an official visit, publicly announced in advance by the State party authorities, cannot be regarded as a demonstration. Insofar as the State party contends that displaying a banner turns their presence into a demonstration, the Committee notes that any restrictions upon the right to assemble must fall within the limitation provisions of article 21. A requirement to pre-notify a demonstration would normally be for reasons of national security or public safety, public order, the protection of public health or morals or the protection of the rights and freedoms of others. Consequently, the application of Finnish legislation on demonstrations to such a gathering cannot be considered as an application of a restriction permitted by article 21 of the Covenant.

Unfortunately, the reasoning in the HRC's only merits decision on article 21 is remarkably opaque.[10] The HRC apparently agreed with Kivenmaa's contention

---

[10] T. Murphy, 'Freedom of Assembly' in D. Harris and S. Joseph (eds.), *The International Covenant on Civil and Political Rights and United Kingdom Law* (Clarendon Press, Oxford, 1995), 443.

that the relevant gathering was not a 'demonstration', and was therefore wrongly interpreted so as to come within the Finnish Act. However, the HRC does not normally question the legal or factual findings of municipal courts.[11] Its reasons for overturning the Finnish Court's decision here are unclear.

[19.07] Some of the deficiencies in the majority decision are highlighted in a vigorous dissent from Mr Herndl:

A. The question of a possible violation of article 21

¶ 2.1. The Committee's finding, that by applying the 1907 Act on Public Meetings (hereinafter called the 1907 Act) to the author—and ultimately imposing a fine on her in accordance with Section 12 of the Act—Finland has breached article 21 of the Covenant, is based on an erroneous appreciation of the facts and, even more so, on an erroneous view of what constitutes a 'peaceful assembly' in the sense of article 21.

¶ 2.3. The legal issue . . . centres on the question whether the author's actions—the fact that she 'and about 25 members of her organization, amid a large crowd, gathered . . ., distributed leaflets and raised a banner' (see paragraph 2.1 of the Views)—ought or ought not to be qualified as a 'public meeting' in the sense of the 1907 Act or, for that matter, as a 'peaceful assembly' in the sense of article 21 of the Covenant.

¶ 2.4. In that respect the Committee observes in paragraph 9.2 (second sentence) of its Views that 'it is evident from the information provided by the parties that the gathering of several individuals at the site of the welcoming ceremonies for a foreign head of State on an official visit, publicly announced in advance by the State party authorities, cannot be regarded as a demonstration'. I am, much to my regret, not able to follow this reasoning.

¶ 2.5. It is not contested by the author that she and a group of people of her organization summoned by her, went to the Presidential Palace explicitly for the purpose of distributing leaflets and raising a banner and thus to publicly denounce the presence, in Finland, of a foreign Head of State whose human rights record they criticized. If this does not constitute a demonstration, indeed a public gathering within the scope of article 21 of the Covenant, what else would constitute a 'peaceful assembly' in that sense, and, accordingly, a 'public meeting' in the sense of the 1907 Act? . . .

¶ 2.7. . . . The decisive element for the determination of an 'assembly'—as opposed to a more or less accidental gathering (e.g. people waiting for a bus, listening to a band, etc.)—obviously is the intention and the purpose of the individuals who come together. The author is estopped from arguing that she (and her group) were bystanders like the other crowd who was apparently attracted by the appearance of a foreign Head of State visiting the President of Finland. She and her group admittedly joined the event to make a political demonstration. This was the sole purpose of their appearing before the Presidential Palace. The State party, therefore, rightly stated, that this was 'conceptually' a demonstration.

[19.08] It is possible that the breadth of the Finnish Act influenced the majority

---

[11] See [14.36].

decision. However, Mr Herndl argued that both the author and the majority conceded the inherent reasonableness of the Act's obligations:

¶ 2.2. In the first sentence of paragraph 9.2 of its Views the Committee rightly observes that 'a requirement to notify the police of an intended demonstration in a public place six hours before its commencement may be compatible with the permitted limitation laid down in article 21 of the Covenant'. A mere requirement, as contained in the 1907 Act, to notify a public meeting to the authorities several hours before it starts, is obviously in line with article 21 of the Covenant which provides for the possibility of legitimate restrictions on the exercise of the right to peaceful assembly 'in conformity with the law and which are necessary in a democratic society in the interests of national security or public safety, public order (*ordre public*), the protection of public health or morals or the protection of the rights and freedoms of others'. The 1907 Act certainly falls in this category. This is, by the way, admitted by the author herself who asserts that she does not contest that restrictions on the exercise of the right to peaceful assembly may be justified, and that prior notification of public meetings is a legitimate form of such restrictions (see paragraph 8.5 of the Views). In her last communication she explicitly states that she is not challenging the validity of the 1907 Act *in abstracto* either. . . .

[19.09] Though the HRC conceded that the Act itself may have come within the permissible limitations to article 21, it apparently felt that application of the Act in the circumstances went beyond the bounds of permissible limitations to article 21. That is, the HRC accepted that prior notice requirements were justifiable for reasons of national security and public order, but the imposition of such requirements on Kivenmaa's gathering was inappropriate due to the minimal 'public order' risks entailed therein. Such a decision arguably relies too much on hindsight. Herndl commented adversely on this aspect of the HRC's decision in the following terms:

¶ 2.8. I [cannot] follow the Committee's argument in 9.2 (4th and 5th sentences) where an attempt is made to create a link between the purpose (and thus the legality) of the restrictive legislation as such and its application in a concrete case. To say that 'a requirement to pre-notify a demonstration would normally be for reasons of national security etc . . .' and then to continue '[C]onsequently, the application of the Finnish legislation on demonstrations to such a gathering cannot be considered as an application of a restriction permitted by article 21 of the Covenant' is, to say at least, contradictory.

¶ 2.9. If the restricting legislation as such—in the present matter the 1907 Act on Public Meetings—is considered as being within the limits of article 21 (a fact not contested by the author and recognized by the Committee) the relevant law must obviously be applied in a uniform manner to all cases falling under its scope. In other words: if the 1907 Act and the obligation therein contained to notify any 'public meeting' prior to its commencement, is a valid restriction on the exercise of the right to assembly, permitted under article 21 of the Covenant, then its formal application cannot be considered as a violation of the Covenant, whatever the actual reasons (in the mind of the authorities) for demanding the notification.

No apparent discretion was given to Finnish authorities regarding the notification requirements as all public meetings were automatically subject to those require-ments. In such circumstances, it seems fallacious for the HRC majority to have distinguished between the Act's requirements and their application.

[19.10] Perhaps the majority decision may be rationalized as a condemnation, albeit poorly executed, of blanket advance notice requirements for public meet-ings. Indeed, Kivenmaa herself had noted that the Act was 'unacceptably broad', as it could potentially apply to 'almost any outdoor discussion between at least three persons'.[12] The Committee's Concluding Comments on Mauritius provide more evidence that such requirements are incompatible with the Covenant. The HRC censured a law requiring seven days' prior notification of public meetings.[13] The requisite notification period was however considerably longer than that required under the Finnish Act in *Kivenmaa* (six hours).

Article 22

1. Everyone shall have the right to freedom of association with others, including the right to form and join trade unions for the protection of his interests.

2. No restrictions may be placed on the exercise of this right other than those which are prescribed by law and which are necessary in a democratic society in the interests of national security or public safety, public order (*ordre public*), the protection of public health or morals or the protection of the rights and freedoms of others. This article shall not prevent the imposition of lawful restrictions on members of the armed forces and of the police in their exercise of this right.
3. Nothing in this article shall authorize States Parties to the International Labour Organi-zation Convention of 1948 concerning Freedom of Association and Protection of the Right to Organize to take legislative measures which would prejudice, or to apply the law in such a manner as to prejudice, the guarantees provided for in that Convention.

MEANING OF 'ASSOCIATION'

[19.11] Freedom of association permits persons formally to join together in groups to pursue common interests. Examples of such groups are political parties, professional or sporting clubs, non-governmental organizations, trade unions, and corporations. The right may be limited to groups that form for 'public' purposes; groups with solely private interests, such as family groups, are probably protected separately under article 17.[14] For example, in *P.S. v Denmark* (397/90), the HRC

---

[12] Para. 8.4.
[13] (1996) UN doc. CCPR/C/79/Add. 60, para. 20; see also Concluding Comments on Belarus (1997), UN doc. CCPR/C/79/Add. 86, para. 18, where a requirement of 15 days' prior notice of a demonstration did not conform to 'the values in art. 21'. See also Concluding Comments on Morocco (1999) UN doc. CCPR/C/79/Add. 113, para. 24.
[14] See generally on privacy Chap. 16.

found that a father's complaint about restrictions on his ability to associate with his son did not raise issues under article 22.[15] It was not clear whether this was because of the nature of the relationship, or whether there were too few people involved to constitute an 'association'.

LIMITS TO FREEDOM OF ASSOCIATION

[19.12] Article 22(2) contains a list of permissible limitations to exercise of the right of freedom of association, which mirrors the lists of limitations in articles 12, 18, 19, and 21. The interpretation of these enumerated limitations with regard to these other provisions would be identical, *viz.* article 22.[16] For example, the requirement that limitations be 'necessary in a democratic society' incorporates a notion of proportionality into the imposition of limits on freedom of association.[17] *M.A. v Italy* (117/81) is a case where restrictions on freedom of association were found to be permissible. The ban on the Italian fascist party was found to be compatible with article 22, presumably for reasons of public order and national security.[18]

[19.13] The last sentence of article 22(2) authorizes 'lawful' restrictions on the exercise of freedom of association by members of the armed forces and the police. This seems to mean that these restrictions need only be prescribed by law, and are not bound by any requirement of proportionality or reasonableness.[19] Furthermore, lawful restrictions can be for any purpose, rather than one of the listed purposes. These measures may have been designed to ensure the compatibility of laws aimed at preserving political neutrality amongst the police and the armed forces with the ICCPR.[20] However, it seems possible under the existing text in article 22(2) to ban, by law, the military and the police from joining opposition political parties in order to induce political fidelity within the enforcement arm of the executive. Perhaps it would have been wise to retain the requirement of proportionality with regard to such restrictions. The HRC has not issued any interpretations of these special rules for the military and the police.

[19.14] In Concluding Comments on Belarus and Lithuania, the HRC has expressed concern over onerous 'registration procedures' for non-governmental organizations and trade unions.[21] Procedural formalities for recognition of associations must not be so burdensome as to amount to substantive restrictions on article 22 rights.

---

[15] Para. 5.3. Other complaints, such as those under arts. 17 (privacy) and 23 (family rights), were inadmissible for failure to exhaust domestic remedies.
[16] See 'Siracusa Principles', above, note 6.   [17] See [18.18] and [19.05].
[18] This case is discussed at [18.29].
[19] Compare commentary at [16.09–16.12] and [11.55–11.56].
[20] Nowak, above, note 1, 397.
[21] Concluding Comments on Belarus (1997) UN doc. CCPR/C/79/Add.86, para. 19; Concluding Comments on Lithuania (1997) UN doc. CCPR/C/79/Add. 87, para. 20.

TRADE UNION RIGHTS

[19.15] Article 22(1) specifically protects membership of particular types of associations, trade unions. Trade unions are employee organizations designed to further the common interests of their members. Their specific mention in article 22(1) is indicative of the historical persecution of trade unions. Advocation and pursuance of labour rights often clash with the interests of big business and governments.

[19.16] Article 22(3) specifically preserves the sanctity of obligations under ILO Convention 87 of 1948. This Convention guarantees certain rights to worker's organizations and their members, so article 22(3) seems to underline the protection offered to trade unions by article 22. In view of article 5(2) however, which prohibits States Parties from using the ICCPR as a pretext to derogate from other treaty obligations, article 22(3) seems superfluous.[22]

[19.17] In Concluding Comments on Senegal, the HRC indicated further elements to trade union protection in article 22:[23]

¶ 16. The Committee is concerned over the lack of full enjoyment of freedom of association, in particular the fact that foreign workers are barred from holding official positions in trade unions, and that trade unions may be dissolved by the executive.

RIGHT TO STRIKE

[19.18] Whilst article 22 guarantees one's right freely to 'form and join trade unions for the protection of [one's] interests', it must be asked to what extent article 22 protects the means by which trade union members may pursue their common interests. *J.B. et al. v Canada* (118/82), the 'Alberta Unions Case', raised the issue of whether article 22 protects the right to strike.

[19.19]   *J.B. et al. v CANADA (118/82)*

The facts of the case are outlined immediately below:

¶ 1.1. The authors of the communication (initial letter dated 5 January 1982 and seven subsequent letters) are J. B., P. D., L. S., T. M., D. P. and D. S., in their personal capacities and as members of the executive committee of the Alberta Union of Provincial Employees, Canada. They are represented by the Alberta Union of Provincial Employees through legal counsel.

¶ 1.2. The authors refer to the prohibition to strike for provincial public employees in the Province of Alberta under the Alberta Public Service Employee Relations Act of 1977 and

---

[22] Nowak, above, note 1, 399–400.
[23] (1997) UN doc. CCPR/C/79/Add. 82.

claim that such prohibition constitutes a breach by Canada of article 22 of the International Covenant on Civil and Political Rights.

The HRC majority decided that article 22 did not incorporate any right to strike.

¶ 6.2. The question before the Committee is whether the right to strike is guaranteed by article 22 of the International Covenant on Civil and Political Rights. . . .

Since the right to strike is not *expressis verbis* included in article 22, the Committee must interpret whether the right to freedom of association necessarily implies the right to strike, as contended by the authors of the communication. The authors have argued that such a conclusion is supported by decisions of organs of the International Labour Organization in interpreting the scope and the meaning of labour law treaties enacted under the auspices of ILO. The Human Rights Committee has no qualms about accepting as correct and just the interpretation of those treaties by the organs concerned. However, each international treaty, including the International Covenant on Civil and Political Rights, has a life of its own and must be interpreted in a fair and just manner, if so provided, by the body entrusted with the monitoring of its provisions.

¶ 6.3. In interpreting the scope of article 22, the Committee has given attention to the 'ordinary meaning' of each element of the article in its context and in the light of its object and purpose (article 31 of the Vienna Convention on the Law of Treaties). The Committee has also had recourse to supplementary means of interpretation (article 32 of the Vienna Convention on the Law of Treaties) and perused the *travaux préparatoires* of the Covenant on Civil and Political Rights. . . . [The HRC then examined the *travaux préparatoires* of article 22, and found no mention of a right to strike] . . . Thus the Committee cannot deduce from the *travaux préparatoires* that the drafters of the Covenant on Civil and Political Rights intended to guarantee the right to strike.

¶ 6.4. The conclusions to be drawn from the drafting history are corroborated by a comparative analysis of the International Covenant on Civil and Political Rights and the International Covenant on Economic, Social, and Cultural Rights. Article 8, paragraph 1 (d), of the International Covenant on Economic, Social, and Cultural Rights recognizes the right to strike, in addition to the right of everyone to form and join trade unions for the promotion and protection of his economic and social interests, thereby making it clear that the right to strike cannot be considered as an implicit component of the right to form and join trade unions. Consequently, the fact that the International Covenant on Civil and Political Rights does not similarly provide expressly for the right to strike in article 22, paragraph 1, shows that this right is not included in the scope of this article, while it enjoys protection under the procedures and mechanisms of the International Covenant on Economic, Social, and Cultural Rights subject to the specific restrictions mentioned in article 8 of that instrument. . . .

¶ 7. In the light of the above, the Human Rights Committee concludes that the communication is incompatible with the provisions of the Covenant and thus inadmissible *ratione materiae* under article 3 of the Optional Protocol. . . .

[19.20] The authors had argued that article 22(3) implied a right to strike within article 22.

¶ 5.1. [The authors] submit that the communication is indeed compatible with the provisions of the Covenant, and refer to the relevance of article 22, paragraph 3 . . . It is implied, they argue, that a denial of the right to strike would prejudice the guarantees of ILO Convention No. 87. Moreover, an interpretation of article 22, paragraph 1, of the Covenant would also have to take into consideration other international instruments, including ILO Convention No. 87, which is an elaboration of the principles of freedom of association in international law. It is submitted that in a series of decisions the Committee on Freedom of Association of ILO has determined that the right to strike derives from article 3 of ILO Convention No. 87 and that it is an essential means by which workers can promote and defend their occupational interests. In particular, the authors point out that, in four cases, the Committee on Freedom of Association has considered the provisions of the Alberta Public Service Employee Relations Act and has found that the statute does not comply with the guarantee of freedom of association contained in Convention No. 87. The Committee on Freedom of Association has accordingly requested the Canadian Government 'to re-examine the provisions in question in order to confine the ban on strikes to services which are essential in the strict sense of the term'. The ILO Committee of Experts on the Application of Conventions and Recommendations it is argued, has also reaffirmed the importance of the right to strike in the non-essential public service.

The HRC's response to this argument confirms the minimal significance of article 22(3) [19.16]:

¶ 6.5. As to the importance which the authors appear to attach to article 22, paragraph 3 (para. 5.1 above), of the Covenant on Civil and Political Rights, the Committee observes that the State party has in no way claimed that article 22 authorizes it to take legislative measures or to apply the law to the detriment of the guarantees provided for in ILO Convention No. 87.

[19.21] A sizeable minority of Mrs Higgins, and Messrs Lallah, Mavrommatis, Opsahl, and Wako dissented in the following terms:

¶ 1. In its decision the Committee states that the issue before it is whether the right to strike is guaranteed by article 22 of the International Covenant on Civil and Political Rights; and, finding that it is not, it declares the communication inadmissible.

¶ 2. We regret that we cannot share this approach to the issues in this case. We note that in Canada, as in many other countries, there exists, in principle, a right to strike, and that the complaint of the authors concerns the general prohibition of the exercise of such right for public employees in the Alberta Public Service Employee Relations Act. We believe that the question that the Committee is required to answer at this stage is whether article 22 alone or in conjunction with other provisions of the Covenant necessarily excludes, in the relevant circumstances, an entitlement to strike.

¶ 3. Article 22 provides that 'Everyone shall have the right to freedom of association with others, including the right to form and join trade unions for the protection of his interests.' The right to form and join trade unions is thus an example of the more general right to freedom of association. It is further specified that the right to join trade unions is for the purpose of protection of one's interests. In this context we note that there is no comma after 'trade unions', and as a matter of grammar 'for the protection of his interests' pertains to 'the right to form and join trade unions' and not to freedom of association as a whole. It is, of course, manifest that there is no mention of the right to strike in article 22, just as there is no mention of the various other activities, such as holding meetings, or collective bargaining, that a trade-unionist may engage in to protect his interests. We do not find that surprising, because it is the broad right of freedom of association which is guaranteed by article 22. However, the exercise of this right requires that some measure of concerted activities be allowed; otherwise it could not serve its purposes. To us, this is an inherent aspect of the right granted by article 22, paragraph 1. Which activities are essential to the exercise of this right cannot be listed *a priori* and must be examined in their social context in the light of the other paragraphs of this article.

¶ 4. The drafting history clearly shows that the right of association was dealt with separately from the right to form and join trade unions. The *travaux préparatoires* indicate that in 1952 the right to strike was proposed only for the draft article on trade unions. This is what we would have expected. It was at that time rejected. They show also that in 1957, when the right to strike (subject to certain limitations) was accepted as an amendment to the draft article on the right to form and join trade unions, such an amendment was neither introduced nor discussed with respect to the draft covenant on civil and political rights. The reason seems to us both clear and correct—namely, that because what is now article 22 of the Covenant on Civil and Political Rights deals with the right of association as a whole, concerning clubs and societies as well as trade unions, mentioning particular activities such as strike action would have been inappropriate.

¶ 5. We therefore find that the *travaux préparatoires* are not determinative of the issue before the Committee. Where the intentions of the drafters are not absolutely clear in relation to the point at hand, article 31 of the Vienna Convention also directs us to the object and purpose of the treaty. This seems to us especially important in a treaty for the promotion of human rights, where limitation of the exercise of rights, or upon the competence of the Committee to review a prohibition by a State of a given activity, are not readily to be presumed.

¶ 6. We note that article 8 of the International Covenant on Economic, Social, and Cultural Rights, having spoken of the right of everyone to form trade unions and join the union of his choice, goes on to speak of 'the right to strike, provided that it is exercised in conformity with the laws of the particular country'. While this latter phrase gives rise to some complex legal issues, it suffices for our present purpose that the specific aspect of freedom of association which is touched on as an individual right in article 22 of the Covenant on Civil and Political Rights, but dealt with as a set of distinctive rights in art-icle 8, does not necessarily exclude the right to strike in all circumstances. We see no reason for interpreting this common matter differently in the two Covenants.

¶ 7. We are also aware that the ILO Committee on Freedom of Association, a body singularly well placed to pronounce authoritatively on such matters, has held that the general prohibition of strikes for public employees contained in the Alberta Public Service Employee Relations Act was not in harmony with article 10 of ILO Convention No. 87 . . . since it constituted a considerable restriction on the opportunities open to trade unions to further and defend the interests of their members.' While we do not at this stage purport to comment on the merits, we cannot fail to notice that the ILO finding is based on the furtherance and defence of interests of trade-union members; and article 22 also requires us to consider that the purpose of joining trade union is to protect one's interests. Again, we see no reason to interpret article 22 in a manner different from ILO when addressing a comparable consideration. In this regard we note that article 22, paragraph 3, provides that nothing in that article authorizes a State party to ILO Convention No. 87 to take legislative measures which would prejudice, or to apply the law in such a manner as to prejudice, the guarantees provided for in that Convention.

¶ 8. We cannot see that a manner of exercising a right which has, under certain leading and widely ratified international instruments, been declared to be in principle lawful, should be declared to be incompatible with the Covenant on Civil and Political Rights.

¶ 9. Whereas article 22, paragraph 1, deals with the right of freedom of association as such, paragraph 2 deals with the extent of the exercise of the right which necessarily includes the means which may be resorted to by a member of a trade union for the protection of his interests.

¶ 10. Whether the right to strike is a necessary element in the protection of the interests of the authors, and if so whether it has been unduly restricted, is a question on the merits, that is to say, whether the restrictions imposed in Canada are or are not justifiable under article 22, paragraph 2. But we do not find the communication inadmissible on this ground.

After consideration of other possible grounds of inadmissibility, the minority found the complaint admissible.

[19.22] In admissibility proceedings, the HRC should have focused on the scope of article 22, which protects all associations. Issues regarding the specific protection of trade unions should not have been considered until the merits stage of proceedings. Therefore, the minority, which focused on the scope of protection for associations *per se* rather than upon determination of the scope of protection for trade unions in particular, exhibited a more coherent method of interpretation.

It is surely doubtful that the minimal protection offered to trade union activities under article 22 by the majority decision translates into minimal protection for the activities of all associations. Otherwise, the majority would be reading article 22 in a very narrow, non-purposive way. The freedom to join an association is fairly narrow if only the existence of the association is guaranteed, but not the necessary activities of the association. On the other hand, there appears to be no justifiable reason for singling trade unions out for special disadvantage as the majority has apparently done.

[19.23] The HRC majority seemed overly concerned to separate the subject matters of the ICCPR and its sister Covenant, the International Covenant on Economic, Social, and Cultural Rights (ICESCR). The right to strike is expressly protected in article 8(1)(d) of the ICESCR. Its classification as an economic and social right seemed to preclude the majority from including the right to strike as an aspect of a civil and political right. In contrast, in later cases decided under article 26,[24] the HRC sanctioned considerable overlap between the subject matters of the two Covenants.

[19.24] The Alberta Unions case was declared inadmissible in 1986. In recent Concluding Comments on Ireland, Guatemala, Germany, and Chile, the HRC has expressed concern about restrictions on the right to strike.[25] This may herald a change of heart regarding the scope of article 22 protection for trade union members.

FREEDOM NOT TO JOIN ASSOCIATIONS

[19.25]   *GAUTHIER v CANADA (633/95)*

The author's complaint related to his exclusion from full membership of the Parliamentary Press Gallery, a private organization. As a consequence of his exclusion, he was denied full access to media facilities at the federal Parliament, as such access was restricted to Press Gallery members by Parliamentary rules. The author submitted that the facts amounted, *inter alia*, to a restriction of his right to freedom of association.[26] The State Party argued:

¶ 11.8. With regard to article 22 of the Covenant, the State party observes that the author is not being forced by the Government to join any association. He is free not to associate with the Press Gallery, nor is his ability to practice the profession of journalism conditioned in any way upon his membership of the Press Gallery.

The HRC majority found that the article 22 claim was unsubstantiated. However, a substantial minority found that the facts constituted a breach of article 22. Mrs Evatt, Mrs Medina Quiroga, Messrs Solari Yrigoyen and Bhagwati, and Lord Colville stated the following, with which Messrs Kretzmer and Lallah essentially agreed:

In regard to article 22, the author's claim is that requiring membership in the Press Gallery Association as a condition of access to the Parliamentary press facilities violated his rights under article 22 read with article 19. The right to freedom of association implies that in general no one may be forced by the State to join an association. When membership of an association is a requirement to engage in a particular profession or calling, or when sanctions exist on the failure to be a member of an association, the State party should be called on to show that compulsory membership is necessary in a democratic society in pursuit of an interest authorized by the Covenant. In this matter, the Committee's deliberations in paragraph 13.6 of the Views[27] make it clear that the State party has failed to show that the

---

[24] See, e.g., decision in *Broeks v Netherlands* (172/84), at [23.08].

[25] Concluding Comments on Ireland (1995) UN Doc CCPR/C/79/Add.21, para. 17; Concluding Comments on Guatemala (1996) UN Doc. CCPR/C/79/Add.63, para. 23; Concluding Comments on Germany (1997) UN doc. CCPR/C/79/Add.73, para. 18; Concluding Comments on Chile (1999) UN doc. CCPR/C/79/Add. 104, para. 25.

[26] See [18.27] for fuller details of this case.   [27] Ibid.

requirement to be a member of a particular organization was a necessary restriction under paragraph 2 of article 22 in order to limit access to the press gallery in Parliament for the purposes mentioned. The restrictions imposed on the author are therefore in violation of article 22 of the Covenant.

[19.26] The HRC majority had initially, *ex officio*, found the article 22 issue to be admissible:[28]

¶ 9.4. The Committee further considered that the question whether the State party can require membership in a private organization as a condition for the enjoyment of the freedom to seek and receive information, should be examined on its merits, as it might raise issues not only under article 19, but also under articles 22 and 26 of the Covenant.

Its subsequent decision that the article 22 claim was unsubstantiated is puzzling. As no reasons are offered for its apparent *volte-face*, the minority opinions in this regard are to be preferred. It is possible that the majority found that the State could not be responsible for article 22 issues arising with regard to membership of a *private* organization.[29] However, application of the Covenant in the private arena has been confirmed with regard to other Covenant rights.[30] Furthermore, the author's complaint related more to the consequences of his exclusion, in which the State was clearly complicit, rather than his exclusion *per se*. In any case, it seems likely, bearing in mind the admissibility decision, that the majority agrees that article 22 guarantees freedom from consequences for failing to join certain associations.

[19.27] Does article 22 prohibit compulsory union membership (i.e. where one is effectively denied employment in a profession unless one joins the relevant trade union)? Compulsory union membership enhances the power of trade unions to protect their members' interests by promoting universal membership; the larger the union the greater its bargaining power. Nevertheless, compulsory union membership may be anathema to one's 'freedom' of association, which implies liberty to join and not to join organizations. In light of the HRC's admissibility decision and the strong dissent in *Gauthier*, it is likely that the HRC would condemn 'closed shop' practices.[31] On the other hand, compulsory union membership could arguably be justified as 'protecting the rights of others', such as the rights to work, or the rights to fair working conditions.[32]

---

[28] The author had not initially raised art. 22, relying instead on the art. 19 rights of freedom of expression.

[29] This was one of the State Party's arguments against admissibility, at paras. 4.3–4.10.

[30] See generally [1.59–1.62].

[31] Such practices have been condemned by the European Court of Human Rights in, e.g., *Young, James and Webster v UK* (1982) 4 EHRR 38.

[32] These rights are guaranteed in, respectively, arts. 6 and 7 of the ICESCR.

Conclusion

[19.28] Unfortunately, articles 21 and 22 have been the subjects of very little HRC jurisprudence. The only case on article 21, *Kivenmaa v Finland* (412/90) exhibits poor reasoning, and is of little help in interpreting the article. The main case on article 22, *J.B. et al. v Canada* (118/82), deals with the rights of trade union members. The majority interpreted article 22 rather narrowly so as to offer minimal protection for the activities, as opposed to the existence, of trade unions. Recent Concluding Comments may however signal a retreat from the conservative reasoning in *J.B.* Finally, *Gauthier v Canada* (633/95) strongly indicates that article 22 also guarantees freedom from coerced association.

One can only presume that limitations to these provisions would be interpreted in similar ways to identical words in other provisions, such as the article 19 guarantee of freedom of expression. In the continued absence of relevant cases, the HRC should issue General Comments to expand on the meaning of these two articles.

Postscript: Please note that General Comment 28 on 'Equality of Rights Between Men and Women', contained in the Addendum at page 634, contains extra information on some of the material in this chapter.

Protection of the Family—Article 23

ARTICLE 23

1. The family is the natural and fundamental group unit of society and is entitled to protection by society and the State.

2. The right of men and women of marriageable age to marry and to found a family shall be recognized.

3. No marriage shall be entered into without the free and full consent of the intending spouses.

4. States Parties to the present Covenant shall take appropriate steps to ensure equality of rights and responsibilities of spouses as to marriage, during marriage and at its dissolution. In the case of dissolution, provision shall be made for the necessary protection of any children.

[20.01] Article 23 guarantees rights of protection to the family. Rights regarding marriage and rights of equality between spouses are also guaranteed. Despite the exalted position it confers on 'the family' as a fundamental societal institution, article 23 does not act as a barrier to protect 'the family' from legitimate interference, such as measures to combat intrafamilial violence,[1] or neglect and abuse of a child.[2]

[20.02]　　　　　　　　***GENERAL COMMENT 19***

¶ 1. Article 23 of the International Covenant on Civil and Political Rights recognizes that the family is the natural and fundamental group unit of society and is entitled to protection by society and the State. Protection of the family and its members is also guaranteed, directly or indirectly, by other provisions of the Covenant. Thus, article 17 establishes a

---

[1] Victims of intrafamilial violence would benefit from countervailing rights, such as those under art. 9(1) (security of the person [11.04]). See G. Van Beuren, 'The International Protection of Family Members' Rights as the 21st Century Approaches' (1995) 17 *HRQ* 732,748–56.
[2] See [21.31].

prohibition on arbitrary or unlawful interference with the family. In addition, article 24 of the Covenant specifically addresses the protection of the rights of the child, as such or as a member of a family. In their reports, States parties often fail to give enough information on how the State and society are discharging their obligation to provide protection to the family and the persons composing it.

[20.03] As stressed in General Comment 19, other Covenant rights also provide family rights. In particular, the article 17 guarantee of privacy prohibits 'arbitrary interferences' with one's family. Article 17(1) guarantees persons a negative right to be free from arbitrary government intervention with their families. Article 17(2) guarantees that people will be protected from 'such interference' by law, so it incorporates a positive obligation.[3] Article 23 appears to take those positive obligations further in guaranteeing families positive rights of protection, such as provision of appropriate financial assistance or tax concessions.[4] However, despite an apparent qualitative difference between the article 17 and 23 guarantees, most cases regarding family rights have concerned violations, or exonerations, of States under both articles.[5]

[20.04]   *GENERAL COMMENT 19*

¶ 3. Ensuring the protection provided for under article 23 of the Covenant requires that States parties should adopt legislative, administrative or other measures. States parties should provide detailed information concerning the nature of such measures and the means whereby their effective implementation is assured. In fact, since the Covenant also recognizes the right of the family to protection by society, States parties' reports should indicate how the necessary protection is granted to the family by the State and other social institutions, whether and to what extent the State gives financial or other support to the activities of such institutions, and how it ensures that these activities are compatible with the Covenant.

[20.05] In *Aumeeruddy-Sziffra et al. v Mauritius* (35/78), the HRC stated, on the scope of article 23:

¶ 9.2(b) 2(ii) 1. . . . The Committee is of the opinion that the legal protection or measures a society or a State can afford to the family may vary from country to country and depend on different social, economic, political and cultural conditions and traditions.

Article 23 may be the only ICCPR right that is 'economically relative', in that the level of entitlement can vary according to the economic circumstances of States Parties.[6] Indeed, it is debatable whether article 23 could ever ground a right to

---

[3] See commentary at [16.18–16.20].

[4] See also M. Nowak, *CCPR Commentary* (N.P. Engel, Kehl, 1993), 406, on the negative/positive distinction between art. 17 and art. 23. However, he concedes that the distinction is 'difficult to maintain in practice'. See also F. Olsen, 'The Myth of State Intervention in the Family' (1985) 18 *Michigan Journal of Law Reform* 835, arguing that the distinction between 'intervention' and 'non-intervention' in the family is meaningless.

[5] Ibid.   [6] See, on economic relativism, [1.73].

financial assistance *per se*. In *Oulajin and Kaiss v Netherlands* (406, 426/90), the HRC found that the State's failure to provide child benefits in respect of the authors' foster children abroad (the authors' nephews), did not raise issues regarding protection of the family under article 17 or, presumably, article 23.[7]

Definition of a Family

[20.06]   *GENERAL COMMENT 16*

¶ 5. Regarding the term 'family', the objectives of the Covenant require that for purposes of article 17 this term be given a broad interpretation to include all those comprising the family as understood in the society of the State party concerned. . . .

GENERAL COMMENT 19

¶ 2. The Committee notes that the concept of the family may differ in some respects from State to State, and even from region to region within a State, and that it is therefore not possible to give the concept a standard definition. However, the Committee emphasizes that, when a group of persons is regarded as a family under the legislation and practice of a State, it must be given the protection referred to in article 23. Consequently, States parties should report on how the concept and scope of the family is construed or defined in their own society and legal system. Where diverse concepts of the family, 'nuclear' and 'extended', exist within a State, this should be indicated with an explanation of the degree of protection afforded to each. In view of the existence of various forms of family, such as unmarried couples and their children or single parents and their children, States parties should also indicate whether and to what extent such types of family and their members are recognized and protected by domestic law and practice.

The HRC, in its General Comment, clearly gives States a certain cultural leeway in determining the definition of the 'family' for the purposes of article 23. However, the last sentence of paragraph 2 indicates that a State Party does not have exclusive jurisdiction over the definition; otherwise the article 23 guarantee could be severely diluted. A State cannot limit the definition by applying structures or values which breach international human rights standards.[8] Furthermore, a State cannot prescribe a narrower definition of 'family' than that adopted within that State's society.[9]

[20.07]   *HENDRIKS v NETHERLANDS (201/85)*

¶ 10.3. The words 'the family' in article 23, paragraph 1, do not refer solely to the family

---

[7] Para. 4.1. See, on this case, [23.55].

[8] Van Bueren, above, note 1, 734–5. There is a wealth of academic material on the meaning of 'family'. For example, see M. Minow, 'All in the Family and in all Families: Membership, Loving and Owing' (1992) 95 *West Virginia Law Review* 278.

[9] See *Hopu and Bessert v France* (549/93) [20.10].

home as it exists during the marriage. The idea of the family must necessarily embrace the relations between parents and child. Although divorce legally ends a marriage, it cannot dissolve the bond uniting father—or mother—and child: this bond does not depend on the continuation of the parents' marriage. It would seem that the priority given to the child's interests is compatible with this rule.

The definition of a 'family' is not therefore confined by the concept of marriage. States may recognize a variety of living arrangements that may constitute a 'family', all of which require protection under the Covenant. The HRC has not however yet confirmed whether gay and lesbian couples, with or without children, constitute a family.[10]

[20.08] While a variety of living arrangements, both within and beyond the nuclear family, come within the concept of 'family', the requisite article 23 protection may differ according to the type of family concerned. For example, in a number of cases, the HRC has rejected complaints from unmarried couples regarding their different treatment, compared to that of married couples, under Dutch welfare laws.[11] One must also note that article 23(2) to (4) confers special rights on married couples and within marriages.

[20.09]   *A. S. v CANADA (68/80)*

In this case the author complained of the failure of Canadian immigration authorities to allow her adopted Polish daughter and grandson to join her as permanent residents in Canada. The State Party objected to the admissibility of the communication on the ground that the facts of the case did not reveal any breach of the rights protected under article 23:

¶ 5.1. . . . As regards article 23, which provides for the entitlement of the family to protection by the State, it is claimed that such protection requires *a priori* that an effective family life between the members of the family must have existed; it could not be concluded that B and her son had shared an effective family life with A.S., since B, after being adopted by A.S. in 1959, lived with her in Canada for two years only, whereafter she left the country in 1961 to return to Poland, where she married and had a son. The fact that A.S. and B have been living apart for 17 years clearly demonstrates that a prolonged family life does not exist and that therefore no breach of article 23 could be claimed by the author.

The HRC agreed with the State Party:

¶ 8.2(b). Articles 17 and 23 provide that no one shall be subjected to arbitrary or unlawful interference with his family and that the family is entitled to protection by the State; these articles are not applicable since, except, for a brief period of 2 years some 17 years ago, A.S. and her adopted daughter have not lived together as a family.

---

[10] Van Bueren has described as 'perverse' the exclusion of gay couples from the definition of 'family' for the purposes of the European Convention on Human Rights, above, note 1, 737.

[11] *Danning v The Netherlands* (180/84), *Sprenger v The Netherlands* (395/90), *Hoofdman v The Netherlands* (602/94). See, on these cases, [23.56].

It is not clear whether the *A.S.* decision was in any way influenced by the fact that B was not A.S.'s biological daughter. Despite the *A.S.* decision, article 23 families may presumably include adopted members.[12]

BALAGUER SANTACANA v SPAIN (417/90)

The facts of this case are outlined below [20.41].

¶ 10.2. The State party has argued that article 23, paragraphs 1 and 4, do not apply to the case, as the author's unstable relationship with Ms. Montalvo cannot be subsumed under the term 'family', and no marital ties between the author and Ms. Montalvo ever existed. The Committee begins by noting that the term 'family' must be understood broadly; it reaffirms that the concept refers not solely to the family home during marriage or cohabitation, but also to the relations in general between parents and child. Some minimal requirements for the existence of a family are, however, necessary, such as life together, economic ties, a regular and intense relationship, etc.

Hence, a formal familial relationship does not suffice to establish a sufficient familial connection for the purposes of article 23. Some degree of effective family life must exist.

[20.10]   HOPU and BESSERT v FRANCE (549/93)

In this case the authors claimed to be victims of violations by France of articles 17 and 23 of the Covenant. The authors submitted the following facts and complaint to the Committee:

¶ 2.1. The authors are the descendants of the owners of a land tract (approximately 4.5 hectares) called Tetaitapu, in Nuuroa, on the island of Tahiti. They argue that their ancestors were dispossessed of their property by *jugement de licitation* of the *Tribunal civil d'instance* of Papeete on 6 October 1961. Under the terms of the judgment, ownership of the land was awarded to the *Société hotelière du Pacifique sud* (SHPS). Since the year 1988, the Territory of Polynesia is the sole shareholder of this company.

¶ 2.2. In 1990, the SHPS leased the land to the *Société d'étude et de promotion hotelière*, which in turn subleased it to the *Société hotelière* (RIVNAC). RIVNAC seeks to begin construction work on a luxury hotel complex on the site, which borders a lagoon, as soon as possible. Some preliminary work—such as the felling of some trees, cleaning the site of shrubs, fencing off of the ground—has been carried out.

¶ 2.3. The authors and other descendants of the owners of the land peacefully occupied the site in July 1992, in protest against the planned construction of the hotel complex. They contend that the land and the lagoon bordering it represent an important place in their history, their culture and their life. They add that the land encompasses the site of a pre-European burial ground and that the lagoon remains a traditional fishing ground and provides the means of subsistence for some thirty families living next to the lagoon. . . .

---

12 Van Beuren, above, note 1, 738.

¶ 3.2. The authors ... claim a violation of articles 17, paragraph 1, and 23, paragraph 1, on the ground that their forceful removal from the disputed site and the realization of the hotel complex would entail the destruction of the burial ground, where members of their family are said to be buried, and because such removal would interfere with their private and their family lives.

In finding for the authors, the HRC gave a broad interpretation to the term 'family'. It made the following comments:

¶ 10.3. The authors claim that the construction of the hotel complex on the contested site would destroy their ancestral burial grounds, which represent an important place in their history, culture and life, and would arbitrarily interfere with their privacy and their family lives, in violation of articles 17 and 23. They also claim that members of their family are buried on the site. The Committee observes that the objectives of the Covenant require that the term 'family' be given a broad interpretation so as to include all those comprising the family as understood in the society in question. It follows that cultural traditions should be taken into account when defining the term 'family' in a specific situation. It transpires from the authors' claims that they consider the relationship to their ancestors to be an essential element of their identity and to play an important role in their family life. This has not been challenged by the State party; nor has the State party contested the argument that the burial grounds in question play an important role in the authors' history, culture and life. The State party has disputed the authors' claim only on the basis that they have failed to establish a kinship link between the remains discovered in the burial grounds and themselves. The Committee considers that the authors' failure to establish a direct kinship link cannot be held against them in the circumstances of the communication, where the burial grounds in question pre-date the arrival of European settlers and are recognized as including the forbears of the present Polynesian inhabitants of Tahiti. The Committee therefore concludes that the construction of a hotel complex on the authors' ancestral burial grounds did interfere with their right to family and privacy. The State party has not shown that this interference was reasonable in the circumstances, and nothing in the information before the Committee shows that the State party duly took into account the importance of the burial grounds for the authors, when it decided to lease the site for the building of a hotel complex. The Committee concludes that there has been an arbitrary interference with the authors' right to family and privacy, in violation of articles 17, paragraph 1, and 23, paragraph 1.

[20.11] In a dissenting opinion, Messrs Kretzmer, Buergenthal, Ando, and Lord Colville made the following comments:

¶ 3. The authors' claim is that the State party has failed to protect an ancestral burial ground, which plays an important role in their heritage. It would seem that this claim could raise the issue of whether such failure by a State party involves denial of the right of religious or ethnic minorities, in community with other members of their group, to enjoy their own culture or to practise their own religion. However, for the reasons set out above, the Committee was precluded from examining this issue. Instead the Committee holds that allowing the building on the burial ground constitutes arbitrary interference with the authors' family and privacy. We cannot accept these propositions.

¶ 4. In reaching the conclusion that the facts in the instant case do not give rise to an interference with the authors' family and privacy, we do not reject the view, expressed in the

Committee's General Comment 16 on article 17 of the Covenant, that the term 'family' should 'be given a broad interpretation to include all those comprising the family as understood in the society of the State party concerned.' Thus, the term 'family', when applied to the local population in French Polynesia, might well include relatives, who would not be included in a family, as this term is understood in other societies, including metropolitan France. However, even when the term 'family' is extended, it does have a discrete meaning. It does not include all members of one's ethnic or cultural group. Nor does it necessarily include all one's ancestors, going back to time immemorial. The claim that a certain site is an ancestral burial ground of an ethnic or cultural group, does not, as such, imply that it is the burial ground of members of the authors' family. The authors have provided no evidence that the burial ground is one that is connected to their family, rather than to the whole of the indigenous population of the area. The general claim that members of their families are buried there, without specifying in any way the nature of the relationship between themselves and the persons buried there, is insufficient to support their claim, even on the assumption that the notion of family is different from notions that prevail in other societies. We therefore cannot accept the Committee's view that the authors have substantiated their claim that allowing building on the burial ground amounted to interference with their family.

¶ 5. The Committee mentions the authors' claim 'that they consider the relationship to their ancestors to be an essential element of their identity and to play an important role in their family life.' Relying on the fact that the State party has challenged neither this claim nor the authors' argument that the burial grounds play an important part in their history, culture and life, the Committee concludes that the construction of the hotel complex on the burial grounds interferes with the authors' right to family and privacy. The reference by the Committee to the authors' history, culture and life, is revealing. For it shows that the values that are being protected are not the family, or privacy, but cultural values. We share the concern of the Committee for these values. These values, however, are protected under article 27 of the Covenant and not the provisions relied on by the Committee. We regret that the Committee is prevented from applying article 27 in the instant case.[13] . . .

¶ 7. We reach the conclusion that there has been no violation of the authors' rights under the Covenant in the present communication with some reluctance. Like the Committee we too are concerned with the failure of the State party to respect a site that has obvious importance in the cultural heritage of the indigenous population of French Polynesia. We believe, however, that this concern does not justify distorting the meaning of the terms family and privacy beyond their ordinary and generally accepted meaning.[14]

Protection of Family Unity

[20.12] Family unification is an important principle under article 23, as demonstrated in this Concluding Comment on Switzerland:[15]

---

[13] France has entered a reservation to art. 27, which precluded consideration of this communication under that guarantee. See [25.08–25.10].

[14] The minority's comments on the meaning of 'privacy' are excerpted at [16.06].

[15] (1996) UN doc. CCPR/C/79/Add.70. See also General Comment 15 at para. 5 [12.08].

¶ 18. The Committee also notes that family reunification is not authorized immediately for foreign workers who settle in Switzerland, but only after 18 months, which, in the Committee's view, is too long a period for the foreign worker to be separated from his family.

[20.13]   *AUMEERUDDY-CZIFFRA et al. v MAURITIUS (35/78)*[16]

The authors, including three women married to aliens, complained about Mauritian legislation that conferred different residential rights on foreign spouses, dependent on their sex. Whereas foreign wives were accorded automatic residential rights, these rights were denied to foreign husbands. The HRC found that the legislation violated a number of ICCPR articles.[17] On article 23, the HRC stated the following:

¶ 9.2(b) 2(ii) 1. . . . each of the couples concerned constitutes also a 'family' within the meaning of article 23 (1) of the Covenant, in one case at least—that of Mrs. Aumeeruddy-Cziffra—also with a child. They are therefore as such 'entitled to protection by society and the State' . . .

¶ 9.2(b) 2(ii) 2. Again, however, the principle of equal treatment of the sexes applies by virtue of articles 2 (1), 3 and 26, of which the latter is also relevant because it refers particularly to the 'equal protection of the law'. Where the Covenant requires a substantial protection as in article 23, it follows from those provisions that such protection must be equal, that is to say not discriminatory, for example on the basis of sex.

¶ 9.2(b) 2(ii) 3. It follows that also in this line of argument the Covenant must lead to the result that the protection of a family cannot vary with the sex of the one or the other spouse. Though it might be justified for Mauritius to restrict the access of aliens to their territory and to expel them therefrom for security reasons, the Committee is of the view that the legislation which only subjects foreign spouses of Mauritian women to those restrictions, but not foreign spouses of Mauritian men, is discriminatory with respect to Mauritian women and cannot be justified by security requirements.

¶ 9.2(b) 2(ii) 4. The Committee therefore finds that there is also a violation of articles 2 (1), 3 and 26 of the Covenant in conjunction with the right of the three married co-authors under article 23 (1).

[20.14] The decision in the *Mauritian Women's Case* was influenced by the discriminatory impact of the law, as it applied different rules to foreign husbands and foreign wives.[18] In Concluding Comments on Zimbabwe, the HRC indicated that non-discriminatory laws which denied automatic residential rights to all foreign spouses would also breach article 23:[19]

---

[16] This case is also known as the *Mauritian Women's Case*.
[17] See also [16.22] and [23.42].
[18] See also individual opinion of Mr Bouziri in *Lovelace v Canada* (24/77).
[19] (1998) UN doc. CCPR/C/79/Add. 89.

¶ 19. The Committee notes with concern that the decision of the Supreme Court in *Rattigan and Others v. Chief Immigration Officer and Others* has been nullified by an amendment to the constitution, the effect of which is to deprive both women and men of the right to have their spouses registered as citizens, who as a consequence may not be allowed to reside in or enter the territory of Zimbabwe. The Committee considers that this amendment is incompatible with articles 17 and 23 of the Covenant. The Committee recommends that steps be taken to bring the law into compliance with the Covenant. . . .

[20.15] The HRC has criticized Canadian policies regarding deportation of long-term alien residents for their failure to take into account article 23 rights.[20] One such deportation order was challenged in the following case.

STEWART v CANADA (538/93)

The author was born in Scotland and emigrated to Canada at the age of seven with his mother. He had always considered Canada to be his home, where he lived with his sick mother and disabled brother. He also had two young children living with his former wife. He considered himself a Canadian citizen, and it was not until immigration officials contacted him that he realized that he was only a permanent resident in legal terms. He was being deported pursuant to the Canadian Immigration Act which allowed for deportation where certain specified offences have been committed. The author argued that the deportation violated a number of articles including articles 17 and 23.[21] The author made the following arguments:

¶ 3.1. The author . . . claims that in respect of article 23, the State party has failed to provide for clear legislative recognition of the protection of the family. In the absence of such legislation which ensures that family interests would be given due weight in administrative proceedings such as, for example, those before the Immigration and Refugee Board, he claims, there is a *prima facie* issue as to whether Canadian law is compatible with the requirement of protection of the family.

¶ 3.2. The author also refers to the Committee's General Comment on article 17, according to which 'interference [with home and privacy] can only take place on the basis of law, which itself must be comparable with the provisions, aims and objectives of the Covenant'. He asserts that there is no law which ensures that his legitimate family interests or those of members of his family would be addressed in deciding on his deportation from Canada; there is only the vague and general discretion given to the Immigration Appeal Division to consider the circumstances of the case, which is said to be insufficient to ensure a balancing of his family interests and other legitimate States aims. In its decision, the Immigration Appeal Division allegedly did not give any weight to the disabilities of the author's mother and brother; instead, it ruled that 'taking into account that the appellant does not have anyone depending on him and there being no real attachment to and no real support

---

[20] (1999) UN doc. CCPR/C/79/Add.105, para. 15: see [21.29].
[21] See also [9.64] (on the similar case of *Canepa v Canada* (558/93)) and [12.30] regarding other claims in this case.

from anyone, the Appeal Division see insufficient circumstances to justify the appellant's presence in this country'.

¶ 3.3. According to the author, the term 'home' should be interpreted broadly, encompassing the (entire) community of which an individual is a part. In this sense, his 'home' is said to be Canada. It is further submitted that the author's privacy must include the fact of being able to live within his community without arbitrary or unlawful interference. To the extent that Canadian law does not protect aliens from such interference, the author claims a violation of article 17.

The State Party responded with the following comments:

¶ 9.2. Articles 17 and 23 of the Covenant cannot be interpreted as being incompatible with a State party's right to deport an alien, provided that the conditions of article 13 of the Covenant are being observed.[22] Under Canadian law everyone is protected against arbitrary or unlawful interference with privacy, family and home as required by article 17. The State party submits that when a decision to deport an alien is taken after a full and fair procedure in accordance with law and policy, which are not themselves inconsistent with the Covenant, and in which the demonstrably important and valid interests of the State are balanced with the Covenant rights of the individual, such a decision cannot be found to be arbitrary. In this context the State party submits that the conditions established by law on the continued residency of non-citizens in Canada are reasonable and objective and the application of the law by Canadian authorities is consistent with the provisions of the Covenant, read as a whole.

¶ 9.3. The State party points out that the proposed deportation of Mr. Stewart is not the result of a summary decision by Canadian authorities, but rather of careful deliberation of all factors concerned, pursuant to full and fair procedures compatible with article 13 of the Covenant, in which Mr. Stewart was represented by counsel and submitted extensive argument in support of his claim that deportation would unduly interfere with his privacy and family life. The competent Canadian tribunals considered Mr. Stewart's interests and weighed them against the State's interest in protecting the public. . . .

¶ 9.4. As to Canada's obligation under article 23 of the Covenant to protect the family, reference is made to relevant legislation and practice, including the Canadian Constitution and the Canadian Charter on Human Rights. Canadian law provides protection for the family which is compatible with the requirements of article 23. The protection required by article 23, paragraph 1, however, is not absolute. In considering his removal, the competent Canadian courts gave appropriate weight to the impact of deportation on his family in balancing these against the legitimate State interests to protect society and to regulate immigration. In this context the State party submits that the specific facts particular to his case, including his age and lack of dependents, suggest that the nature and quality of his family relationships could be adequately maintained through correspondence, telephone calls and visits to Canada, which he would be at liberty to make pursuant to Canadian immigration laws.

The Committee did not find a violation of any of the provisions of the Covenant. The majority made the following comments in relation to articles 17 and 23:

---

[22] See generally Chap. 13.

¶ 12.10. The deportation of Mr. Stewart will undoubtedly interfere with his family relations in Canada. The question is, however, whether the said interference can be considered either unlawful or arbitrary. Canada's Immigration Law expressly provides that the permanent residency status of a non-national may be revoked and that that person may then be expelled from Canada if he or she is convicted of serious offences. In the appeal process the Immigration Appeal Division is empowered to revoke a deportation order 'having regard to all the circumstances of the case'. In the deportation proceedings in the present case, Mr. Stewart was given ample opportunity to present evidence of his family connections to the Immigration Appeal Division. In its reasoned decision the Immigration Appeal Division considered the evidence presented but it came to the conclusion that Mr. Stewart's family connections in Canada did not justify revoking the deportation order. The Committee is of the opinion that the interference with Mr. Stewart's family relations that will be the inevitable outcome of his deportation cannot be regarded as either unlawful or arbitrary when the deportation order was made under law in furtherance of a legitimate state interest and due consideration was given in the deportation proceedings to the deportee's family connections. There is therefore no violation of articles 17 and 23 of the Covenant.

[20.16] There were a number of dissenting opinions.[23] In the opinion of Mrs Evatt and Mrs Medina Quiroga, which was co-signed by Mr Aguilar Urbina and agreed with by Mme Chanet and Mr Prado Vallejo, the following comments about articles 17 and 23 were made:

¶ 10. We agree with the Committee that the deportation of the author will undoubtedly interfere with his family relations in Canada (paragraph 12.10), but we cannot agree that this interference is not arbitrary, since we have come to the conclusion that the decision to deport the author—which is the cause of the interference with the family—was arbitrary. We have to conclude, therefore, that Canada has also violated the author's rights under articles 17 and 23.

[20.17] Despite the HRC's later concerns over Canadian expulsion policy in its 1999 Concluding Comment on Canada [21.29], the HRC majority here did not find Stewart's deportation to constitute an article 23 violation. The *Stewart* decision demonstrates the HRC's willingness to defer to the decision of domestic courts where there is no evidence of procedural flaws in those domestic proceedings.[24] Deportation of family members is therefore permissible under articles 17 and 23, so long as the decision is authorized by law, and is not manifestly arbitrary, and takes into account the effect of the deportation on the deportee's family relationships.

[20.18]   *CANEPA v CANADA (558/93)*

The facts in this case were very similar to those in *Stewart*. The author faced deportation to Italy for a series of offences after having lived in Canada with his

---

[23] These dissents are explored at [12.31].
[24] See commentary at [20.39].

parents and brother since the age of five. The HRC found no violation of either article 17 or 23, in the following terms:

¶ 11.5. The circumstances are that the author has committed many offences, largely of the break, enter and steal kind, and mostly committed to get money to support his [heroin] habit. His removal is seen as necessary in the public interest and to protect public safety from further criminal activity by the author. He has had an almost continuous record of convictions (except for a period in 1987–88), from age 17 to his removal from Canada at age 31. The author, who has neither spouse nor children in Canada, has extended family in Italy. He has not shown how his deportation to Italy would irreparably sever his ties with his remaining family in Canada. His family were able to provide little help or guidance to him in overcoming his criminal tendencies and his drug-addiction. He has not shown that the support and encouragement of his family is likely to be helpful to him in the future in this regard, or that his separation from his family is likely to lead to a deterioration in his situation. There is no financial dependence involved in his family ties. There appear to be no circumstances particular to the author or to his family which would lead the Committee to conclude that his removal from Canada was an arbitrary interference with his family, nor with his privacy or home.

The HRC's statements regarding Canepa's Canadian-based family are unnecessary, judgmental, and insensitive. Is it appropriate to conclude that continued regular family contact would have been unhelpful to Canepa, in view of the insidious nature of his heroin addiction? Indeed, should family rights be altered according to the HRC's judgment of the relevant family's functionality?[25]

Article 23(2): Right to Marry

[20.19]   *GENERAL COMMENT 19*

¶ 4. Article 23, paragraph 2, of the Covenant reaffirms the right of men and women of marriageable age to marry and to found a family. . . . In this connection, the Committee wishes to note that such legal provisions must be compatible with the full exercise of the other rights guaranteed by the Covenant; thus, for instance, the right to freedom of thought, conscience and religion implies that the legislation of each State should provide for the possibility of both religious and civil marriages. In the Committee's view, however, for a State to require that a marriage, which is celebrated in accordance with religious rites, be conducted, affirmed or registered also under civil law is not incompatible with the Covenant. States are also requested to include information on this subject in their reports.

[20.20] Article 23(2) expressly applies only to heterosexual marriages. It is therefore doubtful whether article 23(2) protection extends to same sex marriages.[26] It is also uncertain which sex the HRC would attribute to a transsexual for the

---

[25] 'Dysfunctional' can be distinguished from 'ineffective' family life in that no real family links exist in the latter situation [20.09]. Of course, family rights should be limited where dysfunctionality is severe, as in the case of child or spousal abuse.

[26] See [20.24] below.

purposes of article 23(2), the sex at birth or the reassigned sex after a sex change operation. Ideally, the HRC would take a progressive stance and accept a transsexual's reassigned sex as the relevant sex for such purposes.[27]

[20.21] Article 23(2) is expressed as an absolute right. However, it is likely that certain common restrictions are permissible, such as restrictions on incestuous marriages, or on persons who are already married.[28]

[20.22] As bigamy is prohibited in many States Parties, prohibitions on the right to divorce would deprive one of a right to remarry. Nowak therefore argues that a 'right to divorce' can be construed from the article 23(2) 'right to marry'.[29]

Article 23(2): Right to Found a Family

[20.23]   *GENERAL COMMENT 19*

¶ 5. The right to found a family implies, in principle, the possibility to procreate and live together. When States parties adopt family planning policies, they should be compatible with the provisions of the Covenant and should, in particular, not be discriminatory or compulsory. Similarly, the possibility to live together implies the adoption of appropriate measures, both at the internal level and as the case may be, in cooperation with other States, to ensure the unity or reunification of families, particularly when their members are separated for political, economic or similar reasons.

Hence, coercive methods of population control are incompatible with article 23(2).

[20.24] The article 23(2) 'right to found a family' is guaranteed to those who have a right to marry under the same sub-paragraph. The right to found a family is not however contingent upon marriage, but upon the 'right' to marry.[30] Gay couples are therefore excluded from the right to found a family. A broader 'right to found a family', as well as a right to marry, for gay couples can perhaps be construed from article 23(1) or the article 26 right of non-discrimination.[31]

[20.25] As with the right to marry, no apparent limit is expressed to the right of

[27] However, P. R. Ghandhi doubts that the HRC would take such a stance in light of prevailing ECHR jurisprudence (see, e.g., *Sheffield and Horsham v United Kingdom* (1999) 27 EHRR 163), in 'Family and Child Rights' in D. Harris and S. Joseph (eds.), *The International Covenant on Civil and Political Rights and United Kingdom Law* (Clarendon Press, Oxford, 1995), at 509.
[28] Nowak, above, note 4, 409–10.
[29] Ibid., 411–12. A right to divorce could not be construed from the right to marry in art. 12 of the ECHR in *Johnston v Ireland*, Series A No. 112 (1987) 9 EHRR 203. However, art. 12 ECHR is quite different from the text of art. 23(2) in that it contains a proviso restricting the right 'according to [relevant] national laws'.
[30] Nowak, above, note 4, 412–13.
[31] See A. Burton, 'Gay Marriage—a Modern Proposal: Applying Baehr v Lewin to the International Covenant on Civil and Political Rights' (1995) 3 *Indiana Journal of Global Studies* 177, 204–5.

adult men and women to found a family. Again, however, it is doubtful that the right is absolute. Certain common restrictions are likely to be permissible, such as restrictions on the right to adopt, or on access to artificial procreation methods.[32]

[20.26] Article 23(2) also includes a right of family unity or reunification. Such a right is also subsumed within article 23(1).[33]

Article 23(3): Requirement of Consent to Marriage

[20.27]   *GENERAL COMMENT 19*

¶ 4. . . . [Article 23(3)] provides that no marriage shall be entered into without the free and full consent of the intending spouses. States parties' reports should indicate whether there are restrictions or impediments to the exercise of the right to marry based on special factors such as degree of kinship or mental incapacity. The Covenant does not establish a specific marriageable age either for men or for women, but that age should be such as to enable each of the intending spouses to give his or her free and full personal consent in a form and under conditions prescribed by law. . . .

[20.28] Forced marriages will violate article 23, as demonstrated in the Concluding Comment for Nigeria:[34]

¶ 25. The Committee expresses its concern about the situation of women in Nigeria, particularly as regards their low level of participation in public life and the continued application of marriage regimes which permit polygamy and do not fully respect the equal rights of women. It expresses particular concern about the widespread practices of forced marriage. . . .

[20.29] The Covenant does not set down a 'marriageable age'. However the intending spouse must be able to give free consent, so extremely low ages will be the subject of concern.[35]

Article 23(4): Right of Equality in Marriage

[20.30]   *GENERAL COMMENT 19*

¶ 6. Article 23, paragraph 4, of the Covenant provides that States parties shall take appropriate steps to ensure equality of rights and responsibilities of spouses as to marriage, during marriage and at its dissolution. With regard to equality as to marriage, the Committee wishes to note in particular that no sex-based discrimination should occur in respect of the acquisition or loss of nationality by reason of marriage. Likewise, the right of each spouse to retain the use of his or her original family name or to participate on an equal

---

[32] Nowak, above, note 4, 414.
[33] See *Aumeeruddy-Sziffra et al. v Mauritius* (35/78) [20.13].
[34] (1996) CCPR/C/79/Add.65.
[35] See [21.16].

basis in the choice of a new family name should be safeguarded. During marriage, the spouses should have equal rights and responsibilities in the family. This equality extends to all matters arising from their relationship, such as choice of residence, running of the household, education of the children and administration of assets. Such equality continues to be applicable to arrangements regarding legal separation or dissolution of the marriage. Thus, any discriminatory treatment in regard to the grounds and procedures for separation or divorce, child custody, maintenance or alimony, visiting rights or the loss or recovery of parental authority must be prohibited, bearing in mind the paramount interest of the children in this connection. States parties should, in particular, include information in their reports concerning the provision made for the necessary protection of any children at the dissolution of a marriage or on the separation of the spouses.

It is interesting to note that division of property upon divorce is not mentioned in this General Comment.[36]

[20.31] Article 23(4) is unique in the ICCPR in that its text seems to incorporate a progressive obligation. States are required to 'take appropriate steps' to achieve equality within marriages. The prevailing societal norms in many States undoubtedly impose a hierarchy, husband over wife, within marriage. The text of article 23(4) recognizes that it will take time for States to dismantle these structures within society. However, the same problem arises with regard to other Covenant rights, such as the general right of non-discrimination in article 26, which are nevertheless expressed as immediate obligations. Indeed, it may be that the article 26 guarantee subsumes the article 23(4) guarantee.[37] In any case, the HRC, in General Comment 19, does not acknowledge the apparent progressive nature of article 23(4).[38]

[20.32] The Convention on the Elimination of all Forms of Discrimination Against Women ['CEDAW'] also guarantees equality within marriage in article 16.

ARTICLE 16, CEDAW

1. States parties shall take all appropriate measures to eliminate discrimination against women in all matters relating to marriage and family relations and in particular shall ensure, on a basis of equality of men and women:

(a) The same right to enter into marriage;

(b) The same right freely to choose a spouse and to enter into marriage only with their free and full consent;

(c) The same rights and responsibilities during marriage and at its dissolution;

(d) The same rights and responsibilities as parents, irrespective of their marital status,

---

[36] Cf. art. 16(h) of CEDAW [20.32].
[37] See generally Chap. 23.
[38] However, see below [20.38].

in matters relating to their children; in all cases the interests of the children shall be paramount;

(e) The same rights to decide freely and responsibly on the number and spacing of their children and to have access to the information, education and means to enable them to exercise these rights;

(f) The same rights and responsibilities with regard to guardianship, wardship, trustee-ship and adoption of children, or similar institutions where these concepts exist in national legislation; in all cases the interests of the children shall be paramount;

(g) The same personal rights as husband and wife, including the right to choose a family name, a profession and an occupation;

(h) The same rights for both spouses in respect of the ownership, acquisition, manage-ment, administration, enjoyment and disposition of property, whether free of charge or for a valuable consideration.

[20.33] The CEDAW Committee has issued a General Recommendation on Equality in Marriage and Family Relations. The Recommendation generally recognizes that, without equality with regard to domestic responsibilities, child rearing and family management, the economic, educational, physical and mental well-being of women is unachievable.

CEDAW GENERAL RECOMMENDATION 21

¶ 14. States parties' reports also disclose that polygamy is practised in a number of countries. Polygamous marriage contravenes a woman's right to equality with men, and can have such serious emotional and financial consequences for her and her dependants that such marriages ought to be discouraged and prohibited. The Committee notes with concern that some States parties, whose constitutions guarantee equal rights, permit polygamous marriage in accordance with personal or customary law. This violates the constitutional rights of women, and breaches the provisions of article 5(a) of the Convention.[39] . . .

¶ 39. States parties should also require the registration of all marriages whether contracted civilly or according to custom or religious law. The State can thereby ensure compliance with the Convention and establish equality between partners, a minimum age for marriage, prohibition of bigamy and polygamy and the protection of the rights of children. . . .

¶ 44. States parties should resolutely discourage any notions of inequality of women and men which are affirmed by laws, or by religious or private law or by custom, and progress to the stage where reservations, particularly to article 16, will be withdrawn.

---

[39] Art. 5(a) CEDAW obliges States to combat sexist social and cultural patterns. The HRC has also condemned the practice of polygamy; see Concluding Comments on Nigeria [20.28]; Concluding Comments on Libyan Arab Jamahiriya (1998) UN doc. CCPR/C/79/Add. 101, para. 17; Concluding Comments on Cameroon (1999) UN doc. CCPR/C/79/Add. 116, para. 10.

[20.34] In Concluding Comments on Peru, the HRC expressed concerns over divorce laws which might contravene article 23(4):[40]

¶ 16. The Committee notes with concern that when cases that might lead to a divorce are heard (physical or mental ill-treatment, serious injury and dishonourable conduct), the law instructs judges to take into account the education, habits and conduct of both spouses, a requirement that might easily lead to discrimination against women from the lower socio-economic strata.

[20.35]   *HENDRIKS v THE NETHERLANDS (201/85)*

The author, after a divorce from his wife, was denied access to his young son by reason of the opposition of the former wife. After twelve years of protracted litigation, the Dutch courts failed to issue orders compelling his ex-wife to allow him access to his son on the ground that it would subject his son to unnecessary tension. The author brought a complaint to the HRC, alleging that the State Party had violated his rights to protection of his family relationship with his child. The HRC decided against the author in the following terms:

¶ 10.4. The courts of the States parties are generally competent to evaluate the circumstances of individual cases. However, the Committee deems it necessary that the law should establish certain criteria so as to enable the courts to apply to the full the provisions of article 23 of the Covenant. It seems essential, barring exceptional circumstances, that these criteria should include the maintenance of personal relations and direct and regular contact between the child and both parents. The unilateral opposition of one of the parents, cannot, in the opinion of the Committee, be considered an exceptional circumstance.

¶ 10.5. In the case under consideration, the Committee notes that the Netherlands courts, as the Supreme Court had previously done, recognized the child's right to permanent contact with each of his parents as well as the right of access of the non-custodial parent, but considered that these rights could not be exercised in the current case because of the child's interests. This was the court's appreciation in the light of all the circumstances, even though there was no finding of inappropriate behaviour on the part of the author.

¶ 11. As a result, the Committee cannot conclude that the State party has violated article 23, but draws its attention to the need to supplement the legislation, as stated in paragraph 10.4.

[20.36] A number of individual opinions were appended. Mr Wako concurred in the majority opinion, but submitted the following:

¶ 5. My . . . concern is whether the Netherlands legislation, as applied to the Hendriks family, is compatible with the Covenant. Section 161, paragraph 5, of the Netherlands Civil Code does not provide for a statutory right of access to a child by the non-custodial

---

[40] (1996) UN doc. CCPR/C/79/Add. 72. See also Concluding Comments on Japan (1998) UN doc. CCPR/C/79/Add. 102, para. 16, where the HRC criticized Japanese laws forbidding women to marry within six months of a dissolution or annulment of a previous marriage.

parent, but leaves the question of visiting rights entirely to the discretion of the judge. The Netherlands legislation does not contain specific criteria for withholding of access. Thus the question arises whether the said general legislation can be deemed sufficient to guarantee the protection of children, in particular the right of children to have access to both parents, and to ensure equality of rights and responsibilities of spouses at the dissolution of a marriage, as envisaged in articles 23 and 24 of the Covenant. The continued contact between a child and a non-custodial parent is, in my opinion, too important a matter to be left solely to the judge to decide upon without any legislative guidance or clear criteria, hence the emerging international norms, notably international conventions against the abduction of children by parents, bilateral agreements providing for visiting rights and, most importantly, the draft convention on the rights of the child, draft article 6, paragraph 3, of which provides: 'a child who is separated from one or both parents has the right to maintain personal relations and direct contacts with both parents on a regular basis, save in exceptional circumstances'. Draft article 6, paragraph 2, provides similarly: 'a child whose parents reside in different States shall have the right to maintain on a regular basis, save in exceptional circumstances, personal relations and direct contacts with both parents . . .'.[41]

¶ 6. The facts of this case, as presented to the Committee, do not reveal the existence of any exceptional circumstances that might have justified the denial of personal contacts between Wim Hendriks junior and Wim Hendriks senior. The Netherlands courts themselves agreed that the father's application for access was reasonable, but denied the application primarily on the grounds of the mother's opposition. Although the Netherlands courts may have applied Netherlands law to the facts of this case correctly, it remains my concern that that law does not include a statutory right of access nor any identifiable criteria under which the fundamental right of mutual contact between a non-custodial parent and his or her child could be denied. I am pleased that the Netherlands Government is currently contemplating the adoption of new legislation which would provide for a statutory right of access and give the courts some guidance for the denial of access based on exceptional circumstances. This legislation, if enacted, would better reflect the spirit of the Covenant.

[20.37] Messrs Dimitrijevic, El Shafei, Zielinski, and Mrs Higgins were also distinctly uneasy in their concurring judgment:

¶ 1. The great difficulty that we see in this case is that the undoubted right and duty of a domestic court to decide 'in the best interests of the child' can, when applied in a certain way, deprive a non-custodial parent of his rights under article 23.

¶ 2. It is sometimes the case in domestic law that the very fact of a family rift will lead a non-custodial parent to lose access to the child, though he/she has not engaged in any conduct that would *per se* render contact with the child undesirable. However, article 23 of the Covenant speaks not only of the protection of the child, but also of the right to a family life. We agree with the Committee that this right to protection of the child and to a family life continues, in the parent–child relationship, beyond the termination of a marriage.

---

[41] See art. 9 of the final Convention on the Rights of the Child [21.23].

¶ 3. In this case, the Amsterdam District Court rejected the father's petition for access, although it had found the request reasonable and one that should in general be allowed. It would seem, from all the documentation at our disposal, that its denial of Mr. Hendriks' petition was based on the tensions likely to be generated by the mother's refusal to agree to such a contact—'even to a single meeting between the boy and his father on neutral ground, despite the fact that the Child Care and Protection Board would agree and would have offered guarantees' (decision of 20 December 1978). Given that it was not found that Mr. Hendriks' character or behaviour was such as to make the contact with his son undesirable, it seems to us that the only 'exceptional circumstance' was the reaction of Wim Hendriks junior's mother to the possibility of parental access and that this determined the perception of what was in the best interests of the child.

¶ 4. It is not for us to insist that the courts were wrong, in their assessment of the best interests of the child, in giving priority to the current difficulties and tensions rather than to the long-term importance for the child of contact with both its parents. However, we cannot but point out that this approach does not sustain the family rights to which Mr. Hendriks and his son were entitled under article 23 of the Covenant.

[20.38] The HRC's exoneration of the State Party in spite of the criticisms of all members is perhaps bewildering. Nowak suggests that the decision 'makes sense only when one considers that article 23(4) establishes a progressive implementation duty'.[42]

[20.39] Another reason that the HRC found in favour of the Netherlands was that it deferred to the decision of the Dutch family courts. This is the Committee's common practice in the absence of procedural deficiencies in domestic proceedings.[43] Mr Wako commented upon the consequences of this approach in his separate opinion:

¶ 3. My first concern is that, though the Committee's practice of not reviewing the decisions of local courts is prudent and appropriate, it is not dictated by the Optional Protocol. In cases where the facts are clear and the tests of all relevant orders and decisions have been made available by the parties, the Committee should be prepared to examine them as to their compatibility with the specific provisions of the Covenant invoked by the author. Thus, the Committee would not be acting as a 'fourth instance' in determining whether a decision of a State party's court were correct according to that State's legislation, but would only examine whether the provisions of the Covenant invoked by the alleged victim have been violated.

¶ 4. In the present case, the Committee declared the communication of Mr. Hendriks admissible, thus indicating that it was prepared to examine the case on the merits. In its views, however, the Committee has essentially decided that it is able to examine whether the decisions of the Netherlands courts not to grant the author visiting rights to his son were compatible with the requirements of protection of the family and protection of chil-

---

[42] Nowak, above, note 4, 419.
[43] See generally [14.36], and also *Drbal v The Czech Republic* (498/92), discussed at [21.25–21.26].

dren laid down in articles 23 and 24 of the Covenant. Paragraph 10.3 of the decision reflects the Committee's understanding of the scope of article 23, paragraphs 1 and 4, and of the concept of 'family'. In paragraph 10.4, the Committee underlines the importance of maintaining permanent personal contact between the child and both his parents, barring exceptional circumstances: it further states that the unilateral opposition by one of the parents—as apparently happened in this case—cannot be considered such an exceptional circumstance. The Committee should therefore have applied these criteria to the facts of the Hendriks case, so as to determine whether a violation of the articles of the Covenant had occurred. The Committee, however, makes a finding of no violation on the ground that the discretion of the local courts should not be questioned.

Despite Mr Wako's criticisms, it may be particularly appropriate for the HRC to exercise extreme caution before departing from the decisions of domestic family courts on extremely sensitive matters such as child custody or property settlements. Evidence in Optional Protocol (OP) cases is submitted in writing, so the HRC does not have the advantage of hearing witnesses and evaluating their demeanour. Furthermore, family court disputes are usually between private parties, such as a separated husband and wife. If one party petitions the HRC under the OP, the other party cannot be compelled to participate and give his/her side of the story.[44] It perhaps seems unwise in the highly flammable family law arena for the HRC to overturn family court decisions without hearing from all relevant parties to those decisions.

[20.40] *FEI v COLUMBIA (514/92)*

¶ 2.1. Mrs. Fei married Jaime Ospina Sardi in 1976; in 1977, rifts between the spouses began to emerge, and in 1981 Mrs. Fei left the home; the two children born from the marriage remained with the husband. The author sought to establish a residence in Bogotá but, as she was unable to obtain more than temporary employment, finally moved to Paris as a correspondent for the daily newspaper *24 Horas*. [The author had moved to Italy by the time she submitted the communication.]

¶ 2.2. A Colombian court order dating from 19 May 1982 established a separation and custody arrangement, but divorce proceedings subsequently were also instituted by the author before a Paris tribunal, with the consent of her ex-husband.

¶ 2.3. Under the Colombian court order of May 1982, the custody of the children was granted provisionally to the father, with the proviso that custody would go to the mother if the father remarried or cohabited with another woman. It further established joint parental custody and provided for generous visiting rights. Mr. Rodolfo Segovia Salas, a senator of the Republic, brother-in-law of Mr. Ospina Sardi and close family friend, was designated as guarantor of the agreement.

¶ 2.4. On 26 September 1985, Mrs. Fei's children, during a visit to her mother, were allegedly kidnapped by the father, with the help of three men said to be employees of the

---

[44] Note that Hendriks' former wife never sent any evidence to the HRC in the *Hendriks* case.

Colombian Embassy in Paris, when the author was leaving her Paris apartment. Between September 1985 and September 1988, the author did not have any contact with her children and knew nothing of their whereabouts, as Mr. Segovia Salas allegedly refused to cooperate. The author obtained the good offices of the French authorities and of the wife of President Mitterrand, but these démarches proved unsuccessful. Mrs. Fei then requested the assistance of the Italian Ministry of Foreign Affairs, which in turn asked for information and judicial assistance from the Colombian authorities. The author alleges that the latter either replied in evasive terms or simply denied that the author's rights had been violated. During the summer of 1988, an official of the Italian Foreign Ministry managed to locate the children in Bogotá. In September 1988, accompanied by the Italian Ambassador to Colombia, the author was finally able to see her two children for five minutes, on the third floor of the American School in Bogotá.

¶ 2.5. In the meantime, Mr. Ospina Sardi had himself initiated divorce proceedings in Bogotá, in which he requested the suspension of the author's parental authority as well as an order that would prohibit the children from leaving Colombia. On 13 March 1989, the First Circuit Court of Bogotá ... handed down its judgement; the author contends that in essence, the judgement confirmed the terms of the separation agreement reached several years earlier. Mrs. Fei further argues that the divorce proceedings in Colombia deliberately ignored the proceedings still pending before the Paris tribunal, as well as the children's dual nationality.

¶ 2.6. Mrs. Fei contends that, since September 1985, she has received, and continues to receive, threats. As a result, she claims, she cannot travel to Colombia alone or without protection. In March 1989, therefore, the Italian Foreign Ministry organized a trip to Bogotá for her; after negotiations, she was able to see her children for exactly two hours, 'as an exceptional favour'. The meeting took place in a small room in Mr. Segovia Salas' home, in the presence of a psychologist who allegedly had sought to obstruct the meeting until the very last moment. Thereafter, the author was only allowed to communicate with her children by telephone or mail; she contends that her letters were frequently tampered with and that it was almost impossible to reach the girls by telephone.

¶ 2.7. In May 1989, Mr. Ospina Sardi broke off the negotiations with the author without providing an explanation; only in November 1989 were the Italian authorities informed, upon request, of the 'final divorce judgement' of 13 March 1989. Mr. Ospina Sardi refused to comply with the terms of the judgement. On 21 June 1991, Mr. Ospina Sardi filed a request for the revision of the divorce judgement and of the visiting rights granted to the author, on the ground that circumstances had changed and that visiting rights as generous as those agreed upon in 1985 were no longer justifiable in the circumstances; the author contends that she was only informed of those proceedings in early 1992. Mr. Ospina Sardi also requested that the author be refused permission to see the children in Colombia, and that the children should not be allowed to visit their mother in Italy.

¶ 2.8. The Italian Foreign Ministry was in turn informed that the matter had been passed on to the office of the Prosecutor-General of Colombia, whose task under article 277 of the Constitution it is, *inter alia*, to review compliance with judgements handed down by Colombian courts. The Prosecutor-General initially ignored the case and did not investigate it; nor did he initiate criminal proceedings against Mr. Ospina Sardi for contempt of court and non-compliance with an executory judgement. Several months later, he asked for his disqualification in the case, on the grounds that he had 'strong bonds of friendship' with Mr. Ospina Sardi; the file was transferred to another magistrate. The Italian authorities have since addressed several complaints to the President of Colombia and to the Colombian Ministries of Foreign Affairs and International Trade, the latter having offered, on an unspecified earlier date, to find a way out of the impasse. No satisfactory reply has been provided by the Colombian authorities.

¶ 2.9. The author notes that, during her trips to Colombia in May and June 1992, she could only see her children very briefly and under conditions deemed unacceptable, and never for more than one hour at a time. On the occasion of her last visit to Colombia in March 1993, the conditions under which the visits took place allegedly had become worse, and the authorities attempted to prevent Mrs. Fei from leaving Colombia. Mrs. Fei has now herself instituted criminal proceedings against Mr. Ospina Sardi, for non-compliance with the divorce judgement.

¶ 2.10. In 1992 and 1993, the Colombian courts took further action in respect of Mr. Ospina Sardi's request for a revision of parental custody and visiting rights, as well as in respect of complaints filed on behalf of the author in the Supreme Court of Colombia. On 24 November 1992, the Family Law Division (*Sala de Familia*) of the Superior Court of Bogotá (Tribunal Superior del Distrito Judicial) modified the visiting rights regime in the sense that all contacts between the children and the author outside Colombia were suspended; at the same time, the entire visiting rights regime was pending for review before Family Court No. 19 of Bogotá.

¶ 2.11. Mrs. Fei's counsel initiated proceedings in the Supreme Court of Colombia, directed against the Family Court No. 19 of Bogotá, against the office of the Procurator-General and against the judgement of 24 November 1992, for non-observance of the author's constitutional rights. On 9 February 1993, the Civil Chamber of the Supreme Court (*Sala de Casación Civil*) set aside operative paragraph 1 of the judgement of 24 November 1992 concerning the suspension of contacts between the author and her children outside Colombia, while confirming the rest of said judgement. At the same time, the Supreme Court transmitted its judgement to Family Judge No. 19 [*sic*], with the request that its observations be taken into account in the proceedings filed by Mr. Ospina Sardi, and to the Constitutional Court.

¶ 2.12. On 14 April 1993, Family Court No. 19 of Bogotá handed down its judgement concerning the request for modification of visiting rights. This judgement placed certain conditions on the modalities of the author's visits to her children, especially outside Colombia, inasmuch as the Government of Colombia had to take the measures necessary to guarantee the exit and the re-entry of the children.

¶ 2.13. On 28 July 1993, finally, the Constitutional Court partially confirmed and partially modified the judgement of the Supreme Court of 9 February 1993. The judgement is critical of the author's attitude vis-à-vis her children between 1985 and 1989, as it assumes that the author deliberately neglected contact with them between those dates. It denies the author any possibility of a transfer of custody, and appears to hold that the judgement of Family Court No. 19 is final . . . This, according to counsel, means that the author must start all over again if she endeavours to obtain custody of the children. Finally, the judgement admonishes the author to assume her duties with more responsibility in the future. . . .

¶ 2.14. In December 1993, the author's children, after presumed pressure from their father, filed proceedings pursuant to article 86 of the Colombian Constitution . . . against their mother. The case was placed before the Superior Tribunal in Bogotá (*Tribunal Superior del Distrito Judicial de Santa Fé de Bogotá*). Mrs. Fei claims that she was never officially notified of this action. It appears that the Court gave her until 10 January 1994 to present her defence, reserving judgement for 14 January. For an unexplained reason, the hearing was then advanced to the morning of 16 December 1993, with the judgement delivered on the afternoon of the same day. The judgement orders Mrs. Fei to stop publishing her book about her and her children's story . . . in Colombia.

¶ 2.15. The author submits that her lawyer was prevented from attending the hearing of 16 December 1993 and from presenting his client's defence. Counsel thereupon filed a complaint based on violations of fundamental rights of the defence with the Supreme Court. On 24 February 1994, the Supreme Court (*Sala de Casación Penal*) declared, on procedural grounds, that it was not competent to hear the complaint. . . .

¶ 7.6. . . . [T]he author contends that the violation of article 23, paragraph 4, in her case is flagrant. She describes the precarious conditions under which the visits of their daughters took place, out of their home, in the presence of a psychologist hired by Mr. Ospina Sardi, and for extremely short periods of time. The testimonies of Ms. Susanna Agnelli, who accompanied the author during these visits, are said to demonstrate clearly the violation of this provision.

¶ 7.7. The author further submits that article 23, paragraph 4, was violated because her daughters were forced to testify against her on several occasions in judicial proceedings initiated by Mr. Ospina Sardi, testimonies that allegedly constituted a serious threat to their mental equilibrium. Furthermore, the procedure filed by the children against the author under article 86 of the Constitution is said to have been prompted by pressure from Mr. Ospina Sardi. This, it is submitted, clearly transpires from the text of the initial deposition: according to the author, it could only have been prepared by a lawyer, but not by a child.

The Committee decided as follows:

¶ 8.9. As to the alleged violation of article 23, paragraph 4, the Committee recalls that this provision grants, barring exceptional circumstances, a right to regular contact between children and both of their parents upon dissolution of a marriage. The unilateral opposition of one parent generally does not constitute such an exceptional circumstance. [Views on case No. 201/85 (*Hendriks v The Netherlands*), adopted on 27 July 1988, para. 10.4.]

¶ 8.10. In the present case, it was the author's ex-husband who sought to prevent the author from maintaining regular contact with her daughters, in spite of court decisions granting the author such access. On the basis of the material made available to the Committee, the father's refusal apparently was justified as being 'in the best interest' of the children. The Committee cannot share this assessment. No special circumstances have been adduced that would have justified the restrictions on the author's contacts with her children. Rather, it appears that the author's ex-husband sought to stifle, by all means at his disposal, the author's access to the girls, or to alienate them from her. The severe restrictions imposed by Mrs. Fei's ex-husband on Mrs. Fei's rare meetings with her daughters support this conclusion. Her attempts to initiate criminal proceedings against her ex-husband for non-compliance with the court order granting her visiting rights were frustrated by delay and inaction on the part of the prosecutor's office. In the circumstances, it was not reasonable to expect her to pursue any remedy that may have been available under the Code of Civil Procedure. In the Committee's opinion, in the absence of special circumstances, none of which are discernible in the present case, it cannot be deemed to be in the 'best interest' of children virtually to eliminate one parent's access to them. That Mrs. Fei has, since 1992–1993, reduced her attempts to vindicate her right of access cannot, in the Committee's opinion, be held against her. In all the circumstances of the case, the Committee concludes that there has been a violation of article 23, paragraph 4. Furthermore, the failure of the prosecutor's office to ensure the right to permanent contact between the author and her daughters also has entailed a violation of article 17, paragraph 1, of the Covenant.

The facts in *Fei* may be distinguished from those in *Hendriks* on the basis that the relevant local proceedings in Colombia were blatantly unfair.[45] Thus, the HRC was not disposed to defer to the local courts' decisions. A similar situation would probably arise if the local courts' decisions were based on unjust legislation.

[20.41]   *BALAGUER SANTACANA v SPAIN (417/90)*

The author and María del Carmen Montalvo Quiñones decided to live together in 1983. On 15 October 1985, Ms Montalvo gave birth to a girl, who was recognized by both parents and registered in Barcelona under the name of María del Carmen Balaguer Montalvo. After the birth of the child, their relationship deteriorated. In October 1986 Ms Montalvo left the common household, taking the child with her. Protracted custody disputes ensued. The author submitted the following complaint:

¶ 3. The author claims that he is a victim of a violation of article 23, paragraphs 1 and 4, of the Covenant, because he has been denied family rights and equality of treatment by the Spanish courts in the award of child custody and because of the failure of the courts to act promptly in enforcing a regime of reasonable parental visits. . . . He further claims that Spanish legislation does not sufficiently guarantee the right of access and that the practice of Spanish courts, as illustrated by his own and many other cases, reveals a bias in favour of mothers and against fathers. Although he does not specifically invoke article 26 of the Covenant, the author's allegations also pertain to this provision.

The HRC decided against the author in the following terms:

¶ 10.1. On the merits, the questions before the Committee concern the scope of articles 23, paragraphs 1 and 4; and 24, paragraph 1; i.e. whether or not these provisions guarantee an unqualified right of access for a divorced or separated parent, and a child's right to have contact with both parents. Another issue is whether decisions on custody and access rights in the case have been based on distinctions made between fathers and mothers and, if so, whether these distinctions are based on objective and reasonable criteria, as follows from the application of article 26 of the Covenant. . . .

---

[45] Indeed, the HRC also found a breach of the right to a fair trial [14.30].

¶ 10.3. In the instant case, irrespective of the nature of the author's relationship with Ms. Montalvo, the Committee observes that the State party has always acknowledged that the relations between the author and his daughter were protected by the law and that the mother, between 1986 and 1990, never objected to the author's contacts with his daughter. It was only after Mr. Balaguer continuously failed to observe, and objected to, the modalities of his right of access, that she sought exclusive custody and non-contentious proceedings were suspended. The Committee concludes that there has been no violation of article 23, paragraph 1.

¶ 10.4. The Committee further notes that article 23, paragraph 4, does not apply in the instant case, as Mr. Balaguer was never married to Ms. Montalvo. If paragraph 4 is placed into the overall context of article 23, it becomes clear that the protection of the second sentence refers only to children of the marriage which is being dissolved. In any event, the material before the Committee justifies the conclusion that the State party's authorities, when determining custody or access issues in the case, always took the child's best interests into consideration. This is true also for the decisions of the Third Chamber of the Court of Badalona, which the author has singled out in particular.

[20.42] Article 23(4) also prescribes that adequate provision be made for children at the dissolution of their parents' marriage. No HRC comment has elaborated on this aspect of the article. It is likely that this right is subsumed by the article 24 right of children to protection.

Conclusion

[20.43] The HRC has confirmed that States have onerous protective duties under article 23(1) with regard to 'the family', which has been defined in broad terms. For example, States should take appropriate measures to ensure family unity and reunion. However, these duties are not absolute, as has been evinced by decisions such as *Stewart v Canada* (538/93) [20.15]. Furthermore, the HRC has generally been reluctant to interfere with State family court judgments which have allegedly breached article 23(4) rights. The intimate, personal nature of family law disputes may justify a greater degree of caution on the part of the HRC before disturbing local court judgments. Finally, no Optional Protocol cases have dealt with rights regarding marriage in article 23(2) and (3). The extent of these rights, such as their applicability to gay couples, remains uncertain.

Postscript: Please note that General Comment 28 on 'Equality of Rights Between Men and Women', contained in the Addendum at page 634, contains extra information on some of the material in this chapter.

Protection of Children—Article 24

ARTICLE 24

1. Every child shall have without any discrimination as to race, colour, sex, language, religion, national or social origin, property or birth, the right to such measures of protection as are required by his status as a minor on the part of his family, society and the State.

2. Every child shall be registered immediately after birth and shall have a name.

3. Every child has the right to acquire a nationality.

[21.01] Article 24 accords the special protection to the child required by his/her status as a minor, in addition to those reflected elsewhere in the Covenant. Whilst historically international law may have reflected limited recognition of the civil and political rights of children, this is no longer the case. Children traditionally were defined by their incompetence, rather than as right-holders in international law.[1] However the ICCPR and the Convention on the Rights of the Child demonstrate that civil and political rights are applicable to children, both as 'people' in the general sense and, where appropriate, specifically by virtue of their status as minors. This chapter will focus on the *specific* civil and political rights of children, where children's rights differ from rights accorded in general to children and adults.[2]

---

[1] See G. Van Bueren, *The International Law on the Rights of the Child* (Martinus Nijhoff, Dordrecht, 1995), at 145.
[2] Apart from the comprehensive analysis provided by Van Bueren, ibid., there is a substantial

The Convention on the Rights of the Child

[21.02] The primary international instrument concerning children's rights is the United Nations Convention of the Rights of the Child, 1989 (CRC).[3] The principles underlying the Convention are based on the idea that children, by reason of their physical and mental immaturity, need special safeguards and care, including appropriate legal protection, and the recognition that there are children living in exceptionally difficult conditions in all countries.[4] The CRC has the most States Parties of any of the major UN human rights treaties.[5]

[21.03] The CRC is concerned with four primary aims: participation, protection, prevention, and provision.[6] Thus the Convention covers the range of substantive human rights: civil, political, economic, social, and cultural. A monitoring committee, the Committee on the Rights of the Child (CROC), supervises implementation of the obligations undertaken by States Parties.[7] States' reports are required every five years, and are examined in a public dialogue with CROC.[8] The Optional Protocol monitoring mechanism in place under the ICCPR is not replicated under the CRC, so there is no individual complaints procedure. Furthermore, CROC has so far issued no General Comments or equivalents, which have provided useful interpretations of Convention rights under other UN treaties. CROC does issue Concluding Comments to States Parties to conclude the reporting process, but a lack of comprehensive CROC jurisprudence remains apparent.[9]

body of commentary on the rights of the child under international law; see the *International Journal of Children's Rights*; P. Alston, *The Best Interests of the Child: Reconciling Culture and Human Rights* (Clarendon, Oxford, 1994); P. Alston, S. Parker, and J. Seymour, *Children, Rights and the Law* (Clarendon, Oxford, 1992); M. Freeman, *The Moral Status of Children: Essays on the Rights of the Child* (Martinus Nijhoff, The Hague, 1997); and A. G. Mower, *The Convention on the Rights of the Child: International Law Support for Children* (Greenwood Press, Westport, Conn., 1997).

[3] G.A. Res. 44/25, annex, 44 U.N. GAOR Supp. (No. 49) at 167, U.N. Doc. A/44/49 (1989). See further, Mower, above, note 2; L. LeBlanc, *The Convention on the Rights of the Child: United Nations Lawmaking on Human Rights* (University of Nebraska Press, Lincoln, Neb., 1995).

[4] See Preamble to the CRC.

[5] As at March 2000, only the USA and Somalia had failed to ratify this Convention. See, on the reasons behind the USA's anomalous position (largely right-wing concerns regarding the CRC's potential disempowerment of parents and undermining of 'the family'), S. Kilbourne, 'United States Failure to Ratify the UN Convention on the Rights of the Child: Playing Politics with Children' (1996) 6 *Transnational Law and Contemporary Problems* 437. There are however significant reservations that modify the CRC's application within States Parties. These are comprehensively surveyed and analysed in L.J. Leblanc, 'Reservations to the Convention on the Rights of the Child: A Macroscopic View of State Practice' (1996) 4 *International Journal of Children's Rights* 357.

[6] 'The participation of children in decisions affecting their own destiny; the protection of children against discrimination and all forms of neglect and exploitation; the prevention of harm to children; and the provision of assistance for their basic needs': Van Bueren, above, note 1, at 15.

[7] Art. 43.

[8] Art. 44(2). The operation of the reporting system is extensively analysed in Mower, above, note 2.

[9] However, see J. Todres, 'Emerging Limitations on the Rights of the Child: The UN Convention on the Rights of the Child and its Early Case Law' [1998] *Columbia Human Rights Law Review* 159, detailing how the CRC has been applied in domestic jurisdictions.

[21.04] All States Parties to the CRC undertake the obligation to advance 'the best interests of the child', assessed from the child's perspective, not that of the parents or the State:

ARTICLE 3, CRC

1. In all actions concerning children, whether undertaken by public or private social welfare institutions, courts of law, administrative authorities or legislative bodies, the best interests of the child shall be a primary consideration.

2. States Parties undertake to ensure the child such protection and care as is necessary for his or her well-being, taking into account the rights and duties of his or her parents, legal guardians, or other individuals legally responsible for him or her, and, to this end, shall take all appropriate legislative and administrative measures.

3. States Parties shall ensure that the institutions, services and facilities responsible for the care or protection of children shall conform with the standards established by competent authorities, particularly in the areas of safety, health, in the number and suitability of their staff, as well as competent supervision.

ARTICLE 12, CRC

1. States Parties shall assure to the child who is capable of forming his or her own views the right to express those views freely in all matters affecting the child, the views of the child being given due weight in accordance with the age and maturity of the child.

2. For this purpose, the child shall in particular be provided the opportunity to be heard in any judicial and administrative proceedings affecting the child, either directly, or through a representative or an appropriate body, in a manner consistent with the procedural rules of national law.

The procedural capacity conferred in article 12 of the CRC,[10] and especially the 'best interests' principle set out in article 3, contributes to the conclusion that the international community now 'see[s] children not in terms of charity, but of inherent rights'.[11]

[21.05] The civil and political rights of children are specifically addressed in the CRC, reflecting similar rights accorded in the ICCPR.[12] The CRC, being concerned with the general well-being of children, also contains important

---

[10] In this regard, see also the HRC decision in *De Galicchio and Vicario v Argentina* (400/90), para. 10.3 [21.48]

[11] Mower, above, note 2, at 5.

[12] Thus, art. 13 CRC corresponds with the art. 19 ICCPR on freedom of expression; art. 14 CRC with the art. 18 ICCPR on freedom of religion; art. 15 CRC with arts. 21 and 22 ICCPR freedom of assembly and association; art. 16 CRC with the right of privacy in art. 17 ICCPR; art. 6 CRC with art. 6 ICCPR on the right to life; art. 37 CRC with the protection from torture, and rights to liberty and fair trial in arts. 7, 9, and 14 ICCPR; art. 30 CRC with minority rights protection in art. 27 ICCPR, and the protection in judicial proceedings in art. 40 CRC with art. 14 ICCPR.

economic, social, and cultural rights, so it overlaps substantially with the International Covenant on Economic, Social, and Cultural Rights (ICESCR).[13]

ARTICLE 4, CRC

States Parties shall undertake all appropriate legislative, administrative, and other measures for the implementation of the rights recognized in the present Convention. With regard to economic, social, and cultural rights, States Parties shall undertake such measures to the maximum extent of their available resources and, where needed, within the framework of international co-operation.

The progressive nature of economic, social, and cultural obligations under the CRC reflects the progressive nature of the rights in the ICESCR.[14]

[21.06] The HRC may be expected to be influenced by the CRC in its interpretation of article 24. Therefore, further provisions of the CRC are excerpted, where appropriate, below.

The Ancillary Nature of Article 24

[21.07] Article 2(1) states that the Covenant applies to all individuals within jurisdiction, and thus it must also apply to minors. The ancillary role of article 24 is explained by the HRC:

GENERAL COMMENT 17

¶ 1. Article 24 of the International Covenant on Civil and Political Rights recognizes the right of every child, without any discrimination, to receive from his family, society and the State the protection required by his status as a minor. Consequently, the implementation of this provision entails the adoption of special measures to protect children, in addition to the measures that States are required to take under article 2 to ensure that everyone enjoys the rights provided for in the Covenant. The reports submitted by States parties often seem to underestimate this obligation and supply inadequate information on the way in which children are afforded enjoyment of their right to a special protection.

¶ 2. In this connection, the Committee points out that the rights provided for in article 24 are not the only ones that the Covenant recognizes for children and that, as individuals, children benefit from all of the civil rights enunciated in the Covenant. In enunciating a right, some provisions of the Covenant expressly indicate to States measures to be adopted with a view to affording minors greater protection than adults. Thus, as far as the right to life is concerned, the death penalty cannot be imposed for crimes committed by persons under 18 years of age.[15] Similarly, if lawfully deprived of their liberty, accused juvenile

---

[13] See, e.g., arts. 24, 26–29, and 31 CRC.
[14] See art. 2(2) ICESCR, discussed at [1.11].
[15] See art. 6(5) ICCPR, discussed briefly at [8.24].

persons shall be separated from adults and are entitled to be brought as speedily as possible for adjudication; in turn, convicted juvenile offenders shall be subject to a penitentiary system that involves segregation from adults and is appropriate to their age and legal status, the aim being to foster reformation and social rehabilitation.[16] In other instances, children are protected by the possibility of the restriction—provided that such restriction is warranted—of a right recognized by the Covenant, such as the right to publicize a judgement in a suit at law or a criminal case, from which an exception may be made when the interest of the minor so requires.[17]

[21.08] The General Comment states that 'all of the civil rights' in the ICCPR are applicable to children, perhaps suggesting that children cannot enjoy political rights upheld in the Covenant. Indeed, children are usually denied the article 25 rights to vote and stand for election.[18]

[21.09] Article 24 ensures a child's rights to those measures of protection required of his or her family, society, and the State. This is more than mere reinforcement of the rights guaranteed elsewhere in the Covenant; the laws of a State Party must reflect the special status of a minor and afford special protection to the child.[19] Indeed, it seems that article 24 acts to 'top up' the other civil rights offered to children by the ICCPR's other guarantees by more explicitly requiring positive measures of protection.[20]

Economic, Social, and Cultural Rights and Article 24

[21.10]   *GENERAL COMMENT 17*

¶ 3. In most cases, . . . the measures to be adopted are not specified in the Covenant and it is for each State to determine them in the light of the protection needs of children in its territory and within its jurisdiction. The Committee notes in this regard that such measures, although intended primarily to ensure that children fully enjoy the other rights enunciated in the Covenant, may also be economic, social, and cultural. For example, every possible economic and social measure should be taken to reduce infant mortality and to eradicate malnutrition among children and to prevent them from being subjected to acts of violence and cruel and inhuman treatment or from being exploited by means of forced labour or prostitution, or by their use in the illicit trafficking of narcotic drugs, or by any other means. In the cultural field, every possible measure should be taken to foster the development of their personality and to provide them with a level of education that will enable them to enjoy the rights recognized in the Covenant, particularly the right to freedom of opinion and expression. . . .

---

[16] See [9.120].

[17] See art. 14(4) ICCPR, discussed at [14.107].   [18] See [22.17].

[19] M. Nowak, *UN Covenant on Civil and Political Rights: CCPR Commentary* (N. P. Engel, Kehl, 1993) at 424–5.

[20] See, e.g., *De Gallicchio and Vicario v Argentina* (400/90), para. 10.5 [21.48]; see also *Laureano v Peru* (540/93), para. 8.7, where a violation of the right to life (art. 6) was exacerbated by the fact that it had occurred to a child.

[21.11] Article 24 thus incorporates an economic, social, and cultural element into the protection of children's rights, as is confirmed in Concluding Comments on Canada:[21]

¶ 18. The Committee is concerned that differences in the way in which the National Child Benefit Supplement for low-income families is implemented in some provinces may result in a denial of this benefit to some children. This may lead to non-compliance with article 24 of the Covenant. . . .

¶ 20. . . . the very high poverty rate among single mothers leaves their children without the protection they are entitled to under the Covenant. . . .

See also the following comment on Georgia:[22]

¶ 23. The Committee is concerned at the increase in the number of children affected by poverty and social dislocation and the concomitant increase in the number of street children, delinquents or drug-addicts.

[21.12] In General Comment 17, the HRC states that education is of fundamental importance to the proper development of a child's personality. Although a right to education is an economic and social right, it is essential to ensure the capacity to exercise civil and political rights, and is therefore an important component of article 24 protection. For example, in Concluding Comments on Zambia, the HRC has stated:[23]

¶ 17. The Committee is also concerned that no measures are taken to ensure that pregnancy or parenthood do not affect the continuous education of children.

Similarly, regarding Costa Rica, the HRC stated:[24]

¶ 19. The Committee further notes an increase in child labour and school drop-out, and that no effective remedies are in place.[25]

This analysis also highlights the indivisibility and permeability of economic, social, and cultural rights, and civil and political rights.[26]

[21.13] There is an unresolved issue as to the interplay between rights of education within article 24, and the religious education rights granted to parents by article 18(4) of the ICCPR.[27]

Age of Majority

[21.14] The age of majority is not set out by article 24 ICCPR. The HRC leaves the question of when a child becomes an adult for legal purposes to be determined by each State Party:

---

[21] (1999) UN doc. CCPR/C/79/Add.105.   [22] (1997) UN doc. CCPR/C/79/Add. 74.
[23] (1996) UN doc. CCPR/C/79/Add. 62.   [24] (1999) UN doc. CCPR/C/79/Add. 107.
[25] See discussion at [21.39–21.40], where the HRC links its concerns regarding child labour to the detrimental impact it has on a child's education.   [26] See [1.57].
[27] See G. Van Beuren, 'The International Protection of Family Members' Rights as the 21st Century

GENERAL COMMENT 17

¶ 4. The right to special measures of protection belongs to every child because of his status as a minor. Nevertheless, the Covenant does not indicate the age at which he attains his majority. This is to be determined by each State party in the light of the relevant social and cultural conditions. In this respect, States should indicate in their reports the age at which the child attains his majority in civil matters and assumes criminal responsibility. States should also indicate the age at which a child is legally entitled to work and the age at which he is treated as an adult under labour law. States should further indicate the age at which a child is considered adult for the purposes of article 10, paragraphs 2 and 3. However, the Committee notes that the age for the above purposes should not be set unreasonably low and that in any case a State party cannot absolve itself from its obligations under the Covenant regarding persons under the age of 18, notwithstanding that they have reached the age of majority under domestic law.[28]

ARTICLE 1, CRC

For the purposes of the present Convention, a child means every human being below the age of eighteen years unless under the law applicable to the child, majority is attained earlier.

[21.15] The HRC has expressed concern where the age of criminal responsibility is very low.[29] For example, in Concluding Comments regarding Sri Lanka:[30]

¶ 20. The low age of criminal responsibility and the stipulation within the Penal Code by which a child above 8 years of age and under 12 years of age can be held to be criminally responsible on the determination by the judge of the child's maturity of understanding as to the nature and consequence of his or her conduct are matters of profound concern to the Committee.

Similar statements were made regarding Cyprus:[31]

¶ 13. The Committee is concerned that in a number of key areas children are not

---

Approaches' (1995) 17 HRQ 732, 743–7. There is considerable commentary on the international right to education; see, e.g., D. Hodgson, 'The International Human Right to Education and Education Concerning Human Rights' (1996) 4 *International Journal of Children's Rights* 237, and D. Hodgson, *The Human Right to Education* (Ashgate, Aldershot, 1998). See also [17.28].

[28] A specific age is referred to in art. 6(5) which prohibits the death penalty for persons 'below 18 years of age'. The historical and contemporary standards for defining childhood are reviewed in Van Bueren, above, note 1, at 32–8.

[29] See also Concluding Comments on Belgium (1998) UN doc. CCPR/C/79/Add.99, para. 21; Concluding Comments on Zambia (1996) UN doc. CCPR/C/79/Add. 62, para. 19.

[30] (1995) UN doc. CCPR/C/79/Add. 56.

[31] (1994) UN doc. CCPR/C/79/Add. 39. The concerns had not been addressed by the time new comments were issued on Cyprus: (1998) UN doc. CCPR/C/79/Add. 88, para. 16. See also Concluding Comments on Hong Kong (China), (1999) UN doc. CCPR/C/79/Add. 117, para. 17 (criticizing the age of criminal responsibility being seven years). See also *V v UK* and *T v UK*, judgments of the European Court of Human Rights of 16 December 1999, regarding the rights of accused ju-veniles in criminal trials.

adequately protected under the terms of existing legislation. In particular, the Committee is concerned that marriageable age is defined as the onset of puberty, that criminal responsibility begins at age seven, and that persons between sixteen and eighteen years of age are not considered child or youth offenders, and are subject to penal sanction.

[21.16] The HRC has frequently expressed concern regarding overly young 'marriageable ages'.[32] Regarding Sri Lanka, the HRC stated the following:[33]

¶ 25. The Committee notes that reforms are in place to raise the marriageable age for girls to 18. However, the current legislation permits the marriage of girls from the age of 12. . . .

¶ 38. The Committee recommends that measures be taken to ensure the protection of the child and in this regard the particular attention of the State party is drawn to the Personal Status Act, which permits the marriage of a girl at the age of 12, and its incompatibility with the provisions of the Covenant.

Further, laws that set differing ages of consent for marriage for males and females will breach articles 23 and 24, as seen in the Concluding Comments on Chile:[34]

¶ 21. The minimum age for marriage, 12 years for girls and 14 years for boys, raises issues of compliance by the State party with its duty under article 24, paragraph 1, to offer protection to minors. Furthermore, marriage at such a young age would generally mean that the persons involved do not have the mental maturity to ensure that the marriage is entered into with free and full consent, as required under article 23, paragraph 3, of the Covenant. Therefore: The State party should amend the law so as to introduce a uniform minimum age for marriage of males and females, which will ensure the maturity required in order for the marriage to comply with the requirements of article 23, paragraph 3, of the Covenant.

Regarding France, the HRC stated:[35]

¶ 25. The Committee is concerned that the Civil Code establishes a different minimum age for marriage for girls (15) and for boys (18) and that it sets such a low age for girls. . . .

[21.17] Neither the CRC nor the ICCPR makes any significant express attempt to elicit rights for unborn children. The CRC Preamble does refer to the need for appropriate legal protection applicable 'before as well as after birth'. However, this Preamble essentially represents a compromise on the irreconcilable views of two groups of countries concerning the moment when childhood begins; it is unlikely to be interpreted as a prohibition on abortion.[36] Certainly, HRC

---

[32] See also [20.27–20.29] on art. 23(3). Art. 16(2) of the Convention on the Elimination of all Forms of Discrimination Against Women (CEDAW) also prohibits 'the betrothal and marriage of a child'.

[33] (1995) UN doc. CCPR/C/79/Add. 56.   [34] (1999) UN doc. CCPR/C/79/Add.104.

[35] (1997) UN doc. CCPR/C/79/Add.80. See also Concluding Comments on Cameroon (1999) UN doc. CCPR/C/79/Add. 117, para. 10.

[36] See N. Cantwell, 'The Origins, Development, and Significance of the United Nations Convention on the Rights of the Child' in S. Detrick (ed.), *The United Nations Convention on the Rights of the Child: A Guide to the Travaux Préparatoires* (Martinus Nijhoff, Dordrecht, 1992), at 26.

comments have indicated that the *prohibition* of abortion is more likely to breach the ICCPR than the *permissibility* of abortion.[37]

Right of Non-discrimination

[21.18] *GENERAL COMMENT 17*

¶ 5. The Covenant requires that children should be protected against discrimination on any grounds such as race, colour, sex, language, religion, national or social origin, property or birth. In this connection, the Committee notes that, whereas non-discrimination in the enjoyment of the rights provided for in the Covenant also stems, in the case of children, from article 2 and their equality before the law from article 26, the non-discrimination clause contained in article 24 relates specifically to the measures of protection referred to in that provision. Reports by States parties should indicate how legislation and practice ensure that measures of protection are aimed at removing all discrimination in every field, including inheritance, particularly as between children who are nationals and children who are aliens or as between legitimate children and children born out of wedlock.

ARTICLE 2, CRC

1. States Parties shall respect and ensure the rights set forth in the present Convention to each child within their jurisdiction without discrimination of any kind, irrespective of the child's or his or her parent's or legal guardian's race, colour, sex, language, religion, political or other opinion, national, ethnic or social origin, property, disability, birth or other status.

2. States Parties shall take all appropriate measures to ensure that the child is protected against all forms of discrimination or punishment on the basis of the status, activities, expressed opinions, or beliefs of the child's parents, legal guardians, or family members.

[21.19] Article 2(1) of the CRC adds a further express prohibited ground of non-discrimination compared to those found in the ICCPR, 'disability'. The CRC's concern with disabled children is further defined in article 23, CRC:

ARTICLE 23, CRC

1. States Parties recognize that a mentally or physically disabled child should enjoy a full and decent life, in conditions which ensure dignity, promote self-reliance and facilitate the child's active participation in the community.

Article 23, subparagraphs 2 to 4, CRC spell out positive obligations, such as the provision of appropriate care facilities, designed to address the needs of disabled

---

[37] See [8.47].

children. As with all non-discrimination guarantees, positive measures are necessary truly to redress historical systemic disadvantage.[38]

[21.20] The HRC's General Comment and its Concluding Comments have reflected a particular concern for the treatment of children born out of wedlock, for any distinction based on legitimacy would amount to discrimination by reason of 'birth'. In Concluding Comments on the Libyan Arab Jamahiriya, the HRC stated: [39]

¶ 18. The Committee expresses its concern over the persistence of discrimination in law and practice against children born out of wedlock, which is incompatible with articles 24 and 26 of the Covenant. It recommends that attention be paid to the prompt rectification of this situation with regard to all rights to which children are entitled.

Regarding France, the HRC stated:[40]

¶ 25. ... the Committee recommends that all children born out of wedlock be given the same succession rights as children born in wedlock.

Children's Rights within the Family

[21.21] There is considerable overlap between article 24 and article 23, which recognizes the family 'as being the natural and fundamental unit of society'. Both the HRC and the CRC texts recognize that the family is normally expected to provide the environment for a child's proper development.

GENERAL COMMENT 17

¶ 6. Responsibility for guaranteeing children the necessary protection lies with the family, society and the State. Although the Covenant does not indicate how such responsibility is to be apportioned, it is primarily incumbent on the family, which is interpreted broadly to include all persons composing it in the society of the State party concerned, and particularly on the parents, to create conditions to promote the harmonious development of the child's personality and his enjoyment of the rights recognized in the Covenant.

ARTICLE 5, CRC

States Parties shall respect the responsibilities, rights and duties of parents or, where applicable, the members of the extended family or community as provided for by local custom, legal guardians or other persons legally responsible for the child, to provide, in a

---

[38] Compare [23.77]ff. on 'systemic discrimination' issues regarding the ICCPR and CEDAW.
[39] (1998) UN doc. CCPR/C/79/Add.101.
[40] (1997) UN doc. CCPR/C/79/Add.80; see also Concluding Comments on Iceland (1998) UN doc. CCPR/C/79/Add. 98, para. 11.

manner consistent with the evolving capacities of the child, appropriate direction and guidance in the exercise by the child of the rights recognized in the present Convention.

ARTICLE 18, CRC

1. States Parties shall use their best efforts to ensure recognition of the principle that both parents have common responsibilities for the upbringing and development of the child. Parents or, as the case may be, legal guardians, have the primary responsibility for the upbringing and development of the child. The best interests of the child will be their basic concern.

[21.22] It is common within many societies for both parents to work outside the home. Both the HRC and the text of the CRC have stressed that the State should ensure that proper childcare facilities and other institutional support are available to assist such parents to raise their child.

GENERAL COMMENT 17

¶ 6. ... However, since it is quite common for the father and mother to be gainfully employed outside the home, reports by States parties should indicate how society, social institutions and the State are discharging their responsibility to assist the family in ensuring the protection of the child. ...

ARTICLE 18, CRC

2. For the purpose of guaranteeing and promoting the rights set forth in the present Convention, States Parties shall render appropriate assistance to parents and legal guardians in the performance of their child-rearing responsibilities and shall ensure the development of institutions, facilities and services for the care of children.

3. States Parties shall take all appropriate measures to ensure that children of working parents have the right to benefit from child-care services and facilities for which they are eligible.

Considering the impoverishment of many States Parties, it will be interesting to see how this obligation is interpreted in the context of an OP communication.

[21.23] Both the HRC General Comment and article 9 CRC indicate that a child's access to both parents, in the case of separation, should be guaranteed.

GENERAL COMMENT 17

¶ 6. ... If the marriage is dissolved, steps should be taken, keeping in view the paramount interest of the children, to give them necessary protection and, so far as is possible, to guarantee personal relations with both parents. ...

ARTICLE 9, CRC

3. States Parties shall respect the right of the child who is separated from one or both parents to maintain personal relations and direct contact with both parents on a regular basis, except if it is contrary to the child's best interests.

4. Where such separation results from any action initiated by a State party, such as the detention, imprisonment, exile, deportation or death (including death arising from any cause while the person is in the custody of the State) of one or both parents or of the child, that State party shall, upon request, provide the parents, the child or, if appropriate, another member of the family with the essential information concerning the whereabouts of the absent member(s) of the family unless the provision of the information would be detrimental to the well-being of the child. States Parties shall further ensure that the submission of such a request shall of itself entail no adverse consequences for the person(s) concerned.

[21.24] In *Hendriks v The Netherlands* (201/85), the HRC had to consider the claims of a divorced father who had been denied access to his son by the unilateral opposition of the child's mother. In *Hendriks*, the Committee noted that the State's courts had recognized and considered the child's right to ongoing contact with both parents. The HRC ultimately was unable to find a breach of either article 23 or 24. While the father's 'family' rights were undoubtedly obstructed, the HRC deferred to the domestic courts' opinion that court-enforced paternal contact would subject the child to undue stress. Therefore, the mother's persistent refusal of parental access to the father was a regrettable price paid to ensure the child's continued welfare. Whilst the minority decisions concur in the final result, concerns are clearly expressed therein for the unfortunate position of the father.[41]

[21.25]   *DRBAL v THE CZECH REPUBLIC (498/92)*

¶ 3.3. The author claims that the failure of the Courts to grant him custody of the child, notwithstanding recent expert opinions that the mother is considered incapable to care for the child, constitutes a violation of human rights. He alleges that the Czech authorities are of the opinion that a child should stay with the mother under all circumstances and that they do not protect the interests of the child.

The HRC majority rejected the author's case in the following terms:

¶ 6.3. The Committee . . . notes that the author claims that the courts were biased against him and wrongfully decided to give custody of his daughter to the mother, and not to him, and not to change his daughter's official place of residence. These claims relate primarily to the evaluation of facts and evidence by the courts. The Committee recalls that it is generally for the courts of States parties to the Covenant, and not for the Committee, to evaluate facts and evidence in a particular case, unless it is apparent that the courts' decisions are manifestly arbitrary or amount to a denial of justice. In the instant case, which relates

---

[41] See [20.35–20.39] for excerpts and commentary on *Hendriks*.

to the complex issue of child custody, the information before the Committee does not show that the decisions taken by the Czech courts or the conduct of the Czech authorities have been arbitrary or amounted to a denial of justice. Accordingly, the communication is inadmissible under article 3 of the Optional Protocol.

[21.26] Mr Wennergren issued a dissent:

The author's communication is against the Czech courts' decisions awarding custody of his daughter Jitka, born on 6 March 1983, to her mother Jana Drbalova. The author's complaints are directed primarily against the decisions by the Brno-venkov District Court (P 120/85), the Regional Court in Brno (No. 12 CO 626/86) and the Town Court of Brno (decision 24 June 1991) and the way in which the courts conducted the proceedings. In my opinion, the communication concerns just as much the interests of his daughter.

The author has informed the Committee that Jitka was not well treated by her mother, and that in 1985, a local doctor, Dr. Anna Vrbikova, alarmed the Section for Child Care of the district authorities. While Jitka's mother was later admitted to a psychiatric hospital for care, the author moved to his parents with Jitka and lived there. He asked the Brno-venkov District Court to give him custody of Jitka. Jitka had, after her mother's assumed negligence vis-à-vis her, to be taken into regular care as an outdoor patient at the psychiatric section of the university hospital of Brno, under the supervision of head physician Dr. Vratislav Vrazal. At the court proceedings Dr. Vrazal gave evidence.

According to the author he stated that Jitka was content with her life with the author and that, from a medical point of view, he did not recommend that the child be taken away from her father. Another expert opinion was given by Dr. Vera Capponi, who stated that Jitka's mother was well able to take care of Jitka and that she was better capable of doing it than the author. In its decision on 8 September 1986, the Court decided to give the custody of Jitka to her mother. The Regional Court of Brno confirmed that judgment in its decision of 11 March 1987. The author, however, refused to hand Jitka over to her mother. On 13 July 1988, an attempt was made to enforce the Courts' decisions and have Jitka handed over to her mother, with assistance of the police. A member of the Child Care Section of the Brno-venkov district authorities was present as well as the president of the court and Jitka's mother and her legal adviser. Jitka, then 5 years old, refused to leave her father's home and the attempt was stopped without result. Two months earlier, the author had made a request to the District Court for a change of custody. Two experts in psychiatry and psychology, Dr. Marta Holanova and Dr. Marta Skulova, submitted a report dated 17 July 1989, in which they recognized, according to the author, that he was capable of bringing up his daughter on his own and that in the event of a forcible removal from her father, she would suffer health hazards. The Court forwarded his request for a rehearing to the Town Court of Brno, which rejected his claims on 24 June 1991. Jitka was then 8 years old and is now 11 years old; she still lives with the author and his parents.

It is not apparent from the material that was submitted to the Committee that the courts' decisions were manifestly arbitrary or amounted to a denial of justice. Neither the records from the court proceedings, nor their decisions and the reasons given for them have, however, been available to the Committee. They would in all likelihood not reveal any flagrant misjustice. Instead, what is of real concern to me is that the situation, after the court decisions and the failed enforcement, has developed into a factual anomaly which might jeopardize a healthy, sound and safe development of the child. The author alleges that, as long as the mother has legal custody, his daughter continues to be exposed to possible health damages. She cannot move freely, especially at school, as she constantly runs the risk of an enforced withdrawal to an unknown environment. She does not know her mother. By virtue of all this, she suffers mentally. This anomalous situation is alarming and it is caused, whether inadvertently or not, by the courts' failure to handle the matter, as is now obvious, in an appropriate way. The shortcomings work, in my opinion, to the detriment of the best interests of the child. The communication, in my opinion, therefore raises issues under article 24, paragraph 1, of the Covenant, which entitles every child to such measures of protection as are required on the part of its family, society and the State. I consider the communication admissible in that respect.

Wennergren was the only HRC member to find the *Drbal* case admissible. Considering the apparent seriousness of the situation for the child, it may seem regrettable that the HRC majority deferred to the judgment of domestic courts.[42] On the other hand, *Drbal* and *Hendriks* perhaps confirm that international bodies, which conduct proceedings in writing, remain properly reluctant to 'overrule' domestic courts in such sensitive areas as child access, child custody, or, as indicated in the following case, child maintenance.[43]

[21.27]   *BYRNE and LAZARESCU v CANADA (742/97)*

¶ 6.3. The Committee notes that the authors' main grievance is that as a result of taxation they have paid more towards the maintenance of the child than their former spouses. The Committee observes that the proportional contributions of parents in paying child maintenance are set by the Family Court, not by the tax authorities. In the opinion of the Committee the alleged unequal payments in the authors' cases were the result of the interaction between the child support order providing for the payments and the application of the Income Tax Act. This is to be taken into account by the Court in determining the level of payments. It is not for the Committee to reevaluate the determination of payments by the domestic Courts. In this context, the Committee notes that if the Court did not take the tax consequences into account, as has been suggested by the authors, the authors could have applied for a variance of the order on this basis.

¶ 6.4. The Committee concludes that the facts submitted by the authors do not substantiate their claim that they have been a victim of a violation of article 26, nor of articles 23 and 24 of the Covenant.

[21.28]   *ARTICLE 10, CRC*

1. In accordance with the obligation of States Parties under article 9, paragraph 1, applications by a child or his or her parents to enter or leave a State party for the purpose of family reunification shall be dealt with by States Parties in a positive, humane and expeditious

---

[42] This is the HRC's conventional practice: see [14.36].

[43] See arguments at [20.39]. However, see *Fei v Colombia* (514/92), where the HRC did overrule domestic rulings in a family law matter [20.40].

manner. States Parties shall further ensure that the submission of such a request shall entail no adverse consequences for the applicants and for the members of their family.

2. A child whose parents reside in different States shall have the right to maintain on a regular basis, save in exceptional circumstances personal relations and direct contacts with both parents. Towards that end and in accordance with the obligation of States Parties under article 9, paragraph 1, States Parties shall respect the right of the child and his or her parents to leave any country, including their own, and to enter their own country. The right to leave any country shall be subject only to such restrictions as are prescribed by law and which are necessary to protect the national security, public order (*ordre public*), public health or morals or the rights and freedoms of others and are consistent with the other rights recognized in the present Convention.

[21.29] The HRC has also expressed concerns that States adopt sensitive rules regarding family reunification across borders for the sake of affected children.[44] For example, regarding Canada, the HRC stated:[45]

¶ 15. The Committee remains concerned about Canada's policy in relation to expulsion of long-term alien residents, without giving full consideration in all cases to the protection of all Covenant rights, in particular under articles 23 and 24.

[21.30] State laws must not unnecessarily threaten the stability of a child's family environment. For example, in Concluding Comments on Switzerland:[46]

¶ 19. The Committee is concerned at the requirement for persons who adopt a child abroad under the regime of simple adoption to submit an application for full adoption in Switzerland if they wish the adoption to be recognized in Switzerland. This procedure makes permanent adoption subject to a two-year trial period, during which the adoptive parents may decide not to go ahead with the adoption and the child is entitled only to a temporary and renewable foreigner's residence permit. The Committee expresses its concern since these two factors make the child's position very precarious from both the legal and emotional standpoints. . . .

¶ 30. The Committee recommends that the necessary legislative measures should be taken to ensure that children who have been adopted abroad are granted, as soon as they arrive in Switzerland, either Swiss nationality if the parents are Swiss, or a temporary or permanent residence permit if the parents have such a permit, and that the two-year trial period prior to the granting of adoption should not apply to them.

[21.31] Whilst the family has primary responsibility for caring for children, circumstances regrettably arise where States Parties to the ICCPR and the CRC are required to intervene to protect the child from his/her own family.

---

[44] See discussion of rights regarding family unity at [20.12–20.18].
[45] (1999) UN doc. CCPR/C/79/Add.105; see also Concluding Comments on Denmark (1996) UN doc. CCPR/C/79/Add.68, para. 19.
[46] (1996) UN doc. CCPR/C/79/Add.70

GENERAL COMMENT 17

¶ 6. . . . Moreover, in cases where the parents and the family seriously fail in their duties, ill-treat or neglect the child, the State should intervene to restrict parental authority and the child may be separated from his family when circumstances so require. . . .

ARTICLE 9, CRC

1. States Parties shall ensure that a child shall not be separated from his or her parents against their will, except when competent authorities subject to judicial review determine, in accordance with applicable law and procedures, that such separation is necessary for the best interests of the child. Such determination may be necessary in a particular case such as one involving abuse or neglect of the child by the parents, or one where the parents are living separately and a decision must be made as to the child's place of residence.

2. In any proceedings pursuant to paragraph 1 of the present article, all interested parties shall be given an opportunity to participate in the proceedings and make their views known.

[21.32] When a child has been separated from his/her family, the State has a positive duty to provide suitable alternative care for that child.

GENERAL COMMENT 17

¶ 6. . . . The Committee considers it useful that reports by States parties should provide information on the special measures of protection adopted to protect children who are abandoned or deprived of their family environment in order to enable them to develop in conditions that most closely resemble those characterizing the family environment.

ARTICLE 20, CRC

1. A child temporarily or permanently deprived of his or her family environment, or in whose own best interests cannot be allowed to remain in that environment, shall be entitled to special protection and assistance provided by the State.

2. States Parties shall in accordance with their national laws ensure alternative care for such a child.

3. Such care could include, *inter alia*, foster placement, kafalah of Islamic law, adoption or if necessary placement in suitable institutions for the care of children. When considering solutions, due regard shall be paid to the desirability of continuity in a child's upbringing and to the child's ethnic, religious, cultural and linguistic background.

Child Exploitation

[21.33] It is incumbent upon States to protect children from being exploited by persons taking advantage of their inherent vulnerability.

ARTICLE 19, CRC

1. States Parties shall take all appropriate legislative, administrative, social and educational measures to protect the child from all forms of physical or mental violence, injury or abuse, neglect or negligent treatment, maltreatment or exploitation, including sexual abuse, while in the care of parent(s), legal guardian(s) or any other person who has the care of the child.

2. Such protective measures should, as appropriate, include effective procedures for the establishment of social programmes to provide necessary support for the child and for those who have the care of the child, as well as for other forms of prevention and for identification, reporting, referral, investigation, treatment and follow-up of instances of child maltreatment described heretofore, and, as appropriate, for judicial involvement.

ARTICLE 36, CRC

States Parties shall protect the child against all other forms of exploitation prejudicial to any aspects of the child's welfare.

SEXUAL EXPLOITATION

[21.34] It is clear, as specified in paragraph 3 of General Comment 17 [21.10], that children require special protection from sexual and physical abuse.[47]

ARTICLE 34, CRC

States Parties undertake to protect the child from all forms of sexual exploitation and sexual abuse. For these purposes, States Parties shall in particular take all appropriate national, bilateral and multilateral measures to prevent:

(a) The inducement or coercion of a child to engage in any unlawful sexual activity;

(b) The exploitative use of children in prostitution or other unlawful sexual practices;

(c) The exploitative use of children in pornographic performances and materials.

[21.35] The HRC has expressed concerns regarding Sri Lanka in this respect:[48]

¶ 24. While the Committee welcomes the proposed changes to legislation for offences committed against children, such as incest and the sexual exploitation of children, it is concerned about the situation of the economic and sexual exploitation of children both with respect to the use of children in domestic service and the prostitution of boys.

---

[47] See generally, R. Levesque, 'Sexual Use, Abuse, and Exploitation of Children: Challenges in Implementing Children's Rights' (1994) 60 *Brooklyn Law Review* 959. In July 2000, the General Assembly adopted a new Optional Protocol to the CRC on the Sale of Children, Child Prostitution, and Child Pornography, which will come into force after its tenth ratification.

[48] (1995) UN doc. CCPR/C/79/Add. 56.

The HRC has also stated the following with regard to Japan:[49]

¶ 29. In light of information given by the State party on planned new legislation against child prostitution and child pornography, the Committee is concerned that such measures may not protect children under the age of 18 when the age limit for sexual consent is as low as 13. The Committee is also concerned about the absence of specific legal provisions prohibiting bringing of foreign children to Japan for the purpose of prostitution, despite the fact that abduction and sexual exploitation of children are subject to penal sanctions. The Committee recommends that the situation be brought into compliance with the State party's obligations under articles 9, 17 and 24 of the Covenant.

Finally, regarding Norway, the HRC has stated:[50]

¶ 9. The Committee commends the State party for the new system which was implemented in 1998 with regard to the issue of questioning of child victims of sexual abuse in judicial proceedings. . . .

[21.36] The UN bodies have recognized that child pornography has become a prevalent form of mistreatment and abuse of children worldwide.[51] For example, regarding Belgium, the HRC has stated:[52]

¶ 27. The Committee remains concerned about the production, sale and distribution of paedo-pornography. It urges the State party to take effective measures to curtail the possession and distribution of these criminal materials.

[21.37] Impoverished and/or abandoned children are often in particular danger of sexual abuse. For example, the HRC has stated, with regard to Mexico:[53]

¶ 15. The Committee also deplores the situation of street children, which is constantly worsening. These are the children who are at greatest risk of sexual violence and who are exposed to the practices of sexual trafficking.

The State should take effective measures for the protection and rehabilitation of these children in accordance with article 24 of the Covenant, including measures to end prostitution, child pornography and the sale of children.

[21.38] Child sex tourism was highlighted as a concern regarding Costa Rica:[54]

¶ 18. The Committee is deeply concerned at the high incidence of commercial sexual exploitation of children in Costa Rica, apparently often related to tourism. It notes the creation of a National Board for the Protection of the Child and amendments to the Criminal Code to criminalize the sexual exploitation of children. The Committee urges the State party to take further measures to eradicate this phenomenon, in cooperation as appropriate with other States, through the investigation and prosecution of the crimes in question.

---

[49] (1998) UN doc. CCPR/C/79/Add.102.
[51] Mower, above, note 2, at 41.
[53] (1999) UN doc. CCPR/C/79/Add.109.
[50] (1999) UN doc. CCPR/C/79/Add. 112.
[52] (1998) UN doc. CCPR/C/79/Add.99.
[54] (1999) UN doc. CCPR/C/79/Add.107.

CHILD LABOUR

[21.39] Child labourers are often denied proper payment for their work, and may be concurrently denied the opportunity to undertake education. Their physical and mental health and development may also be diminished.[55]

ARTICLE 31, CRC

1. States Parties recognize the right of the child to rest and leisure, to engage in play and recreational activities appropriate to the age of the child and to participate freely in cultural life and the arts.

2. States Parties shall respect and promote the right of the child to participate fully in cultural and artistic life and shall encourage the provision of appropriate and equal opportunities for cultural, artistic, recreational and leisure activity.

ARTICLE 32, CRC

1. States Parties recognize the right of the child to be protected from economic exploitation and from performing any work that is likely to be hazardous or to interfere with the child's education, or to be harmful to the child's health or physical, mental, spiritual, moral or social development.

2. States Parties shall take legislative, administrative, social and educational measures to ensure the implementation of the present article. To this end, and having regard to the relevant provisions of other international instruments, States Parties shall in particular:

(a) Provide for a minimum age or minimum ages for admission to employment;

(b) Provide for appropriate regulation of the hours and conditions of employment;

(c) Provide for appropriate penalties or other sanctions to ensure the effective enforcement of the present article.

[21.40] Protection of children from economic exploitation is also within the ambit of article 24 of the ICCPR. Whilst it is only implicitly condemned in General Comment 17, the HRC was more forthright in the following criticism of India: [56]

¶ 34. The Committee expresses concern that, despite actions taken by the State party, there has been little progress in implementing the Child Labour (Prohibition and Regulation) Act of 1986. In this respect, the Committee recommends that urgent steps be taken to remove all children from hazardous occupations, that immediate steps be taken to imple-

---

[55] See also Convention concerning Minimum Age for Admission to Employment (ILO Convention 138), 26 June 1973.

[56] (1997) UN doc. CCPR/C/79/Add.81; see also Concluding Comments on Brazil (1996) UN doc. CCPR/C/79/Add.66, para. 31; Concluding Comments on United Republic of Tanzania (1998) UN doc. CCPR/C/79/Add. 97, para. 25.

ment the recommendation of the National Human Rights Commission that the constitutional requirement that it should be a fundamental right for all children under 14 to have free and compulsory education be respected, and that efforts be strengthened to eliminate child labour in both the industrial and rural sectors. The Committee also recommends that consideration be given to establishing an independent mechanism with effective national powers to monitor and enforce the implementation of laws for the eradication of child labour and bonded labour.

With regard to Ecuador, the HRC stated the following:[57]

¶ 17. The Committee is also concerned that, despite the legal requirement of judicial authorization for the employment of children under 14 years of age, there continues to be exploitation of children in employment.

The Committee recommends that the Comité Nacional para la Eradicación Progresiva del Trabajo Infantil be provided with the necessary means to carry out its mandate to eliminate the practice of child labour.

USE IN DRUG TRAFFICKING

[21.41] Children need specific protection from exploitation related to the use of illicit drugs or substances. Children require protection from drug abuse, and from being exploited in the production or trafficking of drugs.[58]

ARTICLE 33, CRC

States Parties shall take all appropriate measures, including legislative, administrative, social and educational measures, to protect children from the illicit use of narcotic drugs and psychotropic substances as defined in the relevant international treaties, and to prevent the use of children in the illicit production and trafficking of such substances.

KIDNAPPING

[21.42] Kidnapping and trafficking in children may take the form of questionable, illegal, or informal adoption practices. These may involve 'sale' of babies by impoverished parents, or outright theft of children.[59]

ARTICLE 11, CRC

1. States Parties shall take measures to combat the illicit transfer and non-return of children abroad.

2. To this end, States Parties shall promote the conclusion of bilateral or multilateral agreements or accession to existing agreements.

---

[57] (1998) UN doc. CCPR/C/79/Add. 92.
[58] See General Comment 17, para. 3 [21.10].
[59] See also the Hague Convention on the Civil Aspects of International Child Abduction 1980.

ARTICLE 35, CRC

States Parties shall take all appropriate national, bilateral and multilateral measures to prevent the abduction of, the sale of or traffic in children for any purpose or in any form.

[21.43] Appropriate laws regarding guardianship and adoption of children are necessary to prevent kidnapping, as demonstrated by these HRC comments directed to Argentina: [60]

¶ 16. The Committee urges the State party to . . . complete urgently investigations into the allegations of illegal adoption of children of disappeared persons, and to take appropriate action.

ARTICLE 21, CRC

States Parties that recognize and/or permit the system of adoption shall ensure that the best interests of the child shall be the paramount consideration and they shall:

(a) Ensure that the adoption of a child is authorized only by competent authorities who determine, in accordance with applicable law and procedures and on the basis of all pertinent and reliable information, that the adoption is permissible in view of the child's status concerning parents, relatives and legal guardians and that, if required, the persons concerned have given their informed consent to the adoption on the basis of such counselling as may be necessary;

(b) Recognize that inter-country adoption may be considered as an alternative means of child's care, if the child cannot be placed in a foster or an adoptive family or cannot in any suitable manner be cared for in the child's country of origin;

(c) Ensure that the child concerned by inter-country adoption enjoys safeguards and standards equivalent to those existing in the case of national adoption;

(d) Take all appropriate measures to ensure that, in inter-country adoption, the placement does not result in improper financial gain for those involved in it;

(e) Promote, where appropriate, the objectives of the present article by concluding bilateral or multilateral arrangements or agreements, and endeavour, within this framework, to ensure that the placement of the child in another country is carried out by competent authorities or organs.

CHILD SOLDIERS

[21.44] *GENERAL COMMENT 17*

¶ 3. . . . Moreover, the Committee wishes to draw the attention of States parties to the need to include in their reports information on measures adopted to ensure that children do not take a direct part in armed conflicts.

---

[60] (1995) UN doc. CCPR/C/79/Add.46.

ARTICLE 38, CRC

1. States Parties undertake to respect and to ensure respect for rules of international humanitarian law applicable to them in armed conflicts which are relevant to the child.

2. States Parties shall take all feasible measures to ensure that persons who have not attained the age of fifteen years do not take a direct part in hostilities.

3. States Parties shall refrain from recruiting any person who has not attained the age of fifteen years into their armed forces. In recruiting among those persons who have attained the age of fifteen years but who have not attained the age of eighteen years, States Parties shall endeavour to give priority to those who are oldest.

4. In accordance with their obligations under international humanitarian law to protect the civilian population in armed conflicts, States Parties shall take all feasible measures to ensure protection and care of children who are affected by an armed conflict.

Even where children appear to volunteer for such duties it is often because they are in need of food, shelter, clothing, and even an identity, which mitigates against the 'voluntariness' of the participation.[61]

[21.45] The recruitment of child soldiers is also prohibited in international humanitarian law. Article 77(2) of the Additional Protocol I to the Geneva Conventions prohibits the recruitment of soldiers under 15 years of age. The Rome Statute of the International Criminal Court, at article 8(2)(b)(xxvi), defines the recruitment or 'use' of soldiers under the age of 15 as a 'war crime'. In June 2000 the UN adopted an Optional Protocol to the Convention on the Rights of the Child, designed to prohibit the recruitment into the armed forces of persons under the age of 18.[62] This Protocol will come into force after its tenth ratification.

[21.46] The HRC has articulated its concerns over child soldiers with regard to Colombia:[63]

¶ 27. The Committee expresses its deep concern at the situation of children in Colombia and at the lack of adequate measures to protect their rights under the Covenant. In this respect, the Committee notes that much remains to be done to protect children from violence within the family and the society at large, from forced recruitment by guerrilla and paramilitary groups and from employment below the legal minimum age, and specifically to protect street children from being killed or otherwise abused by vigilante groups and security forces. . . .

¶ 42. The Committee urges the Government to adopt effective measures to ensure the full

---

[61] See generally S. Maslen, 'The Use of Children as Soldiers: The Right to Kill and be Killed?' (1998) 4 *International Journal of Children's Rights* 455, and I. Cohn and G. Goodwin-Gill, *Child Soldiers* (Clarendon Press, Oxford, 1994).

[62] See Optional Protocol to the Convention on the Rights of the Child on the Involvement of Children in Armed Conflicts.

[63] (1997) UN doc. CCPR/C/79/Add.76.

implementation of article 24 of the Covenant, including preventive and punitive measures in respect of all acts of child murder and assault and protective, preventive and punitive measures in respect of children caught up in the activities of guerrilla and paramilitary groups. The Committee also specifically recommends that effective measures be taken to eliminate employment of children and that inspection mechanisms be established to this effect.

Right to Registration and a Name: Article 24(2)

[21.47] *GENERAL COMMENT 17*

¶ 7. Under article 24, paragraph 2, every child has the right to be registered immediately after birth and to have a name. In the Committee's opinion, this provision should be interpreted as being closely linked to the provision concerning the right to special measures of protection and it is designed to promote recognition of the child's legal personality. Providing for the right to have a name is of special importance in the case of children born out of wedlock. The main purpose of the obligation to register children after birth is to reduce the danger of abduction, sale of or traffic in children, or of other types of treatment that are incompatible with the enjoyment of the rights provided for in the Covenant. Reports by States parties should indicate in detail the measures that ensure the immediate registration of children born in their territory.

ARTICLE 7, CRC

1. The child shall be registered immediately after birth and shall have the right from birth to a name, the right to acquire a nationality and, as far as possible, the right to know and be cared for by his or her parents.

2. States Parties shall ensure the implementation of these rights in accordance with their national law and their obligations under the relevant international instruments in this field, in particular where the child would otherwise be stateless.

ARTICLE 8, CRC

1. States Parties undertake to respect the right of the child to preserve his or her identity, including nationality, name and family relations as recognized by law without unlawful interference.

2. Where a child is illegally deprived of some or all of the elements of his or her identity, States Parties shall provide appropriate assistance and protection, with a view to re-establishing speedily his or her identity.

[21.48] *DE GALLICCHIO and VICARIO v ARGENTINA (400/90)*

The facts are evident from the excerpts and commentary below.

¶ 2.1. On 5 February 1977, Ximena Vicario's mother was taken with the then nine month-old child to the Headquarters of the Federal Police (*Departamento Central de la Policía*

Federal) in Buenos Aires. Her father was apprehended in the city of Rosario on the following day. The parents subsequently disappeared, and although the National Commission on
Disappeared Persons investigated their case after December 1983, their whereabouts were
never established. Investigations initiated by the author herself finally led, in 1984, to
locating Ximena Vicario, who was then residing in the home of a nurse, S.S., who claimed
to have been taking care of the child after her birth. Genetic blood tests . . . revealed that
the child was, with a probability of 99.82 per cent, the author's granddaughter.

Part of the author's complaint related to the circumstances of the child's illegal
adoption. These complaints were inadmissible *ratione temporis*.[64] The following
circumstances also prompted complaints:

¶ 2.3. On 2 January 1989, the author was granted 'provisional' guardianship of the child;
S.S., however, immediately applied for visiting rights, which were granted by order of the
Supreme Court on 5 September 1989. In this decision, the Supreme Court also held that
the author had no standing in the proceedings about the child's guardianship since, under
article 19 of Law 10.903, only the parents and the legal guardian have standing and may
directly participate in the proceedings.

¶ 2.4. On 23 September 1989 the author, basing herself on psychiatric reports concerning the
effects of the visits of S.S. on Ximena Vicario, requested the court to rule that such visits
should be discontinued. Her action was dismissed on account of lack of standing. . . .

¶ 3.1. . . . The fact that the author is denied standing in the guardianship proceedings is
deemed to constitute a violation of the principle of equality before the law, as guaranteed
by article 16 of the Argentine Constitution and articles 14 and 26 of the Covenant.

¶ 3.2. . . . The author also claims a violation of the rights of her granddaughter, who she
contends is subjected to what may be termed psychological torture, in violation of article
7 of the Covenant, every time she is visited by S.S. Another alleged breach of the Covenant
concerns article 16, under which every person has the right to recognition as a person
before the law, with the right to an identity, a name and a family: that Ximena Vicario must
continue to bear the name given to her by S.S. until legal proceedings are completed is said
to constitute a violation of her right to an identity. Moreover, the uncertainty about her
legal identity has prevented her from obtaining a passport under her real name.

The Committee's findings were as follows:

¶ 10.3. As to Darwinia Rosa Mónaco de Gallicchio's claim that her right to recognition as
a person before the law was violated, the Committee notes that, although her standing to
represent her granddaughter in the proceedings about the child's guardianship was denied
in 1989, the courts did recognize her standing to represent her granddaughter in a number
of proceedings, including her suit to declare the nullity of the adoption, and that she was
granted guardianship over Ximena Vicario. While these circumstances do not raise an
issue under article 16 of the Covenant, the initial denial of Mrs. Mónaco's standing effectively left Ximena Vicario without adequate representation, thereby depriving her of the

---

[64] See generally, on the *ratione temporis* requirement, Chap. 2.

protection to which she was entitled as a minor. Taken together with the circumstances mentioned in paragraph 10.5 below, the denial of Mrs. Mónaco's standing constituted a violation of article 24 of the Covenant. . . .

The HRC deferred to domestic court findings regarding the ICCPR compatibility the continued visits to the child of S.S., which were in fact eventually terminated.

¶ 10.4. . . . As to the visiting rights initially granted to S.S., the Committee observes that the competent courts of Argentina first endeavoured to determine the facts and balance the human interests of the persons involved and that in connection with those investigations a number of measures were adopted to give redress to Ximena Vicario and her grandmother, including the termination of the regime of visiting rights accorded to S.S, following the recommendations of psychologists and Ximena Vicario's own wishes. Nevertheless, these outcomes appear to have been delayed by the initial denial of standing of Mrs. Mónaco to challenge the visitation order.

¶ 10.5. While the Committee appreciates the seriousness with which the Argentine courts endeavoured to redress the wrongs done to Ms. Vicario and her grandmother, it observes that the duration of the various judicial proceedings extended for over 10 years, and that some of the proceedings have not yet been completed. The Committee notes that in the meantime Ms. Vicario, who was 7 years of age when found, reached the age of maturity (18 years) in 1994, and that it was not until 1993 that her legal identity as Ximena Vicario was officially recognized. In the specific circumstances of this case, the Committee finds that the protection of children stipulated in article 24 of the Covenant required the State party to take affirmative action to grant Ms. Vicario prompt and effective relief from her predicament. In this context, the Committee recalls its General Comment on article 24, . . . in which it stressed that every child has a right to special measures of protection because of his/her status as a minor; those special measures are additional to the measures that States are required to take under article 2 to ensure that everyone enjoys the rights provided for in the Covenant. Bearing in mind the suffering already endured by Ms. Vicario, who lost both of her parents under tragic circumstances imputable to the State party, the Committee finds that the special measures required under article 24, paragraph 1, of the Covenant were not expeditiously applied by Argentina, and that the failure to recognize the standing of Mrs. Mónaco in the guardianship and visitation proceedings and the delay in legally establishing Ms. Vicario's real name and issuing identity papers also entailed a violation of article 24, paragraph 2, of the Covenant, which is designed to promote recognition of the child's legal personality.

¶ 11.1. The Human Rights Committee, acting under article 5, paragraph 4, of the Optional Protocol to the International Covenant on Civil and Political Rights, is of the view that the facts which have been placed before it reveal a violation by Argentina of article 24, paragraphs 1 and 2, of the Covenant.

[21.49] Concern over the proper legal recognition of a child's name has been expressed by the HRC with regard to Romania:[65]

---

[65] (1999) UN doc. CCPR/C/79/Add.111.

¶ 5. A matter of grave concern to the Committee is the situation of street children and abandoned children, an exceedingly serious problem which remains unresolved in Romania (art. 24).

The State party should take all necessary measures to comply with article 24 of the Covenant, by protecting and rehabilitating these children, by guaranteeing them a name, and by ensuring that all births are duly registered in Romania.

Regarding Uruguay, the HRC stated:[66]

¶ 11. The Committee, while recognizing the progress made by the State party in respect of children's rights and in particular the future Code Relating to Minors (*Codigo del Menor*), remains concerned with the information provided by the delegation, that the future Code discriminates against female minors and fails to protect fully the new born child, as unmarried minor mothers may register their children at any age whereas minor fathers may only do so from the age of 16 onwards. The Committee urges the State party in the course of drafting this Code to bring the whole of it into full conformity with articles 3 and 24 of the Covenant. It wishes to receive the text of the Code when it is enacted.

[21.50] Thus, States Parties have an obligation to expedite recognition of a child's proper name by the provision of verification documentation, in order to facilitate the formal acknowledgment of the child's legal personality, and in order to minimize opportunities for egregious child exploitation.

Right to a Nationality: Article 24(3)

[21.51]   *GENERAL COMMENT 17*

¶ 8. Special attention should also be paid, in the context of the protection to be granted to children, to the right of every child to acquire a nationality, as provided for in article 24, paragraph 3. While the purpose of this provision is to prevent a child from being afforded less protection by society and the State because he is stateless, it does not necessarily make it an obligation for States to give their nationality to every child born in their territory. However, States are required to adopt every appropriate measure, both internally and in cooperation with other States, to ensure that every child has a nationality when he is born. In this connection, no discrimination with regard to the acquisition of nationality should be admissible under internal law as between legitimate children and children born out of wedlock or of stateless parents or based on the nationality status of one or both of the parents. The measures adopted to ensure that children have a nationality should always be referred to in reports by States parties.

[21.52] There is an obligation on States Parties to confer nationality on stateless children within their territory. Nowak argues that this obligation is subsidiary to

---

[66] (1998) UN doc. CCPR/C/79/Add.90.

obligations which may arise in another State Party, if the child has a filial or strong connection to that other State.[67] This is supported by article 7(2) of the CRC [21.47]. Furthermore, the HRC has stated, in Concluding Comments on Ecuador:[68]

¶ 18. The Committee is concerned that the births of children born in Ecuador to undocumented refugees are frequently not registered due to the parents' fear of deportation. This situation prevents the children from claiming Ecuadorian nationality, to which any child born in Ecuador is entitled under Ecuadorian law. The Committee recommends that the State party adopt measures guaranteeing to all children of undocumented refugees born in Ecuador the right to a nationality.

The HRC was more explicit regarding Colombia:[69]

¶ 44. The Committee stresses the duty of the State party to ensure that every child born in Colombia enjoys the right, under article 24, paragraph 3, of the Covenant to acquire a nationality. It therefore recommends that the State party considers conferring Colombian nationality to stateless children born in Colombia.

The HRC has also condemned Zimbabwean laws which denied Zimbabwean citizenship to children born to Zimbabweans abroad.[70]

Conclusion

[21.53] Article 24 provides civil and political rights specifically to children, to top up the rights they receive, in common with adults, from other Covenant guarantees. The text of the CRC has undoubtedly influenced the HRC in its interpretation of article 24. The HRC has dealt with relatively few cases under article 24. However, its General Comment 17 and its Concluding Comments have clarified important aspects of article 24 protection, such as the absolute prohibition on child exploitation, and guidelines for the age of majority. Finally, article 24 and the CRC have opened up the family and its treatment of and responsibilities regarding children to public and international scrutiny.[71] States Parties are obliged to take a sufficiently active role in assisting the development of and ensuring the protection of children within their families. However, it may be that

---

[67] Nowak, above, note 19, 434, In such circumstances, it is indeed arguable that the child is 'within the jurisdiction' of that other State; see generally on jurisdictional requirements, Chap. 4. Furthermore, Nowak questions the extent of this duty where the child has a filial or other claim to nationality against a State which is not party to the Covenant.

[68] (1998) UN doc. CCPR/C/79/Add.92. Similar comments were made regarding Colombia (1997) UN doc. CCPR/C/79/Add.76, para. 44.

[69] (1997) UN doc. CCPR/C/79/Add. 75.

[70] (1998) UN doc. CCPR/C/79/Add. 89, para. 19.

[71] See Levesque, above, note 47, 987–97.

international bodies like the HRC will never feel confident in overruling local family court decisions regarding sensitive matters like child custody.

Postscript: Please note that General Comment 28 on 'Equality of Rights Between Men and Women', contained in the Addendum at page 634, contains extra information on some of the material in this chapter.

22

Rights of Political Participation—Article 25

ARTICLE 25

Every citizen shall have the right and the opportunity, without any of the distinctions mentioned in article 2 and without unreasonable restrictions:

(a) To take part in the conduct of public affairs, directly or through freely chosen representatives;

(b) To vote and to be elected at genuine periodic elections which shall be by universal and equal suffrage and shall be held by secret ballot, guaranteeing the free expression of the will of the electors;

(c) To have access, on general terms of equality, to public service in his country.

[22.01] Article 25 guarantees rights of political participation to citizens of States Parties. Article 25(a) provides a general formulation of the right, and guarantees some democratic accountability on the part of State Party governments.[1] Article 25(b) and (c) relates to specific aspects of political participation, the right to vote and to be elected in genuine elections, and the right of access to the public service.

---

[1] M. Nowak, *UN Covenant on Civil and Political Rights: CCPR Commentary* (N.P. Engel, Kehl, 1993), 441.

Concept of Citizenship

[22.02] Article 25 rights are confined to a State Party's citizens. This contrasts with the other ICCPR rights, which are conferred on all people within a State Party's jurisdiction.

GENERAL COMMENT 25

¶ 3. ... State reports should outline the legal provisions which define citizenship in the context of the rights protected by article 25. No distinctions are permitted between citizens in the enjoyment of these rights on the grounds of race, colour, sex, language, religion, political or other opinion, national or social origin, property, birth or other status. Distinctions between those who are entitled to citizenship by birth and those who acquire it by naturalization may raise questions of compatibility with article 25.

[22.03] The Covenant does not therefore prescribe how a State determines citizenship, though it does prohibit discrimination in such determination. The HRC has also indicated, with regard to Estonia, that citizenship requirements should not be too onerous:[2]

¶ 12. The Committee expresses its concern that a significantly large segment of the population, particularly members of the Russian-speaking minority, are unable to enjoy Estonian citizenship due to the plethora of criteria established by law, and the stringency of language criterion, and that no remedy is available against an administrative decision rejecting the request for naturalization under the Citizenship Law.

[22.04] The HRC went on in its General Comment to concede that municipal rights of political participation can be conferred on non-citizens:

¶ 3. ... State reports should indicate whether any groups, such as permanent residents, enjoy these rights on a limited basis, for example, by having the right to vote in local elections or to hold particular public service positions.

Non-citizen rights of political participation could not be conferred on a discriminatory basis. Although such conferral would not be prohibited by article 25, which protects only 'citizens', it would be prohibited by the Covenant's general non-discrimination provisions.[3]

Article 25(a): General Right of Public Participation

[22.05]   *GENERAL COMMENT 25*

¶ 1. ... Article 25 lies at the core of democratic government based on the consent of the people and in conformity with the principles of the Covenant. ...

---

² (1995) UN doc. CCPR/C/79/Add.59, para. 12.   ³ See generally Chap. 23.

¶ 5. The conduct of public affairs, referred to in paragraph (a), is a broad concept which relates to the exercise of political power, in particular the exercise of legislative, executive and administrative powers. It covers all aspects of public administration, and the formulation and implementation of policy at international, national, regional and local levels. The allocation of powers and the means by which individual citizens exercise the right to participate in the conduct of public affairs protected by article 25 should be established by the constitution and other laws. . . .

[22.06] The General Comment confirms that article 25(a) does not presuppose any particular system of government, so long as the State Party functions as a democracy. Indeed, the modalities of distribution of power and citizens' rights of political participation must be 'established by the constitution and other laws'; article 25 does not strictly dictate the content of those laws. Numerous political systems seem compatible with article 25(a),[4] including Westminster systems, 'presidential' systems, bicameral systems, unicameral systems, unitary systems, and federal systems.

[22.07] The General Comment confirms that 'the conduct of public affairs' is a wide concept, which embraces the exercise of governmental power by all arms of government at all levels. 'The conduct of public affairs' includes, for example, the formulation by central governments of policies regarding defence and foreign affairs, as well as a local council's decisions regarding the frequency of garbage collection.

INDIRECT PARTICIPATION IN PUBLIC AFFAIRS THROUGH ELECTED REPRESENTATIVES

[22.08] Article 25(a) specifies that participation in public affairs may be direct or indirect, through elected representatives. Due to the complexity of modern government, it is virtually impossible for any contemporary State Party to govern solely or even substantially via direct input from citizens. Therefore, article 25(a) effectively dictates that all States Parties provide appropriate avenues for indirect political participation.

[22.09]   *GENERAL COMMENT 25*

¶ 7. Where citizens participate in the conduct of public affairs through freely chosen representatives, it is implicit in article 25 that those representatives do in fact exercise governmental power and that they are accountable through the electoral process for their exercise of that power. It is also implicit that the representatives exercise only those powers which are allocated to them in accordance with constitutional provisions. Participation through freely chosen representatives is exercised through voting processes which must be established by laws which are in accordance with paragraph (b).

---

[4] See H. Steiner, 'Political Participation as a Human Right' (1988) 1 *Harvard Human Rights Yearbook* 77, 87.

Therefore, article 25(a) requires State Party governments to be, in some way, accountable to their citizens.[5] Autocracies, which offer no opportunities for political participation by citizens, do not satisfy paragraph (a).[6] This point is confirmed by the opening paragraph of the General Comment [22.05].

[22.10] The body or bodies elected by the people must 'in fact exercise governmental power'; the elected body cannot be a mere advisory body with no legally enforceable powers. The popularly elected body must either itself play a vital role in governing the State, or be in control of that body.[7] For example, Westminster systems, where the elected legislature itself elects and ultimately controls the executive government, comply with article 25. However, Nowak has noted that it may be difficult to measure the extent of real control exercised by the elected body.[8] For example, in practice in Westminster systems, the executive government, comprising the governing party's leaders, often dominates the legislature if it has a sufficient majority. It does not seem that article 25 is a sufficiently sophisticated mechanism to redress many of the structural flaws in contemporary political systems.[9]

[22.11] Furthermore, undemocratic institutions should not have significant political power. For example, the HRC noted in Concluding Comments on Chile, with regard to Chile's appointed Senate:[10]

¶ 8. The Committee is deeply concerned by the enclaves of power retained by members of the former military regime. The powers accorded to the Senate to block initiatives adopted by the Congress and powers exercised by the National Security Council, which exists alongside the Government, are incompatible with article 25 of the Covenant. The composition of the Senate also impedes legal reforms that would enable the State party to comply more fully with its Covenant obligations.

DIRECT PARTICIPATION IN PUBLIC AFFAIRS

[22.12]   *MARSHALL v CANADA (205/86)*[11]

The authors were representatives of the Mikmaq Indian tribe. The facts and the complaint are outlined immediately below:

---

[5] Nowak, above, note 1, 441.

[6] Ibid.; see also T. Franck, 'The Emerging Right to Democratic Governance' (1992) 86 *American Journal of International Law* 46, 63–4.

[7] See S. Joseph, 'Rights of Political Participation' in D. Harris and S. Joseph (eds.), *The International Covenant on Civil and Political Rights and United Kingdom Law* (Clarendon Press, Oxford, 1995), 543.

[8] Nowak, above, note 1, 454.

[9] See also, below, [22.41] and [22.51].

[10] (1999) UN doc. CCPR/C/79/Add. 104. Many Senators in Chile are members of the former military regime of General Pinochet.

[11] Also known as *Mikmaq Tribal Society v Canada*.

¶ 2.2. By Constitution Act, 1982, the Government of Canada 'recognized and affirmed' the 'existing aboriginal and treaty rights of the aboriginal peoples of Canada' (art. 35(1)), comprising the Indian, Inuit and Métis peoples of Canada (art. 35(2)). With a view to further identifying and clarifying these rights, the Constitution Act envisaged a process which would include a constitutional conference to be convened by the Prime Minister of Canada and attended by the first ministers of the provinces and invited 'representatives of the aboriginal peoples of Canada'. The Government of Canada and the provincial govern-ments committed themselves to the principle that discussions would take place at such a conference before any constitutional amendments would be made and included in the Constitution of Canada in respect of matters that directly affect the aboriginal peoples, including the identification and the definition of the rights of those peoples (articles 35(1) and 37(1) and (2)). In fact, several such conferences were convened by the Prime Minister of Canada in the following years, to which he invited representatives of four national asso-ciations to represent the interest of approximately 600 aboriginal groups. These national associations were: the Assembly of First Nations (invited to represent primarily non-status Indians), the Métis National Council (invited to represent the Métis) and the Inuit Commit-tee on National Issues (invited to represent the Inuit). As a general rule, constitutional conferences in Canada are attended only by elected leaders of the federal and provincial governments. The conferences on aboriginal matters constituted an exception to that rule. They focused on the matter of aboriginal self-government and whether and in what form, a general aboriginal right to self-government should be entrenched in the Constitution of Canada. . . .

The complaint:

¶ 3.1. The authors sought, unsuccessfully, to be invited to attend the constitutional confer-ences as representatives of the Mikmaq people. The refusal of the State party to permit specific representation for the Mikmaqs at the constitutional conferences is the basis of the complaint. . . .

¶ 4.2. The authors contend, *inter alia*, that the restrictions [on participation in the confer-ence] were unreasonable and that their interests were not properly represented at the constitutional conferences. First, they stress that they could not choose which of the 'national associations' would represent them, and, furthermore, that they did not confer on the Assembly of First Nations (AFN) any right to represent them. Secondly, when the Mikmaqs were not allowed direct representation, they attempted, without success, to influ-ence the AFN. In particular, they refer to a 1987 hearing conducted jointly by the AFN and several Canadian Government departments, at which Mikmaq leaders submitted a package of constitutional proposals and protested 'in the strongest terms any discussion of Mikmaq treaties at the constitutional conferences in the absence of direct Mikmaq representation'. The AFN, however, did not submit any of the Mikmaq position papers to the constitutional conferences nor incorporate them in its own positions.

In response, the State party submitted that article 25 'could not possibly require that all citizens of a country be invited to a constitutional conference'.[12]

---

[12] Para. 4.1.

The HRC decided in favour of the State Party:

¶ 5.2. At issue in the present case is whether . . . the authors, or any other representatives chosen for that purpose by the Mikmaq tribal society, had the right, by virtue of article 25(a), to attend the conferences. . . .

¶ 5.4. It remains to be determined what is the scope of the right of every citizen, without unreasonable restrictions, to take part in the conduct of public affairs, directly or through freely chosen representatives. Surely, it cannot be the meaning of article 25(a) of the Covenant that every citizen may determine either to take part directly in the conduct of public affairs or to leave it to freely chosen representatives. It is for the legal and constitutional system of the State party to provide for the modalities of such participation.

¶ 5.5. It must be beyond dispute that the conduct of public affairs in a democratic State is the task of representatives of the people, elected for that purpose, and public officials appointed in accordance with the law. Invariably, the conduct of public affairs affects the interests of large segments of the population or even the population as a whole, while in other instances it affects more directly the interests of more specific groups of society. Although prior consultations, such as public hearings or consultations with the most interested groups may often be envisaged by law or have evolved as public policy in the conduct of public affairs, article 25(a) of the Covenant cannot be understood as meaning that any directly affected group, large or small, has the unconditional right to choose the modalities of participation in the conduct of public affairs. That, in fact, would be an extrapolation of the right to direct participation by the citizens, far beyond the scope of article 25(a).

¶ 6. Notwithstanding the right of every citizen to take part in the conduct of public affairs without discrimination and without unreasonable restrictions, the Committee concludes that, in the specific circumstances of the present case, the failure of the State party to invite representatives of the Mikmaq tribal society to the constitutional conferences on aboriginal matters, which constituted conduct of public affairs, did not infringe that right of the authors or other members of the Mikmaq tribal society. Moreover, in the view of the Committee, the participation and representation at these conferences have not been subjected to unreasonable restrictions. Accordingly, the Committee is of the view that the communication does not disclose a violation of article 25 or any other provisions of the Covenant.

The *Marshall* decision appears to confirm that article 25 does not guarantee a citizen a right of direct participation in public affairs, beyond the specific instances mentioned in articles 25(b) and (c).[13]

[22.13] In General Comment 23, the HRC extrapolated on the minority rights provision in article 27. In paragraph 7 therein [24.19], the HRC recognizes that in addition to the duty to protect minority cultural activities, States must also

---

[13] See M. Turpel, 'Indigenous Peoples and Rights of Political Participation and Self-Determination: Recent International Legal Developments and the Continuing Struggle for Recognition' (1992) 25 *Cornell International Law Journal* 579, 596; see also Joseph, above, note 7, 539. However, see [24.16].

adopt 'measures to ensure the effective participation of members of minority communitities in decisions which affect them'. Interpretations of this phrase in *Länsman v Finland* (511/92)[14] and *Länsman et al. v Finland* (671/95)[15] indicate that minorities, including indigenous peoples, *do* have rights of direct participation in decisions which might impact on their traditional cultural activities. These decisions post-date *Marshall*, and appear to signal a retreat from the conservative position therein adopted. Direct rights of participation may be derived from article 27, if not article 25.

[22.14]   **GENERAL COMMENT 25**

In the General Comment, the HRC noted that there are various ways in which a State *may* provide avenues of direct participation for citizens, beyond those compulsorily prescribed in article 25(b) and (c):

¶ 6. Citizens participate directly in the conduct of public affairs when they exercise power as members of legislative bodies or by holding executive office. This right of direct participation is supported by paragraph (b). Citizens also participate directly in the conduct of public affairs when they choose or change their constitution or decide public issues through a referendum or other electoral process conducted in accordance with paragraph (b). Citizens may participate directly by taking part in popular assemblies which have the power to make decisions about local issues or about the affairs of a particular community and in bodies established to represent citizens in consultation with government.

The HRC added that other provisions of the ICCPR guarantee certain direct modes of political participation:

¶ 8. Citizens also take part in the conduct of public affairs by exerting influence through public debate and dialogue with their representatives or through their capacity to organize themselves. This participation is supported by ensuring freedom of expression, assembly and association.

[22.15] Though a State Party may not be obliged to provide for particular modes of direct political participation under article 25, it incurs obligations if it does in fact provide extra avenues of direct political participation:

¶ 6. . . . Where a mode of direct participation by citizens is established, no distinction should be made between citizens as regards their participation on the grounds mentioned in article 2, paragraph 1, and no unreasonable restrictions should be imposed.

[22.16] The General Comment fails to mention one of the biggest threats to the right of political participation: corruption. Corrupt political processes systematically deny persons the right, on a fair and equal basis, to take part in public affairs. In order fully to comply with article 25, a State Party must take measures to prevent and punish instances of corruption and bribery.

---

[14] Paras. 9.5 and 9.6 [24.26].   [15] Paras. 10.4 and 10.5 [24.28].

Article 25(b): The Right to Vote

RESTRICTIONS ON THE RIGHT TO VOTE

[22.17]   *GENERAL COMMENT 25*

¶ 4. Any conditions which apply to the exercise of the rights protected by article 25 should be based on reasonable and objective criteria. For example, it may be reasonable to require a higher age for election or appointment to particular offices than for exercising the right to vote, which should be available to every adult citizen. The exercise of these rights by citizens may not be suspended or excluded except on grounds which are established by law and which are objective and reasonable. For example, established mental incapacity may be a ground for denying a person the right to vote or hold office. . . .

¶ 10. The right to vote at elections and referenda must be established by law and may be subject only to reasonable restrictions, such as setting a minimum age limit for the right to vote. It is unreasonable to restrict the right to vote on the ground of physical disability or to impose literacy, educational or property requirements. Party membership should not be a condition of eligibility to vote, nor a ground of disqualification.

¶ 14. In their reports, States parties should indicate and explain the legislative provisions which would deprive citizens of their right to vote. The grounds for such deprivation should be objective and reasonable. If conviction for an offence is a basis for suspending the right to vote, the period of such suspension should be proportionate to the offence and the sentence. Persons who are deprived of liberty but who have not been convicted should not be excluded from exercising the right to vote.

[22.18] The deprivation of all political rights, including the right to vote, for a period of fifteen years, to members of opposition parties was found to breach article 25 in *Landinelli Silva v Uruguay* (34/78) and *Pietraroia v Uruguay* (44/79). The HRC has also labelled restrictions on voting for students of military schools as violations of article 25.[16]

[22.19] Regarding restrictions on the voting rights of convicted persons, which are common to many States Parties, the HRC has stated that laws which stripped convicts of their voting rights for up to ten years in Hong Kong 'may be a disproportionate restriction of the rights protected by article 25'.[17]

OPPORTUNITY TO VOTE

[22.20] The preamble to article 25 states that citizens must also have adequate opportunity to exercise their right to vote:

---

[16] Concluding Comments on Paraguay (1995) UN doc. CCPR/C/79/Add.48, para. 23.
[17] (1996) UN doc. CCPR/C/79/Add.57, para. 19.

GENERAL COMMENT 25

¶ 11. States must take effective measures to ensure that all persons entitled to vote are able to exercise that right. Where registration of voters is required, it should be facilitated and obstacles to such registration should not be imposed. If residence requirements apply to registration, they must be reasonable, and should not be imposed in such a way as to exclude the homeless from the right to vote. Any abusive interference with registration or voting as well as intimidation or coercion of voters should be prohibited by penal laws and those laws should be strictly enforced. Voter education and registration campaigns are necessary to ensure the effective exercise of article 25 rights by an informed community.

¶ 12. Freedom of expression, assembly and association are essential conditions for the effective exercise of the right to vote and must be fully protected. Positive measures should be taken to overcome specific difficulties, such as illiteracy, language barriers, poverty or impediments to freedom of movement which prevent persons entitled to vote from exercising their rights effectively. Information and materials about voting should be available in minority languages. Specific methods, such as photographs and symbols, should be adopted to ensure that illiterate voters have adequate information on which to base their choice. States parties should indicate in their reports the manner in which the difficulties highlighted in this paragraph are dealt with.

¶ 13. State reports should describe the rules governing the right to vote, and the application of those rules in the period covered by the report. State reports should also describe factors which impede citizens from exercising the right to vote and the positive measures which have been adopted to overcome these factors.

[22.21] Paragraph 13 expressly confirms that States have positive duties under article 25(b) beyond the provision of electoral facilities. Measures should be taken to ensure that disadvantaged citizens have the opportunity to vote, and have access to information that helps them exercise this right meaningfully. For example, the HRC has recommended that Ireland:[18]

¶ 23. ... undertake additional affirmative action aimed at improving the situation of the 'Travelling Community' and, in particular, facilitating and enhancing the participation of 'travellers' in public affairs, including the electoral process.[19]

QUALITY OF VOTE

[22.22] GENERAL COMMENT 25

¶ 21. Although the Covenant does not impose any particular electoral system, any system operating in a State party must be compatible with the rights protected by article 25 and must guarantee and give effect to the free expression of the will of the electors. The principle of one person, one vote must apply, and within the framework of each State's electoral system, the vote of one elector should be equal to the vote of another. The drawing

---

[18] (1994) UN doc. CCPR/C/79/Add.21.

[19] 'Travellers' live a nomadic lifestyle, and are often perceived as modern-day hippies.

of electoral boundaries and the method of allocating votes should not distort the distribution of voters or discriminate against any group and should not exclude or restrict unreasonably the right of citizens to choose their representatives freely.

Paragraph 21 indicates that numerous electoral systems comply with article 25(b), including proportional representation (PR), constituency voting systems, preferential voting systems, first-past-the-post systems, electoral college systems, and combinations thereof. This is so even though all systems, except pure PR systems, yield allocations of political power that distort the actual voting patterns at elections.[20] The General Comment states only that distorted distributions of voters are prohibited, which probably refers to deliberate gerrymandering;[21] it does not seem to target distorted election outcomes.

[22.23] Article 25(b) prescribes 'equal suffrage'. The General Comment confirms that all votes should have equal value. On this point, the HRC has criticized 'functional constituencies' in pre-transfer Hong Kong, which gave 'undue weight to the views of the business community' and discriminated 'among voters on the basis of property and functions'; functional constituencies violated article 25(b).[22]

[22.24] Electoral systems should not permit significant differences between the numbers of voters in different constituencies.[23] This would indicate that States should not take 'positive discrimination' measures to enhance political representation for less privileged groups or minorities. For example, Scottish and Welsh electors are favoured by lesser populated constituencies in elections for the Westminster Parliament.[24] Electoral boundaries within the state of Western Australia have been drawn so as to favour rural populations.[25] General Comment 25 indicates such measures are impermissible. Though positive discrimination is permitted in some respects under article 25,[26] the text of General Comment 25 does not seem to permit it in the context of the value of one's vote.

[22.25] The General Comment does not state that all votes should have equal 'effect';[27] this would be an impossible requirement in constituency-based

---

[20] Joseph, above, note 7, 543, 555 (notes 56–7); Nowak, above, note 1, 448. See generally, J. Zecca, 'Avoiding "Electoral Dictatorship" in the United Kingdom: Debate on Constitutional and Electoral Reform Through Proportional Representation' (1993) 16 *Hastings International and Comparative Law Quarterly* 425.   [21] See Nowak, above, note 1, 448.

[22] (1995) UN doc. CCPR/C/79/Add.57, para. 19.

[23] In this respect, note the HRC's request to Zimbabwe for more information on the size of constituencies in its electoral system; see Concluding Comments on Zimbabwe (1998) UN doc. CCPR/C/79/Add. 89, para. 23.

[24] Joseph, above, note 7, 547.

[25] The constitutionality of such boundaries was confirmed in *McGinty v Western Australia* (1996) 186 CLR 140.

[26] See, e.g., commentary at [22.31] and decision in *Stalla Costa v Uruguay* [22.45].

[27] See also K. Partsch, 'Freedom of Conscience and Expression, and Political Freedoms' in L. Henkin (ed.), *The International Bill of Rights: The International Covenant on Civil and Political Rights* (Columbia University Press, New York, 1981), 240.

electoral systems where the effect of votes in marginal seats is always greater than the effect of votes in 'safe' seats.

Article 25(b)—Right to Stand for Election

[22.26]   *GENERAL COMMENT 25*

¶ 15. The effective implementation of the right and the opportunity to stand for elective office ensures that persons entitled to vote have a free choice of candidates. Any restrictions on the right to stand for election, such as minimum age, must be justifiable on objective and reasonable criteria. Persons who are otherwise eligible to stand for election should not be excluded by unreasonable or discriminatory requirements such as education, residence or descent, or by reason of political affiliation. No person should suffer discrimination or disadvantage of any kind because of that person's candidacy. States parties should indicate and explain the legislative provisions which exclude any group or category of persons from elective office.

¶ 16. Conditions relating to nomination dates, fees or deposits should be reasonable and not discriminatory. If there are reasonable grounds for regarding certain elective offices as incompatible with tenure of specific positions (e.g., the judiciary, high-ranking military office, public service), measures to avoid any conflicts of interest should not unduly limit the rights protected by paragraph (b). The grounds for the removal of elected office holders should be established by laws based on objective and reasonable criteria and incorporating fair procedures.

¶ 17. The right of persons to stand for election should not be limited unreasonably by requiring candidates to be members of parties or of specific parties. If a candidate is required to have a minimum number of supporters for nomination this requirement should be reasonable and not act as a barrier to candidacy. Without prejudice to paragraph (1) of article 5 of the Covenant, political opinion may not be used as a ground to deprive any person of the right to stand for election.

Note also paragraph 4 of the General Comment, where the HRC indicated that restrictions on the right to stand for election could be more onerous than restrictions on the right to vote [22.17].

[22.27]   *BWALYA v ZAMBIA (314/88)*

The relevant facts are apparent from the HRC's finding of a violation of article 25:

¶ 6.6. As to the alleged violation of article 25 of the Covenant, the Committee notes that the author, a leading figure of a political party in opposition to the former President, has been prevented from participating in a general election campaign as well as from preparing his candidacy for this party. This amounts to an unreasonable restriction on the author's right to 'take part in the conduct of public affairs' which the State party has failed to explain or justify. In particular, it has failed to explain the requisite conditions for participation in the elections. Accordingly, it must be assumed that Mr. Bwalya was detained and denied the right to run for a parliamentary seat in the Constituency of Chifubu merely on account of his membership in a political party other than that officially recognized; in this context, the Committee observes that restrictions on political activity outside the only recognized political party amount to an unreasonable restriction of the right to participate in the conduct of public affairs.

Bwalya confirms that one-party systems are not compatible with article 25.[28]

[22.28] In *M.A. v Italy* (117/81), a ban on the reorganization of the Italian Fascist party was found to be compatible with article 25. Presumably, the threat posed to public order and national security by reorganization of the far right group rendered the ban a proportionate limitation of article 25 rights.[29] In this respect, the reference in paragraph 17 of General Comment 25 to article 5(1) of the Covenant should be noted [22.26]. Article 5(1) states that the Covenant should not be used as a pretext for any group to engage in activities or to perform acts aimed at the destruction of the ICCPR rights of others. The far right has a history of pursuing policies aimed at undermining the civil and political rights of others.[30]

[22.29] The HRC has expressed concern at 'the considerable financial costs' entailed in seeking election to public office in the United States; these costs 'adversely affect the right of persons to be candidates at elections'.[31]

[22.30] General Comment 25, at paragraph 16 [22.26], refers to candidacy restrictions on public servants. Such a restriction was at issue in the following case.

DEBRECZENY v THE NETHERLANDS (500/92)

Mr Debreczeny was a national police sergeant. Due to his employment as 'a civil servant in subordination to local council', he was disqualified from seeking election to a Dutch municipal council.

¶ 3.1. The author submits that the refusal to accept his membership in the local council of Dantumadeel violates his rights under article 25 (a) and (b) of the Covenant. He contends that every citizen, when duly elected, should have the right to be a member of the local council of the municipality where he resides, and that the relevant regulations, as applied to him, constitute an unreasonable restriction on this right within the meaning of article 25 of the Covenant.

¶ 3.2. According to the author, his subordination to the mayor of Dantumadeel is merely of a formal character; the mayor seldom gives direct orders to police sergeants. In support of his argument he submits that appointments of national policemen are made by the Minister of Justice, and that the mayor has authority over national police officers only with

---

[28] See also [18.33].
[30] See also [1.16].
[29] See also [18.29].
[31] (1995) UN doc. CCPR/C/79/Add.50, para. 24.

respect to the maintenance of public order; for the exercise of this authority the mayor is not accountable to the municipal council, but to the Minister of Internal Affairs.

The State Party justified the restrictions on electoral office as follows:

¶ 7.1. By submission of 17 August 1994, the State party reiterates that the Constitution of the Netherlands guarantees the right to vote and to stand in elections, and that section 25 of the Municipalities Act, which was in force at the time of Mr. Debreczeny's election, lays down the positions deemed incompatible with membership in a municipal council. Pursuant to this section, officials subordinate to the municipal authority are precluded from membership in the municipal council. The State party recalls that the rationale for the exclusion of certain categories of persons from membership in the municipal council is to guarantee the integrity of municipal institutions and hence to safeguard the democratic decision-making process, by preventing a conflict of interests.

¶ 7.2. The State party explains that the term 'municipal authority' used in section 25 of the Act encompasses the municipal council, the municipal executive and the mayor. It points out that if holders of positions subordinate to municipal administrative bodies other than the council were to become members of the council, this would also undermine the integrity of municipal administration, since the council, as the highest administrative authority, can call such bodies to account.

¶ 7.3. The State party explains that officers of the national police force, like Mr. Debreczeny, are appointed by the Minister of Justice, but that they were, according to section 35 of the Police Act in force at the time of Mr. Debreczeny's election, subordinate to part of the municipal authority, namely the mayor, with respect to the maintenance of public order and emergency duties. The mayor has the power to issue instructions to police officers for these purposes and to issue all the necessary orders and regulations; he is accountable to the council for all measures taken. Consequently, police officers as members of the municipal council would on the one hand have to obey the mayor and on the other call him to account. According to the State party, this situation would give rise to an unacceptable conflict of interests, and the democratic decision-making process would lose its integrity. The State party maintains, therefore, that the restrictions excluding police officers from membership in the council of the municipality where the officers are posted are reasonable and do not constitute a violation of article 25 of the Covenant.

The HRC decided in favour of the State Party on the merits:

¶ 9.2. The issue before the Committee is whether the application of the restrictions provided for in section 25 of the Municipalities Act, as a consequence of which the author was prevented from taking his seat in the municipal council of Dantumadeel to which he was elected, violated the author's right under article 25(b) of the Covenant. The Committee notes that the right provided for by article 25 is not an absolute right and that restrictions of this right are allowed as long as they are not discriminatory or unreasonable.

¶ 9.3. The Committee notes that the restrictions on the right to be elected to a municipal council are regulated by law and that they are based on objective criteria, namely the electee's professional appointment by or subordination to the municipal authority. Noting the reasons invoked by the State party for these restrictions, in particular, to guarantee the democratic decision-making process by avoiding conflicts of interest, the Committee considers that the said restrictions are reasonable and compatible with the purpose of the law. . . . The Committee observes that the author was at the time of his election to the council of Dantumadeel serving as a police officer in the national police force, based at Dantumadeel and as such for matters of public order subordinated to the mayor of Dantumadeel, who was himself accountable to the council for measures taken in that regard. In these circumstances, the Committee considers that a conflict of interests could indeed arise and that the application of the restrictions to the author does not constitute a violation of article 25 of the Covenant.

[22.31] In Concluding Comments on India, the HRC expressly approved of a constitutional amendment prescribing that women receive at least one third of positions on elected local bodies, as well as the reservation of elected positions for 'members of scheduled castes and tribes'.[32] These 'quotas' are measures of positive discrimination designed to ensure political representation for disadvantaged groups. Reasonable measures of positive discrimination are therefore compatible with article 25 in the context of the right to stand for election, and are also compatible with the specific non-discrimination provisions of the Covenant.[33]

Article 25(b): Periodic Genuine Elections Expressing the Will of the Electors

[22.32]					*GENERAL COMMENT 25*

¶ 19. In conformity with paragraph (b), elections must be conducted fairly and freely on a periodic basis within a framework of laws guaranteeing the effective exercise of voting rights. Persons entitled to vote must be free to vote for any candidate for election and for or against any proposal submitted to referendum or plebiscite, and free to support or to oppose government, without undue influence or coercion of any kind which may distort or inhibit the free expression of the elector's will. Voters should be able to form opinions independently, free of violence or threat of violence, compulsion, inducement or manipulative interference of any kind. Reasonable limitations on campaign expenditure may be justified where this is necessary to ensure that the free choice of voters is not undermined or the democratic process distorted by the disproportionate expenditure on behalf of any candidate or party. The results of genuine elections should be respected and implemented.

¶ 20. An independent electoral authority should be established to supervise the electoral process and to ensure that it is conducted fairly, impartially and in accordance with established laws which are compatible with the Covenant. . . .

[22.33] Numerous measures can be implemented to enhance the genuineness of an election. For example, the HRC suggested, with regard to Mexico, that the

---

[32] (1998) UN doc. CCPR/C/79/Add.81, para. 11.
[33] See also [23.58] ff. See also decision in *Stalla Costa v Uruguay* [22.45], and CEDAW General Recommendation 23 [22.51].

authorities 'accept international observers during the balloting'; this 'would contribute to the transparency of the elections'.[34]

[22.34] The HRC concede at paragraph 19 of the General Comment that restrictions on campaign expenditure may be justified in order to preserve the integrity of the electoral process. In this respect, note the HRC's concerns about excessive campaign expenses in the United States [22.29].

[22.35] State practice indicates that a gap of three to seven years between elections is acceptable.[35]

[22.36] As mentioned above [22.22], all electoral systems except perhaps pure PR systems can distort an electoral outcome so that it does not accurately reflect the 'will of the electors', which may undermine the genuineness of an election. Nevertheless, such distortion, so long as it is not extreme, seems to comply with article 25.

SECRET BALLOT

[22.37] *GENERAL COMMENT 25*

¶ 20. States should take measures to guarantee the requirement of the secrecy of the vote during elections, including absentee voting, where such a system exists. This implies that voters should be protected from any form of coercion or compulsion to disclose how they intend to vote or how they voted, and from any unlawful or arbitrary interference with the voting process. Waiver of these rights is incompatible with article 25 of the Covenant. The security of ballot boxes must be guaranteed and votes should be counted in the presence of the candidates or their agents. There should be independent scrutiny of the voting and counting process and access to judicial review or other equivalent process so that electors have confidence in the security of the ballot and the counting of the votes. Assistance provided to the disabled, blind or illiterate should be independent. Electors should be fully informed of these guarantees.

INFLUENCE OF POLITICAL PARTIES AND THE MEDIA

[22.38] *GENERAL COMMENT 25*

¶ 25. In order to ensure the full enjoyment of rights protected by article 25, the free communication of information and ideas about public and political issues between citizens, candidates and elected representatives is essential. This implies a free press and other media able to comment on public issues without censorship or restraint and to inform public opinion. It requires the full enjoyment and respect for the rights guaranteed in articles 19, 21 and 22 of the Covenant, including freedom to engage in political activity individually or through

---

[34] (1994) UN doc. CCPR/C/79/Add.32, para. 16.
[35] Joseph, above, note 7, 554.

political parties and other organizations, freedom to debate public affairs, to hold peaceful demonstrations and meetings, to criticize and oppose, to publish political material, to campaign for election and to advertise political ideas.

¶ 26. The right to freedom of association, including the right to form and join organizations and associations concerned with political and public affairs, is an essential adjunct to the rights protected by article 25. Political parties and membership in parties play a significant role in the conduct of public affairs and the election process. States should ensure that, in their internal management, political parties respect the applicable provisions of article 25 in order to enable citizens to exercise their rights thereunder.

[22.39] The notion of 'genuine' elections raises some very complex issues. For example, in most States, the likely victors in general elections will come from a limited number of political parties, which have a limited agenda. Does the *de facto* cap on political victors provide genuine choice?[36] Steiner has stated that 'contested elections mean that the people have a choice, but political elites rather than the people decide what that choice is between'.[37] Indeed, the HRC concedes the compatibility of the pervasive influence of political parties with article 25 in paragraph 26 of the General Comment, though it stresses that these parties should conduct themselves in accordance with the Covenant's provisions.

[22.40] In paragraph 25, the HRC recognizes the influence of the media in determining the outcomes of elections. Its comments stress that media should be free of government influence.[38] The General Comment does not target the pernicious influence of private sector media monopolies in moulding public opinion. The HRC has however occasionally commented on how such monopolies undermine rights of freedom of expression under article 19.[39] The importance of full enjoyment of article 19 rights for the enjoyment of article 25 rights is expressly recognized in the General Comment at paragraph 8 [22.14].

[22.41] It seems unlikely that the HRC will conduct the complex enquiry needed to determine whether an election, conducted without procedural flaws, nevertheless suffered from substantive flaws due to the systematic disempowerment of particular persons by the unequal distribution of political and economic power.[40] The HRC may implicitly accept that the complexities of modern government induce or even necessitate the effective exclusion of certain agendas and certain voices. In contrast, the Committee on the Elimination of all Forms of Discrimination against Women, established under the International Convention on the

---

[36] See G. Fox, 'The Right to Political Participation in International Law' 17 (1992) *Yale Journal of International Law* 539, 557, citing S. Mubako, 'Zambia's Single-Party Constitution—A Search for Unity and Development' (1973) 5 *Zambia Law Journal* 82; see also Nowak, above, note 1, 454.

[37] Steiner, above, note 4, 101.

[38] See also Concluding Comments on Armenia (1998) UN doc. CCPR/C/79/Add.100, para. 21.

[39] See also [18.14].

[40] Joseph, above, note 7, 553–4; see also Steiner, above, note 4, 112–13.

Elimination of all Forms of Discrimination Against Women (CEDAW Committee), has exhibited strong awareness of structural problems that impact adversely on the public and political participation of one disadvantaged group, namely women [22.51].

Article 25(c): Equal Access to the Public Service

[22.42]   *GENERAL COMMENT 25*

¶ 23. Subparagraph (c) of article 25 deals with the right and the opportunity of citizens to have access on general terms of equality to public service positions. To ensure access on general terms of equality, the criteria and processes for appointment, promotion, suspension and dismissal must be objective and reasonable. Affirmative measures may be taken in appropriate cases to ensure that there is equal access to public service for all citizens. Basing access to public service on equal opportunity and general principles of merit, and providing secured tenure, ensure that persons holding public service positions are free from political interference or pressures. It is of particular importance to ensure that persons do not suffer discrimination in the exercise of their rights under article 25, subparagraph (c), on any of the grounds set out in article 2, paragraph 1.

As confirmed in *Kall v Poland* (552/93),[41] article 25(c) does not guarantee one an actual job within the public service; it guarantees a fair opportunity to acquire one.

[22.43] Note paragraph 4 of the General Comment [22.17], where the HRC acknowledged that restrictions on the right to be appointed to public office could be more onerous than restrictions on the right to vote. For example, it is reasonable to require certain educational requirements of judges.

[22.44] The HRC has not defined the term 'public service'. It seems to encompass all positions within the executive, judiciary, legislature, and other areas of state administration. For example, schoolteachers and lecturers in public universities have been protected under article 25(c) in, respectively, *Delgado Páez v Colombia* (195/85) [22.49] and *Aduayom v Togo* (422–424/90) [22.46]. Privatization policies reduce the public sector and therefore seem to reduce the scope of article 25(c). Article 25(c) does not prescribe any optimum public/private divide.

In *B.d.B. v The Netherlands* (273/88), the HRC said that a State Party is 'not relieved of obligations under the Covenant when some of its functions are delegated to other autonomous organs'.[42] The relevant 'autonomous organ' was an industrial board made up of representatives of employers' and employees' organizations, which had no formal connection to the government. Though the case did not raise issues under article 25, it potentially indicated that governments

---

[41] Para. 13.2.
[42] Para. 6.6; see also *Lindgren et al. v Sweden* (298–299/88), para. 10.4.

cannot reduce the scope of article 25 by delegating some of their traditional functions to private entities.

Indeed, it is likely that 'public service' has an autonomous meaning that cannot be totally governed by States Parties.[43] For example, it is unlikely that a State could 'privatize' the army or the police force and therefore hold that positions within those bodies were outside article 25(c).

[22.45]   *STALLA COSTA v URUGUAY (198/85)*

The facts are set out immediately below:

¶ 2.1. The author states that he has submitted job applications to various governmental agencies in order to have access to and obtain a job in the public service in his country. He has allegedly been told that only former public employees who were dismissed as a result of the application of Institutional Act No. 7 of June 1977 are currently admitted to the public service. He refers in this connection to article 25 of Law No. 15.737 of 22 March 1985, which provides that all public employees who were dismissed as a result of the application of Institutional Act No. 7 have the right to be reinstated in their respective posts.

¶ 2.2. The author claims that article 25 of Law No. 15.737 gives more rights to former public employees than to other individuals, such as the author himself, and that it is therefore discriminatory and in violation of articles 25(c) and 26 of the International Covenant on Civil and Political Rights.

The HRC dismissed the complaint at the merits stage:

¶ 10. The main question before the Committee is whether the author of the communication is a victim of a violation of article 25(c) of the Covenant because, as he alleges, he has not been permitted to have access to public service on general terms of equality. Taking into account the social and political situation in Uruguay during the years of military rule, in particular the dismissal of many public servants pursuant to Institutional Act No. 7, the Committee understands the enactment of Law No. 15.737 of 22 March 1985 by the new democratic Government of Uruguay as a measure of redress. Indeed, the Committee observes that Uruguayan public officials dismissed on ideological, political or trade union grounds were victims of violations of article 25 of the Covenant and as such are entitled to have an effective remedy under article 2, paragraph 3 (a), of the Covenant. The Act should be looked upon as such a remedy. The implementation of the Act, therefore, cannot be regarded as incompatible with the reference to 'general terms of equality' in article 25 (c) of the Covenant. Neither can the implementation of the Act be regarded as an invidious distinction under article 2, paragraph 1, or as prohibited discrimination within the terms of article 26 of the Covenant. [44]

---

[43] Joseph, above, note 7, 556. See also [9.98–9.99].
[44] See also [23.63].

[22.46] *ADUAYOM et al. v TOGO (422–424/90)*

The authors were detained for political offences in 1986. They were consequently dismissed from their jobs in the Togolese public service for 'having unjustifiably deserted their posts'. They were not reinstated until 1991. The HRC found a breach of article 25(c), as well as article 19 (freedom of expression):

¶ 7.4. In respect of the claim under article 19, the Committee observes that it has remained uncontested that the authors were first prosecuted and later not reinstated in their posts, between 1986 and 1991, *inter alia*, for having read and, respectively, disseminated information and material critical of the Togolese Government in power and of the system of governance prevailing in Togo. The Committee observes that the freedoms of information and of expression are cornerstones in any free and democratic society. It is in the essence of such societies that its citizens must be allowed to inform themselves about alternatives to the political system/parties in power, and that they may criticize or openly and publicly evaluate their Governments without fear of interference or punishment, within the limits set by article 19, paragraph 3. On the basis of the information before the Committee, it appears that the authors were not reinstated in the posts they had occupied prior to their arrest, because of such activities. The State party implicitly supports this conclusion by qualifying the authors' activities as 'political offences' . . . [T]here is no indication that the authors' activities represented a threat to the rights and the reputation of others, or to national security or public order (article 19, paragraph 3). In the circumstances, the Committee concludes that there has been a violation of article 19 of the Covenant.

¶ 7.5. The Committee recalls that the authors were all suspended from their posts for a period of well over five years for activities considered contrary to the interests of the Government; in this context, it notes that Mr. Dobou was a civil servant, whereas Messrs. Aduayom and Diasso were employees of the University of Benin, which is in practice state-controlled. As far as the case of Mr. Dobou is concerned, the Committee observes that access to public service on general terms of equality encompasses a duty, for the State, to ensure that there is no discrimination on the ground of political opinion or expression. This applies *a fortiori* to those who hold positions in the public service. The rights enshrined in article 25 should also be read to encompass the freedom to engage in political activity individually or through political parties, freedom to debate public affairs, to criticize the Government and to publish material with political content.

¶ 7.6. The Committee notes that the authors were suspended from their posts for alleged 'desertion' of the same, after having been arrested for activities deemed to be contrary to the interests of the State party's Government. Mr. Dobou was a civil servant, whereas Messrs. Aduayom and Diasso were employees of the University of Benin, which is in practice state-controlled. In the circumstances of the authors' respective cases, an issue under article 25(c) arises in so far as the authors' inability to recover their posts between 30 June 1988 and 27 May and 1 July 1991, respectively, is concerned. In this context, the Committee notes that the non-payment of salary arrears to the authors is a consequence of their non-reinstatement in the posts they had previously occupied. The Committee concludes that there has been a violation of article 25(c) in the authors' case for the period from 30 June 1988 to 27 May and to 1 July 1991, respectively.[45]

[22.47] Both the *Stalla Costa* and *Aduayom* cases raise issues of discrimination on the basis of political opinion in relation to access to the public service. Both cases indicate that such discrimination is not permitted under article 25. In this respect, also note the following HRC comments regarding Estonia:[46]

¶ 14. The Committee is concerned that the conditions for appointment to or employment in any position in a State or local government agency in particular the automatic exclusion of persons unable to satisfy the requirements of the written oath of conscience regarding their previous activities (under the former regime) may give rise to an unreasonable restriction on the right of access to public service without discrimination.

However, certain public service appointments in all States are influenced by the candidate's political opinion, such as the head of a state's secret service.[47] The HRC has never indicated that such distinctions are permissible,[48] though it is arguable that such distinctions constitute reasonable and justifiable restrictions on article 25 rights.

[22.48] All of the decided cases regarding article 25(c) have confirmed that it guarantees not only access to the public service, but a right of retention in the public service on an equal basis with others.[49] In Concluding Comments on Germany, the HRC reaffirmed the importance, for article 25 compliance, of clear laws to circumscribe conditions of tenure in the public service:[50]

¶ 17. The Committee expresses its concern that the criteria used to evaluate for retaining or dismissing former GDR public servants, including judges and teachers, are vague and leave open the possibility of deprivation of employment on the basis of political opinions held or expressed. The Committee therefore suggests that the criteria for dismissing public servants of the former GDR be made more precise so that no public servant will be dismissed on the ground of political opinion held or expressed by him or her.

[22.49] In *Delgado Páez v Colombia* (195/85), the HRC found that the 'constant harassment and threats against [the author's] person (in respect of which the State Party failed to provide protection) made the author's continuation in public service teaching impossible'.[51] Accordingly, the HRC found a breach of article 25(c).

[22.50] On the facts in *Kall v Poland* (552/93), the author had held a public

---

[45] The violation dates from 1988 rather than 1986, as the former date was the date that the Optional Protocol entered into force for Togo; see generally, on temporal limitations, Chap. 2.

[46] Concluding Comments on Estonia (1996) UN doc. CCPR/C/79/Add.59, para. 14.

[47] Nowak, above, note 1, 451.

[48] Indeed, see the Concluding Comments on Germany at [22.48].

[49] See also decision of Mr Wennergren in *Muñoz Hermoza v Peru* (203/86); the majority decided this case under art. 14 [14.43].

[50] Concluding Comments on Germany (1997) UN doc. CCPR/C/79/Add.73, para. 17.

[51] Para. 5.1; see also, on this case, [11.03].

service position under the communist government before 1990. In 1990, the author's position was classified as being a part of the Security Police. The Security Police were disbanded in 1990, so the author lost his job. The author alleged that his job loss entailed a breach of article 25(c). The author failed to provide enough evidence to show that the State Party's continued failure to re-employ him in another capacity constituted, as he claimed, discrimination on the basis of his leftist political opinions.[52] Both the author and the Committee agreed that the dissolution of the Security Police, which caused many to lose their jobs, complied with article 25(c). The Committee accepted the State Party's contention that the dissolution of the Security Police was necessary to facilitate the State's 'profound political transformation' into a representative democracy, and to restore 'democracy and the rule of law'.[53]

Redressing Systemic Inequality in Public Participation

[22.51] Under-participation in public life causes substantial and continuing disadvantage for the under-represented group; the political interests of under-represented groups are often marginalized and ignored. The CEDAW Committee has issued a General Recommendation addressing discrimination against women in 'political and public life', which is prohibited under articles 7 and 8 of CEDAW.[54]

CEDAW GENERAL RECOMMENDATION 23

¶ 13. The principle of equality of women and men has been affirmed in the constitutions and laws of most countries and in all international instruments. Nonetheless, in the last 50 years, women have not achieved equality, and their inequality has been reinforced by their low level of participation in public and political life. Policies developed and decisions made by men alone reflect only part of human experience and potential. The just and effective organization of society demands the inclusion and participation of all its members.

¶ 14. No political system has conferred on women both the right to and the benefit of full and equal participation. While democratic systems have improved women's opportunities for involvement in political life, the many economic, social, and cultural barriers they continue to face have seriously limited their participation. Even historically stable democracies have failed to integrate fully and equally the opinions and interests of the female half of the population. Societies in which women are excluded from public life and decision-making cannot be described as democratic. The concept of democracy will have real and dynamic meaning and lasting effect only when political decision-making is shared by women and men and takes equal account of the interests of both. The examination of States

---

[52] See para. 13.6.   [53] See paras. 7.2 and 13.3.
[54] Art. 7 requires States to redress sex discrimination in the municipal public and political life of the State; it essentially guarantees art. 25-type rights specifically to women. Art. 8 requires States to redress sex discrimination regarding access to international bodies.

parties' reports shows that where there is full and equal participation of women in public life and decision-making, the implementation of their rights and compliance with the Convention improves.

Temporary special measures

¶ 15. While removal of *de jure* barriers is necessary, it is not sufficient. Failure to achieve full and equal participation of women can be unintentional and the result of outmoded practices and procedures which inadvertently promote men. Under article 4, the Convention encourages the use of temporary special measures in order to give full effect to articles 7 and 8. Where countries have developed effective temporary strategies in an attempt to achieve equality of participation, a wide range of measures has been implemented, including recruiting, financially assisting and training women candidates, amending electoral procedures, developing campaigns directed at equal participation, setting numerical goals and quotas and targeting women for appointment to public positions such as the judiciary or other professional groups that play an essential part in the everyday life of all societies. The formal removal of barriers and the introduction of temporary special measures to encourage the equal participation of both men and women in the public life of their societies are essential prerequisites to true equality in political life. In order, however, to overcome centuries of male domination of the public sphere, women also require the encouragement and support of all sectors of society to achieve full and effective participation, encouragement which must be led by States parties to the Convention, as well as by political parties and public officials. States parties have an obligation to ensure that temporary special measures are clearly designed to support the principle of equality and therefore comply with constitutional principles which guarantee equality to all citizens.

Summary

¶ 16. The critical issue, emphasized in the Beijing Platform for Action,[55] is the gap between the *de jure* and *de facto*, or the right as against the reality of women's participation in politics and public life generally. Research demonstrates that if women's participation reaches 30 to 35 per cent (generally termed a 'critical mass'), there is a real impact on political style and the content of decisions, and political life is revitalized.

¶ 17. In order to achieve broad representation in public life, women must have full equality in the exercise of political and economic power; they must be fully and equally involved in decision-making at all levels, both nationally and internationally, so that they may make their contribution to the goals of equality, development and the achievement of peace. A gender perspective is critical if these goals are to be met and if true democracy is to be assured. For these reasons, it is essential to involve women in public life to take advantage of their contribution, to assure their interests are protected and to fulfil the guarantee that the enjoyment of human rights is for all people regardless of gender. Women's full participation is essential not only for their empowerment but also for the advancement of society as a whole.

Regarding women's appointment by States to international bodies, CEDAW stated:

---

[55] Report of the Fourth World Conference on Women, Beijing, 4–15 September 1995 (A/CONF.177/20 and Add.1), chap. I, resolution 1, annex I.

¶ 39. The globalization of the contemporary world makes the inclusion of women and their participation in international organizations, on equal terms with men, increasingly important. The integration of a gender perspective and women's human rights into the agenda of all international bodies is a government imperative. Many crucial decisions on global issues, such as peacemaking and conflict resolution, military expenditure and nuclear disarmament, development and the environment, foreign aid and economic restructuring, are taken with limited participation of women. This is in stark contrast to their participation in these areas at the non-governmental level.

¶ 40. The inclusion of a critical mass of women in international negotiations, peacekeeping activities, all levels of preventive diplomacy, mediation, humanitarian assistance, social reconciliation, peace negotiations and the international criminal justice system will make a difference. In addressing armed or other conflicts, a gender perspective and analysis is necessary to understand their differing effects on women and men.

The CEDAW extracts can be extrapolated to provide clues as to how chronic under-representation of groups occurs, and how it can be redressed. The causes of chronic under-representation are generally the same as the causes of systemic inequality in other areas of life.[56]

Conclusion

[22.52] Article 25 (a) generally guarantees a right for all persons to be governed democratically by an accountable government. In this respect, the HRC has interpreted article 25 so as to embrace numerous types of political and electoral traditions. Article 25 (b) and (c) guarantees more specific rights, such as the right to vote and the right of appointment to government office. Some of the more complex issues concerning meaningful political participation have not yet been addressed by the HRC. For example, all political systems seem to contain systemic deficiencies that perpetuate the power of certain elites. It is uncertain to what extent such problems can be meaningfully redressed under article 25.

Postscript: Please note that General Comment 28 on 'Equality of Rights Between Men and Women', contained in the Addendum at page 634, contains extra information on some of the material in this chapter.

---

[56] Systemic inequality is discussed at [23.77] ff.

23

Rights of Non-discrimination—Articles 2(1), 3, and 26

ARTICLE 2

1. Each State party to the present Covenant undertakes to respect and to ensure to all individuals within its territory and subject to its jurisdiction the rights recognized in the present Covenant, without distinction of any kind, such as race, colour, sex, language, religion, political or other opinion, national or social origin, property, birth or other status.

ARTICLE 3

The States Parties to the present Covenant undertake to ensure the equal right of men and women to the enjoyment of all civil and political rights set forth in the present Covenant.

ARTICLE 26

All persons are equal before the law and are entitled without any discrimination to the equal protection of the law. In this respect, the law shall prohibit any discrimination and guarantee to all persons equal and effective protection against discrimination on any ground such as race, colour, sex, language, religion, political or other opinion, national or social origin, property, birth or other status.

[23.01] The ICCPR contains comprehensive prohibitions on discrimination in articles 2(1) and 26. These guarantees are reinforced by article 3 (prohibiting sex discrimination), articles 4(1) (prohibiting discrimination in relation to derogations),[1] and articles 23, 24, and 25,[2] which guarantee non-discrimination in relation to particular substantive rights. Finally, one may note that article 20 requires

---

[1] See Chap. 25 on derogations.
[2] See Chaps. 20, 21, and 22 respectively.

States to prohibit various forms of incitement to discrimination.[3] It has been suggested that 'equality and non-discrimination constitute the single dominant theme of the Covenant'.[4] The heavy emphasis on non-discrimination in the ICCPR is appropriate; discrimination is at the root of virtually all human rights abuses.

[23.02] Two other United Nations treaties specifically deal with discrimination: the International Convention on the Elimination of all Forms of Racial Discrimination 1966 (ICERD) and the Convention on the Elimination of All Forms of Discrimination Against Women 1979 (CEDAW). These Conventions go into further detail about the scope of non-discrimination obligations in the areas of race and sex. It is to be expected that the HRC is heavily influenced by ICERD and CEDAW precedents in its interpretation of the relevant ICCPR guarantees, so some reference will be made to the jurisprudence of the respective ICERD and CEDAW Committees. Indeed, it is arguable that the ICCPR obligations essentially subsume those of ICERD and CEDAW, and go substantially further by prohibiting discrimination on more grounds.

Definition of Discrimination

[23.03] *GENERAL COMMENT 18*

¶ 7. The Committee believes that the term 'discrimination' as used in the Covenant should be understood to imply any distinction, exclusion, restriction or preference which is based on any ground such as race, colour, sex, language, religion, political or other opinion, national or social origin, property, birth or other status, and which has the purpose or effect of nullifying or impairing the recognition, enjoyment or exercise by all persons, on an equal footing, of all rights and freedoms.

¶ 13. Finally, the Committee observes that not every differentiation of treatment will constitute discrimination, if the criteria for such differentiation are reasonable and objective and if the aim is to achieve a purpose which is legitimate under the Covenant.

[23.04] Article 3 guarantees a right of 'equality' to men and women. Is 'equality' a substantively different concept from 'non-discrimination'? Linguistically, the notion of equality seems to incorporate more positive obligations than does a notion of 'non-discrimination'.[5]

---

[3] See Chap. 18.

[4] B. Ramcharan, 'Equality and Non-Discrimination' in L. Henkin (ed.), *The International Bill of Rights: The Covenant on Civil and Political Rights* (Columbia University Press, New York, 1981), 246.

[5] Lord Lester of Herne Hill QC and S. Joseph, 'Obligations of Non-Discrimination' in D. Harris and S. Joseph (eds.), *The International Covenant on Civil and Political Rights and United Kingdom Law* (Clarendon Press, Oxford, 1995), 565. See generally, on positive obligations, [23.58] ff. See also Ramcharan, above, note 4, 254.

[23.05] In *Waldman v Canada* (694/96), the impugned discrimination concerned a preference given to Roman Catholic schools compared to schools for other minority religious groups [23.54]. In finding a violation of article 26, the HRC confirmed that one is just as much a victim of discrimination when the advantaged group is a comparable minority as when the advantaged group is a majority.

[23.06] General Recommendation 19, issued under ICERD, confirms that segregation is a form of discrimination [23.85]. The UN bodies will not accept the argument that segregated groups are 'separate but equal'.[6]

Scope of ICCPR Non-discrimination Provisions

[23.07] Article 2(1) prohibits discrimination on certain grounds in the exercise of the Covenant's enumerated rights (i.e. articles 6–27). Article 3 underlines the prohibition on sex discrimination by guaranteeing that all of the Covenant's rights shall be enjoyed equally by men and women. Article 26 extends considerably further than articles 2(1) and 3, as was confirmed in the following case.

[23.08]   *BROEKS v THE NETHERLANDS (172/84)*

The facts are set out immediately below:

¶ 2.3. Mrs. Broeks claims that, under existing law (Unemployment Benefits Act (WWV), sect. 13, subsect. 1 (1), and Decree No. 61 452/IIIa of 5 April 1976, to give effect to sect. 13, subsect. I (1), of the Unemployment Benefits Act) an unacceptable distinction has been made on the grounds of sex and status. She bases her claim on the following: if she were a man, married or unmarried, the law in question would not deprive her of unemployment benefits. Because she is a woman, and was married at the time in question, the law excludes her from continued unemployment benefits. This, she claims, makes her a victim of a violation of article 26 of the Covenant on the grounds of sex and status. She claims that article 26 of the International Covenant on Civil and Political Rights was meant to give protection to individuals beyond the specific civil and political rights enumerated in the Covenant.

The State Party made several responses to Mrs Broeks's allegations of a breach of article 26:

¶ 4.1. In its submission dated 29 May 1985 the State party underlined, *inter alia*, that:

(a) The principle that elements of discrimination in the realization of the right to social security are to be eliminated is embodied in article 9 in conjunction with articles 2 and 3 of the International Covenant on Economic, Social and Cultural Rights;

---

[6] See, e.g., the seminal US Supreme Court case of *Brown v Board of Education* 347 US 483 (1954).

(b) The Government of the Kingdom of the Netherlands has accepted to implement this principle under the terms of the International Covenant on Economic, Social and Cultural Rights. Under these terms, States parties have undertaken to take steps to the maximum of their available resources with a view to achieving progressively the full realization of the rights recognized in that Covenant (art. 2, para. 1);

(c) The process of gradual realization to the maximum of available resources is well on its way in the Netherlands. Remaining elements of discrimination in the realization of the rights are being and will be gradually eliminated;

(d) The International Covenant on Economic, Social and Cultural Rights has established its own system for international control of the way in which States parties are fulfilling their obligations. To this end States parties have undertaken to submit to the Economic and Social Council reports on the measures they have adopted and the progress they are making. The Government of the Kingdom of the Netherlands to this end submitted its first report in 1983.[7] . . .

¶ 8.3. With regard to the scope of article 26 of the Covenant, the State party argues, *inter alia*, as follows:

The Netherlands Government takes the view that article 26 of the Covenant does entail an obligation to avoid discrimination, but that this article can only be invoked under the Optional Protocol to the Covenant in the sphere of civil and political rights, not necessarily limited to those civil and political rights that are embodied in the Covenant. The Government could, for instance, envisage the admissibility under the Optional Protocol of a complaint concerning discrimination in the field of taxation. But it cannot accept the admissibility of a complaint concerning the enjoyment of economic, social and cultural rights. The latter category of rights is the object of a separate United Nations Covenant. Mrs. Broeks' complaint relates to rights in the sphere of social security, which fall under the International Covenant on Economic, Social and Cultural Rights. Articles 2, 3 and 9 of that Covenant are of particular relevance here. That Covenant has its own specific system and its own specific organ for international monitoring of how States parties meet their obligations and deliberately does not provide for an individual complaints procedure.

The Government considers it incompatible with the aims of both the Covenants and the Optional Protocol that an individual complaint with respect to the right of social security, as referred to in article 9 of the International Covenant on Economic, Social and Cultural Rights, could be dealt with by the Human Rights Committee by way of an individual complaint under the Optional Protocol based on article 26 of the International Covenant on Civil and Political Rights.

The Netherlands Government reports to the Economic and Social Council on matters concerning the way it is fulfilling its obligations with respect to the right to social security, in accordance with the relevant rules of the International Covenant on Economic, Social and Cultural Rights. . . .

Should the Human Rights Committee take the view that article 26 of the International Covenant on Civil and Political Rights ought to be interpreted more broadly, thus that this

---

[7] The ICESCR is now monitored by the Committee on Economic, Social and Cultural Rights.

article is applicable to complaints concerning discrimination in the field of social security, the Government would observe that in that case article 26 must also be interpreted in the light of other comparable United Nations conventions laying down obligations to combat and eliminate discrimination in the field of economic, social and cultural rights. The Government would particularly point to the International Convention on the Elimination of All Forms of Racial Discrimination and the Convention on the Elimination of All Forms of Discrimination against Women.

If article 26 of the International Covenant on Civil and Political Rights were deemed applicable to complaints concerning discriminatory elements in national legislation in the field of those conventions, this could surely not be taken to mean that a State party would be required to have eliminated all possible discriminatory elements from its legislation in those fields at the time of ratification of the Covenant. Years of work are required in order to examine the whole complex of national legislation in search of discriminatory elements. The search can never be completed, either, as distinctions in legislation which are justifiable in the light of social views and conditions prevailing when they are first made may become disputable as changes occur in the views held in society. . . .

If the Human Rights Committee should decide that article 26 of the International Covenant on Civil and Political Rights entails obligations with regard to legislation in the economic, social and cultural field, such obligations could, in the Government's view, not compromise more than an obligation of States to subject national legislation to periodic examination after ratification of the Covenant with a view to seeking out discriminatory elements and, if they are found, to progressively taking measures to eliminate them to the maximum of the State's available resources. Such examinations are under way in the Netherlands with regard to various aspects of discrimination, including discrimination between men and women.

¶ 8.4. With regard to the principle of equality laid down in article 26 of the Covenant in relation to section 13, subsection 1(1), of WWV in its unamended form, the State party explains the legislative history of WWV and in particular the social justification of the 'breadwinner' concept at the time the law was drafted. The State party contends that, with the 'breadwinner' concept, 'a proper balance was achieved between the limited availability of public funds (which makes it necessary to put them to limited, well-considered and selective use) on the one hand and the Government's obligation to provide social security on the other. The Government does not accept that the "breadwinner" concept as such was "discriminatory" in the sense that equal cases were treated in an unequal way by law.' Moreover, it is argued that the provisions of WWV 'are based on reasonable social and economic considerations which are not discriminatory in origin. The restriction making the provision in question inapplicable to men was inspired not by any desire to discriminate in favour of men and against women but by the *de facto* social and economic situation which existed at the time when the Act was passed and which would have made it pointless to declare the provision applicable to men. At the time when Mrs. Broeks applied for unemployment benefits the *de facto* situation was not essentially different. There was therefore no violation of article 26 of the Covenant. This is not altered by the fact that a new social trend has been growing in recent years, which has made it undesirable for the provision to remain in force in the present social context.'

The impugned law was in fact amended in 1985, with retrospective effect from 23 December 1984. As Mrs. Broeks's payments had been discontinued in 1980, the amendment provided her with only a partial remedy for her complaint.

The HRC delivered its merits decision in favour of Mrs Broeks:

¶ 12.1. The State party contends that there is considerable overlapping of the provisions of article 26 with the provisions of article 2 of the International Covenant on Economic, Social and Cultural Rights. The Committee is of the view that the International Covenant on Civil and Political Rights would still apply even if a particular subject-matter is referred to or covered in other international instruments, for example, the International Convention on the Elimination of All Forms of Racial Discrimination, the Convention on the Elimination of All Forms of Discrimination against Women, or, as in the present case, the International Covenant on Economic, Social and Cultural Rights. Notwithstanding the interrelated drafting history of the two Covenants, it remains necessary for the Committee to apply fully the terms of the International Covenant on Civil and Political Rights. The Committee observes in this connection that the provisions of article 2 of the International Covenant on Economic, Social and Cultural Rights do not detract from the full application of article 26 of the International Covenant on Civil and Political Rights.

The HRC then noted that the *travaux préparatoires* of the ICCPR were inconclusive as to the scope of article 26:

¶ 12.3. For the purpose of determining the scope of article 26, the Committee has taken into account the 'ordinary meaning' of each element of the article in its context and in the light of its object and purpose (art. 31 of the Vienna Convention on the Law of Treaties). The Committee begins by noting that article 26 does not merely duplicate the guarantees already provided for in article 2. It derives from the principle of equal protection of the law without discrimination, as contained in article 7 of the Universal Declaration of Human Rights, which prohibits discrimination in law or in practice in any field regulated and protected by public authorities. Article 26 is thus concerned with the obligations imposed on States in regard to their legislation and the application thereof.

¶ 12.4. Although article 26 requires that legislation should prohibit discrimination, it does not of itself contain any obligation with respect to the matters that may be provided for by legislation. Thus it does not, for example, require any State to enact legislation to provide for social security. However, when such legislation is adopted in the exercise of a State's sovereign power, then such legislation must comply with article 26 of the Covenant.

¶ 12.5. The Committee observes in this connection that what is at issue is not whether or not social security should be progressively established in the Netherlands, but whether the legislation providing for social security violates the prohibition against discrimination contained in article 26 of the International Covenant on Civil and Political Rights and the guarantee given therein to all persons regarding equal and effective protection against discrimination.

¶ 13. The right to equality before the law and to equal protection of the law without any discrimination does not make all differences of treatment discriminatory. A differentiation based on reasonable and objective criteria does not amount to prohibited discrimination within the meaning of article 26.

¶ 14. It therefore remains for the Committee to determine whether the differentiation in Netherlands law at the time in question and as applied to Mrs. Broeks constituted discrimination within the meaning of article 26. The Committee notes that in Netherlands law the provisions of articles 84 and 85 of the Netherlands Civil Code impose equal rights and obligations on both spouses with regard to their joint income. Under section 13, subsection 1(1), of the Unemployment Benefits Act (WWV), a married woman, in order to receive WWV benefits, had to prove that she was a 'breadwinner'—a condition that did not apply to married men. Thus a differentiation which appears on one level to be one of status is in fact one of sex, placing married women at a disadvantage compared with married men. Such a differentiation is not reasonable; and this seems to have been effectively acknowledged even by the State party by the enactment of a change in the law on 29 April 1985, with retroactive effect to 23 December 1984. . . .

¶ 15. The circumstances in which Mrs. Broeks found herself at the material time and the application of the then valid Netherlands law made her a victim of a violation, based on sex, of article 26 of the International Covenant on Civil and Political Rights, because she was denied a social security benefit on an equal footing with men.

¶ 16. The Committee notes that the State party had not intended to discriminate against women and further notes with appreciation that the discriminatory provisions in the law applied to Mrs. Broeks have, subsequently, been eliminated. Although the State party has thus taken the necessary measures to put an end to the kind of discrimination suffered by Mrs. Broeks at the time complained of, the Committee is of the view that the State party should offer Mrs. Broeks an appropriate remedy.

[23.09]   ***GENERAL COMMENT 18***

The *Broeks* decision was very controversial.[8] However, it was supported in General Comment 18, in which the HRC stated the following:

¶ 12. While article 2 limits the scope of the rights to be protected against discrimination to those provided for in the Covenant, article 26 does not specify such limitations. That is to say, article 26 provides that all persons are equal before the law and are entitled to equal protection of the law without discrimination, and that the law shall guarantee to all persons equal and effective protection against discrimination on any of the enumerated grounds. In the view of the Committee, article 26 does not merely duplicate the guarantee already provided for in article 2 but provides in itself an autonomous right. It prohibits discrimination in law or in fact in any field regulated and protected by public authorities. Article 26 is therefore concerned with the obligations imposed on States parties in regard to their legislation and the application thereof. Thus, when legislation is adopted by a State party, it must comply with the requirement of article 26 that its content should not be discrimi-

---

[8] See M. Schmidt, 'The Complementarity of the Covenant and the European Convention on Human Rights—Recent Developments' in D. Harris and S. Joseph (eds.), *The International Covenant on Civil and Political Rights and United Kingdom Law* (Clarendon Press, Oxford, 1995), at 637–9. See also T. Opsahl, 'Equality in Human Rights Law with Particular Reference to Article 26 of the International Covenant on Civil and Political Rights' in M. Nowak, D. Steurer, and H. Tretter (eds.) *Festschrift für Felix Ermacora* (N.P. Engel, Kehl, 1988), 51.

natory. In other words, the application of the principle of non-discrimination contained in article 26 is not limited to those rights which are provided for in the Covenant.

[23.10] The article 26 guarantee of 'equality before the law' guarantees equality with regard to the *enforcement* of the law. Judges and other legal administrators must not apply legislation in an arbitrary or discriminatory manner.[9] The guarantee of 'equal protection of the law' guarantees *de jure* equality, so that the law dispenses rights and duties to all without discrimination.[10] Non-discrimination in article 26 'is a principle above the law', circumscribing the legitimacy of laws themselves.[11]

[23.11] Article 26 may be distinguished from article 14 of the European Convention on Human Rights, which guarantees non-discrimination only in relation to other Convention rights. In contrast, article 26 is a free-standing guarantee of non-discrimination in relation to all rights. Numerous cases have confirmed the *Broeks* decision that article 26 protects against discrimination in relation to economic and social rights as well as civil and political rights. The HRC has found allegations of discrimination concerning the following 'rights', not independently guaranteed in the ICCPR, to be admissible: the right of conscientious objection (*Brinkhof v The Netherlands* (402/90)),[12] retirement pensions (*Johannes Vos v The Netherlands* (786/97)), severance pay (*Valenzuela v Peru* (309/88)), unemployment benefits (*Broeks, Zwaan-de-Vries v The Netherlands* (182/84), *Cavalcanti Araujo-Jongens v The Netherlands* (418/90), *García Pons v Spain* (454/91)), disability pensions (*Danning v The Netherlands* (180/84), *Vos v The Netherlands* (218/86)), education subsidies (*Blom v Sweden* (191/85), *Lindgren et al. v Sweden* (198–199/88), *Waldman v Canada* (694/96)), employment (*Bwalya v Zaire* (314/88)), veterans' pensions (*Gueye et al. v France* 196/85)), public health insurance (*Sprenger v The Netherlands* (395/90)), survivors' pensions (*Pauger v Austria* (415/90), *Pepels v The Netherlands* (484/91), *Hoofdman v The Netherlands* (602/94)), children's benefits (*Oulajin & Kaiss v The Netherlands* (406, 426/90)), and property rights (*Simunek v Czech Republic* (516/92), *Adam v Czech Republic* (586/94)). A minority found that 'freedom from extradition' could ground a complaint under article 26 in *Kindler v Canada* (470/91); the majority did not comment on this point.[13] Indeed, no article 26 communication has ever been expressly ruled inadmissible for its failure to raise a relevant 'right' (in regard to which discrimination has allegedly occurred).

[23.12] However, a number of minority opinions, excerpted directly below, have challenged the *Broeks* reasoning.

[9] M. Nowak, *CCPR Commentary* (N.P. Engel, Kehl, 1993), 466–7. In so far as this duty applies to judges, it reflects similar rights of 'equality before the courts' in art. 14(1) (see [14.09]).

[10] Lester and Joseph, above, note 5, 566.

[11] Opsahl, above, note 8, 61.

[12] There is conflicting jurisprudence over whether the ICCPR guarantees a 'right' of conscientious objection: see [17.19] ff.

[13] See [8.27–8.31] for commentary on the merits of the *Kindler* case.

SPRENGER v THE NETHERLANDS (395/90)

In *Sprenger*, the author claimed that Dutch law regarding unemployment benefits discriminated against her on the basis of her marital status. The HRC ultimately found no ICCPR violation in this case [23.56]. Messrs Ando, Herndl, and N'diaye appended the following separate opinion regarding the scope of article 26:

While it is clear that article 26 of the Covenant postulates an autonomous right to non-discrimination, we believe that the implementation of this right may take different forms, depending on the nature of the right to which the principle of non-discrimination is applied.

We note, firstly, that the determination whether prohibited discrimination within the meaning of article 26 has occurred depends on complex considerations, particularly in the field of economic, social and cultural rights. Social security legislation, which is intended to achieve aims of social justice, necessarily must make distinctions. While the aims of social justice vary from country to country, they must be compatible with the Covenant. Moreover, whatever distinctions are made must be based on reasonable and objective criteria. For instance, a system of progressive taxation, under which persons with higher incomes fall into a higher tax bracket and pay a greater percentage of their income for taxes, does not entail a violation of article 26 of the Covenant, since the distinction between higher and lower incomes is objective and the purpose of more equitable distribution of wealth is reasonable and compatible with the aims of the Covenant.

Surely, it is also necessary to take into account the reality that the socio-economic and cultural needs of society are constantly evolving, so that legislation—in particular in the field of social security—may well, and often does, lag behind developments. Accordingly, article 26 of the Covenant should not be interpreted as requiring absolute equality or non-discrimination in that field at all times; instead, it should be seen as a general undertaking on the part of the States parties to the Covenant to regularly review their legislation in order to ensure that it corresponds to the changing needs of society. In the field of civil and political rights, a State party is required to respect Covenant rights such as the right to a fair trial, to freedom of expression and freedom of religion, immediately from the date of entry into force of the Covenant, and to do so without discrimination. On the other hand, with regard to rights enshrined in the International Covenant on Economic, Social and Cultural Rights, it is generally understood that States parties may need time for the progressive implementation of these rights and to adapt relevant legislation in stages; moreover, constant efforts are needed to ensure that distinctions that were reasonable and objective at the time of enactment of a social security provision are not rendered unreasonable and discriminatory by the socio-economic evolution of society.

Finally, we recognize that legislative review is a complex process entailing consideration of many factors, including limited financial resources, and the potential effects of amendments on other existing legislation.

In the context of the instant case, we have taken due note of the fact that the Government of the Netherlands regularly reviews its social security legislation, and that it has recently amended several acts, including the Health Insurance Act. Such review is commendable and in keeping with the requirement, in article 2, paragraphs 1 and 2, of the Covenant, to ensure the enjoyment of Covenant rights and to adopt such legislative or other measures as may be necessary to give effect to Covenant rights.

OULAJIN and KAISS v THE NETHERLANDS (406, 426/90)

In this case, the authors complained of discrimination with regard to the allocation of child benefits. The HRC ultimately found no violation [23.55]. Messrs Herndl, Müllerson, N'diaye, and Sadi appended the following separate opinion:

It is obvious that while article 26 of the Covenant postulates an autonomous right to non-discrimination, the implementation of this right may take different forms, depending on the nature of the right to which the principle of non-discrimination is applied.

With regard to the application of article 26 of the Covenant in the field of economic and social rights, it is evident that social security legislation, which is intended to achieve aims of social justice, necessarily must make distinctions. It is for the legislature of each country, which best knows the socio-economic needs of the society concerned, to try to achieve social justice in the concrete context. Unless the distinctions made are manifestly discriminatory or arbitrary, it is not for the Committee to reevaluate the complex socio-economic data and substitute its judgment for that of the legislatures of States parties.

[23.13] J.H.W. v THE NETHERLANDS (501/92)

The complaint in this case concerned alleged sex discrimination with respect to assessment of income tax. In finding the case inadmissible, the HRC stated the following:

¶ 5.2. . . . [T]he Committee notes that the State party, in 1989, adopted measures to abolish the exemption at issue in the present communication. The Committee considers, taking into account that social security legislation and its application usually lag behind socio-economic developments in society, and that the purpose of the abrogated exemption was at its time not generally considered discriminatory, that the issue which the author raises in his communication is moot and that he has no claim under article 2 of the Optional Protocol.

[23.14] Is the *J.H.W.* reasoning consistent with *Broeks*? The decision may constitute HRC endorsement of the more conservative minority opinions in *Sprenger* and *Oulajin and Kaiss*.

However, the *Broeks* reasoning has been supported in more recent decisions such as *Johannes Vos v The Netherlands* (786/97), where married male pensioners were paid a smaller pension than married female pensioners. The HRC found a breach of article 26 entailed in the discriminatory pension laws.[14] Indeed, a violation was

---

[14] Para. 7.6. See also the HRC's recent decision in *Waldman v Canada* [23.54], concerning the allocation of educational subsidies in Ontario.

found even though the relevant provisions conformed to European Union law, which is generally seen as very progressive in the area of sex discrimination.

[23.15] The nature of the right to which the discrimination claim is attached may impact on the HRC's decision whether a distinction is reasonable and therefore permissible under the Covenant. The HRC has not found many distinctions with respect to economic, social, and cultural rights to constitute article 26 violations. This may be due to the ultimate lack of merit in most of the complaints. Alternatively, it may be that the HRC is more willing to defer to a State Party's policies when dealing with complaints of discrimination in the economic field, as is recommended by Mr Ando in a separate opinion in *Adam v The Czech Republic* (586/94) [23.44].

[23.16] Article 1 of both ICERD and CEDAW, and most other substantive articles therein, confirm that both treaties prohibit race and sex discrimination, respectively, with regard to all civil, political, economic, social, and cultural rights.[15]

Prohibited Grounds of Discrimination

[23.17] Article 3 prohibits discrimination on the grounds of sex. Articles 2(1) and 26 go further, and arguably subsume article 3. Both articles contain identical lists of prohibited grounds of discrimination: race, colour, sex, language, religion, political or other opinion, national or social origin, property, birth, or 'any other status'.

[23.18] In a separate opinion in *Vos v The Netherlands* (218/86), Messrs Aguilar Urbina and Wennergren stated the following on the meaning of 'other status':

¶ 1. Article 26 of the Covenant has been interpreted as providing protection against discrimination whenever laws differentiating among groups or categories of individuals do not correspond to objective criteria. It has also been interpreted in the sense that whenever a difference in treatment does not affect a group of people but only separate individuals, a provision cannot be deemed discriminatory as such: negative effects on one individual cannot then be considered to be discrimination within the scope of article 26.

When does a group of separate individuals constitute a distinct group linked by their common 'status'? Would members of a football club or philosophical society constitute a distinct group?

[23.19] The HRC has not issued a detailed consensus comment on the meaning of 'any other status', preferring to decide on a case-by-case basis whether a complaint raises a relevant ground of discrimination.

---

[15] See, e.g., Art. 5(d) and (e), ICERD.

[23.20] *B.D.B et al. v THE NETHERLANDS (273/89)*

The authors in this case complained of disadvantage suffered due to an administrative error.

¶ 6.6. The authors [physiotherapists] complain about the application to them of legal rules of a compulsory nature, which for unexplained reasons were allegedly not applied uniformly to some other physiotherapy practices. . . .

¶ 6.7. . . . The Committee notes that the authors have not claimed that their different treatment was attributable to them belonging to any identifiably distinct category which could have exposed them to discrimination on account of any of the grounds enumerated or 'other status' referred to in Article 26 of the Covenant. The Committee, therefore, finds this aspect of the authors' communication to be inadmissible under article 3 of the Optional Protocol.

The complainants in *B.d.B* failed to establish that they were discriminated against as members of groups united by a common 'other status'.

[23.21] *VAN OORD v THE NETHERLANDS (658/95)*

¶ 8.5. With regard to this claim, the Committee observes that it is undisputed that the criteria used in determining the authors' pension entitlements are equally applied to all former Dutch citizens now living in the U.S.A. . . . According to the authors, the fact that former Dutch citizens now living in Australia, Canada and New Zealand benefit from [higher pension] privileges, entails discrimination. The Committee observes, however, that the categories of persons being compared are distinguishable and that the privileges at issue [Dutch pensions for Dutch citizens abroad] respond to separately negotiated bilateral treaties which necessarily reflect agreements based on reciprocity. The Committee recalls its jurisprudence that a differentiation based on reasonable and objective criteria does not amount to a prohibited discrimination within the meaning of article 26.

¶ 8.6. The Committee finds therefore that the facts . . . do not raise an issue under article 26 of the Covenant. . . .

In *Van Oord*, the HRC gave a clue how 'other statuses' are determined, by indicating that one may be treated differently from another whose status is relevantly 'distinguishable'. In *Van Oord*, relevant distinctions did apparently exist between Dutch citizens resident in the USA, and Dutch citizens abroad in other States, for the purposes of assessing tax on their pensions. However, a test of 'relevant distinction' does not seem any easier to apply than the *Vos* test of belonging to a 'group'. Indeed, the relevance of a distinction would presumably vary according to the 'right' at issue. For example, whilst it may have been reasonable to distinguish between the overseas residences of Dutch expatriates for the purposes of pension taxation, it would not seem reasonable to distinguish between such persons for the purposes of determining their right to vote in Dutch elections.

[23.22] The HRC has found the following to constitute 'other statuses' for the purposes of admissibility of a complaint of violation of the Covenant's non-discrimination provisions: nationality (*Gueye v France* (196/85), *Adam v The Czech Republic* (586/94)), marital status (*Danning v The Netherlands* (180/84), *Sprenger v The Netherlands* (395/90), *Hoofdman v The Netherlands* (602/94)), place of residence within a State (*Lindgren et al. v Sweden* (298–299/88)), a distinction between 'foster' and 'natural' children (*Oulajin & Kaiss v The Nether-lands* (406, 426/90)), a difference between students at public and private schools (*Blom v Sweden* (191/85), *Lindgren et al. v Sweden* (298–299/88)), a difference between employed and unemployed persons (*Cavalcanti Araujo-Jongens v The Netherlands* (418/90)),[16] a difference between persons performing their compulsory national service in a military or in a non-military capacity (*Järvinen v Finland* (295/88), *Foin v France* (666/95)), and a distinction between households shared by close relatives and households shared by others (*Neefs v The Netherlands* (425/90)). However, of these cases, only the *Gueye* [23.45], *Adam* [23.43], and *Foin* [23.48] complaints have been upheld on the merits.

[23.23] *Toonen v Australia* (488/92) concerned an allegation of, *inter alia*, discrimination on the basis of sexual orientation.[17] The HRC found that the reference to 'sex' in Articles 2(1) and 26 is to be taken to include sexual orientation. 'Sexual orientation' however seems more properly classified as an 'other status', rather than as an aspect of one's gender. In more recent Concluding Comments,[18] the HRC has confirmed that 'sexual orientation' is a prohibited ground of discrimination for the purposes of the Covenant. The HRC noted with concern that anti-discrimination laws in Hong Kong did not protect against discrimination on the basis of age, family responsibility, or sexual preference, indicating that these three statuses attract ICCPR non-discrimination protection.[19] Disability too seems likely to be a relevant 'ground' for the purposes of the ICCPR's non-discrimination guarantees.[20]

[23.24]   *H.A.E.D.J. v THE NETHERLANDS (297/88)*

The author was a conscientious objector to military service who was performing alternative civilian service. He complained of the difference between the living allowance paid to him as a performer of alternative sevice, compared to the living allowance paid to ordinary civilians. The alleged ground of discrimination was

---

[16] However, a similar complaint was found inadmissible in *J.A.M.B.-R. v The Netherlands* (477/91) and *A.P.L. v.d.M. v The Netherlands* (478/91).

[17] See, on the merits of *Toonen*, [16.36].

[18] Concluding Comments on Austria (1998) UN doc. CCPR/C/79/Add. 103, para. 13; Concluding Comments on Zimbabwe (1998) UN doc. CCPR/C/79/Add. 89, para. 24; Concluding Comments on Poland (1999) UN doc. CCPR/C/79/Add. 110, para. 23.

[19] (1996) UN doc. CCPR/C/79/Add.57, para. 13. These criticisms were repeated after the handover of Hong Kong to the People's Republic of China in (1999) UN doc. CCPR/C/79/Add. 117, para. 15.

[20] A complaint about discrimination on the basis of disability was ruled inadmissible for failure to exhaust domestic remedies in *Cziklin v Canada* (741/97).

therefore a distinction between the author's status as a conscript (albeit one performing alternative service) and the status of ordinary civilians.

¶ 8.2. The Committee notes that the author claims that he is a victim of discrimination on the ground of 'other status' (article 26 of the Covenant *in fine*), because, as a conscientious objector to military service and during the period that he performed alternative service, he was not treated as a civilian but rather as a conscript and was thus ineligible for supplementary allowances under the General Assistance Act. The Committee observes, as it did with respect to communications Nos. 245/1987 (*R. T. Z. v the Netherlands*) and 267/1987 (*M. J. G. v the Netherlands*), that the Covenant does not preclude the institution by States parties of compulsory national service, which entails certain modest pecuniary payments. But whether that compulsory national service is performed by way of military service or by permitted alternative service, there is no entitlement to be paid as if one were still in private civilian life. The Committee observes in this connection, as it did with respect to communication No. 218/1986 (*Vos v the Netherlands*) that the scope of article 26 does not extend to differences in result of the uniform application of laws in the allocation of social security benefits. In the present case, there is no indication that the General Assistance Act is not applied equally to all citizens performing alternative service. Thus the Committee concludes that the communication is incompatible with the provisions of the Covenant and inadmissible under article 3 of the Optional Protocol.

Similarly, in *R.T.Z. v The Netherlands* (245/87) and *M.J.G. v The Netherlands* (267/87), the HRC ruled inadmissible complaints about the inability of conscripts to appeal summonses from military courts, compared to the ability of civilians to object to civilian summonses. In *Drake and Julian v New Zealand* (601/94), a complaint about distinctions between civilian and military war casualties for the purposes of pension payments was also ruled inadmissible.

[23.25] Do the above decisions indicate that 'military' as opposed to 'civilian' status is never a relevant 'other status' for the purposes of the ICCPR, even if someone is treated unreasonably solely on the basis of their military status? Consider the following case.

VUOLANNE v FINLAND (265/87)

This case largely concerned allegations under articles 7 and 9 regarding the circumstances surrounding the author's military detention.[21] In its reasoning on the merits, the HRC stated:

¶ 9.3. According to article 2, paragraph 1, 'each State party to the present Covenant undertakes to respect and to ensure to all individuals within its territory and subject to its jurisdiction the rights recognized in the present Covenant, without distinction of any kind, such as race, colour, sex, language, religion, political or other opinion, national or social origin,

---

[21] See [9.20] and [11.54].

property, birth or other status'. The all-encompassing character of the terms of this article leaves no room for distinguishing between different categories of persons, such as civilians and members of the military, to the extent of holding the Covenant to be applicable in one case but not in the other.

[23.26] It is arguable that the issue of 'grounds' should be considered as an aspect relating to the permissibility or the reasonableness of the impugned distinction.[22] The definition of 'discrimination' in General Comment 18 [23.03] lends support to this idea with its reference to '*any* grounds'. If so, the 'grounds' issue may become completely subsumed by the issue of reasonableness: an unreasonable distinction may give rise to a violation of article 26 regardless of the grounds upon which that distinction is made. 'Grounds' would remain important to the extent that they help establish or disprove reasonableness. Recent decisions indicate that this may be the strategy generally adopted by the HRC.[23]

[23.27] The HRC would probably view certain grounds of distinction as inherently more suspect and deserving of greater scrutiny than other grounds.[24] In other words, it is likely that violations are more likely to be found with regard to some grounds of distinction than others. It seems intrinsically more important to guard against discrimination on some 'grounds', such as the enumerated grounds, and 'other statuses' such as nationality, sexuality, age, or disability, than it is to protect against discrimination on other grounds such as the distinction between public and private school students. Can common characteristics be ascribed to the most important 'grounds'? Some of the most important grounds, such as one's race or colour, are immutable. It is indeed especially important that one does not suffer discrimination due to characteristics one cannot change. However, other important grounds are inherent characteristics of one's ego, such as one's religion or political opinion, or even one's 'property', if that term is equated with 'wealth' or 'class'. Perhaps the most common characteristic of an important 'ground' is that the 'ground' describes a group which has historically suffered from unjustifiable discrimination.

[23.28]   *GAUTHIER v CANADA (633/95)*

The author complained of his exclusion from the Press Gallery Association, which meant he was denied access to Parliamentary press facilities. The HRC majority found a breach of article 19 on freedom of expression.[25] A minority found a concurrent breach of article 26. Mr Solari Yrigoyen, Mrs Evatt, Ms Medina Quiroga, and Lord Colville, with whom Messrs Lallah and Bhagwati essentially agreed, stated:

---

[22] See, e.g., minority opinion in *Nahlik v Austria* (608/95).   [23] See [23.52–23.57].
[24] A. Bayefsky, 'The Principle of Equality and Non-Discrimination in International Law' (1990) 11 *Human Rights Law Journal* 1, 18–24; Lester and Joseph, above, note 5, 589–90.
[25] See [18.27].

Article 26 of the Covenant stipulates that all persons are equal before the law. Equality implies that the application of laws and regulations as well as administrative decisions by Government officials should not be arbitrary but should be based on clear coherent grounds, ensuring equality of treatment. To deny the author, who is a journalist and seeks to report on parliamentary proceedings, access to the Parliamentary press facilities without specifically identifying the reasons, was arbitrary. Furthermore, there was no procedure for review. In the circumstances, we are of the opinion that the principle of equality before the law protected by article 26 of the Covenant was violated in the author's case.

This minority opinion focuses on the 'arbitrariness' of a government action, and seems to diminish the importance of establishing a prohibited 'ground' of discrimination.[26]

On the other hand, Mr Kretzmer, in another separate opinion, stated:

I do not share [the] view [of the above minority] that a violation of article 26 has . . . been substantiated. In my mind, it is not sufficient, in order to substantiate a violation of article 26, merely to state that no reasons were given for a decision. Furthermore, it seems to me that the author's claim under article 26 is in essence a restatement of his claim under article 19. It amounts to the argument that while others were allowed access to the Press Gallery, the author was denied access. Accepting that this constitutes a violation of article 26 would seem to imply that in almost every case in which one individual's rights under other articles of the Covenant are violated, there will also be a violation of article 26. I therefore join the Committee in the view that the author's claim of a violation of article 26 has not been substantiated.

Kretzmer's opinion cautions against too wide an interpretation of article 26, lest it lose its status as a distinct Covenant guarantee.

Indirect Discrimination

[23.29] Direct discrimination involves the less favourable treatment of the complainant than that of someone else on prohibited grounds in comparable circumstances. Indirect discrimination occurs when a practice, rule, requirement, or condition is neutral on its face but impacts disproportionately upon particular groups.[27] For example, consider the following hypothetical law: only people above six feet can attend university. This law constitutes direct discrimination on the basis of height. It also constitutes indirect discrimination on the basis of sex, as women tend to be shorter than men, and, as a group, are less likely to fulfil the height criterion.

[23.30] The ICCPR does prohibit indirect discrimination. Note the HRC's definition of 'discrimination' in General Comment 18:

---

[26] Messrs Lallah and Bhagwati also found a violation of art. 26, identifying 'membership of a private organization' as the prohibited ground at issue in this case.

[27] Lester and Joseph, above, note 5, 575.

'discrimination' . . . should be understood to imply any distinction . . . based on any ground . . . which has the *purpose or effect* of nullifying and impairing the recognition enjoyment or exercise by all persons, on an equal footing, of all rights and freedoms [emphasis added].

Indirect discrimination occurs when the 'effect' of a law is to discriminate, rather than when discrimination is a law's ostensible 'purpose'.

[**23.31**] The General Comment definition also confirms that prohibited discrimination can occur unintentionally, or without malice.[28] This has been confirmed numerous times, including in *Simunek et al. v Czech Republic* (516/92):

¶ 11.7. The State party contends that there is no violation of the Covenant because the Czech and Slovak legislators had no discriminatory intent at the time of the adoption of Act 87/1991. The Committee is of the view, however, that the intent of the legislature is not alone dispositive in determining a breach of article 26 of the Covenant. A politically motivated differentiation is unlikely to be compatible with article 26. But an act which is not politically motivated may still contravene article 26 if its effects are discriminatory.

[**23.32**] The HRC's case law has not however been consistent regarding the prohibition of indirect discrimination, as is evinced in the following cases.

[**23.33**]   *SINGH BHINDER v CANADA (208/86)*

The facts are set out immediately below:

¶ 1. The author of the communication, dated 9 June 1986, is Karnel Singh Bhinder, a naturalized Canadian citizen who was born in India in 1942 and emigrated to Canada in 1974. He claims to be a victim of a violation by Canada of article 18 of the International Covenant on Civil and Political Rights. A Sikh by religion, he wears a turban in his daily life and refuses to wear safety headgear during his work. This resulted in the termination of his labour contract.

The HRC found the complaint admissible, and summed up the argument in its merits decision:

¶ 6.1. The Committee notes that in the case under consideration legislation which, on the face of it, is neutral in that it applies to all persons without distinction is said to operate in fact in a way which discriminates against persons of the Sikh religion. The author has claimed a violation of article 18 of the Covenant. The Committee has also examined the issue in relation to article 26 of the Covenant.

The decision that the case was admissible seems to confirm that indirect discrimination could violate the Covenant. Though the headgear requirement applied to all relevant labourers, it disproportionately affected Sikhs in the practice of their religion. The author, however, lost on the merits.[29]

---

[28] See also, e.g., *Broeks v The Netherlands* (172/84), para. 16.
[29] See, on the merits, [17.14].

[23.34] *VOS v THE NETHERLANDS (218/86)*

Until the death of her estranged husband, Mrs Vos was eligible to receive a disability pension. After his death, she was disqualified from receiving that pension, as she became eligible for a widow's pension. Mrs Vos claimed that these rules discriminated against her as a disabled widow, as her disability pension had been worth more than her widow's pension. The HRC majority found no violation of the ICCPR.

¶ 12. It remains for the Committee to determine whether the disadvantageous treatment complained of by the author resulted from the application of a discriminatory statute and thus violated her rights under article 26 of the Covenant. In the light of the explanations given by the State party with respect to the legislative history, the purpose and application of the General Disablement Benefits Act and the General Widows and Orphans Act . . ., the Committee is of the view that the unfavourable result complained of by Mrs. Vos follows from the application of a uniform rule to avoid overlapping in the allocation of social security benefits. This rule is based on objective and reasonable criteria, especially bearing in mind that both statutes under which Mrs. Vos qualified for benefits aim at ensuring to all persons falling thereunder subsistence level income. Thus the Committee cannot conclude that Mrs. Vos has been a victim of discrimination within the meaning of article 26 of the Covenant.

The observation that 'the scope of article 26 does not extend to difference of results in the application of common rules in the allocation of benefits' has been repeated in a number of cases.[30] Indirect discrimination occurs precisely when common rules are applied to all yet yield a discriminatory effect on a few.

Does *Vos* conform to the admissibility finding in *Singh Bhinder*? Is the reference to 'allocation of benefits' in *Vos* important in this respect? Perhaps the *Vos* rule applies only when the HRC is considering complaints with regard to unequal access to social security benefits.

[23.35] Messrs Aguilar Urbina and Wennergren delivered the following dissenting opinion in *Vos*, which highlights some of the flaws in the majority's reasoning.

¶ 2. It is self-evident that, as the State party has stressed, in any social security system it is necessary to ensure that individuals do not qualify for more than one benefit simultaneously under different social insurance laws. The State party has admitted that the rule on concurrence which gives precedence to the General Widows and Orphans Act (AWW) is not always advantageous to all widows. It might merely benefit a majority of them. Cases are conceivable in which the award of AWW benefits leads to a decrease in income after cessation of payments under the General Disablement Benefits Act (AAW); this is evidently what happened in the case of Mrs. Vos. The State party has also

---

[30] *P.P.C. v The Netherlands* (212/86), para. 6.3; *H.A.E.d.J. v The Netherlands* (297/88), para. 8.2; *Oulajin and Kaiss v The Netherlands* (406, 426/90), para. 8.2; and *A.P.L.-v.d.M. v The Netherlands* (478/91), para. 6.4.

mentioned that in most cases AWW benefits exceed AAW benefits payable to married women, and that this is attributable to the fact that most married women have worked only part-time and therefore receive only partial AAW benefit in the event of long-term disability. It follows that disabled women with full AAW benefits enjoy higher benefits than women, disabled or not, who receive full AWW benefits because of their status as widows.

¶ 3. In cases where women receive full pensions under the AAW (being disabled and having worked full-time previously), if the husband dies, they will be given the AWW pension instead. This may reduce the level of pension which their physical needs as disabled persons require and which the General Disablement Benefits Act had recognized.

¶ 4. Article 32 of AAW provides in its subsection 1 (b) that the employment disability benefit will be withdrawn when a woman to whom this benefit has been granted becomes entitled to a widow's pension or a temporary widow's benefit pursuant to the AWW. The State party contends that the legislature had to decide whether claimants who were entitled to benefits under both the AAW and the AWW should receive benefits under the one or the other. This is conceivable, but it is not justifiable that this necessarily should be solved by the introduction of a clause which does not allow for a modicum of flexibility in its implementation. An exception should, in our opinion, be made with regard to women who enjoy full AAW benefits, if such benefits exceed full AWW benefits. By failing to make such an exception the legislature has created a situation in which disabled women with full AAW benefits who become widows can no longer be treated on a par with other disabled women who enjoy full AAW benefits. The case cannot be considered as affecting only Mrs. Vos, but rather an indeterminate group of persons who fall in the category of disabled women entitled to full disability pensions. Moreover, the intention of the legislator to grant maximum protection to those in need would be violated every time the law is applied in the strict formal sense as it has been applied in Mrs. Vos's case. The increasing number of cases such as this one can be inferred from the assertion made by the State party that it has seen the need to change the legislation since the early 1980s.

¶ 5. A differentiation with regard to full AAW benefits among disabled women on the sole ground of marital status as a widow cannot be said to be based on reasonable and objective criteria. It therefore constitutes prohibited discrimination within the meaning of article 26. We note that a review of AWW is under consideration and hope that the discriminatory elements will be eliminated and compensation given to those who have been the victims of unequal treatment.

This interpretation of the facts illustrates how differing analyses of the facts can yield differing grounds of discrimination. Here, the dissenters compared Mrs Vos, a disabled widowed woman, to a disabled unwidowed woman. Such a comparison reveals a relevant discriminatory ground of 'marital status', specifically 'widowhood'. A different comparator would yield a different ground of discrimination. For example, if they had compared Mrs Vos's situation to that of a disabled widowed man, they could also have found that the law discriminated on the basis of sex.

[23.26] *CAVALCANTI ARAUJO-JONGEN v THE NETHERLANDS (418/90)*

The HRC's somewhat inconsistent approach to the issue of indirect discrimination is again evinced in the *Cavalcanti* case. The facts were as follows. Under Dutch law, the author, as an unemployed married woman, was refused unemployment benefit between August 1983 and April 1984, in circumstances in which an unemployed married man would have received the benefit, due to the 'breadwinner criterion' in Dutch legislation at the time. Indeed, this law had been successfully challenged before the HRC in the *Broeks* case [23.08].

In 1985, the 'breadwinner' distinction was removed from the relevant legislation, with retrospective effect to 23 December 1984. This date was chosen in order to comply with a relevant European Community Directive. This was of no help to Mrs Cavalcanti.

¶ 3.5. The author claims she suffered damage as a result of the application of the discriminatory provisions in WWV, in that WWV benefits were refused to her for the period of 1 August 1983 to 24 April 1984. She contends that these benefits should be granted to women equally as to men as of 11 March 1979 (the date the Covenant entered into force for the Netherlands), in her case as of 1 August 1983, notwithstanding measures adopted by the Government to grant married women WWV benefits equally after 23 December 1984.

In 1991, whilst the complaint was before the HRC, further amending legislation was enacted.

¶ 5.2. The State party submits that article 13, paragraph 1, subsection 1, WWV, on which the rejection of the unemployment benefit of the author was based, was abrogated by law of 24 April 1985. In this law, however, it was laid down that the law which was in force to that date—including the controversial article 13, paragraph 1, subsection 1—remained applicable in respect of married women who had become unemployed before 23 December 1984. As these transitionary provisions were much criticized, they were abolished by Act of 6 June 1991. As a result, women who had been ineligible in the past to claim WWV benefits because of the breadwinner criterion, can claim these benefits retroactively, provided they satisfy the other requirements of the Act. One of the other requirements is that the applicant be unemployed on the date of application.

¶ 5.3. The State party therefore contends that, if the author had been unemployed on the date of application for the WWV benefit, she would be eligible to retroactive benefits on the basis of her unemployed status as from 1 February 1983. However, since the author had found other employment as of April 1984, she could not claim retroactive benefits under the WWV. The State party emphasizes that since the amendment of the law on 6 June 1991 the obstacle to the author's eligibility for a benefit is not the breadwinner criterion, but her failure to satisfy the other requirements under the law that apply to all, men and women alike.

¶ 5.4. The State party submits that, by amending the law in this respect, it has complied with the principle of equality before the law as laid down in article 26 of the Covenant.

Counsel for Mrs Cavalcanti responded:

¶ 6.2. Counsel submits that, under the amended law, it is still not possible for the author, who has found new employment, to claim the benefits she was denied before. In this connection, she points out that the author failed to apply for a benefit during the period of her unemployment because the law at that time did not grant her any right to a benefit under the WWV. The author applied for a benefit after the breadwinner-requirement for women was dropped as from 23 December 1984, but had by then found new employment. She therefore argues that the discriminatory effect of the said provision of WWV is not abolished for her, but still continues.

The HRC delivered its merits decision in favour of the State Party:

¶ 7.4. The Committee observes that, even if the law in force in 1983 was not consistent with the requirements of article 26 of the Covenant, that deficiency was corrected upon the retroactive amendment of the law on 6 June 1991. The Committee notes that the author argues that the amended law still indirectly discriminates against her, because it requires applicants to be unemployed at the time of application and that this requirement effectively bars her from retroactive access to benefits. The Committee finds that the requirement of being unemployed at the time of application for benefits is, as such, reasonable and objective, in view of the purposes of the legislation in question, namely to provide assistance to persons who are unemployed. The Committee therefore concludes that the facts before it do not reveal a violation of article 26 of the Covenant.

The HRC found the distinction here based on 'present employment' to be 'reasonable and objective' and therefore permissible under the Covenant. However, the HRC did not consider the 'reasonableness' of any latent gender-based distinctions in the law. Did the law not indirectly discriminate against married women? In order to claim retrospective unemployment benefit for a period of time before 23 December 1984, they had to be presently unemployed. No such restriction applied to married men.[31]

Perhaps this complaint evinces direct discrimination against married women. One could argue that the 'breadwinner' criterion, which had directly discriminated against married women, had merely been replaced by the criterion of 'present employment', which again affected only married women. The only difference was that the 'breadwinner' legislation *expressly* applied only to women. This analysis indicates that *Cavalcanti* is not consistent with the *Broeks* decision.

[23.37] The HRC's reasoning in *Cavalcanti* is supported by its decisions in *Vos v The Netherlands* (218/86) [23.34], *J.A.M.B.-R. v The Netherlands* (477/91), and *A.P.L.-v.d.M. v The Netherlands* (478/91). In these cases, 'uniform application' of social security laws resulted in female complainants receiving lesser social security benefits than men in the same position. Perhaps the HRC should have focused

---

[31] See below for a discussion of the relevance and justification for applying the criterion of 'present employment' [23.51].

more on the discriminatory effect of the relevant Dutch legislation, rather than the formally neutral application of the laws.[32]

[23.38]   *BALLANTYNE et al. v CANADA (359, 385/89)*

The authors complained of a Quebec law prohibiting commercial signage in a language other than French. The HRC found no breach of article 26:[33]

¶ 11.5. The authors have claimed a violation of their right, under article 26, to equality before the law; the Government of Quebec has contended that Sections 1 and 6 of Bill 178 are general measures applicable to all those engaged in trade, regardless of their language. The Committee notes that Sections 1 and 6 of Bill 178 operate to prohibit the use of commercial advertising outdoors in other than the French language. This prohibition applies to French speakers as well as English speakers, so that a French speaking person wishing to advertise in English, in order to reach those of his or her clientele who are English speaking, may not do so. Accordingly, the Committee finds that the authors have not been discriminated against on the ground of their language, and concludes that there has been no violation of article 26 of the Covenant.

Is the impugned law in *Ballantyne* a possible example of indirect discrimination? All of the authors were English speakers who argued that their clientele were predominantly English speakers. What if the evidence had shown that English-speaking traders had far more English customers than French-speaking traders?

Perhaps the HRC was mistaken in its analysis. The impugned law in *Ballantyne* possibly constituted direct discrimination on the basis of language, due to its inherent partiality. Consider the following hypothetical law. State X forbids all speech in a language other than German. All persons are therefore forbidden from speaking other languages, including German speakers. Such a law nevertheless is plainly discriminatory, but is it directly or indirectly discriminatory?

[23.39] The ICERD Committee has confirmed that ICERD prohibits indirect discrimination on the basis of race in General Recommendation 14 (1993):

¶ 2. . . . In seeking to determine whether an action has an effect contrary to the Convention, it will look to see whether that action has an unjustifiable disparate impact upon a group distinguished by race, colour, descent, or national or ethnic origin.

For example, in Concluding Comments on Australia in 2000, the ICERD Committee stated the following:[34]

¶ 16. The Committee expresses its concern about the minimum mandatory sentencing schemes with regard to minor property offences enacted in Western Australia and in

---

[32] Lester and Joseph, above, note 5, 576.
[33] See [18.38].
[34] (2000) UN doc. CERD/C/56/Misc. 42/Rev.3. Indirect discrimination is also prohibited under CEDAW. See [23.79] ff.

particular in the Northern Territory. The mandatory sentencing schemes appear to target offences that are committed disproportionately by indigenous Australians, especially in the case of juveniles, leading to a racially discriminatory impact on their rate of incarceration. The Committee seriously questions the compatibility of these laws with the State party's obligations under the Convention. . . .

The mandatory sentencing laws did not directly target aboriginal offenders. However, the laws contravened the Convention due to their discriminatory effect on aborigines.

Permissible Differentiation

[23.40] As confirmed in paragraph 13 of General Comment 18 [23.03], 'reasonable and objective' distinctions do not constitute prohibited discrimination for the purposes of the ICCPR. Hence, proportionate measures designed to achieve a legitimate objective are permissible.[35]

[23.41] The 'reasonable and objective' test is potentially very subjective. The HRC has proceeded on a case-by-case basis. Its jurisprudence in this respect cannot easily be knitted together in order to predict accurately future applications of the test. The following case extracts demonstrate examples of the test in action.

[23.42] *AUMEERUDDY-CZIFFRA et al. v MAURITIUS (35/78)*

The authors complained that Mauritian immigration laws discriminated against Mauritian women, as alien wives were granted automatic residence rights in Mauritius, whereas alien husbands were not.[36]

¶ 9.2(b) 2(ii) 3. [T]he Covenant must lead to the result that the protection of a family cannot vary with the sex of the one or the other spouse. Though it might be justified for Mauritius to restrict the access of aliens to their territory and to expel them therefrom for security reasons, the Committee is of the view that the legislation which only subjects foreign spouses of Mauritian women to those restrictions, but not foreign spouses of Mauritian men, is discriminatory with respect to Mauritian women and cannot be justified by security requirements.

¶ 9.2(b) 2(ii) 4. The Committee therefore finds that there is also a violation of articles 2 (1), 3 and 26 of the Covenant in conjunction with the right of the three married co-authors under article 23 (1).

[23.43]   *ADAM v THE CZECH REPUBLIC (586/94)*

The facts are as follows:

---

[35] Lester and Joseph, above, note 5, 585–6.   [36] See also [16.22] and [20.13].

¶ 2.1. The author's father, Vlatislav Adam, was a Czech citizen, whose property and business were confiscated by the Czechoslovak Government in 1949. Mr. Adam fled the country and eventually moved to Australia, where his three sons, including the author of the communication, were born. In 1985, Vlatislav Adam died and, in his last will and testament, left his Czech property to his sons. Since then, the sons have been trying in vain to have their property returned to them.

¶ 2.2. In 1991, the Czech and Slovak Republic enacted a law, rehabilitating Czech citizens who had left the country under communist pressure and providing for restitution of their property or compensation for the loss thereof. On 6 December 1991, the author and his brothers, through Czech solicitors, submitted a claim for restitution of their property. Their claim was rejected on the grounds that they did not fulfil the then applicable dual requirement of Act 87/91 that applicants have Czech citizenship and be permanent residents in the Czech Republic.

¶ 3. The author claims that the application of the provision of the law, that property be returned or its loss be compensated only when claimants are Czech citizens, makes him and his brothers victims of discrimination under article 26 of the Covenant.

The State Party submitted its defence of the impugned law:

¶ 9.1. The State party also endeavours to explain the broader political and legal circumstances of the case and contends that the author's presentation of the facts is misleading. After the democratization process begun in November 1989, the Czech and Slovak Republic and subsequently the Czech Republic have made a considerable effort to remove some of the property injustices caused by the communist regime. The endeavour to return property as stipulated in the Rehabilitation Act was in part a voluntary and moral act of the Government and not a duty or legal obligation. 'It is also necessary to point out the fact that it was not possible and, with regard to the protection of the justified interests of the citizens of the present Czech Republic, even undesirable, to remove all injuries caused by the past regime over a period of forty years.'

¶ 9.2. The precondition of citizenship for restitution or compensation should not be interpreted as a violation of the prohibition of discrimination pursuant to article 26 of the Covenant. . . .

The HRC decided in favour of Mr Adam:

¶ 12.5. In examining whether the conditions for restitution or compensation are compatible with the Covenant, the Committee must consider all relevant factors, including the original entitlement of the author's father to the property in question and the nature of the confiscation. The State party itself has acknowledged that the confiscations under the Communist governments were injurious and this is the reason why specific legislation was enacted to provide for a form of restitution. The Committee observes that such legislation must not discriminate among the victims of the prior confiscations, since all victims are entitled to redress without arbitrary distinctions. Bearing in mind that the author's original entitlement to his property by virtue of inheritance was not predicated on citizenship, the Committee finds that the condition of citizenship in Act 87/1991 is unreasonable.

¶ 12.6. In this context the Committee recalls its rationale in its Views on communication

No. 516/1992 (*Simunek et al. v The Czech Republic*), in which it considered that the authors in that case and many others in analogous situation had left Czechoslovakia because of their political opinions and had sought refuge from political persecution in other countries, where they eventually established permanent residence and obtained a new citizenship. Taking into account that the State party itself is responsible for the departure of the author's parents in 1949, it would be incompatible with the Covenant to require him and his brothers to obtain Czech citizenship as a prerequisite for the restitution of their property or, in the alternative, for the payment of appropriate compensation.

The *Adam* majority decision essentially upheld the earlier decision of *Simunek v The Czech Republic* (516/92).

[23.44] Mr Nisuke Ando submitted a separate opinion in *Adam*:

Considering the Human Rights Committee's Views on Communication No. 516/1992 [*Simunek v Czech Republic*], I do not oppose the adoption by the Committee of the Views in the instant case. However, I would like to point to the following:

First, under current rules of general international law, States are free to choose their economic system. As a matter of fact, when the United Nations adopted the International Covenant on Civil and Political Rights in 1966, the then Socialist States were managing planned economies under which private ownership was largely restricted or prohibited in principle. Even nowadays not a few States parties to the Covenant, including those adopting market-oriented economies, restrict or prohibit foreigners from private ownership of immovable properties in their territories.

Second, consequently, it is not impossible for a State party to limit the ownership of immovable properties in its territory to its nationals or citizens, thereby precluding their wives or children of different nationality or citizenship from inheriting or succeeding to those properties. Such inheritance or succession is regulated by rules of private international law of the States concerned, and I am not aware of any universally recognized 'absolute right of inheritance or of succession to private property'.

Third, while the International Covenant on Civil and Political Rights enshrines the principle of non discrimination and equality before the law, it does not prohibit 'legitimate distinctions' based on objective and reasonable criteria. Neither the Covenant defines or protects economic rights as such. This means that the Human Rights Committee should exercise utmost caution in dealing with questions of discrimination in the economic field. For example, restrictions or prohibitions of certain economic rights, including the right of inheritance or succession, which are based on nationality or citizenship, may well be justified as legitimate distinctions.

Despite his obvious misgivings, Ando 'did not oppose' the majority decision. This was apparently due to the existence of the *Simunek* precedent.

[23.45] *GUEYE et al. v FRANCE (196/85)*

The facts are evident from the extracts below:

¶ 9.2. The authors are retired soldiers of Senegalese nationality who served in the French Army prior to the independence of Senegal in 1960. Pursuant to the Code of Military

Pensions of 1951, retired members of the French Army, whether French or Senegalese, were treated equally. Pension rights of Senegalese soldiers were the same as those of French soldiers until a new law, enacted in December 1974, provided for different treatment of the Senegalese. Law No. 79/1102 of 21 December 1979 further extended to the nationals of four States formerly belonging to the French Union, including Senegal, the regime referred to as 'crystallization' of military pensions that had already applied since 1 January 1961 to the nationals of other States concerned. . . .

The effect of the 'crystallization' legislation was to freeze Senegalese veterans' pensions as at the rate paid on 1 January 1975. No such freeze applied to pensions for French veterans.

¶ 9.3. The main question before the Committee is whether the authors are victims of discrimination within the meaning of article 26 of the Covenant or whether the differences in pension treatment of former members of the French Army, based on whether they are French nationals or not, should be deemed compatible with the Covenant. In determining this question, the Committee has taken into account the following considerations.

¶ 9.4. The Committee has noted the authors' claim that they have been discriminated against on racial grounds, that is, one of the grounds specifically enumerated in article 26. It finds that there is no evidence to support the allegation that the State party has engaged in racially discriminatory practices vis-à-vis the authors. It remains, however, to be determined whether the situation encountered by the authors falls within the purview of article 26. The Committee recalls that the authors are not generally subject to French jurisdiction, except that they rely on French legislation in relation to the amount of their pension rights. It notes that nationality as such does not figure among the prohibited grounds of discrimination listed in article 26, and that the Covenant does not protect the right to a pension, as such. Under article 26, discrimination in the equal protection of the law is prohibited on any grounds such as race, colour, sex, language, religion, political or other opinion, national or social origin, property, birth or other status. There has been a differentiation by reference to nationality acquired upon independence. In the Committee's opinion, this falls within the reference to 'other status' in the second sentence of article 26. The Committee takes into account, as it did in communication No. 182/1984 [*Zwaan-de-Vries v The Netherlands*], that 'the right to equality before the law and to equal protection of the law without any discrimination does not make all differences of treatment discriminatory. A differentiation based on reasonable and objective criteria does not amount to prohibited discrimination within the meaning of article 26'.

¶ 9.5. In determining whether the treatment of the authors is based on reasonable and objective criteria, the Committee notes that it was not the question of nationality which determined the granting of pensions to the authors but the services rendered by them in the past. They had served in the French Armed Forces under the same conditions as French citizens; for 14 years subsequent to the independence of Senegal they were treated in the same way as their French counterparts for the purpose of pension rights, although their nationality was not French but Senegalese. A subsequent change in nationality cannot by itself be considered as sufficient justification for different treatment, since the basis for the grant of the pension was the same service which both they and the soldiers who remained French had provided. Nor can differences in the economic, financial and social conditions as between France and Senegal be invoked as a legitimate justification. If one compared the case of retired soldiers of Senegalese nationality living in Senegal with that of retired soldiers of French nationality in Senegal, it would appear that they enjoy the same economic and social conditions. Yet, their treatment for the purpose of pension entitlements would differ. Finally, the fact that the State party claims that it can no longer carry out checks of identity and family situation, so as to prevent abuses in the administration of pension schemes cannot justify a difference in treatment. In the Committee's opinion, mere administrative inconvenience or the possibility of some abuse of pension rights cannot be invoked to justify unequal treatment. The Committee concludes that the difference in treatment of the authors is not based on reasonable and objective criteria and constitutes discrimination prohibited by the Covenant.

[23.46] The Dutch legislative scheme in *Vos* [23.34] was designed to prevent persons from drawing two pensions. A blanket rule disqualifying widows from receiving a disability pension was undoubtedly administratively convenient. However, the *Vos* scheme would have been fairer if an individual was refused access to the pension which, in his/her particular circumstances, was worth the least amount of money, even though this would have been a more difficult scheme to administer. As the *Vos* decision appears justifiable only on the basis of administrative convenience, it is not consistent with the decision in *Gueye*. The *Vos* and *Gueye* decisions were made within four days of each other.

[23.47]   *JÄRVINEN v FINLAND (295/88)*

Under new Finnish legislation, conscientious objectors to military service were required to perform alternative civilian service for sixteen months, whereas those who performed military service were required to serve for only eight months. As a conscientious objector to military service, Järvinen argued that this law constituted discrimination on the basis of philosophical opinion.

The rationale for the new law was as follows:

¶ 2.2. . . . 'As the convictions of conscripts applying for civilian service will no longer be examined, the existence of these convictions should be ascertained in a different manner so as not to let the new procedure encourage conscripts to seek an exemption from armed service purely for reasons of personal benefit or convenience. Accordingly, an adequate prolongation of the term of such service has been deemed the most appropriate indicator of a conscript's convictions'.

The HRC favoured the State Party on the merits:

¶ 6.4. In determining whether the prolongation of the term for alternative service from twelve to sixteen months by Act No. 647/85, which was applied to Mr. Järvinen, was based on reasonable and objective criteria, the Committee has considered in particular the *ratio legis* of the Act (see para. 2.2 above) and has found that the new arrangements were designed to facilitate the administration of alternative service. The legislation was based on practical considerations and had no discriminatory purpose.

¶ 6.5. The Committee is, however, aware that the impact of the legislative differentiation works to the detriment of genuine conscientious objectors, whose philosophy will necessarily require them to accept civilian service. At the same time, the new arrangements were not merely for the convenience of the State alone. They removed from conscientious objectors the often difficult task of convincing the examination board of the genuineness of their beliefs, and they allowed a broader range of individuals potentially to opt for the possibility of alternative service.

¶ 6.6. In all the circumstances, the extended length of alternative service is neither unreasonable nor punitive.

In a dissenting opinion in the latter case, Messrs Aguilar Urbina and Pocar stated the following:

The ratio of the law is rather to replace the earlier method of testing the sincerity of an applicant's conscientious objection with a procedure based on administrative convenience, whereby the longer duration of the civilian service results in a sanction against conscientious objectors. Such longer duration constitutes in our view a difference of treatment incompatible with the prohibition of discrimination on grounds of opinion enshrined in article 26 of the Covenant.

Are the *Gueye* and *Järvinen* decisions consistent? Both of the challenged laws were apparently passed to facilitate administrative convenience.[37] However, the *Järvinen* law was found to be valid despite the assertion in *Gueye* at paragraph 9.5 that 'mere administrative inconvenience . . . cannot be invoked to justify unequal treatment'. Perhaps it is important that the victims of discrimination in *Järvinen* gained some advantage from the law (i.e. they no longer had to prove their convictions), whereas Gueye and the other Senegalese veterans received no advantage from the impugned French law. In any case, the HRC appears to depart from its reasoning in *Järvinen* with the following decision.

[23.48] *FOIN v FRANCE (666/95)*

Foin alleged that he was being discriminated against on the basis of his opinions and conscience for the following reasons:

¶ 3.1. According to the author, article 116 (6) of the National Service Code (in its version of July 1983 prescribing a period of 24 months for civilian service) violates articles 18, 19 and 26, *juncto* article 8, of the Covenant in that it doubles the duration of alternative services for conscientious objectors in comparison with military service.

The State Party submitted the following defence of its impugned laws:

¶ 8.3. . . . The State party denies that the length [of alternative service] has a punitive or discriminatory character. It is said to be the only way to verify the seriousness of the objections, since the objections were no longer tested by the administration. After having

---

[37] Bayefsky, above, note 24, criticizes the *Vos* decision at 15.

fulfilled their service, conscientious objectors have the same rights as those who have finished civil national service. . . .

¶ 8.8. In this context, the State party also notes that the conditions of the alternative civil service were less onerous than that of military service. The conscientious objectors had a wide choice of posts. They could also propose their own employer and could do their service within their professional interest. They also received a higher payment than those serving in the armed forces. In this context, the State party rejects counsel's claim that the persons performing international cooperation service received privileged treatment vis à vis conscientious objectors, and submits that those performing international cooperation service did so in often very difficult situations in a foreign country, whereas the conscientious objectors performed their service in France.

¶ 8.9. The State party concludes that the length of service for the author of the present communication had no discriminatory character compared with other forms of civil service or military service. The differences that existed in the length of the service were reasonable and reflected objective differences between the types of service. Moreover, the State party submits that in most European countries the time of service for conscientious objectors is longer than military service.

The HRC found in favour of the author in the following terms:

¶ 10.3. The issue before the Committee is whether the specific conditions under which alternative service had to be performed by the author constitute a violation of the Covenant. The Committee observes that under article 8 of the Covenant, States parties may require service of a military character and, in case of conscientious objection, alternative national service, provided that such service is not discriminatory. The author has claimed that the requirement, under French law, of a length of 24 months for national alternative service, rather than 12 months for military service, is discriminatory and violates the principle of equality before the law and equal protection of the law set forth in article 26 of the Covenant. The Committee reiterates its position that article 26 does not prohibit all differences of treatment. Any differentiation, as the Committee has had the opportunity to state repeatedly, must however be based on reasonable and objective criteria. In this context, the Committee recognizes that the law and practice may establish differences between military and national alternative service and that such differences may, in a particular case, justify a longer period of service, provided that the differentiation is based on reasonable and objective criteria, such as the nature of the specific service concerned or the need for a special training in order to accomplish that service. In the present case, however, the reasons forwarded by the State party do not refer to such criteria or refer to criteria in general terms without specific reference to the author's case, and are rather based on the argument that doubling the length of service was the only way to test the sincerity of an individual's convictions. In the Committee's view, such argument does not satisfy the requirement that the difference in treatment involved in the present case was based on reasonable and objective criteria. In the circumstances, the Committee finds that a violation of article 26 occurred, since the author was discriminated against on the basis of his conviction of conscience.

The decision of the majority appears to overturn the *Järvinen* decision, though this departure from previous jurisprudence is not explicitly recognized.

[23.49] Messrs Ando, Klein, and Kretzmer submitted the following dissenting opinion in *Foin*:

¶ 3. As the exemption from military service may be restricted to conscientious objectors, it would also seem obvious that a State party may adopt reasonable mechanisms for distinguishing between those who wish to avoid military service on grounds of conscience, and those who wish to do so for other, unacceptable, reasons. One such mechanism may be establishment of a decision-making body, which examines applications for exemption from military service and decides whether the application for exemption on grounds of conscience is genuine. Such decision-making bodies are highly problematical, as they may involve intrusion into matters of privacy and conscience. It would therefore seem perfectly reasonable for a State party to adopt an alternative mechanism, such as demanding somewhat longer service from those who apply for exemption. (See the Committee's Views in Communication No. 295/1988, *Järvinen v Finland*). The object of such an approach is to reduce the chance that the conscientious objection exemption will be exploited for reasons of convenience. However, even if such an approach is adopted the extra service demanded of conscientious objectors should not be punitive. It should not create a situation in which a real conscientious objector may be forced to forego his or her objection.

¶ 4. In the present case the military service was 12 months, while the service demanded of conscientious objectors was 24 months. Had the only reason advanced by the State party for the extra service been the selection mechanism, we would have tended to hold that the extra time was excessive and could be regarded as punitive. However, in order to assess whether the differentiation in treatment between the author and those who served in the military was based on reasonable and objective criteria all the relevant facts have to be taken into account. The Committee has neglected to do this.

¶ 5. The State party has argued that the conditions of alternative service differ from the conditions of military service (see paragraph 8.8 of the Committee's Views). While soldiers were assigned to positions without any choice, the conscientious objectors had a wide choice of posts. They could propose their own employers and could do service within their own professional fields. Furthermore, they received higher remuneration than people servicing in the armed forces. To this should be added that military service, by its very essence, carries with it burdens that are not imposed on those doing alternative service, such as military discipline, day and night, and the risks of being injured or even killed during military manoeuvres or military action. The author has not refuted the arguments relating to the differences between military service and alternative service. . . .

¶ 6. In light of all the circumstances of this case, the argument that the difference of twelve months between military service and the service required of conscientious objectors amounts to discrimination is unconvincing. The differentiation between those serving in the military and conscientious objectors was based on reasonable and objective criteria and does not amount to discrimination. We were therefore unable to join the Committee in finding a violation of article 26 of the Covenant in the present case.

[23.50] In *Broeks v The Netherlands* (172/84) [23.08], the HRC rejected arguments that social security payments should differ between men and women on the sexist assumption that men are the 'breadwinners'. 'Breadwinner' legislation was also held to breach article 26 in *Zwaan-de-Vries v The Netherlands* (182/84), a case virtually identical to *Broeks*, and *Pauger v Austria* (415/90). In the latter case, the 'breadwinner' assumption meant that widowed men were treated worse than widowed women under Dutch survivor benefit legislation. This was held to constitute a breach of article 26.[38] Therefore, outmoded assumptions about the financial roles of men and women do not appear to justify *prima facie* sexist distinctions, at least in Western States like the Netherlands. It is possible that the breadwinner distinction is justifiable in a State where women do not generally participate in the paid workforce.

[23.51] Most article 26 cases have involved allegations of discrimination with regard to social security payments. One may speculate that the common reason for the making of legislative distinctions with regard to social security is to save money. The HRC paid scant regard to arguments based on budgetary constraints *per se* in *Broeks* [23.08], and, latterly, *Johannes Vos v The Netherlands* (786/97) [23.14] and *Waldman v Canada* (694/96) [23.54]. However, the impugned distinction in the legislation in the *Cavalcanti* case [23.36] may perhaps be justified only on the basis of pure budgetary constraints. Recapping, the HRC found a distinction between employed and unemployed persons, regarding eligibility for retroactive unemployment benefits for periods of past unemployment, to be reasonable and objective. Why is one's present employment status relevant in determining eligibility for unemployment benefits for a period of past unemployment, especially where the unemployment benefit had originally been refused for sexually discriminatory reasons?

[23.52] As foreshadowed above [23.26], some decisions regarding the reasonableness of a distinction have been linked to the alleged ground of discrimination. This trend is evident in the following cases.[39]

[23.53]   *BLOM v SWEDEN (191/85)*

The facts are evident from the HRC's merits decision:[40]

¶ 10.2. The main issue before the Committee is whether the author of the communication is a victim of a violation of article 26 of the Covenant because of the alleged incompatibility of the Swedish regulations on education allowances with that provision. In deciding whether or not the State party violated article 26 by refusing to grant the author, as a pupil

---

[38] The same author successfully claimed that the State Party had failed adequately to remedy its violation of his rights, and had in fact persisted in similar discrimination, in *Pauger v Austria* (716/96).

[39] See also *Neefs v The Netherlands* (425/90), *Somers v Hungary* (566/93), *Lindgren et al. v Sweden* (298–299/88), para. 10.4; *Debreczeny v The Netherlands* (500/92), para. 9.4; *Drake and Julian v New Zealand* (601/94), para. 8.5, *García Pons v Spain* (454/91), para. 9.5. See also Bayefsky, above, note 24, 18–24.

[40] See also *Lindgren et al. v Sweden* (298–299/88), para. 10.3.

of a private school, an education allowance for the school year 1981/82, whereas pupils of public schools were entitled to education allowances for that period, the Committee bases its findings on the following observations.

¶ 10.3. The State party's educational system provides for both private and public education. The State party cannot be deemed to act in a discriminatory fashion if it does not provide the same level of subsidy for the two types of establishment, when the private system is not subject to State supervision. . . .

[23.54] *WALDMAN v CANADA (694/96)*

Waldman's complaint concerned differing educational subsidies for schools of differing religious faiths. He described his complaint as follows:

¶ 1.2. The author is a father of two school-age children and a member of the Jewish faith who enrols his children in a private Jewish day school. In the province of Ontario Roman Catholic schools are the only non-secular schools receiving full and direct public funding. Other religious schools must fund through private sources, including the charging of tuition fees. . . .

The author detailed the relevant history of school funding in Ontario:

¶ 2.1. The Ontario public school system offers free education to all Ontario residents without discrimination on the basis of religion or on any other ground. Public schools may not engage in any religious indoctrination. Individuals enjoy the freedom to establish private schools and to send their children to these schools instead of the public schools. The only statutory requirement for opening a private school in Ontario is the submission of a 'notice of intention to operate a private school'. Ontario private schools are neither licensed nor do they require any prior Government approval. As of 30 September 1989, there were 64,699 students attending 494 private schools in Ontario. Enrolment in private schools represents 3.3 percent of the total day school enrolment in Ontario.

¶ 2.2. The province of Ontario's system of separate school funding originates with provisions in Canada's 1867 constitution. In 1867 Catholics represented 17% of the population of Ontario, while Protestants represented 82%. All other religions combined represented 0.2% of the population. At the time of Confederation it was a matter of concern that the new province of Ontario would be controlled by a Protestant majority that might exercise its power over education to take away the rights of its Roman Catholic minority. The solution was to guarantee their rights to denominational education, and to define those rights by referring to the state of the law at the time of Confederation.

¶ 2.3. As a consequence, the 1867 Canadian constitution contains explicit guarantees of denominational school rights in section 93. Section 93 of the Constitution Act, 1867 grants each province in Canada exclusive jurisdiction to enact laws regarding education, limited only by the denominational school rights granted in 1867. In Ontario, the section 93 power is exercised through the Education Act. Under the Education Act every separate school is entitled to full public funding. Separate schools are defined as Roman Catholic schools. The Education Act states: '1. (1) "separate school board" means a board that operates a school board for Roman Catholics; . . . 122. (1) Every separate school shall share in the legislative grants in like manner as a public school'. As a result, Roman Catholic schools are the only religious schools entitled to the same public funding as the public secular schools.

¶ 2.4. The Roman Catholic separate school system is not a private school system. Like the public school system it is funded through a publicly accountable, democratically elected board of education. Separate School Boards are elected by Roman Catholic ratepayers, and these school boards have the right to manage the denominational aspects of the separate schools. Unlike private schools, Roman Catholic separate schools are subject to all Ministry guidelines and regulations. Neither s.93 of the Constitution Act 1867 nor the Education Act provide for public funding to Roman Catholic private/independent schools. Ten private/independent Roman Catholic schools operate in Ontario and these schools receive no direct public financial support. . . .

¶ 3.1. The author contends that the legislative grant of power to fund Roman Catholic schools authorized by section 93 of the Constitution Act of Canada 1867, and carried out under sections 122 and 128 of the Education Act (Ontario) violates Article 26 of the Covenant. The author states that these provisions create a distinction or preference which is based on religion and which has the effect of impairing the enjoyment or exercise by all persons, on an equal footing, of their religious rights and freedoms. He argues that the conferral of a benefit on a single religious group cannot be sustained. When a right to publicly financed religious education is recognized by a State party, no differentiation should be made among individuals on the basis of the nature of their particular beliefs. The author maintains that the provision of full funding exclusively to Roman Catholic schools cannot be considered reasonable. The historical rationale for the Ontario government's discriminatory funding practice, that of protection of Roman Catholic minority rights from the Protestant majority, has now disappeared, and if anything has been transferred to other minority religious communities in Ontario. A 1991 census is quoted as indicating that 44% of the population is Protestant, 36% is Catholic, and 8% have other religious affiliations. It is also unreasonable in view of the fact that other Canadian provinces and territories do not discriminate on the basis of religion in allocating education funding.[41]

The State Party defended the impugned Ontario laws as follows:

¶ 4.3.4. Apart from its obligations under the Constitution Act 1867, the State party provides no direct funding to religious schools. In such circumstances, the State party argues that it is not discriminatory to refuse funding for religious schools. In making its decision, the State party seeks to achieve the very values advanced by article 26, the creation of a tolerant society where there is respect and equality for all religious beliefs. The State party argues that it would defeat the purposes of article 26 itself if the Committee was to hold that because of the provisions in the Constitution Act 1867 requiring the funding of Roman Catholic schools, the State party now must fund all private religious schools, thus undermining its very ability to create and promote a tolerant society that truly protects religious freedom, when in the absence of the 1867 constitutional provision, it would have no obligation under the Covenant to fund any religious schools at all. . . .

---

[41] Different constitutional arrangements apply in Quebec and Newfoundland.

¶ 4.4.5. The State party [further argues] that if the province of Ontario were required to fund private religious schools, this would have a detrimental impact on the public schools, and hence the fostering of a tolerant, multicultural, non-discriminatory society in the province, thus undermining the fundamental rights and freedoms of others. According to the State party it has struck the appropriate balance by funding a public school system where members of all groups can learn together while retaining the freedom of parents to send children to private religious schools, at their own expense, if they so desire.

The State's arguments above do not respond directly to the author's complaint. The author was complaining of the distinction between Roman Catholic schools and other minority religious schools, i.e. a distinction between schools and there-fore pupils of different religious persuasions. The State Party, in its arguments above, is addressing the distinction, similar to that which had previously arisen in *Blom* [23.53], between State funding for public secular schools and private reli-gious schools. In further arguments, the State Party addressed the author's complaint more directly:

¶ 8.2. The State party notes that . . . the author . . . indicates that a possible remedy for the alleged discrimination would be the elimination of funding for the Roman Catholic sepa-rate schools. So far, the State party's reply to the author's communication has focused on his claim that the failure to extend funding constituted a violation of the Covenant, not on a claim that the failure to eliminate funding from the Roman Catholic separate school system is violative of the Covenant. . . .

¶ 8.3. . . . In this context, the State party explains that without the protection of the rights of the Roman Catholic minority, the founding of Canada would not have been possible and that the separate school system remained a controversial issue, at times endangering the national unity in Canada. The State party explains that the funding is seen by the Roman Catholic community as correction of a historical wrong.

¶ 8.4. The State party submits that there are reasonable and objective grounds for not eliminating funding to Roman Catholic separate schools in Ontario. The elimination would be perceived as undoing the bargain made at Confederation to protect the interests of a vulnerable minority in the province and would be met with outrage and resistance by the Roman Catholic community. It would also result in a certain degree of economic turmoil, including claims for compensation of facilities or lands provided for Roman Catholic schools. Further, the protection of minority rights, including minority religion and educa-tion rights, is a principle underlying the Canadian constitutional order and militates against elimination of funding for the Roman Catholic separate schools. Elimination of funding for separate schools in Ontario would further lead to pressure on other Canadian provinces to eliminate their protections for minorities within their border.

The HRC found in favour of the author in the following terms:

¶ 10.2. The issue before the Committee is whether public funding for Roman Catholic schools, but not for schools of the author's religion, which results in him having to meet the full cost of education in a religious school, constitutes a violation of the author's rights under the Covenant.

¶ 10.3. The State party has argued that no discrimination has occurred, since the distinction is based on objective and reasonable criteria: the privileged treatment of Roman Catholic schools is enshrined in the Constitution; as Roman Catholic schools are incorpor-ated as a distinct part of the public school system, the differentiation is between private and public schools, not between private Roman Catholic schools and private schools of other denom-inations; and the aims of the public secular education system are compatible with the Covenant.

¶ 10.4. The Committee begins by noting that the fact that a distinction is enshrined in the Constitution does not render it reasonable and objective. In the instant case, the distinction was made in 1867 to protect the Roman Catholics in Ontario. The material before the Committee does not show that members of the Roman Catholic community or any identi-fiable section of that community are now in a disadvantaged position compared to those members of the Jewish community that wish to secure the education of their children in religious schools. Accordingly, the Committee rejects the State party's argument that the preferential treatment of Roman Catholic schools is nondiscriminatory because of its Constitutional obligation.

¶ 10.5. With regard to the State party's argument that it is reasonable to differentiate in the allocation of public funds between private and public schools, the Committee notes that it is not possible for members of religious denominations other than Roman Catholic to have their religious schools incorporated within the public school system. In the instant case, the author has sent his children to a private religious school, not because he wishes a private non-Government dependent education for his children, but because the publicly funded school system makes no provision for his religious denomination, whereas publicly funded religious schools are available to members of the Roman Catholic faith. On the basis of the facts before it, the Committee considers that the differences in treatment between Roman Catholic religious schools, which are publicly funded as a distinct part of the public education system, and schools of the author's religion, which are private by necessity, cannot be considered reasonable and objective.

¶ 10.6. The Committee has noted the State party's argument that the aims of the State party's secular public education system are compatible with the principle of nondiscrimin-ation laid down in the Covenant. The Committee does not take issue with this argument but notes, however, that the proclaimed aims of the system do not justify the exclusive funding of Roman Catholic religious schools. It has also noted the author's submission that the public school system in Ontario would have greater resources if the Government would cease funding any religious schools. In this context, the Committee observes that the Covenant does not oblige States parties to fund schools which are established on a reli-gious basis. However, if a State party chooses to provide public funding to religious schools, it should make this funding available without discrimination. This means that providing funding for the schools of one religious group and not for another must be based on reasonable and objective criteria. In the instant case, the Committee concludes that the material before it does not show that the differential treatment between the Roman Catholic faith and the author's religious denomination is based on such criteria. Conse-quently, there has been a violation of the author's rights under article 26 of the Covenant to equal and effective protection against discrimination.

The *Waldman* case was decided in November 1999. It will be interesting to see the remedy chosen by Canada, in negotiations with Ontario, to redress the violation:

whether to increase funding for all religious schools (which would have a substantial impact on the Ontario budget), whether to permit education for all religious groups within the public school system (contrary to its prevailing secular model), or whether to cease funding for Roman Catholic schools. The latter solution is politically and, in view of section 93 of the Canadian Constitution 1867, legally difficult.[42]

[23.55] *OULAJIN and KAISS v THE NETHERLANDS (406, 426/90)*

The authors complained of a discrepancy in Dutch legislation between child benefit payable for one's natural children and the benefit payable for one's foster children. The authors lived in the Netherlands, while their natural and foster children lived in Morocco. The foster children were nephews of the authors, for whom the authors had financial responsibility. The authors complained about the fact that they received benefits only for their natural children. They had not satisfied the test imposed by the legislation for attaining benefits with regard to their foster children, which required them to prove a sufficiently close relationship with, and to influence the upbringing of, the foster children.

¶ 3.1. [T]he authors argue that an impermissible distinction is made in their case between 'own children' and 'foster children', all of which belong to the same family in Morocco.

¶ 3.2. The authors point out that the actual situation in which the children concerned live does not differ, and that, *de facto*, both have the same parents. The Dutch authorities do pay child benefits for natural children separated from their parents and residing abroad, irrespective of whether the parent residing in the Netherlands is involved in the upbringing. The authors therefore consider it unjust to deny benefits for their foster children merely on the basis of the fact that they cannot actively involve themselves in their upbringing. In their opinion, the 'differential treatment' is not based on 'reasonable and objective' criteria.

¶ 3.3. The authors argue that not only 'Western standards' should be taken into account in the determination of whether or not to grant child benefits. It was in conformity with Moroccan tradition that they had taken their relatives into their family.

The State Party responded to the allegations of violation:

¶ 5.2. The State party submits that the authors' allegations of discrimination raise two issues:

(1) whether the distinction between an applicant's own children and foster children constitutes a violation of article 26 of the Covenant;

---

[42] Amendment of s.93 could occur with the agreement of the province affected and the federal government (para. 5.5). Such amendments have occurred in Quebec and Newfoundland. The Canadian Supreme Court has ruled that the preferential treatment granted to Roman Catholic schools does not breach the Canadian Charter of Rights and Freedoms, as Ontario was constitutionally bound to confer such a preference: see *Reference Re Bill 30, An Act to amend the Education Act (Ont.)* [1987] 1 SCR 1148; *Adler v Ontario* [1996] 3 SCR 609; see also *Waldman* at paras. 2.6–2.11. See M. Valpy, 'Axworthy Draws Flak for Comments on Ontario', *Globe and Mail*, 19 January 2000.

(2) whether the regulations governing the entitlement to child benefit for foster children, as applied in the Netherlands, result in an unjustifiable disadvantage for non-Dutch nationals, residing in the Netherlands.

¶ 5.3. As to the first issue, the State party submits that to be entitled to child benefit for foster children, the applicant must raise the children concerned in a way comparable to that in which parents normally bring up their own children. This requirement does not apply to the applicant's own children. The State party argues that this distinction does not violate article 26 of the Covenant; it submits that the aim of the relevant regulations is to determine, on the basis of objective criteria, whether the relationship between the foster parent and the foster child is so close that it is appropriate to provide child benefit as if the child were the foster parent's own.

¶ 5.4. As to the second issue, the State party submits that no data exist to show that the regulations affect migrant workers more than Dutch nationals. It argues that the Act's requirements governing entitlement to child benefit for foster children are applied strictly, regardless of the nationality of the applicant or the place of residence of the foster children. It submits that case law shows that applicants of Dutch nationality, residing in the Netherlands, are also deemed ineligible for child benefit for their foster children who are resident abroad. Moreover, if one or both of the parents are still alive, it is assumed in principle that the natural parent has a parental link with the child, which as a rule prevents the foster parent from satisfying the requirements of the Child Benefit Act.

The HRC decided in favour of the State:

¶ 7.4. With respect to the Child Benefit Act, the State party submits that there are objective differences between one's own children and foster children, which justify different treatment under the Act. The Committee recognizes that the distinction is objective and need only focus on the reasonableness criterion. Bearing in mind that certain limitations in the granting of benefits may be inevitable, the Committee has considered whether the distinction between one's own children and foster children under the Child Benefit Act, in particular the requirement that a foster parent be involved in the upbringing of the foster children, as a precondition to the granting of benefits, is unreasonable. In the light of the explanations given by the State party, the Committee finds that the distinctions made in the Child Benefit Act are not incompatible with article 26 of the Covenant.

¶ 7.5. The distinction made in the Child Benefit Act between own children and foster children precludes the granting of benefits for foster children who are not living with the applicant foster parent. In this connection, the authors allege that the application of this requirement is, in practice, discriminatory, since it affects migrant workers more than Dutch nationals. The Committee notes that the authors have failed to submit substantiation for this claim and observes, moreover, that the Child Benefit Act makes no distinction between Dutch nationals and non-nationals, such as migrant workers. The Committee considers that the scope of article 26 of the Covenant does not extend to differences resulting from the equal application of common rules in the allocation of benefits.

[23.56]   *DANNING v THE NETHERLANDS (180/84)*

The facts are outlined below:

¶ 2.2. [The author] states that, as a consequence of an automobile accident in 1979, he became disabled and confined to a wheelchair. During the first year after the accident he received payments from his employer's insurance; after the first year, payments were received under another insurance programme for employees who have been medically declared unfit to work. This programme provides for higher payments to married benefi- ciaries. The author claims that since 1977 he has been engaged to Miss Esther Verschuren and that they live together in common-law marriage. Therefore he maintains that he should be accorded insurance benefits as a married man and not as a single person. Such benefits, however, have been denied to him and he has taken the case to the competent instances in the Netherlands. The Raad van Beroep in Rotterdam (an organ dealing with administrative appeals in employment issues) held in 1981 that his claim was ill-founded; he subse- quently appealed to the Centrale Raad van Beroep in Utrecht, which in 1983 confirmed the decision of the lower instance. He claims that this appeal exhausted domestic remedies.

The Dutch government explained the distinction between married and unmarried couples in Dutch disability legislation.

¶ 8.4. With regard to the concept of discrimination in article 26 of the Covenant, the State party explains the distinctions made in Dutch law as follows:

In the Netherlands, the fact that people live together as a married or unmarried couple has long been considered a relevant factor to which certain legal consequences may be attached. Persons living together as unmarried cohabitants have a free choice of whether or not to enter into marriage, thereby making themselves subject either to one set of laws or to another. The differences between the two are considerable; the cohabitation of married persons is subject to much greater legal regulation than is the cohabitation of unmarried persons. A married person is, for example, obliged to provide for his or her spouse's maintenance; the spouse is also jointly liable for debts incurred in respect of common property; a married person also requires the permission or co-operation of his or her spouse for certain undertakings, such as buying goods on hire purchase which would normally be considered a part of the household, transactions relating to the matrimonial home, etc. The Civil Code contains extensive regulations governing matrimonial law concerning property. The legal consequences of ending a marriage by divorce are also the subject of a large number of provisions in the Civil Code, including a provision allowing the imposition of a maintenance allowance payable to the former spouse. The law of inher- itance, too, is totally geared to the individual's formal status. The Government cannot accept that the differences in treatment by the Netherlands law, described above, between married and unmarried cohabitants could be considered to be 'discrimination' within the legal meaning of that term under article 26 of the Covenant. There is no question of 'equal cases' being treated differently under the law. There is an objective justification for the differences in the legal position of married and unmarried cohabitants, provided for by the Netherlands legislation.

The HRC decided in favour of the Netherlands on the merits:

¶ 14. It therefore remains for the Committee to determine whether the differentiation in Netherlands law at the time in question and as applied to Mr. Danning constituted discrim- ination within the meaning of article 26. In the light of the explanations given by the State party with respect to the differences made by Netherlands legislation between married and unmarried couples (para. 8.4 above), the Committee is persuaded that the differentiation complained of by Mr. Danning is based on objective and reasonable criteria. The Committee observes, in this connection, that the decision to enter into a legal status by marriage, which provides, in Netherlands law, both for certain benefits and for certain duties and responsibilities, lies entirely with the cohabiting persons. By choosing not to enter into marriage, Mr. Danning and his cohabitant have not, in law, assumed the full extent of the duties and responsibilities incumbent on married couples. Consequently, Mr. Danning does not receive the full benefits provided for in Netherlands law for married couples. The Committee concludes that the differentiation complained of by Mr. Danning does not constitute discrimination in the sense of article 26 of the Covenant.

Similar decisions were reached in *Sprenger v The Netherlands* (395/90) (regarding differences in Dutch unemployment benefit legislation between married and unmarried couples) and *Hoofdman v The Netherlands* (602/94) (regarding differences in survivors' benefits between married and unmarried couples).

[23.57] However, note Mrs Evatt's reluctant concurring opinion in *Hoofdman*:

While accepting the Committee's decision on this matter, I would like to emphasize that the State party has accepted that cohabitees are to be considered as a family unit for some purposes. This factor needs to be taken into account in examining whether the grounds put forward for maintaining the distinction between married couples and cohabitees are reasonable and objective in regard to the benefit in question. In that regard, I do not find the arguments of the State party based on legal consequences of marriage or inheritance law to be convincing or of particular relevance in regard to the granting of a benefit designed to alleviate, on a temporary basis, the loss of a partner by death. For distinctions between family groups to be regarded as reasonable and objective, they should be coherent and have regard to social reality.

Mrs Evatt's opinion alludes to the fact that 'reasonable' distinctions can become unreasonable over time. For example, the 'breadwinner' distinction between men and women was probably once 'reasonable' for the purposes of determining pension entitlements in the Netherlands. Cases such as *Broeks* and *Pauger* have confirmed that this distinction is now outmoded, and out of step with Dutch social reality [23.50]. Mrs Evatt in *Hoofdman* is warning that the prevailing discrimination against *de facto* couples in Dutch welfare law in the 1990s is also falling out of step with Dutch social mores, and is thus close to crossing the line between 'reasonable' and unreasonable, impermissible discrimination.[43]

Affirmative Action

[23.58] Discrimination in a society may be so firmly entrenched that 'positive' or 'affirmative' action must be taken in order properly to redress the historical

---

[43] Compare the Dutch government's arguments in *Broeks* at para. 8.3 [23.08] and the minority opinion in *Sprenger* [23.12].

disadvantage suffered by some groups. Affirmative action denotes positive steps taken by a State to improve the status of disadvantaged groups. A classic example of affirmative action policy is 'positively' to discriminate in favour of disadvantaged groups. This circumstance is discussed in the next section. However, 'affirmative action' is not synonymous with 'positive' or 'reverse' discrimination. For example, the provision of ramps to allow disabled persons public access is a positive measure which redresses disadvantage for disabled people. It is not however a measure of 'positive discrimination', as the measure does not discriminate against able-bodied people.[44] Similarly, provision of more childcare facilities would tend to redress discrimination against mothers' access to employment. However, such provision does not discriminate against men.

[23.59] The HRC has confirmed that affirmative action is certainly permissible under the Covenant, and may have indicated that, in certain circumstances, it is mandatory for States to take such action.[45]

GENERAL COMMENT 18

¶ 10. The Committee also wishes to point out that the principle of equality sometimes requires States parties to take affirmative action in order to diminish or eliminate conditions which cause or help to perpetuate discrimination prohibited by the Covenant. For example, in a State where the general conditions of a certain part of the population prevent or impair their enjoyment of human rights, the State should take specific action to correct those conditions.

GENERAL COMMENT 3

General Comment 3 deals with State obligations under article 2 ICCPR;

¶ 1. . . . The Committee considers it necessary to draw the attention of States parties to the fact that the obligation under the Covenant is not confined to the respect of human rights, but that States parties have also undertaken to ensure the enjoyment of these rights to all individuals under their jurisdiction. This aspect calls for specific activities by the States parties to enable individuals to enjoy their rights. . . .

GENERAL COMMENT 4

General Comment 4 addresses State obligations under article 3:

¶ 2. Firstly, article 3, as articles 2 (1) and 26 in so far as those articles primarily deal with the prevention of discrimination on a number of grounds, among which sex is one, requires not only measures of protection but also affirmative action designed to ensure the positive enjoyment of rights. This cannot be done simply by enacting laws. Hence, more information

---

[44] Lester and Joseph, above, note 5, 582.
[45] Bayefsky, above, note 24, argues that affirmative action is mandatory under the Covenant, at 30.

has generally been required regarding the role of women in practice with a view to ascertaining what measures, in addition to purely legislative measures of protection, have been or are being taken to give effect to the precise and positive obligations under article 3 and to ascertain what progress is being made or what factors or difficulties are being met in this regard.

[23.60] Affirmative action is permitted under article 1(4) ICERD, and is apparently mandatory 'when the circumstances so warrant' under article 2(2) of ICERD. In General Recommendation 14, the CERD Committee identifies a pertinent positive duty, that training be provided to ensure awareness amongst law enforcement officers of the social evil of racial discrimination. Affirmative action seems permissible rather than mandatory under article 4 of CEDAW. However, other, more specific, CEDAW provisions seem to impose mandatory obligations to undertake affirmative action.[46]

[23.61] The HRC has given some indication of the forms that affirmative action may legitimately take, and the situations in which such action should be taken, in cases and Concluding Comments excerpted in the following sections.

Reverse Discrimination

[23.62]   *GENERAL COMMENT 18*

¶ 10. . . . [Affirmative] action may involve granting for a time to the part of the population concerned certain preferential treatment in specific matters as compared with the rest of the population. However, as long as such action is needed to correct discrimination in fact, it is a case of legitimate differentiation under the Covenant.

[23.63] In *Stalla Costa v Uruguay* (198/1985), the author complained that he was denied access to the Uruguayan public service on an equal basis as Uruguayan law gave preferences to persons who had been dismissed from the public service by the previous government for political reasons.[47] The HRC found that there was no violation of article 26 as the Uruguayan law provided a 'measure of redress' to persons who had previously suffered from discrimination. Therefore, the law was a permissible measure of positive or reverse discrimination.

[23.64]   *BALLANTYNE et al. v CANADA (359, 385/89)*

This case concerned a complaint about laws in Quebec which banned advertising in a language other than French. The government of Quebec, in a submission transmitted through the State Party, argued that these measures were necessary in order to protect the status of the French language.[48] In other words, Quebec

---

[46] See, e.g., art. 12(2) of CEDAW.
[47] The details of the communication are outlined at [22.45].
[48] These arguments are excerpted at [18.38].

argued that the laws constituted affirmative measures designed to protect a vulnerable group, French speakers. Counsel for the authors opposed this argument:

¶ 9.6. In a further comment, counsel to Mr. McIntyre reiterates that Bill No. 178 violates fundamental rights protected by the Covenant. He argues that while Quebec has pointed to figures which show a slow decline in the use of French across Canada, it omitted to point out that, in Quebec, French has been gaining ground on English and the English community is in decline. Furthermore, while Quebec has portrayed the 1982 constitutional amendments as an attack on the French language, it can on the contrary be argued that Section 23 of the amended Charter of Rights and Freedoms has been particularly effective in assisting the francophone population outside Quebec.

¶ 9.7. . . . Furthermore, although French minorities in the rest of Canada have often been treated unfairly in the past, this situation is now improving. As a result, counsel denies that historical or legal arguments would justify the restrictions imposed by Bill No. 178 in the light of articles 19, 26 or 27 of the Covenant.

¶ 9.8. Counsel . . . reiterates that there is no connection between the contested legislative provisions and any rational defence or protection of the French language.

Whilst rejecting Ballantyne's claim under article 26 [23.38], the HRC rejected the affirmative action argument as a defence to a claim of the ICCPR right of freedom of expression.[49] The HRC impliedly accepted the counter-arguments of the authors' counsel.

[23.65] In *Stalla Costa*, the HRC concluded that the measure of affirmative action was proportionate to the end of delivering justice to persons persecuted under a previous regime. In *Ballantyne*, the HRC concluded that the affirmative action measure was disproportionate to its ends; historical discrimination against francophone Québecois did not justify the law in question. As with other distinctions, the permissibility of affirmative action measures is judged by reference to the 'reasonable and objective' test.

[23.66] In *Waldman v Canada* (694/96), the impugned distinction concerned preferential treatment conferred upon Roman Catholic schools compared to other minority religious schools in Ottawa [23.54]. The HRC found that the impugned laws constituted discrimination between Roman Catholics and other minority religions, contrary to article 26. Mr Scheinin, in a separate concurring opinion, stated:

¶ 5. When implementing the Committee's views in the present case the State party should in my opinion bear in mind that article 27 imposes positive obligations for States to promote religious instruction in minority religions, and that providing such education as an optional arrangement within the public education system is one permissible arrangement to that end.[50] Providing for publicly funded education in minority languages for

---

[49] Ibid. See also Ndiaye's dissent at [24.35].
[50] See, on art. 27, Chap. 24.

those who wish to receive such education is not as such discriminatory, although care must of course be taken that possible distinctions between different minority languages are based on objective and reasonable grounds. The same rule applies in relation to religious education in minority religions. In order to avoid discrimination in funding religious (or linguistic) education for some but not all minorities States may legitimately base themselves on whether there is a constant demand for such education. For many religious minorities the existence of a fully secular alternative within the public school system is sufficient, as the communities in question wish to arrange for religious education outside school hours and outside school premises. And if demands for religious schools do arise, one legitimate criterion for deciding whether it would amount to discrimination not to establish a public minority school or not to provide comparable public funding to a private minority school is whether there is a sufficient number of children to attend such a school so that it could operate as a viable part in the overall system of education. In the present case this condition was met.[51] Consequently, the level of indirect public funding allocated to the education of the author's children amounted to discrimination when compared to the full funding of public Roman Catholic schools in Ontario.

The preferential treatment of Roman Catholics arose from a historical agreement, enshrined in the Canadian Constitution, to protect their culture in view of their minority status at confederation (compared to the Protestant majority). The *Waldman* decision indicates that States cannot confer preferences to protect one minority group, even if such preferences were once historically justifiable, without conferring similar preferences on other comparable minority groups. In other words, States must not discriminate with regard to comparable groups when implementing affirmative action programmes.

[23.67] Both ICERD (article 2(2)) and CEDAW (article 4) specify that 'the maintenance of unequal or separate standards' for different groups must be discontinued once the objectives of equality of opportunity and treatment have been met.

[23.68] 'Reverse' or 'positive discrimination' programmes are designed to benefit members of disadvantaged groups. How is an individual identified as belonging to a certain group in borderline cases? For example, would a person with one sixteenth indigenous blood be classified as an 'indigenous person' for the purposes of a relevant positive discrimination programme? The ICERD Committee addressed this issue in the context of racial and ethnic groups in General Recommendation 8 (1990):

such identification shall, if no justification exists to the contrary, be based upon self-identification by the individual concerned.[52]

[23.69] A common reverse discrimination measure is the imposition of quotas for certain groups in certain institutions. The HRC has expressly approved a constitu-

---

[51] The author was Jewish. Clearly there was a sufficient demand for Jewish schools in view of Ontario's substantial Jewish population.

[52] See also [24.13].

tional amendment in India that reserves one third of seats in elected local bodies for women, and the practice of reserving elected positions for members of certain tribes and castes.[53] CEDAW has expressly advocated the imposition of quotas to achieve gender balance in public and political bodies in its General Recommendation 23. For example, at paragraph 29 it urges States Parties to adopt 'a rule that neither sex should constitute less than 40 per cent of members of a public body'.[54]

Measures to Combat Private Sector Discrimination[55]

[23.70] If discrimination in the private sector is permitted to flourish, a society will fail to deliver real equality of opportunity and treatment. The ICCPR definitely prohibits discrimination by state agencies and by state laws. To what extent does the ICCPR oblige States Parties to take positive steps to combat discrimination by private actors? Such a duty can be derived from the obligation in article 2 to 'respect and ensure' all ICCPR rights to all persons, and from article 26: '[t]he law shall prohibit any discrimination and guarantee to all persons equal and effective protection against discrimination'.[56]

[23.71]   *GENERAL COMMENT 18*

The General Comment strongly implies a duty to combat private discrimination.

¶ 9. Reports of many States parties contain information regarding legislative as well as administrative measures and court decisions which relate to protection against discrimination in law, but they very often lack information which would reveal discrimination in fact. When reporting on articles 2 (1), 3 and 26 of the Covenant, States parties usually cite provisions of their constitution or equal opportunity laws with respect to equality of persons. While such information is of course useful, the Committee wishes to know if there remain any problems of discrimination in fact, which may be practised either by public authorities, by the community, or by private persons or bodies. The Committee wishes to be informed about legal provisions and administrative measures directed at diminishing or eliminating such discrimination.

[23.72]   *NAHLIK v AUSTRIA (608/95)*

In this case, the author complained of discrimination entailed in a collective bargaining agreement. The State Party argued against admissibility in the following terms:

---

[53] Concluding Comments on India (1998) UN doc. CCPR/C/79/Add.81, para. 10.
[54] See generally [22.51].
[55] See also [1.59–1.62].
[56] See also Nowak, above, note 9, 475–9.

¶ 4. [The State party] argues however that the communication is inadmissible because the author challenges a regulation in a collective agreement over which the State party has no influence. The State party explains that collective agreements are contracts based on private law and exclusively within the discretion of the contracting parties. The State party concludes that the communication is therefore inadmissible under article 1 of the Optional Protocol, since one cannot speak of a violation by a State party.

The HRC rebuffed the above argument in the following terms:

¶ 8.2. The Committee has noted the State party's argument that the communication is inadmissible under article 1 of the Optional Protocol since it relates to alleged discrimination within a private agreement, over which the State party has no influence. The Committee observes that under articles 2 and 26 of the Covenant the State party is under an obligation to ensure that all individuals within its territory and subject to its jurisdiction are free from discrimination, and consequently the courts of States parties are under an obligation to protect individuals against discrimination, whether this occurs within the public sphere or among private parties in the quasi-public sector of, for example, employment. The Committee further notes that the collective agreement at issue in the instant case is regulated by law and does not enter into force except on confirmation by the Federal Minister for Labour and Social Affairs. Moreover, the Committee notes that this collective agreement concerns the staff of the Social Insurance Board, an institution of public law implementing public policy. For these reasons, the Committee cannot agree with the State party's argument that the communication should be declared inadmissible under article 1 of the Optional Protocol.[57]

[23.73] The reference in paragraph 8.2 of *Nahlik* to the 'quasi-public' sphere is instructive. Whilst the Covenant requires regulation of private-sector discrimination in 'quasi-public' arenas such as employment, housing, or access to publicly available goods and services, it may not require such regulation within the 'totally private' or personal sphere, such as the home or within the family or other private relationships.[58] For example, could a State meaningfully control instances of parental disapproval over the race of a child's spouse? Indeed, discrimination in the totally private sphere is perhaps best addressed by educational measures, rather than by coercive laws.[59] Of course, egregious discrimination or human rights abuse within the personal sphere, such as the perpetration of domestic violence, must be prohibited [23.80].

[23.74] The HRC has recommended that States Parties act to curb discrimination in the private sphere in various Concluding Comments. For example, regarding Mauritius, the HRC stated:[60]

---

[57] The *Nahlik* case was inadmissible due to non-substantiation of allegations.
[58] See Ramcharan, above, note 4, 262. This does not mean that the State itself could pass legislation which compelled or fostered discrimination within the 'totally private' or personal sphere; it means only that the State is not required to regulate discrimination by private persons within that sphere. See, however, [20.30] ff. on duties to foster equality within marriage between spouses.
[59] See, below, [23.86–23.88].
[60] Concluding Comments on Mauritius (1997) UN doc. CCPR/C/79/Add. 60; see also Concluding

¶ 23. . . . It further recommends that [the Mauritian Constitution] be amended to render it compatible with articles 2(1), 3 and 26 of the Covenant and that steps be taken to introduce comprehensive anti-discrimination laws to cover all spheres, public and private, protected by the Covenant.

[23.75] Article 20 ICCPR imposes a specific duty to enact laws against speech which incites discrimination on the basis of race, religion, or nationality.[61]

[23.76] Articles 2(1)(d) of ICERD and 2(1)(e) of CEDAW specifically oblige States Parties to take all appropriate measures to eliminate race and sex discrimination, respectively, by any persons, group, or organization. The duty to redress private discrimination is reinforced by other provisions of both treaties. The ICERD duty is illustrated in the following case.

YILMAZ-DOGAN v THE NETHERLANDS (CERD 1/84)

¶ 9.3. With respect to the alleged violation of article 5(e)(i),[62] the Committee notes that the final decision as to the dismissal of the petitioner was the decision of the Sub-District Court of 29 September 1982. . . . The Committee notes that this decision does not address the alleged discrimination in the employer's letter of 19 July 1982, which requested the termination of the petitioner's employment contract. After careful examination, the Committee considers that the petitioner's dismissal was the result of a failure to take into account all circumstances of the case. Consequently, her right to work under article 5(e)(i) was not protected.

The State Party in *Yilmaz-Dogan* violated article 5(e)(i) of ICERD in failing to take due account of evidence of discrimination by the author's private sector employer, which probably caused her dismissal.

Systemic Inequality

[23.77] All societies are fundamentally influenced by dominant societal values. These values are always male, heterosexual, and able-bodied. They will also reflect a State's prevalent race, religion, and language. For example, in the United States, the United Kingdom, and Australia, the dominant paradigm reflects the values of white Anglo-Saxons, Christians, and English speakers. A State's society will generally reinforce its dominant values through, for example, the perpetuation of customs and the formulation of laws that reflect prevailing values. The reinforcement of dominant norms generates systemic discrimination against, and

Comments on Chile (1999) UN doc. CCPR/C/79/Add. 104, para. 23; Concluding Comments on Costa Rica (1999) UN doc. CCPR/C/79/Add. 107, para. 15.; Concluding Comments on the Republic of Korea (1999) UN doc. CCPR/C/79/Add. 114, para. 10.

[61] See generally Chap. 18.
[62] Art. 5(e)(i) prohibits race discrimination in relation to, *inter alia*, the right to work.

consequent systemic inequality for, persons outside the dominant norm. The causes and effects of systemic inequality may be very subtle and even invisible within parts of society, as such inequality is historically perceived as normal by both the dominant and marginalized people.

[23.78] The causes of systemic inequality are so complex that it is doubtful that systemic inequality could be successfully challenged before the HRC in an Optional Protocol complaint, bearing in mind the inadequacy of some of the HRC's decisions regarding indirect discrimination.[63] It may also be difficult to prove that one is a 'victim' of systemic discrimination. The 'individual' and direct nature of the interpretation of 'victimhood' does not accommodate complaints about fundamental, systemic problems in society.[64] It could be challenged on a macro level during the reporting process, and noted in resultant Concluding Comments. For example, with regard to India, the HRC condemned numerous laws and cultural practices which contributed to the continuing subjugation of women and people of lower castes.[65] Regarding Poland, the HRC noted statistics regarding inequality between the sexes (e.g. that average salaries for women were 70 per cent of those for men).[66] Statistics of themselves, however, would rarely not be enough to prove an individual instance of discrimination.

[23.79] The HRC has acknowledged the problem of systemic inequality in General Comment 18 at paragraph 10 [23.59]. However, of all the UN treaty bodies, CEDAW has exhibited the most awareness of systemic inequality.[67] This is hardly surprising, as women are victims of systemic discrimination in all societies. For example, societal acquiescence in or approval of, or even apathy towards, gender-based violence generates systemic inequality. The CEDAW Committee, in its General Recommendation 19, drew attention to the links between gender-based discrimination and violence against women. It is one of the more detailed General Comments produced by any of the human rights treaty bodies. The Recommendation also highlights the extremely close link between discrimination and other forms of human rights abuse.

[23.80] *CEDAW GENERAL RECOMMENDATION 19: 'VIOLENCE AGAINST WOMEN'*

General comments

¶ 6. The Convention in article 1 defines discrimination against women. The definition of discrimination includes gender-based violence, that is, violence that is directed against a woman because she is a woman or that affects women disproportionately. It includes acts

---

[63] See [23.34–23.38].
[64] See generally, on the 'victim' requirement for OP admissibility, Chap. 3.
[65] (1985) UN doc. CCPR/C/79/Add.81, paras. 15–17.
[66] (1999) UN doc. CCPR/C/79/Add. 110, para. 12.
[67] In this respect, it should be noted that in late 1999 the HRC was in the process of drafting a new General Comment on art. 3: see UN doc. A/54/40, para. 380.

that inflict physical, mental or sexual harm or suffering, threats of such acts, coercion and other deprivations of liberty. Gender-based violence may breach specific provisions of the Convention, regardless of whether those provisions expressly mention violence.

¶ 7. Gender-based violence, which impairs or nullifies the enjoyment by women of human rights and fundamental freedoms under general international law or under human rights conventions, is discrimination within the meaning of article 1 of the Convention. . . .

Specific recommendations

¶ 24. In light of these comments, the Committee on the Elimination of Discrimination against Women recommends:

(a) States parties should take appropriate and effective measures to overcome all forms of gender-based violence, whether by public or private act;

(b) States parties should ensure that laws against family violence and abuse, rape, sexual assault and other gender-based violence give adequate protection to all women, and respect their integrity and dignity. Appropriate protective and support services should be provided for victims. Gender-sensitive training of judicial and law enforcement officers and other public officials is essential for the effective implementation of the Convention;

(c) States parties should encourage the compilation of statistics and research on the extent, causes and effects of violence, and on the effectiveness of measures to prevent and deal with violence;

(d) Effective measures should be taken to ensure that the media respect and promote respect for women;

(e) States parties in their report should identify the nature and extent of attitudes, customs and practices that perpetuate violence against women, and the kinds of violence that result. They should report the measures that they have undertaken to overcome violence, and the effect of those measures;

(f) Effective measures should be taken to overcome these attitudes and practices. States should introduce education and public information programmes to help eliminate prejudices which hinder women's equality (recommendation No. 3, 1987);

(g) Specific preventive and punitive measures are necessary to overcome trafficking and sexual exploitation;

(h) States parties in their reports should describe the extent of all these problems and the measures, including penal provisions, preventive and rehabilitation measures, that have been taken to protect women engaged in prostitution or subject to trafficking and other forms of sexual exploitation. The effectiveness of these measures should also be described;

(i) Effective complaints procedures and remedies, including compensation, should be provided;

(j) States parties should include in their reports information on sexual harassment, and on measures to protect women from sexual harassment and other forms of violence or coercion in the workplace;

(k) States parties should establish or support services for victims of family violence, rape, sex assault and other forms of gender-based violence, including refuges, specially trained health workers, rehabilitation and counselling;

(l) States parties should take measures to overcome such practices and should take account of the Committee's recommendation on female circumcision (recommendation No. 14) in reporting on health issues;

(m) States parties should ensure that measures are taken to prevent coercion in regard to fertility and reproduction, and to ensure that women are not forced to seek unsafe medical procedures such as illegal abortion because of a lack of appropriate services in regard to fertility control;

(n) States parties in their reports should state the extent of these problems and should indicate the measures that have been taken and their effect;

(o) States parties should ensure that services for victims of violence are accessible to rural women and that where necessary special services are provided to isolated communities;

(p) Measures to protect them from violence should include training and employment opportunities and the monitoring of the employment conditions of domestic workers;

(q) States parties should report on the risks to rural women, the extent and nature of violence and abuse to which they are subject, their need for and access to support and other services and the effectiveness of measures to overcome violence;

(r) Measures that are necessary to overcome family violence should include:

    (i)   Criminal penalties where necessary and civil remedies in case of domestic violence;

    (ii) Legislation to remove the defence of honour in regard to the assault or murder of a female family member;

    (iii) Services to ensure the safety and security of victims of family violence, including refuges, counselling and rehabilitation programmes;

    (iv) Rehabilitation programmes for perpetrators of domestic violence;

    (v) Support services for families where incest or sexual abuse has occurred;

(s) States parties should report on the extent of domestic violence and sexual abuse, and on the preventive, punitive and remedial measures that have been taken;

(t) That States parties should take all legal and other measures that are necessary to provide effective protection of women against gender-based violence, including, *inter alia*:

    (i)   Effective legal measures, including penal sanctions, civil remedies and compensatory provisions to protect women against all kinds of violence, including, *inter alia*, violence and abuse in the family, sexual assault and sexual harassment in the workplace;

    (ii) Preventive measures, including public information and education programmes to change attitudes concerning the roles and status of men and women;

(iii) Protective measures, including refuges, counselling, rehabilitation and support services for women who are the victims of violence or who are at risk of violence;

(u) That States parties should report on all forms of gender-based violence, and that such reports should include all available data on the incidence of each form of violence, and on the effects of such violence on the women who are victims;

(v) That the reports of States parties should include information on the legal, preventive and protective measures that have been taken to overcome violence against women, and on the effectiveness of such measures.

[23.81] As noted in paragraph 24(l) of General Recommendation 19, CEDAW had previously condemned the practice of female circumcision in General Recommendation 14, identifying it as a custom which was 'prejudicial to the health and well-being of women and children'.

[23.82] In numerous Concluding Comments, the HRC has reinforced CEDAW's condemnation of gender-based violence. For example, regarding Yemen, the HRC was concerned about reports of female genital mutilation being a common practice in some parts of the country, and 'that the laws of Yemen contain no provision for dealing with domestic violence'.[68] Regarding Guatemala, the HRC 'urge[d] that violence (especially within the home) and acts of discrimination against women (such as sexual harassment in the workplace) be established as punishable crimes'.[69] The HRC was concerned that 'courts in Japan seem to consider domestic violence, including forced sexual intercourse, as a normal incident of married life'.[70] Regarding Poland, the HRC was concerned over 'the shortage of provision of hostels and refuges for family members suffering from domestic violence'.[71] Regarding Cyprus, the HRC recommended:[72]

¶ 12. ... reform of the law of evidence to take into account the possibility of removing obstacles to a spouse providing testimony against another spouse on domestic violence.

[23.83] *GENERAL RECOMMENDATION 13: 'EQUAL REMUNERATION FOR WORK OF EQUAL VALUE'*

¶ 2. [States] should consider the study, development and adoption of job evaluation systems based on gender-neutral criteria that would facilitate the comparison of the value of those jobs of a different nature, in which women presently predominate, with those jobs in which men presently predominate, and they should include the results achieved in their reports to the Committee on the Elimination of Discrimination against Women.

---

[68] (1995) UN doc. CCPR/C/79/Add.51, para. 14.

[69] (1996) UN doc. CCPR/C/79/Add.63, para. 33.

[70] (1998) UN doc. CCPR/C/79/Add. 102, para. 30; see also Concluding Comments on United Republic of Tanzania (1998) UN doc. CCPR/C/79/Add. 97, para. 11, condemning the failure of the State Party to criminalize marital rape and female genital mutilation; Concluding Comments on Uruguay (1998) UN doc. CCPR/C/79/Add. 90, para. 9D, condemning the fact that the subsequent marriage of a rapist and victim will exonerate the rapist, and any other participants in the rape offence.

[71] (1999) UN doc. CCPR/C/79/Add. 110, para. 14.

[72] (1998) UN doc. CCPR/C/79/Add. 88.

This CEDAW Recommendation recognizes that discrimination may occur even in the absence of a specific discriminatory requirement. For example, suppose persons in female-dominated professions are paid less than male-dominated professions, even though those professions are objectively equally 'valuable' or 'skilled'. Discrimination is occurring as a result, though its cause cannot be attributed to specific rules or conditions.[73]

[23.84] *CEDAW GENERAL RECOMMENDATION 17: 'MEASUREMENT AND QUANTIFICATION OF THE UNREMUNERATED DOMESTIC ACTIVITIES OF WOMEN AND THEIR RECOGNITION IN THE GROSS NATIONAL PRODUCT'*

[The CEDAW Committee] . . .

Affirming that the measurement and quantification of the unremunerated domestic activities of women, which contribute to development in each country, will help to reveal the *de facto* economic role of women, . . .

Recommends that States parties:

(a) Encourage and support research and experimental studies to measure and value the unremunerated domestic activities of women; for example, by conducting time-use surveys as part of their national household survey programmes and by collecting statistics disaggregated by gender on time spent on activities both in the household and on the labour market;

(b) Take steps, in accordance with the provisions of the Convention on the Elimination of All Forms of Discrimination against Women and the Nairobi Forward-looking Strategies for the Advancement of Women, to quantify and include the unremunerated domestic activities of women in the gross national product;

(c) Include in their reports submitted under article 18 of the Convention information on the research and experimental studies undertaken to measure and value unremunerated domestic activities, as well as on the progress made in the incorporation of the unremunerated domestic activities of women in national accounts.

Similarly, CEDAW General Recommendation 16 drew attention to the prevalence of unpaid female workers in family enterprises, 'usually owned by a male member of the family'.

[23.85] The Committee on the Elimination of Racial Discrimination identified a particular instance of systemic discrimination in its General Recommendation 19.

---

[73] See also *Enderby v Frenchay Health Authority* [1994] 1 CMLR 8, decision of the European Court of Justice.

CERD GENERAL RECOMMENDATION 19

¶ 3. The Committee observes that while conditions of complete or partial racial segregation may in some countries have been created by governmental policies, a condition of partial segregation may also arise as an unintended by-product of the actions of private persons. In many cities residential patterns are influenced by group differences in income, which are sometimes combined with differences in race, colour, descent and national or ethnic origin, so that inhabitants can be stigmatized and individuals suffer a form of discrimination in which racial grounds are mixed with other grounds.

¶ 4. The Committee therefore affirms that a condition of racial segregation can also arise without any initiative or direct involvement by the public authorities. It invites States parties to monitor all trends which can give rise to racial segregation, to work for the eradication of any negative consequences that ensue, and to describe any such action in their periodic reports.

Educational Duties

[23.86] At paragraph 2 of General Comment 4, the HRC stated that the positive enjoyment of rights under articles 2(1), 3, and 26 'cannot be done simply by enacting laws' [23.59]. This comment may envisage the proper enforcement of laws. It may also refer to a duty to take positive, extra-legal measures to combat discrimination. Such extra-legal measures may include educational or promotional duties to, for example, tackle stereotypical perceptions of disadvantaged groups. Promotional duties are very important in combating discrimination. Legal remedies can go only so far; cases will affect relatively few individuals, and proof of discrimination is always a difficult task. Furthermore, supplementation of legal principles by vigilant promotion of anti-discrimination principles will hopefully prompt fundamental, consensual (as opposed to coerced) non-discrimination within societies.

[23.87] Promotional and educational duties with regard to race and sex discrimination are imposed by ICERD, articles 2(1)(e) and 7, and CEDAW, articles 5 and 10(c).

[23.88] CEDAW's General Recommendation regarding Gender-Based Violence highlights the importance of education campaigns [23.80]. The HRC has also recommended that States undertake promotional campaigns. For example, regarding Mauritius:[74]

¶ 23. It is also recommended that the proposed Equal Opportunity Commission consider whether affirmative action measures, including educational measures, are necessary to overcome remaining obstacles to equality, such as outdated attitudes concerning the role and status of women.

---

[74] (1996) UN doc. CCPR/C/79/Add. 60.

With regard to Finland, the HRC stated:[75]

¶ 16. . . . the Committee recommends that further positive measures be taken to overcome discriminatory and xenophobic attitudes and prejudices, and to foster tolerance.

Equalizing Down

[23.89] Two alternatives seem available to redress violations of the ICCPR's non-discrimination provisions: to raise the rights of the victim to the level of those treated better than him/her, or to lower the rights of those others to the level of the victim. The latter solution diminishes the rights of others whilst often offering little benefit to the original victim.[76] Article 5(2) prohibits a State Party from invoking the Covenant as a pretext to reduce the fundamental human rights of a person within the State. Article 5(2) may prevent States remedying breaches of articles 2(1), 3, and 26 by 'equalizing down'.[77] However, the HRC itself canvassed an option of 'equalizing down' as an appropriate remedy at paragraph 10.6 in *Waldman v Canada* [23.54], so such remedies appear to be valid responses to findings of violation.[78]

Conclusion

[23.90] The HRC, as well as the CERD and CEDAW Committees, has issued a large body of jurisprudence regarding rights of non-discrimination. The ICCPR goes further than ICERD and CEDAW in prohibiting discrimination, as it extends its prohibition beyond the grounds of race and sex. The ICCPR compels States Parties to prevent and remedy invidious discrimination by public bodies, within State laws, and by private entities. In certain circumstances, positive measures, or 'affirmative action', may be needed properly to redress discrimination. Whilst the HRC has arguably been generous in finding discrimination cases admissible with regard to numerous grounds of discrimination, and with regard to the enjoyment of numerous rights, it has been notably reticent to find actual violations. Generally, it has found most instances of alleged discrimination to be justifiable, 'reasonable and objective', distinctions.

However, the HRC may be exhibiting a new radicalism in its interpretations of article 26, as evinced by some decisions of July and November 1999. In *Johannes*

---

[75] (1998) UN doc. CCPR/C/79/Add. 91.

[76] See Lester and Joseph, above, note 5, 594.

[77] Ibid.

[78] In a separate opinion in *Pauger v Austria* (415/90), Mr Ando concedes the possibility of 'equalizing down' as a remedy for art. 26 violations, but suggests that such remedies would hardly be endorsed by the relevant society.

Vos v The Netherlands (786/97), the HRC reinforced the application of article 26 in the socio-economic arena with regard to retirement pensions, despite contrary European Union law [23.14]. In *Foin v France* (666/95) [23.48], the HRC overturned its prior jurisprudence in *Järvinen v Finland* (295/88) [23.47]. Finally, in *Waldman v Canada* (694/96) [23.54], the HRC's decision has posed a challenge to Canadian constitutional arrangements regarding the treatment of minority religions.

Postscript: Please note that General Comment 28 on 'Equality of Rights Between Men and Women', contained in the Addendum at page 634, contains extra information on some of the material in this chapter.

24

Rights of Minorities—Article 27

ARTICLE 27

In those States in which ethnic, religious or linguistic minorities exist, persons belonging to such minorities shall not be denied the right, in community with the other members of their group, to enjoy their own culture, to profess and practice their own religion, or to use their own language.

[24.01] Article 27 protects the rights of minorities; that is it protects individuals belonging to minority groups and that protection is in addition to the rights all individuals have under the Covenant in general.[1] The HRC has explained the supplementary quality to article 27 in General Comment 23:

GENERAL COMMENT 23

¶ 1. . . . The Committee observes that [article 27] establishes and recognizes a right which is conferred on individuals belonging to minority groups and which is distinct from, and additional to, all the other rights which, as individuals in common with everyone else, they are already entitled to enjoy under the Covenant. . . .

¶ 9. . . . The protection of [article 27] rights is directed towards ensuring the survival and continued development of the cultural, religious and social identity of the minorities

---

[1] Cultural rights are given some recognition in the International Covenant on Economic, Social, and Cultural Rights (ICESCR), arts. 3 and 15. Cultural and linguistic rights of minorities are further elaborated in the United Nations 'Declaration on the Rights of Persons Belonging to National or Ethnic, Religious and Linguistic Minorities'. GA Res, 18 December 1992. Minority rights generally are explored in detail in many works: for instance see W. Kymlicka (ed.), *The Rights of Minority Cultures* (Oxford University Press, Oxford, 1995), A. Phillips and A. Rosas (eds.), *Universal Minority Rights* (Institute for Human Rights, Åbo Akademi University, Finland, 1995), and P. Thornberry, *International Law and the Rights of Minorities* (Oxford University Press, Oxford, 1991).

concerned, thus enriching the fabric of society as a whole. Accordingly, the Committee observes that these rights must be protected as such and should not be confused with other personal rights conferred on one and all under the Covenant.

Article 27 and the General Comment make it clear that the right to preserve and defend the identity of minorities is essential. The fundamental components of minority identity, which must be protected, are its cultural, religious, or linguistic manifestations.[2]

Article 27 and other Articles of the ICCPR

[24.02] *GENERAL COMMENT 23*

The distinction between the rights of peoples to self-determination, guaranteed in article 1, and the rights of minorities is explained by the HRC:

¶ 2. In some communications submitted to the Committee under the Optional Protocol, the right protected under article 27 has been confused with the right of peoples to self-determination proclaimed in article 1 of the Covenant. . . .

¶ 3.1. The Covenant draws a distinction between the right to self-determination and the rights protected under article 27. The former is expressed to be a right belonging to peoples and is dealt with in a separate part (Part I) of the Covenant. Self-determination is not a right cognizable under the Optional Protocol. Article 27, on the other hand, relates to rights conferred on individuals as such and is included, like the articles relating to other personal rights conferred on individuals, in Part III of the Covenant and is cognizable under the Optional Protocol.

¶ 3.2. The enjoyment of the rights to which article 27 relates does not prejudice the sovereignty and territorial integrity of a State party. At the same time, one or other aspect of the rights of individuals protected under that article—for example, to enjoy a particular culture—may consist in a way of life which is closely associated with territory and use of its resources. This may particularly be true of members of indigenous communities constituting a minority.

[24.03] Article 27 is therefore distinguished from article 1, *inter alia*, on the basis that the former guarantees individual rather than collective rights. However, as the rights protected under article 27 apply to members of a minority, they may be thought of in part as collective rights, exercisable individually.[3] This would be an equally sustainable argument regarding interpretation of article 1.[4]

[24.04] The General Comment also draws a distinction between article 27 and rights of non-discrimination under articles 2(1) and 26:

---

[2] See P. Thornberry, 'The UN Declaration on the Rights of Persons Belonging to National or Ethnic, Religious and Linguistic Minorities: Background, Analysis, Observations and an Update' in Phillips and Rosas, above, note 1, 20–5.

[3] See General Comment 23, para. 9 [24.01]; see further Thornberry, above, note 1, at 173–6.

[4] See further, on the non-justiciability of art. 1, [7.20–7.21].

¶ 4. The Covenant also distinguishes the rights protected under article 27 from the guarantees under articles 2(1) and 26. [These articles confer non-discrimination rights on individuals within jurisdiction] irrespective of whether they belong to the minorities specified in article 27 or not. Some States parties who claim that they do not discriminate on grounds of ethnicity, language or religion, wrongly contend, on that basis alone, that they have no minorities.

[24.05] Cases under article 25 (rights of political participation)[5] and articles 17 (right of privacy) and 23 (rights of the family)[6] have also raised issues which potentially overlap with minority rights issues. One could also anticipate an overlap with the article 18 right of freedom of religion in relation to religious minorities.[7]

Definition of a Minority

[24.06] There is no fixed definition of what constitutes a minority in article 27. It is clear from the General Comment that a minority is understood in this context to be 'those who belong to a group and who share in common a culture, a religion, and/or a language'.[8]

[24.07]   *BALLANTYNE et al. v CANADA (359, 385/89)*

In this case, the authors sought to argue that Quebec's language laws constituted, *inter alia*, a breach of article 27. The authors were part of the English-speaking minority in Quebec. Out of a total population of 15,600 in the town in question, there were 5,600 English speakers. The law at issue prevented them from displaying commercial signs in English. They alleged disadvantage *vis-à-vis* French-speaking business competitors who were allowed to use their mother tongue without restriction. On the article 27 aspect of the complaint the Committee concluded:

¶ 11.2. . . . that this provision refers to minorities in States . . . Further, article 50 of the Covenant provides that its provisions extend to all parts of Federal States without any limitations or exceptions. Accordingly, the minorities referred to in article 27 are minorities within such a State, and not minorities within any province. A group may constitute a

---

[5] See *Marshall v Canada* (205/86) (also known as *Mikmaq Tribal Society v Canada*), at [22.12].
[6] *Hopu and Bessert v France* (549/93), at [20.10].
[7] See, generally, Chap. 17.
[8] The term 'minority' has been defined elsewhere as 'a group', being:
    'numerically inferior to the rest of the population of a State, in a non-dominant position, whose members—being nationals of a State—possess ethnic, religious or linguistic characteristics differing from those of the rest of the population and show, if only implicitly, a sense of solidarity, directed towards preserving their culture, traditions, religion or language.'
F. Caportori, *Study on the Rights of Persons Belonging to Ethnic, Religious and Linguistic Minorities* (United Nations, New York, 1991), para. 568.

majority in a province but still be a minority in a State and thus be entitled to the benefits of article 27. English speaking citizens of Canada cannot be considered a linguistic minority. The authors therefore have no claim under article 27 of the Covenant.

Thus a minority is a group that is numerically inferior within the state as a whole, and not merely numerically inferior within one province or region.

[24.08] A strong dissent in *Ballantyne* was voiced by Mrs Elizabeth Evatt, co-signed by Messrs Ando, Bruni Celli, and Dimitrijevic:

My difficulty with the decision is that it interprets the term 'minorities' in article 27 solely on the basis of the number of members of the group in question in the State party. The reasoning is that because English speaking Canadians are not a numerical minority in Canada they cannot be a minority for the purposes of article 27.

I do not agree, however, that persons are necessarily excluded from the protection of article 27 where their group is an ethnic, linguistic or cultural minority in an autonomous province of a State, but is not clearly a numerical minority in the State itself, taken as a whole entity. The criteria for determining what is a minority in a State (in the sense of article 27) has [*sic*] not yet been considered by the Committee, and does [*sic*] not need to be foreclosed by a decision in the present matter, which can in any event be determined on other grounds.

[24.09] According to the HRC majority in *Ballantyne* [24.07], a group which forms a majority in a State can never be classified as a minority, though it would probably be classified as a people for the purposes of article 1. A flaw in this reasoning is that the latter rights cannot be enforced under the Optional Protocol [7.20], so the rights of oppressed majorities may be unduly limited by the *Ballantyne* judgment. However, other rights would often be relevantly applicable, such as the rights of non-discrimination and political participation, or, as in *Ballantyne*, freedom of expression.[9]

[24.10] *GENERAL COMMENT 23*

¶ 5.2. Article 27 confers rights on persons belonging to minorities which 'exist' in a State party. Given the nature and scope of the rights envisaged under that article, it is not relevant to determine the degree of permanence that the term 'exist' connotes. Those rights simply are that individuals belonging to those minorities should not be denied the right, in community with members of their group, to enjoy their own culture, to practise their religion and speak their language. Just as they need not be nationals or citizens, they need not be permanent residents. Thus, migrant workers or even visitors in a State party constituting such minorities are entitled not to be denied the exercise of those rights. . . . The existence of an ethnic, religious or linguistic minority in a given State party does not depend upon a decision by that State party but requires to be established by objective criteria.

[24.11] Mrs Higgins, in a separate opinion in *T.K. v France* (220/87), stated:

---

[9] See, on the art. 19 ramifications of *Ballantyne*, [18.38].

The Committee has, in relation to several State parties, rejected the notion that the existence of minorities is in some way predicated on an admission of discrimination. Rather, it has insisted that the existence of minorities within the sense of article 27 is a factual matter; and that such minorities may indeed exist in States parties committed in law and in fact, to the full equality of all persons within its jurisdiction. . . .

Regarding France, the HRC has stated:[10]

¶ 24. . . . The Committee is, however, unable to agree that France is a country in which there are no ethnic, religious or linguistic minorities. The Committee wishes to recall in this respect that the mere fact that equal rights are granted to all individuals and that all individuals are equal before the law does not preclude the existence in fact of minorities in a country, and their entitlement to the enjoyment of their culture, the practice of their religion or the use of their language in community with other members of their group.

In its Concluding Comments on Slovenia, the Committee noted:[11]

¶ 12. . . . that the State party singles out Italians and Hungarians for special protection as minorities, including the right to political representation. Gypsies are also granted certain special protection as a minority. Whilst this protection is welcome, all minorities are entitled to protection of their rights under article 27. Immigrant Communities constituting minorities under the meaning of article 27 are entitled to the benefit of that article.

Finally, in Concluding Comments on Austria, the HRC stated:[12]

¶ 14. The Committee notes with concern that the State party appears to restrict the definition of minorities to certain legally recognized groups. . . .

Thus the Committee has noted its concern at State legislation that limits the definition of minorities,[13] and/or laws which acknowledge only some minority groups within the relevant State. These types of laws often restrict or exclude specific permanent and non-permanent residents from full recognition as minority groups with minority rights.

Membership of a Minority

[24.12]   *LOVELACE v CANADA (24/77)*

This case confirms that States Parties cannot constrict the definition of particular 'minorities', nor can they define membership of a minority. The facts are outlined immediately below:

---

[10] Concluding Comments on France (1997) UN doc. CCPR/C/79/Add.80. France however has benefited from a reservation to art. 27; see, e.g., *T.K. v France* (220/87) [25.08].

[11] (1994) UN Doc CCPR/C/79Add.40; further see the Concluding Comments on Estonia (1995) CCPR/C/79/Add.5, para. 23; Concluding Comments on Russian Federation (1995) U.N. doc. CCPR/C/79/Add.54, para. 23.   [12] (1998) UN doc. CCPR/C/79/Add. 103.

[13] See also Concluding Comments on Ukraine (1995) UN doc. CCPR/C/79/Add.52, para. 18; Concluding Comments on Senegal (1997) UN doc. CCPR/C/79/Add. 5, para. 17; Concluding Comments on Libyan Arab Jamahiriya (1998) UN doc. CCPR/C/79/Add. 101, para. 19.

¶ 1. The author of the communication . . . is a 32-year-old woman, living in Canada. She was born and registered as 'Maliseet Indian' but has lost her rights and status as an Indian in accordance with section 12 (1) (b) of the Indian Act, after having married a non-Indian on 23 May 1970. . . .

The State Party responded as follows:

¶ 5. In its submission under article 4 (2) of the Optional Protocol concerning the merits of the case . . . the State party recognized that 'many of the provisions of the . . . Indian Act, including section 12 (1) (b), require serious reconsideration and reform'. . . . It none the less stressed the necessity of the Indian Act as an instrument designed to protect the Indian minority in accordance with article 27 of the Covenant. A definition of the Indian was inevitable in view of the special privileges granted to the Indian communities, in particular their right to occupy reserve lands. Traditionally, patrilineal family relationships were taken into account for determining legal claims. Since, additionally, in the farming societies of the nineteenth century, reserve land was felt to be more threatened by non-Indian men than by non-Indian women, legal enactments as from 1869 provided that an Indian woman who married a non-Indian man would lose her status as an Indian. These reasons were still valid. A change in the law could only be sought in consultation with the Indians themselves who, however, were divided on the issue of equal rights. The Indian community should not be endangered by legislative changes. Therefore, although the Government was in principle committed to amending section 12 (1) (b) of the Indian Act, no quick and immediate legislative action could be expected.

The HRC decided as follows:

¶ 13.1. The Committee considers that the essence of the present complaint concerns the continuing effect of the Indian Act, in denying Sandra Lovelace legal status as an Indian, in particular because she cannot for this reason claim a legal right to reside where she wishes to, on the Tobique Reserve. . . . In this respect the significant matter is her . . . claim . . . that 'the major loss to a person ceasing to be an Indian is the loss of the cultural benefits of living in an Indian community, the emotional ties to home, family, friends and neighbours, and the loss of identity'.

¶ 13.2. . . . It has to be considered whether Sandra Lovelace, because she is denied the legal right to reside on the Tobique Reserve, has by that fact been denied the right guaranteed by article 27 to persons belonging to minorities, to enjoy their own culture and to use their own language in community with other members of their group.

¶ 14. The rights under article 27 of the Covenant have to be secured to 'persons belonging' to the minority. At present Sandra Lovelace does not qualify as an Indian under Canadian legislation. However, the Indian Act deals primarily with a number of privileges which, as stated above, do not as such come within the scope of the Covenant. Protection under the Indian Act and protection under article 27 of the Covenant therefore have to be distinguished. Persons who are born and brought up on a reserve, who have kept ties with their community and wish to maintain these ties must normally be considered as belonging to that minority within the meaning of the Covenant. Since Sandra Lovelace is ethnically a Maliseet Indian and has only been absent from her home reserve for a few years during the existence of her marriage, she is, in the opinion of the Committee, entitled to be regarded as 'belonging' to this minority and to claim the benefits of article 27 of the Covenant. The question whether these benefits have been denied to her, depends on how far they extend.

¶ 15. The right to live on a reserve is not as such guaranteed by article 27 of the Covenant. Moreover, the Indian Act does not interfere directly with the functions which are expressly mentioned in that article. However, in the opinion of the Committee the right of Sandra Lovelace to access to her native culture and language 'in community with the other members' of her group, has in fact been, and continues to be interfered with, because there is no place outside the Tobique Reserve where such a community exists. On the other hand, not every interference can be regarded as a denial of rights within the meaning of article 27. Restrictions on the right to residence, by way of national legislation, cannot be ruled out under article 27 of the Covenant. This also follows from the restrictions to article 12 (1) of the Covenant set out in article 12 (3). The Committee recognizes the need to define the category of persons entitled to live on a reserve, for such purposes as those explained by the Government regarding protection of its resources and preservation of the identity of its people. However, the obligations which the Government has since undertaken under the Covenant must also be taken into account.

¶ 16. In this respect, the Committee is of the view that statutory restrictions affecting the right to residence on a reserve of a person belonging to the minority concerned, must have both a reasonable and objective justification and be consistent with the other provisions of the Covenant, read as a whole. Article 27 must be construed and applied in the light of the other provisions mentioned above, such as articles 12, 17 and 23 in so far as they may be relevant to the particular case, and also the provisions against discrimination, such as articles 2, 3 and 26, as the case may be. It is not necessary, however, to determine in any general manner which restrictions may be justified under the Covenant, in particular as a result of marriage, because the circumstances are special in the present case.

¶ 17. The case of Sandra Lovelace should be considered in the light of the fact that her marriage to a non-Indian has broken up. It is natural that in such a situation she wishes to return to the environment in which she was born, particularly as after the dissolution of her marriage her main cultural attachment again was to the Maliseet band. Whatever may be the merits of the Indian Act in other respects, it does not seem to the Committee that to deny Sandra Lovelace the right to reside on the reserve is reasonable, or necessary to preserve the identity of the tribe. The Committee therefore concludes that to prevent her recognition as belonging to the band is an unjustifiable denial of her rights under article 27 of the Covenant, read in the context of the other provisions referred to.

Thus the Committee found that Ms Lovelace's access to her indigenous culture and language was unjustifiably restricted by the Indian Act, so a breach of article 27 was made out. This decision was ostensibly confined to apply in the particular circumstances of Lovelace's ostracism, which included the fact of her divorce from her non-Indian husband. However, it is likely that the sexist application of the Indian Act would have breached the Covenant in any case.[14]

---

[14] The provisions would probably have breached art. 27, read in conjunction with the non-discrimination guarantees in arts. 2(1), 3, and 26. See, e.g., [23.42].

[24.13] Canada's Indian Act was subsequently amended to address the issues raised by the *Lovelace* decision. The amendments allowed women who had married non-Indians before 1985 to rejoin their bands, but imposed a restriction on acceptance of children of inter-racial marriages born after 1985. Interestingly, a complaint about this amendment was raised in *R.L. et al. v Canada* (358/89). The author's complaint was that the amendment essentially restricted the band's right to determine its own membership. The complaint was eventually found inadmissible for failure to exhaust local remedies. It is a shame that the HRC was not able to consider the merits of the complaint. Paragraph 5.2 of General Comment 23 states that the classification of minority membership is 'objective' [24.10]. Whilst this objectivity clearly prevents a State from conclusively defining a minority for the purposes of article 27, it probably also precludes a minority group from conclusively defining its own membership.[15]

[24.14] In Concluding Comments on Canada in 1999, the HRC commented on the post-*Lovelace* amendments:[16]

¶ 20. . . . Although the Indian status of women who had lost status because of marriage was reinstituted, this amendment affects only the woman and her children, not subsequent generations, which may still be denied membership of the community. The Committee recommends that these issues be addressed by the State party.

Rights of Indigenous People under Article 27

[24.15] 'Indigenous peoples' in the international context may be understood as 'those living descendants of pre-invasion inhabitants of lands now dominated by others'.[17] In General Comment 23, at paragraphs 3.2 [24.02] and 7 [24.19], the HRC confirms that indigenous peoples are minorities for the purposes of article 7. Indeed, the complaints in *Lovelace* [24.12], *Kitok v Sweden* (197/85) [24.21], and *Ominayak v Canada* (167/87) [24.24] all concerned indigenous minority rights.[18]

---

[15] Such is implied in the decision in *Kitok v Sweden* (197/85) [24.21]. See also [23.68].

[16] (1999) UN doc. CCPR/C/79/Add. 105.

[17] S. J. Anaya, *Indigenous People and International Law* (Oxford University Press, New York, 1996), at 3. Anaya explains that indigenous people 'have been deprived of vast landholdings, and access to life sustaining resources, and they have suffered . . . activ[e] suppress[ion] [of] their political and cultural institutions. As a result indigenous people have been crippled economically and socially, their cohesiveness as communities has been damaged or threatened, and the integrity of their cultures has been undermined', at 4.

[18] In addition to the wide-ranging analysis provided by Anaya, ibid., there is considerable commentary on the nature of the rights of indigenous people at international law; for instance see R. Barsh, 'Indigenous Peoples in the 1990s: From Object to Subject of International Law?' (1994) 7 *Harvard Human Rights Journal* 33; I. Brownlie, *Treaties and Indigenous Peoples* (Clarendon Press, Oxford, 1992); J. Crawford (ed.) ,*The Rights of Peoples* (Clarendon Press, Oxford, 1988), H. Hannum 'Minorities, Indigenous Peoples and Self Determination' in L. Henkin *et al.* (eds.), *Human Rights; An*

[24.16] The HRC has issued a number of Concluding Comments regarding the protection of indigenous peoples' rights under the ambit of article 27. For example, regarding Sweden, the Committee stated the following:[19]

¶ 18. The Committee notes that legislative provisions adopted recently by the Riksdag . . . providing for the right for everyone to fish and hunt on public lands may have adverse consequences on the traditional rights of the members of the Sami people. . . .

¶ 26. The Committee recommends that the recognized customary rights of the Sami people be fully protected in the light of article 27 of the Covenant.

Brazil's treatment of its indigenous peoples generated this Comment: [20]

¶ 15. The Committee is particularly concerned over the existence of racial and other discrimination against black and indigenous persons. It notes that the Government has been pursuing a process of demarcation of indigenous lands in Brazil as a means of addressing the rights of the indigenous communities, but regrets that the process is far from completion.

¶ 32. The Committee recommends that the State party take immediate steps to guarantee the rights of individuals belonging to racial minorities and indigenous communities, especially with regard to their access to quality health services and education. Such steps should ensure greater school enrolment and reduce the incidence of school drop out. It is the view of the Committee that, in light of article 27 of the Covenant, all necessary measures should be taken to ensure that the process of demarcation of indigenous lands be speedily and justly settled.

The HRC stated, with regard to Mexico's treatment of its indigenous people:[21]

¶ 12. Lastly, the Committee has expressed concern about the situation of indigenous populations. Article 27 of the Constitution concerning agrarian reform is often implemented to the detriment of persons belonging to such groups. The delay in resolving problems relating to the distribution of land has weakened the confidence of these populations in both local and federal authorities. Moreover, these persons are subject to special laws, particularly in Chiapas, which could create a situation of discrimination within the meaning of article 26 of the Covenant. . . .

¶ 18. The Committee recommends that the Government should give consideration to more equitable land distribution within the framework of agrarian reform and that it should take into account the rights and aspirations of indigenous populations in that connection. . . . Indigenous populations should have the opportunity to participate in decision-making on matters that concern them.

Agenda for the Next Century (ASIL, Studies in Transnational Legal Policy No. 26,Washington, DC, 1994); S. Pritchard (ed.), *Indigenous Peoples, the United Nations and Human Rights* (Zed Books, London, 1998); S. Pritchard and C. Heindow-Dolman, 'Indigenous Peoples and International Law: A Critical Overview' (1998) 3 *Australian Indigenous Law Reporter* 473–510; and the work of the United Nations Working Group on Indigenous Populations.

[19] Concluding Comments on Sweden (1995) U.N. Doc. CCPR/C/79/Add.58.
[20] Concluding Comments on Brazil (1996) U.N. Doc. CCPR/C/79/Add.66.
[21] Concluding Comments on Mexico (1994) U.N. Doc. CCPR/C/79/Add.32.

The above Concluding Comments confirm that recognition and protection of 'native' or Aboriginal title and land rights for indigenous peoples are an integral part of article 27 compliance.[22]

[24.17] Indigenous peoples are treated as a 'minority' for the purposes of the application of article 27. This is irrespective of assertions by some indigenous peoples that they are not 'minorities' but in fact have a different and special status under international law. Whilst some modern instruments such as the draft Declaration on Indigenous Rights, the ILO Convention Concerning Indigenous and Tribal Peoples in Independent Countries (No 169), and the Convention on the Rights of the Child[23] address indigenous people as discrete groupings, separate from minorities in general, the HRC has not adopted this analysis.

[24.18] The Committee on the Elimination of Racial Discrimination (CERD) has issued a General Recommendation on Indigenous Rights under the International Convention on the Elimination of Racial Discrimination.

CERD GENERAL RECOMMENDATION 23

¶ 3. The Committee is conscious of the fact that in many regions of the world indigenous peoples have been, and are still being, discriminated against, deprived of their human rights and fundamental freedoms and in particular that they have lost their land and resources to colonists, commercial companies and State enterprises. Consequently the preservation of their culture and their historical identity has been and still is jeopardized.

¶ 4. The [CERD] Committee calls in particular upon States parties to:

(a) recognize and respect indigenous distinct culture, history, language and way of life as an enrichment of the State's cultural identity and to promote its preservation;

(b) ensure that members of indigenous peoples are free and equal in dignity and rights and free from any discrimination, in particular that based on indigenous origin or identity;

(c) provide indigenous peoples with conditions allowing for a sustainable economic and social development compatible with their cultural characteristics;

(d) ensure that members of indigenous peoples have equal rights in respect of effective participation in public life, and that no decisions directly relating to their rights and interests are taken without their informed consent;

(e) ensure that indigenous communities can exercise their rights to practise and revitalize their cultural traditions and customs, to preserve and to practise their languages.

---

[22] See also CERD General Recommendation 23, para. 5 [24.18] and Concluding Comments on Japan (HRC) (1998) UN doc. CCPR/C/79/Add. 102, para. 14. See further J. Corntassel and T. Primeau, 'Indigenous "Sovereignty" and International Law: Revised Strategies for Pursuing "Self-Determination" ' (1995) 17 *HRQ* 343, and C. Scott, 'Indigenous Self Determination and Decolonisation of the International Imagination: A Plea' (1996) 18 *HRQ* 814.

[23] See CRC, art. 30.

¶ 5. The Committee especially calls upon States parties to recognize and protect the rights of indigenous peoples to own, develop, control and use their communal lands, territories and resources and, where they have been deprived of their lands and territories tradition-ally owned or otherwise inhabited or used without their free and informed consent, to take steps to return these lands and territories. Only when this is for factual reasons not possi-ble, the right to restitution should be substituted by the right to just, fair and prompt compensation. Such compensation should as far as possible take the form of lands and territories.

In conformity with this General Recommendation, the CERD Committee has criticized Australian legislation which diminished the native title rights of indige-nous Australians:[24]

¶ 6. The Committee, having considered a series of new amendments to the Native Title Act, as adopted in 1998, expresses concern over the compatibility of the Native Title Act, as currently amended, with the State party's international obligations under the Conven-tion. While the original Native Title Act recognizes and seeks to protect indigenous title, provisions that extinguish or impair the exercise of indigenous title rights and interests pervade the amended Act. While the original 1993 Native Title Act was delicately balanced between the rights of indigenous and non-indigenous title holders, the amended Act appears to create legal certainty for Governments and third parties at the expense of indige-nous title. . . .

¶ 11. The Committee calls on the State party to address these concerns as a matter of utmost urgency. Most importantly, in conformity with the Committee's general recommen-dation XXIII concerning indigenous peoples, the Committee urges the State party to suspend implementation of the 1998 amendments and reopen discussions with the repre-sentatives of the Aboriginal and Torres Strait Islander peoples with a view to finding solu-tions acceptable to the indigenous peoples and which would comply with Australia's obligations under the Convention.

Substantive Content: What is Protected under Article 27?

CULTURE

[24.19]   *GENERAL COMMENT 23*

¶ 7. With regard to the exercise of the cultural rights protected under article 27, the Committee observes that culture manifests itself in many forms, including a particular way of life associated with the use of land resources, especially in the case of indigenous peoples. That right may include such traditional activities as fishing or hunting and the right to live in reserves protected by law. The enjoyment of those rights may require

---

[24] Decision 2(54) on Australia: (1999) UN doc. A/54/18. para. 21(2). See [7.17]. See also S. Hoff-man, 'United Nations Committee on the Elimination of Racial Discrimination: Consideration of Australia under its Early Warning Measures and Urgent Action Procedures' (2000) 6 *Australian Jour-nal of Human Rights* 13.

positive legal measures of protection and measures to ensure the effective participation of members of minority communities in decisions which affect them.

The final sentence in paragraph 7 importantly guarantees minority peoples rights of consultation with regard to decisions that might impact on their culture.[25] Indeed, this requirement of direct participation by and consultation with minorities in certain decisions seems to contradict the HRC's earlier decision in *Marshall v Canada* (285/86) regarding the right of political participation in article 25(a) [22.13].

[24.20] In a series of cases concerning the Nordic Sami peoples and their reindeer herding practices, the HRC had to consider whether reindeer husbandry amounted to a cultural activity protected within the scope of article 27. One such case is excerpted directly below.

[24.21]   *KITOK v SWEDEN (197/85)*

The facts are evident from the HRC's decision below:

¶ 9.1. The main question before the Committee is whether the author of the communication is the victim of a violation of article 27 of the Covenant because, as he alleges, he is arbitrarily denied immemorial rights granted to the Sami community, in particular, the right to membership of the Sami community and the right to carry out reindeer husbandry. In deciding whether or not the author of the communication has been denied the right to 'enjoy his own culture', as provided for in article 27 of the Covenant, and whether section 12, paragraph 2, of the 1971 Reindeer Husbandry Act, under which an appeal against a decision of a Sami community to refuse membership may only be granted if there are special reasons for allowing such membership, violates article 27 of the Covenant, the Committee bases its findings on the following considerations.

¶ 9.2. The regulation of an economic activity is normally a matter for the State alone. However, where that activity is an essential element in the culture of an ethnic community, its application to an individual may fall under article 27 of the Covenant. . . .

¶ 9.5. According to the State party, the purposes of the Reindeer Husbandry Act are to restrict the number of reindeer breeders for economic and ecological reasons and to secure the preservation and well-being of the Sami minority. Both parties agree that effective measures are required to ensure the future of reindeer breeding and the livelihood of those for whom reindeer farming is the primary source of income. The method selected by the State party to secure these objectives is the limitation of the right to engage in reindeer breeding to members of the Sami villages. The Committee is of the opinion that all these objectives and measures are reasonable and consistent with article 27 of the Covenant.

¶ 9.6. The Committee has none the less had grave doubts as to whether certain provisions of the Reindeer Husbandry Act, and their application to the author, are compatible with article 27 of the Covenant. Section 11 of the Reindeer Husbandry Act provides that:

---

[25] See [24.26–24.30] for examples of the application of this right.

'A member of a Sami community is:

'1. A person entitled to engage in reindeer husbandry who participates in reindeer husbandry within the pasture area of the community.

'2. A person entitled to engage in reindeer husbandry who has participated in reindeer husbandry within the pasture area of the village and who has had this as his permanent occupation and has not gone over to any other main economic activity.

'3. A person entitled to engage in reindeer husbandry who is the husband or child living at home of a member as qualified in subsection 1 or 2 who is the surviving husband or minor child of a deceased member.'

Section 12 of the Act provides that:

'A Sami community may accept as a member a person entitled to engage in reindeer husbandry other than as specified in section 11, if he intends to carry on reindeer husbandry with his own reindeer within the pasture area of the community.

'If the applicant should be refused membership, the Landsstyrelsen may grant him membership, if special reasons should exist.'

¶ 9.7. It can thus be seen that the Act provides certain criteria for participation in the life of an ethnic minority whereby a person who is ethnically a Sami can be held not to be a Sami for the purpose of the Act. The Committee has been concerned that the ignoring of objective ethnic criteria in determining membership of a minority, and the application to Mr. Kitok of the designated rules, may have been disproportionate to the legitimate ends sought by the legislation. It has further noted that Mr. Kitok has always retained some links with the Sami community, always living on Sami lands and seeking to return to full-time reindeer farming as soon as it became financially possible, in his particular circumstances, for him to do so.

¶ 9.8. In resolving this problem, in which there is an apparent conflict between the legislation, which seems to protect the rights of the minority as a whole, and its application to a single member of that minority, the Committee has been guided by the *ratio decidendi* in the *Lovelace* case, namely, that a restriction upon the right of an individual member of a minority must be shown to have a reasonable and objective justification and to be necessary for the continued viability and welfare of the minority as a whole. After a careful review of all the elements involved in this case, the Committee is of the view that there is no violation of article 27 by the State party. In this context the Committee notes that Mr. Kitok is permitted, albeit not as of right, to graze and farm his reindeer, to hunt and to fish.

[24.22] *Kitok* squarely raises issues regarding the potential clash between the minority rights of an *individual* and the minority rights of a *group*. Indeed, the case illustrates how one's individual minority rights can be validly limited by countervailing minority group rights, although the rights protected under the Convention are generally understood to be rights held by individuals, and not by groups. Thus the group rights protected under article 27 seem subject to a perennial tension.

[24.23] Though ultimately no article 27 violation was found, *Kitok* confirms a broad and flexible interpretation of 'culture' within the scope of article 27. 'Culture' will certainly embrace the maintenance of traditional beliefs and practices, but will also include those social and economic activities that are a part of the group's contemporary culture.[26]

ECONOMIC DEVELOPMENT AND ITS IMPACT ON CULTURE

CHIEF OMINAYAK and the LUBICON LAKE BAND v CANADA (167/87)

[24.24] The Lubicon Lake Cree Indians of northern Alberta in Canada, represented by their Chief, Bernard Ominayak, complained of violation of their rights to enjoy their own culture. They argued that the province of Alberta, and thus Canada,[27] had allowed private oil and gas exploration activities to threaten their way of life, and therefore their culture. The violation was manifested by the threat of destruction of the Band's economic base, and the continuity of its indigenous traditions and practices, thus endangering the Band's survival as a people. On the merits, the Committee found that:

¶ 33. Historical iniquities, to which the State party refers, and certain more recent developments threaten the way of life and culture of the Lubicon Lake Band, and constitute a violation of article 27 so long as they continue. . . .

The *Ominayak* decision is curiously brief.[28] However, it confirmed that economic development projects can be trumped by a State's duty to protect article 27 cultural rights.

[24.25] Mr Ando issued a dissent in *Ominayak*:

In my opinion . . . the right to enjoy one's own culture should not be understood to imply that the Band's traditional way of life must be preserved *at all costs*. Past history of mankind bears out that technical development has brought about various changes to existing ways of life and thus affected a culture sustained thereon. Indeed, outright refusal by a group in a given society to change its traditional way of life may hamper the economic development of the society as a whole. For this reason I would like to express my reservation to the categorical statement that recent developments have threatened the life of the Lubicon Lake Band and constitute a violation of article 27.

Ando's proposed qualification to the nature of the protection offered by article 27 by reference to the needs of the society at large seems to negate the very rationale that underpins the article; that is the protection of that which is unique and

---

[26] See B. Kingsbury, 'Claims by Non-State Groups in International Law' (1992) 25 *Cornell ILJ* 481, at 491. See also para 9.3 of *Länsman v Finland* (511/92) [24.26].

[27] See discussion of the application of the ICCPR in federal States at [1.63–1.64].

[28] See [1.44].

particular to the identity and preservation of the minority group.[29] Indeed, it is quite clear that the proper protection of minority rights often entails reduction in the legal rights of others.[30] However, Ando does raise the issue of whether article 27 rights are absolute. In fact, very few ICCPR rights are absolute, and are normally subject to proportionate limitations.[31] The following cases confirm that article 27 rights may be limited by laws or practices which the HRC find to be proportionate.

[24.26]   *LÄNSMAN v FINLAND (511/92)*

In this case, the authors, Ilmari Länsman and forty-seven other members of the Muotkatunturi Herdsmen's Committee and members of the Angeli local community, claimed to be the victims of a violation by Finland of article 27, when the government authorized quarrying works which disturbed the authors' traditional reindeer herding practices. The HRC decided in favour of the State Party. Pertinent facts are evident from the following excerpts of its decision:

¶ 9.1. The Committee has examined the present communication in the light of all the information provided by the parties. The issue to be determined by the Committee is whether quarrying on the flank of Mt. Etelä-Riutusvaara, in the amount that has taken place until the present time or in the amount that would be permissible under the permit issued to the company which has expressed its intention to extract stone from the mountain (i.e. up to a total of 5,000 cubic metres), would violate the authors' rights under article 27 of the Covenant.

¶ 9.2. It is undisputed that the authors are members of a minority within the meaning of article 27 and as such have the right to enjoy their own culture; it is further undisputed that reindeer husbandry is an essential element of their culture. In this context, the Committee recalls that economic activities may come within the ambit of article 27, if they are an essential element of the culture of an ethnic community. (Views on communication No. 197/1985 (*Kitok v Sweden*), adopted on 27 July 1988, paragraph 9.2.)

¶ 9.3. The right to enjoy one's culture cannot be determined *in abstracto* but has to be placed in context. In this connection, the Committee observes that article 27 does not only protect traditional means of livelihood of national minorities, as indicated in the State party's submission. Therefore, that the authors may have adapted their methods of reindeer herding over the years and practise it with the help of modern technology does not prevent them from invoking article 27 of the Covenant. Furthermore, mountain Riutusvaara continues to have a spiritual significance relevant to their culture. The Committee also notes the concern of the authors that the quality of slaughtered reindeer could be adversely affected by a disturbed environment.

¶ 9.4. A State may understandably wish to encourage development or allow economic

---

[29] Thornberry, above note 1, 141.
[30] See, e.g., para. 18 of Concluding Comments on Sweden at [24.16].   [31] See [1.52].

activity by enterprises. The scope of its freedom to do so is not to be assessed by reference to a margin of appreciation, but by reference to the obligations it has undertaken in article 27. Article 27 requires that a member of a minority shall not be denied his right to enjoy his culture. Thus, measures whose impact amounts to a denial of the right will not be compatible with the obligations under article 27. However, measures that have a certain limited impact on the way of life of persons belonging to a minority will not necessarily amount to a denial of the right under article 27.

¶ 9.5. The question that therefore arises in this case is whether the impact of the quarrying on Mount Riutusvaara is so substantial that it does effectively deny to the authors the right to enjoy their cultural rights in that region. The Committee recalls paragraph 7 of its General Comment on article 27, according to which minorities or indigenous groups have a right to the protection of traditional activities such as hunting, fishing or, as in the instant case, reindeer husbandry, and that measures must be taken 'to ensure the effective participation of members of minority communities in decisions which affect them'.

¶ 9.6. Against this background, the Committee concludes that quarrying on the slopes of Mt. Riutusvaara, in the amount that has already taken place, does not constitute a denial of the authors' right, under article 27, to enjoy their own culture. It notes in particular that the interests of the Muotkatunturi Herdsmen's' Committee and of the authors were considered during the proceedings leading to the delivery of the quarrying permit, that the authors were consulted during the proceedings, and that reindeer herding in the area does not appear to have been adversely affected by such quarrying as has occurred.

¶ 9.7. As far as future activities which may be approved by the authorities are concerned, the Committee further notes that the information available to it indicates that the State party's authorities have endeavoured to permit only quarrying which would minimize the impact on any reindeer herding activity in Southern Riutusvaara and on the environment; the intention to minimize the effects of extraction of stone from the area on reindeer husbandry is reflected in the conditions laid down in the quarrying permit. Moreover, it has been agreed that such activities should be carried out primarily outside the period used for reindeer pasturing in the area. Nothing indicates that the change in herding methods by the Muotkatunturi Herdsmen's' Committee . . . could not be accommodated by the local forestry authorities and/or the company.

¶ 9.8. With regard to the authors' concerns about future activities, the Committee notes that economic activities must, in order to comply with article 27, be carried out in a way that the authors continue to benefit from reindeer husbandry. Furthermore, if mining activities in the Angeli area were to be approved on a large scale and significantly expanded by those companies to which exploitation permits have been issued, then this may constitute a violation of the authors' rights under article 27, in particular of their right to enjoy their own culture. The State party is under a duty to bear this in mind when either extending existing contracts or granting new ones.

The HRC essentially decided that the impugned mining activities did not have an unduly detrimental effect on Sami cultural activities. This decision was prompted by the State Party's evidence that the quarrying occurred only during seasons when reindeer herds were out of the area,[32] and of the relatively small size of the quarry site and the amount of extracted stone.[33]

[24.27] In its defence, the State had submitted the following:

¶ 7.12. The State . . . claims that the Human Rights Committee's Views in the case of *Kitok* (Case No. 197/1985,) imply that the Committee endorses the principle that States enjoy a certain degree of discretion in the application of article 27—which is normal in all regulation of economic activities. According to the State party, this view is supported by the decisions of the highest tribunals of States parties to the Covenant and the European Commission on Human Rights.

¶ 7.13. The State party concludes that the requirements of article 27 have 'continuously been taken into consideration by the national authorities in their application and implementation of the national legislation and the measures in question'. It reiterates that a margin of discretion must be left to national authorities even in the application of article 27: 'As confirmed by the European Court of Human Rights in many cases, the national judge is in a better position than the international judge to make a decision. In the present case, two administrative authorities and . . . the Supreme Administrative Court, have examined the granting of the permit and related measures and considered them as lawful and appropriate'. . . . [T]he authors can continue to practise reindeer husbandry and are not forced to abandon their lifestyle. The quarrying and the use of the old forest road line, or the possible construction of a proper road, are insignificant or at most have a very limited impact on this means of livelihood.

Though the HRC evidently accepted that the mining activities had 'a very limited impact', it rejected the argument that the case could be determined by reference to a 'margin of discretion' for the State Party at paragraph 9.4. Thus, the HRC indicated that it will retain a strong supervisory role in monitoring implementation of article 27.[34] Nevertheless, the HRC also appears willing to give States Parties considerable leeway before finding that development measures pose such a threat to traditional cultures that they breach article 27. This is evinced in the second *Länsman* case, excerpted directly below.

[24.28]   *LÄNSMAN et al. v FINLAND (671/95)*

The Sami of Finland again issued a complaint to the HRC, invoking paragraph 9.8 of the first *Länsman* case [24.26], which they interpreted as a warning to the State Party regarding implementation of new measures affecting the living conditions of local Samis. In the second *Länsman* case, the authors challenged the plans of the Finnish Central Forestry Board to approve logging and the construction of roads in an area covering about 3,000 hectares of the winter herding

---

[32] Para. 7.4.   [33] Paras. 7.5 and 7.9.
[34] On the margin of discretion or the margin of appreciation see [18.21].

grounds of the Muotkatunturi Herdsmen's Committee. The HRC expressed its view as follows:

¶ 10.1. . . . The issue to be determined is whether logging of forests in an area covering approximately 3,000 hectares of the area of the Muotkatunturi Herdsmen's Committee (of which the authors are members)—i.e. such logging as has already been carried out and future logging—violates the authors' rights under article 27 of the Covenant. . . .

¶ 10.3. Article 27 requires that a member of a minority shall not be denied the right to enjoy his culture. Measures whose impact amounts to a denial of the right are incompatible with the obligations under article 27. As noted by the Committee previously in [the first *Länsman* case] however, measures that have a certain limited impact on the way of life and the livelihood of persons belonging to a minority will not necessarily amount to a denial of the rights under article 27.

¶ 10.4. The crucial question to be determined in the present case is whether the logging that has already taken place within the area specified in the communication, as well as such logging as has been approved for the future and which will be spread over a number of years, is of such proportions as to deny the authors the right to enjoy their culture in that area. The Committee recalls the terms of paragraph 7 of its General Comment on article 27, according to which minorities or indigenous groups have a right to the protection of traditional activities such as hunting, fishing or reindeer husbandry, and that measures must be taken to 'ensure the effective participation of members of minority communities in decisions which affect them'.

¶ 10.5. After careful consideration of the material placed before it by the parties, and duly noting that the parties do not agree on the long-term impact of the logging activities already carried out and planned, the Committee is unable to conclude that the activities carried out as well as approved constitute a denial of the authors' right to enjoy their own culture. It is uncontested that the Muotkatunturi Herdsmen's Committee, to which the authors belong, was consulted in the process of drawing up the logging plans and in the consultation, the Muotkatunturi Herdsmen's Committee did not react negatively to the plans for logging. That this consultation process was unsatisfactory to the authors and was capable of greater interaction does not alter the Committee's assessment. It transpires that the State party's authorities did go through the process of weighing the authors' interests and the general economic interests in the area specified in the complaint when deciding on the most appropriate measures of forestry management, i.e. logging methods, choice of logging areas and construction of roads in these areas. The domestic courts considered specifically whether the proposed activities constituted a denial of article 27 rights. The Committee is not in a position to conclude, on the evidence before it, that the impact of logging plans would be such as to amount to a denial of the authors' rights under article 27 or that the finding of the Court of Appeal affirmed by the Supreme Court, misinterpreted and/or misapplied article 27 of the Covenant in the light of the facts before it.

¶ 10.6. As far as future logging activities are concerned, the Committee observes that on the basis of the information available to it, the State party's forestry authorities have approved logging on a scale which, while resulting in additional work and extra expenses for the authors and other reindeer herdsmen, does not appear to threaten the survival of reindeer husbandry. That such husbandry is an activity of low economic profitability is not, on the basis of the information available, a result of the encouragement of other economic activities by the State party in the area in question, but of other, external, economic factors.

¶ 10.7. The Committee considers that if logging plans were to be approved on a scale larger than that already agreed to for future years in the area in question or if it could be shown that the effects of logging already planned were more serious than can be foreseen at present, then it may have to be considered whether it would constitute a violation of the authors' right to enjoy their own culture within the meaning of article 27. The Committee is aware, on the basis of earlier communications, that other large scale exploitations touching upon the natural environment, such as quarrying, are being planned and implemented in the area where the Sami people live. Even though in the present communication the Committee has reached the conclusion that the facts of the case do not reveal a violation of the rights of the authors, the Committee deems it important to point out that the State party must bear in mind when taking steps affecting the rights under article 27, that though different activities in themselves may not constitute a violation of this article, such activities, taken together, may erode the rights of Sami people to enjoy their own culture.

¶ 11. The Human Rights Committee, acting under article 5, paragraph 4, of the Optional Protocol to the International Covenant on Civil and Political Rights, is of the view that the facts as found by the Committee do not reveal a breach of article 27 of the Covenant.

Thus the HRC found no breach on the facts, but warned of the potential for erosion of cultural rights.

[24.29] In Concluding Comments on Chile, the HRC stated:[35]

¶ 22. . . . the Committee is concerned by hydroelectric and other developments that might affect the way of life and the rights of persons belonging to the Mapuche and other indigenous communities. Relocation and compensation may be appropriate in order to comply with article 27 of the Covenant. Therefore: When planning actions that affect members of indigenous communities, the State party must pay primary attention to the sustainability of the indigenous culture and way of life and to the participation of members of indigenous communities in decisions that affect them.

[24.30] The Concluding Comment on Chile again confirms that economic development projects must take account of countervailing article 27 cultural rights. Such projects are more likely to be compatible with article 27 if relevant minorities have been consulted, and their cultural needs at least taken into account. Development projects are however permitted to impose some negative impact on minority rights. This contention is supported by both *Länsman* decisions. However, the negative impacts cannot be too devastating or they will breach the requirement that limits to article 27 be proportionate. For example, the HRC has stated, in Concluding Comment on Ecuador:[36]

¶ 19. The Committee expresses concern at the impact of oil extraction on the enjoyment by members of indigenous groups of their rights under article 27 of the Covenant. In this

---

[35] (1999) UN doc. CCPR/C/79/Add. 104.
[36] (1998) CCPR/C/79/Add.92.

connection, the Committee is concerned that, despite the legislation enacted to allow indigenous communities to enjoy the full use of their traditional lands in a communal way, there remain obstacles to the full enjoyment of the rights protected under article 27 of the Covenant.

The Committee recommends that further measures be taken to ensure that members of indigenous groups be protected against the adverse effects of the oil exploitation within the country and be enabled to enjoy fully their rights under article 27 of the Covenant, particularly with regard to preservation of their cultural identity and traditional livelihood.

RELIGION

[24.31] Article 27 expressly protects religious minorities. The HRC has not extrapolated on this specific element of article 27.[37] Matters relating to religious oppression have been dealt with under the independent guarantee of freedom of religion, article 18. Were a State to prescribe or enforce a State religion upon a minority, a breach of articles 18 and 27 would arise. Arguably then, the protection of religious minorities under article 27 is subsumed by that of article 18.[38]

LANGUAGE

[24.32]　　　　　　　*GENERAL COMMENT 23*

¶ 5.3. The right of individuals belonging to a linguistic minority to use their language among themselves, in private or in public, is distinct from other language rights protected under the Covenant. In particular, it should be distinguished from the general right to freedom of expression protected under article 19. The latter right is available to all persons, irrespective of whether they belong to minorities or not. Further, the right protected under article 27 should be distinguished from the particular right which article 14.3 (f) of the Covenant confers on accused persons to interpretation where they cannot understand or speak the language used in the courts. Article 14.3 (f) does not, in any other circumstances, confer on accused persons the right to use or speak the language of their choice in court proceedings.[39]

---

[37] In *Waldman v Canada* (694/96), Mr Scheinin, in a separate concurring opinion, suggested that 'article 27 imposes positive obligations for States to promote religious instruction in minority religions' [23.66]. The HRC however disposed of this case, which concerned preferential treatment given to Roman Catholics compared to other minority religions in Canada, under art. 26 [23.54].

[38] See generally Chap. 17. See also M. Nowak, *CCPR Commentary* (N.P. Engel, Kehl, 1993), 500; J. Packer, 'The Concept of Minority Rights' in J. Raikka (ed.), *Do We Need Minority Rights? Conceptual Issues* (Martinus Nijhoff, The Hague, 1996); N. Rodney, 'Conceptual Problems in the Protection of Minorities: International Legal Developments' (1995) 17 *HRQ* 48, at 53.

[39] In *Guesdon v French* (219/86) the author claimed the protection of art. 27 regarding his right to address the French courts in the language of his choice. The HRC denied the admissibility of his complaint regarding art. 27, in view of France's reservation concerning that article. The complaint was admissible regarding art. 14, although not upheld on the merits in that case: see [14.102].

[24.33] An example of the language rights protected is found in the HRC's Concluding Comments on Sudan:[40]

20. The Committee is concerned that there is no recognition in law of the right to use local languages in official communications or administrative or court proceedings, and that religious minorities can be adversely affected by a range of discretionary administrative actions which can include the destruction of schools and educational facilities under town planning regulations. Therefore: Emphasis should be given to the need of ethnic and religious minorities, wherever they reside in the Sudan, to pursue and develop their traditions, culture and language, as required by article 27 of the Covenant.

Regarding Algeria, the HRC stated:[41]

15. The Committee notes the statement of the delegation that the intention underlying the Arabic Language Decree which came into force on 5 July 1998 was to reinforce the status which that national language should possess. The Committee notes, however, that the compulsory, immediate and exclusive use of that language in all areas of public activity would have for effect to impede large sections of the population who use Berber or French in the enjoyment of the rights guaranteed under articles 19, 25, 26 and 27 of the Covenant. The Committee recommends that the law should be urgently reviewed so as to remove the negative consequences that it produces.

Regarding Norway, the HRC stated:[42]

¶ 6. The Committee . . . commends the devolution of responsibility to the Sami Assembly (*Sametinget*) with regard to matters affecting the life and culture of members of the Sami community and notes with satisfaction that the Sami language may be used in contacts with public bodies and before the courts.

[24.34] However, article 27 protection of language rights is not without its limits:

C.L.D. v FRANCE (228/87)

In a separate opinion, Mr. Birame Ndiaye stated the following, with the support of Mrs Higgins and Messrs Dimitrijevic, Mavrommatis, Pocar, and Wennergren:[43]

This article [27] certainly does not demand of States parties that they require their postal administrations to issue postal cheques in a language other than the official language nor does it stipulate that the authorities should accept information provided in another language.

---

[40] (1997) UN doc. CCPR/C/79/Add.85.
[41] (1998) UN doc. CCPR/C/79/Add.95.
[42] (1993) UN Doc. CCPR/C/79/Add.27.
[43] The majority found the case inadmissible for failure to exhaust local remedies and did not comment on its art. 27 implications.

[24.35]   *BALLANTYNE et al. v CANADA (359, 385/89)*

In this case, a Quebec provincial law prohibited the exhibition of commercial signs in a language other than French. The authors alleged, *inter alia*, breaches of their minority rights as English speakers in Quebec, and their article 19 rights of freedom of expression. The Quebec government argued that the measures were essential to preserve the cultural identity of French speakers in English-dominated Canada. The HRC majority nevertheless found a breach of article 19, though not article 27 [24.07]. The majority found the measures disproportionate to the aim of protecting the French language. [44] Mr Ndiaye, however, issued a vigorous dissent. He argued that the law essentially upheld *French-speaking* minority rights under article 27, so it constituted a permissible limitation to article 19 rights, in the following terms:

In the cases submitted to the Committee . . ., Quebec considered that 'historical developments since 1763 amply bear out the need for French-speakers to seek protection of their language and culture'. Thus, the goal pursued by the Charter of the French Language, as amended by Bill 178, is the very same as that aimed at by article 27 of the Covenant, to which effect must be given, if necessary by restricting freedom of expression on the basis of article 19, paragraph 3. . . .

The limitations embodied in article 19, paragraph 3(a) and (b), are applicable to the situation of the French-speaking minority in Canada. And as this country has maintained, albeit with too narrow a conception of freedom of expression, 'the Charter of the French Language, as amended . . ., may provide Quebec with a means of preserving its specific linguistic character and give French-speakers a feeling of linguistic security'. This is reasonable and is geared to ends compatible with the Covenant, namely, article 27.

Unfortunately, the Human Rights Committee has not endorsed the State party's view and has not agreed to integrate the requirements of implementation of article 27 in its decision. For the Committee, there is no linguistic problem in Canada or, if it does exist, it is not so important as to merit the treatment which the authorities of that country have chosen to extend to it. I can only disassociate myself from its conclusions.

Positive Measures of Protection

[24.36]   *GENERAL COMMENT 23*

¶ 6.1. Although article 27 is expressed in negative terms, that article, nevertheless, does recognize the existence of a 'right' and requires that it shall not be denied. Consequently, a State party is under an obligation to ensure that the existence and the exercise of this right are protected against their denial or violation. Positive measures of protection are, therefore, required not only against the acts of the State party itself, whether through its legislative, judicial or administrative authorities, but also against the acts of other persons within the State party.

---

[44] See [18.38] for Quebec government arguments and majority HRC decision.

¶ 6.2. Although the rights protected under article 27 are individual rights, they depend in turn on the ability of the minority group to maintain its culture, language or religion. Accordingly, positive measures by States may also be necessary to protect the identity of a minority and the rights of its members to enjoy and develop their culture and language and to practise their religion, in community with the other members of the group. In this connection, it has to be observed that such positive measures must respect the provisions of articles 2(1) and 26 of the Covenant both as regards the treatment between different minorities and the treatment between the persons belonging to them and the remaining part of the population. However, as long as those measures are aimed at correcting conditions which prevent or impair the enjoyment of the rights guaranteed under article 27, they may constitute a legitimate differentiation under the Covenant, provided that they are based on reasonable and objective criteria.

Furthermore, paragraph 7 of General Comment 23 confirms that 'positive legal measures of protection' are needed to preserve traditional activities, such as hunting and fishing [24.19].

[24.37] States are thus obliged to take such positive measures as are necessary in order to make certain that any disadvantages arising out of minority status are remedied, and that assimilationist pressures are counteracted.[45] States have a greater duty than that of guaranteeing tolerance or non-interference with expression of minority rights; 'specific action' must be embraced to address the practical burdens applicable to minority groups.[46] For example, the HRC has recommended that positive steps be taken with regard to protection of the minority rights of Native Americans in the USA:[47]

¶ 25. The Committee is concerned that aboriginal rights of Native Americans may, in law, be extinguished by Congress. It is also concerned by the high incidence of poverty, sickness and alcoholism among Native Americans, notwithstanding some improvements achieved with the Self-Governance Demonstration Project. . . .

¶ 37. The Committee recommends that steps be taken to ensure that previously recognized aboriginal Native American rights cannot be extinguished. The Committee urges the government to ensure that there is a full judicial review in respect of determinations of federal recognition of tribes. The Self-Governance Demonstration Project and similar programmes should be strengthened to continue to fight the high incidence of poverty, sickness and alcoholism among Native Americans.

¶ 38. The Committee expresses the hope that, when determining whether currently permitted affirmative action programmes for minorities and women should be withdrawn, the obligation to provide Covenant's rights in fact as well as in law be borne in mind.

---

[45] See Thornberry, above, note 1, at 24–5.
[46] See also [23.62] ff. on reverse discrimination.
[47] Concluding Comments on the United States of America (1995) UN Doc.CCPR/C/79/Add 50.

Conclusion

[24.38] The case law and General Comment provided by the HRC on article 27 indicate a body of jurisprudence that is supportive of protecting minority identity and valuing diversity as part of the essential 'fabric' of communities and of States. The HRC has made it clear that there are positive obligations on States to secure and strengthen the rights of minorities as fundamental human rights. A number of cases have involved complaints relating to the preservation of culture, particularly that of indigenous groups. Whilst the HRC has accepted that 'culture' has a variety of manifestations which are theoretically worthy of protection, it has demonstrated a reluctance in recent decisions such as the *Länsman* cases to find violations of article 27 on the facts. These decisions confirm that article 27 rights will be balanced against other countervailing interests, such as economic development. However, it is to be hoped that the HRC do not allow this 'balance' to be tipped too far in favour of economic interests.

Postscript: Please note that General Comment 28 on 'Equality of Rights Between Men and Women', contained in the Addendum at page 634, contains extra information on some of the material in this chapter.

Part IV

Alteration of ICCPR Duties

25

Reservations, Denunciations, Derogations

[**25.01**] Upon ratification of the ICCPR, a State Party may limit its legal obligations by entering reservations. After ratification, the State Party may alter its duties by derogating from its ICCPR duties under article 4 in times of public emergency, so long as the rigorous requirements of article 4 are satisfied. However, the HRC has suggested that States Parties cannot abdicate their duties under the ICCPR by withdrawing their ratification by way of denunciation. The following commentary addresses the ability of States Parties to alter their duties under the ICCPR and the two Optional Protocols.

Reservations

[**25.02**] Upon ratification of the ICCPR, a State may enter reservations to some of the provisions. A reservation renders the reserved provisions non-binding. A reservation can also act partially to reduce the effect of a certain guarantee, rather than entirely nullify its application.

[25.03] Reservations undoubtedly dilute the effectiveness of treaties. The permissibility of reservations in international treaty law essentially represents a compromise between the normative strength of a treaty and the maximization of ratifications to a treaty.

[25.04] The HRC has issued a General Comment regarding reservations to the ICCPR. This General Comment has proved controversial. The UK, the USA, and France have submitted formal responses to the HRC's General Comment 24.[1] Furthermore, the International Law Commission (ILC) has issued 'Preliminary Conclusions' regarding 'reservations to normative multilateral human rights treaties including human rights treaties'.[2] These conclusions contradict General Comment 24 to some extent. The ILC is currently awaiting comments from human rights treaty bodies and States on its Preliminary Conclusions, before drafting its final report on the matter.

[25.05]   *GENERAL COMMENT 24*

¶ 1. As of 1 November 1994, 46 of the 127 States Parties to the International Covenant on Civil and Political Rights had, between them, entered 150 reservations of varying significance to their acceptance of the obligations of the Covenant. Some of these reservations exclude the duty to provide and guarantee particular rights in the Covenant. Others are couched in more general terms, often directed to ensuring the continued paramountcy of certain domestic legal provisions. Still others are directed at the competence of the Committee. The number of reservations, their content and their scope may undermine the effective implementation of the Covenant and tend to weaken respect for the obligations of States Parties. It is important for States Parties to know exactly what obligations they, and other States Parties, have in fact undertaken. And the Committee, in the performance of its duties under either Article 40 of the Covenant or under the Optional Protocols, must know whether a State is bound by a particular obligation or to what extent. This will require a determination as to whether a unilateral statement is a reservation or an interpretative declaration and a determination of its acceptability and effects. . . .

¶ 4. The possibility of entering reservations may encourage States which consider that they have difficulties in guaranteeing all the rights in the Covenant nonetheless to accept the generality of obligations in that instrument. Reservations may serve a useful function to enable States to adapt specific elements in their laws to the inherent rights of each person as articulated in the Covenant. However, it is desirable in principle that States accept the full range of obligations, because the human rights norms are the legal expression of the essential rights that every person is entitled to as a human being.

[25.06] The HRC, in General Comment 24, appears to concede that reservations

---

[1] See Observations by the USA on General Comment 24 (1996) 3 IHRR 265 (hereafter 'USA'), Observations by the UK on General Comment 24 (1995) 3 IHRR 261 (hereafter 'UK'), and Observations by France on General Comment 24 (1997) 4 IHRR 6 (hereafter 'France').

[2] UN doc. A/52/10 (1997), para. 157. The final report had not yet been drafted by the time of the issue of the ILC's 1999 report (UN doc. A/54/10).

to the ICCPR are an unfortunate but necessary evil. Indeed, its antipathy towards ICCPR reservations is clearly enunciated in the final paragraph of General Comment 24:

¶ 20. . . . It is desirable for a State entering a reservation to indicate in precise terms the domestic legislation or practices which it believes to be incompatible with the Covenant obligation reserved; and to explain the time period it requires to render its own laws and practices compatible with the Covenant, or why it is unable to render its own laws and practices compatible with the Covenant. States should also ensure that the necessity for maintaining reservations is periodically reviewed, taking into account any observations and recommendations made by the Committee during examination of their reports. Reservations should be withdrawn at the earliest possible moment. Reports to the Committee should contain information on what action has been taken to review, reconsider or withdrawn reservations.

DECLARATIONS

[25.07] As mentioned in paragraph 1 of General Comment 24 [25.05], reservations may be distinguished from other statements made by States Parties upon ratification, often called 'understandings' or 'declarations'. The latter statements essentially give notice of a State's interpretation of the Covenant. They have no legal effect in international law.

GENERAL COMMENT 24

¶ 3. It is not always easy to distinguish a reservation from a declaration as to a State's understanding of the interpretation of a provision, or from a statement of policy. Regard will be had to the intention of the State, rather than the form of the instrument. If a statement, irrespective of its name or title, purports to exclude or modify the legal effect of a treaty in its application to the State, it constitutes a reservation. Conversely, if a so-called reservation merely offers a State's understanding of a provision but does not exclude or modify that provision in its application to that State, it is, in reality, not a reservation.

[25.08]   **T.K. v FRANCE (220/87)**

In this case, the HRC was called upon to decide on the effect of the following statement submitted by France upon its ratification of the ICCPR:

In the light of article 2 of the Constitution of the French Republic, the French government declares that article 27 is not applicable so far as the Republic is concerned.

In *T.K.*, the HRC majority stated the following:

¶ 8.3. . . . The Covenant itself does not provide any guidance in determining whether a unilateral statement made by a State party upon accession to it should have preclusionary effect regardless of whether it is termed a reservation or declaration. The Committee observes in this respect that it is not the formal designation but the effect the statement purports to have that determines its nature. If the statement displays a clear intent on the part of the State party to exclude or modify the legal effect of a specific provision of a treaty, it must be regarded as a binding reservation, even if the statement is phrased as a declaration. In the present case, the statement entered by the French Government upon accession to the Covenant is clear: it seems to exclude the application of article 27 to France and emphasizes this exclusion semantically with the words 'is not applicable'. The statement's intent is unequivocal and thus must be given preclusionary effect in spite of the terminology used. Furthermore, the State party's submission of 15 January 1989 also speaks of a French 'reservation' in respect of article 27. Accordingly, the Committee considers that it is not competent to consider complaints directed against France concerning alleged violations of article 27 of the Covenant.

[25.09] Mrs Higgins delivered a vigorous dissent on this point:

I am not able to agree with the findings of the Committee that it is precluded by the French declaration of 4 November 1980 from examining the author's claim as it relates to article 27 of the Covenant. The fact that the Covenant does not itself make the distinction between reservations and declarations does not mean that no distinction between these concepts exists, so far as the Covenant is concerned. Nor, in my view, is the matter disposed of by invocation of article 2 (1) (a) of the Vienna Convention on the Law of Treaties, which emphasizes that intent, rather than nomenclature, is the key.

An examination of the notification of 4 January 1982 shows that the Government of the Republic of France was engaged in two tasks: listing certain reservations and entering certain interpretative declarations. Thus in relation to article 4 (1), 9, 14 and 19 it uses the phrase 'enters a reservation'. In other paragraphs it declares how terms of the Covenant are in its view to be understood in relation to the French Constitution, French legislation, or obligations under the European Convention on Human Rights. To note, by reference to article 2(1)(d) of the Vienna Convention, that it does not matter how a reservation is phrased or named, cannot serve to turn these interpretative declarations into reservations. Their content is clearly that of declarations. Further, the French notification shows that deliberately different language was selected to serve different legal purposes. There is no reason to suppose that the contrasting use, in different paragraphs, of the phrase 'reservation' and 'declaration' was not entirely deliberate, with its legal consequence well understood by the Government of the Republic. . . .

[25.10] Similar majority and minority opinions on the French statement were delivered in *M.K. v France* (222/87), *S.G. v France* (347/88), and *G.B. v France* (348/89). The majority decisions were again supported, without dissent, in *R.L.M. v France* (363/89) and *C.L.D. v France* (439/90).

INTERPRETATIONS OF RESERVATIONS

[25.11]   *MALEKI v ITALY (699/96)*

The author complained of his trial *in absentia* by the State Party. Italy had made a statement, upon ratification, that the Italian practice governing trial in one's own presence was compatible with the provisions of article 14(3)(d). Italy claimed that this statement was a reservation, protecting it from the author's complaint. The HRC did not decide whether the statement was a declaration or a reservation. It decided as follows:

¶ 9.2. The State party's argument is that its declaration concerning article 14, paragraph 3(d) is a reservation that precludes the Committee examining the author's argument that his trial *in absentia* was not fair. However, that declaration deals only with article 14, paragraph 3(d), and does not relate to the requirements of article 14, paragraph 1. . . . Under this provision, basic requirements of a fair trial must be maintained, even when a trial *in absentia,* is not, *ipso facto,* a violation of a State party's undertakings. These requirements include summoning the accused in a timely manner and informing him of the proceedings against him.

Thus, the State Party's 'reservation' to the specific due process rights in article 14(3)(d) did not preclude examination of compatibility under the more general guarantee in article 14(1).[3] This indicates that the HRC will endeavour to read reservations narrowly.

[25.12] *Hopu and Bessert v France* (549/93) again concerned, *inter alia*, the interpretation of the French reservation to article 27.[4] The authors complained of breaches of their rights in Tahiti, a French colony. The majority interpreted that reservation as applying within France and within all of its dependent territories, including Tahiti, so the article 27 complaint was inadmissible. A minority of Mrs Evatt, Mrs Medina Quiroga, and Messrs Pocar, Scheinin, and Yalden, found that the reservation did not apply in Tahiti.

Whatever the legal relevance of the declaration made by France in relation to the applicability of article 27 may be in relation to the territory of metropolitan France, we do not consider the justification given in said declaration to be of relevance in relation to overseas territories under French sovereignty. The text of said declaration makes reference to article 2 of the French Constitution of 1958, understood to exclude distinctions between French citizens before the law. Article 74 of the same Constitution, however, includes a special clause for overseas territories, under which they shall have a special organization which takes into account their own interests within the general interests of the Republic. That special organization may entail, as France has pointed out in its submissions in the present communication, a difference legislation given the geographic, social and economic particularities of these territories. Thus, it is the declaration itself, as justified by France, which makes article 27 of the Covenant applicable in so far as overseas territories are concerned.

It appears to have been textually possible for the HRC to interpret the French reservation (which the minority insisted on calling a declaration) as having no effect in the French dependent territories. Therefore, the case indicates that the HRC will not always read reservations as narrowly as possible.

---

[3] See [14.76].   [4] See [25.08].

LIMITS TO STATES' RIGHTS OF RESERVATION

[25.13] There are limits to a State's freedom to enter reservations, as outlined in General Comment 24.

GENERAL COMMENT 24

¶ 5. The Covenant neither prohibits reservations nor mentions any type of permitted reservation. The same is true of the first Optional Protocol. . . .

¶ 6. The absence of a prohibition on reservations does not mean that any reservation is permitted. The matter of reservations under the Covenant and the first Optional Protocol is governed by international law. Article 19(3) of the Vienna Convention on the Law of Treaties provides relevant guidance. It stipulates that where a reservation is not prohibited by the treaty or falls within the specified permitted categories, a State may make a reservation provided it is not incompatible with the object and purpose of the treaty. Even though, unlike some other human rights treaties, the Covenant does not incorporate a specific reference to the object and purpose test, that test governs the matter of interpretation and acceptability of reservations.

Article 19(3) of the Vienna Convention on the Law of Treaties 1969 (Vienna Convention) did not come into force until 1980, after the date of entry into force of the Covenant. However, its norms reflect the customary law relating to reservations,[5] so its relevance to reservations under the Covenant is not controversial.

Determination of Incompatible Reservations

[25.14] The HRC has confirmed that States may not submit reservations which are incompatible with the object and purpose of the ICCPR. How is such incompatibility to be determined?

GENERAL COMMENT 24

¶ 16. The Committee finds it important to address which body has the legal authority to make determinations as to whether specific reservations are compatible with the object and purpose of the Covenant. As for international treaties in general, the International Court of Justice has indicated in the *Reservations to the Genocide Convention Case* (1951) that a State which objected to a reservation on the grounds of incompatibility with the object and purpose of a treaty could, through objecting, regard the treaty as not in effect as between itself and the reserving State. Article 20, paragraph 4, of the Vienna Convention on the Law of Treaties 1969 contains provisions most relevant to the present case on acceptance of and objection to reservations. This provides for the possibility of a State to object to a reservation made by another State. Article 21 deals with the legal effects of objections by States to reservations made by other States. Essentially, a reservation precludes the operation, as between the reserving and other States, of the provision reserved; and an objection thereto

---

[5]   See *Reservations to the Genocide Case* [1951] ICJ Rep. 15.

leads to the reservation being in operation as between the reserving and the objecting State only to the extent that it has not been objected to.

¶ 17. As indicated above, it is the Vienna Convention on the Law of Treaties that provides the definition of reservations and also the application of the object and purpose test in the absence of other specific provisions. But the Committee believes that its provisions on the role of State objections in relation to reservations are inappropriate to address the problem of reservations to human rights treaties. Such treaties, and the Covenant specifically, are not a web of inter-State exchanges of mutual obligations. They concern the endowment of individuals with rights. The principle of inter-State reciprocity has no place, save perhaps in the limited context of reservations to declarations on the Committee's competence under article 41.[6] And because the operation of the classic rules on reservations is so inadequate for the Covenant, States have often not seen any legal interest in or need to object to reservations. The absence of protest by States cannot imply that a reservation is either compatible or incompatible with the object and purpose of the Covenant. Objections have been occasional, made by some States but not others, and on grounds not always specified; when an objection is made, it often does not specify a legal consequence, or sometimes even indicates that the objecting party nonetheless does not regard the Covenant as not in effect as between the parties concerned. In short, the pattern is so unclear that it is not safe to assume that a non-objecting State thinks that a particular reservation is acceptable. In the view of the Committee, because of the special characteristics of the Covenant as a human rights treaty, it is open to question what effect objections have between States *inter se*. However, an objection to a reservation made by States may provide some guidance to the Committee in its interpretation as to its compatibility with the object and purpose of the Covenant.

[25.15] The UK and France disputed the HRC's contention that the Vienna Convention rules did not wholly apply to the determination of the validity of ICCPR reservations.[7] So too did the ILC's Special Rapporteur on Reservations to Treaties, in the following terms:

ILC ANNUAL REPORT 1997

¶ 75. . . . the Special Rapporteur wondered whether, on the other hand, special rules would be applicable to the 'special' category of normative treaties formed by human rights treaties. In that regard, he pointed out that, despite the eloquent pleading by human rights specialists for a regime specific to reservations to human rights treaties, none of the arguments offered a convincing basis for such a specific regime. In actual fact, it was the lacunae and the ambiguities of the Vienna regime that were questioned, lacunae and ambiguities of the general regime and not its application to certain categories of treaties.

¶ 76. The Special Rapporteur pointed out that his answer to the question whether there had been crucial reasons for not applying the Vienna regime to human rights treaties had been in the negative for the following reasons:

---

[6] Art. 41 prescribes the interstate complaints procedure, which has not yet been utilized. See discussion at [1.30].

[7] See UK, above, note 1, para. 2; France, above, note 1, para. 6.

(a) The Vienna regime was designed to be applied universally and without exception. Moreover, it should not be forgotten that the point of departure, namely the advisory opinion of the International Court of Justice on reservations to the Genocide Convention, concerned a quintessential human rights treaty;

(b) Since the Vienna Conventions, neither the practice of States *inter se*, nor judicial practice nor even the human rights treaty bodies had contested the applicability of the Vienna regime to human rights treaties. Moreover, the majority of the human rights treaties concluded after the Vienna Conventions either contained express clauses on reservations referring to the Vienna Convention or reproducing the Convention's criteria of the 'object and purpose' of the treaty, or they contained no clauses on reservations, but entailed the effective application of the Vienna regime as an expression of the 'ordinary law', something that was also apparent from the *travaux préparatoires* of those instruments. In that regard, the Special Rapporteur pointed out, even General Comment No. 24 of the Human Rights Committee, which had been challenged on other points, referred on a number of occasions to the Vienna Conventions.

[25.16] The ILC agreed with the Special Rapporteur in its preliminary conclusions:

ILC PRELIMINARY CONCLUSIONS

¶ 1. The Commission reiterates its view that articles 19 to 23 of the Vienna Conventions on the Law of Treaties of 1969 and 1986 govern the regime of reservations to treaties and that, in particular, the object and purpose of the treaty is the most important of the criteria for determining the admissibility of reservations;

¶ 2. The Commission considers that, because of its flexibility, this regime is suited to the requirements of all treaties, of whatever object or nature, and achieves a satisfactory balance between the objectives of preservation of the integrity of the text of the treaty and universality of participation in the treaty;

¶ 3. The Commission considers that these objectives apply equally in the case of reservations to normative multilateral treaties, including treaties in the area of human rights and that, consequently, the general rules enunciated in the above-mentioned Vienna Conventions govern reservations to such instruments;

[25.17] As the HRC believed that State Party objections were an unsuitable means of determining the incompatibility of reservations, it went on to assert its own competence to determine such incompatibility:

GENERAL COMMENT 24

¶ 18. It necessarily falls to the Committee to determine whether a specific reservation is compatible with the object and purpose of the Covenant. This is in part because, as indicated above, it is an inappropriate task for States parties in relation to human rights treaties, and in part because it is a task that the Committee cannot avoid in the performance of its functions. In order to know the scope of its duty to examine a State's compliance under article 40 or a communication under the first Optional Protocol, the Committee has necessarily to take a view on the compatibility of a reservation with the object and purpose of the Covenant and with general international law. Because of the special character of a human rights treaty, the compatibility of a reservation with the object and purpose of the Covenant must be established objectively, by reference to legal principles, and the Committee is particularly well placed to perform this task. . . .

The HRC's position is bolstered by judgments of the European Court of Human Rights and the Inter-American Court of Human Rights, which have used similar reasoning to uphold their own competence to determine the compatibility of reservations to the relevant regional human rights treaties.[8]

[25.18] However, France denied the HRC had the ability to rule on the compatibility of reservations, as such a power had not been expressly conferred by the ICCPR.[9] The views of the UK[10] and the ILC were more conciliatory towards the HRC's position.

ILC PRELIMINARY CONCLUSIONS

¶ 4. The Commission nevertheless considers that the establishment of monitoring bodies by many human rights treaties gave rise to legal questions that were not envisaged at the time of the drafting of those treaties, connected with appreciation of the admissibility of reservations formulated by States;

¶ 5. The Commission also considers that where these treaties are silent on the subject, the monitoring bodies established thereby are competent to comment upon and express recommendations with regard, *inter alia*, to the admissibility of reservations by States, in order to carry out the functions assigned to them;

¶ 6. The Commission stresses that this competence of the monitoring bodies does not exclude or otherwise affect the traditional modalities of control by the contracting parties, on the one hand, in accordance with the above-mentioned provisions of the Vienna Conventions of 1969 and 1986 and, where appropriate by the organs for settling any dispute that may arise concerning the interpretation or application of the treaties;

¶ 7. The Commission suggests providing specific clauses in normative multilateral treaties, including in particular human rights treaties, or elaborating protocols to existing treaties if States seek to confer competence on the monitoring body to appreciate or determine the admissibility of a reservation;

¶ 8. The Commission notes that the legal force of the findings made by monitoring bodies

---

[8] See *Belilos v Switzerland* (1988) 10 EHRR 466, at 485–7; *Advisory Opinion on the Effect of Reservations on the Entry into Force of the American Convention on Human Rights* (1982) 22 ILM 37, at 47; see also W. Schabas, 'Invalid Reservations to the International Covenant on Civil and Political Rights: Is the United States Still a Party?' (1995) 21 *Brooklyn Journal of International Law* 277, 310–16.

[9] See France, above, note 1, para. 7; see also para. 4 of Mr Ndiaye's separate opinion in *C.L.D. v France* (228/87), where he denies the HRC's competence to question reservations.

[10] See UK, above, note 1, paras. 11–12.

in the exercise of their power to deal with reservations cannot exceed that resulting from the powers given to them for the performance of their general monitoring role;

¶ 9. The Commission calls upon States to cooperate with monitoring bodies and give due consideration to any recommendations that they may make or to comply with their determination if such bodies were to be granted competence to that effect in the future;

Thus, the ILC conceded that treaty bodies, such as the HRC, could give opinions on the compatibility of reservations. However, these views have no strict legal force, as is the case with all of the views of UN treaty bodies, as these bodies are not courts.[11]

[25.19] Indeed, their non-judicial role is emphasized in paragraph 12 of the Preliminary Conclusions, where the ILC states that its comments do not apply to 'monitoring bodies within regional contexts'. Clearly, the major relevant difference between UN monitoring bodies and regional bodies is that the latter have a judicial character. It may be noted that the HRC responded to paragraph 12 in the following manner:[12]

[T]he Committee considers that regional monitoring bodies are not the only intergovernmental institutions which participate in and contribute to the development of practices and rules. Universal monitoring bodies, such as the Human Rights Committee, play no less important a role in the process by which such practices and rules develop and are entitled, therefore, to participate in and contribute to it. In this context, it must be recognized that the proposition enunciated by the Commission in paragraph 12 of the Provisional Conclusions is subject to modification as practices and rules developed by universal and regional monitoring bodies gain general acceptance. . . .

Two main points must be stressed in this regard.

First, in the case of human rights treaties providing for a monitoring body, the practice of that body by interpreting the treaty, contributes—consistent with the Vienna Convention— to defining the scope of the obligations arising out of the treaty. Hence, in dealing with the compatibility of reservations, the views expressed by monitoring bodies necessarily are part of the development of international practices and rules relating thereto.

Second, it is to be underlined that universal monitoring bodies, such as the Human Rights Committee, must know the extent of the States parties' obligations in order to carry out their functions under the treaty by which they are established. . . .

The Human Rights Committee shares the International Law Committee's view, expressed in paragraph 5 of its Preliminary Conclusions, that monitoring bodies established by human rights treaties 'are competent to comment upon and express recommendations with regard, *inter alia*, to the admissibility of reservations by States, in order to carry out the functions assigned to them'. It follows that States parties should respect conclusions reached by the independent monitoring body competent to monitor compliance with the instrument within the mandate it has been given.

---

[11] See [1.33]
[12] *Annual Report of the Human Rights Committee*, Part 1, 1999, UN Doc. A/54/40, Annex VI.

[25.20] In issuing General Comment 24, the HRC appears to have posed its greatest challenge to its official non-judicial role. This is compounded by its response to the ILC, where the HRC hints that its twenty years' experience has metamorphosed the legal effect of its practices and rules, so that they equate with the legal status of decisions by regional bodies such as the European Court of Human Rights.

[25.21] The HRC has recently confirmed its belief that it has the authority to determine the validity of reservations in the following case.

KENNEDY v TRINIDAD and TOBAGO (845/99)

Kennedy alleged a number of ICCPR violations entailed in the imposition upon him of a death penalty, and in his detention on death row. The State Party argued against admissibility of the communication, as it had submitted a relevant reservation to the Optional Protocol.[13]

¶ 4.2. The State party submits that because of this reservation . . . the Committee is not competent to consider the present communication. It is stated that in registering the communication and purporting to impose interim measures under rule 86 of the Committee's rules of procedure, the Committee has exceeded its jurisdiction, and the State party therefore considers the actions of the Committee in respect of this communication to be void and of no binding effect.

The HRC issued a vigorous response to the State Party:

¶ 6.4. As opined in the Committee's General Comment No. 24, it is for the Committee, as the treaty body to the International Covenant on Civil and Political Rights and its Optional Protocols, to interpret and determine the validity of reservations made to these treaties. The Committee rejects the submission of the State party that it has exceeded its jurisdiction in registering the communication and in proceeding to request interim measures under rule 86 of the rules of procedure. In this regard, the Committee observes that it is axiomatic that the Committee necessarily has jurisdiction to register a communication so as to determine whether it is or is not admissible because of a reservation. As to the effect of the reservation, if valid, it appears on the face of it, and the author has not argued to the contrary, that this reservation will leave the Committee without jurisdiction to consider the present communication on the merits. The Committee must, however, determine whether or not such a reservation can validly be made.

The HRC's findings regarding the compatibility of the Trinidadian reservation are excerpted below [25.28].

---

[13] See [25.28] and [25.38] regarding the circumstances surrounding this reservation.

What Reservations are Incompatible with the ICCPR?

[25.22]   *GENERAL COMMENT 24*

¶ 7. In an instrument which articulates very many civil and political rights, each of the many articles, and indeed their interplay, secures the objectives of the Covenant. The object and purpose of the Covenant is to create legally binding standards for human rights by defining certain civil and political rights and placing them in a framework of obligations which are legally binding for those States which ratify; and to provide an efficacious supervisory machinery for the obligations undertaken.

[25.23] In paragraph 7 of General Comment 24, the HRC broadly outlines the 'object and purpose' of the Covenant. In subsequent paragraphs, the HRC specifies particular reservations which would defeat that object and purpose.

¶ 8. Reservations that offend peremptory norms would not be compatible with the object and purpose of the Covenant. Although treaties that are mere exchanges of obligations between States allow them to reserve *inter se* application of rules of general international law, it is otherwise in human rights treaties, which are for the benefit of persons within their jurisdiction. Accordingly, provisions in the Covenant that represent customary international law (and *a fortiori* when they have the character of peremptory norms) may not be the subject of reservations. Accordingly, a State may not reserve the right to engage in slavery, to torture, to subject persons to cruel, inhuman or degrading treatment or punishment, to arbitrarily deprive persons of their lives, to arbitrarily arrest and detain persons, to deny freedom of thought, conscience and religion, to presume a person guilty unless he proves his innocence, to execute pregnant women or children, to permit the advocacy of national, racial or religious hatred, to deny to persons of marriageable age the right to marry, or to deny to minorities the right to enjoy their own culture, profess their own religion, or use their own language. And while reservations to particular clauses of Article 14 may be acceptable, a general reservation to the right to a fair trial would not be.

[25.24] The HRC's views regarding reservations to 'peremptory human rights norms' proved controversial.

FRENCH OBSERVATIONS ON GENERAL COMMENT 24

¶ 2. Paragraph 8 is drafted in such a way as to link the two distinct legal concepts of 'peremptory norms' and 'rules of customary international law', to the point of confusing them. . . .

In order to dispel any risk of confusion, France would like to raise the following points:

International custom is proof that a general practice has been accepted as law. It must be acknowledged that it is difficult—however regrettable that may be—to identify practices in the human rights area that fit this definition exactly. It would be premature, to say the least, to claim that all the examples cited in the report fit the definition of international custom cited above.

Although it may be accepted that certain human rights treaties formalize customary principles, this does not mean that the State's duty to observe a general customary principle should be confused with its agreement to be bound by the expression of that principle in a treaty, especially with the developments and clarifications that such formalization involves.

Finally, it goes without saying that the customary rule concept can in no way be equated with a peremptory norm of international law. . . .

It may be noted that France has entered a reservation to article 27, the guarantee of minority rights. Prior to publication of General Comment 24, the HRC had apparently recognized the validity of this reservation by declining to consider complaints of French breaches of article 27 submitted by Bretons in cases such as *T.K. v France* (220/87) [25.08]. Its General Comment indicates that this position could now be reversed. However, the effectiveness of the reservation has been reconfirmed in *Hopu and Bessert v France* (549/93) [25.12].

[25.25]   *US OBSERVATIONS ON GENERAL COMMENT 24*

It is clear that a State cannot exempt itself from a peremptory norm of international law by making a reservation to the Covenant. It is not at all clear that a State cannot choose to exclude one means of enforcement of particular norms by reserving against inclusion of those norms in its Covenant obligations. . . . [14]

The precise specification of what is contrary to customary international law, moreover, is a much more substantial question than indicated by the Comment. Even where a rule is generally established in customary international law, the exact contours and meaning of the customary law principle may need to be considered.

Paragraph 8, however, asserts in a wholly conclusory fashion that a number of propositions are customary international law which, to speak plainly, are not. It cannot be established on the basis of practice or other authority, for example, that the mere expression (albeit deplorable) of national, racial or religious hatred (unaccompanied by any overt action or preparation) is prohibited by customary international law. The Committee seems to be suggesting here that the reservations which a large number of States Parties have submitted to Article 20 are *per se* invalid. Similarly, while many are opposed to the death penalty in general and the juvenile death penalty in particular, the practice of States demonstrates that there is currently no blanket prohibition in customary international law. [15] Such a cavalier approach to international law by itself would raise serious concerns about the methodology of the Committee as well as its authority.

[25.26] The HRC's comments regarding the incompatibility of other specific reservations, outlined below, proved less controversial.

[14] The UK agreed in its comments, above, note 1, at para. 5.

[15] The USA has in fact entered reservations to arts. 20 and 6(5) (which prohibits imposition of the death penalty on juveniles), so its comments were probably partially designed to defend the validity of its own reservations.

GENERAL COMMENT 24

¶ 9. Applying more generally the object and purpose test to the Covenant, the Committee notes that, for example, reservation to article 1 denying peoples the right to determine their own political status and to pursue their economic, social, and cultural development, would be incompatible with the object and purpose of the Covenant. Equally, a reservation to the obligation to respect and ensure the rights, and to do so on a non-discriminatory basis (Article 2(1)) would not be acceptable. Nor may a State reserve an entitlement not to take the necessary steps at the domestic level to give effect to the rights of the Covenant (Article 2(2)).

¶ 10. The Committee has further examined whether categories of reservations may offend the 'object and purpose' test. In particular, it falls for consideration as to whether reservations to the non-derogable provisions of the Covenant are compatible with its object and purpose. . . . A reservation to the provisions of article 4 itself, which precisely stipulates the balance to be struck between the interests of the State and the rights of the individual in times of emergency, would fall in this category. And some non-derogable rights, which in any event cannot be reserved because of their status as peremptory norms, are also of this character—the prohibition of torture and arbitrary deprivation of life are examples. While there is no automatic correlation between reservations to non-derogable provisions, and reservations which offend against the object and purpose of the Covenant, a State has a heavy onus to justify such a reservation.

¶ 11. The Covenant consists not just of the specified rights, but of important supportive guarantees. These guarantees provide the necessary framework for securing the rights in the Covenant and are thus essential to its object and purpose. Some operate at the national level and some at the international level. Reservations designed to remove these guarantees are thus not acceptable. Thus, a State could not make a reservation to article 2, paragraph 3, of the Covenant, indicating that it intends to provide no remedies for human rights violations. Guarantees such as these are an integral part of the structure of the Covenant and underpin its efficacy. The Covenant also envisages, for the better attainment of its stated objectives, a monitoring role for the Committee. Reservations that purport to evade that essential element in the design of the Covenant, which is also directed to securing the enjoyment of the rights, are also incompatible with its object and purpose. A State may not reserve the right not to present a report and have it considered by the Committee. The Committee's role under the Covenant, whether under article 40 or under the Optional Protocols, necessarily entails interpreting the provisions of the Covenant and the development of a jurisprudence. Accordingly, a reservation that rejects the Committee's competence to interpret the requirements of any provisions of the Covenant would also be contrary to the object and purpose of that treaty.

¶ 12. The intention of the Covenant is that the rights contained therein should be ensured to all those under a State's party's jurisdiction. To this end certain attendant requirements are likely to be necessary. Domestic laws may need to be altered properly to reflect the requirements of the Covenant; and mechanisms at the domestic level will be needed to allow the Covenant rights to be enforceable at the local level. Reservations often reveal a tendency of States not to want to change a particular law. And sometimes that tendency is elevated to a general policy. Of particular concern are widely formulated reservations which essentially render ineffective all Covenant rights which would require any change in national law to ensure compliance with Covenant obligations. No real international rights or obligations have thus been accepted. And when there is an absence of provisions to ensure that Covenant rights may be sued on in domestic courts, and, further, a failure to allow individual complaints to be brought to the Committee under the first Optional Protocol, all the essential elements of the Covenant guarantees have been removed.[16] . . .

¶ 19. Reservations must be specific and transparent, so that the Committee, those under the jurisdiction of the reserving State and other States parties may be clear as to what obligations of human rights compliance have or have not been undertaken. Reservations may thus not be general, but must refer to a particular provision of the Covenant and indicate in precise terms its scope in relation thereto. When considering the compatibility of possible reservations with the object and purpose of the Covenant, States should also take into consideration the overall effect of a group of reservations, as well as the effect of each reservation on the integrity of the Covenant, which remains an essential consideration. States should not enter so many reservations that they are in effect accepting a limited number of human rights obligations, and not the Covenant as such. So that reservations do not lead to a perpetual non-attainment of international human rights standards, reservations should not systematically reduce the obligations undertaken only to the presently existing in less demanding standards of domestic law. Nor should interpretative declarations or reservations seek to remove an autonomous meaning to Covenant obligations, by pronouncing them to be identical, or to be accepted only insofar as they are identical, with existing provisions of domestic law. States should not seek through reservations or interpretative declarations to determine that the meaning of a provision of the Covenant is the same as that given by an organ of any other international treaty body.

Reservations to the First Optional Protocol

[25.27] *GENERAL COMMENT 24*

¶ 13. The issue arises as to whether reservations are permissible under the first Optional Protocol and, if so, whether any such reservation might be contrary to the object and purpose of the Covenant or of the first Optional Protocol itself. It is clear that the first Optional Protocol is itself an international treaty, distinct from the Covenant but closely related to it. Its object and purpose is to recognize the competence of the Committee to receive and consider communications from individuals who claim to be victims of a violation by a State party of any of the rights in the Covenant. States accept the substantive rights of individuals by reference to the Covenant, and not the first Optional Protocol. The function of the first Optional Protocol is to allow claims in respect of those rights to be tested before the Committee. Accordingly, a reservation to an obligation of a State to respect and ensure a right contained in the Covenant, made under the first Optional Protocol when it has not previously been made in respect of the same rights under the Covenant, does not affect the State's duty to comply with its substantive obligation. A reservation cannot be made to the Covenant through the vehicle of the Optional Protocol

---

[16] Art. 27 of the Vienna Convention prohibits the invocation of internal law as a justification for breaching treaties. Some ILC members felt that this rule could be transposed to reservations, thus lending support to the HRC's views; UN doc. A/52/10, para. 140.

but such a reservation would operate to ensure that the State's compliance with that obligation may not be tested by the Committee under the first Optional Protocol. And because
the object and purpose of the first Optional Protocol is to allow the rights obligatory for a
State under the Covenant to be tested before the Committee, a reservation that seeks to
preclude this would be contrary to the object and purpose of the first Optional Protocol,
even if not of the Covenant. A reservation to a substantive obligation made for the first time
under the first Optional Protocol would seem to reflect an intention by the State concerned
to prevent the Committee from expressing its views relating to a particular article of the
Covenant in an individual case.

France vigorously disagreed with paragraph 13, stating that 'nothing in international law appears necessarily to prohibit a State from qualifying or restricting its
acceptance of the [First Optional] Protocol'.[17]

[25.28]   *KENNEDY v TRINIDAD and TOBAGO (845/99)*

This case concerned allegations regarding various aspects of the author's death
sentence. In this case, the HRC had to determine the validity of the following
Trinidadian reservation to the First Optional Protocol:

¶ 4.1. In its submission of 8 April 1999, the State party makes reference to its instrument
of accession to the Optional Protocol of 26 May 1998, which included the following reservation:

> '. . .Trinidad and Tobago reaccedes to the Optional Protocol to the International
> Covenant on Civil and Political Rights with a Reservation to article 1 thereof to the
> effect that the Human Rights Committee shall not be competent to receive and consider
> communications relating to any prisoner who is under sentence of death in respect of
> any matter relating to his prosecution, his detention, his trial, his conviction, his
> sentence or the carrying out of the death sentence on him and any matter connected
> therewith.'

The circumstances giving rise to this reservation are described directly below:

¶ 6.2. On 26 May 1998, the Government of Trinidad and Tobago denounced the first
Optional Protocol to the International Covenant on Civil and Political Rights. On the same
day, it reacceded, including in its instrument of reaccession the reservation set out in paragraph 4.1 above.

¶ 6.3. To explain why such measures were taken, the State party makes reference to the
decision of the Judicial Committee of the Privy Council in *Pratt and Morgan v The
Attorney General for Jamaica* 2 A.C. 1, 1994, in which it was held that 'in any case in
which execution is to take place more than five years after sentence there will be strong
grounds for believing that the delay is such as to constitute "inhuman or degrading punishment or other treatment" ' in violation of section 17 of the Jamaican Constitution.[18] The

---

[17] France, above, note 1, para. 4.
[18] The Human Rights Committee has taken a different view from that of the Privy Council on the
human rights compatibility of the 'death row phenomenon': see [9.39] ff.

effect of the decision for Trinidad and Tobago is that inordinate delays in carrying out the death penalty would contravene section 5, paragraph 2(b), of the Constitution of Trinidad and Tobago, which contains a provision similar to that in section 17 of the Jamaican Constitution. The State party explains that as the decision of the Judicial Committee of the Privy Council represents the constitutional standard for Trinidad and Tobago, the Government is mandated to ensure that the appellate process is expedited by the elimination of delays within the system in order that capital sentences imposed pursuant to the laws of Trinidad and Tobago can be enforced. Thus, the State party chose to denounce the Optional Protocol:

> 'In the circumstances, and wishing to uphold its domestic law to subject no one to inhuman and degrading punishment or treatment and thereby observe its obligations under article 7 of the International Covenant on Civil and Political Rights, the Government of Trinidad and Tobago felt compelled to denounce the Optional Protocol. Before doing so, however, it held consultations on 31 March 1998, with the Chairperson and the Bureau of the Human Rights Committee with a view to seeking assurances that the death penalty cases would be dealt with expeditiously and completed within 8 months of registration. For reasons which the Government of Trinidad and Tobago respects, no assurance could be given that these cases would be completed within the timeframe sought.'

The reservation was prompted by a desire to eliminate delays in the execution of persons on death row, so as to accord with a Privy Council decision which had ruled that delays of over five years were unconstitutional in Jamaica (and Trinidad and Tobago). Continued access to the Optional Protocol complaints mechanism for death row inmates *a fortiori* extended their detention on death row, as Trinidad was obliged not to execute persons whilst their complaints were being considered by the HRC.[19]

The HRC majority decided that the reservation was invalid in the following terms:

¶ 6.7. The present reservation, which was entered after the publication of General Comment No. 24, does not purport to exclude the competence of the Committee under the Optional Protocol with regard to any specific provision of the Covenant, but rather to the entire Covenant for one particular group of complainants, namely prisoners under sentence of death. This does not, however, make it compatible with the object and purpose of the Optional Protocol. On the contrary, the Committee cannot accept a reservation which singles out a certain group of individuals for lesser procedural protection than that which is enjoyed by the rest of the population. In the view of the Committee, this constitutes a discrimination which runs counter to some of the basic principles embodied in the Covenant and its Protocols, and for this reason the reservation cannot be deemed compatible with the object and purpose of the Optional Protocol. The consequence is that the Committee is not precluded from considering the present communication under the Optional Protocol.

---

[19] See [8.26]. Trinidad and Tobago defied the HRC's interim request to refrain from executing an OP complainant in *Ashley v Trinidad and Tobago*: see UN doc. A/49/40, paras. 410–1.

[25.29] Messrs Ando, Bhagwati, Klein, and Kretzmer issued a dissenting opinion in *Kennedy*:

¶ 6. . . . . [A]ssumption by a state of the obligation to ensure and protect all the rights set out in the Covenant does not grant competence to the Committee to consider individual claims. Such competence is acquired only if the State party to the Covenant also accedes to the Optional Protocol. If a State party is free either to accept or not accept an international monitoring mechanism, it is difficult to see why it should not be free to accept this mechanism only with regard to some rights or situations, provided the treaty itself does not exclude this possibility. All or nothing is not a reasonable maxim in human rights law.

¶ 7. The Committee takes the view that the reservation of the State party in the present case is unacceptable because it singles out one group of persons, those under sentence of death, for lesser procedural protection than that enjoyed by the rest of the population. According to the Committee's line of thinking this constitutes discrimination which runs counter to some of the basic principles embodied in the Covenant and its Protocols. We find this argument unconvincing.

¶ 8. It goes without saying that a State party could not submit a reservation that offends peremptory rules of international law. Thus, for example, a reservation to the Optional Protocol that discriminated between persons on grounds of race, religion or sex, would be invalid. However, this certainly does not mean that every distinction between categories of potential victims of violations by the State party is unacceptable. All depends on the distinction itself and the objective reasons for that distinction.

¶ 9. When dealing with discrimination that is prohibited under article 26 of the Covenant, the Committee has consistently held that not every differentiation between persons amounts to discrimination. There is no good reason why this approach should not be applied here. As we are talking about a reservation to the Optional Protocol, and not to the Covenant itself, this requires us to examine not whether there should be any difference in the substantive rights of persons under sentence of death and those of other persons, but whether there is any difference between communications submitted by people under sentence of death and communications submitted by all other persons. The Committee has chosen to ignore this aspect of the matter, which forms the very basis for the reservation submitted by the State party.

¶ 10. The grounds for the denunciation of the Optional Protocol by the State party are set out in paragraph 6.3 of the Committee's views and there is no need to rehearse them here. What is clear is that the difference between communications submitted by persons under sentence of death and others is that they have different results. Because of the constitutional constraints of the State party the mere submission of a communication by a person under sentence of death may prevent the State party from carrying out the sentence imposed, even if it transpires that the State party has complied with its obligations under the Covenant. In other words, the result of the communication is not dependent on the Committee's views whether there has been a violation and if so what the recommended remedy is but on mere submission of the communication. This is not the case with any other category of persons who might submit communications.

¶ 11. It must be stressed that if the constitutional constraints faced by the State party had placed it in a situation in which it was violating substantive Covenant rights, denunciation of the Optional Protocol, and subsequent reaccession, would not have been a legitimate step, as its object would have been to allow the State party to continue violating the Covenant with impunity. Fortunately, that is not the situation here. While the Committee has taken a different view from that taken by the Privy Council (in the case mentioned in para. 6.3 of the Committee's views) on the question of whether the mere time on death row makes delay in implementation of a death sentence cruel and inhuman punishment, a State party which adheres to the Privy Council view does not violate its obligations under the Covenant.

¶ 12. In the light of the above, we see no reason to consider the State party's reservation incompatible with the object and purpose of the Optional Protocol. As the reservation clearly covers the present communication (a fact that is not contested by the author), we would hold the communication inadmissible.

[25.30]   *GENERAL COMMENT 24*

¶ 14. The Committee considers that reservations relating to the required procedures under the first Optional Protocol would not be compatible with its object and purpose. The Committee must control its own procedures as specified by the Optional Protocol and its rules of procedure. Reservations have, however, purported to limit the competence of the Committee to acts and events occurring after entry into force for the State concerned of the first Optional Protocol. In the view of the Committee this is not a reservation but, most usually, a statement consistent with its normal competence *ratione temporis*. At the same time, the Committee has insisted upon its competence, even in the face of such statements or observations, when events or acts occurring before the date of entry into force of the first Optional Protocol have continued to have an effect on the rights of a victim subsequent to that date. Reservations have been entered which effectively add an additional ground of inadmissibility under article 5, paragraph 2, by precluding examination of a communication when the same matter has already been examined by another comparable procedure. Insofar as the most basic obligation has been to secure independent third party review of the human rights of individuals, the Committee has, where the legal right and the subject matter are identical under the Covenant and under another international instrument, viewed such a reservation as not violating the object and purpose of the first Optional Protocol.

At the end of paragraph 14, the HRC alludes to the fact that a number of European parties to the Optional Protocol have entered reservations which preclude the HRC from examining a complaint that has previously been examined under the European Convention on Human Rights. These reservations have been found to be compatible with the First Optional Protocol.[20]

---

[20] These reservations are specifically discussed at [5.10] ff.

Reservations to the Second Optional Protocol

[25.31]   *GENERAL COMMENT 24*

¶ 15. The primary purpose of the Second Optional Protocol is to extend the scope of the substantive obligations undertaken under the Covenant, as they relate to the right to life, by prohibiting execution and abolishing the death penalty. It has its own provision concerning reservations, which is determinative of what is permitted. Article 2, paragraph 1, provides that only one category of reservation is permitted, namely one that reserves the right to apply the death penalty in time of war pursuant to a conviction for a most serious crime of a military nature committed during wartime. Two procedural obligations are incumbent upon State parties wishing to avail themselves of such a reservation. Article 2, paragraph 1, obliges such a State to inform the Secretary General, at the time of ratification or accession, of the relevant provisions of its national legislation during warfare. This is clearly directed towards the objectives of specificity and transparency and in the view of the Committee a purported reservation unaccompanied by such information is without legal effect. Article 2, paragraph 3, requires a State making such a reservation to notify the Secretary General of the beginning or ending of a state of war applicable to its territory. In the view of the Committee, no State may seek to avail itself of its reservation (that is, have execution in time of war regarded as lawful) unless it has complied with the procedural requirement of article 2, paragraph 3.

Effect of an Incompatible Reservation

[25.32] The International Court of Justice, in its *Advisory Opinion on Reservations to the Genocide Convention*, said that a State cannot be considered a party to the relevant treaty if it has entered an incompatible reservation.[21] However, the HRC disagreed that this regime applied in the context of the ICCPR.

GENERAL COMMENT 24

¶ 18. . . . The normal consequence of an unacceptable reservation is not that the Covenant will not be in effect at all for a reserving party. Rather, such a reservation will generally be severable, in the sense that the Covenant will be operative for the reserving party without benefit of the reservation.

The HRC's position is supported to some extent by ECHR jurisprudence. In *Louzidou v Turkey*, the European Court found that certain Turkish reservations to the ECHR were incompatible with the ECHR's object and purpose.[22] Nevertheless, Turkey remained a party to the ECHR, and its invalid reservations were severed, leaving the obligations under the 'reserved' provisions intact. In reaching this conclusion, the Court used a test of intention, and found that, upon

---

[21] [1951] ICJ Reports 15, at 29.
[22] (1995) 20 EHRR 99, para. 89.

ratification, Turkey had been willing to remain a State party if such severance occurred.[23]

[25.33] All three responding States objected to the HRC's assertions regarding the effect of an invalid reservation.[24] The ILC also disagreed:

ILC PRELIMINARY CONCLUSIONS

¶ 10. The Commission notes also that, in the event of inadmissibility of a reservation, it is the reserving State that has the responsibility for taking action. This action may consist, for example, in the State either modifying its reservation so as to eliminate the inadmissibility, or withdrawing its reservation, or foregoing becoming a party to the treaty. . . .

[25.34] *KENNEDY v TRINIDAD and TOBAGO (845/99)*

The HRC majority confirmed its beliefs regarding the effect of an invalid reservation in this case by implicitly severing the reservation from Trinidad's acceptance of the First Optional Protocol [25.28]. The dissenting minority (Messrs Ando, Bhagwati, Klein, and Kretzmer) commented in more detail on the effects of an invalid reservation.

¶ 15. In General Comment no. 24 the Committee discussed the factors that make a reservation incompatible with the object and purpose of the Covenant. In para. 18 the Committee considers the consequences of an incompatible reservation and states:

> 'The normal consequence of an unacceptable reservation is not that the Covenant will not be in effect at all for a reserving party. Rather, such a reservation will generally be severable, in the sense that the Covenant will be operative for the reserving party without benefit of the reservation.'

It is no secret that this approach of the Committee has met with serious criticism. Many experts in international law consider the approach to be inconsistent with the basic premises of any treaty regime, which are that the treaty obligations of a state are a function of its consent to assume those obligations. If a reservation is incompatible with the object and purpose of a treaty, the critics argue, the reserving state does not become a party to the treaty unless it withdraws that reservation. According to the critics' view there is no good reason to depart from general principles of treaty law when dealing with reservations to the Covenant.

¶ 16. It is not our intention within the framework of the present case to reopen the whole issue dealt with in General Comment no. 24. Suffice it to say that even in dealing with reservations to the Covenant itself the Committee did not take the view that in every case an unacceptable reservation will fall aside, leaving the reserving state to become a party to the Covenant without benefit of the reservation. As can be seen from the section of General

---

[23] Ibid., paras. 90–8; Schabas, above, note 8, 321–2.
[24] See UK, above, note 1, para. 14; USA, above, note 1 (no para. numbers given), France, above, note 1, para. 7.

Comment no. 24 quoted above, the Committee merely stated that this would normally be the case. The normal assumption will be that the ratification or accession is not dependent on the acceptability of the reservation and that the unacceptability of the reservation will not vitiate the reserving state's agreement to be a party to the Covenant. However, this assumption cannot apply when it is abundantly clear that the reserving state's agreement to becoming a party to the Covenant is dependent on the acceptability of the reservation. The same applies with reservations to the Optional Protocol.

¶ 17. As explained in para. 6.2 of the Committee's Views [25.28], on 26 May, 1998 the State party denounced the Optional Protocol and immediately reacceded with the reservation. It also explained why it could not accept the Committee's competence to deal with communications from persons under sentence of death. In these particular circumstances it is quite clear that Trinidad and Tobago was not prepared to be a party to the Optional Protocol without the particular reservation, and that its reaccession was dependent on acceptability of that reservation. It follows that if we had accepted the Committee's view that the reservation is invalid we would have had to hold that Trinidad and Tobago is not a party to the Optional Protocol. This would, of course, also have made the communication inadmissible.

RESERVATIONS TO OTHER UN CIVIL AND POLITICAL RIGHTS TREATIES

[25.35] Other UN civil and political rights treaties contain express provisions dealing with reservations. Article 20(2) of the International Convention on the Elimination of all Forms of Racial Discrimination 1966 (ICERD) prohibits reservations that are incompatible with the treaty's provisions; such incompatibility arises when two thirds or more States Parties object to it. Article 28 of the Convention on the Elimination of all Forms of Discrimination Against Women 1979 (CEDAW) and article 51 of the Convention on the Rights of the Child 1989 (CRC) also prohibit reservations that are incompatible with the respective treaty's object and purpose. Neither treaty specifies how such incompatibility will be determined, or the consequences of such incompatibility.

Conclusion

[25.36] The HRC's General Comment confirms that States Parties can enter reservations upon ratification which reduce their ICCPR obligations. However, it also identifies numerous instances of incompatibility which render reservations ineffective. Indeed, the General Comment indicates that many existing 'reservations' are actually ineffective, and thus have no impact on the actual extent of the reserving State's ICCPR obligations. The HRC majority has reinforced its faith in the General Comment in its recent admissibility decision in *Kennedy v Trinidad and Tobago* (845/99).[25] However, the persuasiveness of arguments

---

[25] See [25.21], [25.28], and [25.34].

against the General Comment, including its divergence from international law as expressed in the ICJ Advisory Opinion and the Vienna Convention, must be noted.

Uncertainty surrounds the issue of ICCPR reservations. This uncertainty evinces the clear tension between the classical view of treaties creating bilateral and multilateral relations between States, which informs the customary law of reservations, and the modern view that human rights treaties essentially create bilateral relations between States Parties and individuals.

Denunciations

[25.37] Denunciation of a treaty occurs when a State Party withdraws its membership from that treaty. In August 1997, in an unprecedented move, the Democratic People's Republic of Korea (North Korea) purported to denounce the ICCPR, thus terminating its ICCPR obligations.[26] In response, the HRC issued a General Comment dealing with denunciation.

GENERAL COMMENT 26

¶ 1. The International Covenant on Civil and Political Rights does not contain any provision regarding its termination and does not provide for denunciation or withdrawal. Consequently, the possibility of termination, denunciation or withdrawal must be considered in the light of applicable rules of customary international law which are reflected in the Vienna Convention on the Law of Treaties. On this basis, the Covenant is not subject to denunciation or withdrawal unless it is established that the parties intended to admit the possibility of denunciation or withdrawal or a right to do so is implied from the nature of the treaty.

¶ 2. That the parties to the Covenant did not admit the possibility of denunciation and that it was not a mere oversight on their part to omit reference to denunciation is demonstrated by the fact that article 41 (2) of the Covenant does permit a State party to withdraw its acceptance of the competence of the Committee to examine inter-State communications by filing an appropriate notice to that effect while there is no such provision for denunciation of or withdrawal from the Covenant itself. Moreover, the Optional Protocol to the Covenant, negotiated and adopted contemporaneously with it, permits States parties to denounce it. Additionally, by way of comparison, the Convention on the Elimination of All Forms of Racial Discrimination which was adopted one year prior to the Covenant, expressly permits denunciation. It can therefore be concluded that the drafters of the Covenant deliberately intended to exclude the possibility of denunciation. The same conclusion applies to the Second Optional Protocol in the drafting of which a denunciation clause was deliberately omitted.

---

[26] The notification of withdrawal was circulated to all States Parties by the UN Secretariat under cover of C.N.1997.TREATIES–10 of 12 November 1997.

¶ 3. Furthermore, it is clear that the Covenant is not the type of treaty which, by its nature, implies a right of denunciation. Together with the simultaneously prepared and adopted International Covenant on Economic, Social and Cultural Rights, the Covenant codifies in treaty form the universal human rights enshrined in the Universal Declaration of Human Rights, the three instruments together often being referred to as the 'International Bill of Human Rights'. As such, the Covenant does not have a temporary character typical of treaties where a right of denunciation is deemed to be admitted, notwithstanding the absence of a specific provision to that effect.

¶ 4. The rights enshrined in the Covenant belong to the people living in the territory of the State party. The Human Rights Committee has consistently taken the view, as evidenced by its long-standing practice, that once the people are accorded the protection of the rights under the Covenant, such protection devolves with territory and continues to belong to them, notwithstanding change in Government of the State party, including dismemberment in more than one State or State succession or any subsequent action of the State party designed to divest them of the rights guaranteed by the Covenant.

¶ 5. The Committee is therefore firmly of the view that international law does not permit a State which has ratified or acceded or succeeded to the Covenant to denounce it or withdraw from it.

Therefore, according to the HRC, the DPRK's purported denunciation has no effect on its ICCPR obligations. States Parties have no power to extinguish their ICCPR obligations via denunciation. Nor can States Parties denounce the Second Optional Protocol.

[25.38] In contrast, States Parties are expressly permitted under article 12 to denounce the First Optional Protocol. Trinidad and Tobago exercised this right on 26 August 1998, and reacceded to the First Optional Protocol with a new reservation concerning capital punishment on the same date.[27] Guyana withdrew from the Optional Protocol and reacceded, subject to reservations concerning capital punishment, with effect from 5 April 1999. Jamaica withdrew from the First Optional Protocol on 23 October 1997, and has not, as at December 1999, reacceded.[28] All denunciations were impelled by the Privy Council's decision in *Pratt and Morgan v Attorney-General for Jamaica*.[29]

On 27 March 2000, Trinidad and Tobago again denounced the Optional Protocol, in response to the decision in *Kennedy v Trinidad and Tobago* (845/99) [25.28]. This new denunciation took effect from 27 June 2000.

---

[27] The reservation prohibits consideration under the First Optional Protocol of matters arising from imposition of the death penalty. However, the HRC majority determined that the reservation was invalid in *Kennedy v Trinidad and Tobago* (845/99) [25.28].

[28] See generally N. Schiffrin, 'Jamaica Withdraws the Right of Individual Petition under the International Covenant on Civil and Political Rights' (1998) 92 *AJIL* 563.

[29] [1993] 2 AC 1. See *Kennedy v Trinidad and Tobago* (845/99), para. 6.3 at [25.28].

[25.39] *THOMAS v JAMAICA (800/98)*

The effect of the Jamaican denunciation was confirmed in this case. The author's allegations of ill-treatment contrary to articles 7 and 10 of the Covenant were inadmissible as they were 'transmitted to the State party after Jamaica's denunciation of the Optional Protocol came into force'.[30] Mr Solari Yrigoyen dissented in the following terms:

Although the State party denounced the Optional Protocol, a measure which took effect on 23 January 1998, the events described in the author's complaint occurred before that date and are [admissible].

[25.40] Article 21 of ICERD expressly permits denunciation, as does article 31 on the Convention against Torture and other Cruel, Inhuman or Degrading Treatment or Punishment (CAT) 1984 and article 52 of the CRC. CEDAW is silent on the matter. Following the rationale of General Comment 26, it would seem that denunciations are therefore not permitted to CEDAW.

Derogations

ARTICLE 4 OF THE ICCPR

1. In time of public emergency which threatens the life of the nation and the existence of which is officially proclaimed, the States Parties to the present Covenant may take measures derogating from their obligations under the present Covenant to the extent strictly required by the exigencies of the situation, provided that such measures are not inconsistent with their other obligations under international law and do not involve discrimination solely on the ground of race, colour, sex, language, religion or social origin.

2. No derogation from articles 6, 7, 8 (paragraphs 1 and 2), 11, 15, 16 and 18 may be made under this provision.

3. Any State party to the present Covenant availing itself of the right of derogation shall immediately inform the other States Parties to the present Covenant, through its intermediary of the Secretary-General of the United Nations, of the provisions from which it has derogated and of the reasons by which it was actuated. A further communication shall be made, through the same intermediary, on the date on which it terminates such derogation.

[25.41] Under article 4, States may 'derogate' from or limit ICCPR guarantees as a proportionate response to a serious public emergency. The right of derogation, like the right of reservation, may represent a 'necessary evil'. Whilst it is arguable that civil liberties must be curtailed during public emergencies to ensure general public safety,[31] it is also undoubtedly true that some of the most

---

[30] Para. 6.3.
[31] See P. R. Ghandhi, 'The Human Rights Committee and Derogation in Public Emergencies' (1989) 32 *German Yearbook of International Law* 323, at 326.

egregious human rights abuses occur during purported public emergencies.[32] It is therefore important that derogations are strictly monitored, and do not operate as a shield for the 'cynical and calculated destruction of the rights' of government opponents.[33]

[25.42] Despite the undoubted importance of the issue of derogations, the HRC has issued little meaningful jurisprudence on article 4. An early General Comment unfortunately sheds little light on the broader meaning of article 4, and few Optional Protocol cases have concerned derogations.[34] While a number of cases have concerned 'emergency measures', States Parties have rarely invoked derogation as a justification for these measures.[35] Therefore, the commentary below is supplemented by reference to standards which have emerged from expert symposia on human rights derogations, namely the Siracusa Principles[36] and the Paris Standards.[37] Whilst the HRC is not bound to follow these principles, it could be expected to be influenced by them in its future interpretation of article 4.

SUBSTANTIVE LIMITS TO THE POWER OF DEROGATION

Public Emergency Threatening the Life of the Nation

[25.43] The circumstances of derogation are strictly prescribed. First, there must exist a 'public emergency which threatens the life of the nation', such as a war, a terrorist emergency, or a severe natural disaster, such as a major flood or earthquake.

[25.44] It appears that the actual emergency can be geographically limited, as in the case of the UK terrorist emergency in Northern Ireland. Such emergencies can still threaten people throughout the entire nation.[38] Indeed, one may note that numerous terrorist attacks occurred on the UK mainland. It is however unconfirmed whether article 4(1) encompasses emergencies with limited geographical *impact*, such as a localized floods. Siracusa Principle 39 indicates that the whole

---

[32] See D. McGoldrick, *The Human Rights Committee* (Clarendon Press, Oxford, 1994), 301. See also a comprehensive study of human rights in a number of crisis situations by the International Commission of Jurists, *States of Emergency: Their Impact on Human Rights* (ICJ, Geneva, 1983).

[33] Ghandhi, above, note 31, 323.

[34] In 1999, the HRC appointed a *rapporteur*, Mr Scheinin, to draft a new General Comment on art. 4; see UN doc. A/54/40, Vol. I, para. 26.

[35] E.g. the right of derogation was not mentioned in *Polay Campos v Peru* (577/94) [14.48], which concerned special measures for the trial of alleged terrorists.

[36] 'Siracusa Principles on the Limitation and Derogation Provisions in the ICCPR' (1985) 7 HRQ 1, hereafter 'Siracusa Principles'. These principles were formulated at a conference in Sicily attended by 31 distinguished international law experts.

[37] 'Paris Minimum Standards of Human Rights Norms in a State of Emergency' (1985) 79 *AJIL* 1072, hereafter 'Paris Standards'. The Paris Standards were adopted by the International Law Association in 1984.

[38] M. Nowak, *CCPR Commentary* (N.P. Engel, Kehl, 1993), 79.

population must be affected by the emergency.[39] The Paris Standards, however, state the following:

PARIS STANDARDS

(A) 1(b). The expression 'public emergency' means an exceptional situation of crisis or public danger, actual or imminent, which affects the whole population or the whole population of the area to which the declaration applies and constitutes a threat to the organized life of the community of which the state is composed. . . .

(A) 4. The declaration of a state of emergency may cover the entire territory of the state or any part thereof, depending upon the areas actually affected by the circumstances motivating the declaration. This will not prevent the extension of emergency measures to other parts of the country whenever necessary nor the exclusion of those parts where such circumstances no longer prevail.

It is submitted that emergencies with severe yet geographically limited impact should still give States rights to make proportionate derogations. Otherwise, States with large territories such as the Russian Federation or Canada would be prejudiced in this respect.

[25.45] Siracusa Principle 41 states that 'economic difficulties *per se* cannot justify derogation measures'. Public emergencies are inherently extraordinary situations, whereas economic underdevelopment is unfortunately a commonplace situation in many States.

Requirement of Proportionality

[25.46] Permissible derogation measures must limit ICCPR rights only 'to the extent strictly required'. The Siracusa Principles state that:

¶ 51. The severity, duration, and geographic scope of any derogation measure shall be such only as are strictly necessary to deal with the threat to the life of the nation and are proportionate to its nature and extent.

Thus, derogation measures must accord with a strict standard of proportionality. For example, it would normally be disproportionate to deny the right to vote due to the exigencies caused by a flood.

[25.47]   SIRACUSA PRINCIPLES

54. The principle of strict necessity shall be applied in an objective manner. Each measure shall be directed to an actual, clear, present, or imminent danger and may not be imposed merely because of an apprehension of potential danger.

Principle 54 is controversial, as it purports to prohibit derogations designed to

---

[39] See also Ghandhi, above, note 31, 336.

diminish perceived future threats. Many such clampdowns are indeed disproportionate, as they may simply constitute clampdowns by oppressive governments of
legitimate political opposition,[40] or gross overreactions to perceived subversive
elements.[41] However, a question must arise as to how 'imminent' a danger must
be before derogations are permitted, as it is arguably best to prevent the occurrence of a public emergency, rather than to 'cure' a public emergency after it has
erupted.

[25.48] In General Comment 5, the HRC stated that 'measures taken under article 4 are of an exceptional and temporary nature and may only last as long as the
life of the nation concerned is threatened'.[42] Emergency measures must therefore
be terminated upon cessation of the relevant crisis.

Conformity with International Law

[25.49] Article 4 explicitly denies authority to derogate from other international
law measures. This rule is expressed more generally in article 5 of the ICCPR.
Relevant other treaties include the other UN human rights treaties, none of which
includes a derogation provision, as well as the Geneva Conventions on international humanitarian law and ILO Conventions.[43]

Non-discrimination in Derogation Measures

[25.50] Derogation measures may not discriminate 'solely' on enumerated
grounds. The enumerated grounds do not mirror the prohibited grounds of
discrimination under the Covenant's non-discrimination guarantees. For example,
article 4 discrimination seems *prima facie* permissible on the ground of national
origin or political opinion; such discrimination indeed often occurs under emergency laws.[44] Furthermore, the enumerated grounds appear to be exhaustive.[45]
Finally, Roslyn Higgins, a former HRC member, has suggested that the use of the
word 'solely' in the article 4 non-discrimination guarantee means that only deliberate discrimination, rather than inadvertent discrimination is prohibited.[46] For
example, geographically limited emergency measures could impact worse on a
particular racial group; such indirect discrimination would not breach article
4(1).[47]

---

[40] Such clampdowns were evinced on the facts of numerous early Optional Protocol cases against
Uruguay.
[41] E.g. the McCarthyite persecution of Communist sympathizers in the 1950s in the United States.
[42] General Comment 5, para. 3.
[43] Nowak, above, note 38, 85–6; see also Siracusa Principle 66.
[44] Nowak, above, note 38, 86.
[45] Compare the general non-discrimination guarantees, discussed at [23.17] ff.
[46] R. Higgins, 'Derogations under Human Rights Treaties' (1976–7) 48 *BYIL* 281, at 287.
[47] See T. Buergenthal, 'To Respect and to Ensure: State Obligations and Permissible Derogations'
in L. Henkin (ed.), *The International Bill of Rights: The International Covenant on Civil and Political
Rights* (Columbia University Press, New York, 1981), at 83. See, on indirect discrimination, [23.29]
ff.

Non-derogable Rights

[25.51] Article 4(2) specifies certain non-derogable rights: the right to life (article 6); freedom from torture, cruel, inhuman, degrading treatment or punishment, and freedom from medical or scientific experimentation without consent (article 7); freedom from slavery (article 8(1)) or servitude (article 8(2)); the right not to be imprisoned for contractual debt (article 11); freedom from retroactive criminal punishment (article 15); right to recognition as a person before the law (article 16); and freedom of thought, conscience, and religion (article 18).

[25.52]   *GENERAL COMMENT 24*

In its General Comment on Reservations, the HRC offered some observations on the nature of non-derogable rights:

¶ 10. . . . While there is no hierarchy of importance of rights under the Covenant, the operation of certain rights may not be suspended, even in times of national emergency. This underlines the great importance of non-derogable rights. But not all rights of profound importance, such as articles 9 and 27 of the Covenant, have in fact been made non-derogable. One reason for certain rights being made non-derogable is because their suspension is irrelevant to the legitimate control of the state of national emergency (for example, no imprisonment for debt, in article 11). Another reason is that derogation may indeed be impossible (as, for example, freedom of conscience). At the same time, some provisions are non-derogable exactly because without them there would be no rule of law. . . .

[25.53]   *SIRACUSA PRINCIPLES*

The Siracusa Principles indicate that guarantees regarding the administration of justice in articles 9 (right to liberty and security of the person) and 14 (right to a fair trial) may also be effectively non-derogable:

¶ 70. Although protections against arbitrary arrest and detention (article 9) and the right to a fair and public hearing in the determination of a criminal charge (article 14) may be subject to legitimate limitations if strictly required by the exigencies of an emergency situation, the denial of certain rights fundamental to human dignity can never be strictly necessary in any conceivable emergency. Respect for these fundamental rights is essential in order to ensure enjoyment of non-derogable rights and to provide an effective remedy against their violation. In particular:

(a) all arrests and detention and the place of detention shall be recorded, if possible, centrally, and made available to the public without delay;

(b) no person shall be detained for an indefinite period of time, whether detained pending judicial investigation or trial or detained without charge;

(c) no person shall be held in isolation without communication with his family, friend, or lawyer for longer than a few days, e.g., three to seven days;

(d) where persons are detained without charge the need for their continued detention shall be considered periodically by an independent review tribunal;

(e) any person charged with an offence shall be entitled to a fair trial by a competent, independent and impartial court established by law;

(f) civilians shall normally be tried by the ordinary courts; where it is found strictly necessary to establish military tribunals or special courts to try civilians, their competence, independence and impartiality shall be ensured and the need for them reviewed periodically by the competent authority;

(g) any person charged with a criminal offence shall be entitled to the presumption of innocence and to at least the following rights to ensure a fair trial;

(i) the right to be informed of the charges promptly, in detail, and in a language he understands;

(ii) the right to have adequate time and facilities to prepare the defence including the right to communicate confidentially with his lawyer;

(iii) the right to a lawyer of his choice, with free legal assistance if he does not have the means to pay for it;

(iv) the right to be present at the trial;

(v) the right not to be compelled to testify against himself or to make a confession;

(vi) the right to obtain the attendance of defence witnesses;

(vii) the right to be tried in public save where the court orders otherwise on grounds of security with adequate safeguards to prevent abuse;

(viii) the right to appeal to a higher court.

(h) an adequate record of the proceedings shall be kept in all cases, and,

(i) no person shall be tried or punished again for an offence for which he has already been convicted or acquitted.

[25.54] In this respect, the Siracusa Principles are supported by the Paris Standards, which hold the rights in articles 9 and 14 ICCPR to be non-derogable.[48] Furthermore, Paris Standard B3(c) states that:

The guarantees of the independence of the judiciary and of the legal profession shall remain intact. In particular, the use of emergency powers to remove judges or to alter the structure of the judicial branch or otherwise to restrict the independence of the judiciary shall be prohibited by the constitution.

[25.55] In Concluding Comments, the HRC has also indicated that certain judicial guarantees cannot realistically be derogated from, presumably because such

---

[48] See Paris Standards, draft arts. 5, 7, and 16.

derogations could never satisfy the test of proportionality.[49] For example, it has expressed concern over the lack of a clear separation of powers between the judiciary and the executive, which obviously diminished judicial independence, under Egyptian emergency laws.[50] Regarding Sri Lanka, the HRC was 'concerned that courts do not have the power to examine the legality of the declaration of emergency and the different measures taken during the state of emergency'.[51]

[25.56] The democratic rights in articles 1 and 25 are not listed as non-derogable in article 4(2). This is an important omission, as emergency laws usually increase the power of the executive, the coercive arm of government, at the expense of the legislature, the democratic arm of government. The Paris Standards comment on the minimum position of the legislature during times of emergency:

PARIS STANDARDS

(A) 5. The legislature shall not be dissolved during the period of emergency but shall continue to function; if dissolution of a particular legislature is warranted, it shall be replaced as soon as practicable by a legislature duly elected in accordance with the requirements of the constitution, which shall ensure that it is freely chosen and representative of the entire nation. . . .

(B) 3. While assuming or exercising emergency powers every State shall respect the following principles:

(a) The fundamental functions of the legislature shall remain intact despite the relative expansion of the authority of the executive. Thus, the legislature shall provide general guidelines to regulate executive discretion in respect of permissible measures of delegated legislation.

(b) The prerogatives, immunities and privileges of the legislature shall remain intact.

Furthermore, the Siracusa Principles and the Paris Standards require periodic review of emergency measures by the legislature,[52] which presupposes its continued existence. The Paris Standards also recommend that the rights of political participation (article 25 of the ICCPR) be non-derogable.[53]

[25.57] Whilst articles 9, 14, and 25 are not expressly non-derogable under the ICCPR, it is arguable that they are 'functionally' non-derogable, in that their

---

[49] See also A. De Zayas, 'The United Nations and the Guarantees of a Fair Trial in the International Covenant on Civil and Political Rights and the Convention Against Torture, and other Cruel, Inhuman and Degrading Treatment' in D. Weissbrodt and R. Wolfrum (eds.), *The Right to a Fair Trial* (Springer, New York, 1997), at 674.

[50] Concluding Comments on Egypt (1993) UN doc. CCPR/C/79/Add. 23, para. 9.

[51] Concluding Comments on Sri Lanka (1996) UN doc. CCPR/C/79/Add.56, para. 13; see also Siracusa Principle 60. See also Concluding Comments on Israel (1999) UN doc. CCPR/C/79/Add.93, para. 21.

[52] Siracusa Principles, Principle 55; Paris Standards, A3(d).   [53] Ibid., draft art. 15.

guarantees must necessarily be retained to prevent abuse of the right of derogation by the executive.[54]

[25.58] The Paris Standards propose further non-derogable rights in draft articles 10 to 14 respectively, namely rights of minorities (article 27 of the ICCPR), rights of the family (article 23), the right to a name (part of the article 17 right to privacy and the article 24 rights of a child),[55] the rights of the child (article 24), and the right to a nationality (also part of article 24).[56] This extended list is obviously influenced by article 27 of the American Convention on Human Rights 1969, which contains a virtually identical list of non-derogable rights. However, unless such rights are somehow 'functionally' non-derogable, it is difficult to claim them as non-derogable ICCPR rights in the face of their deliberate omission from article 4(2). It may nevertheless be that such rights have become *de facto* non-derogable, as it may be impossible to establish that derogations thereof are proportionate.

PROCEDURAL REQUIREMENTS FOR ARTICLE 4

[25.59] Article 4(1) requires that derogation measures be prescribed for public emergencies that are 'officially proclaimed'. Therefore, States must invoke a domestic procedure to inform their populations of the existence of a relevant emergency. The HRC has confirmed in Concluding Comments that laws governing conditions of states of emergency should be clear and precise.[57] This requirement mirrors the general requirement for permissible limitations to ICCPR rights to be 'prescribed by law'.[58]

[25.60] Article 4(3) requires States Parties to inform the United Nations of any relevant derogations, and the revocation of such derogations. Whereas article 4(1) imposes procedural 'notice' requirements in municipal law, article 4(3) imposes notice requirements at the international level. It must be noted that article 4(3) imposes no express obligation to inform the Committee of relevant derogations, though it can be presumed that the UN Secretary-General would keep the HRC so informed.

---

[54] See J. Fitzpatrick, 'Protection Against Abuse of the Concept of "Emergency" ' in L. Henkin and J. L. Hargrove, *Human Rights: An Agenda for the Next Century* (American Society of International Law, Washington, DC, 1994), 203, at 218. See also A. Svensson-McCarthy, 'The International Law of Human Rights and States of Exception' (Martinus Nijhoff, The Hague, 1998), 445–7, 580–1.

[55] The right to a name is discussed at [16.16] and [21.47–21.50].

[56] See [21.51–21.52].

[57] Concluding Comments on Azerbaijan (1994) UN doc. CCPR/C/79/Add.38, para. 7; Concluding Comments on Nepal (1995) UN doc. CCPR/C/79/Add.42, para. 9; Concluding Comments on Zambia (1996) UN doc. CCPR/C/79/Add.62, para. 11.

[58] See, e.g., [16.11], and, more generally, [1.51] for discussion of the 'prescribed by law' requirement.

[25.61] *SIRACUSA PRINCIPLES*

Siracusa Principle 45 contains recommendations as to the requisite content of a derogation notice under article 4(3).

45 ... In particular, [the notice] shall contain:

(a) the provisions of the Covenant from which it has derogated;

(b) a copy of the proclamation of emergency, together with the constitutional provisions, legislation or decrees governing the state of emergency in order to assist the states parties to appreciate the scope of the derogation;

(c) the effective date of the imposition of the state of emergency and the period for which it has been proclaimed;

(d) an explanation of the reasons which actuated the government's decision to derogate, including a brief description of the factual circumstances leading up to the proclamation of a state of emergency; and

(e) a brief description of the anticipated effect of the derogation measures on the rights recognized in the Covenant, including copies of decrees derogating from these rights issued prior to the notification.

[25.62] *LANDINELLI SILVA v URUGUAY (34/78)*

This case demonstrates the interplay between the substantive and procedural elements of article 4.[59] The author complained of numerous ICCPR breaches. In response, the State Party invoked its right of derogation. The HRC decided against the State Party in the following terms:

¶ 8.1. Although the Government of Uruguay ... has invoked article 4 of the Covenant in order to justify the ban imposed on the authors of the communication, the Human Rights Committee feels unable to accept that the requirements set forth in article 4 (1) of the Covenant have been met.

¶ 8.2. According to article 4 (1) of the Covenant, the States parties may take measures derogating from their obligations under that instrument in a situation of public emergency which threatens the life of the nation and the existence of which has been formally proclaimed. Even in such circumstances, derogations are only permissible to the extent strictly required by the exigencies of the situation. In its note of 28 June 1979 to the Secretary-General of the United Nations (reproduced in document CCPR/C/2/Add.3, p. 4), which was designed to comply with the formal requirements laid down in article 4 (3) of the Covenant, the Government of Uruguay has made reference to an emergency situation in the country which was legally acknowledged in a number of 'Institutional Acts'. However, no factual details were given at that time. The note confined itself to stating that the existence of the emergency situation was 'a matter of universal knowledge'; no attempt

---

[59] See also *Salgar de Montejo v Colombia* (64/79), para. 10.3.

was made to indicate the nature and the scope of the derogations actually resorted to with regard to the rights guaranteed by the Covenant, or to show that such derogations were strictly necessary. Instead, the Government of Uruguay declared that more information would be provided in connection with the submission of the country's report under article 40 of the Covenant. To date neither has this report been received, nor the information by which it was to be supplemented.

¶ 8.3. Although the sovereign right of a State party to declare a state of emergency is not questioned, yet, in the specific context of the present communication, the Human Rights Committee is of the opinion that a State, by merely invoking the existence of exceptional circumstances, cannot evade the obligations which it has undertaken by ratifying the Covenant. Although the substantive right to take derogatory measures may not depend on a formal notification being made pursuant to article 4(3) of the Covenant, the State party concerned is duty-bound to give a sufficiently detailed account of the relevant facts when it invokes article 4(1) of the Covenant in proceedings under the Optional Protocol. It is the function of the Human Rights Committee, acting under the Optional Protocol, to see to it that States parties live up to their commitments under the Covenant. In order to discharge this function and to assess whether a situation of the kind described in article 4(1) of the Covenant exists in the country concerned, it needs full and comprehensive information. If the respondent Government does not furnish the required justification itself, as it is required to do under article 4(2) of the Optional Protocol and article 4(3) of the Covenant, the Human Rights Committee cannot conclude that valid reasons exist to legitimize a departure from the normal legal regime prescribed by the Covenant.

Thus, a State's failure to comply with article 4 procedural obligations will not deprive it of its substantive rights of derogation. Indeed, the HRC has confirmed in cases such as *Weismann and Lanza Perdomo v Uruguay* (8/77) that it will *ex officio* consider the possibility of an article 4 defence in the absence of a State's specific reliance thereon.[60] However, a State's continued failure to provide relevant facts regarding its purported derogation, such as details of the nature and exigencies of the relevant public emergency, means that the State will fail to discharge its burden of proof in justifying those derogations, and will thus be denied any substantive article 4 defence of its actions.

BURDEN OF PROOF AND HRC'S SUPERVISORY ROLE

[25.63] *Landinelli Silva* and numerous other Uruguayan cases confirm that the State bears the burden of proof in justifying purported derogations. In those cases, it was clear that the State Party failed to discharge this burden. It is uncertain how the HRC would react where a State Party had made a *bona fide* attempt to justify its derogations, as this has never occurred in an Optional Protocol case. The

---

[60] Para. 15; see also, e.g., *Torres Ramírez v Uruguay* (4/77), para. 17, and *Pietraroia v Uruguay* (44/79), para. 14. See also Ghandhi, above, note 31, 334–6, and McGoldrick, above, note 32, 311. However, note that the HRC did not consider derogation as a justification in *Polay Campos v Peru* (577/94): see above, note 35, and [14.48].

European Court of Human Rights, in monitoring derogations under article 15 of the European Convention on Human Rights 1950, has stated that States Parties have a wide 'margin of appreciation' in deciding on the existence of and proper response to an emergency,[61] which essentially gives States a strong benefit of the doubt in this regard,[62] substantially easing their burden of proof. It is hoped that the HRC will, in contrast to the European Court, scrutinize the State's justifications for derogation carefully, in view of the propensity of many States to abuse their power during states of emergency.[63]

Conclusion

[25.64] In the absence of substantial HRC jurisprudence, it is presently difficult to draw conclusions on the scope of article 4. Extant HRC statements, as well as the Siracusa Principles and the Paris Standards, appear strictly to limit a State's right of derogation. Indeed, it may be that the permissible limitations of ICCPR rights are so flexible[64] that actual derogation beyond those limits is rarely necessary.[65] For example, the common limits of 'national security' and 'public order' may be enough to cater for the demands of emergency situations.[66] In this respect, it is notable that the more modern human rights treaties have largely limited the right of derogation. For example, while the earlier European Convention on Human Rights 1951 includes a shorter list of non-derogable rights, the American Convention on Human Rights 1969 contains a longer list, and the African Charter of Human and People's Rights 1981 does not even allow for derogation. However, the Arab Charter of Human Rights 1994, perhaps unfortunately, reversed this trend as it includes a derogation provision with a relatively short list of non-derogable rights.[67]

Postscript: Please note that General Comment 28 on 'Equality of Rights Between Men and Women', contained in the Addendum at page 634, contains extra information on some of the material in this chapter.

---

[61] See *Brannigan and McBride v United Kingdom*, Series A, No 258-B (1994) 17 EHRR 539, para. 43.

[62] See T. Jones, 'The Devaluation of Human Rights under the European Convention' [1995] *Public Law* 430, 430–1.

[63] See also the concurring judgment of Judge Martens in *Brannigan and McBride*, above, note 61. Also see Paris Standard A7. See also the discussion of the margin of appreciation doctrine at [18.21]. Svensson-McCarthy, above, note 54, at 580, suggests that the Committee's work indicates it will undertake 'full powers of review' with regard to derogation measures.

[64] See [1.53].

[65] See Siracusa Principles, para. 53.

[66] Ghandhi, above, note 31, 330.

[67] Art. 4(C) of the Arab Charter lists only freedom from torture and degrading treatment, the right to return to one's country, the right of political asylum (a right not guaranteed in the ICCPR (see [9.62]), the right to a fair trial, the prohibition of retrial of the same act, and the principle of legality of crime and punishment.

Addendum

Equality of Rights Between Men and Women: General Comment 28

On 29 March 2000, the Human Rights Committee handed down General Comment 28, on 'Equality of Rights Between Men and Women'. This General Comment is obviously an important addition to HRC jurisprudence on non-discrimination. It also has ramifications for its jurisprudence under other provisions. As publication processes precluded the thorough incorporation of this General Comment within the preceding chapters, it is presented in full below. The footnotes contain appropriate cross-references to other parts of this book. Headings have also been inserted so that information within General Comment 28 regarding the subject matter of the preceding chapters is readily identifiable.

GENERAL COMMENT 28

Non-Discrimination (Chapter 23)

¶ 1. The Committee has decided to update its General Comment on Article 3 of this Covenant and to replace General Comment 4 (thirteenth session 1981), in the light of the experience it has gathered in its activities over the last 20 years. This revision seeks to take account of the important impact of this article on the enjoyment by women of the human rights protected under the Covenant.

¶ 2. Article 3 implies that all human beings should enjoy the rights provided for in the Covenant, on an equal basis and in their totality. The full effect of this provision is impaired whenever any person is denied the full and equal enjoyment of any right. Consequently, States should ensure to men and women equally the enjoyment of all rights provided for in the Covenant.

¶ 3. The obligation to ensure to all individuals the rights recognized in the Covenant, established in articles 2 and 3 of the Covenant, requires that States parties take all necessary steps to enable every person to enjoy those rights. These steps include the removal of obstacles to the equal enjoyment each of such rights, the education of the population and of state officials in human rights[1] and the adjustment of domestic legislation so as to give effect to the undertakings set forth in the Covenant. The State party must not only adopt measures of protection but also positive measures in all areas so as to achieve the effective and equal empowerment of women.[2] States parties must provide information regarding the actual role of women in society so that the Committee may ascertain what measures, in addition to legislative provisions, have been or should be taken to give effect to these obligations, what

---

[1] See [23.86–23.88] on educational duties under art. 26.
[2] See, on 'positive measures' or 'affirmative action', [23.58] ff.

progress has been made, what difficulties are encountered and what steps are being taken to overcome them.

¶ 4. States parties are responsible for ensuring the equal enjoyment of rights without any discrimination. Articles 2 and 3 mandate States parties to take all steps necessary, including the prohibition of discrimination on the ground of sex, to put an end to discriminatory actions both in the public and the private sector which impair the equal enjoyment of rights.[3]

¶ 5. Inequality in the enjoyment of rights by women throughout the world is deeply embedded in tradition, history and culture, including religious attitudes. The subordinate role of women in some countries is illustrated by the high incidence of pre-natal sex selection and abortion of female fetuses. States parties should ensure that traditional, historical, religious or cultural attitudes are not used to justify violations of women's right to equality before the law and to equal enjoyment of all Covenant rights. States parties should furnish appropriate information on those aspects of tradition, history, cultural practices and religious attitudes which jeopardize, or may jeopardize, compliance with article 3, and indicate what measures they have taken or intend to take to overcome such factors.[4]

¶ 6. In order to fulfil the obligation set forth in article 3 States parties should take account of the factors which impede the equal enjoyment by women and men of each right specified in the Covenant. To enable the Committee to obtain a complete picture of the situation of women in each State party as regards the implementation of the rights in the Covenant, this general comment identifies some of the factors affecting the equal enjoyment by women of the rights under the Covenant, and spells out the type of information that is required with regard to these various rights.

Derogations (Chapter 25)

¶ 7. The equal enjoyment of human rights by women must be protected during a state of emergency (article 4). States parties which take measures derogating from their obligations under the Covenant in time of public emergency, as provided in article 4, should provide information to the Committee with respect to the impact on the situation of women of such measures and should demonstrate that they are non-discriminatory.

¶ 8. Women are particularly vulnerable in times of internal or international armed conflicts. States parties should inform the Committee of all measures taken during these situations to protect women from rape, abduction and other forms of gender based violence.

Article 5 (Chapter 1)

¶ 9. In becoming parties to the Covenant, States undertake, in accordance with article 3, to ensure the equal right of men and women to the enjoyment of all civil and political rights set forth in the Covenant, and in accordance with article 5, nothing in the Covenant may be interpreted as implying for any State, group or person any right to engage in any activity or perform any act aimed at the destruction of any of the rights provided for in

---

[3] See, on obligations to counter private discrimination, [23.70] ff.
[4] See, on cultural relativism, [1.65] ff.

article 3, or at limitations not covered by the Covenant.[5] Moreover, there shall be no restriction upon or derogation from the equal enjoyment by women of all fundamental human rights recognized or existing pursuant to law, conventions, regulations or customs, on the pretext that the Covenant does not recognize such rights or that it recognizes them to a lesser extent.

The Right to Life (Chapter 8)

¶ 10. When reporting on the right to life protected by article 6, States parties should provide data on birth rates and on pregnancy and childbirth-related deaths of women. Gender-disaggregated data should be provided on infant mortality rates. States parties should give information on any measures taken by the State to help women prevent unwanted pregnancies, and to ensure that they do not have to undertake life-threatening clandestine abortions.[6] States parties should also report on measures to protect women from practices that violate their right to life, such as female infanticide, the burning of widows and dowry killings. The Committee also wishes to have information on the particular impact on women of poverty and deprivation that may pose a threat to their lives.[7]

Freedom from Torture, Inhuman and Degrading Treatment (Chapter 9)

¶ 11. To assess compliance with article 7 of the Covenant, as well as with article 24, which mandates special protection for children, the Committee needs to be provided information on national laws and practice with regard to domestic and other types of violence against women, including rape.[8] It also needs to know whether the State party gives access to safe abortion to women who have become pregnant as a result of rape.[9] The States parties should also provide the Committee information on measures to prevent forced abortion or forced sterilization.[10] In States parties where the practice of genital mutilation exists information on its extent and on measures to eliminate it should be provided.[11] The information provided by States parties on all these issues should include measures of protection, including legal remedies, for women whose rights under article 7 have been violated.

Freedom from Slavery and Servitude (Chapter 10)

¶ 12. Having regard to their obligations under article 8, States parties should inform the Committee of measures taken to eliminate trafficking of women and children, within the country or across borders, and forced prostitution.[12] They must also provide information on measures taken to protect women and children, including foreign women and children, from slavery, disguised *inter alia* as domestic or other kinds of personal service.[13] States parties where women and children are recruited, and from which they are taken, and States parties where they are received should provide information on measures, national or international, which have been taken in order to prevent the violation of women's and children's rights.

---

[5] See, on art. 5, [1.16].
[6] See, on abortion, [8.47–8.49].
[7] See, on the socio-economic aspects of the right to life, [8.39–8.42].
[8] See, on violence against women, [23.80].
[9] See, on abortion, [8.47–8.49].
[10] See, on sterilization, [9.74].
[11] See, on female genital mutilation, [9.31] and [1.70].
[12] See, on forced prostitution, [10.05], and, on child prostitution, [21.34].
[13] See also [10.06].

Enforced Wearing of Certain Clothing (various chapters)

¶ 13. States parties should provide information on any specific regulation of clothing to be worn by women in public. The Committee stresses that such regulations may involve a violation of a number of rights guaranteed by the Covenant, such as: article 26, on non-discrimination; article 7, if corporal punishment is imposed in order to enforce such a regulation;[14] article 9, when failure to comply with the regulation is punished by arrest; article 12, if liberty of movement is subject to such a constraint; article 17, which guarantees all persons the right to privacy without arbitrary or unlawful interference; articles 18 and 19, when women are subjected to clothing requirements that are not in keeping with their religion or their right of self-expression; and, lastly, article 27, when the clothing requirements conflict with the culture to which the woman can lay a claim.

Freedom from Arbitrary Detention (Chapter 11)

¶ 14. With regards to article 9 States parties should provide information on any laws or practices which may deprive women of their liberty on an arbitrary or unequal basis, such as by confinement within the house. (See General Comment No 8 paragraph 1).[15]

Humane Treatment for Female Detainees (Chapter 9)

¶ 15. As regards articles 7 and 10, States parties must provide all information relevant to ensuring that the right of persons deprived of their liberty are protected on equal terms for men and women. In particular, States parties should report on whether men and women are separated in prisons and whether women are guarded only by female guards.[16] States parties should also report about compliance with the rule that accused juvenile females shall be separated from adults and on any difference in treatment between male and female persons deprived of liberty, such as, for example, access to rehabilitation and education programmes and to conjugal and family visits. Pregnant women who are deprived of their liberty should receive humane treatment and respect for their inherent dignity at all times surrounding the birth and while caring for their newly-born children; States parties should report on facilities to ensure this and on medical and health care for such mothers and their babies.

Freedom of Movement (Chapter 12)

¶ 16. As regards article 12, States parties should provide information on any legal provision or any practice which restricts women's right to freedom of movement as, for example, the exercise of marital powers over the wife or parental powers over adult daughters, legal or *de facto* requirements which prevent women from travelling such as the requirement of consent of a third party to the issuance of a passport or other type of travel documents to an adult woman.[17] States parties should also report on measures taken to eliminate such laws and practices and to protect women against them, including reference to available domestic remedies (See General Comment No 27 paragraphs 6 and 18).[18]

---

[14] See, on corporal punishment, [9.65–9.66].   [15] See [11.07].
[16] See [9.106].   [17] See [12.05].   [18] See [12.05] and [12.23].

Procedural Rights Against Expulsion (Chapter 13)

¶ 17. States parties should ensure that alien women are accorded on an equal basis the right to submit reasons against their expulsion, and to have their case reviewed as provided in article 13. In this regard, they should be entitled to submit reasons based on gender specific violations of the Covenant such as those mentioned in paragraphs 10 and 11 above.

Right to a Fair Trial (Chapter 14)

¶ 18. States parties should provide information to enable the Committee to ascertain whether access to justice and the right to a fair trial, provided for in article 14, are enjoyed by women on equal terms to men. In particular States parties should inform the Committee whether there are legal provisions preventing women from direct and autonomous access to the courts (Case 202/1986, *Ato del Avellanal v Peru* (views of 28 October 1988);[19] whether women may give evidence as witnesses on the same terms as men; and whether measures are taken to ensure women equal access to legal aid, in particular in family matters. States parties should report on whether certain categories of women are denied the enjoyment of the presumption of innocence under article 14, paragraph 2, and on the measures which have been taken to put an end to this situation.

Right to Recognition as a Person (Chapter 10)

¶ 19. The right of everyone under article 16 to be recognized everywhere as a person before the law is particularly pertinent for women, who often see it curtailed by reason of sex or marital status. This right implies that the capacity of women to own property, to enter into a contract or to exercise other civil rights may not be restricted on the basis of marital status or any other discriminatory ground.[20] It also implies that women may not be treated as objects to be given together with the property of the deceased husband to his family. States must provide information on laws or practices that prevent women from being treated or from functioning as full legal persons and the measures taken to eradicate laws or practices that allow such treatment.

Right of Privacy (Chapter 16)

¶ 20. States parties must provide information to enable the Committee to assess the effect of any laws and practices that may interfere with women's right to enjoy privacy and other rights protected by article 17 on the basis of equality with men. An example of such interference arises where the sexual life of a woman is taken into consideration to decide the extent of her legal rights and protections, including protection against rape. Another area where States may fail to respect women's privacy relates to their reproductive functions, for example, where there is a requirement for the husband's authorization to make a decision in regard to sterilization, where general requirements are imposed for the sterilization of women, such as having a certain number of children or being of a certain age, or where States impose a legal duty upon doctors and other health personnel to report cases of women who have undergone abortion.[21] In these instances, other rights in the Covenant, such as those of articles 6 and 7, might also be at stake.[22] Women's privacy may also be

---

[19] See [14.12].   [20] See [10.10].   [21] See also [16.07–16.08].
[22] See paras 10 and 11 of this General Comment, above.

interfered with by private actors, such as employers who request a pregnancy test before hiring a woman. States parties should report on any laws and public or private actions that interfere with the equal enjoyment by women of the rights under article 17, and on the measures taken to eliminate such interference and to afford women protection from any such interference.[23]

Freedom of Thought, Conscience and Religion (Chapter 17)

¶ 21. States parties must take measures to ensure that freedom of thought, conscience and religion, and the freedom to adopt the religion or belief of one's choice—including the freedom to change religion or belief and to express one's religion or belief—will be guaranteed and protected in law and in practice for both men and women, on the same terms and without discrimination. These freedoms protected by article 18, must not be subject to restrictions other than those authorized by the Covenant, and must not be constrained by, *inter alia*, rules requiring permission from third parties, or by interference from fathers, husbands, brothers or others. Article 18 may not be relied upon to justify discrimination against women by reference to freedom of thought, conscience and religion; States parties should therefore provide information on the status of women as regards their freedom of thought, conscience and religion, and indicate what steps they have taken or intend to take both to eliminate and prevent infringements of these freedoms in respect of women and to protect their rights against any discrimination.

Freedom of Expression (Chapter 18)

¶ 22. In relation to article 19 States parties should inform the Committee of any laws or other factors which may impede women from exercising the rights protected under this provision on an equal basis. As the publication and dissemination of obscene and pornographic material which portrays women and girls as objects of violence or degrading or inhuman treatment is likely to promote these kinds of treatment of women and girls, States parties should provide information about legal measures to restrict the publication or dissemination of such material.[24]

Rights Regarding Marriage (Chapter 20)

¶ 23. States are required to treat men and women equally in regard to marriage in accordance with article 23, which has been elaborated further by General Comment 19 (1990). Men and women have the right to enter into marriage only with their free and full consent, and States have an obligation to protect the enjoyment of this right on an equal basis. Many factors may prevent women from being able to make the decision to marry freely. One factor relates to the minimum age for marriage. That age should be set by the State on the basis of equal criteria for men and women.[25] These criteria should ensure women's capacity to make an informed and uncoerced decision. A second factor in some States may be

---

[23] See, on the general obligation to prevent invasions of privacy by private actors, [16.18–16.19].

[24] This is the HRC's first statement indicating an obligation on States to 'control' pornography, where it concerns depictions of adults (see, on child pornography, [21.34–21.36]). Pornography controls are apparently now seen as more than mere permissible limitations to freedom of expression (see [18.25]). General Comment 28 indicates that pornography is a form of free expression, analogous to hate speech, which must be compulsorily controlled. (See generally, on hate speech, [18.41] ff.)

[25] See [21.16].

that either by statutory or customary law a guardian, who is generally male, consents to the marriage instead of the woman herself, thereby preventing women from exercising a free choice.

¶ 24. A different factor that may affect women's right to marry only when they have given free and full consent is the existence of social attitudes which tend to marginalize women victims of rape and put pressure on them to agree to marriage. A woman's free and full consent to marriage may also be undermined by laws which allow the rapist to have his criminal responsibility extinguished or mitigated if he marries the victim.[26] States parties should indicate whether marrying the victim extinguishes or mitigates criminal responsibility and in the case in which the victim is a minor whether the rape reduces the marriageable age of the victim, particularly in societies where rape victims have to endure marginalization from society. A different aspect of the right to marry may be affected when States impose restrictions on remarriage by women as compared to men. Also the right to choose one's spouse may be restricted by laws or practices that prevent the marriage of a woman of a particular religion with a man who professes no religion or a different religion. States should provide information on these laws and practices and on the measures taken to abolish the laws and eradicate the practices which undermine the right of women to marry only when they have given free and full consent. It should also be noted that equality of treatment with regard to the right to marry implies that polygamy is incompatible with this principle. Polygamy violates the dignity of women. It is an inadmissible discrimination against women. Consequently, it should be definitely abolished wherever it continues to exist.[27]

Equality within Marriage (Chapter 20)

¶ 25. To fulfil their obligations under article 23, paragraph 4, States must ensure that the matrimonial regime contains equal rights and obligations for both spouses, with regard to the custody and care of children, the children's religious and moral education, the capacity to transmit to children the parent's nationality, and the ownership or administration of property, whether common property or property in the sole ownership of either spouse. States should review their legislation to ensure that married women have equal rights in regard to the ownership and administration of such property, where necessary. Also, States should ensure that no sex-based discrimination occurs in respect of the acquisition or loss of nationality by reason of marriage, of residence rights and of the right of each spouse to retain the use of his or her original family name or to participate on an equal basis in the choice of a new family name. Equality during marriage implies that husband and wife should participate equally in responsibility and authority within the family.[28]

¶ 26. States must also ensure equality in regard to the dissolution of marriage, which excludes the possibility of repudiation. The grounds for divorce and annulment should be the same for men and women, as well as decisions with regard to property distribution, alimony and the custody of children. The need to maintain contact between children and the non-custodian parent, should be based on equal considerations.[29] Women should also have equal inheritance rights to those of men when the dissolution of marriage is caused by the death of one of the spouses.

---

[26] See also [9.82].
[27] See also [20.28].
[28] On art. 23(4), see [20.30] ff.
[29] See, on equal access to children, [20.35–20.40].

Recognition of the Family (Chapter 20)

¶ 27. In giving effect to recognition of the family in the context of article 23, it is important to accept the concept of the various forms of family, including unmarried couples and their children and single parents and their children and to ensure the equal treatment of women in these contexts (General Comment 19 paragraph 2 last sentence).[30] Single parent families frequently consist of a single woman caring for one or more children, and States parties should describe what measures of support are in place to enable her to discharge her parental functions on the basis of equality with a man in a similar position.[31]

Protection of Children (Chapter 21)

¶ 28. The obligation of states to protect children (article 24) should be carried out equally for boys and girls. States should report on measures taken to ensure that girls are treated equally to boys in education, in feeding and in health care, and provide the Committee with disaggregated data in this respect. States should eradicate, both through legislation and any other appropriate measures, all cultural or religious practices which jeopardize the freedom and well-being of female children.

Right of Political Participation (Chapter 22)

¶ 29. The right to participate in the conduct of public affairs is not fully implemented everywhere on an equal basis. States must ensure that the law guarantees to women article 25 rights on equal terms with men and take effective and positive measures to promote and ensure women's participation in the conduct of public affairs and in public office, including appropriate affirmative action. Effective measures taken by States parties to ensure that all persons entitled to vote are able to exercise that right should not be discriminatory on the grounds of sex. The Committee requires States parties to provide statistical information on the percentage of women in publicly elected offices including the legislature as well as in high-ranking civil service positions and the judiciary.[32]

Non-Discrimination (Chapter 23)

¶ 30. Discrimination against women is often intertwined with discrimination on other grounds such as race, colour, language, religion, political or other opinion, national or social origin, property, birth or other status. States parties should address the ways in which any instances of discrimination on other grounds affect women in a particular way, and include information on the measures taken to counter these effects.

¶ 31. The right to equality before the laws and freedom from discrimination, protected by article 26, requires States to act against discrimination by public and private agencies in all fields. Discrimination against women in areas such as social security laws—Case 172/84, *Broeks v Netherlands* (views of 9 April 1987; case 182/84), *Zwaan-de Vries v The Netherlands*, (views of 9 April 1987); case 218/1986,[33] *Vos v The Netherlands* (views of

---

[30] See also [20.06] ff.

[31] See also [20.05]. General Comment 28 does not support the view that art. 23 guarantees family assistance, such as monetary support, *per se*. It merely states that such assistance should be offered equally to single parents of either gender.

[32] See also [22.51].

[33] *Broeks* is excerpted at [23.08]. *Zwaan-de Vries* was a virtually identical case to *Broeks*.

29 March 1989),[34] as well as in the area of citizenship or rights of non-citizens in a country—Case 35/1978, *Aumeeruddy-Cziffra et al. v Mauritius* (views adopted 9 April 1981),[35] violates article 26. The commission of so called 'honour crimes' which remain unpunished, constitutes a serious violation of the Covenant and in particular of articles 6, 14 and 26. Laws which impose more severe penalties on women than on men for adultery or other offences also violate the requirement of equal treatment. The Committee has also often observed in reviewing States reports that a large proportion of women are employed in areas which are not protected by labor laws, that prevailing customs and traditions discriminate against women, particularly with regard to access to better paid employment and to equal pay for work of equal value. States should review their legislation and practices and take the lead in implementing all measures necessary in order to eliminate discrimination against women, in all fields, for example by prohibiting discrimination by private actors in areas such as employment, education, political activities and the provision of accommodation, goods and services.[36] States parties should report on all these measures and provide information on the remedies available to victims of such discrimination.

Minority Rights (Chapter 24)

¶ 32. The rights which persons belonging to minorities enjoy under article 27 of the Covenant in respect of their language, culture and religion do not authorize any State, group or person to violate the right to equal enjoyment by women of any Covenant rights, including the right to equal protection of the law. States should report on any legislation or administrative practices related to membership in a minority community that might constitute an infringement of the equal rights of women under the Covenant—Case 24/1977 *Lovelace v Canada*, (views adopted July 1981)[37] and on measures taken or envisaged to ensure the equal right of men and women to enjoy all civil and political rights in the Covenant. Likewise, States should report on measures taken to discharge their responsibilities in relation to cultural or religious practices within minority communities that affect the rights of women. In their reports, States parties should pay attention to the contribution made by women to the cultural life of their communities.

---

[34] *Vos* is excerpted at [23.34–23.35]. The HRC did not actually find a violation of art. 26 in *Vos*. This new General Comment indicates that *Vos* would be decided differently in 2000. See also [23.46].
[35] See [23.42].   [36] See [23.72–23.73].
[37] *Lovelace* is excerpted at [24.12].

Appendices

Appendix A

International Covenant on Civil and Political Rights

Adopted and opened for signature, ratification and accession by General Assembly Resolution 2200 A (XXI) of 16 December 1966.

Preamble

The States Parties to the present Covenant,

Considering that, in accordance with the principles proclaimed in the Charter of the United Nations, recognition of the inherent dignity and of the equal and inalienable rights of all members of the human family is the foundation of freedom, justice and peace in the world,

Recognizing that these rights derive from the inherent dignity of the human person,

Recognizing that, in accordance with the Universal Declaration of Human Rights, the ideal of free human beings enjoying civil and political freedom and freedom from fear and want can only be achieved if conditions are created whereby everyone may enjoy his civil and political rights, as well as his economic, social and cultural rights,

Considering the obligations of States under the Charter of the United Nations to promote universal respect for, and observance of, human rights and freedoms.

Realizing that the individual, having duties to other individuals and to the community to which he belongs, is under a responsibility to strive for the promotion and observance of the rights recognized in the present Covenant,

Agree upon the following articles:

PART I

Article 1

1. All peoples have the right of self-determination. By virtue of that right they freely determine their political status and freely pursue their economic, social and cultural development.

2. All peoples may, for their own ends, freely dispose of their natural wealth and resources without prejudice to any obligations arising out of international economic cooperation, based upon the principle of mutual benefits, and international law. In no case may a people be deprived of its own means of subsistence.

3. The States Parties to the present Covenant, including those having responsibility for the administration of Non-Self-Governing and Trust Territories, shall promote the realization

of the right of self-determination, and shall respect that right, in conformity with the provisions of the Charter of the United Nations.

PART II

Article 2

1. Each State Party to the present Covenant undertakes to respect and to ensure to all individuals within its territory and subject to its jurisdiction the rights recognized in the present Covenant, without distinction of any kind such as race, colour, sex, language, religion, political or other opinion, national or social origin, property, birth, or other status.

2. Where not already provided for by existing legislative or other measures, each State Party to the present Covenant undertakes to take the necessary steps in accordance with its constitutional processes and with the provisions of the present Covenant, to adopt such legislative or other measures as may be necessary to give effect to the rights recognized in the present Covenant.

3. Each State Party to the present Covenant undertakes:

(a) to ensure that any person whose rights or freedoms as herein recognized are violated shall have an effective remedy, notwithstanding that the violation has been committed by persons acting in an official capacity;

(b) To ensure that any person claiming such a remedy shall have his right thereto determined by competent judicial, administrative or legislative authorities, or by any other competent authority provided for by the legal system of the State, and to develop the possibilities of judicial remedy;

(c) To ensure that the competent authorities shall enforce such remedies when granted.

Article 3

The States Parties to the present Covenant undertake to ensure the equal right of men and women to the enjoyment of all civil and political rights set forth in the present Covenant.

Article 4

1. In time of public emergency which threatens the life of the nation and the existence of which is officially proclaimed, the States Parties to the present Covenant may take measures derogating from their obligations under the present Covenant to the extent strictly required by the exigencies of the situation, provided that such measures are not inconsistent with their other obligations under international law and do not involve discrimination solely on the ground of race, colour, sex, language, religion or social origin.

2. No derogation from articles 6, 7, 8 (paragraphs 1 and 2), 11, 15, 16 and 18 may be made under this provision.

3. Any State Party to the present Covenant availing itself of the right of derogation shall immediately inform the other States Parties to the present Covenant, through its inter-mediary of the Secretary-General of the United Nations, of the provisions from which it has derogated and of the reasons by which it was actuated. A further communication shall be made, through the same intermediary, on the date on which it terminates such derogation.

Article 5

1. Nothing in the present Covenant may be interpreted as implying for any State, group or person any right to engage in any activity or perform any act aimed at the destruction of any of the rights and freedoms recognized herein or at their limitation to a greater extent than is provided for in the present Covenant.

2. There shall be no restriction upon or derogation from any of the fundamental human rights recognized or existing in any State Party to the present Covenant pursuant to law, conventions, regulations or custom on the pretext that the present Covenant does not recog-nize such rights or that it recognizes them to a lesser extent.

PART III

Article 6

1. Every human being has the inherent right to life. This right shall be protected by law. No one shall be arbitrarily deprived of his life.

2. In countries which have not abolished the death penalty, sentence of death may be imposed only for the most serious crimes in accordance with the law in force at the time of the commission of the crime and not contrary to the provisions of the present Covenant and to the Convention on the Prevention and Punishment of the Crime of Genocide. This penalty can only be carried out pursuant to a final judgment rendered by a competent court.

3. When deprivation of life constitutes the crime of genocide, it is understood that nothing in this article shall authorize any State Party to the present Covenant to derogate in any way from any obligation assumed under the provisions of the Convention on the Prevention and Punishment of the Crime of Genocide.

4. Anyone sentenced to death shall have the right to seek pardon or commutation of the sentence. Amnesty, pardon or commutation of the sentence of death may be granted in all cases.

5. Sentence of death shall not be imposed for crimes committed by persons below eigh-teen years of age and shall not be carried out on pregnant women.

6. Nothing in this article shall be invoked to delay or prevent the abolition of capital punishment by any State Party to the present Covenant.

Article 7

No one shall be subjected to torture or cruel, inhuman or degrading treatment or punishment. In particular, no one shall be subjected without his free consent to medical or scientific experimentation.

Article 8

1. No one shall be held in slavery; slavery and the slave-trade in all their forms shall be prohibited.

2. No one shall be held in servitude.

3. (a) No one shall be required to perform forced or compulsory labour;

(b) Paragraph 3(a) shall not be held to preclude, in countries where imprisonment with hard labour may be imposed as a punishment for a crime, the performance of hard labour in pursuance of a sentence to such punishment by a competent court.

(c) For the purpose of this paragraph the term 'forced or compulsory labour' shall not include

(i) Any work or service, not referred to in subparagraph (b), normally required of a person who is under detention in consequence of a lawful order of a court, or of a person during conditional release from such detention;

(ii) Any service of a military character and, in countries where conscientious objection is recognized, any national service required by law of conscientious objectors;

(iii) Any service exacted in cases of emergency or calamity threatening the life or well-being of the community;

(iv) Any work or service which forms part of normal civil obligations.

Article 9

1. Everyone has the right to liberty and security of the person. No one shall be subjected to arbitrary arrest or detention. No one shall be deprived of his liberty except on such grounds and in accordance with such procedure as are established by law.

2. Anyone who is arrested shall be informed, at the time of arrest, of the reasons for his arrest and shall be promptly informed of any charges against him.

3. Anyone arrested or detained on a criminal charge shall be brought promptly before a judge or other officer authorized by law to exercise judicial power and shall be entitled to trial within a reasonable time or to release. It shall not be the general rule that persons awaiting trial shall be detained in custody, but release may be subject to guarantees to appear at the trial, at any other stage of the judicial proceedings, and, should the occasion arise, for execution of the judgment.

4. Anyone who is deprived of his liberty by arrest or detention shall be entitled to take proceedings before a court, in order that that court may decide without delay on the lawfulness of his detention and order his release if his detention is not lawful.

5. Anyone who has been a victim of unlawful arrest or detention shall have an enforceable right to compensation.

Article 10

1. All persons deprived of their liberty shall be treated with humanity and with respect for the inherent dignity of the human person.

2. (a) Accused persons shall, save in exceptional circumstances, be segregated from convicted persons and shall be subject to separate treatment appropriate to their status as unconvicted persons.

(b) Accused juvenile persons shall be separated from adults and brought as speedily as possible for adjudication.

3. The penitentiary system shall comprise treatment of prisoners the essential aim of which shall be their reformation and social rehabilitation. Juvenile offenders shall be segregated from adults and be accorded treatment appropriate to their age and legal status.

Article 11

No one shall be imprisoned merely on the ground of inability to fulfil a contractual obligation.

Article 12

1. Everyone lawfully within the territory of the State shall, within that territory, have the right to liberty of movement and freedom to choose his residence.

2. Everyone shall be free to leave any country including his own.

3. The above-mentioned rights shall not be subjected to any restrictions except those which are provided by law, are necessary to protect national security, public order (*ordre public*), public health or morals or the rights and freedoms of others, and are consistent with the other rights and freedoms recognized in the present Covenant.

4. No shall be arbitrarily deprived of the right to enter his own country.

Article 13

An alien lawfully in the territory of a State Party to the present Covenant may be expelled therefrom only in pursuance of a decision reached in accordance with law and shall, except where compelling reasons of national security otherwise require, be allowed to submit the reasons against his expulsion and to have his case reviewed by, and be represented for the purpose before, the competent authority or a person or persons especially designated by the competent authority.

Article 14

1. All persons shall be equal before the courts and tribunals. In the determination of any criminal charge against him, or of his rights and obligations in a suit at law, everyone shall be entitled to a fair and public hearing by a competent, independent and impartial tribunal

established by law. The Press and the public may be excluded from all or part of a trial for reasons of morals, public order (*ordre public*) or national security in a democratic society, or when the interest of the private lives of the parties so requires, or to the extent strictly necessary in the opinion of the court in special circumstances where publicity would prejudice the interests of justice; but any judgment rendered in a criminal case or in a suit at law shall be made public except where the interest of juvenile persons otherwise requires or the proceedings concern matrimonial disputes or the guardianship of children.

2. Everyone charged with a criminal offence shall have the right to be presumed innocent until proved guilty according to law.

3. In the determination of any criminal charge against him, everyone shall be entitled to the following minimum guarantees, in full equality:

(a) To be informed and in detail in a language which he understands of the nature and cause of the charge against him;

(b) To have adequate time and facilities for the preparation of his defence and to communicate with counsel of his own choosing;

(c) To be tried without undue delay;

(d) To be tried in his presence, and to defend himself in person or through legal assistance of his own choosing; to be informed, if he does not have legal assistance, of this right; and to have legal assistance assigned to him, in any case where the interests of justice so require, and without payment by him in any such case if he does not have sufficient means to pay for it;

(e) To examine, or have examined, the witnesses against him and to obtain the attendance and examination of witnesses on his behalf under the same conditions as witnesses against him;

(f) To have the free assistance of an interpreter if he cannot understand or speak the language used in court;

(g) Not to be compelled to testify against himself or to confess guilt.

4. In the case of juvenile persons, the procedure shall be such as will take account of their age and the desirability of promoting their rehabilitation.

5. Everyone convicted of a crime shall have the right to his conviction and sentence being reviewed by a higher tribunal according to law.

6. When a person has by final decision been convicted of a criminal offence and when subsequently his conviction has been reversed or he has been pardoned on the ground that a newly discovered fact shows conclusively that there has been a miscarriage of justice, the person who has suffered punishment as a result of such conviction shall be compensated according to law, unless it is proved that the non-disclosure of the unknown fact in time is wholly or partly attributable to him.

7. No one shall be liable to be tried or punished again for an offence for which he has already been finally convicted or acquitted in accordance with the law and penal procedure of each country.

Article 15

1. No one shall be held guilty of any criminal offence on account of any act or omission which did not constitute a criminal offence, under national or international law, at the time when it was committed. Nor shall a heavier penalty be imposed than the one that was applicable at the time when the criminal offence was committed. If, subsequent to the commission of the offence, provision is made by law for the imposition of the lighter penalty, the offender shall benefit thereby.

2. Nothing in this article shall prejudice the trial and punishment of any person for any act or omission which, at any time when it was committed, was criminal according to the general principles of law recognized by the community of nations.

Article 16

Everyone shall have the right to recognition everywhere as a person before the law.

Article 17

1. No one shall be subjected to arbitrary or unlawful interference with his privacy, family, home or correspondence, nor to unlawful attacks on his honour and reputation.

2. Everyone has the right to the protection of the law against such interference or attacks.

Article 18

1. Everyone shall have the right to freedom of thought, conscience and religion. This right shall include freedom to have or to adopt a religion or belief of his choice, and freedom, either individually or in community with others and in public or private, to manifest his religion or belief in worship, observance, practice and teaching.

2. No one shall be subject to coercion which would impair his freedom to have or to adopt a religion or belief of his choice.

3. Freedom to manifest one's religion or beliefs may be subject only to such limitations as are prescribed by law and are necessary to protect public safety, order, health, or morals or the fundamental rights and freedoms of others.

4. The States Parties to the present Covenant undertake to have respect for the liberty of parents and, when applicable, legal guardians to ensure the religious and moral education of their children in conformity with their own convictions.

Article 19

1. Everyone shall have the right to hold opinions without interference.

2. Everyone shall have the right to freedom of expression; this right shall include freedom to seek, receive and impart information and ideas of all kinds, regardless of frontiers, whether orally, in writing or in print, in the form of art, or through any other media of his choice.

3. The exercise of the rights provided for in paragraph 2 of this article carries with it special duties and responsibilities. It may therefore be subject to certain restrictions, but these shall only be such as are provided by law and are necessary;

(a) For respect of the right or reputations of others;

(b) For the protection of national security or of public order (*ordre public*), or of public health or morals.

Article 20

1. Any propaganda for war shall be prohibited by law.

2. Any advocacy of national, racial or religious hatred that constitutes incitement to discrimination, hostility or violence shall be prohibited by law.

Article 21

The right of peaceful assembly shall be recognized. No restrictions may be placed on the exercise of this right other than those imposed in conformity with the law and which are necessary in a democratic society in the interests of national security or public safety, public order (*ordre public*), the protection of public health or morals or the protection of the rights and freedoms of others.

Article 22

1. Everyone shall have the right to freedom of association with others, including the right to form and join trade unions for the protection of his interests.

2. No restrictions may be placed on the exercise of this right other than those which are prescribed by law and which are necessary in a democratic society in the interests of national security or public safety, public order (*ordre public*), the protection of public health or morals or the protection of the rights and freedoms of others. This article shall not prevent the imposition of lawful restrictions on members of the armed forces and of the police in their exercise of this right.

3. Nothing in this article shall authorize States Parties to the International Labour Organization Convention of 1948 concerning Freedom of Association and Protection of the Right to Organize to take legislative measures which would prejudice, or to apply the law in such a manner as to prejudice, the guarantees provided for in that Convention.

Article 23

1. The family is the natural and fundamental group unit of society and is entitled to protection by society and the State.

2. The right of men and women of marriageable age to marry and to found a family shall be recognized.

3. No marriage shall be entered into without the free and full consent of the intending spouses.

4. States Parties to the present Covenant shall take appropriate steps to ensure equality of rights and responsibilities of spouses as to marriage, during marriage and at its dissolution. In the case of dissolution, provision shall be made for the necessary protection of any children.

Article 24

1. Every child shall have, without any discrimination as to race, colour, sex, language, religion, national or social origin, property or birth, the right to such measures of protection as are required by his status as a minor, on the part of his family, society and the State.

2. Every child shall be registered immediately after birth and shall have a name.

3. Every child has the right to acquire a nationality.

Article 25

Every citizen shall have the right and the opportunity, without any of the distinctions mentioned in article 2 and without unreasonable restrictions:

a) To take part in the conduct of public affairs, directly or through freely chosen representatives;

b) To vote and to be elected at genuine periodic elections which shall be by universal and equal suffrage and shall be held by secret ballot, guaranteeing the free expression of the will of the electors;

c) To have access, on general terms of equality, to public service in his country.

Article 26

All persons are equal before the law and are entitled without any discrimination to the equal protection of the law. In this respect, the law shall prohibit any discrimination and guarantee to all persons equal and effective protection against discrimination on any ground such as race, colour, sex, language, religion, political or other opinion, national or social origin, property, birth or other status.

Article 27

In those States in which ethnic, religious or linguistic minorities exist, persons belonging to such minorities shall not be denied the right, in community with the other members of their group, to enjoy their own culture, to profess and to practise their own religion, or to use their own language.

PART IV

Article 28

1. There shall be established a Human Rights Committee (hereafter referred to in the present Covenant as the Committee). It shall consist of eighteen members and shall carry out the functions hereinafter provided.

2. The Committee shall be composed of nationals of the States Parties to the present Covenant who shall be persons of high moral character and recognized competence in the field of human rights, consideration being given to the usefulness of the participation of some persons having legal experience.

3. The members of the Committee shall serve in their personal capacity.

Article 29

1. The members of the Committee shall be elected by secret ballot from a list of persons possessing the qualifications prescribed in article 28 and nominated for the purpose by the States Parties to the present Covenant.

2. Each State Party to the present Covenant may nominate not more than two persons. The persons shall be nationals of the nominating State.

3. A person shall be eligible for renomination.

Article 30

1. The initial election shall be held no later than six months after the date of entry into force of the present Covenant.

2. At least four months before the date of each election to the Committee, other than an election to fill a vacancy declared in accordance with article 34, the Secretary-General of the United Nations shall address a written invitation to the States Parties to the present Covenant to submit their nominations for membership of the Committee within three months.

3. The Secretary-General of the United Nations shall prepare a list in alphabetical order of all the persons thus nominated, with an indication of the States Parties which have nominated them, and shall submit it to the States Parties to the present Covenant no later than one month before the date of each election.

4. Elections of the members of the Committee shall be held at a meeting of the State Parties to the present Covenant convened by the Secretary-General of the United Nations at the Headquarters of the United Nations. At that meeting, for which two thirds of the States Parties to the present Covenant shall constitute a quorum, the persons elected to the Committee shall be those nominees who obtain the largest number of votes and an absolute majority of the votes of the representatives of States Parties present and voting.

Article 31

1. The Committee may not include more than one national of the same State.

2. In the election of the Committee, consideration shall be given to equitable geographical distribution of membership and to the representation of different forms of civilization and of the principal legal systems.

Article 32

1. The members of the Committee shall be elected for a term of four years. They shall be eligible for re-election if renominated. However, the term of nine of the members elected at the first election shall expire at the end of two years; immediately after the first election, the names of these nine members shall be chosen by lot by the Chairman of the meeting referred to in article 30, paragraph 4.

2. Elections at the expiry of office shall be held in accordance with the preceding articles of this part of the present Covenant.

Article 33

1. If, in the unanimous opinion of the other members, a member of the Committee has ceased to carry out his functions for any cause other than absence of a temporary character, the Chairman of the Committee shall notify the Secretary-General of the United Nations, who shall then declare the seat of that member to be vacant.

2. In the event of the death or the resignation of a member of the Committee, the Chairman shall immediately notify the Secretary-General of the United Nations, who shall declare the seat vacant from the date of the death or the date on which the resignation takes effect.

Article 34

1. When a vacancy is declared in accordance with article 33 and if the term of office of the member to be replaced does not expire within six months of the declaration of the vacancy, the Secretary-General of the United Nations shall notify each of the States Parties to the present Covenant, which may within two months submit nominations in accordance with article 29 for the purpose of filling the vacancy.

2. The Secretary-General of the United Nations shall prepare a list in alphabetical order of the persons thus nominated and shall submit it to the States Parties to the present Covenant. The election to fill the vacancy shall then take place in accordance with the relevant provisions of this part of the present Covenant.

Article 35

The members of the Committee shall, with the approval of the General Assembly of the United Nations, receive emoluments from United Nations resources on such terms and conditions as the General Assembly may decide, having regard to the importance of the Committee's responsibilities.

Article 36

The Secretary-General of the United Nations shall provide the necessary staff and facilities for the effective performance of the functions of the Committee under the present Covenant.

Article 37

1. The Secretary-General of the United Nations shall convene the initial meeting of the Committee at the Headquarters of the United Nations.

2. After its initial meeting, the Committee shall meet at such times as shall be provided in its rules of procedure.

3. The Committee shall normally meet at the Headquarters of the United Nations or at the United Nations Office at Geneva.

Article 38

Every member of the Committee shall, before taking up his duties, make a solemn declaration in open committee that he will perform his functions impartially and conscientiously.

Article 39

1. The Committee shall elect its officers for a term of two years. They may be re-elected.

2. The Committee shall establish its own rules of procedure, but these rules shall provide, *inter alia*, that:

(a) Twelve members shall constitute a quorum;

(b) Decisions of the Committee shall be made by a majority vote of the members present.

Article 40

1. The States Parties to the present Covenant undertake to submit reports on the measures they have adopted which give effect to the rights recognized herein and on the progress made in the enjoyment of those rights:

(a) Within one year of the entry into force of the present Covenant for the States Parties concerned;

(b) Thereafter when the Committee so requests.

2. All reports shall be submitted to the Secretary-General of the United Nations, who shall transmit them to the Committee for consideration. Reports shall indicate the factors and difficulties, if any, affecting the implementation of the present Covenant.

3. The Secretary-General of the United Nations may, after consultation with the

Committee, transmit to the specialized agencies concerned copies of such parts of the reports as may fall within their field of competence.

4. The Committee shall study the reports submitted by the States Parties to the present Covenant. It shall transmit its reports, and such general comments as it may consider appropriate, to the States Parties. The Committee may also transmit to the Economic and Social Council these comments along with the copies of the reports it has received from States Parties to the present Covenant.

5. The States Parties to the present Covenant may submit to the Committee observations on any comments that may be made in accordance with paragraph 4 of this article.

Article 41

1. A State Party to the present Covenant may at any time declare under this article that it recognizes the competence of the Committee to receive and consider communications to the effect that a State Party claims that another State Party is not fulfilling its obligations under the present Covenant. Communications under this article may be received and considered only if submitted by a State Party which has made a declaration recognizing in regard to itself the competence of the Committee. No communication shall be received by the Committee if it concerns a State Party which has not made such a declaration. Communication received under this article shall be dealt with in accordance with the following procedure:

(a) If a State Party to the present Covenant considers that another State Party is not giving effect to the provisions of the present Covenant, it may, by written communication, bring the matter to the attention of that State Party. Within three months after the receipt of the communication the receiving State shall afford the State which sent the communication an explanation of any other statement in writing clarifying the matter which should include, to the extent possible and pertinent, reference to domestic procedures and remedies taken, pending, or available in the matter;

(b) If the matter is not adjusted to the satisfaction of both States Parties concerned within six months after the receipt by the receiving State of the initial communication, either State shall have the right to refer the matter to the Committee, by notice given to the Committee and to the other State;

(c) The Committee shall deal with a matter referred to it only after it has ascertained that all available domestic remedies have been invoked and exhausted in the matter, in conformity with the generally recognized principles of international law. This shall not be the rule where the application of the remedies is unreasonably prolonged.

(d) The Committee shall hold closed meetings when examining communications under this article;

(e) Subject to the provision of subparagraph (c), the Committee shall make available its good offices to the States Parties concerned with a view to a friendly solution of the matter on the basis of respect for human rights and fundamental freedoms as recognized in the present Covenant.

(f) In any matter referred to it, the Committee may call upon the States Parties concerned, referred to in subparagraph (b), to supply any relevant information;

(g) The States Parties concerned, referred to in subparagraph (b), shall have the right to be represented when the matter is being considered in the Committee and to make submissions orally and/or in writing;

(h) The Committee shall, within twelve months after the date of receipt of a notice under subparagraph (b), submit a report:

> (i) If a solution within the terms of subparagraph (e) is reached, the Committee shall confine its report to a brief statement of the facts and of the solution reached;

> (ii) If a solution within the terms of subparagraph (e) is not reached, the Committee shall confine its report to a brief statement of the facts; the written submissions and record of the oral submissions made by the States Parties concerned shall be attached to the report.

In every matter, the report shall be communicated to the States Parties concerned.

2. The provisions of this article shall come into force when ten States Parties to the present Covenant have made declarations under paragraph 1 of this article. Such declarations shall be deposited by the States Parties with the Secretary-General of the United Nations, who shall transmit copies thereof to the other States Parties. A declaration may be withdrawn at any time by notification to the Secretary-General. Such a withdrawal shall not prejudice the consideration of any matter which is the subject of a communication already transmitted under this article; no further communication by any State Party shall be received after the notification of withdrawal of the declaration has been received by the Secretary-General, unless the States Party concerned has made a new declaration.

Article 42

1. (a) If a matter referred to the Committee in accordance with article 41 is not resolved to the satisfaction of the States Parties concerned, the Committee may, with the prior consent of the States Parties concerned, appoint an *ad hoc* Conciliation Commission (hereinafter referred to as the Commission). The good offices of the Commission shall be made available to the States Parties concerned with a view to an amicable solution of the matter on the basis of respect for the present Covenant;

(b) The Commission shall consist of five persons acceptable to the States Parties concerned. If the States Parties concerned fail to reach agreement within three months on all or part of the composition of the Commission, the members of the Commission concerning whom no agreement has been reached shall be elected by secret ballot by a two-thirds majority vote of the Committee from among the members.

3. The members of the Commission shall serve in their personal capacity. They shall not be nationals of the States Parties concerned, or of a State not party to the present Covenant, or of a State Party which has not made a declaration under article 41.

4. The Commission shall elect its own Chairman and adopt its own rules of procedure.

5. The meetings of the Commission shall normally be held at the Headquarters of the United Nations or at the United Nations Office at Geneva. However, they may be held at such other convenient places as the Commission may determine in consultation with the Secretary-General of the United Nations and the States Parties concerned.

6. The information received and collated with article 36 shall also service the commissions appointed under this article.

7. When the Commission has fully considered the matter, but in any event not later than twelve months after having been seized of the matter, it shall submit to the Chairman of the Committee a report for communication to the States Parties concerned:

(a) If the Commission is unable to complete its consideration of the matter within twelve months, it shall confine its report to a brief statement of the status of its consideration of the matter.

(b) If an amicable solution to the matter on the basis of respect for human rights as recognized in the present Covenant is reached, the Commission shall confine its report to a brief statement of the facts and of the solution reached;

(c) If a solution within the terms of subparagraph (b) is not reached, the Commission's report shall embody its findings on all questions of fact relevant to the issues between the States Parties concerned, and its views on the possibilities of an amicable solution to the matter. This report shall also contain the written submissions and a record of the oral submissions made by the States Parties concerned;

(d) If the Commission's report is submitted under subparagraph (c), the States Parties concerned shall, within three months of receipt of the report, notify the Chairman of the Commission whether or not they accept the contents of the report of the Commission.

8. The provisions of this article are without prejudice to the responsibilities of the Committee under article 41.

9. The States Parties concerned shall share equally all the expenses of the members of the Commission in accordance with estimates to be provided by the Secretary-General of the United Nations.

10. The Secretary-General of the United Nations shall be empowered to pay the expenses of the members of the Commission, if necessary, before reimbursement by the States Parties concerned, in accordance with paragraph 9 of this article.

Article 43

The members of the Committee, and of the *ad hoc* conciliation commission which may be appointed under article 42, shall be entitled to the facilities, privileges, and immunities of experts on mission for the United Nations as laid down in the relevant sections of the Convention on the Privileges and Immunities of the United Nations.

Article 44

The provisions for the implementation of the present Covenant shall apply without prejudice to the procedures prescribed in the field of human rights by or under the constituent
instruments and the conventions of the United Nations and of the specialized agencies and
shall not prevent the States Parties to the present Covenant from having recourse to other
procedures for settling a dispute in accordance with general or special international agreements in force between them.

Article 45

The Committee shall submit to the General Assembly of the United Nations, through the
Economic and Social Council, an annual report on its activities.

PART V

Article 46

Nothing in the present Covenant shall be interpreted as impairing the provisions of the
Charter of the United Nations and of the constitutions of the specialized agencies which
define the respective responsibilities of the various organs of the United Nations and of the
specialized agencies in regard to the matters dealt with in the present Covenant.

Article 47

Nothing in the present Covenant shall be interpreted as impairing the inherent right of all
peoples to enjoy and utilize fully their natural wealth and resources.

PART VI

Article 48

1. The present Covenant is open for signatures by any State Member of the United Nations
or member of any of its specialized agencies, by any State Party to the Statute of the
International Court of Justice, and by any other State which has been invited by the
General Assembly of the United Nations to become a Party to the present Covenant.

2. The present Covenant is subject to ratification. Instruments of ratification shall be
deposited with the Secretary-General of the United Nations.

3. The present Covenant shall be open to accession by any State referred to in paragraph
1 of this article.

4. Accession shall be effected by deposit of an instrument of accession with the Secretary-
General of the United Nations.

5. The Secretary-General of the United Nations shall inform all States which have signed
this Covenant or acceded to it of the deposit of each instrument of ratification or accession.

Article 49

1. The present Covenant shall enter into force three months after the date of the deposit with the Secretary-General of the United Nations of the thirty-fifth instrument of ratification or instrument of accession.

2. For each State ratifying the present Covenant or acceding to it after the deposit of the thirty-fifth instrument of ratification or instrument of accession, the present Covenant shall enter into force three months after the date of the deposit of its own instrument of ratification or instrument of accession.

Article 50

The provisions of the present Covenant shall extend to all parts of federal states without any limitations or exceptions.

Article 51

1. Any State Party to the present Covenant may propose an amendment and file it with the Secretary-General of the United Nations. The Secretary-General of the United Nations shall thereupon communicate any proposed amendments to the States Parties to the present Covenant with request that they notify him whether they favour a conference of States Parties for the purpose of considering and voting upon the proposals. In the event that at least one third of the States Parties favours such a conference, the Secretary-General shall convene the conference under the auspices of the United Nations. Any amendment adopted by a majority of the States Parties present and voting at the conference shall be submitted to the General Assembly of the United Nations for approval.

2. Amendments shall come into force when they have been approved by the General Assembly of the United Nations and accepted by a two-thirds majority of the States Parties to the present Covenant in accordance with their own respective constitutional processes.

3. When amendments come into force, they shall be binding on those States Parties which have accepted them, other States Parties still being bound by the provisions of the present Covenant and any earlier amendment which they have accepted.

Article 52

Irrespective of the notifications made under article 48, paragraph 5, the Secretary-General of the United Nations shall inform all States referred to in paragraph 1 of the same article of the following particulars:

(a) Signatures, ratifications and accessions under article 48

(b) The date of entry into force of the present Covenant under article 49 and the date of the entry into force of any amendments under article 51.

Article 53

1. The present Covenant, of which Chinese, English, French, Russian and Spanish texts are equally authentic, shall be deposited in the archives of the United Nations.

2. The Secretary-General of the United Nations shall transmit certified copies of the present Covenant to all States referred to in article 48.

Appendix B

First Optional Protocol to the International Covenant on Civil and Political Rights

Adopted and opened for signature, ratification and accession by General Assembly resolution 2200A (XXI) of 16 December 1966

Preamble

The States Parties to the present Protocol,

Considering that in order further to achieve the purposes of the International Covenant on Civil and Political Rights (hereinafter referred to as the Covenant) and the implementation of its provisions it would be appropriate to enable the Human Rights Committee set up in part IV of the Covenant (hereinafter referred to as the Committee) to receive and consider, as provided in the present Protocol, communications from individuals claiming to be victims of violations of any of the rights set forth in the Covenant.

Have agreed as follows:

Article 1

A State Party to the Covenant that becomes a Party to the present Protocol recognizes the competence of the Committee to receive and consider communications from individuals subject to its jurisdiction who claim to be victims of a violation by that State Party of any of the rights set forth in the Covenant. No communication shall be received by the Committee if it concerns a State Party to the Covenant which is not a Party to the present Protocol.

Article 2

Subject to the provisions of article 1, individuals who claim that any of their rights enumerated in the Covenant have been violated and who have exhausted all available domestic remedies may submit a written communication to the Committee for consideration.

Article 3

The Committee shall consider inadmissible any communication under the present Protocol which is anonymous, or which it considers to be an abuse of the right of submission of such communications or to be incompatible with the provisions of the Covenant.

Article 4

1. Subject to the provisions of article 3, the Committee shall bring any communications

submitted to it under the present Protocol to the attention of the State Party to the present Protocol alleged to be violating any provision of the Covenant.

2. Within six months, the receiving State shall submit to the Committee written explanations or statements clarifying the matter and the remedy, if any, that may have been taken by that State.

Article 5

1. The Committee shall consider communications received under the present Protocol in the light of all written information made available to it by the individual and by the State Party concerned.

2. The Committee shall not consider any communication from an individual unless it has ascertained that:

(a) The same matter is not being examined under another procedure of international investigation or settlement;

(b) The individual has exhausted all available domestic remedies. This shall not be the rule where the application of the remedies is unreasonably prolonged.

3. The Committee shall hold closed meetings when examining communications under the present Protocol.

4. The Committee shall forward its views to the State Party concerned and to the individual.

Article 6

The Committee shall include in its annual report under article 45 of the Covenant a summary of its activities under the present Protocol.

Article 7

Pending the achievement of the objectives of resolution 1514(XV) adopted by the General Assembly of the United Nations on 14 December 1960 concerning the Declaration on the Granting of Independence to Colonial Countries and Peoples, the provisions of the present Protocol shall in no way limit the right of petition granted to these peoples by the Charter of the United Nations and other international conventions and instruments under the United Nations and its specialized agencies.

Article 8

1. The present Protocol is open for signature by any State which has signed the Covenant.

2. The present Protocol is subject to ratification by any State which has ratified or acceded to the Covenant. Instruments of ratification shall be deposited with the Secretary-General of the United Nations.

3. The present Protocol shall be open to accession by any State which has ratified or acceded to the Covenant.

4. Accession shall be effected by the deposit of an instrument of accession with the Secretary-General of the United Nations.

5. The Secretary-General of the United Nations shall inform all States which have signed the present Protocol or acceded to it of the deposit of each instrument of ratification or accession.

Article 9

1. Subject to the entry into force of the Covenant, the present Protocol shall enter into force three months after the date of the deposit with the Secretary-General of the United Nations of the tenth instrument of ratification or instrument of accession.

2. For each State ratifying the present Protocol or acceding to it after the deposit of the tenth instrument of ratification or instrument of accession, the present Protocol shall enter into force three months after the date of the deposit of its own instrument of ratification or instrument of accession.

Article 10

The provisions of the present Protocol shall extend to all parts of federal States without any limitations or exceptions.

Article 11

1. Any State Party to the present Protocol may propose an amendment and file it with the Secretary-General of the United Nations. The Secretary-General shall thereupon communicate any proposed amendments to the States Parties to the present Protocol with a request that they notify him whether they favour a conference of States Parties for the purpose of considering and voting upon the proposal. In the event that at least one third of the States Parties favours such a conference, the Secretary-General shall convene the conference under the auspices of the United Nations. Any amendment adopted by a majority of the States Parties present and voting at the conference shall be submitted to the General Assembly of the United Nations for approval.

2. Amendments shall come into force when they have been approved by the General Assembly of the United Nations and accepted by a two-thirds majority of the States Parties to the present Protocol in accordance with their respective constitutional processes.

3. When amendments come into force, they shall be binding on those States Parties which have accepted them, other States Parties still being bound by the provisions of the present Protocol and any earlier amendment which they have accepted.

Article 12

1. Any State Party may denounce the present Protocol at any time by written notification

addressed to the Secretary-General of the United Nations. Denunciation shall take effect three months after the date of receipt of the notification by the Secretary-General.

2. Denunciation shall be without prejudice to the continued application of the provisions of the present Protocol to any communication submitted under article 2 before the effective date of denunciation.

Article 13

Irrespective of the notifications made under article 8, paragraph 1, of the present Protocol, the Secretary-General of the United Nations shall inform all States referred to in article 48, paragraph 1, of the Covenant of the following particulars:

(a) Signatures, ratifications and accessions under article 8;

(b) The date of the entry into force of the present Protocol under article 9 and the date of the entry into force of any amendments under article 11;

(c) Denunciations under article 12.

Article 14

1. The present Protocol, of which the Chinese, English, French, Russian and Spanish texts are equally authentic, shall be deposited in the archives of the United Nations.

2. The Secretary-General of the United Nations shall transmit certified copies of the present Protocol to all States referred to in article 48 of the Covenant.

Appendix C

Second Optional Protocol to the International Covenant on Civil and Political Rights, Aiming at the Abolition of the Death Penalty

Adopted and proclaimed by General Assembly resolution 44/128 of 15 December 1989

Preamble

The States Parties to the present Protocol,

Believing that abolition of the death penalty contributes to enhancement of human dignity and progressive development of human rights,

Recalling article 3 of the Universal Declaration of Human Rights, adopted on 10 December 1948, and article 6 of the International Covenant on Civil and Political Rights, adopted on 16 December 1966,

Noting that article 6 of the International Covenant on Civil and Political Rights refers to abolition of the death penalty in terms that strongly suggest that abolition is desirable,

Convinced that all measures of abolition of the death penalty should be considered as progress in the enjoyment of the right to life,

Desirous to undertake hereby an international commitment to abolish the death penalty,

Have agreed as follows:

Article 1

1. No one within the jurisdiction of a State Party to the present Protocol shall be executed.

2. Each State Party shall take all necessary measures to abolish the death penalty within its jurisdiction.

Article 2

1. No reservation is admissible to the present Protocol, except for a reservation made at the time of ratification or accession that provides for the application of the death penalty in time of war pursuant to a conviction for a most serious crime of a military nature committed during wartime.

2. The State Party making such a reservation shall at the time of ratification or accession communicate to the Secretary-General of the United Nations the relevant provisions of its national legislation applicable during wartime.

3. The State Party having made such a reservation shall notify the Secretary-General of the United Nations of any beginning or ending of a state of war applicable to its territory.

Article 3

The States Parties to the present Protocol shall include in the reports they submit to the Human Rights Committee, in accordance with article 40 of the Covenant, information on the measures that they have adopted to give effect to the present Protocol.

Article 4

With respect to the States Parties to the Covenant that have made a declaration under article 41, the competence of the Human Rights Committee to receive and consider communications when a State Party claims that another State Party is not fulfilling its obligations shall extend to the provisions of the present Protocol, unless the State Party concerned has made a statement to the contrary at the moment of ratification or accession.

Article 5

With respect to the States Parties to the first Optional Protocol to the International Covenant on Civil and Political Rights adopted on 16 December 1966, the competence of the Human Rights Committee to receive and consider communications from individuals subject to its jurisdiction shall extend to the provisions of the present Protocol, unless the State Party concerned has made a statement to the contrary at the moment of ratification or accession.

Article 6

1. The provisions of the present Protocol shall apply as additional provisions to the Covenant.

2. Without prejudice to the possibility of a reservation under article 2 of the present Protocol, the right guaranteed in article 1, paragraph 1, of the present Protocol shall not be subject to any derogation under article 4 of the Covenant.

Article 7

1. The present Protocol is open for signature by any State that has signed the Covenant.

2. The present Protocol is subject to ratification by any State that has ratified the Covenant or acceded to it. Instruments of ratification shall be deposited with the Secretary-General of the United Nations.

3. The present Protocol shall be open to accession by any State that has ratified the Covenant or acceded to it.

4. Accession shall be effected by the deposit of an instrument of accession with the Secretary-General of the United Nations.

5. The Secretary-General of the United Nations shall inform all States that have signed the present Protocol or acceded to it of the deposit of each instrument of ratification or accession.

Article 8

1. The present Protocol shall enter into force three months after the date of the deposit with the Secretary-General of the United Nations of the tenth instrument of ratification or accession.

2. For each State ratifying the present Protocol or acceding to it after the deposit of the tenth instrument of ratification or accession, the present Protocol shall enter into force three months after the date of the deposit of its own instrument of ratification or accession.

Article 9

The provisions of the present Protocol shall extend to all parts of federal States without any limitations or exceptions.

Article 10

The Secretary-General of the United Nations shall inform all States referred to in article 48, paragraph 1, of the Covenant of the following particulars:

(a) Reservations, communications and notifications under article 2 of the present Protocol;

(b) Statements made under articles 4 or 5 of the present Protocol;

(c) Signatures, ratifications and accessions under article 7 of the present Protocol:

(d) The date of the entry into force of the present Protocol under article 8 thereof.

Article 11

1. The present Protocol, of which the Arabic, Chinese, English, French, Russian and Spanish texts are equally authentic, shall be deposited in the archives of the United Nations.

2. The Secretary-General of the United Nations shall transmit certified copies of the present Protocol to all States referred to in article 48 of the Covenant.

Appendix D

States Parties to the International Covenant on Civil and Political Rights

Country	Date of Entry Into Force	Ratification or Accession Date	Signature Date
Afghanistan	24/04/83	24/01/83	
Albania	04/01/92	04/10/91	
Algeria	12/12/89	12/09/89	10/12/68
Angola	10/04/92	10/01/92	
Argentina	08/11/86	08/08/86	19/02/68
Armenia	23/09/93	23/06/93	
Australia	13/11/80	13/08/80	18/12/72
Austria	10/12/78	10/09/78	10/12/73
Azerbaijan	13/11/92	13/08/92	
Barbados	23/03/76	05/01/73	
Belarus	23/03/76	12/11/73	19/03/68
Belgium	21/07/83	21/04/83	10/12/68
Belize	10/09/96	10/06/96	
Benin	12/06/92	12/03/92	
Bolivia	12/11/82	12/08/82	
Bosnia-Herzegovina	06/03/92	01/09/93	
Brazil	24/04/92	24/01/92	
Bulgaria	23/03/76	21/09/70	08/10/68
Burkina Faso	04/04/99	04/01/99	
Burundi	09/08/90	09/05/90	
Cambodia	26/08/92	26/05/92	17/10/80
Cameroon	27/09/84	27/06/84	
Canada	19/08/76	19/05/76	
Cape Verde	06/11/93	06/08/93	
Central African Republic	08/08/81	08/05/81	
Chad	09/09/95	09/06/95	
Chile	23/03/76	10/02/72	16/09/69
Colombia	23/03/76	29/10/69	21/12/66
Congo	05/01/84	05/10/83	
Costa Rica	23/03/76	29/11/68	19/12/66
Côte d'Ivoire	26/06/92	26/03/92	
Croatia	08/10/91	12/10/92	
Cyprus	23/03/76	02/04/69	19/12/66
Czech Republic	01/01/93	22/02/93	
*Democratic People's Republic of Korea	14/12/81	14/09/81	

Country	Date of Entry Into Force	Ratification or Accession Date	Signature Date
Democratic Republic of the Congo	01/02/77	01/11/76	
Denmark	23/03/76	06/01/72	20/03/68
Dominica	17/09/93	17/06/93	
Dominican Republic	04/04/78	04/01/78	
Ecuador	23/03/76	06/03/69	04/04/68
Egypt	14/04/82	14/01/82	04/08/67
El Salvador	29/02/80	30/11/79	21/09/67
Equatorial Guinea	25/12/87	25/09/87	
Estonia	21/01/92	21/10/91	
Ethiopia	11/09/93	11/06/93	
Finland	23/03/76	19/08/75	11/10/67
France	04/02/81	04/11/80	
Gabon	21/04/83	21/01/83	
Gambia	22/06/79	22/03/79	
Georgia	03/08/94	03/05/94	
Germany	23/03/76	17/12/73	09/10/68
Greece	05/08/97	05/05/97	
Grenada	06/12/91	06/09/91	
Guatemala	05/08/92	06/05/92	
Guinea	24/04/78	24/01/78	28/02/67
Guyana	15/05/77	15/02/77	22/08/68
Haiti	06/05/91	06/02/91	19/12/66
Honduras	25/11/97	25/08/97	19/12/66
Hungary	23/03/76	17/01/74	25/03/69
Iceland	22/11/79	22/08/79	30/12/68
India	10/07/79	10/04/79	
Iran (Islamic Republic of)	23/03/76	24/06/75	04/04/68
Iraq	23/03/76	25/01/71	18/02/69
Ireland	08/03/90	08/12/89	01/10/73
Israel	03/01/92	03/10/91	19/12/66
Italy	15/12/78	15/09/78	18/01/67
Jamaica	23/03/76	03/10/75	19/12/66
Japan	21/09/79	21/06/79	30/05/78
Jordan	23/03/76	28/05/75	30/06/72
Kenya	23/03/76	01/05/72	
Kuwait	21/08/96	21/05/96	
Kyrgyzstan	07/01/95	07/10/94	
Latvia	14/07/92	14/04/92	
Lebanon	23/03/76	03/11/72	
Lesotho	09/12/92	09/09/92	
Libyan Arab Jamahiriya	23/03/76	15/05/70	
Liechtenstein	10/03/99	10/12/98	
Lithuania	20/02/92	20/11/91	
Luxembourg	18/11/83	18/08/83	26/11/74

Country	Date of Entry Into Force	Ratification or Accession Date	Signature Date
Madagascar	23/03/76	21/06/71	17/09/69
Malawi	22/03/94	22/12/93	
Mali	23/03/76	16/07/74	
Malta	13/12/90	13/09/90	
Mauritius	23/03/76	12/12/73	
Mexico	23/06/81	23/03/81	
Monaco	28/11/97	28/08/97	26/06/97
Mongolia	23/03/76	18/11/74	05/06/68
Morocco	03/08/79	03/05/79	19/01/77
Mozambique	21/10/93	21/07/93	
Namibia	28/02/95	28/11/94	
Nepal	14/08/91	14/05/91	
Netherlands	11/03/79	11/12/78	25/06/69
New Zealand	28/03/79	28/12/78	12/11/68
Nicaragua	12/06/80	12/03/80	
Niger	07/06/86	07/03/86	
Nigeria	29/10/93	29/07/93	
Norway	23/03/76	13/09/72	20/03/68
Panama	08/06/77	08/03/77	27/07/76
Paraguay	10/09/92	10/06/92	
Peru	28/07/78	28/04/78	11/08/77
Philippines	23/01/87	23/10/86	19/12/66
Poland	18/06/77	18/03/77	02/03/67
Portugal	15/09/78	15/06/78	07/10/76
Republic of Korea	10/07/90	10/04/90	
Republic of Moldova	26/04/93	26/01/93	
Romania	23/03/76	09/12/74	27/06/68
Russian Federation	23/03/76	16/10/73	18/03/68
Rwanda	23/03/76	16/04/75	
Saint Vincent and the Grenadines	09/02/82	09/11/81	09/11/81
San Marino	18/01/86	18/10/85	
Senegal	13/05/78	13/02/78	06/07/70
Seychelles	05/08/92	05/05/92	
Sierra Leone	23/11/96	23/08/96	
Slovakia	01/01/93	28/05/93	
Slovenia	25/06/91	06/07/92	
Somalia	24/04/90	24/01/90	
South Africa	10/03/99	10/12/98	03/10/94
Spain	27/07/77	27/04/77	28/09/76
Sri Lanka	11/09/80	11/06/80	
Sudan	18/06/86	18/03/76	
Suriname	28/03/77	28/12/76	
Sweden	23/03/76	06/12/71	29/09/67
Switzerland	18/09/92	18/06/92	

Country	Date of Entry Into Force	Ratification or Accession Date	Signature Date
Syrian Arab Republic	23/03/76	21/04/69	
Tajikistan	04/04/99	04/01/99	
Thailand	29/01/97	29/10/96	
The Former Yugoslav Republic of Macedonia	17/09/91	18/01/94	
Togo	24/08/84	24/05/84	
Trinidad and Tobago	21/03/79	21/12/78	
Tunisia	23/03/76	18/03/69	30/04/68
Turkmenistan	01/08/97	01/05/97	
Uganda	21/09/95	21/06/95	
Ukraine	23/03/76	12/11/73	20/03/68
United Kingdom of Great Britain and Northern Ireland	20/08/76	20/05/76	16/09/68
United Republic of Tanzania	11/09/76	11/06/76	
United States of America	08/09/92	08/06/92	05/10/77
Uruguay	23/03/76	01/04/70	21/02/67
Uzbekistan	28/12/95	28/09/95	28/09/95
Venezuela	10/08/78	10/05/78	24/06/69
Viet Nam	24/12/82	24/09/82	
Yemen	09/05/87	09/02/87	
Yugoslavia	23/03/76	02/06/71	08/08/67
Zambia	10/07/84	10/04/84	
Zimbabwe	13/08/91	13/05/91	

NB

The Human Rights Committee also considers Kazakhstan to be a party to the ICCPR, by virtue of the principle of succession [1.08]. Furthermore, the ICCPR still applies in the territory of Hong Kong [1.08].

*The Democratic People's Republic of Korea (North Korea) purported to denounce the ICCPR in August 1997. The HRC has determined that denunciation is impermissible (see [25.37]).

Appendix E

States Parties to the First Optional Protocol to the International Covenant on Civil and Political Rights

Country	Date of Entry Into Force	Ratification or Accession Date	Signature Date
Algeria	12/12/89	12/09/89	
Angola	10/04/92	10/01/92	
Argentina	08/11/86	08/08/86	
Armenia	23/09/93	23/06/93	
Australia	25/12/91	25/09/91	
Austria	10/03/88	10/12/87	10/12/73
Barbados	23/03/76	05/01/73	
Belarus	30/12/92	30/09/92	
Belgium	17/08/94	17/05/94	
Benin	12/06/92	12/03/92	
Bolivia	12/11/82	12/08/82	
Bosnia-Herzegovina	01/06/95	01/03/95	01/03/95
Bulgaria	26/06/92	26/03/92	
Burkina Faso	04/04/99	04/01/99	
Cameroon	27/09/84	27/06/84	
Canada	19/08/76	19/05/76	
Central African Republic	08/08/81	08/05/81	
Chad	09/09/95	09/06/95	
Chile	28/08/92	28/05/92	28/05/92
Colombia	23/03/76	29/10/69	21/12/66
Congo	05/01/84	05/10/83	
Costa Rica	23/03/76	29/11/68	19/12/66
Côte d'Ivoire	05/06/97	05/03/97	
Croatia	12/01/96	12/10/95	
Cyprus	15/07/92	15/04/92	19/12/66
Czech Republic	01/01/93	22/02/93	
Democratic Republic of the Congo	01/02/77	01/11/76	
Denmark	23/03/76	06/01/72	20/03/68
Dominican Republic	04/04/78	04/01/78	
Ecuador	23/03/76	06/03/69	04/04/68
El Salvador	06/09/95	06/06/95	21/09/67
Equatorial Guinea	25/12/87	25/09/87	
Estonia	21/01/92	21/10/91	
Finland	23/03/76	19/08/75	11/12/67

The ICCPR

Country	Date of Entry Into Force	Ratification or Accession Date	Signature Date
France	17/05/84	17/02/84	
Gambia	09/09/88	09/06/88	
Georgia	03/08/94	03/05/94	
Germany	25/11/93	25/08/93	
Greece	05/08/97	05/05/97	
Guinea	17/09/93	17/06/93	19/03/75
Guyana[1]	05/04/99	05/01/99	
Hungary	07/12/88	07/09/88	
Iceland	22/11/79	22/08/79	
Ireland	08/03/90	08/12/89	
Italy	15/12/78	15/09/78	30/04/76
Kyrgyzstan	07/01/94	07/10/95	
Latvia	22/09/94	22/06/94	
Libyan Arab Jamahiriya	16/08/89	16/05/89	
Liechtenstein	10/03/99	10/12/98	
Lithuania	20/02/92	20/11/91	
Luxembourg	18/11/83	18/08/83	
Madagascar	23/03/76	21/06/71	17/09/69
Malawi	11/09/96	11/06/96	
Malta	13/12/90	13/09/90	
Mauritius	23/03/76	12/12/73	
Mongolia	16/07/91	16/04/91	
Namibia	28/02/95	28/11/94	
Nepal	14/08/91	14/05/91	
Netherlands	11/03/79	11/12/78	25/06/69
New Zealand	26/08/89	26/05/89	
Nicaragua	12/06/80	12/03/80	
Niger	07/06/86	07/03/86	
Norway	23/03/76	13/09/72	20/03/68
Panama	08/06/77	08/03/77	27/07/76
Paraguay	10/04/95	10/01/95	
Peru	03/01/81	03/10/80	11/08/77
Philippines	22/11/89	22/08/89	19/12/66
Poland	07/02/92	07/11/91	
Portugal	03/08/83	3/05/83	01/08/78
Republic of Korea	10/07/90	10/04/90	
Romania	20/10/93	20/07/93	
Russian Federation	01/01/92	01/10/91	
Saint Vincent and the Grenadines	09/02/82	09/11/81	
San Marino	18/01/86	18/10/85	
Senegal	13/05/78	13/02/78	06/07/70

[1] Guyana withdrew from the First Optional Protocol and reacceded with a new reservation with effect from the given date.

Country	Date of Entry Into Force	Ratification or Accession	Signature Date
Seychelles	05/08/92	05/05/92	
Sierra Leone	23/08/96	23/08/96	
Slovakia	01/01/93	28/05/93	
Slovenia	16/10/93	16/07/93	
Somalia	24/04/90	24/01/90	
Spain	25/04/85	25/01/85	
Sri Lanka	03/01/98	03/10/97	
Suriname	28/03/77	28/12/76	
Sweden	23/03/76	06/12/71	29/09/67
Tajikistan	04/04/99	04/01/99	
The Former Yugoslav Republic of Macedonia	12/03/95	12/12/94	
Togo	30/06/88	30/03/88	
Trinidad and Tobago[2]	26/08/98	26/05/98	
Turkmenistan	01/08/97	01/05/97	
Uganda	14/02/96	14/11/95	
Ukraine	25/10/91	25/07/91	
Uruguay	23/03/76	01/04/70	21/02/67
Uzbekistan	28/12/95	28/09/95	
Venezuela	10/08/78	10/05/78	15/11/76
Zambia	10/07/84	10/04/84	

[2] Trinidad and Tobago withdrew from the First Optional Protocol on 26 August 1998, and re-acceded on the given dates. Trinidad and Tobago again denounced the First Optional Protocol on 27 March 2000, with effect from 27 June 2000. Jamaica withdrew from the First Optional Protocol on 23 October 1997. See [25.38].

Appendix F

States Parties to the Second Optional Protocol to the International Covenant on Civil and Political Rights

Country	Date of Entry Accession	Ratification or Date	Signature Date
Australia	11/07/91	02/10/90	
Austria	02/06/93	02/03/93	08/04/91
Azerbaijan	22/04/99	22/01/99	
Belgium	08/03/99	08/12/98	12/07/90
Bulgaria	10/11/99	10/08/99	11/03/99
Colombia	04/11/97	05/08/97	
Costa Rica	05/06/98	05/06/98	14/02/90
Croatia	12/01/96	12/10/95	
Cyprus	10/09/99	10/09/99	
Denmark	24/05/94	24/02/94	13/02/90
Ecuador	23/05/93	23/02/93	
Finland	11/07/91	04/04/91	13/02/90
Georgia	22/06/99	22/03/99	
Germany	18/11/92	18/08/92	13/02/90
Greece	05/08/97	05/05/97	
Hungary	24/05/94	24/02/94	
Iceland	11/07/91	02/04/91	30/01/91
Ireland	18/09/93	18/06/93	
Italy	14/05/95	14/02/95	13/02/90
Liechtenstein	10/03/99	10/12/98	
Luxembourg	12/05/92	12/02/92	13/02/90
Malta	29/03/95	29/12/94	
Mozambique	21/10/93	21/07/93	
Namibia	28/02/95	28/11/94	
Nepal	04/06/98	04/03/98	
Netherlands	11/07/91	26/03/91	09/08/90
New Zealand	11/07/91	22/02/90	22/02/90
Norway	05/12/91	05/09/91	13/02/90
Panama	21/04/93	21/01/93	
Portugal	11/07/91	17/10/90	13/02/90
Romania	11/07/91	27/02/91	15/03/90
Seychelles	15/03/95	15/12/94	
Slovakia	22/09/99	22/06/99	22/09/98
Slovenia	10/06/94	10/03/94	14/09/93

Country	Date of Entry Accession	Ratification or Date	Signature Date
Spain	11/07/91	11/04/91	23/02/90
Sweden	11/07/91	11/05/90	13/02/90
Switzerland	16/09/94	16/06/94	
The Former Yugoslav Republic of Macedonia	26/04/95	26/01/95	
Uruguay	21/04/93	21/01/93	13/02/90
Venezuela	22/05/93	22/02/93	07/06/90

Appendix G

States which have made the Declaration under Article 41 of the Covenant

State Party	Valid from	Valid until
Algeria	12 September 1989	Indefinitely
Argentina	8 August 1986	Indefinitely
Australia	28 January 1993	Indefinitely
Austria	10 September 1978	Indefinitely
Belarus	30 September 1992	Indefinitely
Belgium	5 March 1987	Indefinitely
Bosnia-Herzegovina	6 March 1992	Indefinitely
Bulgaria	12 May 1993	Indefinitely
Canada	29 October 1979	Indefinitely
Chile	11 March 1990	Indefinitely
Congo	7 July 1989	Indefinitely
Croatia	12 October 1995	12 October 1996
Czech Republic	1 January 1993	Indefinitely
Denmark	23 March 1976	Indefinitely
Ecuador	24 August 1984	Indefinitely
Finland	19 August 1975	Indefinitely
Gambia	9 June 1988	Indefinitely
Germany	28 March 1979	27 March 1996
Guyana	10 May 1993	Indefinitely
Hungary	7 September 1988	Indefinitely
Iceland	22 August 1979	Indefinitely
Ireland	8 December 1989	Indefinitely
Italy	15 September 1978	Indefinitely
Liechtenstein	10 March 1999	Indefinitely
Luxembourg	18 August 1983	Indefinitely
Malta	13 September 1990	Indefinitely
Netherlands	11 December 1978	Indefinitely
New Zealand	28 December 1978	Indefinitely
Norway	23 March 1976	Indefinitely
Peru	9 April 1984	Indefinitely
Philippines	23 October 1986	Indefinitely
Poland	25 September 1990	Indefinitely
Republic of Korea	10 April 1990	Indefinitely
Russian Federation	1 October 1991	Indefinitely
Senegal	5 January 1981	Indefinitely
Slovakia	1 January 1993	Indefinitely
Slovenia	6 July 1992	Indefinitely

State Party	Valid from	Valid until
South Africa	10 March 1999	Indefinitely
Spain	25 January 1985	25 January 1993
Sri Lanka	11 June 1980	Indefinitely
Sweden	23 March 1976	Indefinitely
Switzerland	18 September 1992	18 September 1997
Tunisia	24 June 1993	Indefinitely
Ukraine	28 July 1992	Indefinitely
United Kingdom of Great Britain and Northern Ireland	20 May 1976	Indefinitely
United States of America	8 September 1992	Indefinitely
Zimbabwe	20 August 1991	Indefinitely

Appendix H

Members of the Human Rights Committee (Past and Present)

Name	Country	Tenure
A. Current Members		
Mr Abdelfattah Amor	Tunisia	1999–
Mr Nisuke Ando	Japan	1987–
Mr Prafulla Handra Natwarlal Bhagwati	India	1995–
Mme Christine Chanet	France	1987–
Lord Colville	United Kingdom	1996–
Mrs Elizabeth Evatt	Australia	1993–
Ms. Pilar Gaitan de Pombo	Colombia	1997–
Mr Louis Henkin	USA	1999–
Mr Eckart Klein	Germany	1995–
Mr David Kretzmer	Israel	1995–
Mr Rajsoomer Lallah	Mauritius	1985–
Mrs Cecilia Medina Quiroga	Chile	1995–
Mr Fausto Pocar	Italy	1985–
Mr Martin Scheinin	Finland	1997–
Mr Solari Yrigoyen	Argentina	1999–
Mr Roman Wieruszewski	Poland	1998–
Mr Maxwell Yalden	Canada	1997–
Mr Abdallah Zakhia	Lebanon	1997–
B. Former Members		
Mr Andrés Aguilar	Venezuela	1981–8
Mr Francisco José Aguilar Urbina	Costa Rica	1989–96
Mr Mohamed Al Douri	Iraq	1980–4
Mr Támás Ban	Hungary	1993–6
Mr Mohamed Ben-Fadhei	Tunisia	1976–88
Mr Nejib Bouziri	Tunisia	1979–86
Mr Marco Rulio Bruni Celli	Venezuela	1993–6
Mr Thomas Buergenthal	USA	1995–9
Mr Joseph Cooray	Sri Lanka	1987–90
Ms Gisèle Côté-Harper	Canada	1983–4
Mr Abdulaye Dieye	Senegal	1979–82
Mr Vojin Dimitrijevic	Yugoslavia, Federal Republic of Yugoslavia	1983–94
Mr Omran El Shafei	Egypt	1987–98
Mr Felix Ermacora	Austria	1981–4

Mr Roger Errera	France	1983–6
Mr Ole Mogens Espersen	Denmark	1976–8
Name	**Country**	**Tenure**
Sir Vincent Evans	United Kingdom	1976–84
Mr János Fodor	Hungary	1989–93
Mr Laurel B. Francis	Jamaica	1993–6
Mr Manouchehr Ganji	Iran	1976–80
Mr Bernard Graefrath	German Democratic Republic	1976–84
Mr Vladimir Hanga	Romania	1976–84
Mr Leonte Herdocia Ortega	Nicaragua	1981–3
Mr Kurt Herndl	Austria	1991–4
Mrs Rosalyn Higgins	United Kingdom	1985–96
Mr Dejan Janca	Yugoslavia	1979–82
Mr Haissam Kelani	Syrian Arab Republic	1976–80
Mr Luben G. Koulishev	Bulgaria	1976–80
Mr Rajsoomer Lallah	Mauritius	1976–82
Mr Andreas Mavrommatis	Cyprus	1976–96
Ms. Laure Moghaizel	Lebanon	1997
Mr Joseph A. Moomersteeg	Netherlands	1987–91
Mr Fernando Mora Rojas	Costa Rica	1976–8
Mr Anatoly Petrovich Movchan	USSR	1976–88
Mr Rein Myullerson	USSR, Estonia	1989–92
Mr Birame Ndiaye	Senegal	1983–94
Mr Torkel Opsahl	Norway	1976–86
Mr Julio Prado Vallejo	Ecuador	1976–98
Mr Waleed Sadi	Jordan	1978–94
Mr Fulgence Seminega1	Rwanda	1976–8
Mr Alegandro Serrano Caldera	Nicaragua	1984–92
Mr Walter Surma Tarnopolsky	Canada	1976–83
Mr Christian Tomuschat	Federal Republic of Germany	1976–86
Mr Danilo Türk	Slovenia	1997–8
Mr Diego Uribe Vargas	Colombia	1976–80
Mr S. Amos Wako	Kenya	1984–92
Mr Bertil Wennergren	Sweden	1987–94
Mr Adam Zielinski	Poland	1985–8

Appendix I

Optional Protocol Cases

The following table shows all reported Optional Protocol cases of the Human Rights Committee. It includes all inadmissibility decisions and final views, and other reported decisions, such as interlocutory decisions, admissibility decisions, or decisions to joint communication.

Also note that all reported decisions from the 46th session (October–November 1992) are available from the UN treaty bodies database, at <http://www.unhchr.ch/tbs/doc.nsf>

Communication No.	Author[1]	States Party	Annual Report	Selected Decisions[2]	Date of Decision
1/1976	*A et al.*	S.[3]		1 SD 3, 17, 35[4]	24/10/79
2/1976	L.P.	Canada		1 SD 21	14/8/79
4/1977	Ramírez	Uruguay	80, 123	1 SD 3, 4, 49	23/7/80
5/1977	Ambrosini, Valentini de Massera and Massara	Uruguay	79, 124	1 SD 37, 40	15/8/79
6/1977	Millán Sequeira	Uruguay	80, 127	1 SD 52	29/7/80
8/1977	Weismann, Lanza Perdomo	Uruguay	80, 111	1 SD 45	3/4/80
9/1977	Santullo Valcada	Uruguay	80, 107	1 SD 43	26/10/79
10/1977	Altesor	Uruguay	82, 122	1 SD 6, 105	29/3/82
11/1977	Grille Motta *et al.*	Uruguay	80, 132	1 SD 54	29/7/80
13/1977	C.E.	Canada		1 SD 16	25/8/77
15/1977	D.B.	Canada		1 SD 20	24/4/79
16/1977	Monguya Mbenge *et al.*	Zaire	83, 134	2 SD 76	25/3/83
17/1977	Z.Z.	Canada		1 SD 19	28/7/78
19/1977	C.J.	Canada		1 SD 23	13/8/79
20/1977	M.A.	S.		1 SD 5, 20	24/4/79
21/1977	I.	S.		1 SD 35	24/10/79
22/1977	O.E.	S.		1 SD 5, 6, 35	24/10/79
24/1977	Lovelace	Canada	81, 166; 83, 248	1 SD 10, 37, 83	30/7/81
25/1978	Massiotti and Baritussio	Uruguay	82, 187	1 SD 136	26/7/82
26/1978	N.S.	Canada	82, 212	1 SD 19	28/7/78
27/1978	Pinkney	Canada	82, 101	1 SD 12, 95	29/10/81
28/1978	Weinberger	Uruguay	81, 114	1 SD 57	29/10/80
29/1978	E.B.	S.		1 SD 11, 39	20/10/80
30/1978	Bleier	Uruguay	82, 130	1 SD 109	29/3/82
31/1978	Waksman	Uruguay	80, 120	1 SD 9, 36	28/3/80
32/1978	Sala de Touron	Uruguay	81, 120	1 SD 61	31/3/81

33/1978	Buffo Carballal	Uruguay	81, 125	1 SD 63	27/3/81
34/1978	Llandinelli Silva *et al.*	Uruguay		1 SD 65	8/4/81
35/1978	Aumeeruddy-Cziffra *et al.*	Mauritius	81, 134; 83, 254	1 SD 67	9/4/81
37/1978	Soriano de Bouton	Uruguay	81, 143	1 SD 72	27/3/81
40/1978	Hartikainen *et al.*	Finland	81, 147; 83, 225	1 SD 74	9/4/81
43/1979	Drescher Caldas	Uruguay	83, 192	2 SD 80	9/4/81
44/1979	Pietraroia	Uruguay	81, 153	1 SD 76	27/3/81
45/1979	Suárez de Guerrero	Colombia	82, 137	1 SD 112	31/3/82
46/1979	Fals Borda *et al.*	Colombia	82, 193	1 SD 139	27/7/82
49/1979	Marais Jr.	Madagascar	83, 141	2 SD 82	24/3/83
50/1979	Van Duzen	Canada	82, 150	1 SD 118	7/4/82
52/1979	López Burgos	Uruguay	81, 176	1 SD 88	29/7/81
53/1979	K.B.	Norway		1 SD 24	26/3/80
55/1979	MacIsaac	Canada	82, 150	2 SD 87	14/10/82
56/1979	Celiberti de Casariego	Uruguay	81, 185	1 SD 92	29/7/81
57/1979	Vidal Martins	Uruguay	82, 157	1 SD 122	23/3/82
58/1979	Maroufidou	Sweden	81, 160	1 SD 80	9/4/81
59/1979	K.L.	Denmark		1 SD 24	26/3/80
60/1979	J.J.	Denmark		1 SD 26	31/7/80
61/1979	Hertzberg *et al.*	Finland	82, 161	1 SD 124	2/4/82
63/1979	Sendic Antonaccio	Uruguay	82, 114	1 SD 101	28/10/81
64/1979	Salgar de Montejo	Colombia	82, 168	1 SD 127	24/3/82
66/1979	Campora Schweizer	Uruguay	83, 117	2 SD 90	12/10/82
67/1979	E.H.P.	Canada		2 SD 20	27/10/82
68/1980	A.S., daughter and grandson	Canada		1 SD 27	31/3/81
70/1980	Cubas Simones	Uruguay	82, 174	1 SD 130	1/4/82
72/1980	K.L.	Denmark		1 SD 26	31/7/80
73/1980	Teti Izquierdo	Uruguay	82, 179	1 SD 7, 132	1/4/82

Communication No.	Author[1]	States Party	Annual Report	Selected Decisions[2]	Date of Decision
74/1980	Estrella	Uruguay	83, 150	2 SD 93	29/3/83
75/1980	Fanali	Italy	83, 160	2 SD 99	31/3/83
77/1980	Lichtensztein	Uruguay	83, 166	2 SD 102	31/3/83
78/1980	Mikmaq Tribal Society	Canada	84, 200	2 SD 23	29/7/84
79/1980	S.S.	Norway		1 SD 30	2/4/82
80/1980	Vasilskis	Uruguay	83, 173	2 SD 105	31/3/83
81/1980	K.L.	Denmark		1 SD 28	27/3/81
83/1980	Martinez Machado	Uruguay	84, 148	2 SD 108	4/11/83
84/1981	Ignacio, Barbato, and Dermit Barbato	Uruguay	83, 124	2 SD 112	27/10/82
85/1981	Alfredo Romero	Uruguay	84, 159	2 SD 116	29/3/84
88/1981	Larrosa Bequio	Uruguay	83, 180	2 SD 118	29/3/83
89/1981	Muhonen	Finland	85, 164	2 SD 121	8/4/85
90/1981	Magana ex-Philibert	Zaire	83, 197	2 SD 124	21/7/83
91/1981	A.R.S.	Canada		1 SD 29	28/10/81
92/1981	Almirati Nieto	Uruguay	83, 201	2 SD 126	25/7/83
94/1981	L.S.N.	Canada		2 SD 6	30/3/84
103/1981	Oxandabarat Scarrone	Uruguay	84, 154	2 SD 130	4/11/83
104/1981	J.R.T. and the W.G. Party	Canada	83, 231	2 SD 25	6/4/83
105/1981	Estradet Cabreira	Uruguay	83, 209	2 SD 133	21/7/83
106/1981	Pereira Montero	Uruguay	83, 186	2 SD 136	31/7/83
107/1981	Quinteros Almeida and mother	Uruguay	83, 216	2 SD 11, 138	21/7/83
108/1981	Varela Núñez	Uruguay	83, 225	2 SD 143	22/7/83
109/1981	Gómez de Voituret	Uruguay	84, 164	2 SD 146	10/4/84
110/1981	Viana Acosta	Uruguay	84, 169	2 SD 148	29/3/84
112/1981	Y.L.	Canada	86, 145	2 SD 28	8/4/86
113/1981	C.F. et al.	Canada	85, 217	2 SD 13	12/4/85

Case	Name	Country			Date
115/1982	Wight	Madagascar	85, 171	2 SD 151	1/4/85
117/1981	M.A.	Italy	84, 190	2 SD 31	10/4/84
118/1982	J.B. *et al.*	Canada	86, 151; 87, 47	2 SD 34	18/7/86
121/1982	A.M.	Denmark	82, 212	1 SD 32	23/7/82
123/1982	Manera Lluberas	Uruguay	84, 175	2 SD 155	6/4/84
124/1982	Muteba	Zaire	84, 182	2 SD 158	24/7/84
125/1982	M.M.Q.	Uruguay		2 SD 8	6/4/84
127/1982	C.A.	Italy	83, 237	2 SD 39	31/3/83
128/1982	U.R.	Uruguay	83, 239	2 SD 40	6/4/83
129/1982	I.M.	Norway	83, 241	2 SD 41	6/4/83
130/1982	J.S.	Canada	83, 243	2 SD 42	6/4/83
131/1982	N.G.	Uruguay		2 SD 9	25/7/84
132/1982	Jaona	Madagascar	85, 179	2 SD 161	1/4/85
136/1983	S.G.F.	Uruguay	83, 245	2 SD 43	25/7/83
137/1983	J.F.	Uruguay	83, 247	2 SD 43	25/7/83
138/1983	Mpandanjila *et al.*	Zaire	86, 121	2 SD 164	26/3/86
139/1983	Conteris	Uruguay	85, 196	2 SD 168	17/7/85
146/1983 and 148–154/1983	Baboeram *et al.*	Suriname	85, 187	2 SD 5, 172	4/4/85
147/1983	Arzuago Gilboa	Uruguay	86, 128	2 SD 176	1/11/85
155/1983	Hammel	Madagascar	87, 130	2 SD 11, 179	3/4/87
156/1983	Alberto Solórzano	Venezuela	86, 134	2 SD 183	26/3/86
157/1983	Mpaka-Nsusu	Zaire	86, 142	2 SD 187	26/3/86
158/1983	O.F.	Norway	85, 204	2 SD 44	26/10/84
159/1983	Cariboni	Uruguay	88, 184	2 SD 189	27/10/87
161/1983	Rubio and parents	Colombia	88, 190	2 SD 192	2/11/87
162/1983	Berterretche Acosta	Uruguay	89, 183		25/10/88
163/1984	Group of handicapped persons	Italy	84, 197	2 SD 47	10/4/84

Communication No.	Author[1]	States Party	Annual Report	Selected Decisions[2]	Date of Decision
164/1984	Croes	Netherlands	89, 259		7/11/88
165/1984	J.M.	Jamaica	86, 164	2 SD 17	26/3/86
167/1984	Ominayak and the Lubicon Lake Band	Canada	90, 1[6]		26/3/90
168/1984	V.	Norway	85, 232	2 SD 48	17/7/85
170/1984	E.H.	Finland	86, 168	2 SD 50	25/10/85
172/1984	Broeks	Netherlands	87, 139	2 SD 196	9/4/87
173/1984	M.F.	Netherlands	85, 213	2 SD 51	2/11/84
174/1984	J.K.	Canada	85, 215	2 SD 52	26/10/84
175/1984	N.B. *et al.*	Sweden	85, 236	2 SD 53	11/7/85
176/1984	Peñarietta	Bolivia	88, 199	2 SD 201	2/11/87
178/1984	J.D.B.	Netherlands	85, 226	2 SD 55	26/3/85
180/1984	Danning	Netherlands	87, 151	2 SD 205	9/4/87
181/1984	Sanjuán Arévalo brothers	Colombia	90, 31		3/11/89
182/1984	Zwaan-de Vries	Netherlands	87, 160	2 SD 209	9/4/87
183/1984	D.F. *et al.*	Sweden	85, 228	2 SD 55	26/3/85
184/1984	H.S.	France	86, 169	2 SD 56	10/4/86
185/1984	L.T.K.	Finland	85, 240	2 SD 61	9/7/85
187/1985	J.H.	Canada	85, 230	2 SD 63	12/4/85
188/1984	Martínez Portorreal	Dominican Republic	88, 207	2 SD 214	5/11/87
191/1985	Blom	Sweden	88, 211	2 SD 216	4/4/88
192/1985	S.H.B.	Canada	87, 174	2 SD 64	24/3/87
193/1985	Giry	Dominican Republic	90, 38		20/7/90
194/1985	Miango Muiyo	Zaire	88, 218	2 SD 219	27/10/87
195/1985	Delgado Páez	Colombia	90, 43		12/7/90
196/1985	Gueye *et al.*	France	89, 189		3/4/89
197/1985	Kitok	Sweden	88, 221		27/7/88
198/1985	Stalla Costa	Uruguay	87, 170	2 SD 221	9/7/87

201/1985	Hendriks Sr. and son	Netherlands		88, 230	27/7/88
202/1986	Ato del Avellanal	Peru		89, 196	28/10/88
203/1986	Muñoz Hermoza	Peru		89, 200	4/11/88
204/1986	A.P.	Italy	2 SD 67	88, 242	2/11/87
205/1986	Mikmaq People	Canada		92, 201	4/11/91
207/1986	Morael	France		89, 210	28/7/89
208/1986	Singh Bhinder	Canada		90, 50	9/11/89
209/1986	F.G.G.	Netherlands	2 SD 68	87, 180	25/3/87
210/1986	Pratt	Jamaica	2 SD 3	89, 222	6/4/89
212/1986	P.P.C.	Netherlands	2 SD 70	88, 244	24/3/88
213/1986	H.C.M.A.	Netherlands		89, 267	30/3/89
215/1986	Van Meurs	Netherlands		90, 55	13/7/90
217/1986	H.v.d.P.	Netherlands	2 SD 71	87, 185	8/4/87
218/1986	Vos	Netherlands		89, 232	29/3/89
219/1986	Guesdon	France		90, 61	25/7/90
220/1987	T.K.	France		90, 118	8/11/89
221/1987	Cadoret	France		91, 219	11/4/91
222/1987	M.K.	France		90, 127	8/11/89
223/1987	Robinson	Jamaica		89, 241	30/3/89
224/1987	A. and S.N.	Norway		88, 246	11/7/88
225/1987	Morgan	Jamaica		89, 222	6/4/89
226/1987	Sawyers	Jamaica		91, 226	11/4/91
227/1987	O.W.	Jamaica		88, 250	26/7/88
228/1987	C.L.D.	France		88, 252	18/7/88
229/1987	Reynolds	Jamaica		91, 235	8/4/91
230/1987	Henry	Jamaica		92, 210	1/11/91
231/1987	A.S.	Jamaica		89, 274	21/7/89
232/1987	Pinto	Trinidad & Tobago		90, 69	20/7/90
233/1987	M.F.	Jamaica		92, 330	21/10/91

Communication No.	Author[1]	States Party	Annual Report	Selected Decisions[2]	Date of Decision
234/1987	D.S.	Jamaica	91, 267		8/4/91
236/1987	V.M.R.B.	Canada	88, 258		18/7/88
237/1987	Gordon	Jamaica	93, 5		5/11/92
238/1987	Bolaños	Ecuador	89, 246		26/7/89
240/1987	Collins	Jamaica	92, 219		1/11/91
241–242/1987	Birindwa & Tshisekedi	Zaire	90, 77		2/11/89
243/1987	S.R.	France	88, 263	2 SD 72	5/11/87
244/1987	A.Z.	Colombia	90, 135		3/11/89
245/1987	R.T.Z.	Netherlands	88, 265	2 SD 73	5/11/87
246/1987	N.A.J.	Jamaica	90, 137		26/7/90
248/1987	Campbell	Jamaica	92, 232		30/3/92
250/2987	Reid	Jamaica	90, 85		20/7/90
251/1987	A.A.	Jamaica	90, 141		30/10/89
252/1987	C.J.	Jamaica	88, 267	2 SD 4	26/7/88
253/1987	Kelly	Jamaica	91, 241		8/4/91
254/1987	W.W.	Jamaica	91, 271		26/10/90
255/1987	Linton	Jamaica	93, 12		22/10/92
256/1987	M. and D. MacLean	Jamaica	91, 226		11/4/91
257/1987	L.C. *et al.*	Jamaica	88, 269		26/7/88
258/1987	L.R. and T.W.	Jamaica	90, 145		13/7/90
259/1987	D.B.	Jamaica	90, 149		13/7/90
260/1987	C.B.	Jamaica	90, 153		13/7/90
262/1987	R.T.	France	89, 277		30/3/89
263/1987	González del Rio	Peru	93, 17		28/10/92
265/1987	Vuolanne	Finland	89, 249		7/4/89
266/1987	I.M.	Italy	89, 282		23/3/89
267/1987	M.J.G.	Netherlands	88, 271	2 SD 74	24/3/88
268/1987	M.G.B. and S.P.	Trinidad & Tobago	90, 157		3/11/89

269/1987	Prince	Jamaica	92, 242	30/3/92
270–271/1988	Barrett and Sutcliffe	Jamaica	92, 246	30/3/92
272/1988	Thomas	Jamaica	92, 253	31/3/92
273/1988	B.d.B. *et al.*	Netherlands	89, 286	30/3/89
274/1988	Griffiths	Jamaica	93, 22	24/3/93
275/1988	S.E.	Argentina	90, 159	26/3/90
276/1988	Ellis	Jamaica	92, 257	28/7/92
277/1988	Terán Jijón	Ecuador	92,261	26/3/92
278/1988	N.C.	Jamaica	90, 166	13/7/90
281/1988	C.G.	Jamaica	90, 169	30/10/89
282/1988	Smith	Jamaica	93, 28	31/3/93
283/1988	Little	Jamaica	92, 268	1/11/91
285/1988	L.G.	Jamaica	88, 272	26/7/88
286/1988	L.S.	Jamaica	88, 274	26/7/88
287/1988	O.H.C.	Colombia	92, 334	1/11/91
289/1988	Wolf	Panama	92, 277	26/3/92
290/1988	A.W.	Jamaica	90, 172	8/11/89
291/1988	Inés Torres	Finland	90, 96	2/4/90
292/1988	Quelch	Jamaica	93, 37	23/10/92
293/1988	Hibbert	Jamaica	92, 284	27/7/92
295/1988	Järvinen	Finland	90, 101	25/7/90
296/1988	J.R.C.	Costa Rica	89, 293	30/3/89
297/1988	H.A.E.d.J.	Netherlands	90, 176	30/10/89
298–99/1988	Lindgren *et al.*	Sweden	91, 253	9/11/90
300/1988	J.H.	Finland	89, 298	23/3/89
301/1988	R.M.	Finland	89, 300	23/3/89
302/1988	A.H.	Trinidad & Tobago	91, 274	31/10/90
303/1988	E.B.	Jamaica	91, 278	26/10/90
304/1988	D.S.	Jamaica	91, 281	11/4/91

Communication No.	Author[1]	States Party	Annual Report	Selected Decisions[2]	Date of Decision
305/1988	van Alphen	Netherlands	90, 108		23/7/90
306/1988	J.G.	Netherlands	90, 180		25/7/90
307/1988	Campbell	Jamaica	93, 41		24/3/93
309/1988	Valenzuela	Peru	93, 48		14/7/93
310/1988	M.T.	Spain	91, 284		11/4/91
313/1988	D.D.	Jamaica	91, 287		11/4/91
314/1988	Bwalya	Zambia	93, 52		14/7/93
315/1988	R.M.	Jamaica	91, 290		26/10/90
316/1988	C.E.A.	Finland	91, 293		10/7/91
317/1988	Martin	Jamaica	93, 57		24/3/93
318/1988	E.P. *et al.*	Colombia	90, 184		25/7/90
319/1988	Cañon García	Ecuador	92, 290		5/11/91
320/1988	Francis	Jamaica	93, 62		24/3/93
321/1988	Thomas	Jamaica	94, 1		19/10/93
322/1988	Rodriguez	Uruguay	94, 5		19/7/94
323/1988	Le Bihan	France	91, 219		11/4/91
324–532/1988	J.B. and H.K.	France	89, 303		25/10/88
326/1988	Kalenga	Zambia	93, 68		27/7/93
327/1988	Barzhig	France	91, 262		11/4/91
328/1988	Blanco	Nicaragua	94, 12		20/7/94
329/1988	D.F.	Jamaica	90, 189		26/3/90
330/1988	Berry	Jamaica	94, 20		7/4/94
331/1988	G.J.	Trinidad & Tobago	92, 337		5/11/91
332/1988	Allen	Jamaica	94, 31		31/3/94
333/1988	Hamilton	Jamaica	94, 37		23/3/94
334/1988	Bailey	Jamaica	93, 72		31/3/93
335/1988	M.F.	Jamaica	92, 340		17/7/92
336/1988	Fillastre *et al.*	Bolivia	92, 294		5/11/91

Case	Name	Country	Ref	Date
337/1988	E.E.	Jamaica	93, 178	23/10/92
338/1988	Simmonds	Jamaica	93, 78	23/10/92
340/1988	R.W.	Jamaica	92, 343	21/7/92
341/1988	Z.P.	Canada	91, 297	11/4/91
342/1988	R.L.	Canada	89, 305	7/4/89
343–345/1988	R.A.V.N. *et al.*	Argentina	90, 191	26/3/90
347/1988	S.G.	France	92, 346	1/11/91
348/1989	G.B.	France	92, 351	1/11/91
349/1989	Wright	Jamaica	92, 300	27/7/92
351/1989	N.A.J.	Jamaica	92, 355	6/4/92
352/1989	Douglas, Gentles and Kerr	Jamaica	94, 42	19/10/93
353/1989	Grant	Jamaica	94, 50	31/3/94
354/1989	L.G.	Mauritius	91, 303	31/10/90
355/1989	Reid	Jamaica	94, 59	8/7/94
356/1989	Collins	Jamaica	93, 85	25/3/93
358/1989	R.L. *et al.*	Canada	92, 358	5/11/91
359/1989	Ballantyne and Davidson	Canada	93, 91	31/3/93
360/1989	A newspaper publishing company	Trinidad & Tobago	89, 307	14/7/89
361/1989	A publication and printing company	Trinidad & Tobago	89, 309	14/7/89
362/1989	Soogrim	Trinidad & Tobago	93, 110	8/4/93
363/1989	R.L.M.	France	92, 367	6/4/92
366/1989	Tshiongo a Minanga	Zaire	94, 65	2/11/93
367/1989	J.J.C.	Canada	92, 372	5/11/91
369/1989	G.S.	Jamaica	90, 198	8/11/89
370/1989	G.H.	Jamaica	93, 181	23/10/92
372/1989	R.L.A.W.	Netherlands	91, 311	2/11/90

Communication No.	Author[1]	States Party	Annual Report	Selected Decisions[2]	Date of Decision
373/1989	Stephens	Jamaica	96, 1		18/10/95
375/1989	Compass	Jamaica	94, 68		10/10/93
377/1989	Currie	Jamaica	94, 73		29/3/94
378/1989	E.E.	Italy	90, 201		26/3/90
379/1989	C.W.	Finland	90, 203		30/3/90
380/1989	R.L.M.	Trinidad & Tobago	93, 184		16/7/93
381/1989	L.E.S.K.	Netherlands	92, 374		21/7/92
382/1989	C.F.	Jamaica	92, 378		28/7/92
383/1989	H.C.	Jamaica	92, 381		28/7/92
384/1989	R.M.	Trinidad & Tobago	94, 246		29/10/93
385/1989	McIntyre	Canada	93, 91		31/3/93
386/1989	Koné	Senegal	95, 1		21/10/94
387/1989	Karttunen	Finland	93, 116		23/10/92
389/1989	I.S.	Hungary	91, 316		9/11/90
390/1990	Lubuto	Zambia	96, 11		31/10/95
393/1990	A.C.	France	92, 384		21/7/92
394/1990	C.B.D.	Netherlands	92, 388		22/7/92
395/1990	Sprenger	Netherlands	92, 311		31/3/92
396/1990	M.S.	Netherlands	92, 392		22/7/92
397/1990	P.S.	Denmark	92, 395		22/7/92
398/1990	A.M.	Finland	92, 403		23/7/92
400/1990	Mónaco de Gallichio	Argentina	95, 10		3/4/95
401/1990	J.P.K.	Netherlands	92, 405		7/11/91
402/1990	Brinkhof	Netherlands	93, 124		27/7/93
403/1990	T.W.M.B.	Netherlands	92, 411		7/11/91
404/1990	N.P.	Jamaica	93, 187		5/4/93
405/1990	M.R.	Jamaica	92, 416		28/7/92
406/1990	Oulajin	Netherlands	93, 131		23/10/92

407/1990	Hylton	Jamaica	94, 79	8/7/94
408/1990	W.J.H.	Netherlands	92, 420	22/7/92
409/1990	E.M.E.H.	France	91, 318	2/11/90
410/1990	Párkányi	Hungary	92, 317	27/7/92
412/1990	Kivenmaa	Finland	94, 85	31/3/94
413/1990	A.B.	Italy	91, 320	2/11/90
414/1990	Miha	Equatorial Guinea	94, 96	8/7/94
415/1990	Pauger	Austria	92, 325	26/3/92
417/1990	Balaguer Santacana	Spain	94, 101	15/7/94
418/1990	Cavalcanti Araujo-Jongen	Netherlands	94, 114	22/10/93
419/1990	O.J.	Finland	91, 323	6/11/90
420/1990	G.T.	Canada	93, 190	23/10/92
421/1990	Trébutien	France	94, 250	18/7/94
422–424/1990	Aduayom *et al.*	Togo	96, 17	12/7/96
425/1990	Neefs	Netherlands	94, 120	15/7/94
426/1990	Kaiss	Netherlands	93, 131	23/10/92
427/1990	H.H.	Austria	93, 195	22/10/92
428/1990	Bozize	Central African Republic	94, 124	7/4/94
429/1990	E.W. *et al.*	Netherlands	93, 198	8/4/93
431/1990	Sara *et al.*	Finland	94, 257	23/3/94
432/1990	W.B.E.	Netherlands	93, 205	23/10/92
433/1990	A.P.A.	Spain	94, 269	25/3/94
434/1990	Seerattan	Trinidad & Tobago	96, 25	26/10/95
436/1990	Solís Palma	Panama	94, 274	18/7/94
437/1990	Patiño	Panama	95, 140	21/10/94
438/1990	Thompson	Panama	95, 143	21/10/94
439/1990	C.L.D.	France	92, 424	8/11/91
440/1990	El-Megreisi	Libya	94, 128	23/3/94

Communication No.	Author[1]	States Party	Annual Report	Selected Decisions[2]	Date of Decision
441/1990	Casanovas	France	94, 131		19/7/94
445/1991	Champagnie et al.	Jamaica	94, 136		18/7/94
446/1991	J.P.	Canada	92, 426		7/11/91
447/1991	Shalto	Trinidad & Tobago	95, 17		4/4/95
448/1991	H.J.H.	Netherlands	92, 428		7/11/91
449/1991	Mojica	Dominican Republic	94, 142		15/7/94
450/1991	I.P.	Finland	93, 210		26/7/93
451/1991	Harward	Norway	94, 146		15/7/94
452/1991	Glaziou	France	94, 277		18/7/94
453/1991	Coeriel	Netherlands	95, 21		31/10/94
454/1991	García Pons	Spain	96, 30		30/10/95
455/1991	Singer	Canada	94, 155		26/7/94
456/1991	Celepli	Sweden	94, 165		18/7/94
457/1991	A.I.E.	Libya	92, 430		7/11/91
458/1991	Mukong	Cameroon	94, 171		21/7/94
459/1991	Wright and Harvey	Jamaica	96, 35		27/10/95
460/1991	Simons	Panama	95, 146		25/10/94
461/1995	Graham and Morrison	Jamaica	96, 43		25/3/96
463/1991	D.B.-B.	Zaire	92, 432		8/11/91
464/1991	Peart	Jamaica	95, 32		19/7/95
467/1991	V.E.M.	Spain	93, 214		16/7/93
468/1991	Oló Bahamonde	Equatorial Guinea	94, 183		20/10/93
469/1991	Ng	Canada	94, 189		5/11/93
470/1991	Kindler	Canada	93, 138		30/7/93
471/1991	Barry	Trinidad & Tobago	94,283		18/7/94
472/1991	J.P.L.	France	96, 231		26/10/95
473/1991	del Cid Gómez	Panama	95, 41		19/7/95
475/1991	S.B.	New Zealand	94, 287		31/3/94

476/1991	R.M.	Trinidad & Tobago	94, 291	31/3/94
477/1991	J.A.M.B.-R.	Netherlands	94, 294	7/4/94
478/1991	A.P.L.-v.d.M.	Netherlands	93, 217	26/7/93
480/1991	Fuenzalida	Ecuador	96, 50	12/7/96
481/1991	Ortega	Ecuador	97, 1	8/4/97
482/1991	Peart	Jamaica	95, 32	19/7/95
483/1991	J.v.K. *et al.*	Netherlands	92, 435	23/7/92
484/1991	Pepels	Netherlands	94, 221	15/7/94
485/1991	V.B.	Trinidad & Tobago	93, 222	26/7/93
486/1992	K.C.	Canada	92, 437	29/7/92
487/1992	Veiga	Uruguay	94, 302	18/7/94
488/1992	Toonen	Australia	94, 226	31/3/94
489/1992	Bradshaw	Barbados	94, 305	19/7/94
490/1992	A.S. and L.S.	Australia	93, 227	30/3/93
491/1992	J.L.	Australia	92, 440	28/7/92
492/1992	Peltonen	Finland	94, 238	21/7/94
493/1992	Griffin	Spain	95, 47	4/4/95
494/1992	Rogers	Jamaica	95, 149	4/4/95
496/1992	T.P.	Hungary	93, 230	30/3/93
497/1992	Amisi	Zaire	94, 310	19/7/94
498/1992	Drbal	Czech Republic	94, 312	22/7/94
499/1992	K.L.B.-W.	Australia	93, 234	30/3/93
500/1992	Debreczeny	Netherlands	95, 59	3/4/95
501/1992	J.H.W.	Netherlands	93, 237	16/7/93
502/1992	S.M.	Barbados	94, 318	31/3/94
504/1992	Roberts	Barbados	94, 322	19/7/94
505/1992	Ackla	Togo	96, 57	25/3/96
509/1992	S.R.U.	Netherlands	94, 327	19/10/93
510/1992	P.J.N.	Netherlands	94, 330	19/10/93

Communication No.	Author[1]	States Party	Annual Report	Selected Decisions[2]	Date of Decision
511/1992	Länsman et al.	Finland	95, 66		26/10/94
512/1992	Pinto	Trinidad & Tobago	96, 61		16/7/96
514/1992	Fei	Colombia	95, 77		4/4/95
515/1992	Holder	Trinidad & Tobago	95, 152		19/7/95
516/1992	Simunek et al.	Czech Republic	95, 89		19/7/95
517/1992	Lambert	Jamaica	94, 333		21/7/94
518/1992	Sohn	Republic of Korea	95, 98		19/7/95
519/1992	Marriott	Jamaica	96, 67		27/10/95
520/1992	Könye and Könye	Hungary	94, 336		7/4/94
521/1992	Kulomin	Hungary	96, 73		22/3/96
522/1992	J.S.	Netherlands	94, 342		3/11/93
523/1992	Neptune	Trinidad & Tobago	96, 84		16/7/96
524/1992	E.C.W.	Netherlands	94, 346		3/11/93
525/1992	Gire	France	95, 155		28/3/95
526/1993	Hill and Hill	Spain	97, 5		2/4/97
527/1993	Lewis	Jamaica	96, 89		18/7/96
528/1993	Steadman	Jamaica	97, 22		2/4/97
529/1993	Edwards	Jamaica	97, 28		28/7/97
532/1993	Thomas	Jamaica	98, 1		3/11/97
533/1993	Elahie	Trinidad & Tobago	97, 34		28/7/97
534/1993	H.T.B.	Canada	94, 348		19/10/93
535/1993	Richards	Jamaica	97, 38		31/3/97
536/1993	Perera	Australia	95, 158		28/3/95
537/1993	Kelly	Jamaica	96, 98		17/7/96
538/1993	Stewart	Canada	97, 47		1/11/96
539/1993	Cox	Canada	95, 105		31/10/94
540/1993	Laureano	Peru	96, 108		25/3/96
541/1993	Simms	Jamaica	95, 164		3/4/95

542/1993	Tshishimbi	Zaire	96, 116	25/3/96
544/1993	K.J.L.	Finland	94, 351	3/11/93
546/1993	Burrell	Jamaica	96, 121	18/7/96
548/1993	R.E.d.B.	Netherlands	94, 354	3/11/93
549/1993	Hopu and Bessert	France	97, 70	29/7/97
550/1993	Faurisson	France	97, 84	8/11/96
552/1993	Kall	Poland	97, 105	14/7/97
553/1993	Bullock	Trinidad & Tobago	95, 168	19/7/95
554/1993	LaVende	Trinidad & Tobago	98, 8	29/10/97
555/1993	Bickaroo	Trinidad & Tobago	98, 15	29/10/97
557/1993	X	Australia	96, 235	16/7/96
558/1993	Canepa	Canada	97, 115	3/4/97
559/1993	J.M.	Canada	94, 357	8/4/94
560/1993	A	Australia	97, 125	3/4/97
561/1993	Williams	Jamaica	97, 147	8/4/97
563/1993	Bautista de Arellana	Colombia	96, 132	27/10/95
564/1993	Leslie	Jamaica	98, 21	31/7/98
565/1993	R and M.K.	Italy	94, 360	8/4/94
566/1993	Somers	Hungary	96, 144	23/7/96
567/1993	Poongavanam	Mauritius	94, 362	26/7/94
568/1993	K.V. and C.V.	Germany	94, 365	8/4/94
569/1993	Matthews	Trinidad & Tobago	98, 30	31/3/98
570/1993	M.A.B., W.A.T. and J.-A.Y.T.	Canada	94, 368	8/4/94
571/1994	Henry and Douglas	Jamaica	96, 155	25/7/96
572/1994	Price	Jamaica	97, 153	6/11/96
573/1994	Atkinson et al.	Canada	96, 243	31/10/95
574/1994	Kim	Republic of Korea	99, xx	3/11/98
575–576/1994	Guerra and Wallen	Trinidad & Tobago	95, 172	4/4/95

Communication No.	Author[1]	States Party	Annual Report	Selected Decisions[2]	Date of Decision
577/1994	Polay Campos	Peru	98, 36		6/11/97
578/1994	de Groot	Netherlands	95, 179		14/7/95
579/1994	Werenbeck	Australia	97, 256		27/3/97
583/1994	van der Houwen	Netherlands	95, 183		14/7/95
584/1994	Valentijn	France	96, 253		31/10/95
585/1994	Jones	Jamaica	98, 45		6/4/98
586/1994	Adam	Czech Republic	96, 165		23/7/96
587/1994	Reynolds	Jamaica	97, 157		3/4/97
588/1994	Johnson	Jamaica	96, 174		22/3/96
589/1994	Tomlin	Jamaica	96, 191		2/11/95
590/1994	Bennett	Jamaica	99, xx		25/3/99
592/1994	Johnson	Jamaica	99, xx		20/10/98
591/1994	Chung	Jamaica	98, 55		9/4/98
593/1994	Holland	Ireland	97, 266		25/10/96
594/1994	Phillip	Trinidad & Tobago	99, xx		20/10/98
596/1994	Chaplin	Jamaica	96, 197		2/11/95
597/1994	Grant	Jamaica	96, 206		22/3/96
598/1994	Sterling	Jamaica	96, 214		22/7/96
599/1994	Spence	Jamaica	96, 219		18/7/96
600/1994	Hylton	Jamaica	96, 224		16/7/96
601/1994	Julian and Drake	New Zealand	97, 273		3/4/97
602/1994	Hoofdman	Netherlands	99, xx		3/11/98
603/1994	Badu	Canada	97, 282		18/7/97
604/1994	Nartey	Canada	97, 288		18/7/97
606/1994	Francis	Jamaica	95, 130		25/7/95
607/1994	Adams	Jamaica	97, 163		30/10/96
608/1995	Nahlik	Austria	96, 259		22/7/96
609/1995	Williams	Jamaica	98, 63		4/11/97

610/1995	Henry	Jamaica	99, xx	20/10/98
612/1995	Arhuacos	Colombia	97, 173	29/7/97
613/1995	Leehong	Jamaica	99, xx	13/7/99
614/1995	Thomas	Jamaica	99, xx	31/3/99
615/1995	Young	Jamaica	98, 69	4/11/97
616/1995	Hamilton	Jamaica	99, xx	23/7/99
617/1995	Finn	Jamaica	98, 78	31/7/98
618/1995	Campbell	Jamaica	99, xx	20/10/98
619/1995	Deidrick	Jamaica	98, 87	9/4/98
623–624/1995	Domukovsky and Tsiklauri	Georgia	98, 95	6/4/98
625–626/1995	Gelbakhiani and Dokvadze	Georgia	98, 95	6/4/98
628/1995	Park	Republic of Korea	99, xx	20/10/98
631/1995	Spakmo	Norway	00, xx	5/11/99
632/1995	Potter	New Zealand	97, 294	28/7/97
633/1995	Gauthier	Canada	99, xx	7/4/99
634/1995	Amore	Jamaica	99, xx	23/3/99
635/1995	Morrison	Jamaica	98, 113	27/7/98
638/1995	Lacika	Canada	96, 265	3/11/95
639/1995	Richards and Walker	Jamaica	97, 183	28/7/97
643/1995	Drobek	Slovakia	97, 300	14/7/97
644/1995	Ajaz and Jamil	Republic of Korea	99, xx	13/7/99
645/1995	Bordes and Temeharo	France	96, 267	22/7/96
646/1995	Lindon	Australia	99, xx	20/10/98
647/1995	Pennant	Jamaica	99, xx	20/10/98
649/1995	Forbes	Jamaica	99, xx	20/10/98
650/1995	Perel	Latvia	98, 128	30/3/98
651/1995	Snijders *et al.*	Netherlands	98, 135	27/7/98

Communication No.	Author[1]	States Party	Annual Report	Selected Decisions[2]	Date of Decision
653/1995	Johnson	Jamaica	99, xx		20/10/98
654/1995	Adu	Canada	97, 304		18/7/97
656/1995	V.E.M.	Spain	96, 274		30/10/95
657/1995	van der Ent	Netherlands	96, 276		3/11/95
658/1995	van Oord	Netherlands	97, 311		23/7/97
659/1995	B.L.	Australia	97, 317		8/11/96
660/1995	Koning	Netherlands	96, 278		3/11/95
661/1995	Triboulet	France	97, 319		29/7/97
662/1995	Lumley	Jamaica	99, xx		31/3/99
663/1995	Morrison	Jamaica	99, xx		3/11/98
664/1995	Kruyt-Amesz	Netherlands	96, 280		25/3/96
665/1995	Brown and Parish	Jamaica	99, xx		29/7/99
666/1995	Foin	France	00, xx		3/11/99
668/1995	Smith and Stewart	Jamaica	99, xx		8/4/99
669/1995	Malik	Czech Republic	99, xx		21/10/98
670/1995	Schlosser	Czech Republic	99, xx		21/10/98
671/1995	Länsman et al.	Finland	97, 191		30/10/96
672/1995	Smart	Trinidad & Tobago	98, 142		29/7/98
673/1995	Gonzalez	Trinidad & Tobago	99, xx		23/3/99
674/1995	Kaaber	Iceland	97, 328		5/11/96
676/1996	Yasseen and Thomas	Guyana	98, 151		30/3/98
679/1996	Darwish	Australia	97, 332		28/7/97
680/1996	Gallimore	Jamaica	99, xx		23/7/99
682/1996	Westerman	Netherlands	00, xx		3/11/99
692/1996	A.R.J.	Australia	97, 205		28/7/97
694/1996	Waldman	Canada	00, xx		3/11/99
696/1996	Blaine	Jamaica	97, 216		17/7/97
698/1996	Sánchez	Spain	97, 337		29/7/97

699/1996	Maleki	Italy	99, xx	15/7/99
700/1996	Jarman	Australia	97, 340	8/11/96
702/1996	McLawrence	Jamaica	97, 225	18/7/97
704/1996	Shaw	Jamaica	98, 164	2/4/98
705/1996	Taylor	Jamaica	98, 174	2/4/98
706/1996	T.T.	Australia	98, 184	4/11/97
707/1996	Taylor	Jamaica	97, 234	14/7/97
708/1996	Lewis	Jamaica	97, 244	17/7/96
709/1997	Bailey	Jamaica	99, xx	21/7/99
710/1997	Hankle	Jamaica	99, xx	28/7/99
714/1997	Gerritsen	Netherlands	99, xx	25/3/99
716/1997	Pauger	Austria	99, xx	25/3/99
717/1997	Inostroza	Chile	99, xx	23/7/99
718/1997	Vargas	Chile	99, xx	26/7/99
719/1997	Levy	Jamaica	99, xx	3/11/98
720/1997	Morgan and Williams	Jamaica	99, xx	3/11/98
722/1997	Fraser and Fisher	Jamaica	99, xx	31/3/99
724/1997	Mazurkiewiczova	Czech Republic	99, xx	26/7/99
730/1997	Marshall	Jamaica	99, xx	3/11/98
732/1997	Whyte	Jamaica	98, 195	27/7/98
733/1997	Perkins	Jamaica	98, 205	19/3/98
734/1997	McLeod	Jamaica	98, 213	31/3/98
737/1997	Lamagna	Australia	99, xx	7/4/99
739/1997	Tovar Acuna	Venezuela	99, xx	25/3/99
740/1997	Barzana Yutronic	Chile	99, xx	23/7/99
741/1997	Cziklin	Canada	99, xx	27/7/99
742/1997	Byrne and Lazarescu	Canada	99, xx	25/3/99
744/1997	Linderholm	Croatia	99, xx	23/7/99
746/1997	Menanteau	Chile	99, xx	26/7/99

Communication No.	Author[1]	States Party	Annual Report	Selected Decisions[2]	Date of Decision
748/1997	Silva	Sweden	00, xx		18/10/99
749/1997	McTaggart	Jamaica	98, 221		31/3/98
750/1997	Daley	Jamaica	98, 235		31/7/98
751/1997	Pasla	Austria	99, xx		7/4/99
752/1997	Henry	Trinidad & Tobago	99, xx		3/11/98
754/1997	A	New Zealand	99, xx		15/7/99
755/1997	Maloney	Germany	97, 342		29/7/97
758/1997	Gómez Navarro	Spain	97, 345		29/7/97
761/1997	Singh	Canada	97, 348		29/7/97
768/1997	Mukunto	Zambia	99, xx		23/7/99
775/1997	Brown	Jamaica	99, xx		23/3/99
777/1997	Sánchez López	Spain	00, xx		18/10/99
784/1997	Plotnikov	Russian Federation	99, xx		25/3/99
786/1997	Johannes Vos	Netherlands	99, xx		26/7/99
789/1997	Bryhn	Norway	00, xx		29/10/99
800/1998	Thomas	Jamaica	99, xx		8/4/99
813/1998	Chadee	Trinidad & Tobago	98, 242		29/7/98
816/1998	Tadman *et al.*	Canada	00, xx		29/10/99
830/1998	Bethel	Trinidad & Tobago	99, xx		31/3/99
835/1998	van den Berg	Netherlands	99, xx		25/3/99
844/1998	Petkov	Bulgaria	99, xx		25/3/99
850/1999	Hankala	Finland	99, xx		25/3/99
861/1999	Lestourneaud	France	00, xx		3/11/99
871/1999	Timmerman	Netherlands	00, xx		29/10/99
873/1999	Hoelen	Netherlands	00, xx		3/11/99
883/1999	Mansur and Mansur	Netherlands	00, xx		5/11/99

[1] The name of the victim only is given where the author has submitted a complaint on behalf of the victim.

[2] Selected Decisions Under the Optional Protocol, New York, 1985 and 1990 (Volumes 1 and 2), CCPR/C/OP1 and 2.

[3] Name of State Party not made public.

[4] Where more than one page number is shown, this means that various aspects of the case have been reported at different pages of the same vol. of Selected Decisions.

[5] 1990 references refer to vol. II of 1990 Annual Report. Similarly, references to the 1993, 1995, 1996, 1997, and 1998 reports refer to vol. II of the respective report.

Appendix J

General Comments

Report No.	Sessions and Date Adopted	Article (Topic)
1	13 (28/7/81)	Reporting Obligations
2	13 (28/7/81)	Reporting Obligations
3	13 (28/7/81)	Implementation at National Level
4	13 (28/7/81)	Article 3
5	13 (28/7/81)	Article 4
6	16 (27/7/82)	Article 6
7[1]	16 (27/7/82)	Article 7
8	16 (27/7/82)	Article 9
9[2]	16 (27/7/82)	Article 10
10	19 (27/7/83)	Article 19
11	19 (29/7/83)	Article 20
12	21 (12/4/84)	Article 1
13	21 (12/4/84)	Article 14
14	23 (2/11/84)	Article 6
15	27 (22/7/86)	Position of Aliens under the Covenant
16	32 (23/3/88)	Article 17
17	35 (5/4/89)	Article 24
18	37 (9/11/89)	Non-discrimination
19	39 (24/6/90)	Article 23
20	44 (3/4/92)	Article 7
21	44 (6/4/92)	Article 10
22	48 (20/7/93)	Article 18
23	50 (6/4/94)	Article 27
24	52 (2/11/94)	Reservations
25	57 (12/7/96)	Article 25
26	61 (6/12/97)	Denunciations
27	67 (2/11/99)	Article 12
28	68 (29/3/00)	Article 3

All General Comments are available through the United Nations treaty bodies website:
< http://www.unhchr.ch/tbs/doc.nsf>

[1] General Comment 7 was later replaced by General Comment 20.
[2] General Comment 9 was later replaced by General Comment 21.

Subject Index

The references in this index are to **paragraph numbers,** with the exception of those which appear in *italics*. These italicized references are to **page numbers** in the **addendum** at the rear of the main text of the book.

This 'subject' index also includes references to specific Articles of the *International Covenant on Civil and Political Rights* and to the First and Second Protocols to that Covenant. However, references to specific Articles in other international treaties cited in this book are to be found in the separate **'Table of Treaties'**.